THE

BORDER

SOUTH

STATES

People, Politics, and Power

in the Five Border South States

N EAL R. P EIRCE

W · W · N O R T O N & C O M P A N Y · I N C ·
N E W Y O R K

FIRST EDITION

917.504
Pe

Library of Congress Cataloging in Publication Data
Peirce, Neal R.
    The Border South States.
    Bibliography: p.
    1. Southern States—Politics and government—
1951–   2. Southern States—Economic conditions
—1945–   I. Title.
F216.2.P43   320.9′75′04   74–13731
ISBN 0–393–05531–0

1 2 3 4 5 6 7 8 9 0

THE BORDER SOUTH

Author's Travels

A

Great Lakes and Northeast region:
MINN., Duluth, WIS., St.Paul, apolis, IOWA, Madison, Sioux Falls, Sioux City, Chicago, Des Moines, ILL., Gary, IND., Indianapolis, Lincoln, MO., Springfield, Kansas City, E.St.Louis, St.Louis, Cairo, Lake Superior, Sault Ste.Marie, L.Michigan, MICH., Lansing, Milwaukee, L.Huron, Detroit, L.Erie, Cleveland, OHIO, Columbus, Cincinnati, KY., Frankfort, Louisville, L.Ontario, Rochester, Buffalo, N.Y., Burlington, VT., Montpelier, MAINE, Augusta, Portland, Concord, N.H., Boston, MASS., S., P., H., R.I., CONN., N.H., New York, T., N.J., Philadelphia, Atlantic City, Albany, Scranton, PA., Pittsburgh, Harrisburg, W.VA., W., B., A., MD., Dover, DEL., Washington, Norfolk, VA., Charleston, W.VA., Richmond, Charlotte, N.C., Raleigh, Knoxville, TENN., Nashville, Chattanooga, Memphis, ARK., Little Rock, Tulsa, Dallas, Huntsville, MISS., Birmingham, ALA., Jackson, Selma, Montgomery, GA., Atlanta, S.C., Columbia, Charleston, Savannah, LA., Jacksonville, Tallahassee, FLA., Cape Kennedy, New Orleans, Houston, Gulf of Mexico, Tampa, Miami, Atlantic Ocean

A.–Annapolis
B.–Baltimore
W.–Wilmington
T.–Trenton
N.–Newark
N.H.–New Haven
H.–Hartford
S.–Springfield
P.–Providence

Hawaii inset:
KAUAI, NIIHAU, OAHU, Honolulu, MOLOKAI, MAUI, HAWAII, HAWAII, Hilo, Pacific Ocean, ille

N

MILES
0 50 100 200

THE

BORDER SOUTH STATES

BY NEAL R. PEIRCE

THE MEGASTATES OF AMERICA

THE PACIFIC STATES OF AMERICA

THE MOUNTAIN STATES OF AMERICA

THE GREAT PLAINS STATES OF AMERICA

THE DEEP SOUTH STATES OF AMERICA

THE PEOPLE'S PRESIDENT

For my daughter Andrea

AND

in memory of my traveling companion
and a superb reporter,
Bruce Biossat
1910–1974

CONTENTS

FOREWORD

THIS BOOK IS ABOUT THE Border South States, part of a series covering the story of each major geographic region and all of the 50 states of America in our time. The objective is simply to let Americans (and foreigners too) know something of the profound diversity of peoples and life styles and geographic habitat and political behavior that make this the most fascinating nation on earth.

Only one project like this has been attempted before, and it inspired these books: John Gunther's *Inside U.S.A.*, researched during World War II and published in 1947. Gunther was the first man in U.S. history to visit each of the states and then to give a good and true account of the American condition as he found it. But his book is a quarter of a century old; it was written before the profound economic and population growth and societal change of the postwar era. Before he died, I consulted John Gunther about a new book. He recognized the need for such a work, and he gave me, as he put it, his "good luck signal."

But what was to be a single book became several, simply because I found America today too vast, too complex to fit into a single volume. A first book, *The Megastates of America*, treated America's 10 most heavily populated states. The series of eight regional volumes, completing the exploration of all the states in our time, began with publication of *The Mountain States of America* and *The Pacific States of America*, followed by *The Great Plains States of America*, and the companion volume to this one, *The Deep South States of America*. Separate volumes are to follow on the Mid-Atlantic, New England, and Great Lakes states.

A word about method. Like Gunther, I traveled to each state of the Union. I talked with about 1,500 men and women—governors, Senators, Representatives, mayors, state and local officials, editors and reporters, business and labor leaders, public opinion analysts, clergymen, university presidents and professors, representatives of the Indian, black, and Spanish-speaking communities—and just plain people. Some of the people I talked with were famous, others obscure, almost all helpful.

I went by plane, then rented cars, made a personal inspection of almost every great city and most of the important geographic areas, and must have walked several hundred miles in the process too, insanely lugging a briefcase full of notes and tape recorder into the unlikeliest places. Usually I got names of suggested interviewees from my newspaper friends and other contacts in new states and cities and then sent letters ahead saying I would like to see the people. From the initial interviews, reference to still more interesting people invariably ensued. Rare were the interviews that didn't turn out to be fascinating in their own way; the best ones were dinner appointments, when the good talk might stretch into the late evening hours.

My initial travel and interviewing in the 50 states took a year and a half; there were return visits to some states, and telephone follow-up calls to many sources. The writing was complicated by the need to review hundreds of books and thousands of articles and newspaper clippings I had assembled over time. And then each manuscript, after it had been read and commented upon by experts of the state (often senior political reporters), had to be revised to include last-minute developments, and still once more given a final polish and updating in the galley stage.

Amid the confusion I tried to keep my eye on the enduring, vital questions about each state and its great cities:

What sets it (the state or city) apart from the rest of America?
What is its essential character?
What kind of place is it to live in?
What does it look like, how clean or polluted is it, what are the interesting communities?
Who holds the power?
Which are the great corporations, unions, universities, and newspapers, and what role do they play in their state?
Which are the major ethnic groups, and what is their influence?
How did the politics evolve to where they are today, and what is the outlook for the coming years?
How creatively have the governments and power structures served the people?
Who are the great leaders of today—and perhaps tomorrow?

A word of caution: many books about the present-day American condition are preoccupied with illustrating fundamental sickness in our society, while others are paeans of praise. These books are neither. They state many of the deep-seated problems, from perils to the environment to the abuse of power by selfish groups. But the account of the state civilizations also includes hundreds of instances of greatness, of noble and disinterested public service. I have viewed my primary job as descriptive, to show the multitudinous strands of life in our times, admitting their frequently contradictory directions, and tying them together analytically only where the evidence is clear. The ultimate "verdict" on the states and cities must rest with the reader himself. Nowhere is this more true than in the Southern states, so sensitive about their own identity and place in the nation. As a non-Southerner, I approached them with some trepidation, yet soon found myself swept up in the excitement of their rapidly expanding social and political and economic horizons. Yet the millennium in Dixie is still a distant thing, and if some Southerners are offended by unflattering comparisons I have drawn between their states and other parts of the country, I can only quote a born Savannahan, Chancellor Alexander Heard of Vanderbilt University: "We in the South cannot duck behind the thought that if we show up in the rear ranks in the national ratings, the ratings measure the wrong thing."

For whom, then, is this chronicle of our times written? I mean the individual chapters to be of interest to people who live in the various states, to help them see their home area in a national context. I write for businessmen, students, and tourists planning to visit or move into a state, and who are interested in what makes it tick—the kind of things no guidebook will tell them. I write for politicians planning national campaigns, for academicians, for all those curious about the American condition as we enter the last decades of the 20th century.

From the start, I knew it was presumptuous for any one person to try to encompass such a broad canvass. But a unity of view, to make true comparisons between states, is essential. And since no one else had tried the task for a quarter of a century, I decided to try—keeping in mind the same goal Gunther set for *Inside U.S.A.*—a book whose "central spine and substance is an effort—in all diffidence—to show this most fabulous and least known of countries, the United States of America, to itself."

———

These books had to be, by their very character, a personal odyssey and personal task. But I owe a special word of thanks to those who helped me. In this volume, I am indebted to Michael Barone, co-author of the *Almanac of American Politics*, for assistance in preparation of the North Carolina chapter. My warmest thanks also go to those who read the draft manuscript in its entirety: Evan W. Thomas, my editor at W. W. Norton & Company; Russell L. Bradley; Jean Allaway; Frederick H. Sontag, public affairs and research consultant of South Orange, New Jersey; and copy editor Calvin Towle. Various friends and associates helped with many details of research and proofreading, and for that I am especially indebted to Thomas Ward, Dennis Michaud, Saul Benjamin, Geneva Torrey, F. Rhodes Cook, Barbara Hurlbutt, Prentice and Alice Bowsher, and DeMar and Claudia Teuscher. Credit goes to Russell Lenz, former chief cartographer of the *Christian Science Monitor*, for what I feel is the superb job he did in preparing the state and city maps.

Finally, I would like to express my thanks to the several persons in each state who consented to read and comment on the draft manuscript about their state. The names of these persons appear in the interviewee list at the back of the book; I choose not to list them here lest someone hold them responsible for something said or unsaid in one of the chapters, and of course the full responsibility for that lies with me.

THE
BORDER SOUTH STATES

THE
BORDER SOUTH

AMERICA'S FORGOTTEN REGION

THE BORDER SOUTH STATES—Virginia, North Carolina, West Virginia, Tennessee, and Kentucky—might well be called the forgotten region of 20th-century America. In the beginning they *were* America: the first permanent European settlement on the continent occurred at Jamestown in 1607; Virginia provided the chief architects of American independence and four of the first five Presidents, dominating the national scene clear down to the 1820s; then the nation-building impulse shifted over the mountains to Kentucky and Tennessee, the Golden West of the time, providing creators of the national destiny of the caliber of Andrew Jackson and Henry Clay.

The Civil War ravaged this region of divided loyalties and threw it into a deep spiritual and economic depression, a condition which did not begin to improve substantially until the era following World War II. The waves of vital national growth, it seemed, came from everywhere else—from the industrialized Northeast and Great Lakes regions, from Texas and California, and when the South began to revive in the last quarter century, more from Georgia (because of Atlanta) and Florida.

Through it all, the Border States seemed like an island of quiet. On their eastern flank, the coastal plains of Virginia and North Carolina, the plantation mentality held on tenaciously as both whites and the many blacks toiled through the years for the most meager return. Though it faced the Atlantic, the coastal region was not to have a port of major status from the dawn of the railroad age until Virginia's Hampton Roads area began to boom in the mid-20th century.

In the salubrious climate and natural setting of the Piedmont, the next strip of land moving westward, it was the low-paying, fiercely antiunion textile industry that gradually absorbed the labors of people once engaged in agriculture. Only in the past 25 years have major metropolitan agglomerations appeared in the Piedmont, in North Carolina areas like Charlotte, Raleigh, and Winston-Salem, and in Virginia's "urban corridor," which runs from the Washington, D. C. suburbs down to Richmond, with an easterly extension to the sea at Norfolk. Yet with the exception of the northern Virginia suburbs, this has been a distinctly blue collar economic renaissance, tied to the loom and the workbench at the very moment that the most dynamic parts of the United States were moving into a research- and brains-oriented post-industrial era. In fact, one looked long and hard in the Border States to find the kind of vitality associated with the management centers of the nation's major corporations. By 1972 the region had a total of 19,089,000 people, 9.2 percent of the national total. But of the country's 500 largest industrial firms, only 16, or 3.2 percent, had their headquarters in this five-state area. (Of those, by far the greatest number were in textiles.) The picture was equally gloomy in relation to the nerve centers of the great financial, utility, transportation, or educational institutions of the country.

Through the heart of the Border South, on a north-south axis, run the ancient Appalachian mountains, the "outback" of eastern America, and one of the most physically and culturally isolated regions of the United States. These highlands are peopled by proudly independent, poverty-afflicted mountain folk, some of the hardiest fighters of the American Revolution, among those who suffered the most from the Civil War and its long aftermath. For almost a century, they have seen the timber of their hills, and the mineral wealth beneath them, cruelly usurped by outside corporations. Here, in central Appalachia, lie billions of tons of recoverable coal, and one trembles to think of what the condition of the mountains may be as the process of extraction accelerates in the years ahead.

The pleasant tobacco-producing midlands of central Kentucky and Tennessee, to the west of the mountains, remain deeply rural with the exception of the Louisville and the Cincinnati suburbs (which share in the prosperity of Ohio River commerce), the fast-growing Bluegrass city of Lexington, and Tennessee's progressive capital at Nashville.

Finally, on the region's western flank, lie Mississippi River plantation lands and the city of Memphis, which is as much the capital of the Mississippi Delta as it is of western Tennessee. Here one encounters that typical Deep South phenomenon: poor people on immensely fertile land.

Gloomy Indicators

Of all the Border States, only one—Virginia—comes even close to the average per capita income of Americans in our times. And Virginia would not be much better off than the rest of the region if it were not for the infusion of federal activity that has brought in many out-of-staters.

The table below shows the relative per capita income lag of the Border South, the percentage of homes lacking some or all plumbing facilities (the closest measure one can get from present-day Census figures on the general condition of housing), and the share of families living at or below the federally established poverty line. The figures are taken from the 1970 Census.

	Per Capita Income (% behind national average) (1972)	Plumbing Facilities Lacking (1970)	Families with Poverty-level Incomes (1970)
Virginia	4%	13.4%	12.3%
North Carolina	15	15.7	16.3
West Virginia	20	18.4	18.0
Kentucky	20	20.8	19.2
Tennessee	18	14.9	18.2
United States	—	6.9	10.7

Behind those poor standard-of-living indexes in the Border South lies an educational system which, with few exceptions, has been grossly inadequate over the years. These figures, from the 1970 Census, show the median number of school years completed by the adult population, and the percentage of the adults who never attended school or never went beyond the fourth grade—in other words, functional illiterates. The last column indicates the share of the adult population which completed college:

	Median School Years Completed	Functional Illiterates	College Graduates
Virginia	9.9	7.7%	12.3%
North Carolina	8.9	10.0	8.5
West Virginia	8.8	7.3	6.8
Kentucky	8.7	9.4	7.2
Tennessee	8.8	9.5	7.9
United States	12.1	5.8	10.7

(The reader will note one major exception to the rule in the above figures—Virginia's unusually high percentage of college graduates. This is due almost entirely to the Northern Virginia suburbs, packed with government workers, where about 26 percent of the population has completed college.)

Education, of course, is a prime determinant of the kind of employment for which people can qualify. Thus the abysmally low educational levels of the Border States result in a work force weighted heavily to manual labor and other forms of manufacturing and farm employment. Commensurately, it means less people in white collar, and particularly in professional-level jobs:

	Blue Collar Farm and Service Equipment	White Collar Employment	Scientists per 100,000 Population
Virginia	51.0%	49.0%	140
North Carolina	61.4	38.6	97
West Virginia	59.6	40.4	104
Kentucky	59.8	40.2	77
Tennessee	58.5	41.5	110
United States	51.8	48.2	154

Historic Perspectives and the Regional Character

North Carolina's former Governor Terry Sanford, writing a few years ago of the Border South of marginal farming, ramshackle homes, and poor company-owned mill towns he knew as a boy, commented: "We had crossed the mountains and settled the land, but we had failed to cross a mountain of neglect—neglect of natural resources and neglect of human capacity. . . . In some way, we had let America slip past us."

That condition was all the more tragic when one thought back to the founding centuries of the Border States. Then it was that the first settlers endured incredible hardships to make the first beachheads of European civilization in the New World; when the landed English gentry of the Tidewater and Piedmont created America's first natural aristocracy, sent their agents out to fight the French and Indian wars, and provided the authors of the Virginia Declaration of Human Rights and the Declaration of Independence. George Washington, who was to lead the ragtag troops of the colonies in the Revolutionary War and then be the nation's first President, was perhaps the quintessential man of the region. He was at once the owner of a great plantation and a wilderness explorer and surveyor, a man of natural leadership capacity and one of great physical strength, a passionate fighter, and a winner.

Diversity, rather than unity, was the hallmark of the Border States region from its earliest days. The division was rooted in the class differences of the people, differences which in turn could be traced back to Old World origins, and would later be accentuated by the New World conflict between Tidewater and mountains.

The "first families of Virginia," of course, represented a direct transference of the English aristocracy of the time, and were to be the natural first leaders of the region. But with them came two other groups of quite different background. There were thousands upon thousands of the English common people, the bulk of whom arrived as indentured servants. In many ways, they were an intimidated people. As Kentucky author Harry Caudill pointed out in an interview:

Anyone who's ever been to the Tower of London and seen all that glittering collection of gold plate and the tremendous panoply of powder and magnificence that those old Norman kings and queens built in order to overawe and frighten and intimidate the English common people can begin to get some idea of the impact it must have had. And they had come out of the English countryside where the scaffold stood at nearly every crossroads. And it took them three to four generations to become acclimated to this wild, rough continent. It was not until the Indians were cleared out that the great mass of English stock began to move west.

There was another group of much tougher characteristics in colonial times. It included the Scotch-Irish, who came out of Ulster, a kind of frontier in itself; the Germans, coming out of the crucible of the Thirty Years War; and finally the Huguenot French, who had endured nearly a century of persecution and warfare before they arrived in the New World. "When they reached the New World," Caudill commented, "they were pretty much prepared to go into the wilderness and fight Indians and kill wild beasts." Few of them tarried long in the Tidewater provinces, but instead made their way, as quickly as they could, up to the mountains where they could seize a piece of land as their own. There they lived in virtual isolation for a century, but when the Revolution came, they were to star as its frontier warriors. Indeed, these tough backwoodsmen proclaimed American independence at Mecklenburg Courthouse a year before the nation followed suit on July 4, 1776.

The frontiersmen's brightest hour came at the Battle of Kings Mountain, the dramatic defeat of Lord Cornwallis's troops in 1780. The American roll was made up of some 900 "30-day soldiers" recruited by the separate counties, a group the British derisively called "barbarian squirrel hunters." They faced more than 1,100 splendidly trained and uniformed soldiers of the king. The British fought in classic closed-formation style, while the Americans adopted Indian tactics, using the trees for cover. When the battle was finished, every single one of the British, down to the last scout, was either killed or captured in perhaps the most crushing defeat the English ever suffered in the history of their empire. Only 28 Americans were killed. The most interesting sociological fact about the battle was that the list of American soldiers showed scarcely an English name. Instead, the roster was virtually all Scotch, German, and French.

And it was those people, together with growing numbers of their own and people of English stock flowing down the mountain valleys from Pennsylvania along the Valley Road of Virginia, and across the Cumberland Gap, who would make Tennessee and Kentucky two of the most vibrant states of the Union, the home or birthplace of five of the 11 Presidents of the United States who served between 1829 and 1869. One need mention the names of only two of these—Andrew Jackson and Abraham Lincoln—to appreciate the contribution of the Border States' sons to the development of American democracy in the decades after the first and great Virginia Presidents. Since the 1860s, however, there has been only one President with Border State ties—Woodrow Wilson, born in the Shenandoah Valley in 1856.

In the chapters which follow, the history of each of the five states of this region is traced, in brief form, from their beginnings to the present. With the exception of West Virginia and North Carolina, neither of which has ever really had a golden age, the pattern is strikingly similar: an early period of brilliance in political and economic leadership, followed by a long descent that was halted, in varying degrees, by World War II and its aftermath. With pitifully few exceptions—Harry Byrd of Virginia, Estes Kefauver of Tennessee, Alben Barkley of Kentucky, and Sam Ervin, Jr., of North Carolina are perhaps the most prominent exceptions—one finds few important national leaders of the 20th century coming out of these states. One reason is that the region, with the exception of West Virginia and to a lesser extent Kentucky, has been regarded by Americans as "Southern"—meaning that its leaders suffered under the disadvantage of all Southerners in rising to national leadership for a full century following the Civil War. Another reason has been the deep-seated antigovernment mind set of the region's people. A fiercely individualistic, nonconforming lot, they had to fend for themselves on the early frontier and never took kindly to official interference in their lives. From this stems a distressing resistance to community cooperation, to any subordination of the individual welfare for the common good. The government is identified as "them"—not "us." "Down here," Harry Caudill commented, "people tend to resent any taxes they have to pay. Government is a great, alien, outside force and the people view it with the same suspicion, I'm sure, that their ancestors viewed that great elaborate court in London." One outgrowth of this is a high degree of political violence—in the first 60 years of the 19th century, for instance, there were 27 political duels involving legislators or governors in North Carolina alone. Fabled assassinations darken the political history of Kentucky and Tennessee. Mountaineers in poor Appalachian counties still are known to use the gun in the desperate competition for the few good-paying political jobs. Border state politics, especially in the Appalachian regions, are marked by high degrees of vote stealing and theft of the taxpayer's dollar. Small wonder, then, that for more than a century the region's sons and daughters have rarely made an important mark in national political life.

With rising levels of education and income in the past three decades, the level of political debate and government performance has begun to improve markedly. Corruption is much less than it used to be. Virginia has finally ditched "pay-as-you-go" policies which retarded its development. North Carolina has taken long strides in education. Tennesseeans have learned from the model of the Tennessee Valley Authority that government could accomplish a great deal in improving people's everyday lives.

By national standards, the Border States remain a distinctly conservative region, one slow to innovate. But the differences between the character and governments of these states and the nation as a whole have begun to blur in an era of mass communications and commonly shared problems. For the first time since the Civil War, there is now an opportunity for the Border South and its people to play important roles in national life. Whether it will really seize that opportunity, however, remains an unanswered question in the late 20th century.

The Difficulties of "Prospering Rurally"

Economically, the Border States have been a backwater in 20th-century America. Their disadvantage vis-à-vis the rest of the nation, shown by some of the statistics cited earlier, remains serious, though the gap is not as immense as it was just a decade or two ago. Where real improvement has come, it has been concentrated, by and large, in a few growth centers. The most dynamic of these are Virginia's "urban corridor" (running from Northern Virginia to Norfolk), the Nashville and Memphis metropolitan regions in Tennessee, Kentucky's Louisville and especially the smaller growth city of Lexington, and finally the Piedmont cities of North Carolina which have registered major industrial expansion, albeit with a strikingly low-wage (and anti-union) profile.

The modern growth centers tend to be exceptions to the rule, however. To this date, only a small percentage of the region's people live in metropolitan areas, and scarcely half of them in places one could label "urban." The regional custom of rural living began in early Virginia when the people settled on plantations and small farms rather than in towns. But in West Virginia the rural share of the population is 61 percent, in North Carolina 55 percent, in Kentucky 48 percent, in Tennessee 41 percent, and in Virginia 37 percent.

In modern economics, it is almost axiomatic that rural people earn less income, on the average, than urban people. There may be compensations for rural living—lower costs of living, farmers who feed their own families, and the attractions of woods for hunting, fresh streams for fishing, and quiet places "to bring up kids." Such advantages are cited by many of the workers in the industries—textiles, electronics, furniture, and the like—which have sprung up across the Southern countryside. But the frightful outmigration figures of the Border States since 1940 also indicate that low economic activity means disruption of families and the loss to the region of new generations which head off to more vibrant parts of the nation to make a living. Up to now, only a few parts of the region have been fortunate enough to *prosper rurally* (or at least in a nonmetropolitan way); among these one could name the Kentucky Bluegrass section, the fertile and lovingly husbanded Valley of Virginia, and the sections of the Tennessee Valley where the TVA has had the most beneficial effects.*

---

* The story of TVA is so important as America's shining, lonely example of integrated regional development of human and natural resources that I have devoted a separate chapter to it.

The Plight of Appalachia

The Appalachians, cutting a broad swath through the Border States on a northwest-southwest axis, are not only the Border States' common territory and most unifying force, but also one of the most perplexing problem regions of the country. In a section of the United States most overlooked from the Civil War years onwards, the Appalachian reaches were the most forsaken of all. Outsiders used to scorn the mountain people as backward, ill-tempered "hillbillies," an attitude even reflected by the usually sensitive John Gunther in his *Inside U.S.A.*, written at the end of World War II. The first glimmerings of national recognition of Appalachian problems occurred during Franklin Roosevelt's New Deal—Mrs. Roosevelt, in particular, took an interest in the region's people—but it must have come as quite a revelation to Americans when the famed war correspondent Ernie Pyle, stationed with some East Tennessee boys in England in 1944, detected a positive side to the Appalachian character, altogether unfamiliar to most Americans. "It seems to me," Pyle reported, "that these boys feel more at home over here than any of our other troops. . . . A few have been to college, but some of them cannot read or write. And yet I defy you to find more real gentlemen among our troops than in a camp of these so-called hillbillies. There is a simple genuineness about them that shows in every word they speak. They are courteous, friendly, and trusting—all by instinct."

The task of defining Appalachia—beyond its physical boundaries—is one that the outsider hesitates to undertake, because Appalachia is as much a state of mind as it is a geographic region. All of it seems to lie under a thin blue haze—partly dust, partly smoke, partly moisture, one author has observed—a haze beneath which one finds noble mountains and craggy hills, a labyrinth of winding roads, settlements up hollows and in little towns, magnificent forests and scruffy second-growth, free-flowing streams and sulfurous creeks and black coal mines.

Funson Edwards, an East Tennessee high school principal, penned a description of the Appalachian people that appealed to me especially. They are, he wrote, a race of unique beliefs, attitudes, mores, dialects, and colloquial expressions. . . .

Appalachia is the [land of] steep hills and winding hollows. . . .

Appalachia is the ugly portrait of a naked earth scraped by bulldozer. . . .

Appalachia is the scene of childbirth unattended by medical science but helped along by midwife practices [a now-dying art, one may add]. . . .

Appalachia is the clatter and chatter of gay youngsters as they romp and play in the woods and by-ways but run like turkeys when an outsider appears.

Appalachia is the trudging of a weary people down the creeks and hollows, often barefoot and threadbare, to claim their meager share of "commodities" at the county seat dole-giving center.

Appalachia is the song of distress and despair, written on the faces of the aged and destitute, whose spirit has been broken by unfulfilled promises from landlord and politician.

Appalachia is the small wooden church propped on the vertical land of the scrubby oak and the stunted white pine.

Appalachia is the part of the country which receives only lip-service education. It is that area of the land which secures its direction and counsel from "Big Folks," far away off.

Appalachia is that mass of people endowed with native intellect but trampled into the mire of prejudice, illiteracy, and confusion. . . .

How, Edwards. asked, is one to break through the walls of ignorance and backwardness that pen in so many Appalachian people?

Fence them off from the elite society? Scold them for their backward ways? Direct their thinking from ivory-towered campus and computer rooms of the Federal Building? Experiment with them as we do with white mice and permanently record the findings in file thirteen?

No, these uncouth ones are people. Real people endowed with feelings, aspirations, love, and some gray matter, people created in His image, the same as you, gifted with a certain degree of intellectual know-how which must share human respect.

And this same Appalachia of so many problems, one must add, is also the land of the dulcimer, banjo, guitar, and fiddle, and of haunting mountain folksongs, the land of quaint native arts like quilt-making, weaving of hand-dyed wools, and quaint wood carvings, the only region of America where any number of farmers still till their fields with horse-drawn plow. "Appalachia has what America must regain—a closeness to the earth," one reads in *Mountain Life and Work*, the journal of the Council of the Southern Mountains.

The sad plight of the people of Southern Appalachia over the past century—from the blood feuds which grew out of the Civil War, through the era of the slash-and-run timbermen and the viciously run company coal towns, and down to the assaults on the landscape in our own time—is chronicled in the state chapters which follow, especially those on West Virginia and Kentucky. The story might have been different if Abraham Lincoln had not been assassinated, for in 1864 he had told Colonel O. O. Howard, chief of the Bureau for Freedmen and Refugees, that at the end of the bloody war he intended to seek aid for the poor people of the Southern mountains whose territory had been torn asunder by fierce guerrilla war and foragers of both the Union and Southern sides. But Lincoln died before he could carry out his intention, and in the next half century there developed two quite different Appalachias, described by Harry Caudill:

One, the Appalachia of Power and Wealth, consists of huge land, coal, oil, gas, timber and quarry companies that "recover" the minerals from the earth; rail, barge and pipeline companies that convey the minerals to markets; and steel, refining, chemical and utility firms that convert the minerals to marketable products. This Appalachia, headquartered in New York and Philadelphia, is allied to mighty banks and insurance companies.

The firms of Appalachia One, Caudill noted, have boasted of netting profits of as much as 61 percent of gross income. Then he continued:

The second Appalachia is a land devastated by decades of quarrying, drilling, tunneling and strip mining. Five thousand miles of its streams are silted and poisoned beyond any present capacity to restore them, and many more are being reduced to the same dismal state. Its people are the old, the young who are planning to leave and the legions of crippled and sick.

And Appalachia One, Caudill charged, "routinely raises money to persuade and bribe Appalachia Two to elect candidates acceptable to wealth and power."

The decade of the 1950s, when Appalachia One decided—in the name of economy and efficiency, and with the agreement of John Lewis's United Mine Workers—to automate the coal mines, cutting the employment rolls at a terrifying pace, must be marked down as the most disastrous era for Appalachia in this century. The Appalachian counties of the five Border States suffered a net outmigration of 1,164,651 people—almost 20 percent of their 1950 population of 6,021,273. Portions of the factory cities of Ohio, Michigan, and Illinois began to sprout "little Appalachias" made up of refugee highlanders, who took their fundamentalist churches, their love for hillbilly music, and their ingrown social ways with them. (And whenever they could, even for brief weekends, they returned to the hills and hollows and creeks of their birth, causing huge traffic jams on some of the bridges across the Ohio River. One is hard put to think of a strain of Americans with a more powerful "homing instinct.")

Back home, hundreds of thousands of onetime coal miners, their families, and people who had subsisted on servicing the coal industry were thrown onto the welfare rolls. Had it not been for large-scale distribution of food by the federal government, together with the various forms of the dole, and the fact that central Appalachia was depopulating so rapidly, there might well have been mass starvation in the mountains.

Appalachian Regional Commission: Growth, Complexities, Pro and Con

In the winter of 1966–67 central Appalachia, and East Kentucky in particular, suffered devastating floods which began to draw attention to the region from some congressmen and dedicated Interior Department officials, including economist Howard Forsythe and engineer Gordon Ebersole. John D. Whisman, later to become states' regional representative on the Appalachian Regional Commission, traced the concept of a national corrective effort from events in which he was personally involved. These began with the search for an economic recovery program sparked by the Kentucky Jaycees, which Whisman headed in 1956, and the creation that year of an East Kentucky Economic Development Council. A keen interest in Appalachian problems was shown by Kentucky Governor Bert Combs (himself a mountain man). The first meeting ever of the Appalachian governors to deal with their common problems was called by Maryland's Millard Tawes, and held in Annapolis in the spring of 1960. Combs became head of an ongoing Appalachian governors' group, formed at Annapolis, with Whisman the chief staff person. John F. Kennedy, campaigning in the West Virginia Presidential primary early in 1960, became the first national politician to take note of the incredible hardships which had befallen the mountain people.

Once elected, Kennedy won congressional approval of the Area Redevelopment Administration—a much too piecemeal approach, as it turned out, to make much of a difference in Appalachia or any other depressed region. But the Appalachian governors continued their interest in a program specifically for Appalachia, and after a great flood in 1963 Combs and Whisman, seeking emergency aid at the White House, were able to convince President Kennedy to create a President's Appalachian Regional Commission. Concurrently, in East Kentucky, the unemployed coal miners had become so desperate that they formed roving committees to picket the few coal mines still working—a last, futile effort to restore their jobs. In the fall of 1963 the first major national story on the utter desperation of central Appalachia appeared as Homer Bigart of the New York *Times* wrote a chilling account of children so hungry they were eating mud, and of people's lives in collapsing shacks.

Kennedy died that same autumn, but early in 1965 President Johnson was able to sign, as the first piece of "Great Society" legislation sent him by Congress, the bill creating a statutory Appalachian Regional Commission. The ARC was no ordinary government agency; John Fischer was close to the mark, in fact, when he called it "a wondrously temperamental bastard, sired by state politicians, born out of the federal bureaucracy, and nursed by congressional prima donnas." One could view it as a grand experiment in American federalism, because the 13 Appalachian state governors were given the same voting weight in allocating federal monies as the single federal representative. A regional development plan on this scale had never before been seen in the United States. (The governors thought of the ARC as "theirs," a happy hunting ground in which they could logroll to their hearts' content in the bargaining for federal aid.) Moreover, for a region known for the oft-cantankerous nature of its people and politics, it was an unparalleled model of cooperation, fusing the efforts of Washington, the governors, and the local governments. Finally, ARC was fairly unique (at least at the time of its inception) because it undertook no projects directly, but rather carried on all its activities through the state and local governments.

"This commission is a facilitator," Whisman told me. "We do nothing. But we fund and provide technical assistance." What the ARC had promised at its inception, he said, was to stimulate creation of "a set of institutions" that would make it possible for each of the affected states to deal realistically with their recovery and development problems. As things stood in Appalachia at the start of the '60s, the region was in an alarming downward economic spiral which seemed well nigh irreversible. It was clear that the regular functional agencies of government were unable to devise total or comprehensive resolutions. "We had to tackle the scope of the problem,"

Whisman said, "not by continually trying to get a road from a highway department whose public policies guaranteed we couldn't, or a dam from a Corps of Engineers whose policies guaranteed we couldn't, or to try to get new schools built and teachers paid from state aid based on an inadequate tax base." Thus the problem lay both in getting massive infusions of new aid and, just as important, in coordinating that aid so that it would really make a difference in attacking deeply ingrained problems.

On the state level, the institutional answer was called "program management"—the creation or designation of a single agency for development that could relate the governor's budget functions and state planning with the efforts being undertaken by local jurisdictions. In Kentucky, North Carolina, and Tennessee this became the responsibility of the department of finance and administration; in Virginia the department of administration; in West Virginia the office of state-federal programs. For anyone familiar with the normal disjointedness of state government functions, the program management arms represented a breakthrough to an unheard of level of sophistication.

As a second tier of "new institutions," a series of multicounty development districts was soon created throughout Appalachia. Individual counties lacked the budgets or planning capacity to use federal aid effectively, or even to apply for it, and there were a host of problems, ranging from garbage landfills to vocational training services, that needed to be treated on a regional basis. But saying that groups of counties should cooperate, and getting them to do it, were different problems. "The question," Whisman said, "was how we could get a group of five or so county judges or commissioners, who were like Japanese warlords in their own domains, to work together." The answer was the multicounty development districts, with representatives from all the counties involved, given professional staff and collective power to plan and to review the federal monies coming into their areas. "At some point these five county judges began to see that they could gain more with cooperation than by holding their guns at each other," Whisman said. One could not erase their provincial attitudes, he suggested, but one could raise their sights to a large enough geographic area to make them "practically provincial." In point of fact, many of the development districts did become viable entities, and one beheld many of the fierce antagonisms between communities, which had bedeviled Appalachia so long, beginning to fade away.

As impressive as those organizational achievements sounded, the Appalachian regional effort was shaped and frequently thwarted by broad-scale political problems. The first was the necessity, to gain congressional approval, of including in the program almost 400 counties in 13 states, ranging from New York to Mississippi and containing 18 million people. That meant proportionately less funds and concentrations on central Appalachia (essentially the Border State portion of the region) where the economic indexes were the most depressing and the problems the most difficult.

Secondly, the ARC was designed so that it would pose no threat—indeed, so that it might help—the outside corporations that had fed off the area for so long. There was no provision for public ownership of the region's great wealth in natural resources—neither, in the TVA model, public control of old or new hydroelectric power generating facilities, nor any part of King Coal himself. Visionaries like Gordon Ebersole fought to have the ARC, or better still, publicly owned and controlled economic development districts, given the authority to build dams and coal-burning steam plants which would sell their power at reasonable rates to the region's people or to the eastern power grids.* But the governors and congressmen of Appalachia, many beholden to the private utilities, quashed the proposal.

Instead, the ARC left power generation to the economic royalists and busied itself with building an impressive set of new roads through the region's mountainous terrain. The theory was that until the notoriously poor transportation system was improved, Appalachia could not be "plugged into" the wealthy regions on either side of it, and economic development would be frustrated. In fact, some 1,200 miles of trunk highways—mostly two- or three-lane affairs—had been built or were under construction by 1973, with an additional 760 on the drawing boards. Some criticized the ARC for building the highways of sub-interstate quality, but the visitor to Appalachia has to be impressed by these highways, many constructed through gigantic cuts in the mountains, dramatically reducing travel distances between towns and the area's isolation.

The ARC roads have doubtless been of assistance to many of Appalachia's poor, in creating some new jobs and letting them commute to better-paying jobs (if available) some distance from their homes. But the roads displaced hundreds of impoverished mountaineers, who were not given new homes under the ARC legislation, and they were warmly welcomed by Appalachia One, whose overweight coal trucks began to pound some stretches of the new highways to pieces as soon as they were opened to traffic.

From the start, the lion's share of ARC funds was poured (through the state highway departments) into the road-building program. Much more modest funding went into vocational education, higher education, hospital facilities, nursing homes, mental health centers, libraries, child development programs, and mine area reclamation projects. In 1970 the New York *Times'* Ben A. Franklin, who had taken a keen interest in Appalachia for a decade, reported that the ARC program had "failed to reach the millions of Appalachians who live in poverty 'up the creek,' far from the federal highways and fatalistically certain that no 'Government man' can help them." Yet these were the hill people, he noted, "whose plight had moved President Kennedy to start the program in the first place." Ralph Widener, then execu-

---

* Dams built on the upper tributaries of Appalachia's many streams would not only have provided a new source of public power, but would have done a great deal to control the floods which pose such a grave threat to the region. But as Kentucky author Harriette Simpson Arnow wrote, "the framers of the Appalachian Act wanted everything to be built by free enterprise, and it is much less expensive to produce electricity with coal-fired generators than to build dams for hydroelectric plants. Thus yearly floods continue to destroy life and property in West Virginia, eastern Kentucky, and the mountainous sections of Pennsylvania and Virginia." The Congress for Appalachian Development, organized by Ebersole, Caudill, and others in the mid-1960s to find ways for Appalachia's people to retain some part of the riches their region provides the rest of the world, failed to gain significant support.

tive director of the ARC, acknowledged in an interview with Phil Primack of *The Mountain Eagle* of Whitesburg, Kentucky: "No question about it. Our primary impact has been on towns and highways. The folks at the heads of the hollows have gotten little." As the highways system approached completion, Widener said, more could be done to develop the inaccessible pockets of Appalachia through outreach programs, medical, educational, and other services.

In truth, the ARC focus did appear to shift somewhat to the human services area in the early 1970s. As this occurred, the multicounty development districts began to play an increasingly large role in the implementation of the program. Their power was greatly enhanced by a 1971 directive from the federal Office of Management and Budget, called the A-95 procedure, which gave the development districts the right of review over practically all federal aid flowing into their localities. Unless a proposal fitted into the overall regional development plan, it could be rejected. (Technically, federal agencies can disregard unfavorable A-95 reviews, but in practice they rarely do.) Thus the development districts began to accrue formidable political power—the power of the purse—and to enforce coordinated development plans for their areas.

All this began to arouse complaints, however, because of the composition of the boards of the development districts. Essentially they consisted of elected officials from the local constituencies, plus a number of merchants (the "Main Street crowd"), and a scattering of poor people. Again, the plain mountaineer found himself hopelessly outgunned. The ARC's decision to work with the local elected officials, editor Tom Gish of the *Mountain Eagle* said in an interview, "leaves us where we've been for 200 years. If that worked, our problems would have been solved years ago." That judgment, Gish made clear, was based on his ultra-low assessment of elected officials in the mountains. In a 1972 speech at the Highlander Center, an antiestablishment organization of young activists in East Tennessee, Gish had put the case against the ARC approach in even more extreme form:

> Through local Area Development Districts, the ARC and the federal budget people are bringing into existence a new level of government—regional government—with Kentucky divided into 15 regions, and other states divided much the same way.
> It is a regional government composed of our county judges and our mayors, who, along with a few token citizens, serve as the development group board of directors. And if you think you've never been able to have much influence in city hall or the courthouse, just wait until you start dealing with the Development Districts. . . . They are not elected by the people. They are not responsible to the people. . . . We are regionalizing our police, our schools, our water and sewer systems, our health departments, our garbage collection, our jails and just about every other traditional function of local government, and I don't know how any of us can have a say about any of it. . . . Grass-roots democracy is about gone, replaced by the faceless, the mindless, the heartless bureaucrat who is elected by no one, and is accountable to no one.

The net result of all this, Gish charged, would be ARC-planned "genocide in the mountains"—which he defined as forcing recalcitrant mountaineers, who refused to go along with the plans of the bureaucrats, to leave the hills. As chapter and verse, Gish cited the Kentucky Infant and Pre-School program, planned by the ARC and the federal Department of Health, Education and Welfare. That program, Gish said, would "take the child away from the mountain family and place it in the custody of the state." He also had bitter words for a land use plan to be imposed on his native Letcher County, which was written by University of Tennessee student-planners for the development district in southeastern Kentucky. When local opposition arose, Gish said, "the impression was being passed about that those ignorant hillbillies were opposed to planning and therefore were opposing progress, and just didn't know what was good for them." The local citizens finally killed the plan, but it seemed likely to reemerge in another form.

In Defense of the Mountain Man

There is a kind of desperate romanticism about Gish's stance, a last, desperate call of the mountain people to be left alone in whatever their grandeur or misery may be. One can say that attitude ignores the grinding poverty, the frightful health conditions, the illiteracy of mountain folk who insist on remaining in their isolated hollows. But one cannot ignore the sentiment—in Gish's words:

The glory that is the mountain man, the wonder that is the mountain family, the sheer delight that is the mountain way of life is under attack as never before. Soon there will be no mountain man, no mountain family, no Appalachian resident or no mountaineer in any recognizable form. We will be homogenized, blended, melted down and formed into a uniform mold unless we learn to keep what we want to keep, and to change only what we want to change. . . .

The simple fact is that the overwhelming majority of mountain people are in the mountains because they want to be. They live on a hillside because they like the breezes and the view that goes with hillside living. Or they live in a hollow because they like the coziness, the sense of security that comes with living in a hollow.

More than that, the decision to continue living in the mountains at this point in the 20th century is a conscious decision for almost all mountain people. Most of us have relatives living in Detroit or Cleveland or Baltimore or Houston or Dayton. Most of us have visited those places, and many of us have worked there. We know what big city living is all about, and we have consciously rejected it. We are mountaineers because we want to be—not because we are forced to be.

The same sentiment was turned against the TVA, which—for all it had done to improve the standard of living of the once miserably impoverished Tennessee Valley—was perceived as an autocratic machine out to remake the people's lives, a big utility so intent on getting coal for its great steam power generating plants that it was willing to ravage the hills of Appalachia through strip mining in the process. Gish had been one of those who originally wanted a TVA-like program, controlling natural resources, for areas like East Kentucky. But having viewed what TVA mining programs had done to the landscape in the '60s and early '70s, Gish said he was "almost glad we failed. If TVA could turn into such a destructive animal, an ARC program [controlling basic resources] could be just as if not more destructive."

Predictably, the same sentiments were turned against the efforts of some ARC and development district planners to create urban "growth centers," medium-sized urban centers that would provide economic, educational, and health services to the mountain fastnesses about them. The fear, once more, was that the mountain folk would be forced out of their beloved hollows. The ARC planners replied that they had no intention of forcing people out of the hills against their will, but that families which insisted on living in totally isolated locales could not expect the modern sanitary, health, and school facilities being installed in the growth center towns. It would be many decades, they argued, before there was enough government money to do that.

The argument of native culture versus economic progress, of self-reliance versus modern education and health and employment, of the pristine aboriginal form of life versus cultural homogenization, remains acute in only a few places in America—in Appalachia, in the Ozarks, among the Indians, among the native peoples of Alaska. In the end, the relentless forces of a national economy and of instant national communications will probably decide the case, for each of these peoples, in favor of the modernist, "progressive" side. But Americans would do well to know what they are losing in the process.

Appalachian Economy: Glimmerings of Recovery

Economists and federal planners have been watching carefully to see if their efforts would do something to stem the hemorrhage of Appalachia which assumed such frightening proportions in the 1950s. By the time the 1970 Census results were in, they professed to see some light at the end of the tunnel. The outmigration from Border State Appalachia had subsided from more than a million in the '50s to 531,000 in the '60s, and natural increase had actually made it possible for some counties of the region to register gains in total population. Among these areas were East Tennessee, benefiting (seemingly more every decade) from TVA, and western North Carolina, which was the locus of a booming tourist and second-home industry. Overall, the region's population inched forward by one half of one percent.

Not until the first years of the 1970s, however, did the demographers detect a clear turnaround in the Appalachian Border South. In just two years (1970 to 1972) the Appalachian counties of these five states grew by an average of 3.1 percent.* Dr. J. P. Pickard, chief demographer of the Appalachian Regional Commission, claimed that only 10 percent of the

---

* The new total for the Appalachian counties of the Border South States was 6,043,700 people. The breakdowns: Virginia 485,700, North Carolina 1,068,000, West Virginia 1,781,100, Kentucky 914,200, and Tennessee 1,797,700.

counties of Appalachia "continued to show a significant outmigration."

If Appalachia's long economic tailspin had been reversed, one could assign credit to a number of developments. Among these were (1) increased Social Security and black lung benefits for miners, keeping older residents from leaving; (2) the end of the draft, reductions in military force levels, and the return of the Viet Nam veterans; (3) the reduced supply of good-paying jobs, and housing, in the Northern cities; (4) proliferating retirement homes and recreation developments; and (5) a steady increase in the number of manufacturing jobs. A modest industrial expansion had been evident ever since the early 1960s, and by the early 1970s it was taking on impressive proportions.

Still, most of the manufacturing employment was concentrated in fields like textiles, apparel, leather and wood products, and rudimentary electrical equipment assembly—activities that characterize the early stages of industrial development. Coal mining brought in more income than all manufacturing in many of these Appalachian counties, a unique situation in the United States. The most impoverished area was East Kentucky, which by no accident was also the section with the most coal mining and the least manufacturing relative to the total population. By contrast, mining played the least important role in East Tennessee and western North Carolina, the two central Appalachian areas with the most diversified and extensive manufacturing.

The Appalachian Future

Viewing Appalachia from the vantage point of the mid-1970s, the age-old questions—the fate of the land and the fate of the people—seemed to hang in the balance as much as ever.

The land was endangered by the splurge of strip mining which might be countenanced in the name of coping with the country's energy shortage. Now was the time, the great coal companies said, to relax environmental standards in general, and restrictions on strip mining in particular, to get the quickest possible increase in production of Appalachia's coal reserves. The irony of that situation was that coal prices, along with the prices for all forms of energy, were rising rapidly, so that for the first time one could argue that there was ample money to do a much better job of restoring the land. By the same token, higher energy prices seemed to make feasible an expansion of underground mining with far better precautions for the safety of the miners. (An important caveat, however: although coal produces energy for about half the price of oil or natural gas, the utilities, which are the prime consumers of coal, often prefer oil or natural gas because they can pass the costs along to consumers and also avoid all the air quality problems involved in the burning of coal.) Since the United States' total coal reserves, some 193 billion tons, contain at least four times the energy of all the Arabian oil fields, it seems hard to imagine that the resource will not be used over the coming decades. The open questions in the mid-1970s were when, and how. Deep mining offered the least environmental hazards but required high capital outlays. Strip mining was preferred by the coal companies, but the amount of strippable coal is limited, and some of the attraction of stripping was removed in 1974 when Congress moved toward approval of legislation requiring the return of stripped lands to their approximate original contours, together with a number of other fairly costly environmental protections.

The fate of the common people of Appalachia remained wrapped up in the question of who would speak for them. Because of their intrinsic distrust of government, they had never learned to make local and state government a positive force for their own welfare. Even the politicians most willing to channel government aid into the mountains had been reluctant, over time, to lodge any real power in the hands of the people themselves. Organization of Appalachia's multitudinous poor white folk was forever deterred by their physical isolation—isolation from one state to another, from one county to another, even from one hollow to another—and because of the intrinsically withdrawn and suspicious nature of the people. Church mission groups went into the mountains but limited their nonspiritual activities to immediate needs like food and emergency medical care. The missions did give birth to settlement schools, which tried to overcome the inadequacies of the region's backward and overly politicized educational system; in the end, though, the settlement schools could help only marginally, because the mountain counties offered practically no jobs for educated Appalachian people.

The Appalachian counties had, of course, been a citadel of Border State Republicanism ever since the Civil War—a Lincolnesque Republicanism that abjured the racism of the Tidewater and the delta provinces and was built on the base of deep resentment of exploitation of the hill people by the ruling Democrats and corporate circles of states like Virginia, Tennessee, and Kentucky. But the Republican political cliques of the mountain counties were as prone to corruption as their Democratic counterparts and gradually lost any progressive hue they might once have had.

Appalachia was left with a scattering of groups, labeled as "radical" by the established powers, who were dedicated to transferring power from the economic oligarchies to the people. The seeds of this political rebellion lay in the Populist era, and more particularly in the epic fights for unionization of the coal mines, a struggle that cost many lives from the early part of this century down to World War II. The union struggle spawned a number of courageous mountaineer leaders and immortalized an outsider who came in to help them, Mother Jones, recalled for her lines: "Pray for the dead and fight like hell for the living." By the 1940s, however, the United Mine Workers' leadership made peace with the coal companies at the cost of the miners. Not until the 1960s did any type of "people's politics" seem to take root among the highlanders. The federal antipoverty effort played a major role in awakening the people's consciousness, and a number of former Appalachian Volunteers and VISTA workers returned to the hills to continue organizing work. A few mountaineers, distraught about bulldozers coming in to tear up their land for strip mining, risked their own bodies in the fight to preserve their land. All of this remained largely unfocused activity; as Ernie Mynatt, a native of Harlan, Kentucky, and near-legendary leader of Cincinnati's Appalachian ghetto, said in a New York *Times* interview: "It's a fact that we're years behind the blacks and the Latins. They've gotten together and forced the power structure to deal with them. But we just can't get organized. That's the way we are."

The truth of Mynatt's words seemed to be reflected in the death of organizations like the Congress for Appalachian Development and "Save Our Kentucky." But still, a newly awakened "Appalachian consciousness" seemed to be forming through the mountains. A new wave of interest in Appalachian studies was reported at universities throughout the area, and some of them (like Kentucky's Berea and Alice Lloyd Colleges) began intensive self-help projects for the mountaineers in their areas. A sharp reaction to outside exploitation was evidenced in the growth of the Black Lung Association, Miners for Democracy, and finally the reformers' successful fight for control of the United Mine Workers in the early 1970s. (The UMW story is reviewed in the West Virginia chapter of this book, where note is made of UMW president Arnold Miller's intent to make the UMW an activist force for progressive politics. An indication of how fast things were moving was that when I first interviewed Miller for this book in 1970, he was still working, as he had for 27 years, in a drift mine at Cabin Creek, West Virginia.)

Yet another indication of change was the appearance in 1970 of Appalachia's first public interest law firm, the Appalachian Research and Defense Fund, working in West Virginia and East Kentucky. In the East Tennessee hills, the Highlander Research and Education Center shifted its focus to the organizational problem of Appalachia's common people. Founded in Depression years by Myles Horton, a native Tennessee radical, the Highlander Center (then known as the Highlander Folk School) was first concerned with the labor union movement and then devoted its energies to civil rights problems in the '50s and '60s, conducting workshops for the white and black activists who were to become leading figures in the civil rights movement. This incurred the wrath of the Tennessee state government, which forced the school to close. It was reorganized under its present name and reopened in the mountains near Knoxville. Horton retired and the leadership passed to three dynamic young leaders—Mike Clark, a native North Carolinian who had been seasoned in work for a federal antipoverty campaign; James Branscome, who had come out of the Virginia mountains, worked for the Appalachian Regional Commission, and founded the abortive "Save Our Kentucky" movement; and Buck Maggard, a rough-spoken product "of the mines and industrial sweatshops of southeastern Kentucky." * Maggard had no college education, in contrast to Clark and Branscome, graduates of Berea

* According to an account by John Egerton and Frye Gaillard, "The Mountaineer Minority," in *Race Relations Reporter*, March 1974.

College. The new Highlander leaders were focusing their efforts on weekend workshops on such subjects as TVA and strip mining, Appalachian cultural heritage, mountain schools, and community-controlled health programs.

A startling radicalization came to the 56-year-old Council of the Southern Mountains, which had traditionally consisted of middle-aged educators, ministers, and social workers, interested principally in pastoral guidance and mountaineer arts and crafts. The CSM almost self-destructed, according to a report by North Carolina newsman Dwayne Walls in *South Today*, when a group of poor people and radical youth took it over in 1969, transforming it into a free-swinging, radical organization willing to tackle politics and race relations head on. In its new guise, the CSM fostered a new Black Appalachian Commission which sought to speak for the forgotten among the forgotten—the 1.3 million black people scattered throughout the mountains. After a rocky transition period, the CSM seemed to be settling down by 1973 into a liberal but fairly stable entity, working closely with the new UMW. At its annual conference at Emory, Virginia, the CSM called for "community unions of all poor and working people across the mountains in all areas, learning from each other how to build community." The CSM board provided an interesting list of the Appalachian groups that community unions should "learn from":

—from Citizens for Social and Economic Justice, a multi-issue approach to poor people's organizing and mutual support;
—from Save Our Cumberland Mountains (SOCM), a fight for coal and other wealth control through local taxes for people's development and services;
—like Model Valley, from which we can learn to build and to save our communities;
—from Peoples' Union, a new determination to resist and to stop the strippers together;
—from Mt. Rogers, Virginia, people resisting the Forest Service condemnation of their land;
—from East Kentucky Welfare Rights Organization (EKWRO) and the Mud Creek Health Project, how to control our own clinics and services;
—from West Virginia Welfare Rights Organization how to fight for health rights, consumer rights, strikers food stamps rights, as well as basic rights to income;
—from Black Lung Associations, how to fight for workers' compensation rights and for prevention of occupational slaughter;
—from Pikeville and Richlands hospital strikers, Charleston city workers strikers, and others how to strike and to support strikes with determination for real workers' contol.

(The list might well have included a number of other organizations of similar general purpose, including West Virginia's Disabled Miners and Widows Association, the Council on Religion in Appalachia, the Appalachian Group to Save the Land and People, the Appalachian Student Commission in Blacksburg, Virginia, and a young people's film-making group known as Appalshop.)

Not a single Border State governor, and no more than a handful of congressmen and state legislators from Appalachia were in substantial sympathy with these kinds of activities. "People's politics" was the antithesis of the way that Appalachia, America's prime economic and political colony of the 20th century, had always been run. Through a kept press or electoral manipulation, one felt, Appalachians' innate resistance to change might always be brought to bear against fundamental change in the old order.

But the fresh and independent voices in Appalachia were those of the youth—indeed, many talented young people, for the first time in generations, were electing to remain in the mountains and fight for the kind of society they would like to have. Appalachia was clearly in the process of bridging, however painfully, the gaps of ignorance and indifference that had kept it in bondage so long. One could confidently predict years of intense controversy ahead. A return to the old quiescence seemed quite impossible. But whether, once the process of economic modernization and political awakening had been completed, there would still be the fabled mountaineer of prickly independence, going his own way with little regard to the American mainstream—that was a question which no person, in the mid-1970s, could answer.

VIRGINIA

THE OLD DOMINION GROWS YOUNG

DOUGLAS SOUTHALL FREEMAN, describing the spirit of Virginia in the introduction to the American Guide Series (WPA) volume on the state in 1940, painted a picture of the Old Dominion which illustrates quite vividly—read in the 1970s—the sweep of change that has come over this state in a single generation.

In the Virginia of his time, Freeman wrote, life itself had a different tempo from the nervous *accelerando* of the Northeast:

Life is more leisured. . . . Human relations are somewhat more intimate. . . . Everywhere the dark laughter of the Negro is to be heard. Old houses outnumber modern. . . . From north to south, along the coastal plain, the scenery and the people change scarcely at all. . . .

The elders seldom talk fifteen minutes without some reference to the War between the States. There is a deliberate cult of the past. . . . All eastern Virginians are Shintoists under the skin. Genealogy makes history personal to them in terms of family. Kinship to the eighth degree usually is recognized. There are classes within castes. . . .

By hundreds of thousands, Virginians have gone into other states, but those who have remained in the Old Dominion are of the same stock. . . .

Many rural communities are depressed. Virginia farmers by tens of thousands still seek pathetically to eke a living from eroded or starved land. . . .

Politically, the ominous conditions in Virginia are the gradual atrophy of local self-government, the failure of well-educated, unselfish men and women to partici-pate actively in public service, and the abstention of tens of thousands from the exercise of the franchise. . . .

In 1949 V. O. Key, in his classic book on *Southern Politics*, would call Virginia "a political museum piece." It still was, but Key was writing in the calm before the storm. The fact is that the New Deal and war years set in motion a chain of events—due to climax in the 1960s—that would urbanize Virginia in a few short years, bring in hundreds of thousands of immigrants from other states, shift the commonwealth from controlled to chaotic pol-itics, undermine the authority of the old families, and create the most affluent and open society in the state's history. In the process, the psychological wall of isolation that Virginia had thrown up about itself at the end of Re-construction would be demolished. Now in fact as well as in law, Virginia would rejoin the Union. The commonwealth would also come to share the nation's common problems, especially those of suburbs cannibalizing the land on which they grow, and of environmental quality. It would be a younger, more dynamic, more innovative Virginia than at any time since the late 18th century, when it was the wellspring of a nation. In time Virginians might be able to put behind them the nasty implications of H. L. Mencken's remark that Virginia was the mother of Presidents that hadn't been pregnant in a hundred years. (No likely candidates were in sight at this writing in 1974, however; in fact, the stature of Virginians active in national politics was generally uninspiring, in contrast to the new vitality in state and local government.)

Yet despite all the changes, some things remained constant in Vir-ginia. One certainly found here, in measure rarely equaled in the U.S., pride in state. To be a *born* Virginian remained a special badge of honor in the Old Dominion. Reverence for the past, and for ancestors, was still apparent, albeit in less cloying doses. And one still found an unusual dedication to the principle of integrity in government (a refreshing note in the America of the early 1970s).

What was new in the philosophy of government was a much more careful balance between the rights of the citizen and the greater society than had been apparent throughout Virginia's Civil War century, when the commonwealth had often let the individual suffer at the hands of the col-lectivity. But in its 1971 constitution, Virginia was cautiously righting the balance, juxtaposing rights and responsibilities, the rule of law and the prin-ciples of due process which protect the individual. This section of the revised bill of rights, read with care, speaks volumes about the unique character and explicit values of Virginians, past and present:

That no free government, nor the blessings of liberty, can be preserved to any people but by a firm adherence to justice, moderation, temperance, frugality, and virtue; by frequent recurrence to fundamental principles; and by the recognition by all citizens that they have duties as well as rights, and that such rights cannot be enjoyed save in a society where the law is respected and due process is observed.

(In fact, one of the constitution writers reminded me, the language through the second semicolon was George Mason's of 1776, and what followed was the 1971 addition—the heritage of the Enlightenment fused with a Virginian view of the late 20th century.)

The First Three Centuries: Salient Trends

The Virginia envisaged in the royal charter of 1606 was continental in scope: its eastern boundary was the Atlantic; the northern bound within the territory that would one day become Pennsylvania, its southern limit on the approximate latitude of Columbia, South Carolina, its western bound the Pacific Ocean. In time, these boundaries would shrink drastically to produce a state of a modest 40,817 square miles, less than 35 other states. But over the course of history Virginia established its role as "the mother of states"; its progeny included, among others, Kentucky and Tennessee, the first commonwealths west of the Appalachian barrier, and later West Virginia, cut from the Old Dominion's established borders at the time of the Civil War. In population, in economic power, and most vitally as the generator of the ideas of independence and human rights and nationhood, Virginia was preeminent in America from the moment of its settlement until well into the 19th century.

The fascinating detail of the first settlement at Jamestown in 1607 and the development of Virginia society over the years we must leave to the historians—who, though they have slighted many American states, have treated Virginia with meticulous detail and devoted care.* Our own overview of Virginia in modern times requires, however, a glimpse back through history at the events and movements which shaped this state of particularly deep historic consciousness and tradition.

Virginia's first century, the 17th, Jean Gottmann observed, was the era of the Tidewater. The settlers found four major rivers flowing into the Chesapeake Bay in broad estuaries—the Potomac, the York, the James, and the Rappahannock. They cut the new colony's coastal plain into three strips or "necks," and it was along these that the first settlements and the start of the Old Dominion's great plantations took place. Hunger, disease, and Indian raids took an incredible toll of the first colonists,† in part because

---

    * One of the best books of modern vintage is Virginius Dabney's *The New Dominion,* written by a native with an intensely pro-Virginian point of view. Another, by an insightful outsider, is Jean Gottmann's *Virginia in Our Century.* Gottmann, a Frenchman, was commissioned to study Virginia by philanthropist Paul Mellon. His book is a splendid economic-geographic interpretation that reaches, its title notwithstanding, back to the earliest years.

    † The most gruesome clash with the Indians was Opechancanough's Massacre in 1622, which took the lives of hundreds of colonists. The massacre brought to an abrupt halt work then in progress on what would have been the first college in the colonies, a school for Indians at Henricopolis (near modern Richmond).

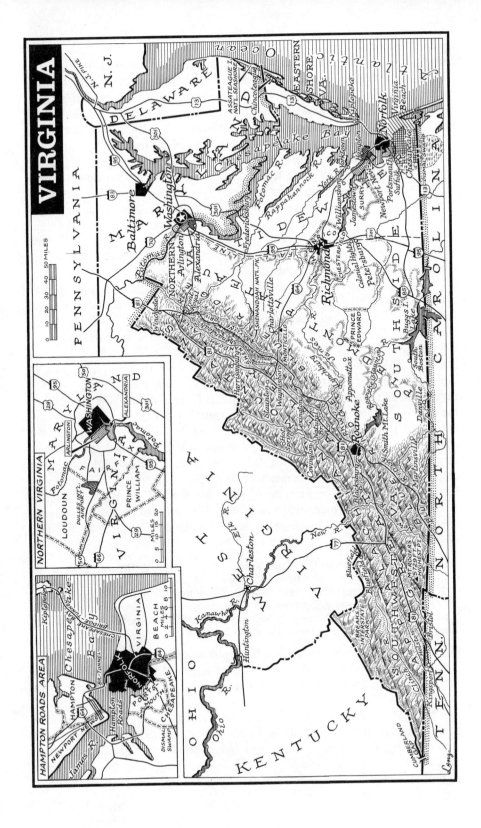

they had in their number so many gentlemen and noblemen of distinguished families, who lacked the practical skills of the artisan or a capacity to work by the sweat of their brow. Before long the immigrant ships contained great quantities of practical working men of more humble origins, many of them indentured servants. But the flow of the "finer" folk—the gentry of the new colony—continued for many years, and set an indelible mark on Virginia. The 1640s brought the founding patriarchs of the Lee, Carter, and Randolph dynasties; about 1670 William Byrd, the first Virginian of that famed family, arrived on the shores of the Chesapeake. (Byrd's grandfather, Thomas Stegg, had come in the 1630s.) Some of the other famous families whose first members arrived in this century were the Masons, Harrisons, Pages, Fitzhughs, Wormeleys, Beverlys, and Nelsons. Virginius Dabney wrote: "As an example of how a single marriage involving such families could affect the life of the colony, the commonwealth and the nation, consider the direct descendants of William Randolph of 'Turkey Island' and Mary Isham of 'Bermuda Hundred,' who were wed in the middle of the 1670s. The list includes Thomas Jefferson, John Marshall, and Robert E. Lee, not to mention 'Light-Horse Harry' Lee, Edmund Randolph, Peyton Randolph, and John Randolph of Roanoke."

The whites were not the only new settlers of 17th-century Virginia. A Dutch man-of-war in 1619 discharged the first black men—20 in number; they came as indentured servants, but 42 years later slavery was legalized in the colony. White indentured servants outnumbered the blacks several times over until the early 1700s, but a fateful trend had begun. These were the golden years of the great Virginia plantations, which depended for economic survival on a steady and dependable flow of slave labor to tend their great crop: tobacco. John Rolfe, secretary of the colony and the husband of Pocahontas, had introduced cultivation of the "joviall weed" in Virginia as early as 1612. The long-term consequences, as with the introduction of slavery, were to be momentous. As Joseph C. Robert wrote in *The Story of Tobacco in America*:

> The staple guaranteed the permanence of the Virginia settlement; created the pattern of the Southern plantation; encouraged the introduction of Negro slavery, then softened the institution; begot an immortal group of colonial leaders; strained the bonds between mother country and Chesapeake colonies; burdened the diplomacy of the post-Revolutionary period; promoted the Louisiana Purchase; and, after the Civil War, helped create the New South.

(Of the medical effects, much has been proven in modern times, but King James had the right idea when, in 1604, he declared tobacco "loathsome to the eye, hateful to the nose, harmful to the brain, . . . dangerous to the lungs.")

Many other events shaped Virginia in its first century, but we may settle for three of special significance. In 1619, in the same year the first blacks touched Virginia soil, Virginians also inaugurated their grand experiment with representative democracy as the house of burgesses, the first democratically elected legislative body of the New World, convened for the first time. In the 1670s Nathaniel Bacon led a rebellion against the Crown's governor, Sir William Berkeley—the first organized and violent resistance to British rule in America. In the same years, the first successful explorations of the land beyond the Blue Ridge, and onto the Allegheny Plateau, began to take place.

In 1700 Virginia began her golden century. It was the century in which her sons would produce some of the most vital statements of human liberty in the history of the world—the Declaration of Independence and the Virginia Statute for Religious Freedom, both from Jefferson's hand, and Patrick Henry's "liberty or death" speech.* It was the time that her George Washington would lead the American Revolution and become the first of an illustrious line of Virginian Presidents. It was the century of the Constitution of the United States, to which so many Virginians contributed, and in particular James Madison. And it was the century in which Virginia would people the opening American "West" in Tennessee, Kentucky, the Northwest Territories, and beyond. Within these 100 years, the population of Virginia would expand from some 72,000 to 880,000.

Yet even in 1700, Virginia had already established a mode of living that would influence its life for more than two centuries to come and eventually diminish its importance in American life. For while the settlers of New England and the other colonies to the North were already establishing towns and cities of substantial import, Virginia had opted for a pattern of widely scattered settlement, consonant with a plantation economy. The consequences of this were many. The plantation had a life of its own, its master a person of unchallenged authority in his own domain. This fostered an aristocratic society, not the more democratic mode of New Englanders in their towns and cities. It discouraged education for the masses, because people lived too far apart for many to attend schools, and the plantation owners could afford private tutors for their own offspring. Education, except for the favored few, would remain a poor stepchild in Virginia until well into the 20th century. Finally, the plantation pattern made Virginia a city of rural residence, not cities. This would cast the mold of life for Virginians, and their politics, straight down to the years after World War II. It was not accidental that the fabled Byrd political organization crumbled not long after urbanization came to Virginia in an important way.

There was, of course, some growth of towns in the 18th century. Jamestown, the first capital, had burned in 1698, and the seat of government was transferred to "Middle Plantation," or Williamsburg, as it came to be called, where the College of William and Mary had been founded in the early 1690s. Williamsburg became a vital center of colonial life in the succeeding

---

* That is only a partial list. To it one can add James Madison's "Memorial and Remonstrance," a classic statement on church and state that the modern-day Supreme Court has often looked to as illustrative of the origins and meanings of the First Amendment. (Madison also moved the original amendments to the Federal Constitution—the Bill of Rights—in the First Congress in 1789.) In addition, the Virginia Constitution of 1776, largely the work of George Mason, was composed when written constitutions in their modern sense were virtually unknown, and thus stands as a significant document in western constitutional development.

decades—though nothing to rival Charleston or Savannah, not to mention the northern cities. But Williamsburg, from a high of about 2,000 people in 1779, dwindled when the capital was transferred to Richmond during the Revolutionary War. (For a century and a half Williamsburg would slumber on as a shopping town for the surrounding country, disturbed only by a fierce battle of the Civil War. Then, starting in 1926, John D. Rockefeller made possible the magnificent Colonial restoration known to so many million Americans.) The 18th century saw the founding of most of Virginia's important cities—Richmond, Roanoke, Staunton, Petersburg, Lynchburg, and Jefferson's Charlottesville; in the same years the Tidewater cities of Norfolk, Portsmouth, and Alexandria received their first significant settlement. But by 1800, the sum total of population in all these towns was only 2.5 percent of the state population, and even at the start of our century, the major cities of Virginia made up only 15 percent of the state total.

The history of 18th-century Virginia was one of constant economic and territorial expansion and frustration with the mother country leading to revolution and independence. Plantations spread from the Tidewater across the Piedmont section of the state's center. Into the Valley of Virginia beyond the Blue Ridge poured thousands of Germans and Scotch-Irish—merchants, yeomen, and peasants—to plant the roots of their farming society. In Tidewater and the Piedmont, the plantation owners built their great Georgian colonial homes; nearby were the small brick or frame houses of the poor white; and increasingly, there were slaves—9 percent of the population in 1700, 25 percent in 1715, 40 percent by the middle of the century. The French and Indian War, begun in 1754, provided a seminar for the Revolution and brought George Washington his first military commands. And the familiar story of increased British economic repression of Virginia and the other colonies, centered on the issue of "taxation without representation," fed the sparks of rebellion that would erupt in the American Revolution in the 1770s.

No historian has ever provided a satisfactory explanation of how it came to be that Virginia produced in the last half of the 18th century the core of leaders who would lead the colonies to independence, fight the successful Revolutionary War, write the Constitution, and provide the Presidents of the United States for 32 of its first 36 years. "Only a political miracle—or an act of God—placed those 10 or 12 monumental leaders there," former Senator William B. Spong commented. "How could Thomas Jefferson, James Madison, and George Mason be at the same place at the same time in history with Patrick Henry, James Monroe, Edmund Pendleton, Richard Henry Lee, John Marshall—and George Washington? Unquestionably they developed each other, which cumulatively gave you the political genius which resulted. But I don't see how you can account for their being there."

The individual stories of these fabulous men are too familiar to require a retelling here. Yet it is interesting to note how greatly they differed, once the Revolution was won, in their chosen direction for Virginia and America.

James Madison, for instance, took such a leading role in the Philadelphia convention of 1787 that he was called the "father of the Constitution." Subsequently he co-authored, with Alexander Hamilton and John Jay, the *Federalist Papers* in support of the new document. Yet when Madison championed ratification in Virginia, he found himself opposed by Patrick Henry, the great spokesman for liberty and erstwhile ally of Madison in fighting British rule. Henry thought the Constitution would usurp the rights of Virginia, and he was against it: "Old as I am . . . I may yet have the appellation of 'rebel.' . . . As this government [the Constitution] stands, I despise and abhor it. The question turns on that poor little thing—the expression We the 'people' instead of the 'states.' I see the awful immensity . . . with which it is pregnant." In terms of the power the Constitution gave the national government, Henry was prescient. Many Virginians helped to make a nation of the United States, but two above all: George Washington, its first President, a living symbol of the national unity, and John Marshall, Chief Justice from 1801 to 1835, who interpreted the Constitution to be the supreme law of the land. Marshall wrote in one of his great opinions: "The constitution and laws of a state, so far as they are repugnant to the Constitution and laws of the United States, are absolutely void." That was precisely what Patrick Henry had feared.

What Henry could not have imagined was that the Constitution, in time, would become the bulwark of individual freedom in America, often by its very power to supersede state laws. And for that, another Virginian could take much of the credit. George Mason had been an outstanding member of the Constitutional Convention, but in an act of immense political courage he had refused to sign the final document because it lacked specific guarantees for individual rights. But Mason returned to Virginia and argued so eloquently at the ratification convention for basic amendments that the agreement was made to amend the new Constitution to insert what would become the Bill of Rights—provisions similar to the Virginia Declaration of Rights which Mason had written himself in 1776. Those first ten amendments to the Constitution were important enough in themselves, but they also created the precedent for the later right-granting amendments, the 14th in particular, which would revolutionize the life of Virginia and all the Southland in the 20th century.

Historians have been particularly fascinated by the contrast between Jefferson, America's man of the Enlightenment, and his shrill critic, Congressman and Senator John Randolph of Roanoke. A man of biting phrase and a master orator of his time, Randolph was so conservative that he opposed the War of 1812, all internal improvements at federal expense, the Missouri Compromise, and the admission of *any* new states to the Union. His most remembered phrase: "I am an aristocrat. I love liberty. I hate equality." Historian Marshall Fishwick observed: "Haughty John Randolph saw that the whole South, threatened by military democracy and finance capitalism, was in what John C. Calhoun called 'a period of transition.' . . . The Jeffersonian emphasis on equality and the natural goodness of man infuriated him. . . . Randolph fought change; Jefferson welcomed it. Randolph wanted to give the people order; Jefferson, light. It is hard to believe that the pessimism of Roanoke and the optimism of Monticello were products of the same society, indeed the same intermarried family—but they were."

Jefferson was deeply committed to education, and in 1825 the doors of the University of Virginia—described by one historian as "the noblest work of Jefferson's life"—opened at Charlottesville. But on the 50th anniversary of the Declaration of Independence, July 4, 1826, Jefferson died at his beloved Monticello. And with his passing, the lights of creativity began to flicker out in the Old Dominion.

Virginia's unhappy decline is illustrated best by its dereliction in the schooling of its young.* Up to the Civil War (indeed, until the Reconstruction era), the legislature obdurately refused to establish a system of state-supported public schools. The shocking results were apparent in the Census of 1840, which showed that one out of every 12 white Virginians was illiterate, compared to one in 164 in Massachusetts, one to 92 in Ohio, and one to 49 in Pennsylvania. A statewide convention pressing the losing cause of public schools declared in 1841 that "22,000 poor children and an indefinite number of thousands who are not poor, do not attend school at all." Those who did attend, the convention said, often did so "in miserable huts scarcely more comfortable than those you provide for your cattle." Quality education, provided largely through tutors, remained the luxury of the few. Virginians' "failure to maintain their 18th century leadership in the nation," Jean Gottmann had written, "was to a large extent due to the feeble numbers of their educated elite."

Inexorably, the locus of power and influence shifted across the Blue Ridge and farther west. The Tidewater and Piedmont, mired in an inefficient plantation and slave economy, plagued by exhausted soil because of the intensive cultivation of tobacco, and offering little in the way of education, held little promise for the aspiring classes of yeomen and merchants. By 1850 the state had many more residents west of the Blue Ridge than to its east, and there were some 388,000 born Virginians living outside the commonwealth, many of them in such states as Kentucky and Tennessee. As early as the 1820s, the national leadership emanating from the Border States came from those transmontane areas, in the hands of such men as Andrew Jackson and Henry Clay. (Clay was a born Virginian, but Jackson was not —an exception to the rule of the times. According to author Park Rouse, Jr., during a 150-year span beginning in 1774, "at least 329 men born within Virginia's present boundaries served other states as delegates to the Continental Congress, United States Senators, and Representatives in Congress."

* This was no accident, when one recalls Governor Berkeley's statement of 1671: "I thank God there are no free schools nor printing [in Virginia], and I hope we shall not have these [for] a hundred years; for learning has brought disobedience, and heresy and sects into the world, and printing has divulged them, and libels against the best government. God keep us from both!" In 1779 Jefferson drafted a Bill for the More General Diffusion of Knowledge which the General Assembly refused to adopt, thus delaying until 1870 the creation of a statewide school system.

Among these were the two great figures of early Texas history, Sam Houston and Stephen Austin.)

Sectional conflicts came to dominate Virginia's politics in the early 19th century, with the Tidewater and Piedmont refusing the demands of the western areas for manumission of slaves, universal manhood suffrage, internal improvements, and legislative reapportionment. The east also resisted an east-west canal system (like New York's Erie Canal), and dawdled when the era of the railroads dawned, leaving the leadership to such competitors as Baltimore and Charleston. The elite continued their gracious lives in eastern Virginia's plantations, seemingly unaware of the vital economic tides of the exuberantly growing nation around them. In the words of Thomas J. Wertenbaker, the historian of Norfolk: "The period for internal improvements was for many states and cities marked by glorious success, by expanding trade, growing wealth, increasing population. For Virginia, . . . it was a time of wasted opportunities and bitter disappointment. The proud Old Dominion, once the undisputed leader in the Union, saw one state after another pass her in all that makes for influence and power."

The Census figures seemed to bear out the point: Until 1820, Virginia had more people than any other state. But in that year's Census she dropped behind New York in population; within four decades Pennsylvania, Ohio, and Illinois would outstrip her too. In 1800, 16.7 percent of the nation's population lived in Virginia; by 1860, the figure had declined to 5.1 percent. In the same years the commonwealth's representation in the United States House dipped from 22 seats out of 142 to just 10 out of an expanded chamber of 243 seats.*

Virginia's failure to come to grips with the issue of slavery was another reason for her decline. Emancipation had been favored by almost all the great Revolutionary period leaders, including Washington, Jefferson, Madison, Mason, and Henry, though a precondition they set down was that a way be found to remove all black people from the commonwealth. But the manpower needs of the plantations, as well as the vastly profitable sale of Virginia slaves to the growing cotton states in the early 19th century, worked against any ideas of manumission. Then there were the frightening slave revolts, highlighted by Gabriel's Insurrection at Richmond in 1800 and Nat Turner's bloody insurrection in the southeastern corner of the state in 1831. Virginians took deep umbrage at the preachings of the northern Abolitionists; in fact by statute they forbade any member of the Abolition Society to enter the state.

As the 1860s approached, Virginia tried to take a "moderate" course, deploring the extremism of the Southern "fire-eaters" on one hand while trying to hold the Union together on the other. History was to show, of course, that slavery was not an issue that could be "moderated," nor could the gut

---

* Virginia's House apportionment has hovered around 10 seats ever since, in a chamber (since 1912) of 435 seats. In the 1970 Census, she had 2.3 percent of the national population, just above her low point of 2.0 percent, recorded in 1930 and 1940.

question of secession. The South Carolinian John C. Calhoun and his secessionist disciples became the region's most powerful leaders, and Virginians seemed to be struck mute with their middling position. The moderates' course was further undercut by John Brown's raid on Harper's Ferry in 1859 (an episode further discussed in our West Virginia chapter).

When the fateful 1860s dawned, Virginians still opposed secession. Indeed, Colonel Robert E. Lee wrote to his son in January 1861: "I can anticipate no greater calamity for the country than a dissolution of the Union." But Robert Lee, sadly, was not the towering and influential figure before the war that he was to be in it. The die for secession was cast when President Lincoln, after the bombardment of Fort Sumter, called for 75,000 volunteers to put down the rebellion. Virginia was not willing to "coerce a sister state," and a convention at Richmond quickly voted for secession, 88 to 55. Rober E. Lee, after turning down the command of the United States Army, reluctantly decided his chief obligation was to Virginia. His genius and honorable conduct as general of the Army of Northern Virginia need no embellishment here.

Four bloody years would intervene before Appomattox, and 15,000 of the 170,000 Virginian men who fought would lie beneath the sod at Manassas, Sharpsburg, Fredericksburg, Chancellorsville, and the many other battle sites within and without the state. As a result of the conflict, Virginia lost its westernmost territory, the new state of West Virginia, and all its slave property (490,865 souls in 1860). But that was not the worst of it. As Gottmann wrote:

> The destruction of the territory of Virginia was frightful, chiefly because of its geographical position. Virginia was the advanced front of the Confederacy facing North, and its proximity to Washington and to such important areas as Maryland and Pennsylvania made it imperative for the South to hold Virginia and for Federal strategy to endeavor to control the area. The capital of the Confederacy was set up in Richmond for both symbolic and political reasons rooted in the history and geography of the Old Dominion. In no other part of the South were the campaigns so long, so frequent, so decisive. . . . The belligerent armies [were] on the march again and again through the same areas, chiefly in the Shenandoah Valley and the Piedmont.

Ravaged by Union General Philip Sheridan's troops, much of the lovely Shenandoah Valley lay in utter desolation. In the words of historian M. P. Andrews, "Stretch upon stretch of the great battle area in eastern Virginia appeared to be entirely deserted by human beings. . . . Returning soldiers found fences burned, cattle and domestic animals gone, with outbuildings and even farm implements destroyed. The counties not directly in the path of the contending armies had suffered from the raids of cavalry detachments bent on errant destruction."

For many months after the end of hostilities and the perceived "Götterdämmerung" of Union victory, Virginians suffered immense depression; many, indeed, fled the state or the country, against the advice of Lee and other cooler heads who knew how desperately able manpower would be needed to rebuild a commonwealth that had lost so much of its treasure, physical and human.*

For five years Virginia had to wait for readmission to the Union, existing under the ignominious title of Military District Number One. The Reconstruction period brought the times of carpetbaggers and scalawags, Northern- and black-dominated government, and fierce white resistance (White League, Ku Klux Klan) typical of the rest of the Confederacy—though the excesses on both sides were less in Virginia than in the Deep South States. The Reconstruction-era constitution did make one great breakthrough for Virginians, by requiring a statewide system of public schools, available to whites and blacks on an equal basis. The result was an increase in the number of children in school from a base of about 60,000 to 184,000 by 1875 and 343,000 in 1891.

Not until the 1960s, however, would Virginia begin to make an investment in primary and secondary education even close to the United States average. That failure can be traced to two roots—Virginia's lingering elitist approach to education and, just as important, the grim financial problems the commonwealth faced in the Reconstruction years. Mired in poverty and her economy in ruins as a result of the war, Virginia was ill equipped to deal with a massive debt it had incurred to finance canals, railroads, and turnpikes in the prewar years. By 1870 the debt, with interest, had mounted to $45 million, and the interest on it alone ($2.7 million a year) was more than the total state budget in many prewar years. Radical Republican control of the state government had been terminated in the 1869 elections, and a coalition dominated by Conservatives (former Democrats and Whigs, soon to become known as Bourbons) came to power and quickly passed a funding act requiring the state to pay off two-thirds of its old debt.† The idea was that debt repayment must come first to maintain the unsullied honor and essential credit of Virginia, even if the repayment required drastic underfinancing of the schools and other state functions to satisfy the demands of out-of-state creditors. Historians point out that many of the Conservatives, together with their allies in the banking and railroad industries, also stood to benefit personally from the funding act and accompanying legislation.

The funding act placed such a burden on the state, however, that a diminutive and eccentric former Confederate general of rare political skills, William Mahone, successfully founded a Readjuster party made up of Republicans, Negroes, and the impoverished small farmers. The Readjusters took control of the state for a few years in the 1880s, giving the Republican party a viability it enjoyed in few states of the postbellum South. Over the outraged opposition of the Bourbons—one of whose leaders had said he would rather see Virginia burn every one of her schoolhouses than to see her repudiate her debt—a downward readjustment of the debt was voted.

---

* Even to this day, Virginia continues to pay some price for its involvement with the Confederacy. In 1973—108 years after the end of the conflict—the commonwealth was still paying pensions to 18 widows and 594 daughters of Confederate soldiers and sailors.

† The theory was that West Virginia would pay the other third.

School expenditures were increased, taxes on corporations raised to more adequate levels, and in a political nod to the Readjusters' black support, the infamous whipping post was abolished.

The Conservatives, who had now adopted the Democratic party as their vehicle, used the race issue to return to power in the mid-1880s. And while they did not seek to undo the Readjusters' reforms, they started to lay the groundwork for permanent political power by rejiggering the election machinery to put it in Democratic hands. The centerpiece of their work was the state constitution, written in a 1901–02 convention. A new charter for the state, advocates had long argued, was needed to correct the unconscionable vote buying and assorted forms of political thievery that had come to mark the commonwealth's elections. But a related and even more important motive was to take the vote away from the black man. Carter Glass, a leading advocate of a new constitution and later a United States Senator, had called Negro enfranchisement "a crime to begin with and a wretched failure to the end." The new constitution instituted a poll tax and literacy tests for registration and provided a legal underwriting for rigid racial separation in the schools. That the document did its work well was illustrated by an immediate shrinkage in the number of registered Negroes from 147,000 to 21,000. Thousands of ill-educated whites, many of them Republicans in the state's western mountains, were also deprived of their right to vote. The total vote for President in 1904 would be only slightly more than half what it had been in 1900. The sharply curtailed electorate, open to easy control by the Democratic organization, would remain a fixture of Virginia politics for 60 years.

In fact, election-day skulduggery did decline sharply under the 1902 constitution. But the constitution itself was a piece of skulduggery, because—contrary to the clear promises of Glass and the legal call for a convention—the document was not submitted to the people for ratification, out of fear that they might reject it. In return for political security, the organization Democrats had subverted democracy and effectively repealed the 14th and 15th Amendments in their application to the Old Dominion.

The Byrd Organization: Rise, Dominion, and Fall

The birth of the Democratic organization with which the name of Harry F. Byrd would become synonymous can be traced back to the election of Thomas S. Martin as U.S. Senator in 1893. Oddly enough, Martin was not one of Virginia's natural-born aristocracy but rather a shrewd railroad lawyer. The 1893 election, according to an account by James Reichley, was "marked by charges of bribery and a lavish expenditure of railroad funds"—a phenomenon prevalent in Virginia since the first postbellum years.

Martin stayed in the Senate and commanded the organization until his death in 1919, aided by such figures as Carter Glass. A brief period of collective leadership ensued, ended when a young apple grower and state senator from the Shenandoah Valley, Harry F. Byrd, challenged the established powers and won election as governor.

Byrd represented a continuity in Virginia public life in two important respects. The first, of course, was familial. We spoke earlier of the first William Byrd's arrival in the colony in 1670. Alden Hatch in *The Byrds of Virginia* breaks down the history of the remarkable family dynasty into several parts. In the first era, 1670–1777, the Byrds—William I, William II, and William III—left a deep imprint on the colony's growth, rising to positions of great wealth in the process. But as the era approached its end, William III was in desperate financial straits and found his unfailing allegiance to the crown had alienated his friends of the Revolutionary period. On January 1, 1777, he took his own life.

For nearly a century and a half thereafter, the Byrds drifted into relative obscurity. Thomas Taylor Byrd, a son of William III, settled on 1,000 acres in the Shenandoah Valley and eventually one of his descendants, Richard Evelyn Byrd, overcame the poverty of his early life to become a successful newspaper publisher in Winchester and speaker of the House of Delegates. One of his sons was Rear Admiral Richard Evelyn Byrd, Jr., who achieved world renown for his explorations of the Arctic and Antarctic. Another was Harry Byrd, who as a boy of 15 had left school to help salvage his father's newspaper, then in such dire financial straits that young Harry had to arrange to have the newsprint for each day's edition delivered on the day of publication, paying cash for it. Within five years, he had made the paper profitable and had begun to branch out into the apple orchard business around Winchester—an activity that would lead to the world's largest one-family apple growing, packing, and processing operation. Thus a hallmark of the Byrd era in Virginia, according to J. Harvie Wilkinson III,* was to be a "cash-drawer frugality."

In like fashion, the financial hardships of the Byrd family paralleled those of Virginia during the years that it was laboring to free itself of the staggering Civil War debt. From this came an abhorrence of public debt that Byrd reflected in his real debut in statewide politics—a campaign to defeat a $50 million bond issue for the construction of highways. The "establishment" of the time (1923) favored the bond issue, but farmers feared that they would bear the brunt of paying off the debts, just as they had been encumbered by the 19th-century debt payment. For the first but not the last time, Harry Byrd spoke up for a "pay-as-you-go" approach in Virginia. And the bond issue, in a popular referendum, was decisively defeated.

Two years later, running as something of an insurgent candidate, Harry Byrd was elected governor of Virginia, and his long dominion began in earnest.

Friend and foe agree that Byrd was the most outstanding governor Virginia had had—or was to have—for many years. A rambling structure of al-

* In his excellent book, *Harry Byrd and the Changing Face of Virginia Politics,* 1945–1966.

most 100 bureaus, boards, and departments, largely independent of the governor, had previously directed the state's affairs; under Byrd it was all consolidated into fourteen departments headed by his appointees and responsible to him. And the number of statewide elective offices was reduced from seven to three—all in accordance with the maxim of Woodrow Wilson, often quoted by Byrd, that the most simplified and visible government was the best.

On the fiscal front, Byrd put "pay-as-you-go" into practice and managed to convert a million-dollar state deficit to a generous surplus by the time he left office in 1930. He consistently favored farmers in tax matters, abolishing the state tax on land. To force lower consumer rates and prices, according to Virginius Dabney, Byrd "moved with great effectiveness against certain corporations, notably the oil companies and the Virginia subsidiary of the American Telephone and Telegraph Company." Byrd also promoted rural electrification, conservation, and the tourist trade, and sponsored the first law in any state to make all members of a lynch mob subject to murder charges. As newspaperman Guy Friddell later wrote, Byrd "had a whole state to set straight. He rushed Virginia, as breathless as a girl going to her first ball, into the 20th century. He gave the Old Dominion a new deal before the New Deal."

Byrd's regime as governor was virtually free of corruption, and so it was to be during the following decades of his organization's rule—an exceptional record of unblemished integrity in American politics, and an astounding phenomenon in the Border States. Even hostile observers, like William Manchester in a 1952 article in *Harper's Magazine*, characterized the organization as "forthright, incorrupt, and almost offensively virtuous." Bribery of legislators and low deals with contractors, Manchester wrote, were virtually "unheard of" among the gentry who ran the Byrd organization.

The long dominion of the Byrd organization was made possible in part by a set of ingenious institutional relationships. A state compensation board, established in 1934, fixed the salaries and office budgets for the principal county officials across the state, and for years it was headed by E. R. Combs, Byrd's most powerful associate. Combs also served at times as clerk of the state senate and Democratic National Committeeman. Opponents said the compensation board used its power of the purse to punish any recalcitrant local officials, but generally that power did not need to be exercised. As one observer told V. O. Key in the late 1940s, the mere fact of the power in Combs' hands kept local officials in "an understanding and sympathetic frame of mind." Until his retirement in 1950, Combs was "the man to see" for any young Democrat hopeful of running for office in the state.

At the county level, the organization's strength was anchored in its control of the major elected officials. The circuit court clerk, with an eight-year term, was often the most powerful local figure, but even his authority was often overshadowed by the circuit judge, who had appointive power over the persons running the local election machinery. The organization controlled the selection of circuit judges absolutely, because they were chosen by the state legislature. Thus even in Republican or anti-organization areas, the Byrd clique had a powerful voice.

Arm-twisting and brute use of patronage power, however, were not the secret of the Byrd machine's success. "What has been overlooked," Harvie Wilkinson wrote, "was the remarkable similarity of viewpoint among organization members, which, in the long run, unified them far more effectively and fundamentally than any pressure or patronage tactics ever could have." John S. Battle, the organization's candidate for governor in 1959, said: "As for this so-called iniquitous [Byrd] machine, it is nothing more or less than a loosely knit group of Virginians . . . who usually think alike, who are supremely interested in giving Virginia good government and good public servants, and they usually act together." "It's like a club," Governor J. Lindsay Almond once said, "except it has no bylaws, constitution, or dues. It's a loosely knit association, you might say, between men who share the philosophy of Senator Byrd."

And that philosophy included a love for balanced budgets, loyalty to the cause of states' rights, an aversion to "wild federal spending," a Jeffersonian-like dedication to rural dominance, and a determination among the white organization cadres to maintain the racial status quo in the Old Dominion. It was significant that the bulwarks of Byrd organization support were in the counties and independent cities with a large Negro population—in an era when few Negroes voted, but when the whites thought they had reason to fear what might happen if they did. Most of these biracial counties were centered in Southside and Piedmont Virginia, which turned in overwhelming margins for Byrd machine candidates in each election. But at least until the era of "massive resistance" in the late 1950s, when it felt its own power threatened, the organization brooked no resort to crude, vocalized racism in campaigns. To be considered for high office, Key noted, one had to enjoy relatively high social status. "In a word, politics in Virginia is reserved to those who can qualify as gentlemen. Rabble-rousing and Negro-baiting capacities, which in Georgia or Mississippi could be a great political asset, simply mark a person as one not of the manner born."

While virtually every organization candidate for governor hailed from the rural areas—usually Southside Virginia—and adhered to Harry Byrd's rigid conservatism, there were some who failed to live up to the high degree of decorum V. O. Key suggested. A prime example was Governor William M. Tuck (1946–50), a 235-pound bear of a man known for "shoot-em-up" conservatism and rather buffoonish manners that gave Byrd some pause. But Tuck was such a likable and lovable politician, and hobnobbed so intensively with his cronies from one end of Virginia to the other, that he was an unstoppable force in elective politics. Byrd had no reason to be concerned about Tuck's philosophy. He became known as the Virginia politician "most likely to succeed," flailing the national Democratic leadership as "Washington wastrels," "political vultures," and "tormenting minions of vice and venality."

A concomitant of the organization's strength was the incredibly small number of people who actually voted. The winning organization candidate for governor triumphed in the decisive primaries with the votes of no more than 11.2 percent of the adult population between 1925 and 1945, V. O. Key showed. One year the figure was a minuscule 6.2 percent. The poll tax and restrictive registration requirements stemming from the constitution of 1904 were generally held responsible for this, but the reasons appear to have run much deeper. Virginia had a one-party system which effectively isolated it from the stimulation of national campaigns. Apathy and general civic indifference became a way of life, because the "better people" ran the government, and since they seemed to be honest, upstanding gentlemen, the mass of the people saw no reason to distrust them—especially in a state so steeped in tradition. Even in the late 1950s, there were more than a million Virginians who had paid their poll taxes but still didn't bother to vote.

Given a limited, stable, and quite predictable electorate, it was not difficult for the Byrd organization to reach a consensus on the candidates it would like to run for office. A high degree of practical "democracy" actually entered into this process. Aspirants loyal to the organization felt free to travel the state and try to win support from the machine's cadre of about 1,000 politically influential persons. A candidate who could demonstrate broad local support would then be in a strong position to win endorsement from the top leadership. And who were those statewide leaders endowed with the ultimate power of decision? According to the late Ralph Eisenberg, a leading political scientist at the University of Virginia, the group was hard to identify but did include the legislative leaders, some congressmen, some local organization leaders, and elected state officials. "The figure who stood *primus inter pares*, however, from 1926 until his retirement from office in 1965, was Harry F. Byrd, first as governor and then as United States Senator." Once the high command gave "the word" in any election season, the favored candidate would receive miraculously rapid and unanimous endorsement from the organization cadre in courthouse after courthouse across Virginia. His nomination in the Democratic primary, tantamount to election in those years, would be virtually assured.

There were some exceptions to the rule of final candidate decision by the organization, when struggles for nominations between organization stalwarts broke out into the open. The organization did have some factions opposed to its rule, especially in the Hampton Roads area and Southwestern Virginia. For years it had to accept congressmen from the Southwestern Highlands who voted far more in accord with liberal-labor positions than Senator Byrd would have liked. Occasionally a slightly maverick organization man would maneuver himself into position to win election, even on a statewide basis. But such deviations were rare indeed.

Over the years, there were some bitter opponents of the organization's rule. They accused it of stifling healthy political opposition through the compensation board and the patronage ring surrounding the circuit judge, of holding hostile attitudes toward Negroes and labor, and of depriving Virginia, in the name of fiscal frugality, of desperately needed money for education, welfare, and health.

Those complaints, however, were to be of little avail until the years after World War II. As a result of the war and subsequent pressures from the federal courts and Congress, Virginia was drawn back into the mainstream of American life, and political change became inevitable. The relevant developments, all closely related, may be defined as urbanization-suburbanization and a decline of the rural redoubts, population-based reapportionment, a broadened franchise for blacks and poor whites alike, the civil rights revolution, emerging Republicanism, greater strength in organized labor, and a hardening of the organization's arteries as its leaders grew old and less flexible.

All this did not occur overnight, and there were many fits and starts in the Byrd machine's decline. The process began with a number of seemingly quixotic assaults on the old order in the late 1940s and early 1950s, but the *coup de grace* would not be administered for another decade and a half.

A growing minority vote against organization candidates had been apparent through the mid-1940s, and in 1948 Senator Byrd had raised the hackles of Virginians loyal to the national Democratic party by drawing up a piece of legislation that would have made it possible for the state's Democratic electors to withhold their votes from President Truman.* This gave impetus to the 1949 insurgent candidacy of Francis Pickens Miller, a World War II intelligence officer and former antiorganization member of the state legislature from Arlington. Miller plunged into the campaign with a frontal attack on the organization as a "political clique of backward-looking men" responsible for inadequate government services. Byrd, Miller said, was the "absentee landlord" of Virginia politics who ran things through "overseers." (Byrd responded by calling Miller "the CIO-supported candidate.")

To carry its banner, the organization picked state senator John S. Battle. In the end, Battle was to win—but with only 43 percent of the vote, contrasted to Miller's 35 percent. The result was significant in that the organization, for the first time, had been forced to exert its every effort to hold power.

Battle, as governor, did respond to the need for new schools to meet the postwar school-age population explosion, approving large construction grants to local communities, a startling innovation for the normally parsimonious Byrd organization. But Byrd's son, Harry Byrd, Jr., had entered the state senate and introduced restrictive funding legislation. The Byrd bill

* Byrd's opposition to Harry Truman's reelection was to prove a precursor to his famous "golden silence" in the Presidential elections of the 1950s. Many Byrd organization types went along with the Senator in opposing the national Democratic party, but not all. J. Lindsay Almond, later to be the organization's successful candidate for governor in 1957, campaigned for Truman and Barkley and defined Virginia's predicament. "The only sane and constructive course to follow," Almond had said, "is to remain in the house of our fathers—even though the roof leaks and there may be bats in the belfry, rats in the pantry, a cockroach waltz in the kitchen, and skunks in the parlor. . . . We cannot take our inheritance and depart into a far country. Where shall we go and to what shall we return?" Oddly enough, the question Almond posed seems as relevant at this writing, in the mid-1970s, as it did a quarter century ago.

passed, but not without the opposition of a group of nonconformist younger members of the General Assembly. Four years later, in 1954, the revolt from within the organization's own ranks blossomed out into a full-scale "Young Turk" movement. The Young Turks lost by a narrow margin in an effort to repeal the poll tax, but they did tie up the whole General Assembly past its adjournment date fighting to use a budget surplus for education and health. They wrung some major concessions from the organization majority, prompting one state paper to proclaim a "political revolution now in the making."

One could argue that the Byrd organization made a grave error in not accommodating itself to the Young Turks. As William Spong, then a Young Turk and later U.S. Senator, noted in a conversation I had with him years later: "The organization could have reformed itself to the degree that younger people were welcomed into the party, voting was made easier, and the growing urban problems of the state recognized. The result would have been a more moderate Democratic party—one not on all fours with the national party, but one more responsive to the needs of an expanding state."

Certainly, the Byrd organization should have been able to read the political tea leaves well enough to see that its statewide margins were dwindling dangerously. In the 1953 general election for governor its candidate was opposed by Republican Ted Dalton, an eloquent and tireless campaigner from Virginia's Southwestern Highlands. Dalton's platform was remarkably similar to that of the Young Turks—poll tax repeal, higher salaries for teachers, and more state aid for hospitals. Byrd's candidate, Thomas B. Stanley, rarely opened his mouth except to say he would remain true-blue to the organization's long-standing policies of fiscal conservatism. Dalton got 45 percent of the vote, and the best showing of any Republican gubernatorial candidate in the 20th century.

Having repulsed a progressive Republican attack with difficulty, and barely holding in check the Young Turks in its own ranks, the Byrd organization seemed in dire peril by 1954. Clearly, it was becoming increasingly out-of-tune with a more urban state that found its gentlemanly conservatism, however principled, inadequate for the times.

But then, in the nick of time, an issue intervened which quickly made it possible for the Byrd machine to postpone the day of its demise. The issue was school integration, occasioned by the Supreme Court's May 1954 decision in *Brown vs. Board of Education*. The Byrd organization's answer —in a phrase coined by the Senator himself—was "massive resistance." As Virginia was whipped up to a racial frenzy over the school issue, a top organization leader was quoted as saying: "This will keep us in power another 25 years." In point of fact, the issue, by diverting Virginians' attention from the basic issues of state services that were undermining the Byrd organization, probably did delay the day of reckoning for the machine by about a decade. But the organization prevailed only by a naked display of power that exposed its weaknesses and precluded, finally and definitively, any moderation in its stands that could lead to development of a centrist Democratic party in Virginia.

It had not been inevitable that the organization would react to the school integration problem with massive resistance. The first reaction of then-Governor Stanley, in fact, had been to endorse and carry through the legislature and popular referendum a plan that permitted some integration, on a local-option basis, and set up a tuition grant fund for parents who refused to send their children to integrated schools. But Harry Byrd, at one of his famed annual orchard picnics in the summer of 1956, declared that Virginia must fight the Supreme Court decision "with every ounce of energy and capacity." "If Virginia surrenders," Byrd warned, "the rest of the South will go down too." As a result of this, Stanley changed his position and the legislature, in special session, enacted the full massive resistance program, including a requirement that the governor close any schools directed by court order to integrate, or alternatively cut off all state funds for school districts that broke the color line.

Senator Byrd was the leading force behind the massive resistance decision, but he did not act alone. In Southside Virginia, where Negro populations were the highest and the organization's strength the greatest, an organization known as "Defenders of State Sovereignty and Individual Liberties" was formed and became such strong spokesmen for defiant segregationist sympathy that the organization, in Harvie Wilkinson's words, was "pushed from token compliance to massive resistance." At the same time, a philosophic base for massive resistance was provided by the young editor of the Richmond *News Leader*, James Jackson Kilpatrick, Jr. A gifted phrasemaker, Kilpatrick made his point by disinterring the doctrine of Interposition used by Calhoun and others in antebellum times, asserting the right of a state to resist actions of the federal government it considered unconstitutional.

The effort to impose massive resistance had not gone unopposed in the General Assembly. A group of moderates, including most of the Young Turks, tried to insert a local option provision in the fund cutoff bill and attracted substantial minority support in both houses. And it would be a mistake to say that members of the oldest Virginia families were all with Byrd in the massive resistance camp; indeed the ranks of legislators opposed to it included the direct lineal descendants of such Virginia greats as Robert E. Lee, George Mason, and J. E. B. Stuart.

While this scenario was being played out in the legislative halls at Richmond, Virginia held its 1957 gubernatorial election and chose the organization candidate, state Attorney General J. Lindsay Almond. For the year, Almond seemed to be a perfect choice. By contemporary accounts, he was "a pink-faced, white-maned orator of the old school" who caught the mood of the times by promising to fight the Supreme Court's iniquitous edict "from here to eternity." Ted Dalton was the Republican candidate again, and he spoke out clearly against massive resistance. Any chances Dalton might have had were submerged when President Eisenhower dispatched federal troops to Little Rock that September. "Little Rock knocked me down to nothing," Dalton said later. (He got only 36.5 percent of the vote.)

In his inaugural address, Almond continued his all-out support of massive resistance, saying that "integration anywhere means destruction everywhere" and that no compromise was possible. Nine months later, however, Virginians discovered that all the talk of last-ditch resistance and school closings had been more than oratory. Under federal court orders, several schools integrated, and under the Virginia law, Almond closed them immediately. Four months later, on January 19, 1959—Robert E. Lee's birthday—two court orders delivered body blows to massive resistance. The Virginia Supreme Court of Appeals said the closing laws violated the state constitution, and a federal court in Norfolk found massive resistance in violation of the 14th Amendment.

A day later, Almond went on statewide radio, as bombastic and defiant as ever. Almond, however, was a good lawyer as well as a good politician, and he had known for some time that massive resistance stood on very shaky legal grounds. Moreover, he had been approached by leading Virginia businessmen who told him massive resistance and closed schools were doing great harm to the state's economic growth and future prospects. Even Kilpatrick had backed down a bit in his editorials, suggesting that some kind of compromise might have to be found.

So it was that Lindsay Almond went before a somewhat incredulous General Assembly, just a week after the court orders, to call for new laws that in effect repealed massive resistance and allowed integration of the schools. On February 2, 1959, the first school integration in Virginia's history took place in Norfolk and Arlington. J. Harvie Wilkinson, in his excellent account of this era, said that Almond was a pivotal figure in the history of the Byrd organization. "His decision to abandon massive resistance marked the first major policy matter on which Senator Byrd, Southside Virginia, and courthouse conservatism did not have their way." In time, Wilkinson added, "massive resistance came to seem more and more a political nightmare. Its architects gained little stature. . . . Instead a newer Virginia saw massive resistance as the end of an era—an era which ended in aberration."

Nevertheless, as the 1960s dawned the outward appearances would have led one to believe that the Byrd organization could look forward to more years of easy dominion. For a while there seemed to be an "era of good feeling" between the state's Democrats as they recovered from the trauma of the school integration battle. Concern about rising Republican strength at the local level also appeared to unify the Democrats to a degree.

The decade was to bring, however, a rush of events—all beyond the control of the state's politicians or government—which would forever alter the face of Virginia politics. Preeminent was the rapid shift from a fundamentally rural to a basically urban society, creating a new electorate little impressed by the state's traditional modes of politics. The new urbanites were hardly enamored of the idea of hoary "Virginia gentlemen" ruling their affairs, and they were anxious for more and more government expenditures to meet the problems of their fast-growing communities. In the 1950s, the South-side and other rural areas had been the pivot of Virginia voting; by the end of the 1960s, the metropolitan areas were casting a substantial majority of the vote.

A second event was the Supreme Court's 1962 reapportionment decision, *Baker v. Carr*, and the quick shift to equally populated legislative districts which ensued. Up to 1950, when the rural areas enjoyed a comfortable population edge, Virginia traditionally employed legislative districts of relatively equal population. But after that year the General Assembly began to give the urban areas less than their due—an obvious stratagem to prolong Byrd organization control. The first court-forced redistricting on an equal population base took place in 1964, and while the organization was able to retain control of the legislative leadership, a new climate was created. Politically, Ralph Eisenberg noted, one-man one-vote "signaled the end of the rural base of the organization."

In January 1964 the 24th Amendment to the United States Constitution took effect, outlawing the use of the poll tax in federal elections and thus knocking another prop out from beneath the Byrd organization. The impact on the size of the electorate was immediate and dramatic, just as the poll tax's institution in 1902 had been. More than a million Virginians voted for President in 1964, a rise of 35 percent over the 1960 level. By 1972 the state's total vote for President would rise to 1,457,019 votes—almost twice the 1960 total. The poll tax was completely obliterated when the U.S. Supreme Court in 1966 found its use unconstitutional in state as well as federal elections. The impact of that decision was to be felt in 1969, when the vote for governor rose 63 percent above the preceding election. The small, controlled vote of the Byrd machine's heyday had become a mere memory of a bygone day, even though the melody lingered on in the form of one of the nation's lowest voting participation levels.

Even before the removal of the poll tax, the pool of registered Negroes in Virginia had been rising steadily, from about 5 percent of the black adults in 1940 to 23 percent in 1960. The city black vote was the first to expand significantly. William Thornton, a black Richmond podiatrist, explained that after the 1956 massive resistance referendum, it was discovered that only 4,000 Negroes were registered in Richmond, and that less than 2,000 of them had voted in that election so vital to their interests. The result was formation of the Crusade for Voters, which he headed. Enlisting the support of black lawyers, doctors, professors, businessmen, and union leaders, the Crusade set itself the objective of increasing the black voting pool in Richmond to 20,000 in five years. (Originally the group operated without membership lists, to prevent the type of harassment from state legislative committees to which the NAACP had been subjected.) The registration campaign was tough going at first, but by the late 1960s there were 30,000 registered blacks in Richmond and the Crusade for Voters had expanded its operations to cover the entire state. Allied groups were the NAACP,

SCLC (Southern Christian Leadership Conference), and black Elks, Masons, PTAs, and churches.

The poll tax repeal, combined with application of the federal Voting Rights Act of 1965 and the cumulative weight of the registration campaigns, produced startling results. The number of registered blacks in Virginia leapt from some 100,000 in 1960 to 250,000 in the latter part of the decade. The figure remained fairly constant into the early 1970s. It represented about 50 percent of the voting-age black people in the state, and roughly 12 percent of the total electorate of two million. Moreover, the blacks were the most cohesive voting block in Virginia, casting as much as 95 percent of their vote for candidates endorsed by the Crusade for Voters and other black organizations. In several primary and general election races, the black vote was to spell the difference between victory and defeat for one candidate or another. This was first evidenced in 1964, when Johnson defeated Goldwater for President in Virginia by a margin of 76,704 votes. At least 160,-000 blacks participated in that election, and they cast well over 90 percent of their vote for Johnson, easily his margin of victory.

The Democratic coalition of 1964, an amazing assemblage of Byrd organization cadres, party moderates, and even the liberal wing, carried over into the 1965 gubernatorial election. Mills E. Godwin, Jr., an organization stalwart who had led the fight for massive resistance in the legislature, surprisingly faced no primary opposition. One reason was Godwin's promise of a progressive administration, including advances in education. The disgruntled ultraconservatives broke off to form their own Virginia Conservative Party, which garnered 13.4 percent of the statewide vote, chiefly from the Southside. The Republican nominee was Linwood Holton, an attractive young candidate from Roanoke who linked the excesses of massive resistance to the state's pressing needs in public education. But the Crusade for Voters in this election decided to stay with the Democrat Godwin, hoping, as Thornton put it, "that he would realize we'd help him to win and therefore do something for us." Godwin, like LBJ the year before, could thank the blacks for his margin of victory—57,319 votes, far less than the black vote in his behalf.

Godwin proved to be an exceptionally progressive governor, ending many antiquated policies and moving the state forward in vital public policy areas—a record we will review later. Because he had been a Byrd organization man so many years, the rural crowd in the legislature trusted him and went along with his precedent-shattering sales tax and other programs. At no time since the 1920s had Virginia government made such impressive forward steps; indeed one might say that the finest hours of the Byrd organization were its first and its last—Byrd's term as governor in the 1920s and Godwin's in the 1960s.

Although Godwin was respected by Virginians, he lacked the communicative skills and either the warmth or will to be a political leader of Harry Byrd's caliber. Moreover, the problems of superannuation were beginning to plague the Byrd organization and became an unspoken but vital factor in the 1966 Senate and House elections, the real day of reckoning for the Byrd Democrats. The old Senator himself, sick with a brain tumor, had resigned in 1965, and died in 1966. With his passing, all the old restraints seemed to be gone. Harry Byrd, Jr., had been appointed to his father's vacant seat, but he did not command the devoted organization support his father had. He was challenged in the 1966 primary by former state senator Armistead Boothe of northern Virginia, who had been a Rhodes Scholar in his youth and the most important leader of the Young Turks in the 1950s. Byrd won—but by a perilously close margin of 8,225 votes out of 434,217 cast.

The seat of 79-year-old Senator A. Willis Robertson was at stake in the same 1966 primaries, and he was not as fortunate as Byrd Jr. William B. Spong, another erstwhile Young Turk, defeated him for renomination. Spong's victory was razor-thin—a mere 611 votes. But it did symbolize a new balance of power in the Democratic party, and it clearly would have been impossible without the heavy black vote in his favor.

On the same primary election day another great oak in the Byrd forest fell—veteran Congressman Howard W. Smith, the nationally famed chairman of the powerful House Rules Committee. Age was a factor in Smith's defeat; he was 83 at the time. Even more vital was the fact that congressional redistricting to equalize district populations had added a large chunk of fast-growing suburban Fairfax County, outside Washington, to Smith's district. It was not the kind of area likely to be impressed by Smith's lifetime fealty to the Democratic organization, or his old-style brand of conservatism. (In the autumn of 1966, however, the district rejected liberal Democrat George C. Rawlings, Jr., Smith's primary vanquisher, and elected a young, rigidly conservative Republican, William L. Scott, to the seat. Six years later Scott would advance to the U.S. Senate.)

By 1968 the Virginia Democratic party was literally coming apart at the seams. Three factions were fighting for dominance, and none seemed to have much desire to compromise with another. On the right flank there were the old organization men, lacking strong leadership from either Godwin or Harry Byrd, Jr. The left flank, consisting of ideological liberals, the statewide AFL-CIO leadership, and the blacks, looked to a feisty populist from Norfolk, state senator Henry E. Howell, Jr., as their leader. Sitting uneasily in the middle were the moderates, a varied crowd of fairly progressive people (including many of the "Young Turks" of yore) who rejected both the organization in its old form and what they regarded as the extremism of Howell and the left wing.

Meanwhile, the Republicans were marching forward and by the end of the 1968 election year—in which Nixon easily defeated Humphrey in Virginia—they held five of the state's 10 seats in the U.S. House. Yet the Republicans remained a fairly small minority in the legislature and local offices throughout the state. And they too were split ideologically. On one side was the group described by journalist Charles McDowell as "the hereditary Republicans who kept the party alive for a century in the hills and hollows of the western part of the state," where they had "fought, endured, and resented the power of the Democratic planters, banks, railroads, and the Byrd government that controlled key offices even in Republican counties." These mountain Republicans were racial moderates, too, based on a legacy handed down from Civil War days and the gubernatorial campaigns of Ted Dalton and Linwood Holton. Counterposed, and growing rapidly in power, were a group of "new" Republicans, most of them refugees from the Democratic right, who had been nurtured in the Goldwater campaign and were as conservative on racial matters as they were on economics.

So the stage was set for the utterly chaotic and seemingly formless politics of Virginia in the post-Byrd era. Yet even as Harry Byrd was laid in his grave in 1966, young J. Harvie Wilkinson penned, to end his book on the Byrd years, an epitaph which would come—especially in the wake of Watergate and the floodtide of public disillusionment about American leadership in the early 1970s—to have more meaning than he might have imagined:

> Harry Byrd and his organization were rich and valuable parts of any Southern uniqueness of history and humanity. Byrd was born of the somber side of Southern history. His organization, notwithstanding its faults, was truly coined from the mint of its time. If it was parsimonious, it emerged from a period when Virginia had little to give. If it feared deficits, it remembered the state's staggering Reconstruction debts. If it was oligarchic, it was so by reason of long inheritance. If it was regionally oriented, it bore still the scarred tissue of the Civil War. If it was rurally flavored, it respected the power of the farmer's franchise and the state's agrarian heritage. If it was slow—too slow—to change, Virginia had long been changeless. . . .
>
> Harry Byrd's Virginia would soon seem but yesteryear's quaint and curious memento. But Byrd's personal cause—his honesty, his courtesy, in short, his humanity—was not tied to time. The greatest men have often urged dated or debatable specifics. George Washington warned against foreign alliances; Thomas Jefferson dreamed of an agrarian utopia; Woodrow Wilson warned against bigness in American life; Robert E. Lee struggled valiantly for a divided nation. History values men as much for what they are as for what they espouse. Let not its view of balanced budgets determine its judgment of Harry Byrd.

Virginia Politics: The Chaos Now

The end of one-party politics in Virginia was confirmed by the first two governorship elections after Harry Byrd's death. In 1969 the three Democratic factions fought such a divisive and bitter primary battle that they lost the governorship for the first time in the 20th century. In 1973 the Democratic party's prestige had sunk so far that it did not even offer a candidate.

The Byrd organization made a final, brave attempt in the 1969 Democratic primary, running candidates for each of the three major posts in contention—governor, lieutenant governor, and attorney general. But it lost ignominiously in each contest; in fact its candidate for governor received only 23 percent of the primary vote, and failed to qualify for the runoff. The contest was then between the candidates of the Democratic left and center, Henry Howell and William C. Battle respectively. Battle, whose father had been the organization candidate who defeated Francis Pickens Miller 20 years before, edged Howell in the runoff. But the margin was only 19,000 votes, boding ill for the autumn contest against Linwood Holton, again the Republicans' nominee.

From their home in Washington, Francis Miller and his writer wife, Helen Hill Miller, watched with delight as their son Andrew, former head of the state's Young Democrats, swamped the organization candidate in the runoff and went on to win election as Virginia's attorney general. Another moderate-liberal Democrat, J. Sargeant Reynolds, a state senator from Richmond and wealthy scion of the Reynolds Aluminum Company family, won nomination without a runoff and then election as lieutenant governor. Reynolds, in particular, seemed destined for a major role in Virginia's late 20th century history. A vibrant person given to appealing wit about his personal wealth, he evidenced (as I discovered in a 1970 interview) a superb understanding of Virginia's history and future potential. Reynolds won the support of many conservatives, despite his personal liberalism, and as the Washington *Post*'s Helen Dewar noted, he seemed "the only foreseeable catalyst for the state's strife-torn Democratic party," a personal leader with skills comparable to those of Harry Byrd, Sr. But in 1971, still only 34 years of age, he died as a result of an inoperable brain tumor.

Reynolds would in all likelihood have won the governorship in 1973 and probably gone on to the Senate after that. Andrew Miller proved to be an able attorney general and was to win reelection by a landslide in 1973. But Miller was not the crusader his father had been.

Linwood Holton's election as governor in 1969 represented a natural culmination, on the state level, of the victories which the Republicans had been enjoying in Presidential elections since Dwight Eisenhower's breakthrough victory in 1952. Under Senator Byrd's famed "golden silence" approach to national campaigns, the state went Republican for Eisenhower in both his campaigns and for Nixon in 1960; the stage was thus set for heavy Republican victories in 1968 and again in 1972. Until the 1960s, however, the Virginia Republican party, in the words of one observer, "had always been the poor victim of Harry Byrd, Sr.'s flirtations with the national Republican party." As a national leader of the Republican-Southern Democrat "conservative coalition," Byrd had been able to court the generally conservative state Republicans when he needed their support in tight primaries (such as Francis Pickens Miller's 1949 race) and ignore them the rest of the time. The Senator's golden silences, however, had helped to legitimatize Republican voting. In the 1960s, as the Byrd organization declined and the voting population increased so rapidly, especially in suburban areas, the Republicans came into their own. They were turning sharply to the right by the late 1960s, as many Byrd organization men filtered into their ranks, and they nominated Linwood Holton in 1969 with marked reluctance but in full knowledge that he was the only member of their party with a chance of winning.

Holton carried several advantages into his November 1969 race against William Battle. Invigorated by their 1968 Presidential victory, the Republicans had a strong organization. The chaos of the Democratic primary had left 200,000 Democratic votes that Holton could shoot for. This he did, picking up support from both the right and left factions of the Democrats. Some 500 conservative businessmen and professional people, principally from Richmond, broke with their old pattern of being Presidential Republicans and state Democrats by shifting their endorsement (and campaign money) to Holton.

Holton's support from the Democratic left was even more dramatic and crucial. The Virginia AFL-CIO and the Crusade for Voters both combined their predictable support for Democrats Reynolds and Miller with precedent-shattering endorsements of the Republican gubernatorial nominee. The endorsement of Holton was not based so much on positive feeling for him—although Holton did have a strong civil rights record, and had not opposed labor in the past. Rather, the unions and blacks were interested in electing a Republican governor because Battle, the Democrat, had Godwin's endorsement, and they wanted to "drive the last nail" into the coffin of the Byrd organization.

Both groups, of course, had reason to detest the Byrd organization. The blacks recognized that they had been subjected to less overt repression than in many other Southern states, but they knew the poll tax had been principally a device to keep black people from the polls and that the Byrd organization had shown its true colors in the massive resistance era. Organized labor had long been used and abused by the organization. The Virginia AFL had been chartered in 1900, and eventually came under the domination of the Byrd machine through the offering of patronage plums to some leaders (a situation akin to Chicago Mayor Richard Daley's control of organized labor in Chicago). New and more militant unionism, with the first organization of women and blacks, came with the formation of the CIO in 1937 —a development that was anathema to the rurally based, conservative Byrd Democrats, and provided its orators with a handy whipping boy. During World War II, the AFL broke away from the Byrd organization's control. A wave of Byrd-inspired anti-unionism swept the state at the end of the war and led to enactment of a right-to-work statute in 1947. The unions were unable to organize workers on a numerical level comparable with the North, but were on a par with the South as a whole. Unionization grew apace with industrialization, and especially as the number of city jobs grew. Back in the rural areas, where Virginians tended to view themselves as "members of one big family" and were wary of outsiders, unionization had remained very difficult; in the context of urban life it became easier, so that overall union membership in the state rose from 68,000 before Pearl Harbor and 156,000 in 1953 to 230,000 at the end of the 1960s. The merged AFL-CIO became a vocal opponent of massive resistance after 1955, even though many of its members personally opposed any kind of school integration. Then, in the 1960s, the AFL-CIO began broad voter registration and political education campaigns and became a factor to be reckoned with, not only in its areas of greatest strength, like the Hampton Roads section, but in statewide elections as well.

Shortly after the 1969 election I talked to both black and labor leaders in Virginia, and they were outspoken about their reasons for supporting Holton. "Back in 1965," Dr. Thornton of the Crusade for Voters said, "we felt that by supporting Godwin he would realize we'd helped and therefore do something for us. But he turned his back on us. I actually cast the deciding vote for Godwin in our 1965 endorsement meeting, and I kicked myself for it for four years. In 1969 we felt that Battle would still be controlled by the Byrd organization. And we knew the Byrd organization would not give us what we wanted—not even a black state trooper or Negro judge. Holton promised he would put blacks into important state jobs." Julian F. Carper and Brewster Snow, president and secretary-treasurer respectively of the state AFL-CIO, expressed similar disillusionment with Godwin and fear that Battle would have been more of the same. The Democrats, they said, had been desperate to stop the Virginia labor movement from endorsing a split ticket—an unusual move for any state AFL-CIO. The national AFL-CIO, and even Senator Edward M. Kennedy, put pressure on them to endorse Battle. "Our reply," Carper said, "was simply this: 'We've been waiting a lifetime to kill the Byrd machine, and this is our chance, and we're going to do it.' "

When the returns of the November 1969 balloting were in, Linwood Holton was elected governor with 52 percent of the vote and a lead of 65,174 votes over Battle. An essential base of his victory was the large majority he received in the traditional enclaves of Republican support in the Valley of Virginia and the Southwestern Highlands. But Holton's margin of success was in the clear pluralities he received in urban Virginia, especially the Tidewater cities, Richmond, and the Richmond and Northern Virginia suburbs. It was a new Virginia, so different from Harry Byrd's. The new base of negotiable conservative votes was no longer rural but in the metropolitan areas, especially the suburbs, which had 31 percent of the statewide vote, giving Holton a strong majority. Moreover, any Democrat who hoped to win had to do especially well in the cities (23 percent of the state vote), with their growing numbers of black and union-oriented voters. But Holton cut deeply into the normally Democratic black vote, winning about 40 percent of it, did well in the union areas, and emerged the urban winner.

One could well say it was Democrats who made Republican Holton the governor of Virginia, but the increasingly relevant question was whether any party held the loyalty of a significantly large share of the Virginia electorate. The political chaos of Virginia elections in the '60s, and most particularly the bitter internecine fights among the Democrats, had created a remarkably fluid and unstable electorate. A poll in 1971 would show less than 60 percent of the state's people willing to identify themselves with either party. And since the state has no registration by party and the ballot does not even show the partisan affiliation of candidates, Virginians feel quite free to split their tickets at random and vote as they please.

Senator Harry F. Byrd, Jr., showed a clear understanding of the new situation when he announced in the spring of 1970 that he would desert the Virginia Democratic party with which his father's name had so long been synonymous and run for reelection as an independent. "Party labels mean less and less in Virginia," Byrd said. Byrd's ostensible reason for taking the independent route was a loyalty oath to the national Democratic nominee for President in 1972, imposed by the state party committee; a likelier reason, however, was that Byrd feared he might be defeated in the Democratic primary. Whatever the reasons, his decision was a sound one for him politically. In the autumn Byrd won reelection with 53.5 percent of the vote, compared to only 31.2 percent for liberal Democrat George C. Rawlings, Jr., and a minuscule 15.3 percent for Ray Garland, the Republican nominee backed by Governor Holton. Byrd's famous name may have helped him achieve his landslide, but he also benefited from the thinly veiled neutrality of the Nixon administration, which withheld any support from Garland.* Byrd did sound like the model Nixonian Republican in his reelection race, opposing busing to integrate the public schools, the growth of federal welfare benefits, left-leaning jurists, and campus unrest.

Byrd, through his 1970 campaign, had made the idea of nonparty candidacy viable in Virginia, and the next year the same technique was seized on by a contender of a quite different stripe—Henry Howell—to win a special election for the lieutenant governorship vacated by Sargeant Reynolds' death. Howell is the kind of candidate an outsider would scarcely expect to find in a patrician state. His father was a traveling lumber salesman and Henry was once a water boy at a sawmill. Fresh out of law school, he made his political start in Norfolk by supporting Francis Pickens Miller against the Byrd machine. "I did it," Howell told me in an interview, "when it was said that if I did, I wouldn't be able to record a deed or get a divorce processed thereafter. People said I was likely to die of political cancer." But in 1953 he was

* Holton had insisted on running a Republican candidate against Byrd, after the Senator refused to switch parties, in order to continue the GOP party-building process in the state. But President Nixon told Holton, in so many words, that he supported Byrd rather than Holton's candidate. By his move, the President cut the political ground out from under Holton, despite the fact that Holton had been an earlier organizer of Nixon's own Presidential campaign and continued to support him enthusiastically thereafter. Political and personal loyalty to Holton was dispensable if he failed to conform to the White House's "Southern strategy" and "game plan" of the year.

Holton later claimed that he had acted correctly in resisting the pressures of the right-wing Republicans, including Congressman Joel Broyhill, to back Harry Byrd without a party conversion on Byrd's part. "If I had let the Republican party abdicate in 1970, the same forces that sought abdication would have been back in 1973, saying that you have to do for Mills Godwin what you did for Harry Byrd." Thus the party, Holton claimed, was strengthened in the long run, although he admitted it had a much more conservative tinge, in the short run, than he liked.

alive enough to run for the legislature in an old hearse with a sign on its side: "Bury the Poll Tax." He lost that time but won in 1959. Howell turned out to be the kind of legislator who often won in court the battles he lost in the legislature. His suits covered reapportionment and challenges to the public utilities and insurance companies before the courts and the state corporation commission—an extraordinarily powerful agency mandated by the Virginia Constitution, which has regulatory power over such disparate fields as trucks, banks, auto, and life insurance companies.

When he got ready to run statewide, Howell was thus ready to present himself as a "people's candidate" pledging to "keep the big boys honest." (The "big boys," according to Howell, include an interlocking directorate of powers including the Virginia Electric Power Company, the Virginia Manufacturers Association, the state chamber of commerce, and the railroads—"a shortsighted group that fights things like a minimum wage, not seeing the necessity to put money into folks' pockets, for their own long-term benefit.") He also became a vocal champion of the unions, calling the state's antilabor philosophy "a throwback to the plantation philosophy—'I'll tell you what I'm going to pay you, you're lucky to have a job.' " By the early 1970s Howell had a statewide constituency of liberals, blacks, working people unionists, small farmers, racial moderates, and national Democrats. He won the lieutenant governorship in a split field, with only 41 percent of the total vote, but it was enough to send shivers through the old-line business-political establishment.

By the late '60s and early '70s, the state's Democratic party seemed to be occupying politically untenable ground on the far left of the Virginia spectrum. The 1968 and 1972 Presidential campaigns had both put the party in that position, as Hubert Humphrey and George McGovern won only 32.5 and 30.1 percent of the state respectively. Primaries had weeded out of the party most of its one-time conservative core, leaving the competition—and it was to prove a fierce one—between the moderate and liberal wings, which regularly undercut each other in general elections, making possible the election of Republicans and independents. The moderates viewed leaders like Howell as ideologues and nonelectables, while Howell complained: "The Spongs and Battles should listen to us. We feel we've been the ones walking the dusty roads, delivering the newspapers in the rain, in good days and poor. But there's no give and take."

The liberals, however, left a lot to be desired as party unifiers themselves. A prime example was the battle for delegates to the Democratic National Convention of 1972. The liberals, including many newly enfranchised young people, turned out in record numbers at the local delegate-selection meetings—actually "packing" them in many cases—and routed the Democratic regulars. The McGovernites captured a strong majority of the convention to Miami Beach, clearly not an accurate reflection of Democratic party sentiment in Virginia. "The liberal steamroller in the party convention in Roanoke," the Washington *Post* noted editorially, "was awesome to see and ruthless in its domination. It rolled over the party's conservatives and moderates just like the old Byrd machine once rolled over the liberals." In the autumn, regular Democrats deserted McGovern in droves, and Mills Godwin ended up as a leader of the Virginia Committee to Re-elect the President.

On the Republican side, by contrast, the Holton brand of moderate politics was suffering one reversal after another. About the only thing Holton was able to accomplish was to demand that Mills Godwin, who emerged from political retirement to run for governor again in 1973, do so as a Republican rather than as an independent (as Godwin would doubtless have preferred to do). The Godwin conversion, however skin-deep it may have been, climaxed the successful move of philosophic and racial conservatives to take over the Virginia Republican party.

Along with the breakdown of party loyalty in Virginia, there has been a marked tendency for the voters to coalesce around strong personalities or strong issues. "The corollary to this fluid state of politics," Howell lieutenant John T. Schell suggested in *New South*, "is that when a mediocre personality without any strong ideological stands runs against a strong conservative or liberal, he generally loses." A prime example of this was said to be the defeat of Senator William Spong, a reasoned, soft-spoken moderate, in his 1972 reelection race against Republican Congressman William Scott. A conservative ideologue of scant distinction, Scott had little to recommend him for the United States Senate. Scott was undoubtedly aided by Nixon's landslide in Virginia, and by a saturation television advertising campaign (financed by a $200,000 loan from a little-known conservative millionaire, J. D. Stetson Coleman) which distorted Spong's positions on such emotional issues as gun control. Yet it was also true that Spong conducted a lackluster campaign and had failed to cultivate the grass roots during his six years in office.

(Spong's own explanation of why he failed to hit the hustings earlier was an interesting commentary on the problems of being simultaneous legislator and campaigner in the era of elongated congressional sessions. "I had been assigned responsibility for legislation on toxic substances, clean drinking water, endangered species, and the treaty concerning international drug control," Spong later told the *Virginian Pilot* of Norfolk. "I believed it my duty to remain until that legislation had been acted upon. Perhaps I didn't realize that I was among the endangered species.")

Race, class, populism, Watergate, credibility, and nostalgia for the Byrd era all played vital roles in the Godwin-Howell gubernatorial contest of 1973, one of the most curious in the annals of American politics. A. E. Dick Howard of the University of Virginia Law School characterized it as "a textbook illustration of magnolia against the red galluses; in some ways, the classic Bourbon Democrat against the populist Democrat." The description was apt, except that the Bourbon Democrat was running as a Republican, and the populist Democrat as an independent. And many of the "predictables" of the contest ended up being stood on their head by the time the returns were in and Mills Godwin had won by an uncomfortably small margin of 14,972 votes out of more than a million cast.

Considering the fact that Virginia had a thin populist tradition at best, Howell ran a remarkably strong campaign. The pitch of his campaign was somewhat mellower than his first try for governor four years before, when he had been tagged "Howling Henry" for his verbal bludgeoning of the opposition. But Howell in 1973 was still classic populist, seizing on one issue—the sales tax on food and nonprescription drugs—and putting his opponent on the defensive with it. (Godwin had been governor when the overall sales tax was passed in 1966.) "I believe the people of Virginia are ready," Howell said, "to take the tax off bread and put it on bank stock dividends, . . . to take the tax off patent medicines for colds and coughs and for people who are crippled and add it to corporate income taxes." Howell stuck with the slogan—"Keep the Big Boys Honest"—he had first adopted in 1971. The fighter against the utilities and big corporations hoped to capitalize on a year of consumer revolt to "send them a message," Wallace style, and defeat Godwin, the "Republocrat" and "big boy."

All of this threw Mills Godwin, the wealthy corporate lawyer who sat on the boards of six corporations, somewhat off balance at the start. Godwin had hoped to campaign on "law and order" and bring in Nixon and Agnew to champion his cause—until Watergate and other scandals made that impossible. The next tack was to work on the theme of Howell the "McGovernite" and "free spender," and worst of·all, a "pawn of the union czars . . . he wears their mantle and collar." It was true that Howell enjoyed the enthusiastic backing of Virginia's AFL-CIO, both in money and manpower, and that national unions sent personnel in to work on his behalf. But for most Virginians, labor was no longer the bogeyman of yore, and Howell had defended his flank by getting the state AFL-CIO to say it would not press for a repeal of right-to-work if he were elected. (In much the same way Howell had arranged for the state Democratic party to "commend" his candidacy without endorsing or nominating him, thus avoiding a primary and preserving the independent position he thought necessary to assemble the remarkable coalition at which he was aiming—blacks, white-collar liberals, blue-collar workers, and Wallaceites.)

Godwin resorted to a thinly veiled racism, summed up in one little but hyper-controversial word: "busing." Howell expressed no enthusiasm for busing, and indeed it was hardly a relevant issue since it was in the hands of the federal courts anyway. But a year before Howell had indeed said that merger of suburban and inner-city schools might be "the only tool for integrating the school system"—a statement Godwin never let him forget, even though Howell had said he was against the "extremes" of busing and that the "consent of the governed" in an 80-percent white society had to be considered.

In the eyes of some voters, Howell thus appeared to have waffled on a gut issue. His credibility was further brought into question when he advanced a complex tax and questionable budget ceiling plan to make up for the loss of revenue from the sales tax change. These issues gave Godwin an opportunity to dwell on the themes of trustworthiness and reliability, to accuse Howell of deviating from "the integrity and clean dealings which have always characterized government in Virginia." Thus, as Virginian Thomas C. Ward suggested in an article for the *Harvard Political Review*, "nostalgia" for the Byrd regime and its rectitude, especially in the year of Watergate, impelled many swing voters to stay with Mills Godwin, the symbol of stability and continuity, even though Godwin was running on the ticket of the party of Watergate. Writer Jack Bass reported that Godwin privately held the same view, and appreciated the irony of it.

Had it not been for the busing issue in particular, however, Godwin would have lost. His uninspired campaigning (punctuated with chauvinistic appeals to love of Virginia) were no match for Howell's scrappy campaign. Howell did write modern-day political history by forging an alliance of the underprivileged—blacks, who gave him more than 90 percent of their vote, and low-income whites in such George Wallace strongholds as the Southside and the Tidewater cities of Portsmouth and Chesapeake. But busing caused Howell to lose by huge margins in the race-conscious suburbs (especially those around Richmond), and the predictable polarization along class lines, because of the differential in voting participation between the rich and poor, worked to his ultimate disadvantage.*

Godwin's narrow victory gave little hope to the Republicans or the promise of party realignment. The GOP on the same day suffered a serious erosion of its minority strength in the legislature. And while the voters returned Mills Godwin, symbol of the Byrd organization, to power, they simultaneously voted for the sons of the Byrd regime's two most prominent opponents in the statewide races of the early postwar era. Andrew Miller, who had made his mark as an aggressive, consumer-oriented attorney general, was reelected as a regular Democrat with a landslide margin of more than 350,000 votes. John Dalton, Ted Dalton's son and a moderate-conservative Republican from the Southwestern Highlands, was elected lieutenant governor with a solid 156,000-vote plurality.

Clearly, the early 1970s had failed to pierce the fog of political confusion lying over Virginia—the balance of power within either party, the problems raised by independent candidacies, the tension between Byrd-style conservatism and Howell-style populism. As a Virginia historian once noted, the Old Dominion still "wanders between two worlds, one dying, the other powerless to be born."

---

* A survey by WRC-TV in Washington showed that 73 percent of the people with incomes exceeding $15,000 voted for Godwin, while 74 percent of those with incomes of less than $6,000 voted for Howell. Middle-income voters gave Godwin a slight two-percentage point lead. In all this, turnout was the key. Godwin's affluent, white supporters turned out in somewhat greater numbers than the blacks and working class people who supported Howell. Howell's whole campaign, as Helen Dewar of the Washington *Post* suggested, had been aimed at motivating "the common man . . . to shed his traditional inactivism and vote." In the end, Howell did motivate enough of the common folk to get 525,075 votes. It was an amazing performance for a maverick politician without a precinct organization to back him up, but it was not quite enough.

State Government: Brighter Years and
a New Constitution

If a society is to be measured by its responsiveness to the needs of the broad masses of its people, then the years since 1965 must be called the brightest era in the history of the Old Dominion. No one would call Virginia a paragon of progressive government, but the form and substance of public policy has improved immeasurably—concurrent with, and one might even say precisely because of, the disintegration of the old political order. Good leadership has been part of the reason for this; another reason, I would venture, is that Virginians saw they could not join the mainstream of 20th-century American life without a fundamental reordering of their public priorities. Once they made that determination, the changes came with startling rapidity.

The man responsible for many of those changes was Mills Godwin in his first term as governor (1966–70). In area after area, Godwin made up for the gross neglect of his predecessors. It was, indeed, a remarkable performance for this lieutenant of the old and dying Byrd organization, who had been an eloquent opponent of progressive programs during his years in the General Assembly. By 1965, he recognized, the pressures for more adequate schools and colleges and mental health facilities and other state services could simply not be denied. Accurately judging the temper of the time, Godwin was able to put through precedent-shattering legislation, as James Latimer of the Richmond *Times-Dispatch* wrote, "with an amazing minimum of opposition, rancor, and political flak."

As the fiscal cornerstone of his program Godwin persuaded the legislature to enact the first sales tax of Virginia's history, a measure which he and the other organization stalwarts had fought bitterly in earlier years. The new tax was soon bringing in hundreds of millions of dollars each year and making it possible for Virginia to at least begin "catching up" with her sister states in the financing of public services. In addition, Godwin won approval of an $81 million bond issue to finance capital outlays for mental hospitals and higher education, thus jettisoning Harry Byrd's sacrosanct policy of pay-as-you-go.

Leading the fight for massive resistance in the 1950s, Godwin had declared that "integration, however slight, would be a cancer eating at the very life blood of our public school system." But now, as governor, he became the first chief executive in the South to speak out firmly against the Ku Klux Klan and appointed, for the first time, a number of Negroes to state positions. He allowed the symbols of massive resistance—the pupil placement board and the tuition grant program—to be repealed. Virginia's peculiar commission on constitutional government, created by the legislature at the height of the massive resistance frenzy to foster the cause of states' rights and push the doctrine of Interposition, was also abolished during the Godwin governorship.* After racial disturbances racked American cities in the late 1960s, Godwin said he was especially proud of the fact "that Virginia is one of the few states on the Eastern seaboard, if not the only state, which hasn't had to call out the National Guard to maintain order."

The improvements in education made in the Godwin years were to have a tremendous impact on Virginia, one of the Union's two or three most derelict states in support of schools and universities. At the start of the 1960s the state had one of the nation's highest school drop-out and illiteracy rates, and there were gross disparities between the funding for schools in affluent and poor communities. The sales tax had a rapid, beneficial effect on the public schools, so that per pupil expenditures, in relation to personal income, rose from last place among the 50 states in 1961 to a figure almost exactly the national average a decade later. State support for kindergartens was provided for the first time under Godwin, and the high school drop-out rate began to decline.

Godwin was also the father of an ambitious community college program to give thousands of Virginians an opportunity for higher education not otherwise open to them. As Sargeant Reynolds said in a talk I had with him before his death: "If it hadn't been for the community colleges, there would be no college education for those young people; if it hadn't been for the sales tax, there would have been no community colleges; if it had not been for Godwin, there would have been no sales tax." As a result of the expansion in higher education begun by Godwin, enrollment jumped from 64,000 in the mid-1960s to 150,000 in 1973. (There were some questions about the quality of planning in all this, however. According to a 1974 report of a Virginia legislative commission, "Over the years, the institutions of higher education have proceeded according to their own inclinations—some toward national preeminence, some toward almost self-defined excellence, and others toward complacent mediocrity—but none has based its direction on a comprehensive determination of the public need and how to serve it.")

The start of a community mental health program was also made under Godwin. "The state has a sorry record," Reynolds said. "They wait 'til you go crazy, then set up a monster central institution and stick you in it forever." By the early 1970s, some of the old snake pits had been demolished and more than 30 local clinics set up to work with patients released from the larger institutions. Reynolds said, however, that Godwin had not funded mental health sufficiently and that it remained "the stepchild of Virginia public service."

The final contribution of Godwin's first term as governor was to lay the groundwork for sounder Virginia government in future years through major

* The commission had a fairly respectable side in its publications committee, originally headed by James Jackson Kilpatrick, but drew public ridicule when its chairman, David J. Mays, called Pennsylvania Governor William Scranton a "pink" and urged formation of vigilante-like "home guard" units to quell possible riots.

constitutional revision. A blue-ribbon constitutional commission was created by the General Assembly, at Godwin's urging, in 1968. The chairman was former Governor Albertis S. Harrison, Jr., and the members included such figures as former Governor Colgate W. Darden, Jr. (an outstanding governor of the 1940s), Ted Dalton (by then a federal judge), and Lewis F. Powell, Jr. (former president of the American Bar Association, later to become a Justice of the United States Supreme Court). The commission did include one black (Oliver W. Hill, an NAACP attorney), but essentially it was a group of older, "establishment"-type white males. (Not a single woman was included.) It was the kind of group from which an outsider could have expected a very cautious approach, but it turned out to be a very open-minded commission. Part of this was undoubtedly due to an exceptionally able staff, headed by A. E. Dick Howard, the young associate dean of the University of Virginia Law School and former clerk to Justice Hugo Black.

Once the commission had completed a draft constitution, its work was submitted to the General Assembly, which reviewed and revised the document in a special session. "I feared the legislature might well add provisions benefiting special interest groups," Howard told me later. "But I found, generally, a very high sense of purpose in the General Assembly, a lack of venality and special-interest pleading. On balance, I think they improved the document."

After the legislature had twice ratified the new constitution, it was submitted to the people. Godwin and Linwood Holton, who by then had become governor, led a vigorous, bipartisan drive for ratification, organized again by Dick Howard. Approval came by a two-to-one margin in a November 1970 referendum.

Constitution writing is approached with characteristic care and reverence in Virginia. One is, after all, treading on sacred ground. In 1776 Virginia had written the country's first state constitution in an assemblage that included such greats as George Mason, Patrick Henry, James Madison, and Edmund Randolph. That initial document was an essentially conservative one, severely restricting the right to vote and presenting the existing malapportionment of the General Assembly to the advantage of the Tidewater counties (thus arousing scathing criticism from Thomas Jefferson). The early framers, remembering the excesses of George III, also made the governor totally dependent on the legislative branch. But the document did include the Virginia Declaration of Rights, which would find its way into the Bill of Rights of the U.S. Constitution.

The Virginia constitution was drafted anew in 1830, 1851, 1869, and 1902, with major amendments under Harry Byrd in 1928—thus following Jefferson's recommendation of periodic revisions because "the earth belongs always to the living generation." One of the most interesting assemblages was the convention of 1829–30, which included two former Presidents (Madison and Monroe), a future President (John Tyler), the Chief Justice of the United States (John Marshall), seven past, present, or future U.S. Senators,

26 sometime Congressmen, and countless other notables. Virginia opted then, however, as it would for more than a century afterwards, for a strictly limited, "negative" government, following the advice of Governor William Branch Giles: "That the only rightful purpose of government, was to secure to man two great objects, which man in his natural state could not secure to himself—safety and justice. . . . After effecting these great objects, the less government has to do in human affairs the better."

The convention of 1850–51 would be remembered for reducing legislative malapportionment, broadening the suffrage, and making the governor, for the first time, elected by the people. The 1870 document, in Reconstruction times, contained the first education article. The 1902 document, as we noted earlier in this chapter, was aimed at depriving the black man of his right to vote. The revision of 1928 enhanced the governor's power, created the "short ballot," and gave Byrd's pay-as-you-go philosophy the sanctity of constitutional mandate.

It remained for the 1971 constitution to reverse, finally, the "negative government" focus of Virginia's long history and adopt a positive attitude toward government responsibility in bringing services to the people. This was accomplished most dramatically in regard to Virginia's perennial dark island, public education. For the first time in the history of the commonwealth, education was declared a fundamental right of Virginians and was included in the state's bill of rights. The constitution guaranteed every child of school age an education of "high quality" and imposed a judicially enforceable responsibility on the General Assembly to see to it that such an education was provided, even if a locality should default in its responsibility. This constituted a radical break with Virginia's past. The education clause of the old constitution had been so emasculated by the massive resistance laws and court interpretations that any county could terminate public education altogether and still be within the letter of the law. (The most egregious case was that of Prince Edward County, where the dominant whites, rather than submit to integration, closed down the schools completely, and left them closed for several years until 1964, when the U.S. Supreme Court ordered them reopened.)

Former Governor Darden, interestingly, was the man responsible for the inclusion of education in the revised bill of rights, and for structuring the education article to create the vehicle for achieving quality education. It was a fitting capstone to the career of a man who had long fought for better education.

Along the same lines, the bill of rights was enriched by a guarantee against "any governmental discrimination upon the basis of religious conviction, race, color, sex, or national origin." The new document also recognized the goal of a decent environment and included the first consumer protection clause in any U.S. state constitution. While the realities of the 20th century were thus given recognition, some antediluvian provisions of the old document—including a provision on dueling and one regulating the rates of canal companies—were expunged. The new constitution also decreed annual (rather than biennial) sessions of the legislature, and required reapportionment of the state legislative and congressional seats, according to population, every 10 years. A great deal of statutory detail was removed from the constitution, thus enhancing clarity and consistency; the result was a more easily comprehended organic law of some 18,000 words, compared to 35,000 in the old constitution.

Because "pay-as-you-go" had so long been a shibboleth in Virginia, the constitution writers approached the questioning of state bonding authority with marked trepidation. They did seize the nettle to the degree of permitting the state to put its full faith and credit behind revenue bonds (for such self-liquidating projects as college dormitories), thus making substantial savings possible in lower interest rates. And they did enlarge the state's capacity to issue general obligation bonds for projects like new hospitals and college buildings, although they set a strict limit on the amount and required a public referendum on each issue. But the legislators were so nervous about these assaults on old Harry Byrd's sacred cow that they submitted them to the people as separate proposals. The caution was apparently unnecessary, because the bonding questions received almost as high a vote of approval as the main body of the new constitution itself.

Over the years, Dick Howard said, Virginia had indeed paid a high price for pay-as-you-go. Countless opportunities had been missed to build sorely needed facilities, especially in the areas of mental health and education. Beyond narrow limits set out in the old constitution, all state-financed capital construction had to be paid for out of current income. But by the time the new constitution was written, Howard pointed out, Virginia was "actually over the watershed on the question of pay-as-you-go." In the first place, the doctrine had not applied to the counties and cities, which had issued up to $1 billion in bonds, mostly for schools and highways—albeit at higher interest rates, because the bonds lacked the state's full faith and credit. Moreover, the $81 million bond issue proposed by Governor Godwin and approved by the voters in 1968 had been a dramatic break with the spirit if not the letter of pay-as-you-go. "The new constitution in fact just expanded the existing capacity to borrow," Howard said. But many critics said the new limits still represented a stingy recognition of Virginia's future needs.

While there was general agreement that the changes in the new constitution were solid and worthwhile, the document did not reflect the bold spirit of innovation which had characterized the great Virginia leaders of the 18th century. Political scientist Albert L. Sturm of the Virginia Polytechnic Institute and State University suggested a number of shortcomings in the document. These included, as he saw it, continued limitations on legislative sessions and powers, retention of the ban against two successive terms in the governorship, failure to opt for a nonlegislative body to carry out the decennial apportionments, and failure to give the governor authority to initiate administrative reorganizations of the state government, subject to legislative veto. Sturm noted that the sections on the legislature, local government, and taxation had not received the same thorough revision accorded the article on the judiciary—an inevitable consequence, perhaps, of entrusting the constitution writing to a body made up mainly of lawyers. He also criticized leaving the *sole* authority for suggesting future amendments in the hands of the legislature, a body with its own vested interests. (An alternative provision allowing the citizens, through an initiative process, to propose amendments or at least force calling of a constitutional convention would certainly have made the constitution a more democratic document.)

Virginia, however, was leary about plunging into reforms of textbook perfection which could unsettle the society or make ratification more difficult. Old institutions were retained where possible, and the dictum of the 19th-century British statesman Lord Macaulay was oft quoted: "Reform, that you may preserve."

Throughout their deliberations, the Virginia constitution writers kept a careful eye on the very recent failures of two sister states of the Eastern Seaboard, Maryland and New York, to win the people's approval for new constitutions. In Maryland, Howard observed, the talented and high-minded people who wrote a new constitution in convention "let their zeal for reform outstrip their political judgment." In New York, by contrast, rank partisanship and a probably superfluous ban on aid to parochial schools contributed to eventual rejection. Virginia was more successful, Howard said, because it produced a moderate document that took care of the state's basic needs without entering into areas which seemed to threaten the jobs of officeholders or vital interests of segments of the society. The commission and staff brought substance to the new document, the legislature through its review provided a legitimate test of political acceptability, and finally the central core of the new document was protected by submitting to the people as separate questions the potentially controversial sections, such as those on bonds and lotteries. The result was not a "model" constitution. But it was far·superior to the old document, it was a good constitution by national standards, and after generating support from every political leader from Mills Godwin to Henry Howell, it passed. The whole performance, one had to conclude, was quintessentially *Virginian.*

Virginia Government in the '70s

By the time Linwood Holton became governor in January 1970, most of the spectacular legal breaks with Virginia's tradition-encrusted conservatism had been made. A number of progressive laws were to be passed during the Holton years. But the historic contribution of this first Republican governor of modern times lay, in his own words, with "the development of an attitude of reconciliation between Virginians on the racial question." Holton wasted no time in setting the new tone for the Old Dominion of Confederate leadership and massive resistance fame. In his inaugural address, he proclaimed:

The era of defiance is behind us.

As Virginia has been a model for so much else in America in the past, let us now endeavor to make today's Virginia a model in race relations. Let us, as Lincoln said, insist upon an open society "with malice toward none, charity for all."

To succeed, this quest for an open society must involve all of us, not just the leaders of government. We earnestly ask the active participation of our business and professional leaders, the heads of our schools and universities, our labor chiefs and legislators, our local governments, leaders of minorities, and all individual citizens. Let our goal in Virginia be an aristocracy of ability, regardless of race, color, or creed.

Holton believes, probably with some justification, that the break with Southern tradition enunciated in that address paved the way for later and more publicized statements for racial moderation from such Dixie governors as John West of South Carolina, Reubin Askew of Florida, Dale Bumpers of Arkansas, and Winfield Dunn of Tennessee—a new form of Virginian leadership among the old Confederate states.

As his first official act as governor, Holton issued an exceedingly tough executive order on racial discrimination in state employment. "I will not tolerate nor will any state official tolerate racial or ethnic prejudice in the hiring or promotion of state employees," he declared. The number of blacks on state employment rolls increased about 25 percent during his administration, to approximately 18 percent of the total, a level comparable with the 18.5 percent black share of the total state population. Starting with a black as one of his executive assistants and the first black statewide Selective Service director in the nation, Holton went beyond tokenism to appointment of black people to a substantial number of policy-making positions, including all of the major state boards and commissions.

Holton was also able to exert subtle but effective pressure on private business to open employment opportunities for blacks. As an example, he named a Richmond bank "that started six years ago with two black clerks and today has two black officers and is proud of it." The major point in racial reconciliation, Holton said, was to open up job opportunities for black people "and let them use their full talents."

Holton's commitment to a biracial society was put to its severest test in the autumn of 1970 when intense antibusing fervor had erupted in the capital city of Richmond. As governor, Holton could have enrolled his school-age children in the most exclusive private school in town. But instead he chose to send them to the local schools called for under the court-ordered busing plan—even though those schools were then 96 percent black in enrollment. And so, on the front page of the New York *Times* and newspapers across the land, a picture appeared of the governor of Virginia escorting his daughter to a school the white world of America considered a typical ghetto institution. That event, Colgate Darden later wrote to Holton, was "the most significant happening in this commonwealth during my lifetime." As if that praise from Virginia's most respected elder statesman and former Democratic governor were not enough, Holton, on leaving office three years later, received a letter from J. Stanley Pottinger, Assistant U.S. Attorney General for Civil Rights, praising him for his "courageous leadership in the field of school desegregation." Pottinger told Holton his effort was particularly remarkable "because of your willingness to lead by personal example and to risk serious political disadvantage in order to achieve a fair and stable resolution to the problem."

Holton indeed suffered for his action, one of the reasons he had lost control of the Virginia Republican party by the time he left office. But his children, the object of so much interest at the time, apparently did not. While he and his wife were seriously abused verbally, Holton said, "we saw immediately after putting our youngsters into that situation what a great experience it was for them. They were given an opportunity at a young age to accept a major responsibility. They accepted it knowing their mother and I had confidence in their ability to handle it. It was a tremendous maturing experience for them."

Black Virginians considered Holton the first governor of the century really attuned to their needs. "He's been a very healthy influence," William P. Robinson, one of the three blacks in the 140-member General Assembly, told a reporter at the end of Holton's term. "He knew he would get a lot of guff, but he stood tall."

Actually, only one civil rights bill passed the Virginia legislature during Holton's term. It was important enough, however: the first state open housing law in the old Confederacy. Holton had not proposed it, because he feared the time was not ripe. But he backed the legislation and hailed its passage as the Old Dominion's most significant act since the Civil War.

Holton was never to become a master of the intricacy of Virginia government and legislative process on a level comparable with his predecessor and successor, Mills Godwin. (Even Holton's own aides, reporter Helen Dewar noted, described his first months in office as "on-the-job" training.) But Holton did bring a remarkably open style of leadership to the office, in refreshing contrast to the aloof, close-to-the-vest style of many of his Democratic predecessors, Godwin included. For example, groups like organized labor and the blacks felt they had channels of communication with the governor they had never before enjoyed. A glimpse of the new atmosphere was provided by AFL-CIO president Julian Carper, who described Holton as "the most human governor we've had in ages—a very personable man, outgoing, a person who doesn't stand on ceremony because of his position. He'd see me down a hallway and walk up and give me a big slap on the back—'Julian, I'm having barrels of fun. Ho, ho, ho.'" (An example of Holton's "fun" was his rejoinder to criticism, especially from Virginia Republicans, that he was hiring too many top administrative personnel from outside the state. Virginia, Holton replied, "no longer can afford to maintain an isolationist attitude toward the rest of the nation." He said he intended to keep right on luring talent from elsewhere.)

Holton's frankness and boyish enthusiasm helped him get cooperation from the 70,000-person state bureaucracy, filled with officials who had come in during the earlier Democratic regimes. During his first year in office he called some 35 agency heads together at Williamsburg for what was called an "organizational development" session but really amounted (with the advice of psychologists) to a variant of sensitivity training. With an emotional inspiration-type speech at the end of the conference, Holton was able to win a rare degree of cooperation for a governor of a state's "other" political party.

His success was not total. A lot more than personal charm would have been required to change the conviction of the veteran state highway commissioner, Douglas B. Fugate, that what Virginia needed in the field of transportation was roads, roads, and more roads. A son of rural, mountainous Pulaski County, Fugate had joined the state highway department in 1927 when getting Virginia "out of the mud" was a kind of holy mission. The suggestion of areas like Northern Virginia that there were already quite enough superhighways, with attendant bumper-to-bumper congestion and air pollution, fell on deaf ears with Fugate. Through his almost total control of road funds, Fugate wielded tremendous influence with the General Assembly and was able to kill proposals for diverting a part of gas taxes for mass transit,* or one of Holton's pet projects, a proposed state department of transportation (which would have diminished Fugate's power).

A significant reorganization of state government was effected in 1972 when the legislature approved Holton's proposal for a governor's cabinet, to consist of six secretaries assigned respectively to the major areas of government concern (administration, commerce and resources, education, finances, human affairs, and transportation and public safety). Previously, Virginia had an unmanageable group of 95 agencies reporting directly to the governor. That meant, Holton noted, "that no one reported to the governor" and that his predecessors had traditionally singled out one area of concentration (Godwin in education, Harrison in industrial development), and let a great deal else slip.

Following up on the recommendations of a management study, Holton in 1970 organized six task forces of department heads. With that precedent, he was able to get the legislature—by an exceedingly close vote—to approve the cabinet system in 1972. The new secretaries, who had no line agency responsibilities, became a direct extension of the governor's authority because they acted as the conduit for information from and instructions to all the separate departments, as well as meeting as a cabinet with the governor. "The device involves no great staff or super-level of government," Holton said. "The agencies retain substantive responsibility and to a degree can be autonomous units, but are coordinated by the appropriate cabinet secretary. I think my reorganization will go down in history on a basis comparable to the last major one of Virginia government, carried out by Governor Byrd

---

* Not until 1974 did the legislature, for the first time, free some highway money for use on mass transit—a step greeted with great joy in northern Virginia.

in the 1920s." Critics, however, said the individual departments retained, to large degree, their semiautonomous decision-making capacity.

Despite his own Republicanism and the overwhelmingly Democratic composition of the General Assembly, Holton enjoyed fairly good relations with the state legislators. But it was a totally different relationship from earlier years, when Byrd organization governors enjoyed a tight—and dominant —relationship with Byrd men in the leadership posts of the legislature. One vital factor was that the General Assembly itself was changing, both because of reapportionment and because of the timely retirement of many older legislators in the early 1970s. As Helen Dewar noted in 1970, "This session of the General Assembly is writing the epitaph to Virginia's long reign of rural patriarchs, the chieftains of the Byrd organization who ran the state from the tobacco lands of Southside Virginia, the apple orchards of the Shenandoah Valley and the courthouse squares that dot the landscape from the Chesapeake Bay to the Cumberland Gap." As this occurred, the balance of power shifted decisively from the rural to the urban areas of the state. Without a Democratic governor in office, the legislators felt free to act much more independently, thus restoring an executive-legislative balance notably missing since the early days of Harry Byrd. (Most comparative studies identify the governor of Virginia as one of the nation's strongest modern-day state executives, because of the lack of constitutional encumbrances with which he must cope, his broad appointive authority and full veto powers, budget-framing responsibilities, and the like. One should not, of course, discount the role of the lobbies, which in the 1974 legislative session reported spending more than $320,000—or about $2,300 for each of the 140 state legislators, under a loophole-ridden reporting law. Prominent in the lobby group are utilities, developers, banks, merchants, and labor unions.)

Governor Holton was sufficiently nonpartisan, and also sufficiently urban-oriented to win substantial cooperation from the resurgent legislature. He was rebuffed on several proposals, including no-fault auto insurance, a rebate to the poor for the sales tax on food, and legislation to authorize the state's 22 planning districts to provide regional services (an idea that conjured up the racial fears connected with city-county school consolidation). But Holton and the legislators did agree on enough innovative bills to suggest that Virginia government in the 1970s was taking on a progressive cast unlike anything the Old Dominion had ever known. Court reform, the issuance of some $300 million in bonds for capital improvements, increased expenditures for mental health, and a breakthrough appropriation to equalize educational opportunities in the state's public schools were all cases in point. Many of these reforms were made possible by the new state constitution written during the Godwin years, the new bonds and school equalization in particular. But it was chiefly because of Holton's leadership that the legislature in 1973 began seriously to fulfill the constitution's promise of quality education for all Virginia youngsters, even those in the poorest counties. Some $25 million was pumped into the poor school systems, together with a requirement that school systems which could afford it pay more to maintain adequate schools.

When Holton left office in 1974 * the legislature had still not given final approval to his proposal for a consolidated department for all conservation and environmental affairs. Holton had, however, appointed citizen and scientist activists to the state's pollution control boards and had begun the pumping of hundreds of millions of dollars into sewage control projects on Virginia's long-polluted and neglected rivers. Paper mills and other polluting industries were also forced to clean up their operations. Holton said that Norman Cole, a Northern Virginian nuclear physicist whom he appointed to the water control board, had as chairman of the group "built fires under the localities of Virginia" to break with their old lethargic ways in water control. Referring to local opposition to pollution control, Holton said: "Every damn river in Virginia was so political you couldn't get near it. But by the time the new facilities we're requiring are built, practically all our rivers are going to be swimmable again. We really cracked down—and we got cooperation."

When Mills Godwin returned to the governorship in January 1974—the first man since William ("Extra Billy") Smith, during the Civil War, to serve a second term in that office—the indications were that he would continue the generally progressive direction of his own earlier term, albeit more in a consolidating than an innovative mode the second time around. The force of circumstances—a major upheaval in the long scandal-ridden prison system of Virginia—suggested that if education had been the hallmark of the first Godwin term, corrections would be the major activity of his second. But it promised to be a much harder problem to cope with. Court decisions and independent evaluations had long identified the Virginia penal system as one of the most inhumane in the United States, but conservative and progressive administrators alike had failed to come to grips with the problem.† Godwin's new term was only a few days old when a circuit court grand jury indicted six of Virginia's highest current and former prison officials, including the cabinet secretary for human affairs, on a charge that they "unlawfully and willfully committed misconduct in office." The indictments, as a matter of law, were highly questionable, and were soon dismissed. But the fact of gross mismanagement over the years seemed all too apparent.

Godwin in his second term did promise to offer an interesting case study of how a man changes (if any) after he switches parties in Virginia. The answer to that question was likely to be "very little" because Godwin found himself faced by a legislature in which the Democrats still claimed 33 of the 40 senate seats and 70 of 100 in the house. Godwin said he expected to steer

---

* Holton became Assistant Secretary of State for Congressional Relations.

† A state crime commission in January 1974 detailed a pattern of homosexual rapes, prisoner control of discipline, and gross administrative shortcomings in the 275-year-old maximum security in Richmond. It concluded that life for the prison's 900 inmates had been reduced to a "struggle for survival that is devoid of any of the moral and ethical standards usually associated with western civilization."

his program through a bipartisan coalition, and would give no special preference to Republicans. (So much for the great political "conversion"!) In fact, the first legislative session in Godwin's second term, while quite harmonious, accomplished little of long-term note.*

Virginia was fortunate to have a steadily increasing tax yield through economic growth, due to a well balanced system of taxation. The personal and corporate income taxes, which dated back to 1915–16, were unique in the South in that they represented a relatively high portion of the total tax yield. The more regressive sales tax, enacted under Godwin in 1966 and pegged at 4 percent, took a smaller share of people's income than the national average. All Virginia's taxes, however, would probably need upward revision if the commonwealth ever decided to invest more heavily in public services. As a percent of personal income, the total state and local tax bite in Virginia ranked only 41st among the states in the early 1970s. The commonwealth continued to rank low among the states in many service areas— 48th in its financial support and care of the mentally ill, 45th in welfare, and 40th in higher education, for instance. The figures suggested that as far as Virginia had come in the post-Byrd years, it still had a long way to go.

The Congressional Delegation: Constancy and Decline

Until two liberal Democrats won surprise victories in Northern Virginia districts in 1974, the Virginia congressional delegation had remained true, to a man, to the Byrdian tradition. The Virginians on Capitol Hill were almost monolithically conservative and included not a single person who reflected the growing progressivism of so many Southern delegations in our time. Virtually every voting study confirmed the Virginians' rightward bent; in 1973, for instance, the delegation's average level of support for President Nixon's position was the highest of all state delegations.

There is a great difference from the past, however: with few exceptions, Virginia's congressmen today lack the seniority and stature to wield the power exercised in the heyday of Harry Byrd, Sr., and before. A related factor is that in a Congress controlled by Democrats, Virginia has one Senator who is an independent (Harry Byrd, Jr.) and one who is a Republican (William L. Scott), and a U.S. House contingent in which Republicans control half the 10 seats.

The long Senate career of Harry Byrd, as Harvie Wilkinson wrote, "represented a sustained attempt to cut federal expenditures and slash executive budgets." In the long run it would be a losing battle, but the power of Byrd in his heyday was formidable indeed. He was one of the great Southern patriarchs in the era of Dixie committee dominance, when one could speak

---

* The most important 1974 accomplishments were mass transit funds for Northern Virginia and permitting localities to exempt themselves from the state's rather ludicrous set of "blue laws."

of Congress as "the only place in the country where the South did not lose the war." (As such, Wilkinson suggested, "the organization and its leaders were not archaic misfits in national politics.") From his platform as chairman of the Joint Committee on the Reduction of Federal Expenditures, Byrd could preach the doctrine of fiscal frugality to a profligate nation. And as chairman of the Senate Finance Committee, he had immense concrete power over legislation. When asked about his influence, Byrd was graciously modest. "Why, I'm just an apple merchant myself," he told a reporter in 1952. "I just offer a little advice now and then."

The organization's stable strength provided Byrd with able and willing colleagues. In 1955, the same year that he ascended the Finance throne, his colleague Howard Smith took charge of the Rules Committee of the House of Representatives. In 1959 they were joined in the chairmanship ranks by another Byrd loyalist, A. Willis Robertson, chairman of the Senate Banking and Currency Committee. Among them these three Virginians held a major collective authority over almost all taxation, currency, social security, banking, and housing measures before the Congress. Howard Smith's power, as chairman of the Rules Committee with its life-or-death power of decision on which bills reached the House floor, was even greater. He was the unofficial head of the conservative coalition of some Republicans and Southern Democrats which had its way with so much legislation from the '30s to the '60s. If it ever appeared to Smith that a majority of the Rules Committee might go against him, he would quietly retire to his pleasant acreage in northern Virginia and thereby suspend the deliberations of the committee, as if by act of God. Business could not proceed without the chairman present. Not until 1961, when the Kennedy Administration, liberal-moderate House Democrats, and a small band of progressive House Republicans combined to expand the Rules Committee membership to give the Democratic leadership a precarious majority, did Smith's power begin to decline.

Byrd, Robertson, and Smith all disappeared from the scene in 1965–66, and Virginia since then has had a delegation that is conservative without clout. Three Virginians sit on the House Armed Services Committee, assiduously cultivating military progress that will benefit the state (especially the big Naval concentration in the Hampton Roads area). None of the three has much seniority, however.

Republican William C. Wampler of the "Fighting Ninth" district in the Southwestern Highlands in 1974 became ranking Republican on the House Agriculture Committee; his overall voting record could be characterized as standardly conservative, and he has not shown any of the sparks of independence of his Democratic predecessor, W. Pat Jennings, who cast a courageous vote in 1961 to expand the membership of Howard Smith's Rules Committee. (Defeated by Wampler in 1966, Jennings became—and remained—Clerk of the U.S. House.)

Another figure of some power in the House was Republican Joel Broyhill, who in 1952 won a newly created congressional seat in the northern Virginia suburbs and kept his grip on it, despite repeated liberal Democratic assaults, until 1974. The Arlington-Fairfax-Loudon County area Broyhill represented is heavily laden with federal workers; in fact, 31 percent of its working population is on the government's payroll, a large proportion of them for the Pentagon and other military installations. This creates a much more conservative constituency than, for instance, Maryland's Montgomery County, which has many residents working for the National Institutes of Health. I have heard stories of military personnel assigned to the Pentagon who consider the District of Columbia such a citadel of blacks and cauldron of crime that they *never* cross the Potomac to Washington during their stays in Northern Virginia. It is on the fears of the Virginia suburbanites concerning Washington that Broyhill preyed through his 22-year career. From the vantage point of a seat on the House District Committee, he was a longtime opponent of home rule, pressed for crackdowns on welfare chiselers and "lawlessness" in the ghettos, and fought proposals for a commuter tax on suburbanites working in the District. The Washington *Post*, his old political enemy, once accused Broyhill of "attempting to strangle the District of Columbia, politically, economically, and socially." But even that paper had to acknowledge "the remarkably high level of service he provides his constituents," an especially vital role in a district where so many people are dependent, in one way or another, on the federal government. Broyhill finally lost when he was obliged to reveal his net worth of several millions in real estate and banking, and voters became convinced he was in Congress more to serve "special interests," including his own, than theirs.

In the Senate, Harry Byrd, Jr., truly reflects his father's philosophy but is hardly more than a cameo of the old man's influence or stature. The conservative hard line is also reflected in Senator William L. Scott, a teetotaling Methodist Sunday school teacher from the Washington suburbs. Drawing heavily on a critical review of Scott in the *Washingtonian* magazine, the Ralph Nader Congress Project report said "the bulk of Scott's reputation, by far, seems to consist of grotesque tales of harsh temper, ingratitude, niggardliness, quixotic disciplinarianism, and summary mistreatment" of staff and some visitors. The *Washingtonian* also quoted Scott as saying, "The only reason we need zip codes is because niggers can't read." Appointment to the Senate Armed Services Committe gave Scott a chance to deliver on installations for Virginia, but when a reporter asked him what the highlight of his first year in the Senate was, he replied: "Being sworn in was perhaps the highlight of the year." Scott's problems with the press seemed never to end. When the left-leaning *New Times* in 1974 declared him "the dumbest congressman of them all," he said he would like to sue but would not do so for fear that he might be unable to prove malice and thus lose the case, so that people would conclude he truly was the dumbest member of Congress. Despite all this, Scott's popularity with Virginian voters is not to be gainsaid. Only time will tell whether his style and philosophy will become synonymous with Virginia congressional politics.

Perhaps the most able of the modern-day Republican Congressmen, Richard H. Poff of Roanoke, retired in 1972, after 20 years service, to accept a state court appointment. The year before Poff had been at the top of President Nixon's list for appointment to a Supreme Court vacancy. It was an appointment that Poff, a senior Republican on the House Judiciary Committee and a conservative with a keen, flexible mind, could have fulfilled admirably. But some civil rights and labor groups raised opposition to his prospective appointment, and Poff was afraid of a bruising confirmation fight and its possible effects on his family. His withdrawal deprived the court of a potentially outstanding Justice, and Virginia of a chance to place one of its sons at the highest level of federal service. Another opportunity soon came, however, when Nixon appointed Lewis Powell, Jr., a highly regarded Richmond lawyer, to the court. Poff's successor in the U. S. House, M. Caldwell Butler, a former law partner of Linwood Holton, was appointed to the Judiciary Committee. There—in a move interpreted at the time as one of real political courage—he cast a vital Republican vote for the impeachment of President Richard Nixon.

Economy and Growth: The Perplexities of Progress

One is hard put to think of a state which has enjoyed an economic rejuvenation comparable to Virginia's in our time. Widely diversified industry (including substantial foreign investment), high government employment, a thriving tourist business, and rapid urbanization are all part of the picture. No matter what measure one takes in hand, the picture is the same. Virginians' per capita income, just 62 percent of the national average in 1929, was up to 79 percent in 1948, 89 percent in 1967, and 96 percent in 1973. It has been many years since the unemployment rate in the state even approached the national average.

Some say Virginia's economic resurgence can be traced to the 1920s, when the state began building highways that "pulled it out of the mud" and made possible later development. More important, I would say, are fortuitous factors well beyond the capacity of any state government to control. And chief among these is location. Virginia has not been considered part of the east coast megalopolis stretching from Boston to Washington, but it has certainly been close enough to service its markets through manufacturing. It also has superb harbor facilities in the Hampton Roads area, and well watered valleys and flatlands well suited to modern industrial development. The build-up of Naval facilities on the coast has provided a powerful economic impetus in a century of world wars and increasingly constant military preparedness.

And of immense importance is the state's location alongside Washington, D.C. "Madison and Jefferson," author Guy Friddell wrote, "bargained with Hamilton to have the Capitol placed on the Potomac where Virginia could keep an eye on her daughter, the nation." But they could never have imagined, in an era of minimal service government, what that decision would mean for nearby Virginia. In fact, it was not until the administration of

Franklin D. Roosevelt that the federal government began its rapid modern-day expansion of activity and personnel. When it did, the activity quickly spilled over to the Virginia side of the river. Northern Virginia, together with Hampton Roads, was a major reason that by 1972 almost 27 percent of Virginians' income—in salaries, welfare, veterans' benefits, grants, contracts, and the like—came from the federal government. Except for Alaska and the District of Columbia itself, it was the highest figure in the nation. (The national average was 14 percent.)

The rise in manufacturing (now an output of more than $5 billion a year) is impressive, both for the sharp rise in employment it has brought about, and for its broad diversity. Wood, textiles, and chemicals lead the list, but none could be called dominant. The largest textile mill in the world is located at Danville, for instance, but textiles account for only 12 percent of the state's factory jobs, compared to 38 percent in North Carolina. Richard S. Gillis, Jr., executive director of the state chamber of commerce, said Virginia business leaders had adopted a deliberate policy of diversification—both in types of industry and in geographic location. The industrial map of the commonwealth shows a broad sweep of industry concentrations—substantial tobacco production in Richmond and Petersburg, for instance, transportation in the Hampton Roads area, textiles and furniture in the South Side and Roanoke areas, food products and electrical equipment all up and down the Valley of Virginia. A number of blue-ribbon national firms have joined the industrial parade in recent years, and many have substantial research activities in their Virginia installations.

The growth and diversity of manufacturing activity is illustrated by these figures, covering the change in a 22-year period ending in the early 1970s:

Type of Manufacturing	1950 Employment	1972 Employment	Change
All manufacturing	229,500	378,000	+ 64.7%
Lumber and furniture	43,200	49,300	+ 14.1
Metals and machinery	16,300 *	32,800	+101.2
Electrical equipment	5,800 *	28,400	+389.7
Transportation equipment	11,000	34,000	+209.1
Food products	33,800 *	36,700	+ 8.6
Textiles	40,600	43,000	+ 5.9
Apparel	16,300	38,800	+138.0
Paper	10,000	14,300	+ 43.0
Chemicals	34,100	39,000	+ 14.4

* Figures for 1958, the earliest year for which figures are available.

So it appears that Virginians have spurned, once and for all, Jefferson's admonition to send raw materials from the New World to Europe for processing, rather than setting up factories in America and risking the rise of cities and all their attendant evils. "The loss by transportation of commodities across the Atlantic will be made up in happiness and permanence of government," Jefferson wrote. "The mobs of great cities add just so much to the support of pure government, as sores do to the strength of the human body." What would Jefferson have to say, though, to the fact that the urbanization of Virginia, when it finally came, was as much due to the employment rolls of the national government he helped to found as to the growth of manufacturing?

The master of Monticello would probably be pleased to know, however, that forests occupy more than three-fifths of Virginia's land area in our time, and that with the rising affluence of recent decades, the areas of rural landscape with a manicured look, offering pleasant pastures, well managed farms, and woodlands, have grown significantly. The plantation era belongs to history now, and so does the era of hundreds of thousands of small, marginal farm operations. But the cultivation of the land is still immensely important and more diversified than ever before. On the Eastern shore the visitor finds truck farms producing fresh vegetables and fresh fruits. Inland from Norfolk, fields of peanuts* and soybeans provide new agricultural prosperity (cotton having disappeared almost entirely), and the breeding of purebred swine, a factor in modern Virginia's bid for an important role in world trade, has risen sharply. Tobacco remains important in Southside Virginia, and in the Shenandoah Valley one discovers one of the country's most important apple-growing areas (Byrds and others), together with a thriving poultry industry. In recent times field crops have diminished in importance, to be replaced by fat cattle pasturing on rich fields in the Valley of Virginia and parts of central Virginia.

Agriculture is a $700 million a year business in the Virginia of the 1970s, and the great fisheries of the commonwealth's Atlantic Coast, the Chesapeake Bay, and the tidal rivers bring in a catch third among the states in terms of volume. But all this is less important than tourism, a $1 billion-plus a year industry in modern-day Virginia. The reasons are clear enough: from Jamestown and Williamsburg to Richmond, Alexandria, and Charlottesville, by virtue of great battlefields and plantation and town houses rich with lore, Virginia seems to the outsider to be one great historic park. Then there are the natural attractions: the Virginia seashore, the Shenandoah National Park and the Skyline Drive, state and national forests, and enough placid countryside to sooth the spirit of any jaded urbanite. A drive through Virginia in the early spring, when dogwood and azalea and forsythia and countless flowers bloom, and all the earth is green and pulsating with life, is one of the most beautiful sights I have seen anywhere on this continent. Official Virginia has cleverly exploited all this with an official slogan, "Virginia is for lovers," thought up by a Richmond advertising agency in the late 1960s. One can interpret the slogan as he or she chooses, but surveys in places like Long Island and Pittsburgh have shown more than 70 percent of the people familiar with it. The only sour note to report is that Florida's garish Disney World quickly outstripped Mount Vernon as the prime tourist attraction of the American Southland.

The vitality, and especially the urbanization, of present-day Virginia

---

* Southampton County, on the North Carolina border, produces more peanuts than any other county in the country.

mark a dramatic departure from the past. Until World War II, Jean Gott-mann noted, the Old Dominion deserved its nickname, featuring the tradi-tional hallmarks of an "old" country: "an essentially rural society and econ-omy, low standards of living, abundant and cheap labor, emigrating surplus population, predominance of a peasantlike psychology resisting innovation." The population figures illustrated the point: mired in its post-Reconstruction doldrums, Virginia lost a third of its natural population increase to other states between 1880 and 1930. The outmigration reached a crescendo in the 1920s, and then abated rapidly and reversed as the Depression made job op-portunities elsewhere scarce and the federal government began its massive new civilian and then military activity within the state. The tables of popu-lation growth have been turned dramatically in the past three to four decades, as Virginia has drawn hundreds of thousands of immigrants from out of state and consistently exceeded the national population growth rate:

Population Growth	1880s	1900s	1920s	1930s	1940s	1950s	1960s
Virginia	9.5%	11.2%	4.9%	10.6%	23.9%	19.5%	17.2%
U.S.	25.5	21.0	16.2	7.3	14.5	18.5	13.3

The result of the population surge, Attorney General Andrew Miller observed, is that "Virginia has been nationalized." In fact, immigration has been so strong that the 1970 Census found that more than a third of the people living in Virginia had been born elsewhere. Virginia's "fresh blood" index was far in advance of neighboring West Virginia and North Carolina (albeit less than in the District of Columbia and Maryland). The Old Dominion, Gottmann concluded, had "grown young."

The population growth figures for Virginia are even more dramatic if one analyzes where they have occurred. One could not imagine a more com-plete reversal of the commonwealth's traditional preference for the rural way of life. While the cities and suburbs have ballooned in population, there are many counties, especially in Southside Virginia, the western mountain counties, and on the Eastern Shore, where population has declined steadily for the past three decades. In the 1960s alone, the 49 most rural counties decreased by 17,693 in population, while the rest of Virginia grew by 676,-153 (to a new statewide total of 4,648,494). The rural population of the state, which had been 68 percent of the total on the eve of Pearl Harbor, dropped to 37 percent by 1970. The flight from the land is underscored by the drop in the rural farm population, from 22 percent of the state to-tal in 1950 to a mere 4 percent in 1970.

The urban areas have absorbed the bulk of Virginia's rural refugees, plus thousands of people from other states. Back in 1940, the total popula-tion of Virginia's metropolitan areas * was 955,579 people—36 percent of the state total. By 1970, that figure had increased almost threefold, to 2,-846,034, making up 58.5 percent of the population. The great bulk of this was in a much talked-of "urban corridor" running from the northern Vir-

* The metropolitan areas, with their 1970 populations: Northern Virginia suburbs 921,237, Richmond, 518,319, Norfolk-Portsmouth 680,600, and Newport News-Hampton 292,159, Roa-noke 181,436, Lynchburg 123,474, and Petersburg-Colonial Heights 128,809.

ginia suburbs in the Washington orbit to Richmond, and thence easterly to the Hampton Roads area. The rapidity of this section's growth is illustrated by the fact that Jean Gottmann, an expert on the concept of megalopolitan concentrations, did not even notice that of the urban corridor in the first edition of his *Virginia In Mid-Century*, published in 1955. In recent years, however, the idea of the urban corridor has taken a firm hold on the mental set of Virginians about their own state. One finds it constantly referred to in the press, in politics, in industrial planning, and in state publications. By 1960, the urban corridor accounted for 52 percent of Virginia's population: according to one estimate, three out of five Virginians will live within it by 1980.

Thus one notes the emergence of two very different Virginias in our time—a metropolitan Virginia, sharing fully in the affluence of the United States in the post-World War II period, and an "old" Old Dominion, still chiefly of the land, a rural backwater in its time. The 1970 Census throws the differences into bold relief. Urban Virginians turned out to have much higher levels of educational attainment than their rural counterparts, to have a younger average age, to include practically all the latter-day migrants to the state (making for a greater cultural mix), to be much more heavily engaged in white collar jobs (58 percent versus 33 percent in the rural areas), to live in housing of much superior quality, and to enjoy an average family income 31 percent above that of rural families.

This is not to suggest that urban Virginia is free of poverty, especially in some of the core cities. But the rural poverty problem is much greater. One finds it, among blacks and whites alike, in some of the wretched coal mining towns and farming areas of Appalachia, in Southside Virginia where the vestiges of sharecropping linger on, and even in the midst of the posh hunt country of Loudon County not far from Washington. Henry Howell recalled the conditions he found near Petersburg, on the Southside:

> There are six or seven dwellings built many decades ago to support a stave mill (barrel factory). The factory is gone, but the houses are still there, renting for $10 a month. They have no indoor or outdoor plumbing. In one house I found there were 12 children. They have to go into the woods to relieve themselves. To get water, the mother has to go with a bucket to a common well. Now the kids are going to an integrated school. This has traumatized the white people, because what was behind the bushes emerges to mix with their children in a unitary school system. You have to ask, how clean can kids without running water or toilets be?
>
> The man who owns those houses was on the county board of supervisors for 20 years. And there are little pockets like this, with no one caring, all over Virginia.

The income and population imbalance between Virginia's metropolitan and urban areas has begun to cause major problems for both. The urban areas are facing mounting crime rates, air and water pollution, congested streets, and failing or nonexistent public transit systems. Some of the ecological consequences of the urban corridor, for instance, were spelled out in a 1970 University of Virginia study:

> As the Corridor's population grows, development will impinge directly upon Virginia's coastal wetlands, a resource of unquestioned value to the Common-

wealth. Aside from their primary productivity, the coastal wetlands are an essential link in the often tenuous ecological chain of plant, fish, animals, and, ultimately, human life. . . .

Another special feature of the Urban Corridor is its geographical relation to the Chesapeake Bay. The Bay and its tributaries have long been recognized as one of Virginia's most threatened resources. . . . Virginia's Corridor and the southern reaches of the Boston-Washington corridor, between them, form a crescent which acts like a pincer around the Bay. That pincer is the source of industrial effluents, human wastes, soil silts, and other forms of pollution which kill fish, taint oysters, and in other ways inflict measurable harm on the Bay, its economy, and those who live around it.

In addition, fearsome urban sprawl has come to characterize many of the areas within the urban corridor. The interstate highways, the lifeline of the corridor, facilitate the sprawl, even into placid rural counties once thought beyond the reach of metropolitanization. The 1970 Census revealed the astounding fact that 47 percent of Virginians worked outside their city or county of residence.

The rural counties, by contrast, have to grapple with mounting public needs even as outmigration depletes their tax revenues. A study by the state's rural affairs commission showed that lack of economic opportunity was a salient rural problem, and one tied in turn to the lack of services. Rural areas, plagued by a dearth of trained workers, inadequate water and sewage systems, poor schools, a shortage of physicians and health facilities, and large numbers of substandard houses, are inevitably in a weak position when they try to attract new industries. Yet 50 of the 95 Virginia counties, almost all rural, do not even have zoning ordinances. Furthermore, modern-day problems like pollution cannot be contained, either practically or economically, within old jurisdictional boundaries. Thus, as Dale Patrick reported to the Southern Growth Policies Board in 1973, there is "a growing feeling among educators, planners, and state officials that the real mechanism for obtaining solutions is some form of regionalization, a concept that has traditionally been opposed at all levels of government in Virginia." A commission appointed by Governor Godwin in the mid-1960s recommended dividing the state into multicounty planning districts, together with a mechanism for setting up regional service organizations in such areas as water supply, waste disposal, and health care. The legislature did approve the planning districts, which hired professional planning staffs. But the mechanism for establishing service districts was made so politically complex—requiring approval of all the governments involved, plus a favorable public referendum in each locality involved—that none was established by 1973. Virginia has a long tradition of strength, independence, and sometimes important innovation in local government.* Independent cities, for instance, are administratively separate from the counties in which they are geographically located. (The counties, in turn, fear annexation by the cities, which has occurred with fair frequency.) All of this perpetuates a degree of parochialism dangerous to the orderly development

---

* The city of Staunton, for instance, conceived and instituted a city manager form of government in 1908, a plan later followed by hundreds of cities across the nation.

of the state, to effective land use planning, and to a more uniform pattern of population growth—the problems with which Virginians must cope if they are to protect, in the most prosperous of all the Old Dominion's eras, the heritage of their commodious and fair land.

Places and People: Tidewater and Southside

"*What Is It About Virginia?*" Norfolk newspaperman Guy Friddell asked in a book of that title. Then he proceeded to offer an answer:

> There is the name.
> Virginia. . . .
> It sings itself. . . .
> In the sweet, undulating roll of Virginia, you catch the soft folds of the Blue Ridge mountains in the morning mist, the giddy, gaudy green Easter Egg hills billowing around Albemarle, the lazy James embracing Richmond, the dark green tobacco fields somnolent in the Southside sun, and the long, pale green combers rolling in white thunder on Virginia Beach. . . .
> The contour of the State offers every scenery—seacoast, tidewater, piedmont, mountains—as if to say, beguilingly, stay, it's all here, all that earth can afford.

Perhaps we could leave it at Friddell's lilting description, but there is more to say about the great geographic divisions and their people in our time.

We do well to start, in the manner of the history we traced earlier, with Tidewater—the low, flat, sandy plain that stretches from the sea some hundred miles inland to the fall line, where the upland streams descend from the Piedmont. Along the Chesapeake Bay's western shores there are the long peninsulas, or "necks," formed by the great Tidewater rivers, mostly very rural regions with agriculture and active fishing and oystering. There is, of course, the great urban concentration in the southwestern corner of the Tidewater, around Hampton Roads, to which we will turn shortly. And close by, on the peninsula formed by the York and the James, lie Virginia's great historic treasures—Williamsburg, Jamestown, and the Yorktown battlefield, receiving a steady year-round flow of tourists from all over the United States and many foreign countries. Industry is coming to the Williamsburg area, too, but of an apparently well planned type. Anheuser-Busch in 1970 began construction of a huge brewery complex there, eventually to be part of an industrial park with satellite industries and gardens to draw tourists, at a total cost of some $200 million.

Across the Chesapeake Bay are the two Virginia counties of the Delmarva Peninsula, the Old Dominion's "Eastern Shore." The state actually extends 62 miles up the peninsula, in a rich vegetable and fruit area, deeply rural in complexion. The Eastern Shore used to be accessible to Norfolk and the rest of the Tidewater only by ferry or a 400-mile auto trip through Maryland. This was corrected in 1964 with completion of the 17.6-mile, $200 million Chesapeake Bay Bridge-Tunnel, hailed as a marvel of modern engineering. The drive *is* an exciting one, especially on hazy days when land drops from sight. But the bridge has been battered by a series of marine mishaps that have closed it for months on end. Traffic on this, the world's longest bridge-tunnel, has never reached early projections. The Eastern Shore has its attractions, including the magnificent stretches of unsullied beach and the nature preserve at the new Assateague Island National Seashore. Close by the seashore is the town of Chincoteague, where the wild ponies make their famed swim from Assateague on "Pony Penning Day" each summer. (Some controversy has swirled around the allegedly callous treatment of the horses, whose ancestors are said to have swum ashore to Assateague Island from a shipwrecked galleon. The greater cruelty of the Eastern Shore, however, has long been the subhuman living conditions in some of the migrant labor camps which take in a heavy population during the summer harvesting season.) Finally, we should mention Wallops Island and its NASA rocket-launching facility, which has cost the taxpayers a fraction of the cost of the Kennedy Space Flight Center at Cape Canaveral but may have achieved, through the scientific findings of its many launchings, a lot more of benefit to mankind. A rocket fired from Wallops, for instance, enabled Dr. James Van Allen to discover the two great belts of radiation which encircle the globe and now carry his name.

The southern reaches of the Tidewater, close by the North Carolina border, are the locus of Hampton Roads, the greatest natural seaport between New York and Rio de Janeiro, the home of some one million people, more than a fifth of Virginia's population. The urban concentration—and the people—are quite *un*Virginian. Except for a narrow strata of the blue blood aristocracy that can trace familial roots back to the early days of the Old Dominion, the cities are peopled largely by blue-collar working folk and those birds of passage, the military. Former Senator Spong, himself a native of Portsmouth, noted that Hampton Roads was the nearest thing in Virginia to a cross-section of urban America, and especially the great cities of the North and Midwest. He suggested that Richard Scammon and Ben Wattenberg (coauthors of *The Real Majority*) "would have a field day" analyzing the working class people of these Tidewater cities, "who were for Wallace in '68, for Nixon in '72, and [in 1973–74] are raising more hell about Watergate than anyone else."

In addition, there is the cosmopolitan tone associated with any great seaport. Henry Howell described it happily as "the tides coming in and going out, storms and ships and sailors and sealing wax." Hampton Roads, he continued, "has very average people—this is a big hamburger and toys area. But the government pays good blue-collar wages, and there's less poverty. The spirit is quite democratic. It's the only place in Virginia where I could have survived politically." He recalled that the Norfolk papers had shown courage in their opposition to massive resistance.* Hampton Roads was one of the first areas to break with the Byrd organization, and for good reason, because it was afflicted with major school closings and for years there was

---

* Many Virginians, not only in the Hampton Roads area, consider *The Virginian Pilot*, published at Norfolk, the state's most outstanding newspaper.

talk of "The Lost Class of 1959." In addition, the state's dry laws (forbidding liquor by the drink until the late 1960s) put a big crimp in the bar, nightclub, and restaurant businesses, all "naturals" for port cities. And pay-as-you-go in building highways with state funds obliged the Hampton Roads communities to finance many local toll roads, with exorbitant costs because the state's full faith and credit could not be put behind the bonds. Howell was an early leader of the campaign to let Norfolk, Hampton Roads, and eventually all of Virginia "out of the Byrd cage."

One finds the greatest population in the cities on the southern flank of Hampton Roads—Norfolk, which had 307,951 in 1970 (up from 144,332 in 1940 and the highest total of any Virginia city), Portsmouth with 110,963, fast-growing Virginia Beach with 172,106, and Chesapeake with 89,580 people. But the people count is heavy enough across the waters of Hampton Roads to the north—Newport News with 138,177, and Hampton with 120,-779 (cities which had a combined population of just 42,960 in 1940). Some of the growth figures are distorted by annexations, but the total metropolitan population of the Hampton Roads area grew from 352,280 in 1940 to 927,759 in 1970—a rise of 163 percent.

The gods of war were chiefly responsible for starting the Hampton Roads area on its way to being a great world port. With World War I, and especially during World War II and the Cold War years which ensued, a fantastic array of military facilities was channeled into Hampton Roads. The headquarters of the Navy's Atlantic Fleet and 22 other Navy commands are in Norfolk and the nearby areas—the largest concentration of naval installations in any country, anywhere. (Taking the Navy out of Norfolk, one state official suggested to me, would "be like taking the plug out of a bathtub." The largest employer not engaged primarily in government work, he pointed out, was a Ford plant with fewer than 1,900 employees.)

One of the most interesting stories revolves about the unending efforts of the Hampton Roads communities to make the military feel totally and permanently at home in their midst. Active duty personnel are welcomed into local civic groups and chambers of commerce and enjoy annual gala military-civilian dinners in their honor. Civilian officials of the Navy and Air Force bases serve on official boards and commissions of local governments. Numerous museum displays are done in cooperation with the military. Hampton built an $8.5 million coliseum in the late 1960s because, in the words of one local official, "we wanted to give the military the kind of entertainment they expect in view of their worldwide experience." In Norfolk, the chamber of commerce greets U.S. ships returning from extended tours, providing refreshments for dependents waiting on the pier and distributing small American flags to the children. On occasion, entire high school bands turn out to greet the returning ships. The locals have good reason to exert themselves so enthusiastically, because the Department of Defense each year spends no less than $1.2 billion in the Hampton Roads area. In addition, there are NASA expenditures (largely for the Langley Research Center) of more than $125 million a year.

Numerous manufacturing and R & D plants prosper in the military's shadow in the Hampton Roads area. The Norfolk Shipbuilding and Dry-dock Company is one of the most important. But the granddaddy of them all is the Newport News Shipbuilding and Dry Dock Company, the world's largest privately owned shipyard. Close to 500 ships, ranging from tugs and passenger liners (including the United States) to aircraft carriers and Polaris submarines, have been built at the yards since their founding as the "little Virginia sideline" of millionaire industrialist Collis P. Huntington in 1886. In 1972 the firm did $485 million worth of business for the U.S. government. It had a peak employment of 31,000 workers during World War II, but with 20,000 in the early '70s it still had the most employees of any shipyard in the world.

The most interesting development in Hampton Roads in recent years, however, has been the transformation, as journalist Carl Bernstein put it, "from a military-oriented port into a true world trade center." For many years, Hampton Roads had been an important export point for coal and, to a lesser extent, tobacco. But in the early 1960s the various port cities decided to invest heavily in docks that could handle containers—the large boxcar metal shipping devices that can be transferred, unopened, from ships to railroad flatcars or tractor-trailer trucks for direct land delivery. As an advanced container port, Hampton Roads began to export and import widely diversified types of goods. More than 5,000 ships a year now call at Hampton Roads, carrying in their holds everything from Indian fabrics and Indonesian spices to Australian lumber and meat from Holland. A quarter million Virginians owe their jobs, directly or indirectly, to industries that are dependent on shipping their goods and materials through the Roads. Hampton Roads is second only to the Port of New York (especially northern New Jersey) as a container port on the Atlantic Coast, and it continues to lead all Atlantic and Gulf Coast ports in total export tonnage. By the early 1970s, 28 foreign governments had established consulates in Norfolk, and the city was also becoming a major center for international banking, marine insurance firms, and customs house brokers. In addition, since 1970 the port has become a significant embarkation point for cruise ships to the Caribbean.

The irony of all this is that the established leaders of Virginia never planned it. The idea of developing the commonwealth's sea frontier was somehow foreign to a state preoccupied with its internal concerns for well over a century. The possibilities should, of course, have been obvious, because Hampton Roads enjoys immense natural advantages. It is only 18 miles from the open sea; it is easily reached by rail (and now by interstate road) from points north, west, and south in the U.S. at a midpoint on the Atlantic seacoast; and the way had been shown by the rail lines built especially to carry coal from Appalachia to the sea at Norfolk. But not until the 1950s did the state of Virginia appropriate a single dollar for capital expenditures to develop its ports, and not until the 1970s did it begin to bring them under unified control—the *sine qua non*, economists say, for successfully competing with other large ports. (Public subsidization of docks and cargo landing facilities is necessary because they are not in themselves generally profitable operations. Yet they greatly enrich any area because of the jobs and commerce they generate.)

The hell-bent-for-election growth of Hampton Roads has brought a lot of tasteless urban sprawl. Guy Friddell, for instance, wrote of his own home town of Norfolk as

a city of shopping centers, one merging into another, sometimes so vast that when thoroughfares intersect the motorist knows the eerie sensation of knowing no street boundaries, simply cruising an unlimited asphalt bay, in which he could just as easily be going any one of four ways.

Some find the scene sterile, but riding through the jumping, jittery neon night by bold, flamboyant signs of weird off-color colors of red, green, and orange is like driving through a three-dimensional Stuart Davis painting.

Friddell also characterized Norfolk's makeup as "a blend of N's—Navy, NATO, natives and newcomers, especially North Carolinians." The city, he added, "operates largely on nerve." Just after World War II, according to other accounts, Norfolk was beset by the infirmities of a down-at-the-heels sailor's town, including rampant prostitution and streets going to pot. This situation sparked a reform crusade that brought in a new city manager and many civic improvements. Norfolk became one of the nation's first and model cities in the use of federal urban renewal funds, and also built quantities of well designed and well run public housing units in clusters of town houses scattered around the city. Major downtown development came in the 1960s with a new $32 million convention center, new bank-owned high rise buildings, and the like. But retailing was still fleeing to suburbia, and the city (with a 28 percent black population) was struggling with court-imposed desegregation plans, requiring racial balance in the schools and busing. Many whites fled the city schools as a result, although city board chairman Vincent J. Thomas candidly admitted in 1971 that black children were receiving a much better education than they had before integration, and that if it had not been for the NAACP and the federal courts, "we never would have done any of this [desegregation]—and that's true throughout the South."

Historic Portsmouth, Norfolk's neighbor across the Elizabeth River, seemed to be plunging into ecomomic *rigor mortis* in the 1950s when a new highway tunnel to Norfolk siphoned away a huge portion of its downtown business. The county government and other offices started to move away from the city, with the familiar suburbs-only growth pattern. Local leaders embarked on a two-pronged renewal program of private and public expenditures to revive the downtown, however, with success eventually noted in terms of demolished slums, new life for historic old neighborhoods, and new commercial buildings dotting the skyline. Portsmouth still suffers, however, from having practically half its real property off the tax rolls because it is owned by some level of government or charities—by far and away the highest percentage of any Virginia city.

The most astounding growth story of the Hampton Roads orbit is that of Virginia Beach, traditionally—as Guy Friddell wrote—the summertime "main street of Virginia," now on the way to becoming a major city. In fact, if the regional planners are right, it will rise from 200,000 population in the early '70s to almost 400,000 in 1985, thus outranking Norfolk as the largest city in the entire commonwealth. Yet on the eve of Pearl Harbor, the combined population of Virginia Beach and neighboring Princess Ann County (with which it was to consolidate in the early 1960s) was only 20,000. Highways have made the growth possible—the interstate roads linking Hampton Roads with all of the commonwealth, the Chesapeake Bay Bridge-Tunnel providing easy access from the metropolitan centers of the Northeastern U.S., and finally the highway link to Norfolk, which has made commuting easy and prevalent.

Virginia Beach has an exceptionally young, affluent, and white (91 percent) population. An illustration of the youth theme was the choice of a city manager in his early thirties, Roger M. Scott, in the 1960s. (At the time, Scott was the youngest man in the top administrative position of any American city in the 100,000-population range.) A nationally known consulting firm was hired to plan for future development and conceived a code, which was adopted, bringing land use, occupancy, and construction under unified control (the first of its kind in the United States). One trusts all of this is working to bring order, eventually, out of the heady rush to build more and more motels, subdivisions, and shopping centers.

The city of Chesapeake, on Norfolk's southern side, is actually a curious mixture of rural area, swamp, villages, and sprouting shopping centers—covering 341 square miles—hardly one's picture of a typical urban area. The overall population has grown smartly over the past several years, however (to 89,580 in 1970). Chesapeake will be making industrial history in the next several years, because a Swedish auto manufacturer, Volvo-Penta, in 1973 announced plans to build there the first U.S. assembly plant of a foreign auto maker. Unions already have their strongest hold anywhere in Virginia in the Hampton Roads area, and the addition of up to 4,000 workers for the Volvo plant could be expected to have a significant political impact.

Until recently, the path of rapid development from the Hampton Roads area posed a dire threat to the great Dismal Swamp, which actually extends into Chesapeake and neighboring North Carolina counties. The swamp was not always recognized as the unique ecological treasure it is. Colonel William Byrd II, who surveyed the state line through the swamp in 1728, had called it a "horrible desart [sic] . . . nor indeed do any birds care to fly over it . . . for fear of the noisome inhalations that rise from this vast body of dirt and nastiness." What Byrd apparently failed to notice was that 75 species of birds nest in the swamp, and that many more use it on their annual migrations. In addition, the swamp has great numbers of raccoons, muskrats, snapping turtles, river otter, flying squirrels, silver-haired bats, cottontail and nutria, and its own unique species, the Dismal Swamp short-tailed shrew. It is actually the northernmost of the chain of great swamps which begin with the Everglades, offering animal and plant life rarely seen so far north in the country. Dismal has been subject to assault ever since George Washington, who owned a portion of it, started a drainage ditch. The water level has dropped seriously over the years, and by the early 1970s ecologists warned that the wilderness might not have much more than a decade to go before the bulldozers and drainage ruined it forever. The Union Camp Corporation, owner of some 50,000 acres in the very heart of the swamp which it had not logged for many years, then came to the rescue by donating all its land there to the federal government, using the Nature Conservancy as an intermediary. "A refuge is the only right thing for this land, the only right thing," Union Camp's president said. "I hope the conservancy can get the other companies to cough up the rest of it."

Virginia's broad Southside area, the Old Dominion's brush with the Old South, runs along the North Carolina border from Dismal Swamp on the east to the mountains on the west and northward through the Piedmont to a point a bit northwest of Richmond. We have already touched on this region in connection with the political wars, in which it was always the firmest bastion of the Byrd organization. The New York *Times*' Cabel Phillips, a native Virginian, once called the Southside "a bleak country of red clay and scrub pine; of somnolent small towns; of marginal, worked-out farms; of much poverty, ignorance, and prejudice." This is the Virginia where the plantation psychology never really let go, the Virginia with the most black people, the Virginia of drowsy little county seats with their Confederate memorials, and the Virginia of Smithfield hams, tobacco and peanut fields, and, these days, more and more soybeans.

Most of the Southside is rural in the extreme, but there are exceptions. On the region's eastern flank a 1974 merger combined the city of Suffolk with surrounding Nansemond County, making a new "city" of 45,024 people, the fifth largest in the U.S. in land area. Just south of Richmond, one finds the fast-growing Petersburg-Colonial Heights metropolitan area. On the North Carolina border is Danville (1970 population 46,391), of textile fame. Danville has a history of taut race relations, and so does the manufacturing city of Lynchburg (54,083), to the northwest at the point of contact with the Blue Ridge. The Lynchburg establishment is symbolized by the segregationist morning *News* and evening *Advance*, owned by the descendants of the late Senator Carter Glass, known as "the Unreconstructed Rebel" and "Father of the Federal Reserve System." Glass, who had also served as Secretary of the Treasury in the Wilson administration, ran Lynchburg as a kind of oligarchy for more than 40 years; after his death in 1946 things remained much the same. The city's most famous personality of recent decades has been a Baptist minister, Jerry Falwell, an apostle of "saturation evangelism" whose weekly "Old-Time Gospel Hour" is carried each week by some 400 television stations around the world. (Falwell, son of a well-to-do local businessman and onetime sheriff, took over the Thomas Road Baptist Church in 1956, when it had 35 members, and by the early '70s had built it to a congregation of 12,000, almost a quarter of Lynchburg's population. Hoping to learn Falwell's secret, some 5,000 Baptist church workers from all over America came to Lynchburg in 1972 for a symposium on "How to Build a Super-Aggressive Local Church.")

Surry County, located directly across the James River from Jamestown, is a Southside cameo and also a caricature of the region's worst problems. The great river plantations still stand; the rurality and poverty go deep; blacks make up 65 percent of the population of 5,800; and until recently, absolute governmental control was held by a ruling elite of white landowners, politicians, lawyers, and businessmen. When court-ordered desegregation finally came in 1963, the whites simply withdrew en masse to a segregation academy and let the public schools, suddenly 99 percent black, atrophy through lack of funds or attention. Things began to change in 1971, however, when blacks won three of the five posts on the five-man county board of supervisors. "All we want is a role in our own destiny," one of the new supervisors, factory and farm worker Walter N. Hardy told a reporter. "We don't want to dominate anybody or take anything away from the whites that's rightfully theirs. But we *do* want to have a say in how the school system's run, how the taxes are set up, who works in the county jobs—all the things nobody ever asked us about before." The words were hauntingly reminiscent of what one has heard through Deep South States like Mississippi and Alabama in recent times: newborn black pride, but still a touching regard for white people, and a determination not to return an eye for an eye.

Two years after the blacks took control in Surry County, they elected their first mayor of this century in Petersburg, a tobacco belt city of 36,-000 just south of Richmond. By 1970, according to an account by Virginia State College faculty member Carey Stronach, Petersburg had become the relatively compact urban core of a much larger metropolitan area including the industrialized city of Hopewell, the lily-white and Klan-infested bedroom city of Colonial Heights, and the Fort Lee military base. Middle-class whites had departed Petersburg in droves, leaving a 55-percent black majority. With black political control appearing imminent, the controlling whites sought to annex enough white suburbs to restore a white majority in Petersburg. Another, apparently legitimate reason was to expand the city tax base. The annexation was finally effected in 1972, and the whites quickly ordered at-large elections for the expanded city, apparently figuring no blacks would be elected that way. But because Virginia fell under the Voting Rights Act of 1965, local blacks were able to petition the U.S. Justice Department for a review of the new statute, claiming that the at-large plan for council elections would deny them representation. Surprisingly, the Nixon-controlled Justice Department took their side, and the local whites, appealing the case through the courts all the way to the Supreme Court, lost each time. A ward plan was then ordered into effect, and through intensive campaigning and a fortuitous set of circumstances in the elections, the blacks were able to win four of the seven council seats. They promptly named one of their councilmen, Hermanze E. Fauntleroy, Jr., as mayor.

Petersburg's whites regained control of the council in 1974 elections, but the rise of black political power in the city appeared to have two major implications. The first, as the Lawyer's Committee for Civil Rights noted, was that the court decisions represented "the first crack in the crumbling wall of at-large elections which have in the past blocked many blacks from widespread political power." The other was reflected in the post-1973 election comment of a young, white Petersburg businessman-politician to journalist Helen Dewar. White people, he said, "just don't get involved in Petersburg. They have their golf games and their bridge games and that's the extent of their civic involvement. Their children are in private schools [the public school system is about 70 percent black] and they don't participate in city recreation programs. So long as they get their garbage picked up, they don't have a stake." For black people—like the immigrants to the great Northern cities before them—local government and politics of course impinge very directly on personal well-being. Thus while black political control of public offices remains at a minimal level, both in the Southside and across Virginia, the seeds may have been planted for a major black political flowering in the years to come.

Richmond vs. Its Suburbs

Economically, Virginia's capital region at Richmond was in robust shape at the start of the 1970s, with the prospect of many good years to come. The metropolitan area population had grown at a healthy clip (58 percent since 1950), topping the half-million mark. Per capita income was well over the statewide average, and in fact higher than the U.S. average. Overall employment was up 73 percent in 20 years. Nearly 600 plants, employing 52,000 people, made the Richmond area a major manufacturing center, with chemicals, tobacco (the city had long called itself the "cigarette capital of the world," with plants of almost all the major producers), metals, printing, and publishing leading the list. Blue-chip national companies like Reynolds Metals, Du Pont, and the Ethyl Corporation all had major research-manufacturing or headquarters installations in Richmond. State and local government payrolls provided jobs for some 38,000 people, more than double the figure of a decade before.

Most of the postwar population and economic growth had been channeled into the suburban hinterlands of Henrico and Chesterfield County, and by 1960 downtown Richmond had not had a single major new office building since 1929. The chamber of commerce admitted that "a trickling flow of businesses from the central city to suburban locations threatened to become a flood, washing away all hopes for a prosperous future for downtown Richmond." In the early 1960s, however, the city's business and political leadership was able to "get it together" and spark an important downtown renewal. By 1970, well over $100 million had been invested in downtown construction, especially in new office buildings along Main Street, the banking-finance center of the state of Virginia. There was also a new $23 million coliseum, a new city hall, and, for the first time, a number of major downtown apartment buildings.

An important change in tone and leadership had also come to the old capital of the Confederacy. Writing of Richmond in the early 1950s, Harvie Wilkinson had observed:

> Richmond's heart was in the past. Behind its industry and trade lay a "land of gracious living" where the old manners and the old leisure still remained. Symbols of the golden age graced the streets, as in stately leaf-laced Monument Avenue where equestrian statues of the Confederate greats still stalked the land. In central Richmond stood the state Capitol, designed by Thomas Jefferson, the White House of the Confederacy, and the homes of John Marshall and Edgar Allen Poe. Fashionable clubs, small, pillared houses, and antebellum grace existed beside a restless suburban and industrial sprawl.

The next 20 years, however, were to witness an historic "opening up" of Richmond's power structure. The city's West End with its great, old encrusted wealth and social caste system remained, but the aristocracy no longer held in its hands the virtually complete political, economic, social, and intellectual power of the city. Richmond had become so diversified that the old power structure, while still in place, simply didn't matter as it used to. The social power had become divorced from the political and economic power, and the latter was more dispersed (a development which had taken place much earlier in the Northern cities, through the impact of the foreign ethnic groups). The power points of Richmond in the early 1970s ranged from David Tennant Bryan, publisher of the conservative Richmond *News Leader* and *Times-Dispatch* (whose family had dominated the city's journalism over several generations), to the cigarette industry, the Richmond banks and insurance and stockbroker firms, the big department stores, the major manufacturers of chemicals and metals, and for the first time in the city's history, its black people through the unified voice of the Crusade for Voters.

What the growth and prosperity of Richmond masked, up to the early '70s, was the growing wall of hostility between the old city proper and Henrico and Chesterfield, which must rank as some of the most conservative—perhaps reactionary would be a better word—suburbs in the United States. The voting patterns are even more conservative than those of the Southside. Why this is so is not clear; I was never able to get a very adequate explanation from Richmondites. A contributing factor is that they stretch out in a vast pattern of sprawl that bears little relation to the mother city. Henrico in 1970 had 166,000 people in 232 square miles with a single high-rise building, Chesterfield 73,000 in 442 square miles. Moreover, the Richmond area lacks the leavening and often liberalizing influence of people born in other states than Harry Byrd's Virginia. Only 22 percent of its population was born outside Virginia, compared to 44 percent in the Hampton Roads area and an astounding 63 percent in Northern Virginia. The Richmond area's median age is also significantly higher than in the other metropolitan concentrations of the urban corridor.

The picture which emerges is of a suburban population, drawn largely from the Virginia countryside rather than Richmond itself, which has achieved a fair degree of affluence in a setting of low crime rates, low taxes, and higher incomes than Richmond proper—and is determined at all costs to keep its distance. The city, by contrast, had a population about 50 percent black by 1970, and substantial areas of poverty within it. Court-ordered racial balancing in the city schools, which took effect in 1970, quickly drove the black percentage there up to 69 percent. In the wake of the busing plan, there were widespread reports of muggings, harassment, and educational deficiencies in Richmond. ("These problems had always been there in the all black schools," Thomas C. Little, the city's school superintendent said. "But who gave a damn? But mix things up [racially] and they sure surface fast.")

Alarmed by the white flight from its schools, Richmond asked the federal courts to effect a school merger with the overwhelmingly white (91 percent) school districts of Henrico and Chesterfield. U.S. District Judge Robert H. Merhige, Jr., ordered the consolidation, which would have brought with it widespread cross-boundary school busing. His decision sparked a torrent of angry protest from Henrico and Chesterfield. Parents formed protest groups and marched on the Capitol. The Ku Klux Klan, dormant in the area for years, enjoyed a new lease on life. Ugly invective was directed against Merhige, together with threats on his life (necessitating around-the-clock guards). And the Richmond papers printed frequent, long antibusing editorials and ran frequent letters to the editor decrying the "puppet courts throughout America" and the "Communist trend overtaking the nation." *

Merhige's decision was eventually reversed by the Fourth U.S. Circuit Court of Appeals, and the reversal was allowed to stand by an equally divided U.S. Supreme Court. Thus one of the most emotionally volatile political issues of modern-day Virginia (and America) seemed to have been defused. But as reporter Ken Ringle of the Washington *Post* wrote in the wake of the Supreme Court's rebuff to Richmond:

> Virginia's capital city drifts toward lonely years of . . . uncertainty among the shoals of urban decay and continuing white flight.

* With more progressive newspapers, Richmond might today have better race relations and a more open spirit, on the Atlanta model. Linwood Holton suggested to me that Virginius Dabney, a Pulitzer Prize winner and for 33 years editor of the *Times-Dispatch,* "could have been the Ralph McGill of Virginia if he had not been silenced in the mid-1950s for his stand against massive resistance." Editorials, Holton observed, may not affect people directly, "but if a politician can see editorial approval, he's a whole lot bolder." The moderate politicians of Richmond have rarely received that kind of support from the city's papers, although on state issues like mental health, education, and highways, the papers have taken some strong progressive stands. And in all fairness, it should be noted that their news coverage is straightforward and objective. Outstanding reporters like James Latimer, Virginia's leading political writer, and Charles McDowell, who covers Washington, have never been muzzled.

Both the *Times-Dispatch* and *News Leader* are under the corporate umbrella of Media General, Inc., of Richmond, the group which purchased, and then soon let die, the Newark (New Jersey) *News,* that state's leading newspaper, in the early 1970s. According to a *Business Week* account, Media General's business image "is that of a low-performance, labor-busting conglomerate that frequently bites off more than it can chew." But paradoxically, the news budgets and reporter pay scale of MG's Southern papers are higher than many competitors who bask in warm publicity generated by their liberal editorials while pinching pennies on staff and news coverage.

The uncertainty comes from the long history of social and political fragmentation of the Richmond metropolitan area, which has increasingly estranged black from white, city dweller from suburbanite, and rich from poor.

The questions facing the city will delineate its future: Is it too late to keep Richmond from becoming a city of the old, the poor, and the black, as are so many urban areas in the nation?

Northern Virginia: Suburban Nightmare

Washington's Northern Virginia suburbs must be judged a veritable Eden on the Potomac—that is, if one adheres to the demographic measures of "progress" most in vogue in modern America (measures which, I must confess, are employed heavily in these books, largely because the alternative science of "social indicators" and gauges of the "quality of life" remains in its infancy). Consider, though, the Northern Virginia evidence. Two of the region's counties—Fairfax and Arlington—rank second and ninth respectively on the list of the wealthiest counties in the United States. The region as a whole had an average family income of $15,347 in 1970, compared to a figure well under $9,000 for the rest of the Old Dominion. The 1970 Census showed a remarkable 72.5 percent of Northern Virginia's work force in white collar jobs, contrasted to 49.4 percent for Virginia as a whole.* Twenty-seven percent of all adults had completed college or postgraduate education, more than twice the statewide average. The percentage of families living below the poverty line was 4.4 percent in these Washington suburbs, contrasted to a statewide level of 12.3 percent. For years, unemployment in the region has been almost nonexistent. Strong waves of in-migration have not abated since the start of the New Deal, and from a base of just over 600,000 in 1950, the total population, by one projection, will reach 1,300,000 by the end of the 1970s.

Moreover, there are spots of great charm and beauty in Northern Virginia. One thinks of General Lee's home and the Arlington National Cemetery, of Mount Vernon and the quaint, cobbled streets and townhouses of old Alexandria, of the magnificently planned George Washington Parkway along the Potomac, of the charming hill and dale about Great Falls, and one of the architectural masterpieces of the 20th century, Eero Saarinen's terminal for the Dulles International Airport, an edifice fused with grace, strength, and drama. A still later addition was Wolf Trap Farm Park, with its superb open-air auditorium, opened in 1971 as the United States' first national park for the performing arts.

Sadly, one must put all these things down as the exception to the rule in Northern Virginia in our time. For the most part, this area is a suburban nightmare, an example of pell-mell development gone wrong, devastating a

---

* The white collar phenomenon, reflecting a highly trained and highly paid population, is not a completely unmitigated blessing. Wealthy Fairfax County, for instance, suffers from an acute shortage of blue collar workers in trades and service industries, simply because they cannot afford the county's sky-high housing prices.

region of great natural beauty. But let the indictment not come from me, but from a Virginian, the late Lieutenant Governor Sargeant Reynolds, in a speech he gave in 1970:

We are on the threshold of becoming a sister state to the great sprawl of the industrial Northeast. If we are not careful, the Virginia that is distinctive for her loveliness—her tidewaters, her mountains and valleys and streams—will become one solid urban mass, whose revered history will be crowded among the nooks and crannies that are left when concrete and metal dominates the topography all around us.

If you think that is farfetched—if you think your panoramic views of lake and forest are secure—take a trip to northern Virginia and have a good look: the sprawling suburbs that have swept away trees and hills and all that is green from the path of "progress"; the choking arteries of highways that feebly try to feed Washington its daily work force; the glass jungle of Rosslyn; the pervading massive development of Crystal City.

Northern Virginia suffers from "excess opportunity"—from more demand for houses, highways, hospitals, utilities, office and commercial buildings than the area has been able to supply with the abortiveness of time for planning and financing. . . .

We have not developed methods of coping with mass transportation, the need for high-rise living, capital requirements for rapidly developing communities, and zoning requirements that eliminate competition between contiguous areas to attract the quick-turn developer who uses a bulldozer as the great leveler.

(To Reynolds' credit, he had the courage to give that speech to an association of home builders. In postwar Northern Virginia, some of the most powerful politicians have been real estate developers, and some of the pressure they have placed on local governments for zoning and sewer changes to open the way for their bulldozers have been case studies in the subversion of public policy for private profit.)

Up through the 1940s, the Northern Virginia suburbs were chiefly a bedroom area for government workers who commuted daily to jobs in Washington. Detached single-family homes dominated the scene, complemented by garden-type apartments. But the monstrous Pentagon building had been built during World War II, funneling 30,000 workers into a single facility daily, and during the 1950s the trend toward decentralization of federal offices to the suburbs began to accelerate. (An example was the huge Central Intelligence Agency headquarters, which until the 1970s had no identifying sign—a bit of petty secretiveness which may have fooled some tourists but certainly not the Soviets nor Washingtonians.)

By the 1960s the pressure for federal office space had become so intense that massive, ill-planned clusters of towering office buildings began to sprout along the Potomac, offering rental space to the feds. One of these was the Jefferson Davis Corridor, on U.S. Route 1 near the National Airport, including the great monolith called Crystal City. (By 1990 the Jefferson Davis Corridor is expected to have 15,000 apartments and 16 million square feet of office space, providing space for a resident population of some 25,000 and close to 100,000 daytime employees.) Or consider Rosslyn, across the Key Bridge from Washington. In 1962 it was a melange of one-story buildings, gas stations, pawnshops, and the like. Then the highrises began to poke up into the sky, set at awkward angles to each other in tasteless profusion. They provide working space for 28,000 people. All along the major arteries, fighting for space with the shopping centers and apartment buildings (some of gargantuan proportions), the office buildings have risen—with crest after crest of development, farther from the Potomac and deep into suburbia. More office-apartment complexes, in the multi-hundred million dollar cost range, were on the drawing boards by the start of the '70s.

As a result of this, Arlington County—the mother suburb of them all, directly opposite Washington—had more apartment units than single-family homes. The subdivision developers were not idle, however, responding to the population surge by pushing their stereotyped plans out through Fairfax County, to the outer reaches of Alexandria, and on into hitherto-placid counties like Prince William and Loudoun. And no one could say where it all might stop (if ever).

Traffic estimates made in the early 1970s showed that close to half a million automobiles were crossing the Potomac to and from Washington and nearby points each day.* (Washingtonians had had enough, and were stoutly resisting the efforts to throw more bridges across the river.) The traffic density on the roads of Arlington, Alexandria, and Fairfax ranged from four to eight times the state average, on a vehicle-per-mile basis. Monumental daily traffic jams were the inevitable result. (As a Washington *Post* writer commented in 1971: "For thousands of Northern Virginians who have traveled and suffered Shirley Highway [I-95] over the years, the road's creator is Dante. No mortal highway engineer, no mere planner of urban sprawl, could have possibly concocted such a heinous scheme." The road had been widened time and again, to ever more lanes, yet the traffic tie-ups only got worse.)

Not all the Northern Virginian traffic was headed to the District, however. A complex cross-metropolitan work and traffic pattern had evolved, showing that of 425,000 persons either living or working in Northern Virginia, 36 percent commuted to work elsewhere, 21 percent commuted *into* Northern Virginia (from the District, Maryland, or other Virginia counties), and that a surprising 43 percent both lived *and* worked in Northern Virginia. But whichever way their movement went, it was overwhelmingly by private automobile, and the congestion and air pollution was getting worse and worse, year by year.

It came as little surprise, then, when Northern Virginia voters in 1968 voted 78 percent in favor of the concept of Metro—the Washington area subway-surface rapid transit system finally approved by Congress, after years of effort, in 1969. Construction began that same year, but the total system of 98 miles—30 of them in Virginia, including 20 Virginia stops—was not expected to be completed until the early 1980s. The "Metro" system was

---

* That was the equivalent of a single column of autos 1,700 miles long, enough to produce a bumper-to-bumper traffic jam from Northern Virginia to Key West and back to about Jacksonville, or a column of cars 17 abreast from the Potomac to Richmond.

projected to carry 132,000 riders across the Potomac each day.* As a stop-gap measure, express bus lanes were set up on some of the major arteries feeding into Washington from Northern Virginia. Looking forward to Metro, former Fairfax County Supervisor Frederick A. Babson said that there was "no other solution to the traffic problems facing this region." But the heavy tide of cross-suburban commuting patterns would not be helped much by Metro.

With their high educational level, one might have expected the people of Northern Virginia to insist on sound land use planning as the population shot upward in the postwar era. Two factors worked against this, however. First, a high degree of transiency and the lack of any established, accepted political hierarchy mitigated against region-wide consensus. In elections it was every man for himself, and no political party long held power. Second, many of the most skilled residents worked for the federal government and were prohibited by the Hatch Act from taking part in partisan political activity.

To complete the Northern Virginia picture, a quick rundown of the major areas is in order:

Arlington (1970 population 174,284) used to be a pastoral summer retreat for Washingtonians. Then it became the best-known bedroom boomtown of World War II. Today the bulk of its population is made up of lifetime government workers. Jack Fraser, in an excellent account for the *Washingtonian* magazine, summed up Arlington as "a shrine, a paradox, a mess, and a surprise." One can depict it as an aging suburb, bypassed by booming Fairfax County. But if it is suburb, it is also a city in its own right; after all, some 100,000 people migrate *into* it for work everyday. "It is too close to downtown Washington to remain only a bedroom, too valuable to speculators in office space to evade rezoning pressures, too strategic to avoid freeways," Fraser noted. (It did, however, win an apparent victory in the early '70s in stopping a proposed 14-lane extension of Interstate 66 from the south, which would have cut through its very heart.)

Arlington never accepted urban renewal and never built any public housing—the problems of the ghetto, if you please, are to remain in Washington. (The black percentage of Arlington in 1970 was 6 percent, compared to 72 percent in the District.) And who have been the most famous citizens of this massive suburb? Fraser's answer: "The dead at Arlington Cemetery and American Nazi Party leader George Lincoln Rockwell, extinguished near a neighborhood laundromat."

The city of Alexandria (110,938) dates its first settlement back to 1695. It has many historic buildings of the 18th century, when George Washington considered it his "home town" and helped to lay out the streets. Washington also drilled his troops there in 1754 before marching them against the French and Indians, and the people of Alexandria feasted him when he passed through on his way from Mount Vernon to Philadelphia

* The Metro system will be discussed in full in a subsequent book in this series, *The Mid-Atlantic States*, which will include chapters on the District of Columbia and Maryland.

to take office as the first President of the United States in the spring of 1789. The city enjoyed a flourishing trade with the interior in early times, and until the railroad lines went west from Baltimore and preempted its role, it was an important port.

Now it has been more than a century since Alexandria measured its prosperity by the tonnage of its cargoes, and the old waterfront, sunken into desolation and blight, has been a major point of controversy over proposals for renewal. The Federal Records Center, a bleak, gray building covering several blocks of the waterfront, is scheduled to go down in this decade.* But Congress has yet to resolve some of the problems of disputed land ownership, clouded by land swaps that began in 1791, high water marks and bulkhead lines, and changes in the river's configuration over many years. Proposals for a towering "Watergate II" apartment complex along the waterfront were scotched in the early '70s on the basis of citizen protests. One hopes the whole matter can be resolved, for close onto the waterfront is historic "old" Alexandria, a townhouse area splendidly preserved and redeveloped, a competitor to Washington's Georgetown for gracious urban-style living in the metropolitan area. Close by are Banker's Square and Market Square, the heart of the city's tastefully executed urban renewal program.

Alexandria has had its problems with racial disorders, neighborhoods in transition, and a rate of serious crime that shot up beyond the District of Columbia level in 1972. The city's black people, whose roots go back to the town's slave-trading days and who presently make up 14 percent of the population, have long felt excluded from the vital policy decisions of the city. But in 1970 they did elect their first city council member in history.

The major population increase of the city since World War II has come in its more suburban areas, around traffic-glutted growth centers like the Landmark Shopping Center (which boasts a 4,000-car parking lot.) The developers also hope to put up some Crystal City-scale developments in the next few years, one to cost as much as $800 million.

In 1974 the Washington Center for Metropolitan Studies suggested that Alexandria and Arlington had become, with the District of Columbia, part and parcel of the Washington metropolitan area's "real central city." All three jurisdictions, it was noted, shared characteristics more typical of central urban areas than suburbs, including close-in land being converted from primary residential to office/industrial uses, higher density levels in the remaining land, and high percentages of adult "singles" and childless couples in renter-occupied units. "Perhaps it is not coincidental," according to the study, "that Arlington, Alexandria, and the District were originally parts of the 'ten-mile-square' section carved out of the states of Maryland and Virginia to serve as the Nation's Capital. Although Alexandria and Arlington

---

* Other cheerless waterfront structures are the chief storehouse point for Interarms, the biggest private dealer in surplus military weapons on the international market. The Interarms operations were given a thorough airing in *The War Business*, by the late George Thayer (New York: Simon and Schuster, 1969).

were later returned to the state of Virginia, and even though they are separated from the District by the Potomac River, they now appear to be pursuing a common urban destiny with the city of Washington."

Fairfax County, which encircles Arlington and Alexandria to the west and south, is the wunderkind of Northern Virginia's modern-day growth. The county had 40,929 inhabitants in 1940, 275,002 in 1960, and an estimated 533,000 in 1973—an increase of 1,200 percent in 32 years. Its year 2,000 population has been projected at 1,300,000. Land area has a lot to do with the growth to date and the future potential. For while Arlington has only 26 square miles, and Alexandria 15, Fairfax's total is 399.

For years the county government tended to be dominated by the developers and their toadies, who did everything in their power to expedite the relentless march of the subdivisions across Fairfax's fair fields and forests. Then, at the end of the 1960s, the people began to look carefully at their overcrowded schools, clogged highways, and mounting sewage problems and began to wonder if the growth—and especially its pace—was such a good idea. Environmentally-conscious supervisors were elected to office, pledged to slow the growth. In 1971 the new board created a task force, headed by supervisor Rufus Phillips, a professional planner, to develop an effective land use program. "We researched everything that is going on here and abroad," Phillips later told *Time* magazine. "We sat down with city planners. . . . We looked at British and Scandinavian efforts, where the governments largely control development planning. Then we turned to the citizens, sent out questionnaires through the county, held open workshops and public hearings." The result was a 161-page primer for planning, calling for a new master plan and zoning ordinance, an inventory of all the county's resources (natural and man-made), and requiring environmental impact statements from developers. The land use program, Phillips claimed, "puts Fairfax County in a new realm where planning and zoning will be meaningful and not just a paper mirage."

The new supervisors went a step further by requiring that all developments exceeding 50 units must include some housing for low- and moderate-income groups.* And over the angry protest of developers, they put moratoriums on sewer connections for most of the county because the treatment plants serving Fairfax were operating at capacity and threatened the discharge of untreated waste into the Potomac. (As noted in the discussion of Lexington, in the Kentucky chapter of this book, sewers are one of the most effective planning mechanisms a government can use.)

One has to admire the courage of some of Fairfax's new leaders, especially its women. It was Supervisor Audrey Moore who identified existing zoning practices for what they were—"just an invitation to bribery, corruption and abuse and bad land use, . . . inequitable and unfair." And Jean

---

* A meager five percent of Fairfax's people subsist at income levels even near the poverty line. Only 3.5 percent of the population is black—and even at that, there have been celebrated cases of excluding black residents from private community swimming pools and cross-burnings on the lawns of Negroes who dared to impinge in lily-white subdivisions.

R. Packard made the transition from citizen activist to chairman of the board of supervisors on a pledge to be Fairfax's first full-time chairman. "We're a county with a budget of over $355 million. It's ridiculous not to have a full-time chairman," she said.

Most of the place names in Fairfax are studies in obscurity. (If you don't agree, try Annandale, Bailey's Crossroads, Jefferson, Seven Corners, and Long Branch for size.) Shopping centers tend to be the only meaningful landmarks. There are two exceptions, however—one very old, one very new. The old is McLean, which includes the hill where James and Dolly Madison stood in August 1814 to view the burning of Washington. McLean's modern-day residents include Ethel Kennedy and Edward M. Kennedy and many of Washington's political-business elite. A subdivision with homes valued as high as a quarter million dollars began there in the late 1960s.

The very new is Reston, conceived by Robert E. Simon, Jr., in the early 1960s as an antidote to haphazard suburban sprawl, a totally "new town" that would be its own self-contained entity of housing, stores, schools, and cultural and recreational facilities. In an idea radical for its time, Simon devised a system in which the standard detached suburban house would be replaced by clusters of townhouses, leaving the large tracts of land for green space and extending residents' living patterns through copious walkways and common open spaces. With good reason, architectural critics jumped with joy at the town center of futuristic townhouses and a highrise on the shores of man-made Lake Anne, with a semicircle of stores topped by apartments, facing a community plaza on the water's edge. The "pioneer" residents of Reston seemed to be a new type, too—in the words of one local leader, an "urbane, activist, sophisticated, artsy-craftsy" group of people.

Much of that was to remain into the 1970s, creating a fresh suburban atmosphere for Reston's professional-technical population and higher grade government workers (who commute to Washington by bus each day). But Simon got into financial hot water in 1967, a result of a tight money market, management deficiencies, and the high cost of his type of development. He was bought out by the Gulf Oil Company, a major early investor, and the new housing switched to a more conventional model, generally single-family homes undistinguishable from standard suburbia and often miles from the shops to which Reston's residents, by original plan, were to be able to walk. But Gulf had "saved" the town financially, and its population was up to 25,000 by 1973 (and headed for some 80,000 by the end of the decade). Only 5 to 7 percent of the residents were black, and even they tended to be high-income professional people. Gulf-Reston began to construct housing, however, for a large number of blue collar and less affluent people. (Reston's management was often criticized for the lack of moderate- or low-income housing, but the record showed it had tried from the start, only to find its applications for FHA assistance sidetracked and pigeonholed by federal bureaucrats, who made the silly argument that lower income people would not want to live there.)

With its share of hippie and drug problems in the late '60s and early

'70s, Reston was said to have "lost its innocence." Many of the new residents failed to understand the peculiar social outlook of the FFR (first families of Reston). But Reston still had a special ambiance, and it had provided an invaluable national model of the potentialities and pitfalls of private new town development in the United States.

Within the past decade the hot game of speculation and development has spilled over into Prince William and Loudoun Counties, rural innocents in the path of progress. The *National Observer's* James Perry visited Prince William one day and was told by Ralph A. Mauller, one of the supervisors: "You know, not long ago all we had to do was housekeeping. We'd buy a new lawnmower every so often. Now we've got these big bankers, builders, and developers, and they look at us and they rub their hands in glee."

The rural county folk are not altogether without sophistication, however. In 1973, for instance, Loudoun County enacted a new zoning ordinance that required any builder seeking permission to erect housing at increased densities to put up the money for required new schools and facilities, to the extent that the new residents' taxes would not cover the costs. (County officials pointed out that Loudoun's population had increased by 51 percent in the 1960s, but that the county budget had gone up 10 times as much, largely to pay the bills associated with population expansion.)

Prince William County, historically a quiet, rural, agricultural community where the biggest events ever were the two Battles of Bull Run in the Civil War, has been impacted even more heavily by Washington area spillover. Its population increased 121 percent, to 111,102 in the 1960s, with huge, dull subdivisions accounting for most of the growth.

Loudoun and Prince William have a long way to go, of course, before they become replicas of Fairfax or resemble the urban concentration of the inner suburbs. In another few decades, however, it is not hard to imagine the urban corridor packed with people all the way to Richmond. All of this northern Piedmont region might one day be endangered. The vanguard of a new era came years ago—Jean Gottmann noted in the 1950s that parts of the Piedmont, including the areas around towns like Leesburg, Middleburg, and Warrenton, were "becoming a sort of beautiful country club, the members of which still work or have some interest in Washington, and among whom one could find an impressive repertory of names famous in American industry, finance, or politics." This is the famous Virginia hunt country, given largely to woodlands and grassy meadows for pasturing; there are still many indigenous farmers, but the choicest land has long since passed into the hands of those who nurture the land for fun and beauty (the "station-wagon farmers," the saying goes). The phenomenon is even noted as far southwest as Albemarle County, surrounding Charlottesville, an area of beautiful estates and much affluence. (Charlottesville itself is one of the most appealing towns of the United States, offering the visitor the sight of the University of Virginia campus with its central buildings designed by Jefferson, as well as the lovely homes of Presidents—Jefferson's own Monticello and James Monroe's Ashlawn.)

One can only say that if great stretches of the still-placid northern Piedmont eventually fall before the developers' bulldozers, the travesty will not have been one that came without warning. As Sargeant Reynolds said, the close-in Northern Virginia suburbs were already a warning light of what might come.

From the Blue Ridge to Cumberland Gap

Western Virginia is a world to itself, a region of mountains and valleys quite distinct from Tidewater and Piedmont, a "puzzle of compartments" with differing natural and human characteristics. The eastern flank of the region is the lovely Blue Ridge, which rises as a line of low hills in western Loudoun County, near the Potomac, and widens southwestward, boasting the highest peaks in the state, and encompasses whole counties near the North Carolina line. On the western slope of the Blue Ridge lies the Great Valley, a long, fertile furrow in the mountains running from the Potomac to the Tennessee border in the south. The broad northern section is known as the Valley of Virginia, the most famous section of which is the fabled Shenandoah Valley. West of the valley rise the mountains of the Allegheny region. Finally, there are the Southwestern Highlands, a triangular wedge between Kentucky and Tennessee that ends at the historic Cumberland Gap.

The hollows of the Blue Ridge were settled in the late 1700s by mountain folk who remained there for generation after generation, in a kind of suspended animation, while the rest of America changed. This is one of the regions where a dialect close to Elizabethan English survived into our century. As recently as 1928–29, children were found in the Blue Ridge who had never seen the American flag and had no idea of the world beyond their mountains. Roads, motorcars, and generally improved communications began to break down the wall of isolation in the 1930s, and many of the mountain folk were forced to move when the Shenandoah National Park, stretching from Front Royal to Waynesboro and topped by the Skyline Drive, was created. Further south, many Blue Ridge areas were made into national forests. But to this day Franklin County, south of Roanoke, remains one of the great moonshining counties of America. (In a recent year revenue agents seized 424 stills in Virginia and destroyed 23,000 gallons of "white lightning." The value of Virginia moonshine at illegal retail outlets was estimated at $1 million a year.)

The Skyline Drive and the park areas along it, within easy motoring distance of Washington, are heavily used by visitors and represent one of the prime recreational areas of the eastern United States. The park itself is a splendid example of the opportunities for recycling heavily used land to create islands of peace and beauty in easy reach of megalopolis. As George B. Hartzog, then director of the National Park Service, said in 1971: "Look at Shenandoah National Park. It was created from an area that was heavily utilized. They had cut every stick on it. They plowed every acre that was fit for plowing. But then it was set aside for a national park. Nature has healed the land, and here we are proposing some 65,000 acres of it for wilderness classification."

A very new but grave threat to the fringes of the Blue Ridge and nearby areas of Shenandoah Valley has been posed by an explosion in sales of mountain and riverfront acreage for vacation retreats or "second homes" for the people of the metropolitan areas. No one saw much problem in the early trickle of city people who sought out scattered sites for vacation homes. But starting in the late 1960s, a new and more ominous development occurred: the arrival of real estate speculators who carved up mountain acreage into half- or quarter-acre lots, selling them at inflated prices. Whole second-home subdivisions, vacation villages, and ski slopes began to sprout. Real estate values were driven up so rapidly that the natives of these counties often found they could not afford to buy land for their own homes. On Massanutten Mountain, a dramatic 35-mile-long mountain that rises out of the floor of the Shenandoah Valley, there were 27 developments by 1973. They ranged from a $50 million Del Webb project, complete with ski slopes and sewage treatment facilities, to one real estate development of half-acre lots devoid of roads, sewerage, or utility easements. The ecological hazard involved in all of this was apparent enough; moreover, the arrival of suburbia-in-the-mountains could ruin the natural beauty the purchasers had hoped to find in the first instance.

The Great Valley, stretching some 360 miles southwesterly from the Potomac, is a land in many ways blessed. The mountains on each side provide a superb setting; the lime-rich soil is excellent for farming; there are many rivers and streams; and the string of cities along the valley floor has developed modestly, providing a fine balance between human settlement and open space. In recent years industry has arrived, chiefly in food processing, wood working, textiles, light machinery, and the like, providing employment for the surplus farm labor but not in great enough concentrations to imperil the environment. And of course there is the romance, especially of the Shenandoah Valley—

> O Shenandoah, I long to hear you,
>   Away, you rollin' river.
> O Shenandoah, I long to hear you,
>   Away, I'm bound away,
>   'Cross the wide Missouri.

The song obviously originated with people who had known the valley but had then gone farther westward in the migrations of the republic's early years. Among the pioneer families had been ones bearing the names of Lincoln and Houston. John Sevier, destined to be the "father of Tennessee," founded the valley town of New Market in 1761. Later the valley would be the birthplace of Woodrow Wilson, and of course the famous Byrd brothers.

The land has been well husbanded, ever since the early settlement of the Shenandoah Valley by the Germans coming southward from Pennsylvania, bringing with them superior agricultural skills. To this day, even the casual traveler can see how well the farm resources of the Valley of Virginia are managed. Winchester, in the north, is the great apple-growing center; as one moves southward, one comes on great poultry (chicken and turkey) farms, and a wide diversity in grains, cattle, and hogs. Tourism is also of great importance, for this valley has great caverns honeycombing its limestone floor, the famed Natural Bridge (a limestone wonder Jefferson called "the most sublime of Nature's works"), and the national forests which draw millions of visitors each year. To the north, where the Shenandoah meets the Potomac, lies historic Harper's Ferry; at Winchester, which exchanged hands 70 times in the Civil War, are the side-by-side headquarters of Confederate General "Stonewall" Jackson and Union General Philip Sheridan, and the surveying office used by George Washington in 1784. Near Harrisonburg the traveler finds Mennonites in their black suits and long dresses; Staunton is the site of the Presbyterian manse where Wilson was born; Lexington has the contrasting elegance of Washington and Lee University and the stark buildings of the Virginia Military Institute.

The people of the valley tend to be a thrifty, debt-fearing, hardworking lot, many still descended from or related to the Pennsylvania Dutch. In politics they are staunch fiscal (but not racial) conservatives. They seem to care little whether a candidate runs under Democratic or Republican colors, as long as he exhibits a frugality and opposition to big government in the mode of Winchester's late Harry F. Byrd.

Roanoke, crowded up against the Blue Ridge well to the south in the Great Valley, is the only city of any real size (92,115 in 1970) in this part of the state. I was amazed to find how very mountainous its setting is. The city sprang up in the 1880s, the creation of the Norfolk and Western Railway. Over the years it successfully sought a wide range of industries, and its go-getting spirit gave it the reputation of being Virginia's most "Midwestern" city. (The image was reinforced by Roanoke's status as the only major Virginia city founded after the Civil War, thus free of the psychic scars of that conflict.) A series of grave economic reversals for the city began in 1958, when the N & W shops stopped making steam locomotives, throwing 2,000 men out of work. But the local boosters went to work and recruited many new plants, and while the center-city population declined, the suburbs expanded at a good clip. Roanoke is also the trade and service center for a wide area, not only all of the southern part of the valley but also for virtually all of southwestern Virginia as well.

Population is light and prosperity an elusive factor in the rugged Allegheny Mountain province, west of the Great Valley and along the West Virginia line. (The Allegheny Plateau actually continues westward, one ridge after the other, to the valley of the Ohio; as Jean Gottmann pointed out, "the commonwealth includes only the façade, often very shallow, of this vast mountain world.") The best known industry of the Alleghenies within Virginia is the giant plant of the West Virginia Pulp and Paper Company at Covington, infamous both for its pollution of the Jackson River and for the harsh sulfurous smell it throws over the town. In the early '70s the pollution was gradually being brought under control, and of course Covington remained thankful for a factory that had been its economic lifeblood for seven decades and still provided 2,000 jobs. Hardscrabble farming in the hollows characterizes this region, but by way of contrast there is also Hot Springs with its sumptuous 17,000-acre resort, The Homestead, where 900 employees look after the comfort of 900 guests at American plan rates averaging close to $50 a day.

The Southwestern Highlands, locale of Virginia's famous "Fightin' Ninth" congressional district, is the commonwealth's poorest, least-educated, most poorly-housed area—in the words of one observer, a "rural slum." * Race is not the reason, because blacks make up a meager 2.4 percent of the population. The region has a scattering of cattle and burley tobacco farms, but there are scarcely any other districts in the United States where agricultural methods are so primitive (sickles, scythes, and horse-drawn plows down to the last few years) and where the farmers' standard of living is so abysmally low. Based on the 1959 Census of Agriculture, for instance, a farm operator level-of-living index was developed, measuring farm prosperity in terms of average sales per farm, value of land and buildings, how many farms had telephones, freezers, and automobiles. The Virginia Ninth ranked fourth from the bottom in the entire country, trailing only the two congressional districts of neighboring East Kentucky and one district in Mississippi.

The highlands have a scattering of industry, but the most important income comes from the relatively limited but rich coal fields there. Virginia coal production, the great bulk of which is in this region, rose from 18 million tons in 1950 to 35 million tons in the early 1970s, about 6 percent of the U.S. production. The industry provides an annual payroll of some $100 million, and one shudders to think what would become of the typical Appalachian folk of these Southwestern Highlands if it were not for coal. Not that mining itself is a very safe or desirable line of work, at least by most people's standards. In one recent year 27 Virginia miners died in accidents in the mines, including 10 from roof falls. The mile-deep Beatrice Mine at Keen Mountain is a constant concern of the mine safety inspectors, since it is one of the most gassy coal mines anywhere, "liberating" some three million cubic feet of volatile methane gas each day.

Unemployment has been high in the coal fields ever since the postwar automation, and there are many counties where more than a third of the families earn less than $4,000 a year. Thousands of the highlanders have deserted their region for better jobs, especially in the Hampton Roads shipbuilding complexes and the Detroit auto plants. But still, many return whenever they get a chance, in the prototypal Appalachian mountaineer fashion.

The dying coal mine town of St. Charles, close to the Kentucky border

* In 1970, for instance, 28 percent of the 9th's homes lacked plumbing facilities, a higher figure, even, than the Southside. (The state average was 11.6 percent.)

in Lee County, provides a picture of the saddest part of the highlands in our time. As reported by journalist Paul G. Edwards:

St. Charles is a picture postcard no one would want to print. It lies near the head of a hollow, where sooty, two-story brick buildings line both sides of the narrow, twisting main street. Many storefronts are boarded over. A half-dozen dimly lit snack bars and grocery stores are open seven days a week. On a Sunday, the townspeople drift from one to another, talking, playing pinball machines and drinking coffee.

Chickens strut in the empty lots between buildings, scratching the site of a now demolished hotel or grocery store that disappeared with the mining heyday that ended with World War II.

And then there are depressing stories like that of Tazewell, where the town's biggest industry, which employed 1,000 people producing electrolytic capacitors for television sets, suddenly closed in the early 1970s. General Instrument Co., the multinational conglomerate that owned the plant, decided that because of labor costs and tariff concessions it would be cheaper to move the whole manufacturing facility to Taiwan and Portugal. The Tazewell workers were left in jobless desperation.

On the bright side, a startling economic recovery has begun around the town of Duffield, on the Clinch River, sparked by the planners of the TVA's tributary area division—a story reviewed in the TVA chapter of this book (page 362). And the city of Bristol, which sits cheek-by-jowl with a Tennessee city of the same name on the state border ("State Street" is the official boundary), has some reason for hope because it abuts the newly thriving Bristol-Kingsport-Johnson City area of eastern Tennessee.*

The Southwestern Highlands—and our story—end at Cumberland Gap, that dramatic notch in the mountains through which the first white man, Dr. Thomas Walker, passed on March 6, 1750. The date was almost a century and a half after the first settlers had landed at Jamestown, almost 400 miles to the east. Some years later Walker's path would be trod again by Daniel Boone, blazing the famed Wilderness Road into Kentucky, the American West of its day. In time, thousands would make the same trek westward, up and over Cumberland Gap, or over the Great Valley Road into Tennessee. And many of those pioneers, or their descendants, would later push to the end of the primeval forest, onto the open prairies and then across the Mississippi and the Missouri, and over the Great Plains to the Southwest and the Pacific. The restless progeny of an Old Dominion too settled in its ways to accommodate them, even in its first centuries, their destiny would be to people a continent.

* The two Bristols, incorporated by their respective state legislatures in 1856, came close to an armed clash in 1889 as a result of a dispute over where the boundary ran. The controversy was finally decided by the U.S. Supreme Court. According to political scientist C. P. Curcio, a local resident, "Each city has separate post offices, court systems, educational systems, prisons, courthouses, and police and fire departments. The separation of these services has caused much discussion and speculation about the possibility of consolidating at least some of these services in order to avoid duplication. No way has been found, however, to overcome the barrier of the state boundary line." In 1970, Virginia's Bristol had 14,857 people, and Tennessee's 20,064.

NORTH CAROLINA

PROGRESSIVE PARADOX

WHEN THE NORTH CAROLINA SENATE refused to ratify the Equal Rights Amendment in March 1973, feminist writer Kate Millett, apparently surprised, lamented that the state "used to lead the South in liberalism and the progressive social ethic." Ms. Millett, whose field of expertise is far removed from Southern and Border State politics, nonetheless reflected the longstanding conventional wisdom about this state.

A quarter century ago, V. O. Key in *Southern Politics* was able to report that North Carolina "enjoys a reputation for progressive outlook and action in many phases of life, including industrial development, education, and race relations." John Gunther, after his brief stop in the state for *Inside U.S.A.*, was fairly gushing: "That North Carolina is by a good deal the most liberal southern state will, I imagine, be agreed to by almost everybody." Key, more judiciously, added that North Carolinians themselves are the first to point out that their state does not entirely deserve its progressive reputation; and that is still the case today. The local monthly which printed Ms. Millett's lament also reported that North Carolinian women's rights supporters, "more aware of the true climate of repression, . . . were not so surprised at the senate's action."

"Repression" is not the right word, but "progressive" gives North Carolina too much credit. For this is a state of paradoxes: behind every fact which can be cited as proof of its progressiveness lurks another which suggests just the opposite. Take industrial development, one of the progressive factors mentioned by Key. North Carolina continues to lead all Southern and Border States except Texas in value-added by manufacturers and new capital expenditures. Yet North Carolina industrial workers in 1971 earned a pathetic $104 a week—a figure lower than in any other state but Mississippi.

North Carolina is proud, and in many respects justly so, of its system of public education. North Carolinians like to recall Charles B. Aycock, a turn-of-the-century politician who is still remembered as the "education governor"; they are less fond of recalling that Aycock, a Democrat, beat a Republican-Populist fusion on the platform of disenfranchising the Negro. But after years of effort, most adult North Carolinians have not finished the 11th grade, and the state ranks near the bottom, ahead only of West Virginia, Arkansas, South Carolina, and Kentucky, in terms of the number of school years completed. North Carolina likes to think of itself as more sophisticated, more mature than other Southern and Border States; but in 1973 it still voted down, and by a large margin, liquor-by-the-glass (while supporting a fair-sized moonshine industry in the hills).

Finally, we should mention that this is a state that has long prided itself on its racial tolerance. Yet for a while in the 1960s it was the home of the most heavily peopled and virulent Ku Klux Klan in the United States, headed by Bob Jones of Granite Quarry, who finally went to prison for several months rather than turn over Klan records to the House Un-American Activities Committee. According to a report in the *Race Relations Reporter,** the "glory days" of the modern Klan were in the mid-1960s "when rallies in cow pastures and corn fields would draw thousands of believers and Jones was treated like the godfather of white supremacy. . . . He was able to drum up blood-curdling fervor from the traditional supporters of the Klan: farmers, laborers, working-class people, a smattering of sheriff's deputies, small-town businessmen and work-toughened mill hands." The North Carolina Klan claimed at least 6,000 dues-paying members. By 1973, however, even the most optimistic measure of state Klan membership was only 500, and Bob Jones was thinking of a new career in elective politics.

And however progressive North Carolina leaders may claim their state to be on the race issue, there were several cases in the early 1970s in which black rights activists were pursued with suspicious fervor by law enforcement officers and, after conviction on questionable charges, sentenced to astonishingly long prison sentences.

How to explain these paradoxes? One clue is that North Carolina has never had a golden age—or much of a revolution. When Virginia was producing democratic aristocrats like Washington, Jefferson, Madison, and Marshall, North Carolina was a land of fiercely independent small farmers, many of them Scotch-Irish, and few slaves. When John C. Calhoun of South Carolina was promulgating the doctrine of nullification, North Carolina was supporting—for a while—as many abolitionist societies as any state in the Union. North Carolina, unlike Kentucky and Tennessee, did not enjoy flourishing

---

* "Farewell to the Grand Dragon," by Luisita Lopez and Frye Gaillard, *Race Relations Reporter,* November 1973.

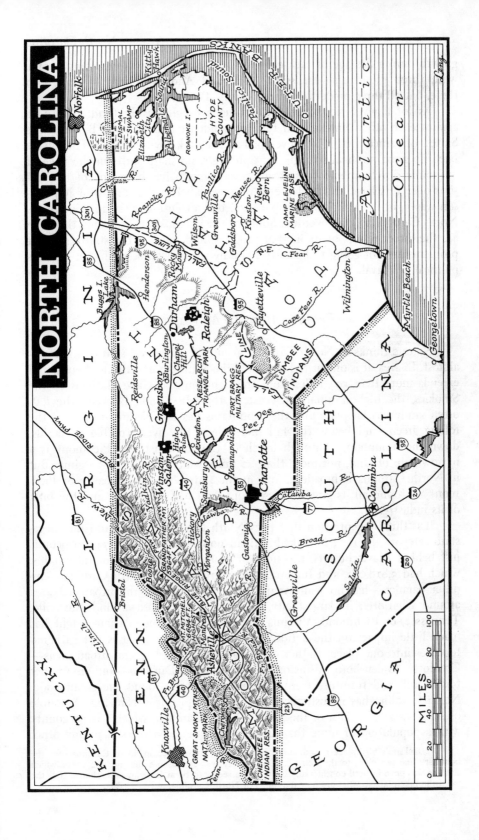

growth during the age of Jackson and Clay. Rather, it was exporting people west; three Presidents—Jackson,* Polk, and Andrew Johnson—were born there, but all three made their careers from Tennessee.

As for a revolution, North Carolinians fought lustily (and sometimes against each other) in the War for Independence and the War Between the States. But since then it has developed at a remarkably even pace. There have been no great political struggles or upheavals, no sharp shifts in the pace of economic development. This steady, even growth has been one of the reasons observers have attached the progressive label to the state. But if Jefferson was right in saying that people needed a revolution every 20 years or so, North Carolina is long overdue. Some of the paradoxes that plague the state are the direct results of its inertial progress, and most of the state's greatest problems are not going to be solved rapidly without an economic or perhaps political upheaval.

People: Almost a Megastate

No one thinks of North Carolina as one of our largest states, but it is—almost. In area, it is one of the largest of the Southern and Border States, and extends more than 500 miles from the lighthouse at Cape Hatteras to the Smokies, the highest mountains east of the Mississippi. Between the flat, often sandy coastal plain and the mountains lies the Piedmont. This is the rolling green land below the fall line, where the rivers tumble in rapids, down the mountains. Through much of the southeast, the Piedmont is a narrow strip of land, not more than 40 miles wide in northern Virginia. But in North Carolina it broadens, and in the state's 200-mile expanse of Piedmont are found all its largest cities, more than half its people, and the bulk of its industry.

It is this concentration that puts North Carolina almost into the megastate category. In 1973 it ranked 12th in population, with 5,273,000 people, just behind Massachusetts, the smallest of the ten big states or megastates, which had 5,818,000, and Indiana, with 5,316,000. Yet North Carolina—another paradox—has no really major metropolitan area; the urbanized area around Charlotte, its largest city, is smaller than those around Nashville, Tennessee, or Richmond, Virginia. North Carolina's population weight has made little impact on the national consciousness because it is not gathered together into one place. Rather, it is scattered around several urban areas—Charlotte, Greensboro, Winston-Salem, Raleigh, Durham—and in smaller textile mill and furniture factory towns, and even around the countryside. North Carolina has industrialized without completely urbanizing. A couple of statistics give an idea of the results. North Carolina, which has no county with a population of more than 400,000, has more counties than any other

* Jackson's birthplace is sometimes considered to have been in South Carolina, but the boundary line ran close to the house and his family was so obscure that no one cared which state he was born in until considerably later. There seems to be at least an even chance that the event did take place in what are now the limits of North Carolina.

state in the nation (28) with populations between 50,000 and 100,000. And North Carolina, next to California and Florida, has more mobile homes than any other state in the nation. These are not so much the homes of retirees or itinerants; they are the shelter for the people who work in the state's factories who cannot afford a regular home, or still wish to live on a larger than city-sized lot.

Of North Carolina's Atlantic beaches and verdant mountains, we will have more to say later. They are what tourists are wont to see, but the real history of how North Carolina came to be what it is today takes place mostly in the Piedmont. And most of the story is not of intellectual statesmen or of brave revolutionists or gallant Confederates. North Carolina's golden age, if any, is yet to come, and its history properly focuses on the brute forces of economics.

An Economic History of the Tar Heel State

As a colony, North Carolina could legitimately be called what it has liked to be referred to as ever since, "a vale of humility between two mountains of conceit." It never had the advantages of Virginia or South Carolina: there was no good port here (Wilmington, the best, was not even established till the 1730s); there was only a pathetically small planter aristocracy; there were few slaves and, for quite a time, very few settlers at all. The Roanoke Island settlement financed by Sir Walter Raleigh in the 1580s vanished with no trace but the word "Croatoan"—name of a local Indian tribe—carved on a tree; this was the famous Lost Colony, whose story, largely imagined, is enacted for tourists each summer. North Carolina was settled principally overland from Virginia and South Carolina, mostly by Scotch and Scotch-Irish farmers, and their stock still populates the state, for there has been relatively little immigration, from foreign countries or even other states, since the Revolution. In 1970 North Carolina had the lowest percentage of residents of first- or second-generation foreign stock—a mere 1.5 percent—of any state in the union. And in the same year, 79 percent of all North Carolinians were natives of the state, a figure exceeded by only five other states.

From all accounts, the early North Carolinians were a feisty lot. They were fighting the British, albeit on an unorganized basis, before Lexington and Concord, and they declined to ratify the Constitution—missing the first Presidential election—until assured that it would include a bill of rights. The state held out against secession until the guns began blazing over Fort Sumter and Virginia had seceded; but North Carolina soldiers made up one-quarter of the Confederate dead.

Up until the Civil War, North Carolina was an unrelievedly agricultural, and mostly poor, state. In 1860 it had fewer slaves than any other Confederate state except Tennessee, and fewer big plantations. In the early years of the 1800s, the golden age of Kentucky and Tennessee, North Carolina became known as the Rip Van Winkle state; its population increased only sluggishly, as thousands of North Carolinians made their way west over the mountains. At the outbreak of the Civil War, this state of small farmers had no city of even 10,000 population.

In the war, North Carolina lost many young men. But its land was not ravaged like Virginia's, and emancipation did not destroy the wealth of the state—for there were not that many large slaveholders here—as it did in South Carolina. North Carolina was ready to move toward what many were seeing as the panacea for the South: industrialization.

The most important industry in North Carolina from the Revolution to the Civil War was the production of turpentine; it was distilled from pine sap and was the only nonagricultural product exported from the state.* But even in the antebellum years, there were cotton textile mills. These were not sophisticated factories. The leading mill owner of his day, Edwin Michael Holt, built a cotton mill and water wheel with slave labor in 1837 on Great Alamance Creek; in addition, he operated a gristmill, distilled whiskey, and ran several plantations. But from these crude beginnings, local capitalists were building up the expertise and familiarity with the industry that would fuel the post-Reconstruction boom. From 1880 to 1900, an average of six new cotton mills was built each year in North Carolina—almost all of them in the Piedmont—and the value of goods produced increased eleven-fold. This was the beginning of what has become the largest textile industry of any state in the union.

Why this concentration of textiles in the Carolina Piedmont? In the years just after the Civil War, one main reason was inexpensive water power; the mills were located on the fast-falling waters of rivers like the Yadkin or the Catawba or their tributaries, at or above the fall line. Another reason, clearly, was cheap labor. Continually, for the past hundred years, mechanization and often lower prices have been driving North Carolina farmers off the land. In addition, the textile industry from the beginning employed more women and children than adult males—and, of course, paid them lower wages. (Average textile wages in 1900: $216 for men, $157 for women, $103 for children—per *year*.) The availability of raw materials (chiefly cotton) may have been a factor in the early years, but is significant no longer. Transportation—Piedmont North Carolina is crossed by the major north-south rail lines—surely facilitated development.

Two factors not present in those first postbellum years were northern capital and "runaway industries." It was not until the 1920s that the big textile mills of Massachusetts were abandoned for cheaper-labor sites in North and South Carolina. And in those first years, it was local businessmen, on their own or in partnership, who put together the capital for the first mills. Why didn't this happen in Virginia or Georgia or other states with the same advantages? No one knows for sure; it seems to be one of those accidents of

---

* The nickname "Tar Heel State" is not derived from this industry, however. It stems from an incident of the Revolutionary War when Cornwallis' soldiers crossed a North Carolina river into which tar had been poured, emerging with the substance stuck to their heels.

local entrepreneurship and financing of the type that gave Detroit the bulk of the auto industry or Akron the rubber factories.

But the greatest story of North Carolina capitalism is in the tobacco industry, and it is largely the personal story of James B. "Buck" Duke. At the end of the Civil War, Duke's father, a Confederate soldier, walked 137 miles from where he had been mustered out to his home in the Piedmont. With 50 cents cash he processed a small quantity of tobacco and sold it in eastern North Carolina. Eight years later Washington Duke had a small factory in Durham, a postwar tobacco boom town already famous for Bull Durham, a competing brand of chewing tobacco. In 1884, Buck Duke, then 27, bought one of the first cigarette-making machines and launched a frontal attack on the bigger tobacco companies. With shrewd promotion and advertising and lower costs, Duke soon dominated the national market. In 1890 he set up the American Tobacco Company, combining under his control manufacturers of 90 percent of the cigarettes in the United States. Then Duke set out to outsell or to absorb the major manufacturers of pipe and chewing tobacco, snuff, and cigars. All the time, Duke promoted cigarette smoking, to his great enrichment. In 1911 the Supreme Court ordered Duke's tobacco trust dissolved, and it was broken into four companies—American Tobacco (now American Brands), R. J. Reynolds, P. Lorillard, and Liggett & Myers. They still dominate the industry, and all have a major share of their operations in North Carolina.

It is no mystery why the tobacco industry became concentrated in North Carolina, for Duke was not the only early tobacco capitalist in the state; he simply absorbed the others. This is an industry which has grown up close to its raw material. There are two kinds of tobacco used mainly by American cigarette makers. The chief constituent is flue-cured bright leaf tobacco, grown mainly in eastern and northern North Carolina, as well as South Carolina and Georgia. The other is burley, used chiefly for flavoring; it is grown in North Carolina, Kentucky, and Tennessee. In 1972 North Carolina grew 40 percent of the nation's tobacco, and it has grown at least as large a share since Duke's time.

Proximity of raw materials also helps to explain the growth of North Carolina's third major industry, furniture. The raw material, of course, is wood, abundant on the moist slopes of the Smokies and the hills of the western Piedmont. The post-Reconstruction furniture industry was concentrated in the western Piedmont and scattered among many towns; the capital, once again, was raised locally, and the industry grew at a healthy enough rate so that it became a national, rather than just local, supplier.

These three great industries have grown, not at spectacular, but at healthy, steady rates ever since. Tobacco grew as entrepreneurs like R. J. Reynolds (Camels) and George Washington Hill (Lucky Strikes) made smokers of millions of Americans. Textiles grew as plants fled high-wage New England, with its antiquated mills, for modern, low-wage North Carolina. Furniture grew as the nation's population and prosperity surged and demand rose. This is reflected in the population growth rate of North Carolina's Piedmont, where all three industries are concentrated. (Tobacco is grown chiefly in the eastern part of the state but manufactured mainly in Durham, Winston-Salem, Greensboro, and Reidsville in the Piedmont.) The Piedmont grew 18 percent in population between 1900 and 1910, 19 percent in the next decade, 33 percent in the booming '20s, and 14 percent in the Depression '30s. Since 1940, Piedmont growth has been 17 to 18 percent per decade —compared to the national average of 15 percent. Today North Carolina is number one among the states in textiles ($8 billion in annual shipments),* number one in tobacco, and number one in furniture. In 1970, 15 percent of all American textile workers were North Carolinians. Nine percent of all furniture workers and 52 percent of all persons employed in the manufacture of cigarettes were likewise North Carolinians, all in a state with 2.5 percent of the nation's population.

North Carolina has reached for, and gained, the panacea of the visionaries of a New South in the late 19th century. It has industrialized—more than any other state. In the early 1970s, 40 percent of all employed North Carolinians held manufacturing jobs, the highest level in the nation. Yet the panacea has not produced the bounteous society that was hoped for. The North Carolina Fund, a nonprofit research and program development corporation, pinpointed the problem in 1967: "Current economic development policy relies heavily on industrialization as a means to increase income in North Carolina. Yet, while this policy has been in effect we have seen North Carolina shift from a poor agricultural state to a poor industrial state. We have experienced industrialization without development."

This paradox of overindustrialization and underdevelopment leaves North Carolina in the position of exporting relatively inexpensive goods to the rest of the United States—textiles, furniture, tobacco—and importing almost everything else.

North Carolina industrial wages are close to the lowest in the country. In 1970 the average hourly wage in North Carolina's factories and mills was $2.46, barely ahead of Mississippi and behind the other 48 states. One can make the case that North Carolina wages did make some progress in the '60s; they rose from 68 percent of the national average to 73 percent. (By the same token, the state's overall per capita income rose from 70 percent to 85 percent of the national average between 1960 and 1972.) But in 1961 the average North Carolina production worker was making 74 cents an hour less than the national average, and by 1970 he or she was 90 cents behind the

* The chief North Carolina-headquartered textile firms, with their most recent annual sales totals: Burlington Industries, Greensboro, $2.1 billion; Akzona, Asheville, $704 million; Cone Mills, Greensboro, $372 million; Cannon Mills, Kannapolis, $355 million; Fieldcrest Mills, Eden, $291 million; Hanes, Winston-Salem, $276 million; Texfi Industries, Greensboro, $179 million; Chadbourn Inc., Charlotte, $130 million; Textiles of Gastonia, $107 million. Other major textile employers in the state include such firm names as J.P. Stevens, duPont, Chatham, Washington Mills, Glen Raven, Springs Mills, Wiscassett Mills, Kayser-Roth, and Highlander.

Many of the big firms are the result of gradual agglomerations of smaller family-owned mills. Today the management, research and development work, and struggle for survival of the big textile firms present some of the most difficult challenges for business leadership in any U.S. industry. (See discussion in the South Carolina chapter of *The Deep South States of America*, pp. 417–18.)

national average. For all the state's progress in attracting industry, North Carolina factory workers were making an average weekly wage of only $97 in 1970.

Why such low wages? The reasons, again, can be summed up in the three words which dominate the economic history of the Tar Heel state: textiles, furniture, tobacco. Of the three, only tobacco pays above the national hourly average, and it is by far the smallest. The average wage in the furniture factories and the textile mills was $93 a week in 1970. With so many of its workers making so little money, it is clear why North Carolina has failed to develop a healthy, balanced economy.

Textiles, Unions, and the Drive
for Diversification

Throughout North Carolina, the visitor finds people dissatisfied with the state's economic position and concerned about the dominance of low-wage industries, particularly textiles. "Textiles have been the Achilles heel of North Carolina since the day of their inception," state representative Claude deBruhl, a mountain Democrat from Asheville, told me vehemently. Similar sentiments, in more muted tones, were expressed by leaders at the top of the power structure. A top state officeholder lamented the "lack of diversification" and low wages, and Luther Hodges, Jr., son of the former governor and chairman of the multi-billion dollar North Carolina National Bank, said with obvious distaste that for many years "all we were getting was more textiles."

Indeed, the major culprit in North Carolina's low-wage quandary is the textile industry. Of all the nation's major industries, textiles pay the lowest wages—and are the least unionized. And of all the 50 states, North Carolina is the least unionized. Only 7.5 percent of the nonagricultural workers in the state were union members in 1972, a figure that had remained static for many years. Until the Textile Workers Union, in a possibly historic breakthrough, managed to organize seven J. P. Stevens Company plants at Roanoke Rapids in 1974, virtually none of the state's textile mills was organized, and precious few of the furniture factories. Textile wages would probably not be very high even with unionization, since most of the work requires little skill and there is the pressure of heavy foreign competition.

Unions have made sporadic attempts to organize North Carolina mills; there was even a Communist-led strike in Gastonia in 1929. But the last massive drive was in the late 1950s, and it ended in disaster for the union. The Textile Workers Union struck a cotton mill in the town of Henderson and not only lost the strike; the union's Carolinas director was sentenced to two to ten years in prison for conspiracy to commit violence, on what seems to have been questionable evidence. Besides management intransigence, North Carolina's low unionization is also due to an oversupply of low-skill labor and the fierce independence, even orneriness, of its working people. The

rising number of black mill hands may change this, though; they are less adverse to unions and figured importantly in the 1974 union victory at J. P.
Stevens. It may be true, as Governor James Holshouser suggested to me, that
"unions in textiles would drive many companies out of the business." And
most observers agree with George Esser, former head of the North Carolina
Fund, who told me that union leadership in the state is very weak.* But the
primary reason for North Carolina's low rate of unionization is surely business hostility. As Joe Doster, managing editor of the Winston-Salem *Journal*,
said, "One of the unchanging political goals of industry is: let's not encourage unions."

It is easier to see what unions are up against when one takes a look at
an operation like Cannon Mills, which produces half the nation's towels and
a fifth of all its sheets. For 50 years, until his death in 1971, Cannon was
run autocratically by Charles Cannon, known as "Mr. Charlie" everywhere
in North Carolina. Mr. Charlie did not like outsiders looking into his business, and he allowed his stock to be taken off the New York Stock Exchange
rather than reveal information as the Exchange rules require. His family
owned more than half the company's stock, and the company owned almost
all of the unincorporated town of Kannapolis (1970 population 36,293),
renting stores to local tradesmen and houses to Cannon Mills workers. Mr.
Charlie, of course, would never have tolerated a union, and there never has
been a significant attempt to organize Cannon Mills.

Cannon is an atypical case, of course; power there was more highly concentrated in one man's hands than in most North Carolina mill towns. But
the companies are helped in their battles against unions by the geographic
dispersion of textiles across the state. There is surprisingly little textile employment in North Carolina's major cities, although Cone has large mills in
Greensboro and Hanes in Winston-Salem. But aside from these, the largest
textile employment is in and around Piedmont towns like Kannapolis, Gastonia (population 47,182), Burlington (35,390), Hickory (20,569), Eden
(15,871), and Asheboro (10,797). It takes little imagination to see how the
giant textile makers, with their huge sums of capital and absolute control
over workers' jobs, can have things pretty much as they want in such communities. "Mill village culture is now largely a thing of the past," Elizabeth
Tornquist, a liberal journalist, has written. (Cannon's Kannapolis is still an
exception.) Nevertheless, the vestiges of company town atmosphere are
still apparent. A number of textile mill owners have managed to persuade
local governments and chambers of commerce to repel investors who wanted
to build new factories. The reason is fairly obvious: personnel turnover in

---

* The weakness of organized labor may be indicated by its almost pathetically small impact on electoral politics. The president of the state AFL-CIO, Wilbur Hobby, ran for governor
in the Democratic primary in 1972. He finished fifth in a field of six, with 7 percent of the votes.
Or, as one close observer of North Carolina campaigns said, you would like labor's support, but
you certainly don't want their endorsement. But—another paradox—the legislature in 1973 did
approve one of labor's highest political goals: a $1.80 minimum wage, the highest in the South.
But this may just be testimonial to a general awareness that North Carolina is suffering because
of its low-wage economy.

textile mills is high, and the presence of higher-paying jobs would attract workers from the mills and tend to drive up wages.

The textile industry is not about to change its low-wage spots in the foreseeable future, and so if North Carolina is going to get the high-wage economic base it needs, the change will have to come through economic diversification. Yet it was not so many years ago that concern about North Carolina's economic mix did not exist at all. In the early 1950s the state seemed to be basking in the kind of proud glow that led Gunther to write that its "industry is decentralized and diversified." * The initial impetus for change, when it came, originated with Luther Hodges, Sr., who fortuitously served almost seven years as governor, from 1954 to 1961. (North Carolina limits its governors to one four-year term. Hodges, a successful businessman, was elected lieutenant governor in 1952. Within 48 hours of the inauguration the governor suffered a stroke. He died the next year. Hodges succeeded to the office and was easily returned to a full term in 1956.) Hodges used much of that long tenure to travel around the country and even to the nations of the Common Market, selling businessmen on North Carolina. It was not an effort that paid off immediately; an early *Time* magazine report on a supposed North Carolina boom in the 1950s was, like Mark Twain's obituary, a bit premature. But probably more important, Hodges seems to have sold the state on the idea of diversification, and there is not a politician or a well-known businessman around today who does not pay at least lip service to it.

Another contribution by Hodges was the creation of Research Triangle Park, set up in the 1950s near Durham and halfway between Chapel Hill and Raleigh. This location gave it access to the state's three major universities (Duke, the University of North Carolina, and North Carolina State). The plan was to sell or lease land to corporations and governmental units for research facilities. It succeeded handsomely—and in both senses of the word, for the new, tastefully designed buildings occupy only 15 percent of the land companies acquire, and the rest is kept in second-growth North Carolina pines. By 1970, there were 28 buildings put up by 18 corporations and governmental units on the 5,000 acres of the park. Some 5,500 people worked in park facilities, earning two and a half times the average North Carolina wage. The total value of facilities in the park climbed toward the $100 million mark in the early '70s, including laboratories or plants of the National Environmental Health Sciences Center, Chemstrand Research Corporation (lured to North Carolina from Alabama during the racial turmoil of the 1950s), Beaunit Fibers, IBM, the National Center for Health Statistics, HEW's Regional Education Laboratory, and the like. From the perspective of the entire South, the most important addition of the early 1970s was that of the headquarters of the Southern Growth Policies Board, a joint creation of the

* Gunther added, a sentence later, that North Carolina "runs its public relations better than any state I know." It surely did. North Carolina's industry may have been spread all over the Piedmont, but it was even less diversified than it is today.

governors and legislatures of the region's states initially proposed by former North Carolina Governor Terry Sanford. By 1974, 13 states were participating and the organization was advanced enough to write a statement of South-wide economic goals relating to regional transportation, land and natural resources, human resources and public services, and growth management policies.

Among the services of the Research Triangle Park is an instantaneous computer service, sponsored jointly by the three nearby universities. There is no question that the park has brought thousands of high-paying jobs and upgraded the economy of central North Carolina, with statewide benefits. (Even after his return to North Carolina after four years as U.S. Secretary of Commerce, Luther Hodges, Sr., continued to play an active role as chairman of the Research Triangle Foundation. "They offered to pay me $1 a year, and I asked to be paid quarterly," Hodges said.)

North Carolina's diversification effort, after the first steps of the '50s, continued into the following decade under Governor Sanford. And as the '60s rolled on, results began to become visible. In 1955, Hodges' first full year as governor, textiles still accounted for 51 percent of North Carolina's manufacturing employment. By 1973, according to figures compiled by the state, that percentage had declined to 38. The trio of textiles-furniture-tobacco had accounted for 63 percent of the manufacturing jobs in 1955; in 1973, that figure was 51 percent. It is clear that North Carolina still does not have a diversified economy, but it is moving in the right direction.

What kind of new industries are coming to North Carolina? Robert Leak, the head of the state's office of Industrial, Tourist, and Community Resources, gave the answer at the beginning of 1974—chemicals, metal working, auto parts. Among service industries there have also been notable advances; one shining example is trucking. Many large national firms that started as one- or two-man operations in North Carolina have grown phenomenally, including Akers Motor Lines, McLeans (now part of Reynolds' Sea Land operations), and Pilot Freight.

The new economic enterprises pay better than textiles—almost every industry does—but North Carolina's low wages and lack of unionization are clearly attractive to many employers. Leak insisted: "We're not selling low wages or lack of union activity." But he does like to point out that North Carolina is always among the states with the lowest number of work-days lost by work stoppages—a statistic which, not surprisingly, is closely related to low rates of unionization. What is perhaps more remarkable about North Carolina's diversification efforts, as former Governor Sanford stressed, is that the state has granted no tax concessions to incoming industry. This is in vivid contrast to South Carolina, whose achievements have been more spectacular but depend heavily on such inducements.

But North Carolina's diversification efforts still face serious problems. Too many of the industries coming in either pay low wages or demand higher skills than possessed by the bulk of the state's labor pool. In either case, there is a delay in creating new jobs for North Carolinians. To get a better look at these problems, it will be helpful to focus on the geographic area where they are most acute, the coastal plain east of Raleigh.

The Underdeveloped East

So far our economic picture of North Carolina has focused almost entirely on the Piedmont, from Raleigh to the foothills of the Smokies. This is where the vast majority of the textile mills, the furniture and cigarette factories are; it is the site of all the state's major cities and of most of its economic growth. But in 1970, 37 percent of the state's population—nearly 1.9 million people—still lived in the counties east of the fall line; that is about as many people as live in the entire state of Arkansas.

Eastern North Carolina has not had as high a rate of population growth as the Piedmont since the Civil War. Its cities are small; the largest are Wilmington (1970 population 46,169), the state's largest port, which has always been overshadowed by Charleston and Norfolk, and Fayetteville (53,510). The latter is almost a tributary of the Army's giant Fort Bragg, home of the 82nd Airborne; the four-lane highway which connects the fort and the city is one of the most garish in America, and in addition to the usual fast-food franchises and shopping centers can boast numerous risqué go-go joints and pornographic movie palaces. Fayetteville also contains a couple of Vietnamese restaurants, patronized largely by servicemen who picked up a taste for the cuisine in "Nam." Military bases, like Bragg and the Marine Corps's Camp Lejeune, have been the centers of much of the recent population growth of eastern North Carolina.

The litany of the problems of the East is strikingly similar to that of the South Carolina Low Country and south Georgia, described in the *Deep South States* volume of this series. Nor will it come as a surprise to anyone with a passing acquaintance with Southside Virginia. One statistic tells a lot of the story: eastern North Carolina in 1972 was producing the nation's highest percentage of volunteers for the Army. These young men apparently find prospects for education and employment far more attractive in the military than in their home region.

Outmigration, indeed, has been the dominant demographic fact in the east for decades. And most of that migrating is done by blacks. To the extent that North Carolina ever had a plantation culture, it was in the east, and to this day the region has a higher proportion of blacks than any other part of the state.* But it would be much higher if so many had not left. Census statistics show that more than three-quarters of all whites born in North Carolina still live there, but only two-thirds of North Carolina-born blacks

---

* Thirty-three percent of the residents of eastern North Carolina in 1970 were black. The corresponding figure for the Piedmont was 20 percent and for the mountains five percent. More than half—51 percent—of all North Carolina blacks lived in the east.

do. Most of the rest have moved to the ghettos of Washington, Baltimore, Philadelphia, Newark, and New York. There are 126,000 North Carolina-born blacks in New York, 57,000 in New Jersey, 46,000 in Pennsylvania, and 47,000 in Washington, D. C.—a full 6 percent of the capital city's population. The difficulties and unpleasantness of Northern ghetto life need no repetition here, but despite those difficulties literally thousands of blacks have left. In parts of eastern North Carolina, there have been cases of *entire* high school graduating classes leaving, looking for jobs. So many left each summer that in the '60s the Seaboard Coast Line Number 76 train became known as the "Chickenbone Special," because the young travelers usually carried a picnic lunch of fried chicken. The migration patterns from the Carolinas followed the northbound train tracks; the process was best explained by former Charlotte *Observer* reporter Dwayne Walls in *The Chickenbone Special,* published by the Southern Regional Council. Walls gives us the perspective of a black funeral home owner:

> That was the way it usually went. First one member of a family would go to a northern city; then he would be followed to the same place by a brother or a sister or a cousin, and eventually the parents and the neighbors. My God, he thought. We're being bled dry in this county and it don't seem to be anything we can do about it. Not just this county. . . . All the farming country.
>
> That was the trouble. It was farming country, with little farms where a man was lucky just to be able to hang on. Tobacco was shot, and tobacco's what kept the little farms going. Jobs in industry were pitifully few and most of them were for the whites. All of them had been for whites until three or four years earlier.

One reason the outmigration has been so large, Walls pointed out, was that many black children, born of young parents recently migrated to the North, are sent back to relatives in the South to be brought up. When they finish school, they naturally gravitate to the North, as their parents had.

Outmigration seems to have lessened in the late '60s and early '70s. But it continues, and in eastern North Carolina it is linked inextricably with the crop that dominates the area's—and the state's—agriculture: tobacco.* Flue-cured tobacco is a crop which requires intensive care. The leaves on each stalk mature at different times, and so each row of tobacco must be harvested three or four times. Then the tobacco must be hung in barns for curing by artificial heat. Tobacco is so labor-intensive that it is cultivated only in small plots; a 20-acre allotment from the Department of Agriculture can provide a farmer a living, albeit not a grand one. (I am indebted to my traveling companion, the late Bruce Biossat, for pointing out that only three counties in the nation have a farm population density of more than 40 persons per square mile; all are in the tobacco belt of eastern North Carolina.) Of course many blacks, and a considerable number of whites, in eastern North Carolina do not own the tobacco land they work; some are still sharecroppers, and even many landowning farmers find themselves perpetually in debt to tobacco warehousemen. With such a marginal economic situation, it is natural

* There is also considerable tobacco growing in the row of Piedmont counties just south of the Virginia border.

that many tobacco farmers leave the land each year, and that their children disappear on the Chickenbone Special when school is out.

Moreover, long-term trends are not good news for tobacco farmers. Cigarette smoking has not risen as fast as population in the decade since the Surgeon General's warning that smoking may be dangerous to health—despite unusually large numbers of people in the age groups when smoking habits start. Tobacco allotments were reduced in 1973 and 1974 by the Department of Agriculture, effectively limiting the acreage tobacco farmers plant. And in the late 1960s, agricultural experts developed a system for mechanical harvesting of tobacco. By the mid-1970s, this had not eclipsed the pattern of small tobacco holdings; because of the allotment system, mechanization was not yet profitable for most tobacco farms. But the specter remains. "I have almost a nightmare," Joe Doster, managing editor of the Winston-Salem *Journal* said, "about someone developing artificial tobacco. Eastern North Carolina would become a desert almost overnight." The consequences of mechanization, if it comes, will not be quite so disastrous, but they will be drastic enough in an economy based on the small tobacco-grower. Thousands of poorly educated tobacco farmers, totally unaccustomed to the patterns of urban life, would have to look elsewhere to make their living. It could be the last great surge of Southern black migration to the teeming ghettos of the North's cities.

What the east needs, one hears constantly, is what the Piedmont already has had: industrialization. And it seems to be occurring; many of the new plants being built in the state are in the east. But what kind of industry? Too often the answer is apparel; eastern North Carolina seems to be the destination for many cut 'n' sew shops, as they are called, running away from the high-wage northeastern states. The location, of course, makes sense—near the center of the American textile industry, in an area where plenty of people are ready to work for low wages and nobody thinks much about joining a union. But one wonders how much of a good thing is an industry which paid weekly wages, as late as 1973, of $84.87. The cut 'n' sew shops can get away with this because they hire mainly women,* a large percentage of them black, many of whose husbands are still trying to eke out a living on the farm.

If the apparel shops are clearly not the salvation of eastern North Carolina, then perhaps education—particularly skills training—is. Here the efforts of the state government and of some segments of the North Carolina business community seem to merit the progressive label which has so long been applied to the state. The moving force in this regard, as in many others, was Governor Terry Sanford. During his four years in office, he prodded the legislature into setting up industrial education centers and, in 1963, expanding them into a system of community colleges and technical institutes. By 1972 there were 17 state community colleges and 41 technical institutes, with a total enrollment of 51,000—with 18,000 in the east. These schools are

---

* Altogether, 46.5% of North Carolina women over 16 are in the labor force, a percentage exceeded only in the District of Columbia, Hawaii, and Nevada. This is no triumph for women's liberation, perhaps the contrary; most of them work in unskilled jobs for low wages.

scattered throughout the state, so that only in the farthest reaches of the western mountains or on the Outer Banks is a potential student more than an hour's drive away from such a school.

Another effort certainly worth notice is that of the North Carolina Manpower Development Commission, a nonprofit group funded by business and government grants. Its Chairman is Luther Hodges, Jr., and it is run by George Autry, an alumnus of Sam Ervin's staff in Washington. Autry's goal is to rechannel much of the outmigration from the east from the Chickenbone Special to the tight labor markets of North Carolina's Piedmont. But simply getting people to move, and even getting them jobs, is not enough. As Autry described the problem:

> We've found people who moved to Greensboro on their own, who've been in the city for four years without even using the bus system. They're afraid of it, scared of that bus driver. They even walk, or in an emergency take a cab. They're used to working from sunrise to sunset, in the tobacco fields. Learning to work by the clock is a difficult problem—regimentation for very independent people. Even the lowliest tenant farmer had his farm, without somebody telling him what to do every minute.

But Greensboro, Autry said, is surely a far less alien environment to North Carolina farmers than the slums of Baltimore or Bedford-Stuyvesant. MDC has developed programs which use tape recorders, both to impart basic information and reading skills and to develop mental discipline and concentration. MDC also runs programs, much in demand by business, training management personnel in how to get along with the workers they supervise; it also conducts courses at many of the state's community colleges. This is not intended to create a permanent empire for the agency; the purpose is more to show what can be done, in the hopes that others—state agencies, private industry—will follow. But these efforts do reach to the heart of one of the state's major problems: the need to upgrade the skills of North Carolinians, particularly those from the east, to the point where they can fill the kind of high-paying jobs which will provide a solid base for the state's economy.

And change is coming—slowly—to the east. If the bulk of its new jobs have been in cut 'n' sew shops, there are also chemical plants rising around Wilmington, near Pamlico Sound. Outmigration in the early '70s had been much less than it was in the '50s, and apparently less than in the '60s. Some eastern North Carolinians have been heading west on the interstates to Greensboro and Charlotte rather than to the North. But a region with nearly two million people—at least this one—is hardly going to be transformed overnight. We should perhaps conclude our look at the east with some notes on the racial situation, for this is still where most North Carolina blacks live.

Back in the days of segregation, North Carolina was considered the most racially liberal of the southern states. Interestingly, the first lunch counter sit-ins were at the downtown Woolworth's in Greensboro. But rural eastern North Carolina, unlike parts of the Mississippi Delta and the Black Belt of Alabama, was not the scene of intensive civil rights organizing. Today, blacks can get jobs at apparel factories and can eat in once all-white restaurants. They have the vote, and in five eastern counties they are a majority.*

But the trend in eastern North Carolina today, as in so much of the nation, seems to be less toward integration than toward a separate development of the black community. A major example is Soul City, the black-owned development in Warren County, near the Virginia border. The driving force here is Floyd McKissick, who has had an interesting career: he went all the way up to the U.S. Supreme Court in the 1950s to gain admission to the University of North Carolina Law School; as national head of CORE (Congress of Racial Equality) in the mid-'60s, he increasingly took a separatist line; in 1968 and 1972, he supported Richard Nixon for President. (Soul City has been the recipient of federal grants, and at its opening ceremonies in 1973, Governor Holshouser, a Republican, appeared.) Soul City's first economic enterprises (a stereo cabinet factory and a related electronics company) were due to open early in 1975. McKissick's goal is an economically self-sufficient and prosperous, predominantly black community of some 40,000 persons by the 1990s. He expects the project to be the largest single minority-owned enterprise in the United States and the first new town that will not be a satellite of larger cities. Eventually this could mean an end to the days of the Chickenbone Special as blacks find an opportunity to make a good living, and to run their own community, at home in eastern North Carolina.

A more poignant story is what happened when school integration came in the late 1960s to Hyde County, a desolate, empty stretch of swampy flat land along Pamlico Sound. When the small rural schools were consolidated, and several black schools closed, blacks, with Southern Christian Leadership Conference assistance, started a boycott which lasted for months. One older woman, asked why she opposed the closing of a black school, told a reporter, "Why I can remember picking blackberries to raise money for the curtains in the schoolhouse. When you put your blood and sweat into something like this, you hate to see it go. Every time I see those swings out there, I think of my little ones on them, swinging sweet as angels."

But according to Joe Doster, of the Winston-Salem *Journal*, who told me the story, her children had long since gone north. Consolidation was clearly desirable—Hyde County is dying; in 1970 it had only 60 percent of its 1900 population—and integration will surely provide a better education for black and white children. Eastern North Carolina is never going to be what it once was, and on the whole this is a welcome development. But progress has its price.

One place in the east where "progress" has made little imprint is the Outer Banks, the string of sandy islets that separates Albemarle and Pamlico Sounds from the ocean. The waters here are treacherous, and among sailors the name of Cape Hatteras (the tip of the elbow that the Banks stick out into the Atlantic) is still feared. Off Hatteras the warm waters of the Gulf

* The five are Bertie, Gates, Hertford, Northampton, and Warren. But their total population is only 92,400, 1.8 percent of the state total. In two other counties, Robeson and Hoke, blacks plus Lumbee Indians have a majority, but they do not necessarily act as a unit.

Stream meet colder currents from the north, and there have been more than 700 shipwrecks, some of them recent. Perhaps the most famous of all was that of the Union's U.S.S. Monitor, which sank in a gale less than 10 months after its duel with the Merrimack of the Confederacy in history's first clash between ironclad vessels, at Hampton Roads on March 9, 1862. The remains of the Monitor, long lost, were finally discovered in 220 feet of water some 15 miles southeast of the cape by an oceanographic researcher at Duke University in 1974.

The Banks were also the site of the Wright brothers' first flight at Kitty Hawk, and close by is Roanoke Island, where Sir Walter Raleigh tried to start a colony in 1587. One of the leaders returned to England for more provisions, and when he came back three years later he found no trace of the colonists except for the word "Croatoan," the name of a local Indian tribe, carved on a tree. Among those lost was Virginia Dare, the first English baby born in North America. What became of this Lost Colony? No one knows. There are numerous stories; some say that the colonists intermarried with the Indians and were the ancestors of the Lumbees, who still live between Wilmington and Fayetteville.

For years, the Outer Banks were isolated from the rest of the state, and the Bankers, as its residents are called, retain the speech patterns and vocabulary of the 17th century. Those on Ocracoke Island, connected to the mainland only by ferry, have held most tenaciously to their heritage. Bridges have made the Banks, with their miles of sandy beaches, into prime vacationland. There is a happy absence of high-rise developments, and most of the beach is protected by National Seashore designation. In fact, the federal government, which has dredged and filled to preserve the shoreline since the 1930s, has now decided to let nature take its course. The turbulent Atlantic will carve new inlets between the Banks, and fill others with silt; even the Cape Hatteras lighthouse will probably be undermined. But the Banks will retain their sunny, majestic emptiness.

The Piedmont and the Press

North Carolina's urban growth has not centered on one city, as in Georgia. Instead, it is concentrated in the cities and suburbs of what is known as the Piedmont crescent. Roughly following Interstate 85 from northeast to southwest—and thus forming the eastern anchor of the vital growth line of the new South, which stretches on through the South Carolina Piedmont cities and on to Atlanta and finally Birmingham—they are, with their 1970 metropolitan area populations: Raleigh (228,453), Durham (190,388), Greensboro-Winston Salem-High Point (603,895), and Charlotte (409,370).

Why, one asks, did cities grow here in the first place? One hears, again and again, that they developed at the fall line, although none straddles a major river. The more likely explanation for their growth is that they developed as headquarters of major economic interests. Greensboro is the headquarters of Burlington Industries, Winston-Salem of R. J. Reynolds Tobacco (both city names used as names for cigarette brands), Durham for the Duke tobacco interests, Raleigh for state government, Charlotte for numerous banking and insurance interests. None of these cities had a population of 20,000 in 1900; their fastest early growth was in the Piedmont's boom decade of the 1920s (excepting Winston-Salem, in the 1910s); since World War II both the suburbs *and* the cities of the Piedmont have experienced vigorous growth, a notable exception to the suburbs-only expansion pattern of much of the United States. An important reason for this is that none of these cities is surrounded by incorporated suburbs, and each has been annexing its environs as developers turn farmland into new subdivisions.

There is little to distinguish the Piedmont cities from one another. Even in their physical layouts they are similar. Each spreads out from a downtown which has some gleaming new skyscrapers (Durham is an exception) but diminishing retail trade (it is all going to the new enclosed shopping malls). Each has a black quadrant, roughly pie-shaped and spreading from downtown to the city limits, and a well-to-do white quadrant. To a Northerner, the racial patterns seem unusual. Blacks rather rarely move into white neighborhoods; instead, they push farther out, toward or beyond the city limits, into neighborhoods that have always been black or into new subdivisions which been built for blacks—and often by black developers. Consequently, there is less block-busting activity than in the North, which may be why Raleigh was willing to elect a black mayor—and why Charlotte reacted so negatively to the threat of busing. But let us look at the major cities one by one.

Charlotte (1970 population 241,178). Every Monday morning, 30,000 salesmen pour out of Charlotte, I was told; this is a city of branch offices, banks, insurance companies, trucking firms. It seems to have its eyes constantly on Atlanta; though it will never eclipse that city, it will surely remain the largest in the state. Charlotte is a Republican town; it was part of the district which elected Republican Congressman Charles Jonas for 10 terms, starting in 1952, and elected a Republican to succeed him in 1972. It has not supported a Democrat for President since 1948.

But what Charlotte is most known for these days is the Charlotte-Mecklenburg County school desegregation case. In 1970, federal Judge James McMillan ordered extensive busing of school children in the consolidated city-county school district as the only means of providing full desegregation. His decision was reversed on appeal, then reinstated by the Supreme Court in a landmark decision. The busing plan went into operation in the fall of 1970; there was some racial fighting in the schools a few months later, and the offices of Julius Chambers, the black attorney who prosecuted the suit, were firebombed in February 1971. Brawls in the schools, quite prevalent that year, were still erupting occasionally in 1974 and opposition to busing remained strong on the part of the school board, most parents, and many students (both white and black). In many cases, however, the high school students themselves were taking the initiative to make the system work, and in the 1974 school board elections, most of the candidates told the voters it was time to shift focus from legal stratagems to upset busing orders to a chief emphasis on improving classroom teaching. Indeed, the quality of education offered in the schools had improved markedly, and the system even offered "open" schools and was preparing to open one "traditional" school (based on an old-style academic curriculum emphasizing fundamental skills and disciplines). In the words of Reese Cleghorn, editor of the Charlotte *Observer* editorial pages, "given the ossification of the old school bureaucracy, these things would not have happened." Forty "segregation academies" had sprouted, he said, but the white flight from the public schools was a "steady trickle," not a "massive erosion" on the scale of an Atlanta or Memphis. In 1973–74, when an ambitious program called "Dimensions for Charlotte-Mecklenburg" was launched—modeled on the famed "Goals for Dallas" program—the citizen-participants listed "educational excellence" as a major goal, stating: "We must maintain an integrated system of education."

There were some ironies in the Charlotte situation. Judge McMillan was a pillar of the community, of conservative bent, hardly the man to make such a revolution. And back in the 1950s, North Carolina, proud of its school consolidation and transportation programs, had called itself the "school-busingest" state in the nation.

Winston-Salem (132,913). This is the headquarters of Reynolds Tobacco and the Wachovia Bank, the state's largest until the early '70s, when Charlotte's North Carolina National barely eclipsed it. The bank's name comes from a name applied to the area by early settlers, the Moravian sect which bought the land and settled the area in the 1750s and '60s. Little trace of the Moravians remains today, except for place names (Salem, Bethania) and the restored village of Salem just a mile south of the gleaming Wachovia tower. Winston-Salem is a manufacturing town (Reynolds cigarettes, Hanes textiles), and there is plenty of old money here. In the 1950s, the Reynolds family financed the transfer of Wake Forest University from its namesake town near Raleigh, building a university almost singlehandedly, as James B. Duke had done many years before in Durham.

Greensboro (144,076). This is more of a headquarters town, like Charlotte. Burlington, the biggest textile firm, has its main offices here; so do other large textile firms like Cone, Blue Bell, Glen Raven. Greensboro also has the Lorillard tobacco factory (Kents), but it is prouder of the giant Western Electric installations which have come in more recently. For North Carolina, the city has a quite well diversified economic base.

Durham (95,438). Buck Duke's town: Chesterfield cigarettes, Duke University. The latter is one of the two or three most distinguished private universities in the Border States, with excellent medical and law schools. But Durham as a whole is a factory, not a university town, and it is notable mainly for its large black population (30 percent of the total, the highest figure for any of North Carolina's large cities). Perhaps the most attractive high-rise building in Durham's skyline is the North Carolina Mutual Building, headquarters of a black-owned and operated insurance company which has been in business since 1898 and by 1972 had a billion dollars of insurance in force and well over $100 million assets. Durham also has a black-owned bank, founded in 1908, with $37 million in deposits in 1972. Durham's black community is well organized politically. Curiously, it has never come close to winning control of the city government, but it makes Durham the strongest Democratic city in North Carolina.

One of the strangest political developments of recent times occurred in the early 1970s when C. P. Ellis, president of the Durham chapter of the United Klans of America, agreed to become a member of the Durham Human Relations Commission. Apparently Ellis, also president of an integrated union of maintenance workers at Duke University, became convinced that the affluent white leadership of Durham was using the Klan to do its dirty work while continuing to hold poor whites and blacks alike in a kind of economic servitude.

Raleigh (121,577). An almost entirely nonindustrial city, it is dominated by state government and North Carolina State University, and benefits, as Durham does, from the nearby presence of the Research Triangle Park. What makes Raleigh unusual these days is that in 1973 it elected a black mayor. It was the second North Carolina city to do so; Chapel Hill (population 25,537) had elected Howard Lee in 1971. But Chapel Hill is a university town, which went for George McGovern in 1972, while Raleigh is only 26 percent black and has been voting increasingly for conservatives in recent years. What brought victory to Clarence Lightner, owner of a funeral home and veteran member of the City Council, was the environmental issue. Raleigh has been growing rapidly, and some of the new subdivisions have lacked proper drainage; the giant Crabtree Creek shopping mall, at the northwest end of town, has been submerged by floods. The developers had generally had their way with the council, and Lightner's opponent was head of the Raleigh Merchants' Bureau—a position he said he would retain if elected mayor. Lightner, who had not been conspicuously antideveloper in the past, closed ranks with whites unhappy with the city's patterns of growth, and won fairly easily. What is remarkable is that race played little part in the outcome. There were not even those interminable statements, like those heard in places like Detroit the same year, denying that race had anything to do with the outcome when in fact practically all the voting was on racial lines. Lightner carried the black vote heavily, but he also ran 2–1 ahead in white middle-class precincts where antideveloper feeling was strong. His victory was a signal that issues other than race can determine municipal elections,* and that even prosperous middle-class Americans are beginning to question the progress they have traditionally favored.

The Newspapers. North Carolina has a collection of daily newspapers which, to my mind, compare favorably with any other Southern or Border State's. *The News and Observer* of Raleigh, one of the few large independents

---

* Of course, everyone knew that blacks were not, presently or prospectively, a majority in Raleigh, and so white voters could rest comfortable in the knowledge that Lightner, if he wanted reelection, would have to remain responsive to an overwhelmingly white electorate.

left in the South and the only one in North Carolina, blankets both the capital city and much of eastern North Carolina. This is a Democratic paper with a capital "D"; it was run for many years by Josephus Daniels, who was Secretary of the Navy (and Franklin D. Roosevelt's boss) in the Wilson Administration, and his son Jonathan, who served as FDR's press secretary for a while during World War II. The present publisher is Frank Daniels, Jr.; the editor is Claude Sitton, who covered the South for the New York *Times* during the tumultuous late '50s and early '60s, served as national editor in New York, and then came back South again (a rare reversal of the one-way flow of talent from the Southland to the *Times*).

Exceeding *The News and Observer's* circulation (but not by much) is the Charlotte *Observer*, a part of the Knight chain and a paper known for its fine reporting on both North and South Carolina. Then there is the Winston-Salem *Journal*, whose managing editor, Joe Doster, is a wealth of wisdom and information on North Carolina politics and mores, and the Greensboro *Daily News*, known particularly for its fine editorial page. None of these papers is quite of national stature, and they are sometimes necessarily parochial (decreased tobacco allotments mean banner headlines). The *Journal* was acquired recently by the Richmond conglomerate, Media General (see page 99), and has turned rightward on its editorial page but improved, through high budgets and Doster's leadership, in news coverage. The *Daily News* is now a property of the Norfolk-based Landmark Publications. Traditionally, all of these papers were well ahead of public opinion on civil rights, and focused their readers' attention on problems they might prefer to ignore. Competition helps, too. Most Southern and Border States have one good paper; but with four solid dailies in the field, as Joe Doster, an old statehouse hand, put it, "you could never sit on a story."

North Carolina's Mountains: The Gem of Appalachia

In his 1973 statement announcing his retirement from the Senate, Sam J. Ervin, Jr., said that he intended to do a little fishing and sit around home in Morganton and watch "the indescribable glory of the sun setting behind Hawksbill Mountain." As it happens, Hawksbill Mountain, just west of Morganton and about 50 miles west of Charlotte and Winston-Salem, is part of the Blue Ridge that rises from the hilly Piedmont and signals the beginnings of North Carolina's mountain country. We think of the west as a sort of promised land, where people gravitate, but the mountains in North Carolina have had another function. The great wave of western migration following the Revolutionary War went over the mountains, into Tennessee and Kentucky. The mountains did begin to fill up during this period, but their greatest growth awaited the industrial boom before and after the turn of the century, when furniture factories and, to a lesser extent, textile mills located there. Today, only about 10 percent of all North Carolinians live in the mountains, and many of the winding roads lead into quiet backwaters where English is still spoken in Elizabethan accents.

The statisticians will tell you that the Smokies of North Carolina are the highest mountains east of the Mississippi. But their fascination for me is not in their height but in their haunting appearance: it is as if deep green velvet were draped loosely over the earth, rising and falling in curving folds, sometimes reflecting the light of the sun and sometimes absorbing it till they seem almost black. In the distance, the velvet seems to disappear in the smoky haze that has given the mountains their name. Yet close by, these mountains also have a profound fascination in the weird, almost exotic shapes—ridgelines straight out of a fairy tale. As one who has spent most summers of his life in New Hampshire, it is a hard confession to make, but I must say that for me, the Smokies of North Carolina are the gem of the Appalachians.

These are some of the oldest mountains in North America. Their contours have been worn down through millions of years, and their slopes covered with vegetation because of the plentiful rainfall and temperate climate. As far back as we know, this land was peopled by the Cherokee Indians. This remarkable tribe, which spread south into South Carolina, Georgia, and Alabama, adapted well to the white man's ways and, under the great chief Sequoyah, even developed its own alphabet and literature. But in the 50 years following 1785, the Cherokee signed 37 treaties, each ceding more land to the white man. The crowning blow was the Treaty of New Echota, in 1835. A small group of Cherokees agreed to give up their remaining lands in return for $5.6 million and territory in what now is Oklahoma. Most of the Cherokees resisted these terms. But President Van Buren, mindful that whites wanted the Indians' land, sent General Winfield Scott in to drive them west. Nearly one-quarter of the Cherokees died on the Trail of Tears to the arid lands they had been granted; it was perhaps the lowest moment of Jacksonian democracy.

But a little more than a thousand Cherokees had remained behind. As the story goes, an Indian named Tsali, who had killed a white soldier, gave himself up to a sympathetic colonel on condition that the rest of the tribe be allowed to remain. (This incident is commemorated throughout each summer in the open-air production of the drama, "Unto these Hills.") And for once, a promise to the Indians was kept. The continuing difficulties over the Eastern Bank of Cherokees' legal status is too complex to recount here. But the upshot is that there are now about 6,000 Cherokees in western North Carolina, most of them in the large reservation just south of the entrance to the Great Smokies National Park.*

The Smokies Park receives more visitors each year than any other national park in the United States, and the chief business of the Indians is tourism. The tribal government holds all lands in common and gives use rights to individuals; it also operates an excellent modern motel (Boundary Tree Lodge at Cherokee); a crafts store; factories producing leather prod-

---

* There are even more Indians in eastern North Carolina. Most of them are Lumbees, who live in and around Robeson County, south of Fayetteville, and who may or may not be descendants of the Lost Colony of Roanoke. The Lumbees have not lived on reservations, although at one time Robeson County maintained three sets of segregated schools, for whites, Indians, and blacks. Altogether, North Carolina had 44,406 Indians in 1970, the largest number east of the Mississippi, exceeded only by Oklahoma, Arizona, California, and New Mexico.

ucts, quilting, and hair accessories; full municipal services at Cherokee, including a water and sewer system; and a fish and game service. Altogether, Chief John Crowe said, the Cherokee tribal government and enterprises have a budget of about $1 million a year. Unemployment is very low in the summer tourist season, sometimes as low as 1 percent; in the winter, however, it may rise to 15 or 20 percent.

In 1973, at the same time I spoke with Chief Crowe, I attended a meeting of the tribal council. The debate was free-wheeling and irreverent; several women (including a precious cameo of indeterminate older years) were members; and there was an interpreter present for the few council members who speak only the Cherokee language. In the last years, the Cherokee schools have been teaching the language to children in the primary grades—another example of that growing pride in special heritages that one senses all over the country.

Up through the 1940s, western North Carolina was one of the most isolated sections of eastern America. Then came tourism, industrialization, and the growth of mountain-based educational institutions. In the 1960s Terry Sanford defined the mountains' future as "an educational factory, a retirement land, a recreational paradise, leavened by appreciative industrial neighbors."

Now that the wall of isolation has been broken, however, thoughtful people of the region speak with deep concern of the head-over-heels tourist development, soaring land prices, the bulldozing off of mountains to make way for condominiums and ski resorts and golf courses, and the arrival of the plastic civilization of hamburger and fried chicken stands and gas stations and all the rest. The once placid little city of Boone and its environs is one example of that kind of growth. With tourism and the growth of the Appalachian State University there, Boone's population jumped 138 percent, to 8,754, during the 1960s. The university's enrollment is close to 10,000. Just as alarming, in terms of poor development, is the once exquisite Magee Valley, west of Asheville, now full of snake farms and the like. "It's a mess," one local leader said, "and unfortunately the zoning can't be made retroactive."

There has also been poorly controlled development in the town of Cherokee, strategically located at the entrance to the Great Smokies National Park. In 1946 Cherokee had a post office in a store, three trading posts, and a filling station. About 50 tourist cars passed by each day, Chief Crowe recalled. By the early 1970s (at least before the energy crisis struck) some eight million tourists a year were going through Cherokee. The town had spawned what seemed like dozens of souvenir shops, restaurants, and gas stations, the whole not quite as garish as Gatlinburg, Tennessee, across the mountains, but a bit more tawdry. The most attractive offerings of the town were those of the Cherokee Historical Association—the Oconaluftee Indian Village, with a splendid portrayal of early Cherokee life, and the nightly performances of "Unto These Hills."

For all the growth, there are some bright spots to the modern-day development of the mountain section. The national park and the Blue Ridge Parkway—notwithstanding exceedingly heavy use—are well maintained by the government. Among private scenic developments, few are as tasteful or impressive as Grandfather Mountain near Boone, which is owned and run as a tourist attraction by a leading local politician-businessman, Hugh Morton. Morton's grandfather bought the mountain, the highest in the Blue Ridge, in 1889, and he has fought repeated attempts by the National Park Service to take it over. "I'm seen in the hills as an oddity—the only man who ever licked the federal government," Morton said. "But I really don't feel the mountain is mine. It's mine in trust to protect." He showed me a dazzling set of slides (his own photography) of the mountain at all seasons of the year, and of its flora and fauna—fitting competition for any National Park Service presentation. Grandfather Mountain is 120 million years old, and has some of the oldest rock formations in America.

With the rising tide of tourism and the large number of retirement and vacation condominium developments, western North Carolina desperately needs careful planning lest it become, in one native's words, a "Miami Beach in the mountains." But in 1973 the legislature failed to pass a state land-use planning law, and the future of the mountains remained unclear.*

Until now, there has been something very special about North Carolina's Appalachia, a place where the historic memory is not altogether erased, the last frontier of the old mountaineers. In the dying hours of a golden summer day, I spent several hours talking with journalist John Parris on the porch of his lovely farm retreat near the town of Sylva. Parris was a son of the mountains who could (as so many have) led an exciting life in the greater world. A distinguished Associated Press correspondent in London during World War II, and later at the United Nations, he was offered any AP correspondent's job he would like, anywhere in the world. But Parris chose instead to return to the mountains, to write a column for the Asheville *Citizen* in which he might capture the flavor of a fast-fading civilization. (When the first book of his columns was published, Parris was a guest on Ed Murrow's CBS show and Murrow—also a North Carolina native—said that Parris had the best job in the world, and got paid for it.)

It is scarcely possible to capture, in a paragraph or two, the essence of Parris's columns and books (*Roaming the Mountains; My Mountains, My People; Mountain Bred; These Storied Mountains*), because they deal with the minutiae of everyday life that give it its warp and woof. From Clear Creek he reports "She's Still Hoein' Corn at 102." From Bryson City he tells the story of Sarah Palestine Kirkland, who "for 70 years, in rain and snow and dark of night, has followed the stork wherever it flew—the last of the old-time mountain midwives." (Until 1928 or 1930, Parris told me, practically everyone was delivered by a midwife or doctor at home in the hills.) Another column is entitled "Quiltin' Sparks Marriage-Talk"; another "Squirrel and Dumplings"; others "Old Man Conner's Coffin" and "Autumn's Glory Spreads Across the Hills." And these are not just tales for old folks who like

* A watered-down land-use plan was passed by the 1974 legislature, but it applied only to the state's coastal areas.

to reminisce; I discovered that my own nine-year-old daughter, Andrea, was avidly reading *These Storied Mountains,* catching a touch of their bitter-sweet nostalgia and common humanity.

"Western North Carolina," Parris observed as we sipped bourbon and chewed on pickled ramps, "is the last of the pioneer's preserve. The frontier has passed us by but this is the last isolated section to buckle under to modern times. Each day I find little pockets of this pioneer life unchanged—especially among the older people, despite the great changes all around them." The change does worry Parris. There has been more of it in the mountains in the past 20 years, he observed, especially the better roads and schools and communications. But he notes with alarm the loss of conversation, recalling how when he was a youngster "we visited with grandfathers and grandmothers and other relatives on Sundays, and everyone sat around and talked, and you had conversations at the table at every meal, and you didn't just sit down with a TV dinner and keep your mouth shut." His own grandfather, Parris said, had such a skill as a storyteller, and at remembering details, "that you could take his words and go ahead and make things." In those days, Parris observed, family history really meant something, and "you learned who your great-, and great-great grandparents were, and who begat so and so." The same loss of history is perpetrated in the schools, he said. "We've skipped so much history—put it aside as if it didn't mean anything. We sloughed off the state histories. What the kids get in school isn't humanized—there's no flesh put on the bones."

There is a fierce mountain defensiveness, even in as well traveled a mountaineer as John Parris. He rejects out of hand a view of the mountain people, either in times past or now, as an ignorant or debased type. "Many of the people who came into these mountains could speak the forgotten language of Latin, and they had the books they brought over from England with them, the classics and all, and some of these things were handed down to us." Even in Asheville, Parris said, people say to him: "Aren't you afraid to go back into the hills?" They have, he noted, "the same misconceptions about the people who live back in the hollows as people in the North who think every man down here is a gallused guy with a jug of whiskey in one hand and a rifle in the other. People ask me: 'Where can I see a mountaineer?' And I answer: 'I'm one.'"

Up in the mountains, in the village of Montreat, near Asheville, is the home of evangelist Billy Graham. From his comfortable house notched in the Smokies, Graham has gone forth to preach to huge crowds almost all over the world. Since 1947, 1.5 million people have come forward and made decisions for Christ at Graham rallies (his public relations department in Atlanta keeps count); many may have backslid, but Graham has undoubtedly changed thousands of people's lives. His fame was due initially to his vibrant, emotion-charged preaching style, but his place in American life today is due more to his closeness to men of power. He has been on friendly terms with Presidents Truman, Eisenhower, Kennedy, Johnson, and Nixon; sometimes he seems to have been a sort of ambassador to Presidents from that huge segment of America that is evangelical Christianity. Graham's strongest imprecations over the years have been directed at sexual immorality and god-lessness; he was silent for years on the evils of racial segregation and never said a word against the American bombing in southeast Asia. Nor was his a voice of prophetic judgment when the depredations associated with Watergate were revealed; about the best he could muster was a mild rebuke of his friend Richard Nixon for "isolation" and poor judgment, and a suggestion that the crisis might deepen Nixon's character as the agonies of the Civil War made Lincoln the great man that he was (as if one might one day hear a mellowed Richard Nixon speak from the heart of "malice toward none, charity toward all.") Graham said: "I just can't imagine . . . how Mr. Nixon got caught in this Watergate buzzsaw, . . . because I always thought of him as a man of great integrity, of great patriotism, of great love of family, with deep religious roots." In a way, Graham was reflecting the disillusion-ment of his constituency, which had always wanted to see Nixon as a pillar of patriotic morality. One was tempted to say that Billy Graham, disciple of the simple carpenter from Nazareth, had supped too often at the tables of the mighty.

Economically, the mountains have suffered from many of the same prob-lems of the east, including low-paying industry and outmigration. But the mountains are surely better off than the east. Race is not much of a problem, if only because there are few blacks (about 5 percent of total population). The mountains are not wedded to a crop like tobacco. Nor has western North Carolina experienced the boom-and-bust coal mining development that has so scarred other Appalachian regions. In fact, some western North Carolinians were resentful of their inclusion in the Appalachia program.

The leading city in the west is Asheville (population 57,681), the fifth largest in the state. But both Hugh Morton and state representative Claude de Bruhl of Asheville said that the city had given little leadership to the re-gion. Asheville has not been much of a growth center of late; its population in 1970 was just 7,000 more than in 1930. It is situated in a valley along the French Broad River, which flows across the mountains to the Tennessee; there is a lack of space, really, to grow. Asheville had its own little golden age around the turn of the century, when its cool climate and beautiful scenery made it a fashionable resort for well-to-do Southerners. It also attracted Mr. George W. Vanderbilt, who bought 130,000 acres of mountain land around the city, appointed a youthful Gifford Pinchot (later Theodore Roosevelt's Secretary of the Interior) as superintendent of his forests, and built the Bilt-more mansion. This house covers four acres and has dozens of rooms; it was designed by Richard Morris Hunt and is reminiscent of the French chateaux of Blois and Chambord.

It was about the same time, in 1900, just five years after the Biltmore mansion was completed, that the novelist Thomas Wolfe was born in Ashe-ville. In his prose he poured forth the memories of early life in Asheville and of how "mile-away hills reeked protectively above the town." A critique of Wolfe, western North Carolina's most brilliant son of letters, is beyond our scope here, but Wilma Dykeman and James Stokely, friends of the Wolfe family, summed it up well when they said "he captured as did no one else the essence of his region's countryside and town, mountaineers and middle class, terror and tomfoolery." Wolfe passed away very early—at the age of 38 —but one is haunted too by what he said of life at the start of *Look Homeward, Angel:* "Naked and alone we came into exile. In her dark womb we did not know our mother's face; from the prison of her flesh have we come into the unspeakable and incommunicable prison of this earth. Which of us has known his brother? Which of us has looked into his father's heart? . . . Which of us is not forever a stranger and alone?"

Tar Heel Politics—and State Government

We have come this far without mentioning, except in passing, politics or the state government. It has not been an accident. What has shaped North Carolina—what has determined how people live, where they work—is not so much government or politics as the face of the land and the raw economic power of the big textile, tobacco, and furniture companies, the utilities, and the big banks.* But politics has played some part, and a few politicians who chanced to become governor or Senator have provided much of what reason there is for the state's progressive reputation. What really matters in North Carolina politics is the governorship, and so any study of North Carolina politics is interwoven with matters of state government.

The importance of the governorship—universally subscribed to by politicians and reporters—is another North Carolina paradox, for the governor here has less formal power than in any other state. He (North Carolinians have yet to elect women to any office higher than state senator) is prohibited from seeking a second consecutive term (until recently he could *never* run again); he has no veto; he must share administrative powers with a tribe of nine other elected officials. Withal, it is surprising that North Carolina governors have been able to accomplish much of anything; in fact, over the years, only a few of them have. The good reputation of the series of governors who held office for the 50 years from 1904 to 1954 derives mainly from the fact that they were personally honest and conducted reasonably efficient regimes free of gross corruption.

Then the state had two outstanding governors: Luther Hodges and Terry Sanford. We have already seen how Hodges, who later served as Secretary of Commerce in the Kennedy and Johnson administrations, was granted an unusually long term, and how Hodges and Sanford, who is now president of

* North Carolina allows banks to build branches anywhere in the state. As a result, this state with no giant cities has several giant banks. Three North Carolina banks are among the nation's 50 largest, and two others had in 1973 deposits of more than $750 million. Wachovia Bank & Trust Company, long the state's largest, had deposits of $2.4 billion and assets of $3.7 billion in 1973; North Carolina National Bank, formed in 1960 largely to compete with Wachovia, passed it in both categories in 1973. Competition is vigorous, probably more than it would be if banking in small cities and towns were dominated by banks owned by complacent local notables.

Duke University and chairman of the national Democratic Party's charter commission, got the state moving toward economic diversification. Much of North Carolina's current reputation for political progressivism rests on their achievements. But there are some paradoxes here, too. Consider the Pearsall Plan, which was the Hodges administration's response to the Supreme Court's 1954 school desegregation decision. Backed by Hodges and passed by the legislature, the plan authorized school closings and tuition payments for private schools. But Hodges' main theme was "let's keep the schools open"; in 1969 he told me the Pearsall Plan (which was later ruled unconstitutional) had been "safety valve legislation" which he never intended to enforce. There was no massive resistance in North Carolina, as there was in Virginia; no schools closed; and the token integration of the late '50s and early '60s went off peacefully. Back in the 1950s, Hodges said, he had been obliged to take ostensibly anti-civil rights positions "in order not to lose the bulk of the people of the state." Some years later, in 1968, Hodges would show his true colors by offering to give up his seat to the 1968 Democratic National Convention so that Negroes could have more representation.

Sanford's main contribution was in the realm of education, particularly in building up the community college and technical institute system. He also sponsored experimental antipoverty programs, such as those funded by the North Carolina Fund, before the national antipoverty program was proposed. Sanford had been manager of W. Kerr Scott's successful Senate campaign in 1954, and had assembled a diverse group of supporters for his own 1960 campaign—including Mr. Charlie Cannon and the president of the state AFL-CIO. Once in office, he showed that he could employ some of the traditional wheeler-dealer powers of the governorship to make almost startling innovations. An example was the North Carolina School of the Arts, located in Winston-Salem, with programs in ballet, voice, and instrumental music. Rural legislators called it a "toe-dancing school," but Sanford was able to ram it through by horsetrading road projects (the state has a monopoly on road-building) and appointments the legislators dearly wanted. Today, North Carolina even has a state art gallery and a state-supported symphony—unlikely institutions in a state of its sociological composition (and rare enough in any state, for that matter). But there is another side of the Sanford record. In order to support his massive education spending program, Sanford got the legislature to pass a sales tax on food—just about the most regressive tax there is. (North Carolina already had, and has, a moderately progressive income tax.)

The governors who followed Hodges and Sanford were less distinctive. Dan Moore, a Democrat elected in 1964, was an easygoing conservative who now serves on the state supreme court. Robert Scott, elected in 1968, seemed more promising; the son of a former governor, he combined a rural orientation and progressive rhetoric. But Scott made many enemies. For one thing, he pushed through a two-cents-per-pack tax on cigarettes; North Carolina was the last state to hold out against taxing the weed, for obvious reasons, and howls went up from the tobacco farm regions and the cigarette factory towns.

And he was not able to fulfill his spending promises to the North Carolina teachers' organization, which is by general agreement considered the state's most powerful lobby, both in the legislature and at the polls.

So in 1972, the Tar Heel state, which has had a tradition of unusual political continuity and seeming contentedness, was eager for change and ready for a minor political revolution. It came in the form of statewide Republican victories for President, Senator, and governor—the first, of course, in years. North Carolina had last supported the Republican Presidential ticket in 1928, when the dominant Democratic politicians opposed Catholic Al Smith; it had last elected a Republican governor in 1896, when the GOP formed a fusion with the Populists.

But the political revolution of the early 1970s, if a long time coming, was clearly foreseeable. Up through the 1950s, the Republicans had been a regional party, centered in the same counties in the northwest Piedmont and western mountains which had opposed secession most steadfastly in 1861. Even in the New Deal, this regional Republican party was electing a few legislators and winning as much as 33 percent of the statewide vote against Franklin D. Roosevelt. But the national Democratic ticket dipped below 60 percent in 1948 and stayed at about that level through the 1964 landslide; then it dropped to a miserable 29 percent in 1968 and 1972. Even Terry Sanford admits that the national Democratic party will have trouble in North Carolina as long as the electoral college system is in effect, since there is little reason for Democrats to work for more votes when they are sure to lose the state anyway.

The erosion of the state Democratic party came more gradually, of course, but even in 1960, when Sanford ran for governor, it was apparent. Despite his great attractiveness as a candidate, Sanford got only 54 percent of the general election vote. Conservative Dan Moore did better in 1964, with 57 percent, but Bob Scott slipped to only 53 percent in 1968. So it should not have come as a complete surprise in 1972 when Republican state representative (and party chairman) James Holshouser won the governorship with 51 percent of the votes and television and radio commentator (and ultraconservative) Republican Jesse Helms won a U.S. Senate seat with 54 percent of the votes. The Republican triumph was a long time coming, and in 1972 it just finally happened.

The 1972 elections signaled other changes in North Carolina politics. For years, elections had been matters of lining up support from local courthouse politicians, who were deemed capable of delivering their counties' votes. There are still a few who can, but most of these local bosses—almost all of them are Democrats, of course—have precious few votes to barter any more. In 1972 there was a heavy shift to media campaigning. Senate candidate Helms was familiar to thousands, particularly in the east, from his editorials on WRAL-TV (Raleigh) and his radio broadcasts on the Tobacco Network (a hook-up of small North Carolina stations). As a Republican, Holshouser of course relied more on media than local power brokers, and so, even more, did his Democratic opponent, Hargrove "Skipper" Bowles. Bowles started his campaign early, in the fall of 1971, with heavy TV advertising, and beat the winter-book Democratic favorite and Scott administration heir apparent, Lieutenant Governor Pat Taylor, in the primary. Bowles employed the services of professional campaign consultant (and coauthor of *The Ticket-Splitter*) Walter De Vries, a recent Michigan transplant and ex-campaign counselor to George Romney. A half dozen other major political consultants and media packagers were involved in 1972 North Carolina campaigns. This is a far cry from Senator Sam Ervin's favorite campaign tactics—get into his Chrysler, drive around, and chat to any gathering of voters he finds—and it is probably the wave of the future in North Carolina as in most of the rest of the country.

Another notable fact about the 1972 gubernatorial race was the small difference between the candidates. Both Holshouser and Bowles could probably be described as conservative progressives (or progressive conservatives); the main difference between them seems to have been how money should be spent on education. Holshouser favored higher teachers' salaries, which got him the support of the teachers' lobby (and which he delivered on in 1973), while Bowles favored a career-education program. Greater differences could be perceived between Holshouser and his ticket-mate Jesse Helms. This is really a reflection of a geographical split in the Republican Party. Holshouser is from the town of Boone in the mountains (which is also the home of Rufus Edmisten, who was the young deputy counsel of the Watergate committee and 1974 Democratic candidate for attorney general). Helms is from Raleigh, and won largely because he managed to carry the traditionally heavily Democratic eastern counties. Holshouser's mountain Republicanism has a moderate, if not populist, cast; Helms is a former Democrat who appeals to registered Democrats who supported segregationist candidates in the past. (On television over the years, Helms had excoriated the courts and others responsible for school integration, attacked welfare, foreign aid, and trade with the Communists countries, and even accused President Nixon of "appeasement" in his détente with China.) The difference between the two Republican camps was reflected in the struggle over the state Republican chairmanship in late 1973. Holshouser wished to oust the ultraconservative incumbent, Frank Rouse, who had openly backed his eastern-based opponent in the 1972 primary. Helms officially stayed neutral, but strong Helms backers naturally supported Rouse. Holshouser won the fight, but only with the help of party members who respected his patronage powers.

Which way would the Republican Party go in the future? It seemed unclear in 1974. Holshouser was greatly aided in 1972 by the fact that he was both state party chairman and head of his party's joint legislative caucus; he was therefore the party's chief spokesman on most issues and well versed in the minutiae of state government. No similarly well known and knowledgeable figure had emerged from either the Holshouser-mountain or Helms-eastern wing of the party. In general, the Republicans suffer from a lack of back-bench talent warming up for the majors. The great bulk of legislative seats, for instance, remain in Democratic hands. In most eastern counties which Jesse Helms carried in the 1972 election, there was no Republican legislative candidate at all. Even in the Piedmont, Republicans do not necessarily run slates. The successful young businessmen who might win as Republicans seem more interested in climbing the corporate ladder than in spending several months in Raleigh. (As one young Charlotte insurance man who had become active in some antipoverty campaigns told me, "My impression is that the state legislature's just a damned waste of time.") Thus while the long-term trends point to increasing Republican victories, one wonders where the candidates will come from.

As his party's first governor in 76 years, Holshouser clearly demonstrated that the state would not fall apart in Republican hands. But he did not rise to the stature of a Hodges or a Sanford either. One reason was probably unpreparedness. Few people expected him to win, and even after a year in office, he had still left many key appointive posts unfilled. There was no throng of Republicans eager for places on the public payroll, as there always had been under the Democrats.

Holshouser did use his appointive authority and his control of road building to win enough Democratic votes to stop a move to strip him of highway patronage, traditionally a mainstay of Tar Heel governors' political strength. His most substantive achievements were in extending the school year to ten full months and instituting a full kindergarten program—victories won with the help of the teacher's lobby. The major criticism of Holshouser's program and the Democratic legislature's response was not that they lacked some progressive aspects, but that they were conventional—just more funding of traditional programs. Where no organized lobbies appeared to back major bills, such as measures to set up a coastal management act and establish a state land-use policy, next to nothing happened.

The legislature, even under Holshouser, did little more than respond to the governor's proposals, in the manner of legislatures through the prior three-quarters of a century of Democratic governors. Moreover, the North Carolina experience seems to prove that fancy facilities alone do not a legislature make. A few years ago the house and senate moved out of the old state Capitol into a splendid new marble and glass legislative building designed by Edward Durell Stone. The close proximity of legislative chambers, committee rooms, and legislators' individual offices makes for probably the most convenient working environment for state legislators in the nation. With its red carpets, fountains, and airy mezzanines, the legislative building is also— with the notable exception of Hawaii's architecturally magnificent new Capitol—the most pleasant place for legislators to work in the United States. The facility has diverted a lot of the important decision-making from sessions in smoky Raleigh hotel rooms. Still, the Citizens Conference on State Legislatures in 1971 ranked North Carolina's 47th among the 50 on a general scale of accountability, information sources, independence, and representativeness. An unmanageably large number of committees and gross deficiencies in professional staff were among the chief drawbacks noted. Since then, the legislature has experimented with annual (instead of every-other-year) sessions, and made some other marginal improvements. And slowly reapportionment—taking seats away from the east, adding them to the Piedmont —has had its effect. At first, one legislator told me, "the Piedmont sent people who didn't know where the water closets were—or the skeletons in them." Another problem was that the east and west often teamed up against the Piedmont, and that Piedmont legislators rarely stayed in office very long. This situation is changing, but slowly.

One should recognize some of the modernization prompted by Piedmont legislators. State senator Herman A. Moore of Charlotte told of how "I came into the legislature from a lifetime in business, and I was one frustrated son-of-a-bitch when I got down here and found no staff, no planning, no aids. I damn near quit after my first session." But over the opposition of many older members, Moore was able to get a legislative reform commission created and to persuade the legislature to install a computer which stores all past statutes and makes possible quick printing of amended bills with insertions and deletions from the original text.

What of the Democratic party? One Democrat I know called it a "leaderless mob," and while the "mob" may be an exaggeration, "leaderless" is not. There is no party organization to speak of; although the Republicans have been competitive for years now, every Democratic candidate still campaigns on his own. In 1972 the party chose its most liberal Senate candidate in years, Congressman Nick Galifianakis (in a state with only a minuscule number of Greek-Americans), and he was pretty soundly beaten (in part because of the drag on Democratic races caused by the McGovern Presidential campaign).* Former Governor Sanford, the embodiment of North Carolina progressivism, ran in the state's 1972 Presidential primary; he won only 37 percent of the state's votes, as against George Wallace's 50 percent. (It might have been much closer were it not for Congresswoman Shirley Chisholm, whose 7.5 percent vote in North Carolina was her best showing in the nation.) In 1974 the Democrats were able to hold Sam Ervin's old Senate seat, in part because the Republicans, in the wake of the Nixon-Watergate scandals, were unable to persuade their strongest potential candidate, Congressman Wilmer "Vinegar Bend" Mizell, to risk a loss. Moreover, the Democrats were blessed with a strong candidate in Attorney General Robert Morgan, described by political columnists Rowland Evans and Robert Novak as "a throwback to shrewd courthouse Democratic politicians of the old one-party South—canny, nonideological, and supremely flexible." Back in 1960, Morgan had managed segregationist I. Beverly Lake's campaign for governor against Terry Sanford; later he defended North Carolina's repressive law banning Communists and fellow-travelers from speaking at state universities. Twice elected attorney general, however, he built a reputation as a consumer advocate, fighting higher utility and milk prices. He also hired blacks for his staff and won the endorse-

* Galifianakis won the 1972 Democratic Senate nomination by beating the mild-mannered textile millionaire who had held the seat since 1958, B. Everett Jordan, who was 74 years of age at the time and in ill health. Jordan had won some national notice as chairman of the Senate Rules Committee, in which post he headed the investigation of Bobby Baker, former Secretary to the Senate Majority and Lyndon Johnson protegé.

ment of some major black organizations in the state's larger cities. On the other hand, Morgan had defended the Nixon administration's Vietnam policy, and it was impossible for the Republicans to pin on him the "liberal" tag that had sunk Galifianakis.

Long-range Democratic prospects, however, did not seem bright. Republicans won between 41 and 45 percent of the votes for all the lesser statewide offices in 1972—an indication they may be able to win some in the near future. And for the first time, the Republicans in 1972 received more votes than Democrats in contested U.S. House races (some Democrats were unopposed). Walter De Vries, through polling, has shown that the large Democratic lead in registration is meaningless, since 51 percent of the registered Democrats in the early '70s were persons who ordinarily voted straight Republican or habitually split their tickets. The large cities, where population growth is most rapid, have been trending Republican for years; all with populations over 100,000 sent at least some Republicans to the legislature in the early 1970s.* And among young voters, the trend seemed to be—as it is in Tennessee, for example—toward Republican voting habits. North Carolina Democrats seem to be stuck with either a courthouse politician or a liberal image at a time when most North Carolinians no longer identify with either one.

Even the elections of Hodges and Sanford seem, in retrospect, to be somewhat accidental. Hodges, of course, moved up from the lieutenant governorship; who can say whether he would have won on his own? And Sanford was aided in the 1960 primary by a split of the middle-of-the-road Democratic vote between two candidates; he was able to beat segregationist I. Beverly Lake in the runoff, but he might well have lost to either of the two moderates. That is more or less what happened to Richardson Preyer, Sanford's heir apparent, in the 1964 contest. Dr. Lake was eliminated in the first primary, and virtually all his support went to Dan Moore, who won the runoff against Preyer easily.

What strikes one most forcefully about this ferment in partisan politics is its irrelevance to the major problems the state faces. One has the sense that this giant state runs largely on inertia these days. "Education" has been a watchword of North Carolina politics since Charles B. Aycock was elected governor in 1900 and became known as the great "education governor." Here North Carolina is still a leader. Its average teacher's salary in 1973 was $9,076, higher than in any Southern or Border State except Virginia, Florida, or Louisiana. And it is the state government which pays 80 percent of the cost of elementary and secondary education, including a base salary for all teach-

---

* In North Carolina, one hears again and again that this Republican trend in the cities is due in large part to an influx of Northern-bred management and technical personnel. The Yankee transplants may indeed provide a fresh supply of Republican political talent, but their overall influence is vastly overstated. Eighty-nine percent of all North Carolinians were either born in the state, or in other parts of the South, Maryland, or Delaware. In the Greensboro-Winston-Salem metropolitan area, only 5 percent of the residents were born outside the South; in the Charlotte metro area, the Yankee-born number only 7 percent. This is not enough to make a political trend. The constantly increasing—at least until 1972—number of Republican votes comes almost entirely from native North Carolinians and other born Southerners.

ers. The University of North Carolina at Chapel Hill is surely the most distinguished public institution of higher learning south of the Mason-Dixon line, and the state's higher education system as a whole, including 15 other universities and the community colleges and technical institutes, is at least a match for any other in the region.*

On the other hand, North Carolina spends considerably less per capita than the Southern and Border State average on welfare and health (and on highways, for that matter). There is no lobby as powerful as the teachers to push these items, and they have caught no governor's imagination. One might argue that this is a regressive pattern of spending. Most North Carolinians over 16 have not completed the 11th grade, and only 8.5 percent of the state's residents over 25 were graduated from college; higher education is a benefit which accrues largely to those already affluent. This is not quite fair, for it overlooks the efforts the state has made to draw in undereducated people to its technical programs and community colleges. Nonetheless, there are prominent North Carolinians today who are uttering the heresy that the state is spending too much on education and too little on other things.

North Carolina in Congress

Considering the fact that North Carolina is the 12th largest state, it has made surprisingly little impact on our national politics. No North Carolina politician has ever been elected President, though, as I noted at the beginning of the chapter, three North Carolina-born Tennesseeans—Jackson, Polk, and Johnson—made it to the White House after moving west. But search your mind for the name of a 20th-century national leader from North Carolina; except for Terry Sanford, Luther Hodges, and Sam Ervin, you will not think of any. To understand why, just consider the career of Furnifold McLenden Simmons, a member of the United States Senate for 30 years (1901–31). In all that time, Simmons made little impact in Washington; his place in history is due solely to the fact that he was generally able to deliver the Democratic gubernatorial nomination until he made the mistake of op-

* During the Scott administration, the state set up a higher education board to set priorities for the growth of the entire state university system. This was resisted by some Chapel Hill boosters, but its main problems have come from East Carolina University at Greenville and its president, Leo Jenkins. A New Jersey native with a penchant for promotion—he gave me his pitch one evening in a lobbyists' and legislators' hangout in Raleigh—Jenkins wants to build East Carolina into a major institution and has carefully cultivated support from legislators from the east and other regions of the state. As a result in 1973 the legislature set up a reserve fund for a medical school at ECU—although such an institution would be more costly than expanding Chapel Hill's fine medical school, and although the higher education board was dead set against the project. Jenkins argued that the placement of a medical school in the East would increase the number of doctors located there (and the region does need more). But there is no assurance that young M.D.'s from East Carolina would not do what most of their fellow physicians do, which is to head for a lucrative practice in a large metropolitan area, of which there are none in eastern North Carolina.

The reader should not be deceived into thinking that all North Carolina leaders approve the education-intellectual thrust of state policy. Luther Hodges, Sr., told me the perhaps apocryphal story of a medical school dean who grew a beard and got a call from a state legislator who told him: "That'll cost you $10 million, you s.o.b."

posing Al Smith in 1928. It is the governorship which has always mattered in North Carolina politics. People seem to give little consideration to congressional elections, and politicians seldom take great pains to become a Congressman or Senator.

Having said that, I should add that North Carolina sent one of its undeniably distinguished sons, Frank Porter Graham, to the Senate, back in 1949. But Dr. Graham, who had been president of the University of North Carolina, was merely appointed to fill a vacancy; in 1950, after a scurrilous campaign redolent of McCarthyism and racism, Graham was defeated in the Democratic primary. (One of those working for his opponent was a young journalist named Jesse Helms, who now holds the seat Graham lost.) And we may also note that from late 1950s into the early '60s, thanks to the inexorable workings of the seniority system, there were several committee chairmen in the North Carolina House delegation; none of them, however, had the stature of, say, Wilbur Mills. Probably the most powerful was Harold Cooley of Agriculture; he shepherded the complex and lucrative sugar quota bill through the House and after his surprise defeat in 1966 went to work as a lobbyist for sugar interests. Graham Barden of Education and Labor was a crusty conservative who refused to let the number two Democrat on the committee, Adam Clayton Powell, ask questions of witnesses. (Powell, as Harlem's congressman, represented thousands of blacks who had been brought up in Barden's eastern North Carolina district.) Herbert Bonner headed Merchant Marine and Fisheries, a body often of little interest except for those to whom it siphons subsidies from the federal treasury. Perhaps a more significant footnote in history should be accorded Carl T. Durham, who served twice as chairman of the Joint Committee on Atomic Energy during his 22-year House career (1939–61). Durham deserved credit, along with Connecticut's Senator Brien McMahon, for influencing President Truman's decision to develop the hydrogen bomb and, even more important for future U.S. policy, pressed to have the Atomic Energy Commission made a civilian rather than a military-directed agency of the government.

For many years, North Carolina's congressional districts were gerrymandered against Republicans. Traditional GOP counties in the mountains were linked to more heavily populated Democratic territory in the Piedmont. But in 1952, Charles Raper Jonas, Jr., managed to ride the Eisenhower landslide to victory in a district that included Charlotte; he was the first Republican to win a House seat in the state since his father had ridden to victory in the Hoover landslide of 1928. Jonas, Sr., lasted only one term, but Jonas, Jr., confounded the Democrats by hanging on, despite repeated adverse redistrictings. He was joined by another Republican, James T. Broyhill, in 1962, and by 1972, when Jonas retired, there were four Republicans in a delegation of 11, and the party just missed capturing a fifth seat. Jonas may have been the most important member of the delegation his last few years; a firm believer in government economy, he was ranking Republican on the House Appropriations Committee. Currently, the class of the House group is

Greensboro's Democrat Richardson Preyer, scion of a wealthy family, a former federal judge, and Terry Sanford's candidate to succeed him in 1964. Preyer is highly respected for intelligence and integrity; he won 94 percent of the votes against an American Independent Party candidate in 1972. His voting record is sometimes liberal, but like the rest of the North Carolina delegation, he makes few waves in Washington.

The exception, of course, was the man who in 1974 retired as the state's senior Senator, Sam J. Ervin, Jr. At the beginning of 1973 Sam Ervin was no more a household word than was the Watergate office and apartment complex. Within six months, all that had changed. The Watergate coverup had been blown wide open, and television brought Sam Ervin and his Watergate Committee hearings into just about every living room in America. College students began wearing Uncle Sam Ervin T-shirts, and Midwestern women tourists cooed as they saw "him" (always taller than they had expected) shamble through the Capitol. People remembered his country yarns, and his habit of quoting the Bible, the Constitution, and random bits of poetry that occurred to him.

But beneath the fustian there was steel. It is hard to remember now, but in the spring of 1973 President Nixon, invoking executive privilege, announced he would forbid all his aides from testifying before Ervin's committee. Senator Sam responded by saying that he would recommend sending marshals out to arrest the aides. In the face of this and the unfolding revelations, Nixon backed down. The Ervin Committee did its duty and exposed the crimes of the Committee to Reelect the President, and even the malfeasance of the President himself, to the nation.

Some liberals had been disappointed when Senate Majority Leader Mike Mansfield appointed Ervin to head the probe. Wasn't he, they tried to remember, the man who had made all those pesky arguments against civil rights bills? Hadn't he used his position on the Judiciary Committee to oppose the Equal Rights Amendment? Hadn't he voted down the line with Johnson and Nixon on Vietnam? And while a Senator, hadn't he come forward and argued in the Supreme Court with gusto the case for textile millionaire Roger Milliken, who closed down one mill when the workers voted for a union?

The answer to all these questions was yes. But what the liberals—and the White House—would learn was that Sam Ervin could not be stuffed into a neat ideological pigeonhole. He was also a man who had served on the committee that recommended the censure of Joe McCarthy. And in the late 1960s, he began a series of crusades against what he considered the overweening power of the executive branch. He probed into Army spying on civilians and into abuses of government data banks. He led the Senate opposition to the no-knock law. He was one of the leading opponents of Presidential impoundment of appropriations voted by Congress. Ervin did not take up these causes because he sympathized with the people being spied on or because he favored high government spending. But, as *The Almanac of American Pol-*

itics—1974 put it, "It is a measure of Sam Ervin's devotion to the Constitution that he has spent many of his years in the Senate defending the rights of people whose ideas he does not share."

It is the Constitution which Ervin reveres, and like the late Justice Hugo Black—with whom he often disagreed—he always carried a dog-eared copy of the document around with him. Ervin spent the six years before his appointment as Senator as a justice of the North Carolina supreme court, and in the Senate slowly earned the reputation as the chamber's foremost constitutional scholar. Perhaps the classic confrontation in the Watergate hearings came between him and former presidential aide John Ehrlichman. Ervin asked the witness whether he believed that the Constitution prohibited unreasonable searches of a man's person or home, and he cited William Pitt's stirring declaration that though the wind and rain may pierce the walls of a freeman's shabby tenement, yet the King of England cannot cross his doorstep. Ehrlichman condescendingly replied that that principle had been rather eroded lately; it was a sharp lawyer's reply, accurate at least in part, and quite contemptuous of the right the Constitution sought to protect. It was really a confrontation between the eternal verities of the Founding Fathers and the amorality of a clever maneuverer. Threatened by strong primary opposition, Sam Ervin announced that he would not run for reelection in 1974; he would be 78 on election day and 84 when another term would expire. Ervin would be missed in Washington, but he could return to Morganton in the firm knowledge that he had capped his career with an example of principled public service all too rare in American political life of the late 20th century.

WEST VIRGINIA

THE SADDEST STATE

I TRAVELED TO WEST VIRGINIA hoping to find, through talks with the people and leaders there, fresh rays of hope for a chronically depressed state. More than a decade had passed since John F. Kennedy's Presidential primary campaign, with all its bright promises. Hundreds of millions of dollars of federal aid had poured in. The miners and their friends had staged the great Black Lung revolt, wringing concessions from a reluctant state legislature. The same reform movement had propelled a straightforward and utterly honest veteran of 27 years service in the West Virginia mines, Arnold Miller, to the presidency of the decadent United Mine Workers. Finally, there had been the emergence of reform-minded political leaders like John D. (Jay) Rockefeller IV, Congressman Ken Hechler, and the late Virginia House Speaker Ivor Bioarsky.

Despite those signs of a quickening of the democratic spirit in the body politics, however, I still found West Virginia the saddest of all American states. Here is a province, especially in its eastern reaches, of pristine mountain beauty and rolling countryside so splendid that it will surely one day be a place of respite for the huddled millions of the eastern megalopolis (and also, hopefully, a place of better opportunities for its native people). But viewing West Virginia as a whole, one has to conclude that its liabilities—physical, economic, political, and human—remain overwhelming and discouraging in the extreme.

Some of the grim specifics are these:

■ Afghanistanism. When the federal planners in the early 1960s delineated the counties of Appalachia, West Virginia turned out to be the only state in which *every* county was included. And for good reason. Among the 50 states, this is indubitably the most mountainous. Level land is hard indeed to find: in the narrow flood plains of the river bottoms, the broadest of which, in the Ohio Valley, is nowhere more than two miles wide; a few plateaus in the mountain ranges; and in the eastern panhandle, which includes some of the Shenandoah Valley spilling over from Virginia. But all this encompasses a very small percentage of the total land area. Otherwise the landscape is uneven and ragged, filled with jumps, gulleys, quick falls, and rises, a configuration that reaches its most extreme form in some of the southern coal counties.

The historic consequences of this geographic configuration have been minimal agriculture, poor communications, fierce sectionalism, and severely constrained industry. The inaccessibility of much of West Virginia has been broken down some in recent years by 511 miles of interstate highway and 427 miles of the companion developmental roads built by the Appalachian Regional Commission. ("All of this construction," one observer commented, was "going on in a state where until recently it could take five hours to drive 100 miles on mountainous roads as winding and dark as licorice.") But the highway building was cut and fill all the way (interstates can cost as much as $4 million a mile through the mountains), and many areas are still unreached by decent highways.

Even where the new roads go, the problems of a ragged upland terrain remain. Not long ago the planners in McDowell County, in the southern coal fields, looked around for flat land for industrial development. The biggest tract they could find was 14 acres—and that involved moving a railroad track and a road. In McDowell County, 92.4 percent of the land is more than a 40-degree slope. The situation is not unusual in West Virginia, where an old saying goes, "Flatten the whole thing out and it would be bigger than Texas." Another saying attributed to a native son, in disparaging the state slogan of "Switzerland of America"—"Switzerland, nothing! It's more like Afghanistan!"

■ Misery among riches. Nature endowed West Virginia with great riches, which it has been mining assiduously for more than a century. In the early '70s mineral production rose to $1.4 billion a year. Of that, 88 percent was from coal. Despite the fact that 7 *billion* tons of coal have been extracted over the years, 100 billion still remain in the ground—so much, it was once estimated, that if it was stacked into a monument one acre square, it would make a sort of pylon for astronauts more than 17,000 miles high. West Virginia also produces more natural gas than any other state east of the Mississippi. Its proven reserves of petroleum are over 100 million barrels, of natural gas two quadrillion cubic feet. The state has major reserves of salt brine (a major base of its chemical industry), immense sand deposits (therefore famed West Virginia glass), lime, and clays. Only three other states exceed it in mineral production. Primordially, West Virginia was also covered with mag-

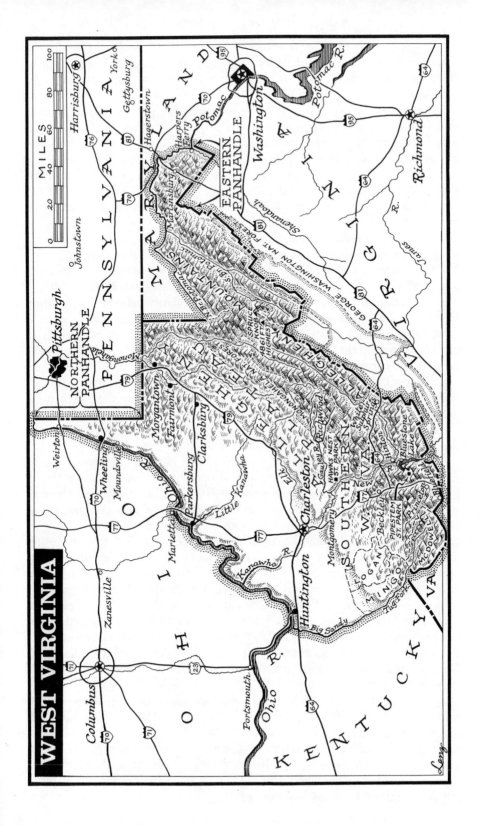

nificent forests; sad to report, however, most of the best growth was taken by slash and run methods early in the century, and the amount sawed in 1909 has not since been equaled.

The people of West Virginia themselves do not profit much from all of this. In 1960 their per capita income was 28 percent below the national average, and in the early 1970s it still lagged 22 points behind, on a par with states like South Carolina and Arkansas. Unemployment has soared far above the national average in recent times, to a frightful peak of 13.5 percent in 1961, though the gap has been less in recent years. There are West Virginia counties where a fourth of the people are on welfare. A few years ago, there were reports of actual cases of starvation.

Paul J. Kaufman, a former state senator, put it well when he said: "West Virginia is not a poor state. It is a rich state inhabited by poor people."

▪ Colonialism. The inability of West Virginians to better their own lot is grounded in the fact that they control such a small portion of the wealth of their own state. Several writers have noted the similarity between 20th-century West Virginia and the colonial domains of Great Britain and other imperial powers in the 19th century. The situations are strikingly parallel: outside capital, extracting the natural wealth of a colony, treats the natives as a lowly, expendable, cheap source of labor; to protect investments, it is deemed necessary to control the government, and this is accomplished by payoffs, threats, or the use of brute force (such as West Virginia witnessed in the bloody mine union wars of the 1920s). Where any rival force becomes too potent, and cannot be repressed, it is co-opted—the fate of the United Mine Workers in the '50s and '60s.

Predictably, the overriding interest of the outside corporations is to maximize profits from their West Virginia operations. One way to do that is to minimize any state taxes they must pay. It is not the distant stockholders who must suffer from the shoddy services—substandard schools, poor hospitals, inadequate welfare—that come from underfinanced state and local government. Through the inordinate influence of the coal industry and other major corporate interests on the state legislature, the tax system has been kept so regressive that government services are doomed to remain inadequate. Until recently, Kaufman pointed out, the entire coal industry paid less in taxes to the state of West Virginia than the state collected in cigarette taxes. Long overdue corporate and severance taxes have been imposed in the last few years, but their yield is a fraction of what is gathered from the regressive sales tax. The tax concessions, my friend Don Marsh of the Charleston *Gazette* noted, have been "just enough to keep the natives sullen rather than mutinous."

Vast stretches of West Virginia are in the hands of absentee landlords, who have little motivation to conserve resources of the land. When a progressive outside corporation does try to take a pro-people or pro-environment stand, it may find the internal West Virginia establishment opposed. As an example, Monsanto was opposed by the state government in the early 1970s when it placed environmental and land-usage restraints on a piece of property it was selling in West Virginia.

The extent of outside land holdings was suggested in testimony by Paul Kaufman before the U.S. Senate Anti-Trust and Monopoly Subcommittee in 1972:

The nine southernmost counties contain approximately 30 percent of the state's total population and produce about 70 percent of the state's coal. Nine corporations own more than 33 percent of these nine counties with real estate holdings worth over 90 million dollars at grossly underassessed values. The top 25 landowners in the nine counties control more than one-half the total land area through their collective ownership of more than 1,600,000 acres. Of these nine corporations, only one is a West Virginia corporation doing business principally within the state. The others include Pocahontas Land Corporation, a wholly owned subsidiary of the Norfolk and Western Railway Company; the mammoth Georgia-Pacific Corporation; Western Pocahontas Corporation, a wholly owned subsidiary of the Chesapeake and Ohio Railway Company; Island Creek Coal Company, a wholly owned subsidiary of the Occidental Petroleum Corporation; Berwind Corporation, a diversified company holding huge tracts of land; Union Carbide Corporation, one of the world's largest chemical combines; Beaver Coal Corporation; and Bethlehem Steel Corporation, a major national metals producer.

Ten coal companies produce roughly 51 percent of the coal mined in the nine counties. Seven of these 10 companies maintain their principal offices outside of West Virginia.

The giant corporations amount to a "private government" with assets and revenues that dwarf those of West Virginia itself. The state government's total revenues, about $1.1 billion a year at latest count, are less than those of several outside corporations active in the state. Among these are Union Carbide and Bethlehem Steel (each about $3 billion in annual sales), Occidential Petroleum ($2.4 billion), and Georgia Pacific ($1.5 billion). Union Carbide employs 12,000 West Virginians—three quarters as many as the state government itself. From its privately owned hydroelectric and coal-burning plants in West Virginia, Union Carbide produces enough electricity to supply a city of a million people. It draws heavily on the state's irreplaceable resources of natural gas as well as coal. The corporation does spend about $125 million a year on goods and services in West Virginia. But its *profits* in one recent year averaged out to $3,800 for each of its workers. This is more than the *total income* of more than 200,000 families and unrelated persons in West Virginia.

Rarely have the big outside corporations been pressed hard to pay a fair share of the cost of government in West Virginia. In Union Carbide's case there was a fascinating exception in the tiny and impoverished town of Anmoore, which took bit in teeth in 1970 and raised the taxes on the local Union Carbide plant some 400 percent. The factory is Anmoore's only resource, occupying 132 acres of land and employing 900, of whom only 40 are actual Anmoore residents. The company's lawyers had negotiated in earlier years to hold the taxes on the plant to a meager $20,000 a year. But the town council, egged on by Ralph Nader's West Virginia field agents, raised the assessment to about $100,000 a year. Mayor Buck Gladden—himself a $3-an-hour laborer—called the action a blow to "corporate colonialism." And when Union Carbide said the town was raising the tax without examining its real budget needs, city councilwoman Margaret Golden replied: "We know our budget needs only too well. Just walk through this town. The mud is every-where. We have no sewer system so the cesspools overflow into the streets. Our kids walk in it. We have no parks, no health clinic, no children's play-ground. All of this not even mentioning the black soot smell that is every-where, thanks to the factory. How can they ask us to examine our budget needs? What needs examining around here is the conscience of Union Car-bide."

The despoliation of the once pristine Appalachian environment, largely for the profit of outside interests, is one of the most appalling aspects of the West Virginia story. The ravages of the coal industry are best known: slag heaps and gob piles that often catch on fire and pollute the air with smoke and stench, acid mine drainage, silted streams, and gouged-out hills from strip mining. Lawyers for the Appalachian Research and Defense Fund in Charleston said they had discovered four o'clock in the morning was the favorite time for coal mines to pollute the streams with black water or for major chemical factories to blow their stacks and pollute the air—all illegal actions, of course. Until the start of the 1970s, one Union Carbide plant was pouring more particulates (solid matter) into the West Virginia skies than all the boilers of New York City. One can imagine the harm done over the years to the ecological balance of fish and wildlife as a result of discharges from the thick concentration of chemical plants along the 12-mile industrial stretch of the Kanawha River at Charleston. By the late 1960s there were more than 2,000 refuse pipes leading into the river. And the list goes on and on.

It is not difficult to define the reasons for a tax system slanted outrage-ously for corporations, for laughably low assessments on big factories and coal mines, and for lackadaisical environmental and mine safety control. They can be traced directly to the massive infiltration of the corporate interests and their minions into the political structure, from the county level on up. Paul Kaufman assembled this sample list of convenient combinations of cor-porate interests and public jobs. Many of the connections may be totally incidental and innocent, but the cumulative weight does suggest a picture. (I have changed the list somewhat, based on later information).

BUSINESS ROLE	PUBLIC ROLE
President, Amherst Coal Company	Member and former chairman, W. Va. Air Pollution Control Commission
Executive vice president, Continental Oil-Consolidation Coal	Former W. Va. tax commissioner
Executive secretary, W. Va. Coal Assoc.	Former speaker, W. Va. House of Delegates
Former executive secretary, W. Va. Coal Association	Former president, W. Va. Senate
Director of Environmental Conservation, Continental Oil	Former director, W. Va. Department of Natural Resources
Distributor for Union Oil; oil and gas entrepreneur	Chairman, W. Va. Senate Committee on Natural Resources
Partner to above as oil and gas entrepreneur	Former president, W. Va. Senate

Director, American Electric Power; director, Consolidation Coal (now retired)	President, W. Va. Board of Regents; Former speaker, House of Delegates; Former chairman, W. Va. Senate Judiciary Committee; Former Democratic national committeeman
Law partner to above; director First National Bank of Belle (W. Va.)	Chairman, W. Va. Senate Judiciary Committee; Senate majority leader; Prime candidate for Senate presidency
Organizer and first executive director of the W. Va. Surface (strip) Mining Association	Former chief of W. Va. Department of Natural Resources, Reclamation Division

In addition to this, the West Virginia governor's office has long served as a springboard to the corporate boardroom, whence a politician is still free to use his political influence. Governor John J. Cornwell became general counsel of the Baltimore & Ohio Railroad, Homer A. Holt general counsel of Union Carbide, Clarence Meadows a board member of Investors Stock Fund, and Cecil Underwood vice president of the Island Creek Coal Company.*

Against these formidable "interlocking directorates," the people are at an overwhelming disadvantage. In the environmental field, for instance, there is no organized citizens group that operates 24 hours a day as the Surface Mining Association and other industrial groups do, with their full-time counsel, publications, and advertising campaigns. There has, however, been a rising tide of agitation to protect the environment, centered especially around the colleges and universities. Slowly, the people are awakening to the very low property taxes on coal lands, an issue popularized by young people, especially those connected with universities. An important force has been the Charleston-based Appalachian Regional Research and Defense Fund, the only public interest law firm in Appalachia. (The organization was founded by Paul Kaufman in 1970 to provide, as he explained it to me, "a countervailing force to the heavy influences of the special interest groups and to provide access to government to the disadvantaged people of our region who are denied it.") Yet when it comes to concrete, fundamental change in this most colonial of all American states, the discussion seems forever mired in the future tense.

- Population drain. While out-of-state corporations have been making money off of West Virginia, huge numbers of its people have been leaving. Jay Rockefeller pointed out that "70 percent of our young people are gone by the time they're 24—and that includes all too many of the best. It's almost an ethic of departure. They all know it's not an exciting or promising place to grow."

According to the Census, West Virginia's population rose slightly in the 1940s and then, over the following two decades, plunged downward at a rate without parallel in any other state at any time in the history of the country. The 1950s brought a net population loss of 145,000, or 7.2 percent and the 1960s a further loss of 116,000, or 6.2 percent, leaving 1,744,237 people in the Mountain State. The loss would have been even greater if it had not been for

* Underwood later became president of Bethany College in Bethany, West Virginia.

the excess of births over deaths. The state has actually suffered a net population loss to other states of 950,000 people since 1940. The loss has been the most severe in the central mountain counties and in the southern coal counties, where automation idled thousands of miners in the 1950s, but it has also afflicted the cities. In the 1960s, only Morgantown among the state's eight cities of 20,000 people or more failed to lose population. The 1970 Census also showed only 39 percent of West Virginia's people living in towns or cities of 2,500 people or more—making the state, except for Vermont, the most rural of the entire country. Many of those who remained were the aged and infirm, living back in the hollows.

The stagnant nature of West Virginia's population pool is underscored by the fact that only 15 percent of its people were born in another state, the fifth lowest average of outsiders (and thus fresh blood) in the Union. Across the country, the 1970 Census takers found 2.5 million people who said they had been born in West Virginia—but 1.1 million of them were living somewhere else. The West Virginia emigrants were heavily concentrated in the Midwest, with 345,700 in Ohio alone. Other states found to have heavy numbers of West Virginia expatriates were Maryland (89,000), Florida (82,000), Pennsylvania (70,000), California (61,000), and Michigan (52,000). The result of all this can be seen in the "little Appalachia" sections of Chicago, Cleveland, Detroit, Dayton, and other cities.

West Virginia officials noted with some hope that the population drain was much less in the last half of the 1960s than the first half, and that a gain of 50,000 in total population was actually estimated by the Census Bureau for the 1970 to 1973 period. Part of the gain might be attributed to returning Vietnam veterans, but it was the state's first ray of hope in many years.

West Virginia still faces a grievously long list of economic impediments in our time. Because outside industry has left so few of its profits in the state, for instance, there is a dearth of decent schools, hospitals, libraries, or even adequate water and sewage facilities—prerequisites for attracting diversified industries and their personnel. The state also suffers from an antiquated banking system under which branch banks are forbidden and there are few pools of equity to help young entrepreneurs. I talked with two academicians at the West Virginia Institute of Technology at Montgomery who put the case most poignantly:

The key to our problems would be to get our population relatively stabilized. Then our merchants might be more venturesome. But look at this town. It's just going to seed, even though we have a strong college here and coal is booming.

There are towns in this state that have lost a third, sometimes almost a half of their population in a decade or two. Why, people reason, should one put in a sewer system or invest in a place that has already lost a huge chunk of its population and may decline even more?

Ever since 1870, there's been a feeling in the southern counties of this state that you're here temporarily. You come in from Virginia or Pennsylvania, you're going to take that coal out, and take that long green dollar and go to Florida with it. This demoralizes people if they want to do anything about their communities.

We have to get over the fear that we're going down and down and down. If we can reverse that, maybe growth in secondary and tertiary industries will come. Many young people would have stayed around if they could have found decent jobs.

The wealth is here, but it's in the banks. It's not being applied. Our real hang-up is a deep-set lack of confidence.

Ostensibly to draw tourists, but probably just as much a device to restore West Virginians' confidence in their own state, the administration of Governor Arch A. Moore, Jr., in the late 1960s began an intensive public relations campaign on the themes—"Almost heaven . . . wild, wonderful West Virginia." Psychologically, the campaign probably did make many of the people feel better about their home state. But there were few positive improvements to be noted in the everyday lives of the people.

▪ Debased politics. There is probably little hope for West Virginia until its politics undergo radical and complete reform. Just as extractive industry dominates the economy, an appallingly large number of state's politicians have learned to be extractive—to take out of the system far more than they put in. Theodore H. White in his *The Making of the President: 1960*, put West Virginia in "that Jukes family of American politics" where politics are "the most squalid, corrupt, and despicable." (The other states White included then were Indiana, Massachusetts, and Texas; today one would certainly delete Massachusetts from the list but quickly add New Jersey and Maryland. In 1960 it was not yet clear how quickly suburban-type political corruption would rise to compete with the old rural form symbolized by West Virginia.)

Sheer greed has a lot to do with the state's corrupt politics; one is hard put to find another reason why William Wallace Barron, West Virginia's governor in the early '60s, was only one of a dozen Democratic officials and hangers-on who went to jail for bribery, tax evasion, or, in Barron's case, paying a $25,000 bribe to the foreman of a jury when he was on trial for collecting more than $200,000 in kickbacks from companies receiving state contracts. Barron pleaded guilty to the jury-tampering charge and was sentenced to 25 years in federal prison. The "Statehouse Gang" he led in the 1961–65 period fleeced West Virginians of millions of dollars—all in addition to the longstanding and legal system of "voluntary" monthly contributions from state employees to the "flower fund," otherwise known as the Democratic State Committee. Even Republican Governor Moore, elected in 1968 on a pledge to restore "honesty and integrity in the governmental affairs of West Virginia," was alleged to have omitted many thousands of dollars of taxable income from his federal tax returns.*

---

* There appears to have been little doubt that Moore was in some trouble with the Internal Revenue Service, even though he labeled columnist Jack Anderson a "muckraking liar" and denied any problem after Anderson reported in 1970 that the IRS was after Moore for allegedly pocketing $80,000 in 1968 campaign contributions. Investigative reporter James A. Haught of the Charleston *Gazette* later discovered that IRS agents had wanted Moore prosecuted for nonpayment of tax on nearly $200,000, including the campaign funds. Moore obtained the services of a well-known Washington criminal lawyer, William Hundley, who succeeded in having the case quashed—apparently on the personal decision of then Attorney General John Mitchell. Hundley later told Haught the case "was some turkey" and "should never have been brought." But disgruntled IRS agents told the reporter it was a "strong case," "double-checked and triple-checked," and intimated Mitchell quashed it on political grounds.

On the local level, the corruption is just as endemic but probably caused as much by simple hunger as undue avarice. Lucky is the man who can get elected sheriff or county assessor, doubling or tripling his income in the process. School board elections are especially bitter, since they provide countless possibilities for contract favoritism and all sorts of jobs for members' friends and relatives, often the only visible alternative to the dole. The election fraud all this occasions is staggering. As recently as 1968, for instance, graveyard registrations and the like had pushed the number of registered voters higher in number than the total voting-age population in 33 of the 55 counties. In Mingo County in southern West Virginia, there were 29 percent more registered voters in 1964 than the total of the actual adult population. The election day syndrome of West Virginia includes absentee voter abuses, "a swaller and a dollar" (half pints of whiskey and cold cash that encourage citizens to let poll watchers "assist" them in marking their ballots), incredibly long and complex ballots, and finally candidate "slates" endorsed by local machines in exchange for money or favors. The citizen tends to think of the politician as a character who comes around every four years promising to fix his road but never does. Corruption and inept performance in office are accepted fatalistically, a situation in which the expectation becomes father to the fact.

■   *Depression of the spirit.* Not many years ago a young man who had emigrated to Akron, Ohio (along with thousands of his fellow West Virginians) wrote back to his hometown paper to complain about the second-rate roads and ugly auto dumps and polluted streams of his native state. West Virginia, he said, was "remote, backward, and dangerously provincial." There is a depressing weight of evidence to sustain this point, and the excuses do not come easily. Faculty members at the West Virginia Institute of Technology suggested to me that "corruption may be inevitable in a state with few opportunities," a situation they said had made a lot of cynical youngsters who "see themselves growing up in a totally corrupt state and hate it."

If the problems are that deep for the educated young, they are compounded many times over for the mountaineers. A young man who went to West Virginia as a VISTA worker in the 1960s described to me the difficulties in getting himself accepted, or any self-help projects going for the mountain people:

At the first number of meetings we had, the men wouldn't come into the hall. Many impoverished communities are quite matriarchal, because the women don't feel the guilt of not having produced. Finally the men came into our meetings, but for a long time they would literally squat facing the corners.

When we had our elections, the three officers elected were the first three who spoke—an assumption that just being willing to speak made a person a leader.

On the sides of those mountains you see incredible personal habits of introversion and resignation and cynicism and aloneness. It's a family orientation as opposed to a community orientation. These are almost impossible things to overcome.

Yet the shell of suspicion about the outside world has been broken in many communities in West Virginia, and once the horizons have been broadened, one discovers qualities of loyalty rarely matched in the United States. The "mountaineers take a long time to make up their mind about a person or idea," Jay Rockefeller commented. "But once they've decided, they stick with their convictions. You can go into houses and still see pictures of Franklin Roosevelt and John Kennedy on the wall. You can argue that Kennedy did very little for West Virginians except make them feel better. But, by God, they would have gone anywhere with Jack Kennedy, or later with Bob Kennedy." *

West Virginians have also been willing to go anywhere in the service of their country; in fact, there is no state where a higher percentage of the young men have enlisted under the colors. In the Vietnam War, 711 West Virginians lost their lives—again the highest proportion, relative to population, of any state. Based on my own travels, I would not dispute Theodore H. White's conclusion that West Virginians are "the best-mannered and most courteous in the nation." They are also a people remarkably free of racial or religious bigotry. The tragedy lies in what outsiders have done to them, and in their perplexing and lasting failure to take control of their own destiny. Reviewing the gloomy political and economic prognosis for West Virginia in the last decades of this century, one of the state's leading journalists suggested to me that the best solution might be partition: parceling out the various sections of the state to neighbors like Pennsylvania, Ohio, and Kentucky. It is hard to see how the people of West Virginia could see their lot worsened by partition. Conceivably, their chances for responsive politics and a better economic future might be greatly enhanced by the process.

Frontier Society and Independence; Partisan Trends and the Unique "Southern" Counties

The stamp of a quintessential frontier society was on the western mountain territory of Virginia from the 1670s, when the first white exploration occurred, clear down to the Civil War and separation from the mother state. The fur trade, part of an effort for diversification by wealthy Virginia tobacco planters, accounted for much of the early interest in the area. Later, Virginia saw these western lands as a valuable buffer between itself and the French and Indians, and encouraged settlement for that reason. Germans were strongly represented among the early settlers, and then great quantities of Scotch-Irish. All suffered greatly from life-and-death struggles with the Indians, a problem not resolved until the 1790s. West Virginia remained primarily a place of small-scale farming in isolated settlements until the War of 1812. Even though the coming of the railroads and coal mining promised a future based on industry, most of the state was in a semi-frontier condition until the Civil War.

* Jack Kennedy, Rockefeller argued, raised expectations for West Virginia but then failed to insist on getting more done than giving an occasional new road or the like. "Jack was an older style politician," Rockefeller said. "But Bob was changing—to more and more responsiveness—and I believe he would really have produced for West Virginia."

West Virginia's decision to break off from Virginia and become a separate state was quite predictable from the historic evolution of the region. Mountainous in territory, with only a handful of slave-holding areas, the section had long chafed under what it regarded as a form of colonial exploitation by the government at Richmond. Unfair taxes, unequal representation in the legislature, and the refusal of Virginia to build the internal improvements the west needed—turnpikes, canals, and railroads—were all part of the smoldering resentment that had prompted mutterings of secession ever since the Revolution. A sample of the opinion in 1861 was provided by the Tyler County *Plaindealer:* "We are for secession at once. No ties bind us to Eastern Virginia but the unjust laws they have made." The *Star* at Morgantown echoed the same theme: "We have been hewers of wood and drawers of water for Eastern Virginia long enough." And aside from the classic split between Tidewater and the mountain people, there was the fact that the mountains largely cut the western counties off from regular communication with the main body of Virginia. The west looked rather to the great Ohio-Mississippi river system as its economic outlet. And from the help they received in suppression of the hostile Indians to the later construction of the National Road to Wheeling, the western counties had entertained a strong loyalty to the federal government at Washington.

Thus the delegates from the west lined up strongly against Virginia's move into the Confederacy and the region's people voted 3—1 against secession from the Union. The way was then paved for a series of conventions that set up an independent government, loyal to the Northern cause, and the passage of a statehood bill for West Virginia which President Lincoln signed in 1863.*

The stand for the Union taken by the people of West Virginia, Edward C. Smith wrote in *The Borderland in the Civil War*, had a profound impact on the outcome of the conflict. It reduced the military potential of the South by preventing the Confederate armies from defending the line of the Ohio River, and it provided a mountainous buffer district that protected Ohio and Pennsylvania so that those states could concentrate their military resources for invasions of the South. Psychologically, the effect was also great, because it provided inspiration for West Virginians' mountain kinsmen in the hills of North Carolina, Tennessee, Alabama, and Georgia to resist the Confederate authorities.

West Virginia was lucky enough to come through the Civil War without a single major battle having been fought on its soil. But the cruel divisions that afflicted the other Border States, between neighboring hollows and even within families, were present here too. In all, some 36,000 West Virginians served with the Union Army, about 12,000 with the Confederate. And the Radical Republicans showed so little compassion for Southern sympathizers

* The state-makers were faced with the delicate problem of getting around Article 4, Section 3 of the U.S. Constitution, which provides that "no new state shall be formed or erected within the jurisdiction of any other state." The device used was to let the western counties of Virginia reorganize the Virginia state government as an entity loyal to the Union, a step the Confederate state government at Richmond was in no position to resist. Once officially recognized, the pro-Union government then gave its consent to dismemberment.

immediately after the war, seeking first to disenfranchise them, that the Democrats had returned to power by the early 1870s. A burning question between 1863 and 1877 was the location of the new state's capital, with the Republicans generally favoring Wheeling in the north, the Democrats in favor of Charleston with its more southerly location. Twice the state government was moved back and forth between these locations on steamboat packets, until the people finally chose Charleston in a referendum.

West Virginia has had two-party politics since the Civil War, but in a pattern called "cyclically competitive"—infrequent shifts which go all the way to one party or the other. From 1863 to 1871 and later from 1896 to 1932, the Republican party dominated the scene. The Democrats, on the other hand, controlled the state's politics from 1871 to 1896 and again almost solidly since the advent of the New Deal, holding strong state legislative and congressional seat majorities even in the few years the Republicans held the governorship (1957–61 and since 1969).

Democratic strength in the state comes first from the counties—mostly along the state's long southeastern border, but a few in the west as well—which had large slave holdings at the time of the Civil War, with a resultant Southern orientation. In addition, the Democrats are exceedingly strong in the central and southern counties, which include many coal counties that shifted to the Democrats during the New Deal. The Democrats are also dominant in most of the industrialized areas. The Republicans' traditional base of strength was among poor mountain folk and in the counties along the Ohio River and in the Northern Panhandle. Since the last years of the 19th century, the Republicans have also attracted a conservative vote in the metropolitan centers of the state.

Prior to 1940, the Democratic party was controlled by the so-called Bourbon faction—conservative, with its roots in Southern, rural, former slaveholding counties. With the growth of the United Mine Workers and the liberal ideology the union espoused in its early years, conflict was inevitable. The UMW became convinced that the last Bourbon governor, Homer A. Holt in the late 1930s, was out to destroy the union. And in the 1940 election, Senator Matthew Neely—a crafty veteran who had been in Congress almost continuously since 1913—announced he was giving up his Senate seat to return home and run for governor. Neely won UMW and other middle-of-the-road Democratic support and defeated the Bourbon candidate. And he promptly established a kind of dynasty, with his selected successors following him to the governor's chair until his death in 1958. This so-called Statehouse faction dominated the state's politics through a combine of state employees (mainly highway and liquor store workers), the familiar collection of businessmen and others favored by state business, interests groups like the UMW which were allied with the machine, and cooperative county courthouse people. The organization's electoral support had little to do with the cohesive social aims of its adherents. As John H. Fenton wrote in his 1957 book, *Politics in the Border States*, it stemmed from the machine's "position astride the feed troughs of political preferment."

Fenton's words were prophetic, because W. W. Barron, the inheritor of the organization as governor in the early 1960s, brought so many tawdry types to the feed trough that several landed in jail with him.

Governors with a deep sense of the people's needs have been a rarity in West Virginia politics. One legitimate champion of the people, according to political scientist Otis K. Rice, was Democrat Emmanuel Willis Wilson, an almost entirely self-educated native of Harper's Ferry. Wilson won the governorship in 1884 in a campaign in which he flayed the monopolies and trusts and railroads for their discrimination against West Virginians. Another was Republican Henry D. Hatfield, a member of the famous feuding clan which clashed with the Kentucky McCoys in such bloody fashion in the years after the Civil War. Hatfield was governor between 1913 and 1917, when the Progressive movement was at its peak, and his accomplishments included a primary election law to replace the old convention method of nomination and a bipartisan public service commission to regulate the utilities. As a physician in the southern West Virginia coal fields, Hatfield had become sympathetic with miners' problems and as governor was responsible for creation of a state department of health and a state bureau of labor. When provoked, Hatfield could erupt with the same temper for which his clan was famous. Shortly after his inauguration, in a period of fierce strikes and tensions in the coal fields, he spent two days in the strike zone, treating the sick and trying to create an atmosphere of peace and order. When the coal operators accused Hatfield of "toadying to the damned strikers" and sent a delegation to dress him down for his action, Hatfield gave the operators' chief spokesman a clout on the side of his head that sent him sprawling, and then ordered the man out of his office.

Hatfield's progressivism was a startling exception in a Republican party which Fenton described as always "conservative in character, or 'standpat' to use its own terminology." The rarely disputed leader of West Virginia Republicans from 1928 until the late 1950s was Walter Hallanan, a millionaire oil and gas man who was twice vice-chairman of the Republican National Committee while also chairman of the National Petroleum Council. Hallanan was the prototype of the likable, safe "manager" for a party out of power. He controlled most of the federal patronage dispensed to Republicans in the state, had time and his personal fortune to spend on development of the state organization, and was a well-liked figure. His chief concern was to retain patronage control of his own party, and thus he often collaborated with the Democrats to prevent one of his Republican foes from winning election. But when it came to national politics, Hallanan showed little flexibility. His conservatism prompted him to back Robert Taft for the 1952 Republican Presidential nomination, preventing the Eisenhower insurgents from making any real headway in the state's Presidential primary.

No matter which decade of modern West Virginia politics one looks at, he is struck by the vital importance of the southern coal counties with their machine-controlled vote in primaries and general elections. They were simultaneously the heart of Neely's majority coalition and of Hallanan's grip on the minority Republicans. In 1960 John F. Kennedy's political operatives, seasoned in the rough-and-tumble of political organization in Massachusetts, knew instinctively how to handle the coal counties, and they assured JFK's victory there. Hubert Humphrey, nurtured in Minnesota's issues-first politics, was at a loss to cope with the situation. In the 1972 gubernatorial election, a drastic fall-off in the normal Democratic vote in the same southern coal counties helped to doom Jay Rockefeller's attempt to oust Arch Moore. The influence of the coal operators, concerned about Rockefeller's stand against strip mining, had a lot to do with the results.

In primaries, the trick in the counties is to "get slated" by the faction likeliest to win. This means money, since enough precinct workers have to be mobilized to deliver the printed slate of favored candidates to the voters. The poorer the county, the more vital the money is, because putting a man on an election-day payroll will be vitally important to him, and also be likely to deliver a dozen or so of his relatives. In Mingo and Logan Counties, a political practitioner from that area told me, each faction takes at least $80,000 for delivering the vote.

The dominant faction in a county is often headed by the most powerful local politician—sometimes a state senator, sometimes the clerk of the county court, often the sheriff. "Being a sheriff of a small county," a politician who had once held that office in southern West Virginia said, "means being a social worker, a welfare worker, a detective to smell out stills, and a dog catcher. The good part about it is that you collect not only a salary but two and a half percent of all taxes collected over 85 percent of the assessment."

Southern West Virginia is a much more civilized place now than it was during the decades of the mine wars in the early part of this century, but it is worthwhile recalling the atmosphere of those years because the aroma of political bossism allied with coal operators lingers on. A frequent practice from 1910 onwards was for the sheriff or other dominant power to hire, with money provided by the companies, scores of mine guards, or deputy sheriffs, whose job it was to keep out the unions by any means they chose. The most famous boss was Sheriff Don Chafin of Logan County. In his book, *Bloodletting in Appalachia*, former West Virginia Attorney General Howard B. Lee described Chafin as "a short, stockily built, dark complexioned mountaineer." When clothed with power in his heyday, Lee wrote, Chafin "was a hard-drinking, swaggering, bragging, bullying gunman, who ruled his 'Kingdom of Logan' with a mailed fist." Chafin had dozens of heavily armed deputies allegedly financed by a royalty of 10 cents a ton for all coal mined which the operators paid to keep out the unions. According to Lee,

During the early years of Chafin's rule, there were no roads in the county, and the only means of ingress and egress were by railroad. He guarded his domain against union organizers by keeping one or more of his deputy-gunmen at every railway station. It was openly charged that when a stranger got off the train he was approached by these "merry gentlemen," who demanded to know his name and business in the county. If the replies were not satisfactory, he was told to get back on the train and leave the county. If he refused, he was arrested and taken to the county jail as a "vagrant." If he resisted arrest, he was sometimes soundly beaten and his limp form tossed back on the train, to be carried out of the county, more dead than alive.

Chafin's rule of Logan was so total that the union forces countenanced armed march by thousands of their followers on the county in 1921. According to Rice's history, they met a force of some 1,200 state police, deputy sheriffs, mine guards, and "volunteers" in the battle of Blair Mountain, which was fought on a 25-mile front and continued for four days. Many lives were lost, and successful unionization of Logan County's mines was still 15 years away. Chafin's power began to crumble when treason trials against the union organizers, instituted after the battle of 1921, failed to produce convictions. He was convicted of conspiracy to violate the national prohibition law, served a few months in prison, and finally was forced to leave Logan County in 1934. When he died some years later in Huntington, he was said to have left an estate of more than a million dollars.

Illegality as a way of life still exists in Logan County. It is one of the worst counties in America for vote fraud; indeed some say there is not a single precinct within it where some fraud is not practiced on election days. The situation in neighboring Mingo County is not much different; there, in one primary of the late 1960s, 90 percent of the people who asked for absentee ballots in the circuit clerk's office pretended to have forgotten their glasses or whatever and asked for assistance from the "impartial" personnel in the clerk's office. Frequently these votes were paid for at a rate of $3 to $5 each, and there were widespread allegations of intimidations (threats of physical violence or loss of jobs) suffered by opponents of the local political boss, state senator Noah Floyd. Floyd and three others were eventually prosecuted by the U.S. Government for vote fraud, but they were acquitted. Jay Rockefeller, however, led a successful crusade to defeat Floyd in the 1970 election. Mingo, he told me in an interview, is "a classic machine county, utterly depressing and corrupt in its politics."

Situated across the Tug Fork of the Big Sandy River from Pike County, Kentucky, Mingo is a land of precipitous wooded mountains, split apart by narrow hollows with swift creeks, of destitute people and little hope. In 1965 unemployment for men in the county stood at 16 percent, compared to 4.5 percent nationally. The Selective Service Board rejected two out of every three young men it examined for military service. Nearly half the adult population had less than an eighth-grade education. The people were fleeing so rapidly that by 1970 the county would have only 32,780, 31 percent less than lived there 20 years before.

The federal poverty program came to Mingo County in 1965. The local courthouse crowd and dominant political clans, who had traditionally depended on patronage jobs and welfare programs to buy the votes of the poor and keep their own hand in the public trough, at first welcomed the poverty project with its prospective $2 million in federal money. They designated Huey L. Perry, then 29 years of age and a member of one of the county's most politically powerful families, to head the program. It proved to be a serious miscalculation, a story fairly and colorfully told by Perry in his later book, They'll Cut Off Your Project. For whatever its other failings may have been, the poverty program did succeed in arousing and mobilizing the political consciousness of the long downtrodden people of counties like Mingo on a scale few would have thought possible. The people began to realize how they had been exploited and denied decent schools and services by the political powers, and they started to raise Cain with the local Democratic machines. The reaction of Okie Ray, who raised hogs in the Rock House fork of Pigeon Creek in Mingo County, was not unusual: "Somebody has done messed with my civil rights, and we're agonna git 'em." Noah Floyd's courthouse crowd first tried strongarm tactics to stop the insurgency and, when that failed, made an all-out effort to defang the poverty program by having its direction transferred to the county government.* Noah Floyd wrung a promise from his political ally and the last of the old-style Democratic governors, Hulett Smith, to do just that. But the outpouring of protest from the poor folk and their friends in Mingo was so intense that both candidates for governor that year promised to keep control in the hands of the poor themselves, through the regular local antipoverty agency. Noah Floyd's political power was not ended, but at least there was the potentiality of legitimate democracy in a county where the process had been so appallingly debased for so many years.

Labor in West Virginia

The struggle of the workers of West Virginia to organize in unions dates back to the 1830s; it is a history replete with hard-won advances, periodic reversals, and an incredible amount of bloodshed. Today the victory of organized labor would seem to be as complete in West Virginia as in any state of the Union. There were 221,000 workers in unions in 1972, representing 41.3 percent of the work force—the highest level in the country. In terms of numbers, the United Mine Workers of America are the greatest force. They have some 45,000 working members in the state—far less than the 125,000 figure in 1948, before the mechanization of the mines and the switch from coal to other fuels for home heating and powering trains. But the UMW is a much more important force now under its revitalized leadership than it was over most of the postwar era. There are also large numbers of unionized workers in the iron and steel, chemical, and glass industries. The chief geographic areas of intensive unionization, outside of coal, are the valleys of the Kanawha, Monongahela, and Ohio Rivers, plus the northern end of the Shenandoah Valley where such industrial giants as 3M, Corning Glass, and General Motors have all built plants. Some 68,000 workers are in unions belonging to the West Virginia Labor Federation, AFL-CIO, which was headed, until his untimely death in 1974, by Miles C. Stanley, a competent and socially conscious chief.

* Such takeovers had been facilitated by 1967 antipoverty legislation which contained an amendment, authored by Oregon's Democratic Congresswoman Edith Green, requiring that all local community action funds be controlled by local officials. The legislation included an escape clause, however, which gave OEO and the state governors a measure of discretion in cases where the local government failed to develop a satisfactory anti-poverty plan.

The first of the momentous labor disputes which dot West Virginia's history came in 1877 when railroad workers of the Baltimore and Ohio at Martinsburg struck in protest against a cut in their wages, triggering a nation-wide walkout. Rioting and burning ensued and eventually President Ruther-ford B. Hayes ordered in federal troopers to restore order.

In 1890 the United Mine Workers of America was organized and it was in that union's dogged pursuit of the right to organize, not to be won until the 1930s, that the greatest labor-associated turbulence in the state's history occurred. The early mine operators were a hardbitten lot willing to use any means—legal and more often illegal—to keep the unions out and maintain their feudal proprietorship of the ill paid miners who lived in rapacious company towns and died by the hundreds in unsafe mines. Howard B. Lee named six principal methods of defense and attack used by the coal operators: (1) court injunctions; (2) martial law; (3) suzerainty over county government; (4) elaborate spy systems; (5) coercion and intimidation of workers by the use of mine guards and private detectives; and (6) blacklisting of all miners who favored the Union. Yet another device was to bring in Negroes and unwitting foreigners as scabs.

It was in 1912–13, at coal mines in the narrow gorges of Cabin Creek and Paint Creek in the Kanawha Valley, not far from Charleston, that the first great coal strike and worst labor war of all took place. Some 7,500 coal-begrimed miners were involved, and during the course of the strike the workers were evicted from their homes and forced into tent colonies along the highways. In one great pitched battle, 12 miners and four mine guards were killed. According to Bill Blizzard, a strike leader whose name would become legend among the miners, "at least 50 men died violent deaths in those desolate gorges, while the death toll among women and children from malnutrition was appalling." A leading figure in the strike was Old Mother (Mary) Jones, then 82 years of age and one of the fieriest, most fearless, and sometimes profane labor agitators of all history. At a meeting on the steps of the Capitol at Charleston, she warned that unless the governor got rid of the mine guards at Paint and Cabin Creeks, "there is going to be a lot of bloodletting in these hills." To drive the point home, she screamed to the assembled miners: "Arm yourselves, return home and kill every goddamned mine guard on the creeks, blow up the mines, and drive the damned scabs out of the valleys."

There were softer sides to Mother Jones, who had been born in Ireland, in 1830, came to America at the age of five, married and had four children, and taught school for many years before she became a labor organizer. Once she asked a small boy at a mine, "Why don't you go to school?" "I ain't lost no leg," he replied proudly, looking at his little legs. "I knew what he meant," Mother Jones wrote later—"that lads went to school only when they were hurt by accidents." Mother Jones finally died in Maryland, at the age of 100. But her final words about West Virginia are worth recording: "Medieval West Virginia! With its tent colonies and the bleak hills! With its grim men and women! When I get to the other side, I shall tell God Almighty about West Virginia!"

The First World War, which produced a great demand for coal and intense labor shortages, enabled the UMW to increase its West Virginia membership from about 7,000 to about 50,000. The craft unions experienced similarly dramatic gains. But in the 1920s, with manpower ample again, the mine operators and factory owners began to return to nonunion status. This was the decade of some of the most gruesome mine wars—including the Matewan massacre in "Bloody Mingo" County, the armored train that brought strikebreakers into the valleys, and of the hated Baldwin-Felts mine guards. During the Depression unionization declined even further, so that in 1931 the State Federation of Labor, AFL, which then included the UMW, was left with a paltry 3,000 dues-paying members. Soon afterwards the New Deal came to the unions' rescue. Labor's right to bargain collectively, together with a ban on yellow dog contracts, was written into legislation approved by Congress during President Roosevelt's first 100 days in office. Membership in West Virginia unions promptly soared to more than 100,000 and continued to rise through the 1930s. By the 1940s organized labor, and most particularly the UMW, had formed an alliance with Neely's statehouse machine and was regarded by many as the most powerful single influence in West Virginia politics.

Even at the peak of its political power in the Neely era, however, the UMW exhibited what Miles Stanley described to me as "a rather narrow, parochial kind of interest," concentrated on such issues as workmen's compensation and unemployment compensation. The merger of the AFL and CIO in 1957 brought a union leadership more attuned to broad issues of public policy, but the UMW was not part of it, and thus it lacked the power to accomplish what a unified labor movement might have done. Moreover, the AFL-CIO, like the old UMW, has more often than not made the mistake of endorsing candidates who are "yes" men for its stands, rather than supporting more competent and independent contenders. The result has been to perpetuate mediocrity in West Virginia public life and to lose the opportunity for constructive influence that organized labor should be able to exert in the nation's most heavily unionized state.

Until his retirement in 1960, the UMW *was* John L. Lewis—a figure splendidly described by James Humphreys, a native West Virginian on the staff of the Southern Regional Council:

John L. Lewis, the enigmatic man who spoke with the authority and cadence of an Old Testament prophet, the Republican who was a favorite of Coolidge and was offered the Vice-Presidency under his close friend, Herbert Hoover, the labor militant who built the CIO largely with socialist and communist organizers and brazenly called strikes in the country's coal fields during World War II, the understanding co-operator who silently allowed automation and fuel substitutes to shrivel the union membership from 95 percent of the total mining force to 65 percent and from 650,000 to 70,000, he did it all, and much more, by his own hand and without the interference of internal dissent or loyal opposition.

Lewis, and after 1960 his hand-picked successor, W. A. (Tony) Boyle, ran the UMW in an incredibly autocratic and dictatorial manner. Dissenters were ejected from union office, the miners in their often isolated communities read only the official line in the *United Mine Workers Journal,* 19 of the 23 UMW districts were placed under trusteeship, duly elected officers were replaced by sychophantic individuals loyal to Lewis or Boyle, and strongarm tactics were employed against any opponents. At election-time suspect returns from "paper locals" made up chiefly of retirees helped to swell the totals for the national leadership. And Lewis and Boyle became suspiciously cozy with management. The UMW welfare and retirement fund had a vested interest in uninterrupted production, since it received a 40-cent (and later 80-cent) a ton royalty. Automation was accepted without thought for the displaced miners and their families or the communities in which they lived. (To its credit, the welfare and retirement fund did, in the 1950s, build eight miners' hospitals in Appalachia, bringing quality medical care to the mountains for the first time. But when the expenses became too great, the UMW unloaded ownership of the hospitals to a nonprofit regional organization financed by church and government leaders.) The UMW also seemed to be moving to the management side when it invested millions of dollars in coal mines through the National Bank of Washington, which it controlled. In negotiating sessions during the 1960s, Boyle did get smartly increased wages for miners. But the union failed to ask for significant new safety regulations in this exceedingly high-risk industry. Twice in the 1960s, the UMW was found guilty of antitrust conspiracy with large coal operators. To top it all off, Boyle and his cohorts granted themselves royal salaries, fat expense accounts, and sumptuous pensions.

The chain of events that would lead to the toppling of this corrupt *ancien régime* began in the predawn hours of November 20, 1968, when a massive explosion shook a mine of the Consolidation Coal Company at Farmington, in the placid green countryside of rural northern West Virginia.* As 78 men lay dead or dying in the mine, Tony Boyle appeared at the burning portal to tell reporters that such is the way of coal mining, and that Consolidation Coal had a fine safety record. To extinguish the fire and save the salable coal, the company, with the permission of the UMW and the state and federal governments, sealed the mine with the bodies of the 78 miners still inside. Not long after Boyle said the UMW "will not abridge the rights of mine operators in running the mines. We follow the judgment of the coal operators, right or wrong."

The reaction to Farmington of West Virginia's Congressman Ken Hechler was of a quite different order. Outraged at the lackadaisical official response to the disaster, Hechler sat down at a battered old typewriter in his Capitol Hill office and composed a statement that would alter his own career, affect the attitude of official Washington, and send ripples of revolutionary change out across the coal fields:

Coal miners [Hechler wrote] don't have to die. In a civilized society, it is nothing short of criminal to allow the present conditions to continue in the coal

---

* The UMW story from Farmington through the Boyle-Yablonski election, with special attention to the political and environmental impact of the coal industry on West Virginia, is told in fine detail in Brit Hume's book, *Death and the Mines: Rebellion in the United Mine Workers* (New York: Grossman, 1971).

mines. Federal and state mine-safety laws are weak, most coal companies seem to know when the inspectors will appear, enforcement of safety standards is weak and entangled in red tape, the union leaders seem more interested in high wages than in health and safety, there is no aggressive attack on the health hazards of coal dust which cause black lung, the coal miners and their families have been steeled to take a fatalistic attitude toward death and injury and both Congress and the general public have been complacent and apathetic.

From Monongah to Mannington, the same script is grimly familiar. The national searchlight is focused on a disaster. The company officials promise that everything possible is being done. The families wait stoically. The union leaders say that everything possible is being done. The surviving coal miners and their sons say that, of course, they will go back into the mines. Soon everybody goes back to the status quo until the next disaster strikes in the coal mines.

Coal miners have a right to live, to breathe, and to be protected by twentieth-century safety standards. The nation must rise up and demand that strong and effective mine-safety legislation be passed by Congress.

The miners' own response to Farmington, as James Humphreys wrote, "was the quick emergence of *ad hoc* organizations dedicated to doing what their union would not do—protect the health of the men who descend beneath the green earth's surface into the black bowels to rip out the shiny dark coal." In December 1968 a group of West Virginia miners formed the Black Lung Association to demand that the state legislature make workmen's compensation available for victims of black lung, the popular name for pneumoconiosis, a gradual form of lung debilitation that results from prolonged inhaling of coal dust particles.* Among the leaders was Arnold Miller, a simple but eloquent miner from Cabin Creek who had started out hand-loading coal on mine cars in the early 1940s and was partially disabled by black lung himself. Three outspoken physicians—Donald Rasmussen, the late I. E. Buff, and Hawley Wells—began to tour the state speaking on the miners' behalf. A wildcat strike began at the Winding Gulf Mine in Raleigh County in February 1969, spreading in five days to encompass almost all of West Virginia's miners. For 23 days, virtually no coal was mined.

The UMW tried to discourage this strike, and the AFL-CIO showed little interest. But the rank-and-file coal miners did, exhibiting a spontaneous and rarely matched militancy. A thousand of them marched angrily on the State Capitol. They began to flex their political muscle, talking of an early political demise for their legislative opponents. ("We found out that the black janitors at the Capitol were former miners," Miller told me later. "They reported to us which politicians were ripping us in private.") When the strike began, the existing state's workmen's compensation law, written by legislators pliant to the coal industry, made it exceedingly difficult for a miner to prove his pneumoconiosis came from work in the mines, so that he would be eligible for disability benefits. When the miners had finished exerting their pressure, West Virginia had perhaps the best workmen's com-

---

* There is no known treatment for pneumoconiosis, which can leave a man choking for breath, blue from lack of oxygen, and doomed to an early death. Black lung is by no means a new disease. More than a century ago Emile Zola described it in his novel, *Germinal*, in which a blood-spitting miner declared: "I've got enough coal in my carcass to warm me 'til I die." To avoid high workmen's compensation claims, U.S. coal operators always argued that black lung didn't exist, or wasn't really harmful, or wasn't job-related.

pensation bill in the world. Any impairment of lung function experienced by a man who had spent more than 10 years mining coal was declared evidence of black lung, making him eligible for benefits. A victim could receive a high proportion of his average weekly salary for life with no dollar limits. A reluctant Governor Arch Moore signed the black lung bill into law, capping an historic breakthrough for West Virginia's long neglected miners.

The three physicians, and especially Dr. Buff, a Charleston heart specialist endowed with fierce perseverance and a gift for inflammatory rhetoric, got the lion's share of thanks from the miners for their victory. But Miller also gave major credit to a young VISTA worker named Craig Robinson, who had come from Buffalo, New York, to work in a small town near Beckley. Robinson became interested in black lung and quietly carried the word to thousands of miners of how they were being shortchanged. "He was as responsible as anyone for getting the movement going, and then he helped to write the law," Miller said.

Spurred by its great West Virginia victory, the Black Lung Association pressed through Ken Hechler and others in Washington for a major new Federal Coal Mine Health and Safety Act, passed in 1969 with little or no help from the UMW leadership. The law was signed grudgingly by President Nixon. Tacked onto the legislation was a supposedly temporary program to pay federal benefits to black lung victims—thus relieving either the states or the coal industry of the cost, which may add up to a staggering $3 billion to $4 billion by 1981. (The federal black lung law was written so sloppily that lawyers were able to collect scandalously high fees in pressing claims. One lawyer in Pikesville, Kentucky, received more than $1 million in fees in 1972 alone).

Back in the coal fields, the great excitement of 1969 was an election for the United Mine Workers presidency. To his amazement—and outrage— Boyle suddenly found himself faced with an opponent—Joseph A. (Jock) Yablonski, former president of District 5 in the Pittsburgh area and supposedly a stalwart of the Boyle regime. For years, Yablonski had silently balked at what he considered misrule of the union and neglect of rank-and-file miners. A key figure in persuading him to run for the presidency was Ralph Nader, and a key part of the package was Nader's assurance that Joseph Rauh, a brilliant Washington attorney and Democratic leader, would be his campaign manager and legal brains. The Yablonski campaign had an electrifying effect on thousands of miners who had never thought anyone would have the courage to oppose Boyle's iron regime. Yablonski was a volatile, colorful personality who relished his rebel's role. He was for union democracy, for tough safety legislation, for a fair pension system (many miners had been denied pension or disability rights on flimsy technicalities), and for an end to "sweetheart ties" between the UMW and the coal industry.

The Yablonski-Boyle campaign was marked by appalling bribery, intimidation, fraud—and violence. At a campaign appearance in Illinois, Yablonski was knocked unconscious by a karate chop to the neck. He regarded the incident as a calculated attempt on his life. Rauh lodged repeated complaints with the U.S. Labor Department, which discounted them all and said, in a tortured interpretation of the Landrum-Griffin Act, that it had a policy of never investigating a union election until it was all over and the result certified. Boyle got just a bare majority of the reported active miners vote in that December 1969 election. Yablonski immediately challenged the result, charging a stolen election. Twenty-two days later, the bodies of Yablonski, his wife, and his young daughter were found in his Clarksville, Pennsylvania, home—all shot to death. Only then did the Labor Department prepare to enter the case.

In death, Yablonski became a near-legendary figure to rebels within the UMW. He had never been the world's most saintly man, but now he was lionized. A movement called Miners for Democracy sprang up in western Pennsylvania; its official head was Mike Trbovich, a flamboyant, uneducated miner from Clarksville (given to arm-waving, purple shirts, and yellow ties); the real leader, however, was Yablonski's son, Joseph, an attorney in Washington, D.C., who took on the cause as a near-holy one. Miners for Democracy made Pennsylvania one cockpit of a major revolt against the UMW leadership. The other principal base was in West Virginia, where the Black Lung Association was joined by a new group, the Disabled Miners of West Virginia, protesting the progressive reductions in medical benefits and pensions from the UMW's welfare and retirement fund. The leader of this group was Robert Payne, a disabled 45-year-old black coal miner from Itmann, West Virginia. Circulating with roving pickets, his organization in 1970 pulled 200,000 miners off the job in West Virginia, eastern Ohio, and western Pennsylvania. Injunctions finally stopped the wildcat walkout. But by this time the UMW, once revered as the militant spokesman for America's coal miners, was reeling with charges of graft, collusion with management, and cold lack of concern for its own members.

A whole variety of legal actions were begun against Tony Boyle and the UMW power structure, charging gross mismanagement of union funds, illegal campaign contributions, and a usurpation of power through the trusteeship system over union locals. Eventually—but not until 1973, after his defeat as UMW president—Tony Boyle himself was indicted for murder in the Yablonski case, allegedly having arranged through intermediaries for the cold-blooded assassination of his rival. At the trial, held in Pennsylvania, William Turnblazer, president of UMW District 19 in East Kentucky, testified that Boyle told him and Albert Pass, secretary-treasurer of District 19, "We're in a fight. We've got to kill Yablonski, take care of him." After Boyle had given those instructions, he arranged for union money to be used to pay for the murder. The blood money passed through the hands of Turnblazer and Pass to Silous Huddleston, the president of an all-pensioner UMW local in East Tennessee. Huddleston's son-in-law and an accomplice carried out the actual killing. The jury convicted Boyle, and he received the mandatory sentence of life imprisonment.*

Several months after the Boyle-Yablonski election and Yablonski's mur-

---

* Except for Boyle himself, the murderers and go-betweens were an "all-Appalachian" cast, including Huddleston's daughter and the gunmen, who were living at the time in a section of Cleveland, Ohio, heavily populated with Appalachian emigrants.

der, a federal court finally decided there was enough evidence of fraud in the voting to warrant ordering a new election, this one to be conducted under careful supervision of the Labor Department. The Miners for Democracy met at Wheeling, West Virginia, to pick a slate to run against Boyle and his cohorts. Mike Trbovich campaigned intensively for the nomination for UMW president, but eventually he was rejected, perhaps because he was too much of a dandy, perhaps also because he was so close to the Yablonski faction. The nomination went instead to Arnold Miller, an unassuming man of quiet virtue who also exhibited qualities of determined militancy so often lacking in modern-day labor leaders. Trbovich was nominated for vice president while Harry Patrick, a young Fairview, West Virginia, miner who had been co-chairman of Miners for Democracy back in 1969, was chosen for secretary-treasurer. The MFD campaign started in eastern Kentucky, a region so "tough" that Yablonski had feared to campaign there in person. But now the insurgents had Labor and Justice Department protection, the *Mine Workers Journal* was required by the court to give equal space to both slates, and union funds were monitored to prevent the old-type manipulation. When the votes from the December 1972 balloting were in, Arnold Miller had won a solid 55.5 percent victory, with Trbovich and Patrick close behind.

The fresh winds of democracy came rushing through the house of labor John L. Lewis had built. Boyle's cronies—including most of his hand-picked directors in the districts under trusteeship—were promptly deposed. (Interestingly enough, many of the Boyle clique took jobs with the coal operators or on the related nonemployee side, suggesting where their hearts had been all along.) Miller then ordered democratic elections. He immediately lopped half a million dollars off the union's annual payroll, trimmed his own salary from the $50,000 Boyle had received to $35,000, and cut the salaries of other top staffers by 40 percent. Joseph "Chip" Yablonski, the martyred reformer's son, was installed as UMW chief counsel. Missouri Democratic politician and financier True Davis, the $142,000-a-year president of the National Bank of Washington controlled by the UMW, was forced to resign. (Davis had approved a huge collateral-free loan to keep Boyle out of jail after Boyle's spring 1972 conviction for making illegal political contributions.) Finally, Miller cut Boyle's annual pension from $50,000 to $16,000.

The method of leadership of Miller and his colleagues, it quickly became apparent, would differ as day and night from the Boyle approach. The *UMW Journal* began to report candidly on union affairs and provide space for members' criticism. The old cozy relationship with the mine operators evaporated virtually overnight, with Miller warning that the new UMW would trust neither the coal companies nor the U.S. Bureau of Mines to see to it that miners' health and safety was assured. (In the last 30 years, Miller said, 16,000 men had lost their lives in coal mines and more than three-quarters of a million had been injured. "Coal miners in West Virginia and Kentucky and Pennsylvania, and in the other coalfields, are tired of dying so that men in board rooms in New York and Boston and Pittsburgh can get rich.")

A degree of openness and democracy unknown since the founding days of the UMW was apparent in the way the Miller group ran the day-to-day operations of the union and particularly the UMW's convention in Pittsburgh in December 1973. The convention, writer Phil Primack noted, was "a welcome reversal from the days of Boyle's white-helmeted goons suppressing dissidents on the convention floor." A democratically run organization, however, is prone to opposition within its own ranks. When Miller ordered direct election of officers in the old trusteeship districts, many of his backers lost those contests. There were some rumblings of discontent about the long hair and life styles of many of the young men Miller brought into UMW headquarters from the Miners for Democracy movement. And, as Primack commented, the new UMW leadership was perhaps more progressively minded than much of its membership. In Appalachia, he noted, the miners earned an average of more than $40 a day and constituted a coal-field middle class not naturally oriented to social activism or friendly to the MFD's allies in welfare groups and organizations pressing for an abolition of strip mining. (Once a strip-mining foe himself, Miller seemed to soften his position once he became UMW president. There are many UMW members who work in strip pits.)

The Pittsburgh convention rebuffed Miller on a few key issues, including a strike fund he wanted to back him up in dealing with the coal operators before a scheduled contract expiration in November 1974. The convention did approve Miller's request for authority to move the UMW headquarters out of the imposing, ornate Washington headquarters the union has occupied since 1934 to a location "closer to the coal fields." Tom Bethell, Miller's planning and research director, was quoted as saying of the old greystone façade where John L. Lewis had ruled in regal splendor, and Tony Boyle after him: "This rockpile is part of the past, when the UMW had 600,000 members and a big treasury. The union is down to 200,000 members, of whom only 120,000 are working in the mines. The rest are either disabled or retired, or both. The truth is, we're no longer that wealthy, and there's no question but that the union would be a lot better off if it were headquartered where its membership live and work." Enough of the union's executive board disagreed, however, to block Miller in several efforts to carry out the convention's mandate and actually move to a proposed site between Charleston and Huntington.

As the new UMW leadership headed for its first serious contract negotiations with the operators, the union took an important step toward union democracy by deciding that a poll of the rank-and-file membership would be required for final approval of any contract. The move created the potential for a rebuff to the leadership, but it did underscore the Miller group's essential posture—respect for, and concern about, the individual miner. Through legal challenges, for instance, the UMW reformers had been able to open the union's welfare and retirement fund to thousands of disabled miners and their widows who had been unconscionably closed out in earlier years. But the fund's reserves were dwindling to a peril point, and Miller announced he would press the operators for a 300 percent increase in the per-ton royalties.

Further than that, the UMW faced serious problems in organizing the fast-expanding numbers of strip miners, particularly in the scattered mining sites across the Mountain States. The vast revenues that could come to the union's welfare and retirement fund if the Western miners were thoroughly organized would make a real difference in the UMW's future viability.

Miller's team proved immensely successful in negotiating a new contract with the operators in 1974, including a cost-of-living pay escalator and improved mine safety guarantees. The new UMW was certain to be a vital force in Appalachia in the '70s and '80s. And especially in the long-contrived and controlled politics of West Virginia, the unfettered UMW could play a leading role in elections and changing the policies of state government. This is not a new idea for Arnold Miller; in 1970 he told me, "every problem we have here goes back to the political structure." Under Miller's leadership, a new Coal Miners Political Action Committee (COMPAC) was formed in 1973 to replace the old Labor's Non-Partisan League. Run on contributions from the UMW membership, COMPAC was to lobby for specific legislation and help candidates friendly to union's views win office. Congressman Hechler, a close friend of the new UMW leadership, predicted that COMPAC would be "terrifically effective" and make a real difference in toppling the company-owned politicians and building a responsive West Virginia state government.

Perils of a One-Horse Economy

Even in an era when Americans are starting to question the value of "growth for growth's sake," it is difficult to write in very cheerful tones of the economy of a state in which the increase in total personal income between the late '40s and early '70s lagged 43 percent behind the national average. The transformation of so many communities into near-ghost towns, the dearth of decent job opportunities that could keep young people in their home state, the high unemployment and welfare and poverty rolls—all testify to a severely ailing society. No matter what sector of the West Virginia economy one looks to, the story tends to be one of stagnation if not actual decline.

Consider manufacturing industries, for example. The number of jobs opened in the state's big industrial groups—chemicals, iron and steel, glass, and pottery—has barely balanced the losses suffered from factories pulling up their stakes to move out of state, or folding entirely, in the years since World War II. West Virginia factories, at their employment peak in 1949, provided jobs for 142,000 workers. In recent years the figure has hovered around 130,000. A sharp upturn in dollar investment in new plants was reported in 1973, together with some new jobs. But for any substantial increase in employment in recent times, one has to look to retailing, service industries, and —of course—government. And even with modest growth in those sectors, the proportion of West Virginians working in white-collar jobs, with their traditionally higher salaries, is the lowest of any state outside the Deep South and Kentucky.

Farming does little to brighten the economic picture. It is limited by the sharp terrain, with the only operations of any substantial size in the Eastern Panhandle and Greenbrier Valley areas. The quantity of livestock and crops taken to market has declined markedly in recent years, together with a precipitous drop in the number of farms. Only 2 percent of the work force makes its living off agriculture. And the lumbering industry, despite the harvesting of some 400 million board-feet a year, provides only 8,000 jobs.

A somewhat brighter note is struck in tourism, which brings in some $700 million a year from visitors to the many state parks and recreation areas, the Monongahela and George Washington National Forests, and such famous places as Harper's Ferry and White Sulphur Springs with its beautiful and sumptuous hotel, The Greenbrier. To foster tourism, the state over the years has built many handsome resort lodges in its parks, including the Pipestem Resort and Hawk's Nest Lodge, both in exciting mountain territory. But even though tourism provides jobs for about 19,000 West Virginians, it is seriously imperiled by the ravages worked on the land by strip mining—an industry with a payroll only a third as large.

For better, and often worse, coal is the economic lifeblood of West Virginia. When strikes close the mines, 1,350 coal mines operated by 900 separate companies, scattered from one end of the state to the other, are affected. And it is not only the 45,000 coal miners who are suddenly without income; a coal strike also means layoffs for some 6,000 railroad workers and numerous employees of other support industries, some 10 percent of the entire work force. The wholesaling and retail structure of the state also starts to decline. And just in directly attributable revenues, the state government loses a quarter of a million dollars each day.

Coal mining in West Virginia got underway on a serious scale in the latter part of the 19th century as company towns, with their paternalistic and exploitive way of life, sprang up like weeds across the mountains. In 1870 only 600,000 tons of coal were mined in the state; by 1912 the figure was up to 66,732,000 tons. Today the annual figure is around 150 million tons. West Virginia vies each year with Kentucky for the greatest coal production in the country. About a quarter of the nation's bituminous coal is extracted from the mines spotted through 36 of the state's 55 counties. This output has been growing and seems certain to expand to help meet the energy shortages projected for the remainder of the 1970s and beyond.

West Virginia has always had to pay a gruesome price for its coal riches. We spoke earlier of the colonial-style economy and brutalized politics stemming from coal; now mention must be made of the perils to the health and safety of the miners, and the threat to the environment.

The carnage in the mines has prompted many a haunting folk song, like these words of a little girl to her father in a ballad popular in the southern Appalachians:

> *O Daddy, don't work in the mines today,*
> *For dreams have so often come true.*
> *O Daddy, my Daddy, please don't go away,*
> *I never could live without you.*

A line in another folk song, this one written in the 1950s, summed it up well: *Bone and blood are the price of coal.* West Virginia is living proof of the allegation. The worst disaster in the history of coal mining occurred at Monongah in 1907, when an explosion took the lives of 361 men. At Eccles, in 1914, 183 died; at Layland a year later, 112 were killed; at Benwood in 1924, there was a mine disaster that cost 119 men their lives. Then there was the Farmington disaster of 1968, which killed 78. What these "disaster statistics" omit is the ongoing carnage from smaller mine mishaps, and the thousands upon thousands of men who have been grievously injured by accidents in the mines. One placid spring evening I sat with Dr. Jack Robertson of the West Virginia Institute of Technology on the porch of his home, overlooking a lovely sweep of the Kanawha River. Across the river, the trains were winding up the valley with their cars laden with coal from the southern coal fields. "For every 200-car train that goes by here," Robertson said bitterly, "there's been an accident in the mines—crushed hands, broken joints, or whatever. For every several trains, there's a death. Eighty to 90 men lose their lives from mining accidents in West Virginia each year."

The Farmington explosion prompted a young West Virginian in his mid-twenties, J. Davitt McAteer, to undertake an 18-month study of the health and safety problems of mining in the state, financed by $9,000 advanced by consumer advocate Ralph Nader, state officials, two private foundations, and others. A number of college students were recruited to help McAteer in his work. The result was a 689-page study, released in 1970 and later published by Praeger (*Coal Mine Health and Safety—The Case of West Virginia*). West Virginia, the report said, had the highest rate of mining deaths and injuries in the United States. For this, blame was placed on the coal operators, the United Mine Workers leadership, state and federal agencies charged with safety enforcement, the governor and legislature of West Virginia, and the President of the United States.

"Coal mines can be made safe," the report declared, "if the companies are willing to pay for it. Time after time, we found specific instances of coal operators ignoring minimum safety standards in order to maximize production." The report demanded revamping of West Virginia's "grossly inadequate" mining laws, which McAteer said "so blatantly favor the coal operator and disregard the miner that one must assume that it is by design."

After his report was released, McAteer spent two years working for Ralph Nader in Washington and then, in 1973, became solicitor for the safety division of the new UMW under Arnold Miller's leadership. Some time after he had taken over his union duties, I asked McAteer how, on the basis of his widened experience, he would rate West Virginia's mine safety laws in comparison to those of the other coal-producing states. "West Virginia is almost as bad as Kentucky, but it's worse than all the rest," he replied. The best state on safety enforcement, he said, was Pennsylvania. The reason? "Pennsylvania had a divergent economy," McAteer said. "The people could shift off, working in the steel mills, for instance. They had options. West Virginia, by contrast, was basically a one-horse economy. And in a one-horse town you just don't fool with the man. Especially in southern West Virginia there are three places for employment—the mines, the schools, and the government. And if you're not working there you're going to Detroit or Cincinnati or Cleveland to get a job." McAteer also said Pennsylvania had traditionally had strong UMW locals—"strong in an enlightened sense, not just as a bullheaded old union"—which kept their autonomy and had leaders of Yablonski's quality, of a caliber rarely found in the old West Virginia UMW.

There is strong evidence to indicate that underground mining could be made a lot safer if the operators were willing to make the appropriate investment of time and money. The two big steel companies which have large numbers of "captive" mines supplying their needs have exceptionally good safety records, compared to the rest of the industry. Between 1968 and 1971, for instance, these were the rates of injury per million man-hours in the 10 biggest coal producers:

U.S. Steel mines	2.7
Bethlehem Steel mines	12.3
Consolidation Coal	18.7
General Dynamics mines	38.7
Peabody Coal	46.9
Old Ben Coal	47.4
Amax Coal	48.2
Pittston	56.6
Eastern Associated Coal	62.5
Island Creek Coal	72.1

The differences in actual fatalities per million man-hours were found to be almost as striking, ranging from 0.3 in U.S. Steel mines to 1.1 in Pittston mines and 1.5 in Consolidation mines. The reason for the superior safety records of the steel company mines appears to be, quite simply, that for decades they have poured far more money into safety programs than the regular coal companies. In defense of the other companies, it is often said that they must be more competitive in their coal prices and thus can't afford the safety measures. Yet the fact is that U.S. Steel and Bethlehem do sell a portion of their coal on the open market, at competitive prices. In the words of one steel executive, "we can mine coal at the same price and run the mines safely at the same time." The conclusion seems inescapable that the poor safety record of most coal producers stems from cost-cutting to appease stockholders, callousness, or both. And in a state like West Virginia, they find it cheaper to subvert the political process than to submit to effective safety regulation.

Often that subversion reaches directly into the federal government and its safety control programs, as the first years' experience with the Federal Coal Mine Health and Safety Act of 1969 clearly demonstrated. The legislation, made possible by the wave of national publicity in the wake of the Farmington disaster, appeared on its face to be the first really tough federal mine health-and-safety law in U.S. history. It imposed far stricter controls than ever before on methane gas, restricted permissible dust levels in the mines, spelled out specific requirements for shielding and grounding of electric equipment, and other safety precautions.

Yet after threatening to veto the legislation, President Nixon and his administration seemed to go out of their way to sabotage it and appease the coal companies (many of which are owned by oil companies that were major Nixon campaign contributors). Nixon began by firing John F. O'Leary, because he seemed to be too tough a regulator as director of the Bureau of Mines. Then he permitted the office to remain vacant for seven months and tried to name a new director so patently inadequate and blatantly wedded to the coal industry that his name had to be withdrawn. The job eventually went to Elburt F. Osborn, a Penn State geologist. At the same time Nixon appointed Edward Failor, an Iowa lawyer and political hack (GOP fund-raiser and publicist, worker with the ultraconservative Young Republicans) to oversee coal mine safety enforcement. Failor had no mining experience of any kind. Failor, in turn promptly hired Harry Treleaven, one of President Nixon's top media image men from the 1968 campaign, to conduct a publicity campaign putting the onus on the miners themselves, rather than the operators, for mine safety. As if all that were not enough, the administration also packed the board to oversee coal mine safety research with political hacks or persons with close ties to the mine operators. It then came as little surprise when the General Accounting Office three times accused the Bureau of Mines of thoroughgoing negligence in enforcing the 1969 safety act.

Another problem was the obvious conflict of interest in which the Bureau of Mines found itself when it was simultaneously directed to enforce safety standards and do everything possible to maximize the production of coal—two frequently conflicting objectives. In 1973 the Interior Department finally recognized this and transferred responsibilities for the 1969 safety law to a new mine enforcement administration. The prospects for conscionable safety enforcement did seem to brighten a bit. But the coal operators, while complaining bitterly that the 1969 act increased their costs and cut their production, refused to pay close to $20 million in assessments for safety violations and invited time-consuming court actions to force collections. Thus the thrust of the law—to impose such sharp assessments that it would simply be too expensive for an operator to maintain an unsafe mine—was being frustrated by the defiance of the operators, countenanced by the executive branch of the federal government.

Only the most naive would fail to see the direct tie between the lawlessness of West Virginia's early coal operators and that of the present-day companies. As the coal fields opened up in the last decades of the 19th century and the first of the 20th, the operators looked first to the native Appalachian people for manpower. But the labor demands were so great that they also cast their nets far afield for workers. Agents were sent into the Deep South to lure able-bodied blacks with promises of "free transportation, steady work at good wages, and company houses in which to live." Usually the agents were mine guards, and they took with them Negro "recruiters" who deceitfully and eloquently told the blacks of the glories of work in the mines. Labor trains were provided, and once the recruits were aboard, the trains were sealed and guarded until they reached the coal fields. Men who tried to escape from the trains were frequently shot. Likewise, recruiters went to Europe and distributed foreign language pamphlets that spoke glowingly of the opportunities in the mines of America. Thus thousands of Europe's peasants came by steerage to New York, where they were quickly herded onto labor trains and transported to West Virginia.

The story of life in the company coal towns is a familiar one, an appalling chapter in American history. In some towns the housing was little better than cow stables; starvation wages were often paid; and the operators resorted to the oppressive and illegal tactics which led to the bloody labor uprisings we discussed earlier in this chapter. In 1946 the Secretary of the Interior asked the U.S. Navy's Bureau of Medicine and Surgery to make a study of housing and sanitary conditions in the coal fields, and received this report:

Ninety-five percent of the houses are built of wood, finished outside with weather board, usually nailed direct to the frame with no sheathing. Roofs are of composition paper. Wood sheathing forms the inside finish. The houses usually rest on posts with no cellars. . . . The state of disrepair at times runs beyond the power of verbal description or even of photographic illustration since neither words nor pictures can portray the atmosphere of abandoned dejection or reproduce the smells. Old, unpainted board and batten houses, batten gone or going and boards fast following, roofs broken, porches staggering, steps sagging, a riot of rubbish, and a medley of odors.

There is the ever present backyard privy, with its foul stench—the most common sewage disposal plant in the coal fields. Many of these ill-smelling back-houses, perched beside roads, along alleys, and over streams, leave their human waste exposed, permeate the air with nauseating odors, and spread disease and death. . . .

Then there is the camp dirt—a mixture of coal dust, dust from the dirt roads, smoke from the burning "bone pile," which blend into a kind of grime that saturates the atmosphere, penetrates houses and even clothing, and sticks tenaciously to human bodies.

Before strip mining was even thought of, the blot on the landscape from deep mines was ugly enough. Gaunt skeletal tipples (loading machinery) were set up at the mine mouths. As the guts of the hillsides were dug out, huge quantities of slate and other refuse, mingled with coal, was simply dumped into the hollows to form mountains of grey slag. By spontaneous combustion, many caught on fire—fire that no one knew how to, or cared to, put out. More than 200 of these burning refuse piles, which emit noxious gases, have been counted in West Virginia. Then there is the dangerous run-off of acid drainage from the mines, turning countless streams yellow-red, and subsidence of the ground over underground mines which has caused some degree of cave-in over hundreds of thousands of acres in the state's bituminous coal fields. The coal towns today are blighted with the rotting tipples, buildings of abandoned mines, and rusting worn-out mining machinery clogging the rutted roads.

Strip mining, the modern-day controversy swirling about the coal industry, presents the same problems of denuded landscape, hideous highwalls, sliding overburden, and silted streams typical to all of Appalachia. The arguments are also familiar. From Ken Hechler, a staunch advocate of a total ban on surface mining: "Billions of tons of valuable topsoil, trees, rocks, the habitat for wildlife and the hills themselves are being chewed and churned up because it's so cheap to make a quick killing when you can pass the environmental costs on to future generations." And from Edwin R. Phelps, president of Peabody Coal, the country's largest stripper: "Beauty is in the eye of the beholder and impossible to define. Nature created the Badlands of South Dakota and they were made a national monument, but if any surface miner duplicated them, even on a small scale, it would be called a national disgrace." A balanced accounting was provided to the West Virginia legislature by the Stanford Research Institute in 1972. Continued stripping in the state, at an annual rate of 27 million tons a year, would cause 6 to 10 million tons of sediment eroding each year. If stripping were banned, the Stanford report indicated, about 8,000 persons would be temporarily unemployed and the state's economy would suffer a loss in the neighborhood of $200 million a year.

The enemies of stripping lost their battle for a total ban in a major fight in the West Virginia legislature in 1971, and Jay Rockefeller's defeat in 1972 seemed to settle the issue even more definitively. In the meantime, the state's enforcement of the strip mining limitations that were enacted in 1971 has been clearly pro-industry and antiprotection. Few states have less effective protection measures. In Hechler's opinion, "competitive economic blackmail pressure from state to state makes the whole question of state regulation a defective one, since the companies always threaten that if environmental or safety regulations are too tough, they'll pull out." And the scope or effectiveness of new federal legislation was put in a shadow as the well oiled publicity machinery of the coal industry capitalized on the energy crisis mounting in 1973–74 to attack environmental and safety regulations as the problem that caused the energy shortage in the first place. The argument, however specious, placed the once fair hills of West Virginia in more peril than ever.

One hesitates to make light of such a grievous problem as strip mining, but I was amused by the suggestion put forth by two friends of Charleston *Gazette* writer Mary Walton after it was discovered that some hardy mountaineers in Wise County were growing marijuana plants on an abandoned strip mine: "Dump solid waste on worked out strip mines, and then plant marijuana. Not only would the state have a cash crop, but the young people would be kept here."

On the grimmer side, one is obliged to recall yet another disaster brought on West Virginia's people by the coal industry. At one minute past eight on the morning of February 26, 1972, a massive coal-waste dam at the head of Logan County's 17-mile-long Buffalo Creek Hollow suddenly collapsed. A great wall of water—some 21 million cubic feet of it—went roaring down the narrow valley, taking the lives of 125 people, destroying almost 500 homes, and causing some $50 million in property damage. It was the worst flood in the state's history and, worse than that, one due entirely to the negligence of Buffalo Mining Company and its corporate parent, Pittston Coal, the largest independent producer of coal in the United States.

Since 1946 a great coal tipple had been operating at the head of Buffalo Creek. By 1972 it was processing about 5,200 tons of raw coal each day from five underground and three strip mines which Pittston operated in the vicinity. Some 4,200 tons of cleansed coal were produced daily and sent on their way in the trains of the Chesapeake and Ohio. But, as in all tipple operations, an immense amount of waste was removed from the coal—"slag" or "gob," as it is familiarly known. Year-in, year-out it had accumulated at the rate of some 1,000 tons a day, forming a gob pile of fantastic proportions almost 500 feet thick. Eventually part of the pile began to burn, creating a stinking, smoking hill. In 1964 Buffalo Mining faced another problem: it needed a reliable, year-round source of water (some half a million gallons a day) to use in the cleaning-separating process. And it faced state clean waters regulations that meant the company could no longer sluice the contaminated black wash directly into Buffalo Creek. So the decision was made to use the slag heap as a dam to create a series of settle ponds, which would both purify the water to some degree and create a reliable supply of water that could be pumped back uphill to use in the tipple. The problem with all this, as Tom Bethell and Davitt McAteer pointed out in a muckraking *Washington Monthly* article on Buffalo Creek, was that the dam was "built of nothing but junk, standing on a foundation of slime and silt and dead trees. . . . No civil engineer in his right mind would permit the construction of a dam from such materials." But no civil engineer trained in dam construction, it would appear, was ever consulted.

February of 1972 brought heavy snows and rain to Logan County—nothing uncommon for the region, the state meteorologist later said, but enough to start the water behind the dam rising at a precipitous rate, and then to cause the entire dam structure to collapse. The water caused a great explosion as it cascaded into the burning part of the slag heap, and then it went roaring down the valley, carrying with it untold quantities of mud and rock and coal wastes. Five thousand people lived in the cramped confines of Buffalo Creek Hollow, and it is a wonder that many more of them did not die, since the company had informed only a few that there was any real danger of flooding. (The idea that the whole 80,000-ton slate dump could just collapse, like a sand castle, apparently occurred to no one. Later it turned out that the required state licenses had not been obtained for any of the coal companies' "dams.") As the black mass of water and sludge surged down the valley, it careened from one mountain wall to the other, obliterating some communities, skirting others entirely. In three hours the carnage was finished, but it would take months to find all the bodies of the dead, the ruins of houses, and people's lifetime possessions.

The strengths and weaknesses of American society were mirrored in what happened afterwards. The immediate relief steps were magnificent—quick removal by the U.S. Army Corps of Engineers of 300,000 cubic yards of flood debris, preparation of 599 mobile homesites for refugees and the supply of rent-free trailer parks by federal housing authorities, $8 million in direct assistance to survivors by the American Red Cross, 200,000 free meals from Salvation Army mobile canteens, rapid reconstruction of the road through the hollow by the state and federal highway authorities. By late spring the valley had been restored enough to grow a new grass cover.

The longer-term fate of Buffalo Creek and its people provided less grounds for cheer. In the words of Tom Nugent, author of *Death at Buffalo Creek* (W. W. Norton, 1973):

> Most of the flood victims were uprooted from the land on which they had lived for generations, and resettled among strangers, in rows of identical government trailers. Many of them began to develop psychological problems, irrational phobias and guilts which psychologists say are directly traceable to the killer flood. Some of the survivors said they had been forced to haggle, endlessly and unfuriatingly, with tight-fisted company adjusters who refused to make fair payment for property losses.
>
> Worst of all, perhaps, the vast majority of Buffalo Creek's former inhabitants were required to sit in their temporary trailers, helplessly idle, while a whole portfolio of ambitious, elegantly drawn government plans to rebuild their valley first faltered, then stalled, then virtually died in a snarl of red tape.

More than a year after the flood, Senator Jennings Randolph said assistance from the federal government had deteriorated so far "that the lack of progress in the rebuilding effort is a disaster in itself."

And again, one must return to the responsibility of Pittston Coal, an immensely profitable corporation which also has one of the worst safety records in the U.S. coal industry. No less than three government reports concluded that the dam had been built in violation of several laws, using absurdly unscientific methods, and that Pittston and its subsidiary had shown "flagrant disregard for the safety of the residents of Buffalo Creek."

More than two years after the great flood, there were well over 100 coal refuse impoundments spotted around West Virginia with the same potentiality for collapse as Buffalo Creek. And neither the state nor federal authorities were doing much to protect the lives of the people living below them.

The rank exploitation of West Virginia's people is not, of course, confined to the activities of the coal companies alone. The 1930s witnessed another episode, not related to coal, which I think must go down as one of the most gruesome examples in American history of the free enterprise system gone amok. The story was told by a young author, Hubert Skidmore, in *Hawk's Nest*—a book effectively suppressed after its 1941 printing by Doubleday and Company. Finally, in the late 1960s, it was reprinted in *West Virginia Heritage*, a collection of readings prepared by Jim Comstock, editor of an unconventional weekly, *The Hillbilly*, at Richwood, West Virginia. In a discussion late one evening in his office, Comstock brought *Hawk's Nest* to my attention, and I still remember the chill of horror at the first telling.

The setting of the story, which Skidmore wrote in novel form but based on facts, was several miles southwest of Charleston, where three rivers meet and Hawk's Nest peak has long been a prime tourist attraction. There in Depression years the West Virginia Power Commission licensed a contractor for Union Carbide and Carbon Company to drive a long tunnel, 32 to 44

feet in width, through Gauley Mountain, the purpose being to divert water
from the steeply downsloping New River to a hydroelectric plant.* Five thousand workers were brought in to dig the tunnel. As Skidmore described their
arrival:

> Down the Gauley River they came, down the New River gorge or up the
> broad Kanawha from Charleston. Rickety trucks, jalopies crammed with bedclothes
> and household furnishings, wagons, road-dusty and creaking over the hard high-
> ways, and some by bus, their belongings tied in paper, their work clothes bound
> together with rope. Negroes and sharecroppers from the South, Polacks and Italians
> and Slovaks from Pennsylvania, from bituminous fields and bootleg mines, men
> from Ohio and Michigan and Indiana, off the farms and out of the factories, and
> some from Missouri and Arkansas, from the lead and zinc mines; men who came
> down from the Ozark Mountains their tongues still strange with a language cen-
> turies old, their frames tall and lean and angular with the way they had lived.
> Work-hungry they plodded into the head of the great Kanawha Valley, want-
> ing nothing more than a job, nothing more than a little money to send their
> women and kids. The memory of bare, oil-cloth-covered kitchen tables made them
> silent. Some did not even ask what they would be earning.

Construction camps of crude shacks were thrown up and the mountain
soon reverberated with drilling and explosions as the muckers did their work.
The tunnel was provided with a single ventilator fan which soon proved defective and unable to carry away the thick clouds of dust from the drills and
blasting. Even with the best safety precautions, the result of the tunneling
might have been disastrous. For the rock—as the construction company must
have known from its first test drillings—contained a thick stratum of almost
pure silica. In fact, the silica rock was hauled away to use in steel processing,
even while the miners labored on in the dust-laden tunnel in round-the-clock
shifts. Apparently the construction company hoped to finish up the job and
get the men out of town before the inevitable occurred: widespread cases of
silicosis, shortening the lives of a vast portion of the Depression-hungry workers, bringing rapid death for many of them. But the disease began to take its
gruesome toll before the drilling was even completed, and the body of one
miner after another was lowered into mountain graves.

Author Skidmore has one of the widows cry out in indignation—"But
they didn't give the men masks to wear and fix the ventilators. Why didn't
they do that, if they knew it was killing the men?"

"They didn't give a hoot," came the reply.

Jay Rockefeller: A Fresh Breeze

At least on the surface, the entry of John D. Rockefeller IV into West
Virginia public life bore a striking resemblance to the impact on Arkansas of
his uncle, Winthrop Rockefeller, who spent the last 20 years of his life in his

---

* It was the contractor, Rinehart and Dennis of Charlottesville, Virginia, which threatened
a libel suit against Doubleday, forcing the publisher to try to recall all copies of the book before the publication date. But some copies evaded the recall net, and eventually brought prices
of as much as $80.

adopted state and served as its governor from 1967 to 1971.* Both these Rockefellers grew up in the rarified atmosphere of their famous family's New York state life; both grew restless and broke off their educations for distant adventures (Winthrop in the Oklahoma oilfields, Jay by an extended sojourn in the Orient); both, at the suggestion of friends, were finally drawn to small, provincial states in which they would use the family fortune, along with their personal skills, to make a profound mark; and both would be rebuffed in their initial races for governor.

But there were differences between the two Rockefellers, which went a lot further than Winthrop's decision to remain with the familial Republican allegiance and Jay's move over to the Democratic party after he reached West Virginia. Winthrop's personal life, starting with his unhappy and nationally publicized first marriage, was a sad one; Jay's, symbolized by his marriage to Sharon Percy, the charming and articulate daughter of the Illinois Republican Senator, seemed quite the opposite. Winthrop was unscholarly and shy and something of a family black sheep in his youth; Jay was academically proficient, naturally outgoing, and an obvious "star" from the start. Winthrop was an average-enough looking man (until he grew his wonderful Hemingwayesque beard in the last year of his life); Jay, by contrast, was endowed with a six-foot, six-inch frame and a natural air of authority. Most of all, one had to notice the generational difference. Jay spoke with the idiom of the youth of the '60s and '70s, and when our conversation touched on the trials and tribulations his uncle Winthrop was having with the Arkansas legislature, Jay commiserated and said quite simply: "I love my uncle." Men in Winthrop's generation, it occurred to me, would not have gone further than a word like "fond." Jay's hallmarks seemed to be clear, strong emotions, and a startling ingenuousness—which would eventually get him into political trouble.

It was in 1964 that Jay Rockefeller, then 27 years of age, strolled into Emmons, a community of some 200 impoverished souls strung out along a hollow a few miles southwest of Charleston, to begin his West Virginia career. From Emmons, it is four miles over a rutted dirt road to the nearest store, and most of the people are jobless and on welfare. As a poverty worker there over the next two years, Rockefeller got an insight into poor people's lives that rich men rarely acquire. "Emmons became a total challenge, an absolute, total obsession for two years," Rockefeller said later. "It took me six months just to sell myself, to get the people to trust me. Then it took another year to get them to trust their own power as a community. . . . I can look at what I was able to accomplish at Emmons and, in retrospect, be very depressed. But I can look back at what I was able to do for a few individual people and feel it was all worthwhile."

In 1966, having become a Democrat, Rockefeller won election to the West Virginia House of Delegates from Kanawha County (Charleston). Two

* The Winthrop Rockefeller story was extensively treated in the Arkansas chapter of the previous book in this series, The Deep South States of America.

years later he ran for secretary of state, but even before the voters had a chance to ratify his election (by an overwhelming majority), articles were appearing in the national press hailing John D. Rockefeller IV as a potential future President of the United States.

Assuming the secretary of state's job in 1969, Rockefeller quickly made it apparent that he would not limit his activities to record-keeping or his constitutionally mandated responsibility as "Keeper of the Great Seal." There was a contest for speakership of the House of Delegates between J. E. (Ned) Watson, a bedfellow of the coal and other moneyed interests, and Ivor Boiarsky, a millionaire bank president and diametrically opposite type. ("Watson," as Rockefeller put it, "was terribly warm, cuddly, fun to be with, and very smart; Boiarsky was Jewish, uncuddly, ultra-knowledgeable, a poor smiler, awful to people a lot of the time, but a man of total integrity.") Rockefeller put his weight behind Boiarsky, who, contrary to expectations, won the speakership.

Rockefeller then turned his attention to election reform, proposing laws aimed particularly at the southern counties known for the worst fraud and corruption. But his reform proposals were derailed in the senate's fair election committee, headed then by none other than Mingo County's Noah Floyd. And even if the statutes were made more stringent, Rockefeller acknowledged, they would do little good if the Republicans and Democrats were in collusion in any given county: "The Republicans say to the Democrats, 'You go ahead and pile-drive your people the way you want. We won't bother you if you let us do the same—or give us so many jobs at the county court or in the board of education office.' That amount of patronage is helpful to the weak Republican party in the southern counties. And it's a type of corruption hard to reach by law."

The only way to get at the problem, Rockefeller decided, was to purge some of the politicians most connected with the special interests or unsavory election practices. So he took the politically risky choice of campaigning publicly for the defeat of several, including Floyd (who lost by fewer than 400 votes). "Mystically, Floyd's defeat helped a great deal," Rockefeller said. "Even though he retained control of the Mingo County Court and the local election machinery, his defeat encouraged people tired of corruption and of the old style of politics." Several other incumbents whom Rockefeller disliked but did not openly oppose, including Lloyd Jackson, president of the state senate, were turned out of office in the same 1970 primaries.

Late in 1970 Rockefeller took a position that would turn out to be as harmful to his political future as the enduring enmity of the more corrupt county machines. Based on a thorough study of strip mining and its effects, he came to the conclusion that reclamation of stripped lands was impracticable and that surface mining was ruining the long-term economic prospects of the state. He had become convinced, Rockefeller announced, "that strip mining of coal in West Virginia must be prohibited by law, completely and forever." Strip mining, he explained later in defense of his stand, is a "cancer of the earth" that mutilates the hills "like a knife slash through a painting." To make up for the loss in coal production and jobs, he urged an expansion of deep mining with its higher manpower requirements. "When I see one stripper working," he said, "I see three deep miners out of work."

Democratic State Chairman William E. Watson, a Rockefeller ally, later said it was characteristic of Jay that he never seriously considered the political dangers of his strip mining stand when he announced it—perhaps because "he was operating on the premise that his immense political strength afforded him the luxury of allowing his conscience to be his political guide." And, for a while, it looked as if Rockefeller would succeed at his new tack. Although the legislature turned down the proposed ban on strip mining in favor of far more limited controls, the spring 1972 primaries found Rockefeller swamping his Democratic primary opponents. Legislative candidates who supported abolition of strip mining won a number of contested primaries. Ken Hechler, the leading congressional opponent of stripping, swept to an easy victory over another incumbent Representative, James Kee, in southern and southwestern West Virginia counties joined in a new district. (Kee, whose father and mother had represented the southern counties in Congress before him in a line of succession dating back to 1932, was a toady of the coal interests and won some notoriety for a statement defending stripping because the breaks created in the forest give animals an opportunity to sun themselves, and because "the only argument I've ever heard against strip mining is that it destroys the land.")

The strip operators, however, were merely lying back in the bushes and waiting for the crucial general election contest against Rockefeller. Governor Arch A. Moore, Jr., was seeking reelection—the first West Virginia governor able to do so, because of a constitutional change made in 1970. (Rockefeller had supported the change because he thought Moore was no threat, and he hoped to serve two terms himself.) A successor to Walter Hallahan as the "Mr. Republican" of West Virginia politics, Moore had served six terms in the U.S. House from the state's northernmost (Panhandle) district before winning the governorship in 1968. He had been obliged to make repeated denials of unethical conduct while a member of Congress, but nonetheless capitalized on the massive voter disenchantment about the proven corruption of past Democratic regimes to eke out a narrow victory over Democrat James M. Sprouse in the 1968 election. (Ironically, Sprouse had been a fresh, young face in Democratic ranks, the party's first gubernatorial nominee not of the Neely dynasty or the entrenched Democratic politician type.)

Imagewise, Arch Moore was no match for Jay Rockefeller. Just short of age 50, he had a round face, white hair, and a height almost a foot short of Rockefeller's. But he was a tough, shrewd politician who had run an efficient administration in which budgets were balanced, some 200 new business firms allegedly brought into the state, welfare rolls reduced, and great forward strides made in completion of the interstate highways (permitting many publicized ribbon-cutting ceremonies). In addition, Moore had the all-out backing of the strip mining industry, which pumped substantial amounts of money into his reelection campaign and made it possible for him to match the Rockefeller wealth—or at least to the extent he felt he had to. (When the final campaign expenditure reports were in, Moore's committee was shown to have spent $696,000, compared to Rockefeller's expenditures of $1,535,000. Rockefeller's contributors included many nationally known persons and members of the Rockefeller family; Moore's included a number of the state's most prominent strip operators.)

Between them, Moore and the Strip Mining Association were able to convey the impression that Rockefeller's stand on strip mining was really an attack on "King Coal" itself and the prelude to an assault on the bulwarks of the state's economy, including deep coal mining, steel, and chemicals. According to Democratic Chairman Watson, it was also common on election day for mining companies and related industries to give their employees the day off and instruct them to vote for Moore. In addition, Watson charged, "many previously loyal Democratic supporters were afraid openly to show their support for Rockefeller because of economic ties with the coal industry. This was especially true in the case of lawyers, bankers, and sellers of mining equipment and trucks." The results of all this were especially apparent in several southern coal counties, normally bastions of Democratic strength, which registered a vastly reduced Democratic vote.

Rockefeller ran a strong Populist-type campaign, claiming: "There's quick service [in state government] for anyone with big money and lobbies—but a mess of regulations for the people who need help most. I can change all that." He also tried to turn the issue of his wealth to advantage by asserting: "The big, special interests and machines can't buy or control me. I can afford to be independent and fair." Moore's campaign, however, was able to exploit with great effectiveness the "carpetbagger" issue about a native New Yorker only eight years resident in the state. Moore also made a skillful appeal to West Virginia chauvinism. "You never heard Arch Moore run the state of West Virginia down one time," he told one campaign crowd in Mingo County. "I've listened to the rhetoric of this campaign and all they say—that's the opposition—is 'poor West Virginia' this and 'poor West Virginia' that. Well, we don't have to put up with that kind of designation any more. We're on the move in this state and we're doing it ourselves." * The message, of course, underscored the image of Rockefeller the outsider, merely using his family's familiar prerogative to use the state, like a convenient province, for personal advancement.

Under the circumstances, it helped Rockefeller little to suggest that Moore was the real outsider since he was the captive of the coal interests in Pittsburgh, New York, and Cleveland. Nor did Rockefeller's promise of 50,000 new jobs and 20,000 miles of improved secondary roads for West Virginia make much impact in the emotionally charged atmosphere of the campaign. (In a style reminiscent of his uncles Nelson and Winthrop and his father John D. Rockefeller III, former head of the Rockefeller foundation,

---

* According to the Charleston *Gazette,* Moore had channeled substantial state patronage to Rockefeller's old Mingo County enemy, Democratic boss Noah Floyd. Despite the county's traditional heavy Democratic vote, Floyd was able to deliver it for Moore.

Jay had assembled a staff of 30 and spent $300,000 on an 18-month study of the state economy.)

In addition, Rockefeller's personal support for the unpopular campaign of George McGovern—who captured only 36.4 percent of the West Virginia vote—probably harmed his cause. The Nixon landslide contributed to a strong Republican tide, especially considering West Virginia's normally strong Democratic habits. Although Senator Jennings Randolph and the state's four Democratic Congressmen won easy victories, in every statewide race where there was a strong Republican challenger, the Democrat either lost or the outcome was very close. Republicans were elected secretary of state, auditor, and to the state supreme court for the first time since the 1920s.

Finally, Rockefeller may have lost because he was running against a well regarded incumbent governor. When the votes were counted, Moore was the victor with a solid 73,355-vote plurality—54.7 percent of the total.

If the voters thought a single defeat would drive Jay Rockefeller out of the state, however, they were mistaken—just as some Arkansans had made the wrong assumption that Winthrop Rockefeller would flee after losing to Orval Faubus in his first race for governor in 1964. Rockefeller accepted the presidency of West Virginia Wesleyan College at Buckhannon, remained politically active, and appeared ready to try again for the governorship in 1976. By then, the carpetbagger issue would have faded more, and there would be no incumbent governor to oppose. Rockefeller's 1972 defeat had clearly postponed any shift to a West Virginia government less shackled by coal and the other special interests, and taken the wind out of the movement to ban strip mining. But for the young, intensely idealistic and ambitious candidate, the defeat might have contributed to a maturing and mellowing process from which he would benefit over the longer span of his career.

State Government: Governor and Legislature, Taxes and Services, Welfare and Prisons

Considering the general climate of state politics, West Virginia state government is not much better—or worse—than one might expect. The state constitution written in 1872 and repeatedly amended remains in effect and makes the governor one of the country's weakest. Six other offices are elected statewide and independent of the governor. Until 1969 the authority to draw up a state budget was in the hands of a seven-man board of public works of which the governor was but one member. (That situation, which led to incredible log-rolling, has now been corrected with budget-making authority transferred to the governor's office.)

The state legislators are also strictly circumscribed by the constitution in what they can do. (They are forbidden, for instance, to relocate county seats or to create new counties except under special circumstances.) It came as something of a surprise when the Citizens Conference on State Legislatures in 1971 gave West Virginia as high a rank as 25th among the states in terms of efficiency, accountability, information-gathering facilities, and independence. At the time, the legislators earned a scant $1,500 a year (since raised to $3,000)—a sum, as Jay Rockefeller pointed out, that could be used up in Charleston on a hotel room alone. Legislative sessions are only 30 to 60 days a year; staff facilities are very limited; no private offices for the legislators are available. Lobbyists keep the legislators so busy with parties that it is hard to see when they have any time to reflect on the 600-odd bills they must approve or disapprove within a few weeks' time. Yet as Paul Kaufman testified, "lobbyists for the private government of the corporate giants are paid upwards of $25,000 per year and are supported by lawyers, researchers, and experts in abundance."

Both houses of the legislature have been said to become more independent, and less controlled by the lobbies, in recent years. Some relatively progressive measures have passed, including the state's first significant severance tax on minerals, the first public kindergartens, and funding for three educational television channels which cover the entire state. But in 1972 the legislators were unable to override Governor Moore's veto of a rather good consumer protection bill. The reason: intense pressure from the banking lobby. The number of good bills which never even make it out of the committee, due to lobby pressure, is legion. A corollary to all this is found in the state's ineffectual and/or industry-dominated regulatory agencies. Most of them are required by law to include corporate representatives on their governing boards, appeal boards, or advisory panels. The public service commission, which has responsibility for all public utilities and common carriers, is required by law to get its funding from the industries it is supposed to regulate. Environmental protection is split up between a number of regulatory bodies. Safety inspections of mines, dams, and bridges are remarkably ineffectual. This has been one reason for a staggering series of preventable disasters. Farmington, Buffalo Creek, and less publicized mishappenings—all are matters of very recent history and suggest a negligent attitude toward people's lives for which the state government bears a heavy responsibility.

The only area in which modern-day West Virginia state government has excelled, as far as I could discover, has been welfare. Under Democratic aegis in the early 1960s, important beginnings were made in WPA-work type programs and then work-incentive programs for fathers of welfare families, enabling those with higher IQ's to find jobs in industry. More improvements came under Governor Moore, who instituted—with his welfare commissioner, Edwin F. Flowers—a system to reduce the number of people on the welfare rolls while substantially increasing benefits to those who remain on them. "In many respects," then Deputy Undersecretary of Health, Education and Welfare Richard Nathan said in 1972, "West Virginia is at the very forefront nationally in doing the kind of things that many federal agencies are contemplating in terms of how programs should operate under a reformed welfare system."

An early step was to remove the county governments from all welfare responsibilities. All record-keeping was tied to a central computer operation in Charleston headquarters, with the number of local welfare offices cut drastically. As a result, it became possible to issue a first check for a new welfare applicant within a week, compared to the six weeks or more previously required. West Virginia also originated the sale of food stamps by mail, with the cost deducted from relief checks—an especially important advantage for people living in the remote hollows. Then, the state required that mothers of school-age children on welfare must register for work or job training. It was a profound shock for many women so accustomed to the welfare syndrome that they had never worked in their lives, but many were placed successfully in work training programs or actual jobs. When men came in to apply for welfare, the first step was to talk to them about a job rather than a relief check. An employment service unit, set up within the welfare department, scoured the local communities to find job openings. Yet in cases of urgent need, even "satellite" welfare offices were authorized to write emergency checks.

The result of the various reforms was to reduce the number of fathers on relief from 5,400 to 900 in five years and to reduce the number of persons collecting AFDC (Aid to Families with Dependent Children) from 97,000 in 1970 to 69,000 in 1973—a drop of 29 percent during a period when the U.S. total rose 33 percent. The typical recipient of AFDC benefits in West Virginia moved off the rolls in six months, compared to a national median of nearly 20 months. At the same time benefits for those legitimately in need and unable to find work or jobs were increased to a point at which —according to the claims of state welfare officials—"total basic human needs" could be met. Many of these reforms, first tried in West Virginia, were later to be written into federal law and tested or implemented across the country.

The 1971 passage of a severance tax was of major symbolic importance in West Virginia, because it marked an important advance in the state's long and tortuous path toward the taxation of the vital sources of income within its borders. Back in 1933 the state had adopted its first sales tax (since increased to 3 percent, with no exemption for food), in 1931 its business and occupation tax (the major source of business taxation), in 1961 a personal income tax, and rather belatedly, in 1967, its first corporate income tax. But there never was a severance tax on natural resources, an omission in West Virginia once likened to a failure to tax coffee in Brazil. In 1953 a newly elected Democratic governor, William C. Marland, had proposed a severance tax on minerals—some say at the urging of John L. Lewis.

Marland seemed to have a promising public career ahead of him. At 34, he was the youngest governor in the state's history and had enjoyed a meteoric rise in politics. But the proposed severance tax caused an immediate war with the extractive industries, headed by coal. Marland seemed to have formidable support for the tax—the then potent United Mine Workers with 115,000 members in the state, educators, and all but one member of the congressional delegation. Senator Matthew Neely actually traveled back to Charleston to argue for the measure. The battle raging over the severance tax, Neely declared, "is largely between absentee captains of industry on the one hand and the men, women, and children of West Virginia on the other."

In addition to the coal operators, strong opposition came from most of the West Virginia press. The Charleston *Gazette*, then under the editorial direction of a conservative managing editor, Frank A. Knight, said John L. Lewis was "the real mastermind" of the severance tax effort and would use it to get control of the coal industry, the state police, and by implication, the entire state government. Marland responded by pointing out in a letter to the editor that a member of the *Gazette*'s editorial board was Carl Andrews, secretary of the West Virginia Coal Operators Association. The real battle, however, was in the Democratic-controlled legislature, where the coal interests quickly applied enough pressure to kill the severance tax. Governor Marland found his relationships with the legislators permanently ruined by the battle, and his promising governorship turned into a nightmare. (Marland subsequently lost two races for the U.S. Senate, became an alcoholic, disappeared from the state, and was finally discovered in 1965 driving a taxicab in Chicago and trying—as a member of Alcoholics Anonymous—to rehabilitate himself. He was offered and took a job with a prominent West Virginia thoroughbred horse raiser, but died late in 1965 of cancer.)

After Marland's defeat on the severance tax issue, no West Virginia politician was about to try again for many years to come. But the arguments for it remained strong, and when the independent-minded and brilliant Ivor Boiarsky rose to power in the house in the 1960s, becoming speaker in 1969, the climate began to change. The rationale was explained by state AFL-CIO president Miles C. Stanley:

I'm convinced a severance tax on irreplaceable natural resources is not only economically right but morally right, because these resources—the coal under the ground of West Virginia—don't really belong to the Pittsburgh Consolidation Coal Company or any other. They really belong to all the people. If a company is going to extract irreplaceable resources, then I think that in addition to paying a tax for the privilege of doing business, it should pay the people in the form of a severance tax for what belongs to the people and will never be returned.

The studies of the tax structure initiated by Boiarsky in the late 1960s had shown that the coal industry was not paying its fair share of the costs of state government. And in a 1971 bill increasing the overall business and occupation tax, he was able to insert a modest severance tax on coal. The coal lobby was thrown off balance that year by the fight over attempted banning of strip mining, and it accepted the severance tax without much of a fight. Boiarsky died not long after, however, and there was soon a notable relaxation of the effort to continue reform of West Virginia's tax structure to make it less regressive and more directed toward the immensely profitable coal industry.

The overall state and local tax collections of West Virginia government ranked only 42nd in the country in the early 1970s, or 33rd as a percentage of personal income. The results, in terms of expenditures, were not hard to imagine: fifth among the states for highways (so expensive to build, so prone to corruption and political debt-paying), 32nd for health and hospitals, and

42nd for education. Long overdue changes in education have been made, however, including some increase in teachers' salaries, a board of regents to oversee the higher education program, and perhaps most important, an attempt to catch up with other states through building a series of vocational training schools more attuned to the state's blue-collar job market. A reevaluation of West Virginia's whole educational system has been in order for some time—finding ways to cope with the problems of many children coming out of the public school system without basic reading or math abilities, and devising a college curriculum geared to the advancement of hillbilly kids as well as the middle class. Often, West Virginia has merely exported its trained young people. In the mid-1960s the president of the state medical association pointed out that only 20 of the first 150 graduates of the West Virginia University Medical School were practicing in the state.

It may seem unfair to fault West Virginia, with all of its other problems, for its prisons, but the fact stands out that the fortress-like penitentiary at Moundsville in the Northern Panhandle, built in the 1860s and holding more than 500 prisoners, is a gruesome (though certainly not unique) example of American penology gone awry. Homosexual rapes, shakedowns, robberies, assaults, and frequent murders all take place behind the ancient prison's grimy walls. According to W. Thomas Gall, the prosecuting attorney of Marshall County, in which the prison lies, "I wouldn't now ask the court to sentence a man to the penitentiary unless I consider him a complete loss, an irrevocable loss to society. . . . Frankly, I would personally rather be dead than to be incarcerated in that place." In 1967 a number of faculty members at nearby Bethany College, a private liberal arts school founded in 1840 (West Virginia's first), began an imaginative program of courses for the inmates, ranging from modern political ideology to genetics. But it was just a drop of water compared to the prison's problems. In 1973 several hundred of the inmates took part in an uprising, holding guards as hostages, and yet another death-behind-bars was added to the roster of Moundsville's fatalities.

By contrast, the $10 million Robert F. Kennedy Youth Center near Morgantown, a federally run correctional center for young offenders found guilty of serious crimes, is one of the most splendidly equipped penal institutions in the United States. Opened in 1969, it has no walls, offers many courses, and helps to maintain a human touch by having women on its staff. The center has been called "the most elaborate effort in the U.S. to turn incipient criminals into productive, law-abiding citizens."

West Virginia and the National Scene

The political course of the United States is rarely thought to hinge on West Virginia. There was, however, the great exception during the spring of 1960 when the national eye focused on the audacious race by John F. Kennedy in the West Virginia Presidential primary. "If our political disputes are ever remembered as our battlefields are now, West Virginia will become a national shrine," Arthur Edson of the Associated Press wrote after Kennedy had finally secured his party's nomination for President. Everyone, including the Kennedy forces, "agree this was the turning point," Edson observed.

The reason Kennedy entered West Virginia was not to corral its 25 delegate votes—in fact, the primary was nonbinding.* Rather, he wanted to demonstrate that the people of a heavily Protestant, heavily unionized Border State would vote for a Roman Catholic for President. And he had good reason to believe West Virginia would do just that; advance polls conducted on his behalf by Louis Harris had shown him winning by as much as 70 percent of the vote.

Kennedy's forces had a fledgling campaign organization going in a majority of the state's counties, organized by state campaign manager Robert P. McDonough (the owner of a Parkersburg printing plant), long before Kennedy even intimated that he might run in the state's primary. What was needed was (1) an opponent, and (2) an effective dramatization of the religious issue. The first was provided by Hubert Humphrey, who decided his liberal, prolabor record was tailor-made for West Virginia. The second was provided by the Wisconsin primary, a few weeks before West Virginia's, which showed substantial resistance to Kennedy among Protestant voters. Political writers were quick to predict that Kennedy's Roman Catholicism might sink him in West Virginia, where Catholics make up only 5 percent of the population. "It will be a miracle if the outcome in West Virginia shows there is no religious issue which divides seriously the people of this country," columnist Walter Lippmann wrote. The same theme was echoed in countless other news reports.

In fact, the religious issue was not particularly well posed in West Virginia at all. As one Protestant minister supporting Kennedy commented, "There is no large minority of Catholics here agitating for public aid to parochial schools, censoring books and movies, and opposing birth control." In addition, there was the fact that church membership in the state was only half the national average, and that the Bible Belt religionists of the state put a huge gulf between their intensely personal religious experiences—the world of baptism in a cold-water creek, traumatic conversions, and even sometimes handling of rattlesnakes and copperheads—and any kind of application to their own daily lives, not to mention public life. Moreover, competent observers of the sociology of Appalachia had found remarkably little bigotry in West Virginia, much less than in most states of the country.

One would never have dreamed this during the campaign, as outside reporters found a bigot behind every shack. Kennedy himself became concerned that the word of his Catholicism, spreading from Wisconsin and through the media, might harm him. So a direct counterattack was decided upon, with the candidate reaffirming his support of separation of church and state, pointing out that the Constitution forbids religious tests for public

* For much of the ensuing account I am indebted to Harry W. Ernst for his incisive monograph, *The Primary that Made a President: West Virginia 1960*, Eagleton Institute Cases in Practical Politics, McGraw-Hill, 1962.

office, and asking: "Is anyone going to tell me I lost this primary the day I was born?" This line of attack worked so well that a Charleston newspaper columnist soon suggested a rapid spread of "the popular psychology which suggests that a West Virginia vote against Senator Kennedy is a vote for bigotry." This infuriated Humphrey's supporters, whose candidate had been one of the leading champions of equality and tolerance in American life. But there was little they could do about it. In the final vote little difference could be noted between the counties with the most and the least Catholics, a measure which in Wisconsin had showed the clear impact of the religious issue.

From start to finish, Humphrey was thoroughly outgunned by the superior Kennedy campaign organization—Robert Kennedy and Lawrence F. O'Brien acting as the chief field generals, Theodore Sorenson in charge of the image-making, and the West Virginians McDonough and Matthew A. Reese serving as in-state coordinators. McDonough and O'Brien had the key task of getting Kennedy "slated" by the county organizations. They did their job so well, a former sheriff from one of the southern counties told me, that they often got *both* factions in a county to slate JFK. After the primary there were allegations that the Kennedy forces had actually bought the election through underhanded use of political money. There was no question that Kennedy had outspent Humphrey many times over—his expenditures were over $250,000 compared to the Minnesotan's meager $30,000. A lot of the Kennedy money was judiciously used with county factions, and there is little doubt that some of it ended up in "bought" votes in the classic West Virginia manner. But W. E. Chilton, then assistant publisher of the Charleston *Gazette,* summed it up well when he said: "The Massachusetts Senator bought a landslide, not an election."

Part of the Kennedy money went into a blitzkreig advertising effort to drive home the Kennedy campaign themes. One of these, according to Harry Ernst's summary, was to "link John F. Kennedy and Franklin Delano Roosevelt, no pauper himself and a patron saint in the coal fields because of his liberalism, and to prophesy that JFK represented FDR's second coming." To this end Franklin D. Roosevelt, Jr., was brought in to campaign intensively for Kennedy, and campaign material boosting Kennedy was sent to thousands of West Virginia Democrats with the postmark of Hyde Park, New York, the Roosevelt home. The voters came to regard Kennedy as an important rich man who might actually do something for their state, not just a "smoothie" out after their votes.

A second Kennedy theme was to suggest that West Virginians would be foolish to vote against him, because national polls showed he stood an excellent chance to be elected President and could then look after the state's crushing problems. The message was that Humphrey had scarcely a chance, even to win the Democratic nomination. Repeated reference was made to Kennedy's colorful "PT Boat 109" war record, in invidious comparison to Humphrey's 4-F experience—a telling point with the patriotic Mountain State people.

There is still an element of pathos in the story of how Hubert Humphrey, the grand workhorse liberal of his era, had to struggle and even demean himself to scrape together enough money to keep his campaign barely afloat. His savings had already been depleted by the Wisconsin primary, he had scarcely any money for television or newspaper advertising, and in his campaigning he was subjected to the vagaries of commercial airline travel while Kennedy shuttled back and forth from Washington in his private plane. Humphrey was telling the truth when he said that his campaign boiled down to "pitting my body, my ideals, and my faith against the wealth of my opponent." And the Kennedys, adding insult to injury, used foul methods to see that Humphrey did not get the money he needed. Theodore H. White in his *The Making of the President: 1960* tells the shocking story of how Kennedy's Connecticut ally, Democratic party boss John Bailey, informed former U. S. Senator William Benton, publisher of the *Encyclopedia Britannica,* that if he continued to finance Humphrey, "he would never hold another elective or appointive job in Connecticut as long as he, Bailey, had any say in Connecticut." The episode is a sobering reminder, especially in the post-Watergate era, that political strongarm tactics did not originate with the Nixonites.*

Yet another keen disappointment for Humphrey was that organized labor, whose cause he had so long championed, remained neutral in the primary. Even the black vote, which Humphrey might have expected to get in view of his early and courageous stand on civil rights, went 75 percent for Kennedy.

The final returns showed Kennedy the victor with 60.8 percent of the vote—236,510 to Humphrey's 152,187. Even as the returns poured in that May night, Humphrey went before the television cameras to announce he was no longer a candidate for the nomination. John Kennedy, on the other hand, had indeed won "the primary that made a President."

In all the years of the West Virginia primary, first instituted in 1915, there has never been a contest in any way as important as the 1960 fight. Hubert Humphrey ran again in 1972, announcing he had "come back to West Virginia to pick up the fallen torch of President Kennedy." Only George Wallace filed against him, and Humphrey won with 67 percent of the vote. Wallace may have thought he could do well in West Virginia because of its predominantly blue-collar profile, but the returns seemed to indicate that his style of populism, without a racial ingredient, had little to offer. Dennis McCamey of CBS News wrote a preview of the contest that also does well as conclusion:

Wallace may have made a serious miscalculation in going into West Virginia. . . . There are just not enough blacks—only 73,931 out of 1,666,870—for whites to feel threatened or angry. School busing for racial integration is simply not a problem. There are not enough jobs or decent housing for anyone, white or black. Some relatives who have moved to Chicago, Cleveland, Akron, Washington, or Baltimore may write back their newly conceived prejudice against blacks. [But] any racially-motivated vote for Wallace will be small indeed.

* Benton, a man of high integrity and skill, contributed some to Humphrey anyway. "I don't sell out either for money or in response to threats," he told friends. "I've been threatened by better people than the Kennedys. I won't yield. I have to live with myself."

Once in U.S. history there was a Presidential candidate from West Virginia—John W. Davis, the Democrats' choice to oppose Calvin Coolidge in 1924. Davis had deep roots in the state. His father was a Clarksburg lawyer who had been an outspoken Union sympathizer in the Virginia legislature when the Civil War began and subsequently became a leader of the West Virginia statehood movement. But the younger Davis, an attorney of high integrity and intellect, had been drawn away from the state after terms in the legislature and Congress. He served as President Woodrow Wilson's Solicitor General and then as Ambassador to the Court of St. James, and was a member of a Wall Street law firm when he ran for the Presidency. A strong states' rights Democrat reared in the Jeffersonian tradition of honest and limited government, Davis lacked the skill or will to ignite national indignation about social injustice or the corruption of the Teapot Dome era. It was the age of normalcy, and he carried only 12 states—not including West Virginia.

Davis' political philosophy, in fact, was not untypical of many Border State political leaders in the earlier part of this century, old-style Jeffersonian Democrats who saw the times pass them by. Davis ended up opposing the New Deal and backing Republican Presidential candidates from 1940 onward. Just before he died in 1955, he unsuccessfully defended South Carolina's school segregation laws before the Supreme Court. "On the surface," political writer F. Rhodes Cook observed, "this seems to be a radical philosophical transformation for a prominent Wilsonian. But Davis had changed little; political thinking in the United States had moved and, as a result, Davis, who was a little left-of-center in the Wilson years, was on the far right by the time of his death."

An interesting modern-day parallel to John Davis is provided by U.S. Senator Jennings Randolph, a septuagenarian who has qualified for many years as a patriarch of West Virginia politics. As a freshman Congressman, Randolph was one of the mass that huddled in the mist and wind before the Capitol on March 4, 1933, to hear Franklin Roosevelt say, "This nation asks for action, and action now." It was a time for the expenditure of vast amounts of money to pull the country out of the Depression, and Randolph voted for all the historic New Deal measures. In recent years a new breed of liberals has emerged, people who want to attack and change the institutions they feel are preventing social change. But Randolph remains the prototype of the New Deal liberal, hewing still to the idea that problems are solved by extracting money from the Treasury. He is chairman of the Public Works Committee, keeper of the traditional pork barrel. Even in his freshman term in Congress, when Randolph joined the House Committee on Roads, he perceived the need for a national superhighway system. "I was so bold as to draw lines on a map outlining where it would go," he has said. In time, the superhighways came to be in the form of the interstate highway system, and Randolph became the chief defender of the highway trust fund, fighting to prevent tapping of the multi-billion dollar fund for mass transit.

Understandably, Randolph became the darling—some say even the product—of the highway lobby. Between leaving the House in 1947 and his election to the Senate in 1958 he was not only an official of Capital Airlines for some time but also a representative of the American Road Builders Association. Randolph pays scant attention to the modern-day attacks on superhighways as part and parcel of the nation's environmental ills and energy crisis. He is also a very polite man who takes offense at the hot rhetoric of some of his younger colleagues. John Kramer, the young head of the antifreeway Highway Action Coalition, was quoted as saying in 1973: "Every time [Connecticut Senator] Lowell Weicker comes within 20 feet of Randolph, his jowls start quivering. When Weicker starts in about children dying in school bus accidents and highways for the rich and paving the country with asphalt, Randolph nearly goes into cardiac arrest."

Highways, of course, do seem to make more sense for mountainous, rural West Virginia than modern forms of mass transit. And no one has ever faulted Randolph as a superb service Senator for his state or a staunch liberal by his own lights. But his efforts to please all constituents, including the corporate interests, have sometimes gotten him into trouble. A classic example came in 1969 when he said he was for mine safety but then introduced a set of 40 weakening amendments to that year's mine safety act. Consumer advocate Ralph Nader accused Randolph of seeking to "hamstring" the legislation by imbedding in the law "the fossil-age mentality of the coal barons." Nader also said Randolph had been "inspired to such depths of irresponsibility" by Stephen F. Dunn, president of the National Coal Association, the industry's largest trade association. Randolph never sought to refute the charge, but he did step gingerly away from his own proposals to water down the bill to coal industry specifications.

West Virginia's other Senator, Robert C. Byrd, is an even more fascinating type—the "embodiment of Poor White Power," as Robert Sherrill once wrote, and simultaneously the odds-on favorite to succeed Montana's Mike Mansfield as the Majority Leader of the United States Senate sometime during the 1970s.

Robert Byrd's story is quintessentially West Virginian. He was born in North Carolina in 1918, but his mother died that year and his carpenter father had no interest in raising him, so he was sent to live with his aunt and uncle in Stotesbury, a dreary southern West Virginia company town. His foster father drifted between coal mining jobs, and there was so little money that there were many nights that the family had virtually nothing to eat. As a boy Robert went from house to house in the hollow collecting garbage for his uncle's pigs, which he was allowed to shoot when slaughtering time came around. He was the class valedictorian when he graduated from high school at the age of 16, but there was no money to send him to college. So he worked variously at screening coal, filling gas tanks, in the Baltimore shipyards during the war, and running a butcher shop at Crab Orchard, just over the hill from Stotesbury, in the years afterwards. Byrd and his wife—a coal miner's daughter he had married when he was 17—lived above the butcher shop with their two young daughters.

In 1946 Byrd decided to run for the state legislature, and the first reporter ever to interview him—Thomas Stafford, then with the newspaper in nearby Beckley—talked to Byrd while he cut meat for a customer. "He was somewhat pontifical," Stafford said, but also "the most ambitious fellow I ever met. He has never wasted a moment in his life. . . . To be corny about it, he is the Horatio Alger of West Virginia." Neither the UMW nor the coal companies helped Byrd in those days. He made his own way, visiting virtually every home in his legislative district and, to warm the folks up, playing hillbilly tunes on a fiddle (probably the closest thing to a good time Robert Byrd has ever had). He served two terms in the West Virginia house and then one in the senate, going to college in his spare hours.

A vital part of Byrd's constituency, in those days and later ones, were the God-fearing, fundamentalist, church-going folk of his region. From the base of the Baptist congregation at Crab Orchard, he became a favored preacher and broadcast a popular "Robert C. Byrd Bible Class" from the Beckley radio station. He still enjoys giving sermons, sometimes punctuating his talk with handclaps: "I believe in a personal God (clap)—one who hears my prayers (clap)—and one who punishes the wicked (clap). . . . I praise God for ministers (clap) who stick to the job of winning souls (clap) and leave political activity to the politicians. Winning souls is a full-time job. Pastors who devote full time to winning souls (clap) don't have time to go out and lie in the streets and break laws and get themselves hauled away in police wagons (clap). . . ."

In 1952 Byrd decided to try for Congress, and his political career almost came to an abrupt halt on the issue of his former membership in the Ku Klux Klan, revealed by a primary opponent. Byrd replied with a radio speech heavy with religious and anticommunist overtones:

I belonged from mid-1942 to early 1943. . . . Being only 24 at the time, I joined the order because it offered excitement and because it was strongly opposed to communism. After about a year I became disinterested, quit paying my dues, and dropped my membership in the organization. During the nine years that have followed I have never been interested in the Klan, but on the other hand I have directed my energies toward upholding my community, my church, and my fellow citizens of every race, creed, and color.

The reply got Byrd through the primary, but a lack of candor—or memory—became apparent when his general election opponent produced a letter from Byrd to the Klan's Imperial Wizard Samuel Green, dated April 8, 1946, in which Byrd said he was "a former Kleagle of the Ku Klux Klan" and declaring: "The Klan is needed today as never before and I am anxious to see its rebirth here in West Virginia. . . . It is necessary that the Order be promoted immediately and in every state in the Union." West Virginia's Democratic governor demanded that Byrd withdraw as a candidate for Congress, but he refused, rode out the storm, and went on to six rather undistinguished terms in the U.S. House.

In 1958 Byrd bid for a seat in the U.S. Senate, winning by an overwhelming margin as he has in all his contests (though he has never faced a really formidable opponent). After eight years of night classes, he won a law degree (cum laude) from American University in 1963. And Byrd continued to show the attention to his constituents which has made him an apparently unstoppable force in West Virginia politics. Driving himself relentlessly, denying himself any real social life, he was home in West Virginia campaigning weekend after weekend. Letters to his Senate office were answered instantly, and he acquired a card file of some 2,500 prominent people in the state—editors, ministers, party people, county judges, and the like—whom he telephoned at least once a year, to ask how they were doing and what their problems were. His Senate staff kept track of dozens of federal projects he lined up for West Virginia. In fact, Byrd drove the staff so hard that the turnover was exceptionally high.*

It would be fair to say that no burning sense of the American purpose impelled Robert Byrd to claw his way up from the bleak coal camps of West Virginia to the inner circle of the United States Senate. Certainly it was not personal charisma that persuaded the voters to send Byrd to Washington— he is a man of dour visage, never known to tell a joke, whose physical appearance was aptly summarized by Jack Anderson: "A rather pale man of medium height, with an undershot jaw, a pompadour, sideburns shaved off, and dressed inconspicuously." Byrd seems to have entered politics in the first instance because it was the only way out of the poverty of his youth. Later he delighted in telling his own story in terms of how a poor orphan boy could rise to the seats of the mighty.

Achieving all that required a keen sense of power, which Byrd quickly showed in the Senate when he cultivated then Majority Leader Lyndon Johnson and especially the patriarch of the powerful Southerners, Richard Russell of Georgia. This quickly won him positions on the Appropriations and Armed Services Committee, two of the most powerful in the Senate. Russell became Byrd's mentor, and Byrd returned the favor by joining the fight against the landmark Civil Rights Act of 1964, at one point filibustering for 14 hours to stop the bill. "Men are not created equal today, and they were not created equal in 1776, when the Declaration of Independence was written," Byrd said. "Men and races of men differ in appearance, ways, physical power, mental capacity, creativity, and vision. . . . As citizens of this nation, our people are men and women who are unequal. Some of us are among the 'haves,' and some of us are among the 'have-nots.' Some of us succeed, and some of us fail. So it has always been, and so it will ever be."

Through most of the 1960s Byrd was chairman of the District of Columbia Appropriations Subcommittee and won national notice for the way he

---

* The Ralph Nader Congress Project compiled an eye-boggling list of facilities and projects Byrd acquired for the state. Just a few examples: forest products marketing laboratory at Princeton; expansion and remodeling of Bureau of Mines Building at Mount Hope; coal fly-ash research at West Virginia University; planning funds for an $800,000 Eagle Lake recreation facility; reconstruction of streets in Harpers Ferry National Historical Park; $400,000 for air traffic control tower at Greenbrier County Airport. . . . The list goes on and on. Senator Randolph's list of federal benefits for the state would be equally impressive. But the stagnation of the state's economy, all these stimuli notwithstanding, raises the question if anything short of fundamental political and social change can really pull West Virginia out of its economic morass.

badgered local welfare officers about the vigor of their enforcement of the man-in-the-house rule. He railed against the rates of illegitimacy and venereal disease of Washington's welfare population—the overwhelming majority of whom, of course, were black. Milton Viorst wrote caustically: "Some Senators, in the course of their careers, make their reputations as authorities on the armed services, on taxation, on foreign relations, on housing, on science and technology, on medical care. Senator Robert C. Byrd has made his reputation as an authority on the mating habits of Washington's underprivileged." Viorst also wrote of Byrd: "A Darwinist in fundamentalist clothing, he sneers at all but the fittest."

At the same time Byrd made war on Washington's welfare recipients, he did show a fine grasp of the intricacies of the District budget, supported higher federal appropriations for the city, and pressed for libraries, playgrounds, and swimming pools. But rank racism seemed to show through when he urged, at the time of the 1968 rioting after Martin Luther King's assassination, that looters be shot, "swiftly and mercilessly." He was just as aroused by antiwar demonstrations, which he called "a sickening spectacle, senseless, diabolical, disgraceful, abominable, and hurtful." He found the Supreme Court's busing decisions "monstrous and costly madness" and said "the Marxists, in their own godless scheming, could hardly have asked more from our Supreme Court than they have received." This record was apparently in President Nixon's mind when he spoke to Byrd in October 1971 about the possibility of taking a seat on the Supreme Court. Byrd toyed with the idea, then decided he was not interested. (Heated opposition was in sight, not only because of Byrd's record on civil rights and liberties but because he had no judicial or practical legal experience.)

By the early 1970s Byrd had amassed immense power in the U.S. Senate, with the prospect of more to come. In 1967 he had defeated Pennsylvania's Joseph Clark to become Secretary of the Democratic Caucus, and four years later he startled the country by upsetting Massachusetts' Edward Kennedy for the post of Democratic Whip. Byrd's formula for success was the same he applied to constituent relations: grinding, hard work, and attention to detail. He volunteered to do any kinds of jobs his fellow Democratic Senators wanted done—inserting items in the *Congressional Record* for absent colleagues, scheduling debate for their convenience, arranging pairs, acting as the Senate's parliamentary policeman. All this drudgery Byrd raised to high political art, and whenever he did a favor for a fellow Senator, he would send notes saying he had been pleased to help and looked forward to assisting in the future. After his defeat of Kennedy, these notes were often signed "Your Obedient, faithful Whip."

Byrd's eyes were clearly set on the Majority Leadership, which Mike Mansfield was expected to relinquish in 1976. That required some moves to the political center, however, and starting in 1972 Byrd moved in that direction by opposing Richard Kleindienst's nomination as Attorney General (in the wake of hearings that touched on political peddling by ITT), attacking Presidential budget cuts, and calling for a U.S. resumption of relations with

Cuba. When L. Patrick Gray was nominated to head the FBI, Byrd evoked the answer from Gray that White House counsel John Dean had "probably lied" to him about Watergate conspirator E. Howard Hunt. The questioning was a major factor in dissolving the White House cover-up and breaking open the Watergate scandal. In the 1974 hearings on Nelson Rockefeller's nomination to be Vice President, Byrd starred in questioning the nominee on how his immense wealth and oil stock holdings might influence his actions if Rockefeller ever advanced to the Presidency.

Whichever way the political winds blew in the mid- and late-1970s, one could predict with confidence that Byrd would be moving with them, forever advancing the political fortunes of the poor white boy from Crab Orchard.

Population losses have cut West Virginia down to four seats in the U.S. House, compared to the five it had from the 1910s through the 1950s. As chairman of the House Interstate and Foreign Commerce Committee, silver-crowned Harley O. Staggers, who represents the eastern part of the state, must be considered the most powerful man on the delegation. His committee's jurisdiction includes virtually all of the independent regulatory agencies of the government, consumer affairs, broadcasting and communications in general, petroleum and natural gas matters, and many others. In 1971, however, Staggers suffered a severe rebuke to his authority when the full House refused to vote the contempt citation he had sought against CBS and its president, Frank M. Stanton, for the network's refusal to supply untelevised material involving the controversial CBS documentary "The Selling of the Pentagon." The defeat also was a landmark in the slow and general decline of committee chairmen in the House.

The most interesting member of the delegation is unquestionably Ken Hechler, whose district encompasses several Ohio River counties and the grimly depressed southern part of the state. Before he even arrived in West Virginia in 1957, Hechler had gone through a varied career as a Budget Bureau official, professor at Columbia and Princeton, World War II combat historian and author of *The Bridge at Remagen,* assistant in the Truman White House, and research director of Adlai Stevenson's 1956 Presidential campaign. A widely circulated story—which Hechler, for the record, denies—is that he wanted to serve in Congress, had his students at a Long Island college survey the country for districts with weak Republican incumbents, and settled on West Virginia's 4th where an 82-year-old obstetrician, Dr. Will Neal ("I delivered the voters, you deliver the votes") seemed a likely target. The fact is that Hechler took a teaching assignment at Marshall College in Huntington and 14 months later, having become well known as a commentator on a local television station, announced for the Democratic nomination for the U.S. House. Congressman Neal had little to say in the race except that no foreigner should be allowed to represent the district. Hechler campaigned from dawn to evening in a red and white jeep with his name emblazoned on the side, got backing from a small army of students dedicated to his cause, and despite a meager budget was able to capitalize on the recession of 1958 to win a narrow victory.

Once ensconced in office, Hechler endeared himself to his West Virginia constituents by assiduous attention to their letters and requests, frequent home visits, and a steady supply of campaign stunts to keep his name in their minds. Among his House colleagues he got a reputation as a maverick, one might almost say oddball. A bachelor, he had no hobbies and worked prodigious hours. He wore rumpled suits and old scuffed shoes. His desk was forever piled with mountains of paper, reflecting a generally messy confusion throughout his office suite. He even insisted on writing every statement that went out over his name, a rare habit in the modern-day Congress. No matter what the legislative task, he "did his homework." When I asked to interview him for this book, he requested a question outline in advance so that he could use a few days to develop full and responsive answers. When we did talk, there was scarcely a question on which he waffled.

Yet through his first 10 years in Congress, as Brit Hume noted, Hechler hardly distinguished himself outside of his work on the Science and Astronautics Committee. He remained a generally obscure figure in Washington until the catalyzing event—the Farmington mine disaster. Then it was that Hechler made the bold statement about mine safety which I quoted earlier in this chapter. Before long he had led the successful battle which resulted in the Coal Mine Health and Safety Act of 1969, won the undying enmity of his old allies in the coal industry and Tony Boyle's UMW, and became a leading national spokesman for the banning of all strip mining. He campaigned for Joseph Yablonski and subsequently Arnold Miller for UMW president, risking his own personal safety in the process. In 1972 he survived a hostile redistricting that forced him into a race against another incumbent. Hechler's critics called him an outrageous ham; his friends said he was the most courageous Congressman West Virginia had had in a long time. And both were unquestionably right.

Notes on Places and the Press

The shape of West Virginia, John Gunther suggested, is rather like that of a squid or other odd marine animal. It is the only state with *two* panhandles. The Northern Panhandle cuts up like an arrow between Pennsylvania and Ohio, coming to a point northwest of Pittsburgh; it is heavily industrialized (great steel plants, chemicals along the Ohio River) and counts a large number of beer-drinking, muscular steelworkers in its population, many of them of Polish, Italian, Czech, and German stock.

The Eastern Panhandle is placid and rural by contrast; it consists of four counties that "overhand" Virginia and are only part of West Virginia because, during the Civil War, they included the Baltimore and Ohio Railroad line and thus controlled the westerly approaches to Washington. The most famous town is legendary Harper's Ferry, where the Civil War was made inevitable by John Brown's insurrection in October of 1859. Colorfully set between high mountains where the Shenandoah River meets the Potomac, and where three states (West Virginia, Maryland, and Virginia) converge,

Harper's Ferry today is a national historic park and retains much of its pre-Civil War appearance.*

Roughly speaking, West Virginia can be considered as a state of four broad regions. There is the Northern Panhandle and the counties just below it, fairly indistinguishable from nearby Pennsylvania and Ohio, a land of some coal mining, substantial industry and urbanization, and less poverty than in any other part of the state. The chief cities are Wheeling (population 48,188), a grimy steel town with one of the finest municipal parks in the U.S., and Morgantown (29,431), home of West Virginia University, problems with wide-open gambling, and the U.S. Department of Transportation's problem-plagued experimental rapid transit system, constructed in the early 1970s. The idea of the transit system was to relieve Morgantown's frequent and massive traffic jams, caused in large part by students going from one campus to another over the narrow streets of the mountainous town. The system was to operate with eight-passenger fiberglass cars, directed by computer, running along a 3.2-mile track. A lavish dedication of the system was indeed held in October 1972 after officials rushed to score points for the Nixon administration with urban voters in what one participant later called "an election-year hysteria." But the system, in effect, was built before it was fully designed. By 1974 it was not only not yet operational but had become a research and development nightmare. Federal and university officials were arguing about whether to complete the system at a cost of as much as $125 million (compared to the original estimate of $13.5 million), or to tear down the elevated track and write off the project as one of the great political-technical miscalculations of our time.

Eastern West Virginia contains both the panhandle of that name and a long string of rural counties where farming and cattle or sheep grazing are an important business. There is little coal mining, a minor amount of industrialization, and a substantial number of people living on some type of government check: payroll, welfare, veteran's benefits, social security, or unemployment. The east also contains the vast Monongahela National Forest, recently protected from clear-cutting in a landmark court victory by the environmentalists. (The decision was handed down by Federal Judge Robert E. Maxwell, a native West Virginian taking a courageous stand in his own state.) Tourism is important in this eastern region, anchored on the north by Harper's Ferry, on the south by White Sulphur Springs.

Of southern West Virginia, with its dozens of sad coal towns, depressed

* The story of how John Brown and his 18 abolitionist companions seized the federal arsenal at Harper's Ferry and held it for 36 hours, failing to attract the support they hoped for but sending tremors of fear through the white Southland and galvanizing the abolitionist cause, is beyond our scope here. I would commend to readers Truman Nelson's brilliant 1973 book, *The Old Man: John Brown at Harper's Ferry,* in which Nelson throws into sharp relief the indomitability and heroism of Brown and his men and expounds the thesis that Brown's real intent was a classic coup, as distinguished from either insurrection or revolution. Brown hoped to repair, after the assault, to a base in the Virginia mountains where a limited number of escaped slaves and whites would gather, creating a situation in which the white abolitionists of the North would be compelled to use arms or political means to achieve their liberation and that of all slaves. Brown's last written words, just before he was executed at Charles Town, underscore the point: "I John Brown am now quite *certain* that the crimes of this *guilty land* will never be purged *away,* but with Blood. I had *as I now think: vainly* flattered myself that without *very much* bloodshed, it might be done."

living conditions, and vicious and vacuous county political machines, we have written earlier in the chapter.

Finally, there is the western part of the state, which includes the state capital at Charleston (population 71,505), the industrialized Kanawha Valley, and then a number of cities facing the Ohio River. The two largest of these, Huntington (74,315) and Parkersburg (44,208), have a distinctively Midwestern flavor and remain—despite major steel and chemical plants—two of the state's most attractive urban centers. One looks across the river from these towns to the bluffs on the Ohio side, views the busy river commerce, and forgets the feeling of isolation prevalent in so much of West Virginia.

The city of Charleston has a special grace by virtue of its dramatic river setting—the combination of relatively flat center-city terrain surrounded by craggy hills, the grand view along the Kanawha with its several bridges, the stately homes to be seen in the hills, and especially the State Capitol, a magnificent design by Cass Gilbert in Italian Renaissance style, its dome glowing in a rich gold so incongruous for poor West Virginia. A part of the center city has been renewed in recent years, and a handful of towering new office buildings put up by the major banks give an aura of progress and modernity.

Charleston is alive and stimulated because it is West Virginia's seat of government and the financial center of the state, and because its population lacks the static quality of so many West Virginia places. The big chemical companies—DuPont, Union Carbide, FMC, and Monsanto—are chiefly responsible for this, because, in varying degrees, they bring a constant infusion of scientists and skilled technicians.

Withal, it is a city with problems. The rich supply of natural resources in the Great Kanawha Valley, including brine, coal, sulphur, oil, and gas, made it possible for Charleston to become one of the world's great chemical centers. But in recent years the chemical industry has shifted markedly to areas where gas is more plentiful and harbor facilities superior—i.e., to places like the Texas and Louisiana Gulf Coast. Some major chemical and glass companies withdrew from Charleston or curtailed their operations there during the 1960s—a principal reason for the city's 17 percent loss of population in that decade. New industry is discouraged by the valley's narrow confines, which make usable land expensive and building sites scarce. Moreover, the area has suffered from a poor press and negative image in the national business community. To reverse the trend, a "Committee of 100" with broad support from local industry and labor, was formed in 1970. Its first president was Angus Peyton, a forceful young attorney and former state commerce commissioner. The idea was to let the outlying areas develop new manufacturing jobs while Charleston became the regional financial-service-medical-cultural center. Peyton acknowledged, however, the immense difficulties in reversing the area's perceptible economic decline.

Then there is the question of pollution in the Kanawha Valley: I have yet to meet anyone, except an official of the industry, who suggests that chemical plants make pleasant neighbors. One misty morning in 1970 I drove through the valley toward Charleston, witnessing for the first time the succession of chemical plants exuding smoke and steam and fumes at every pore, the emissions of many colors, the smell oppressive. Pollution controls have begun, however belatedly, to ameliorate the problem, but a return visit three years later suggested it may be a long time before the chemical pollutant problem is licked.

Charleston has a median family income figure some $2,000 over the state average, but there are pockets of wretched poverty within the county and inside the city itself, especially the black Triangle neighborhood "at the back end of town." The people of Triangle rose up in angry protest in the early '70s in an attempt to stop a proposed six-lane interstate road from taking their homes and splitting their community. One of Charleston city's worst civic headaches of recent years was a determined and bitter strike of mostly black garbage collectors and street department workers seeking union recognition—shades of Memphis in a state proud of its record for tolerance.

Then, in autumn 1974, the schools and even the mines of Kanawha County were shut down for several days in a dispute over new school textbooks which fundamentalist ministers and blue-collar parents alleged were "un-Christian, unpatriotic, and pornographic." The protesters said the books were deliberately designed to question the infallibility of God and undermine parental authority. The protest was a unique arising in America—except in racial incidents—of the class of hard-working, conservative folk, deeply suspicious of the mores of the mass media and other opinion makers, who have rarely had a way to make their voice heard. In Charleston, however, their roving picket lines proved extraordinarily effective and forced an at least temporary withdrawal of some $500,000 worth of books from the schools. The byproducts of the protest movement were boycotts of businesses, arrests, threats, beatings and a shooting.

One bright point in Charleston has been the evolution of the *Gazette*, its leading paper, away from the conservative and property-oriented stance it had in the early 1950s. Under publisher W. E. (Ned) Chilton III and editor Harry Hoffman, the *Gazette* has developed into a progressive and sometimes crusading force; these days, in fact, the conservatives regularly accuse the paper of giving only one (i.e., the liberal) side of the news. Quite the opposite ideological slant, however, is apparent in most of West Virginia's other daily newspapers. Except for the *Gazette* and Charleston's other paper, the *Daily Mail*, only the Huntington *Herald-Dispatch* even bothers to send its own reporter to cover the legislature. All the others depend on the understaffed AP and UPI bureaus. And not a single West Virginia paper, not even the *Gazette*, has a full-time correspondent in Washington. Byrd and Randolph and the others can run their affairs by press release—and do. So the miasma of West Virginians' ignorance about their own leadership and government continues, and one can easily despair about the consequences for public life in poor, beleaguered, exploited West Virginia—the state the times passed by.

KENTUCKY

DIVERSE, GENTEEL, AND VIOLENT

HORSES, COAL, BOURBON WHISKEY, BORDERLAND, a state of Ohio River ports sharing the industry of the Midwest and fields of tobacco beckoning Southward, a land marked at once by Bluegrass gentility and mountaineer feudin' and destitution—Kentucky has always meant many things to America.

But first it was the "Eden of the West," and in the 1760s and '70s, as Daniel Boone and the other first explorer-settlers penetrated the barrier of the Appalachians, there was a widely believed legend that they were moving into a land of milk and honey spread from the Cumberland Gap to the waters of the Ohio. In reality, of course, they were moving into an uncharted wilderness, a hard and treacherous land fraught with Indian perils.

Most of Kentucky was virginal forest, and no more so than in the East Kentucky mountains, where a surprising number of the unskilled English and Scotch-Irish settlers stopped after they had passed over the Wilderness Road leading westward from the Cumberland Gap. Ancestrally dirt-poor, they instinctively claimed as their own the first land they could find—no matter how inhospitable. There they hunkered down in narrow hollows between interminable hillcrests, bred and inbred, chopped away enough of the forest to start hardscrabble farming, and lost much contact with the outside world. There, on the Cumberland Plateau, they may still be found in amazing numbers, indentured not as their ancestors were to affluent Tidewater farmers, but rather to the behemoth of coal.

There was also in Kentucky, however, land worthy of Boone's description of "a second paradise." This was the fabulous Bluegrass region in the state's center, pleasant and rolling country enriched by decaying beds of limestone that produced grasses so rich in calcium and phosphorous that they strengthened the bones of livestock and would soon foster growth of some of the world's most magnificent horses. The more knowledgeable Revolutionary War veterans pressed westward until they found these lands, and here sprang up cities like Lexington, soon to become known as "the Athens of the West" through Transylvania Seminary (later College), the first institution of higher learning beyond the Appalachians. Lexington and the Bluegrass in general soon proved a powerful magnet for aristocratic Virginians and Marylanders, whose gentlemanly and worldly ways, as distinctive as the inward-looking ways of the mountaineers, survive to our day.

And then there was Louisville, and the river. Down the Ohio, to the place where General George Rogers Clark, the Indian fighter, had put up a blockhouse fort, came the servants, the livestock, and the implements of land-hungry opportunists of every stripe. The port became a bustling, bawdy site, on its way to being Kentucky's greatest city.

From Golden West to Classic Border State

Through the last years of the 18th century and the first of the 19th, Kentucky was the booming golden West, the California of its day. In 1792, when its divorce from Virginia was final and Congress admitted Kentucky as the first state west of the Alleghenies, the territory held 74,000 people. By 1820 that figure had swelled to 564,000—larger than five of the original 13 states. In 1820, in fact, almost 6 percent of the population of the United States lived in Kentucky, a figure never again to be equaled. (In 1970 the figure was 1.6 percent.) Early in the 19th century its borders were extended clear to the Mississippi in the "Jackson Purchase" lands, bought from the Chickasaw Indians by a commission headed by Andrew Jackson. The Indian problem, so grave in Kentucky's first days, had largely subsided by the time of statehood; after the Battle of Fallen Timbers, in 1794, there would never again be an Indian attack.

The lion's share of those hundreds of thousands of new settlers put their roots down in the land, placing an agrarian stamp on Kentucky society that is still distinguishable. Far into the early 19th century, Kentucky was one of America's leading states in the sale of mules, in production of hemp and corn and hogs, and in that other distinctive regional crop—tobacco. The English and Scotch-Irish settlers had brought tobacco seeds with them from Virginia and North Carolina, and to this day tobacco remains the mainstay of Kentucky agriculture, grown in every county of the state.

The "master farmer" of early Kentucky was none other than Henry Clay, the state's leading national figure from the early 1800s to his death in 1852. Thomas D. Clark points out in his splendid volume, *Kentucky: Land of Contrast*, that Clay's estate near Lexington was "a model farm for his day." There Clay grew hemp, fine livestock, and, of course, tobacco. His scientific interest in livestock breeding was so keen that he might have become a major figure in U.S. agricultural history if public life had not been his major concern.

Clay was as important to Kentucky—and, in a way, to the entire United States—as Andrew Jackson was for Tennessee in its formative years. As United States Senator, Speaker of the House, Secretary of State, and several times an actual or potential candidate for the Presidency, Clay fought for internal improvements to build the young nation, championed Latin American freedom, and, through his early leadership of the Whigs, contributed to development of the two-party system in American politics. Most important of all, he moved heaven and earth in one attempt after another to compromise the issue of slavery that threatened to tear the fledgling nation apart. He was the author of the compromises of 1820 and 1850, earning the title of the "Great Pacificator." Clay might have been able to win the Presidency, as Jackson did, if he had not become so identified with the moneyed upper class of his time.

Kentucky was never again, in fact, to play as vital a role in national affairs as it did in the early 19th century and up to and through the Civil War. Caught up in the expansionist frontier spirit, Kentucky's Clay and Congressman Richard M. Johnson were leaders of the "Young War Hawks" who wanted to annex Canada and attack the British a year before the War of 1812. Some 25,000 Kentuckians—five times the number requested—fought in that war. Legion were the Kentuckians, great and obscure, whose adventuring spirit took them to Ohio and to the Indiana, Illinois, and Missouri territories, and on to the far West, while Kentucky itself was still green behind the ears. Even Daniel Boone paddled on to a new home in Missouri. The Sublettes, from Dick's River Valley, became some of the most famous fur traders of the trails leading west from St. Louis. Christopher (Kit) Carson of Kentucky's Madison County was famed for many a Western venture, including his role as scout and guide for John C. Fremont's expedition. Alexander William Doniphan of Madison County commanded militiamen against the Mormons (but saved the life of Joseph Smith). Doniphan's 1st Missouri Mounted Volunteers made a fabled overland march, from Fort Leavenworth to Santa Fe, Chihuahua, and Matamoros, 3,600 miles overland and 2,000 by water. Alexander Majors organized an historic overland freighting firm across the Western ranches, and also the famed pony express.

And as Americans were later to discover, two births of profound significance took place, less than a year apart, on Kentucky frontier farms. Abraham Lincoln was born to Tom Lincoln and his young wife Nancy Hanks in a simple log cabin on Sinking Spring farm, on the waters of the Nolin River, in 1809—only three decades after Tom's father, a Revolutionary vet-

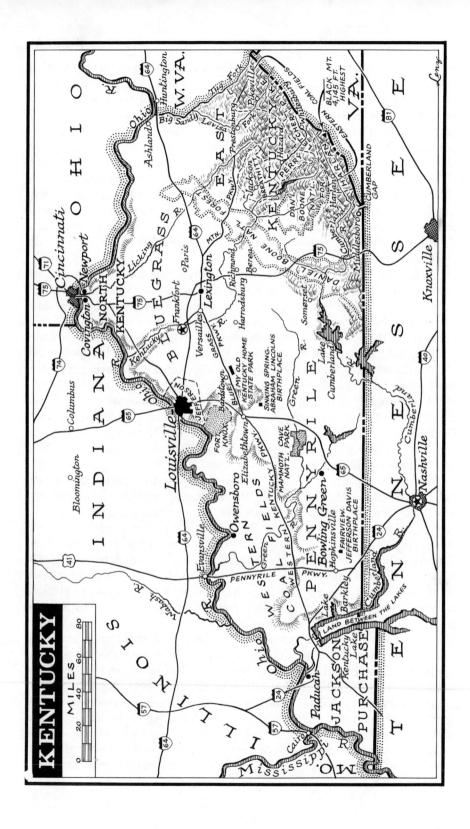

eran, had left Virginia, coming over the Cumberland Gap to take up farming in the "Eden of the West." Jefferson Davis, the tenth child of Samuel Davis, an emigrant from Georgia, was born in a fertile valley of the Pennyroyal section. While the future Union and Confederate Presidents were still small boys, their families were swept up in the movement to lands thought more promising. The Lincolns moved to Indiana, and eventually to Illinois; the Davises went downriver and settled in the rich cotton lands of Mississippi. "This fortuitous parting of the ways of two backwoods families," Thomas Clark wrote, "was no doubt one of the most exciting ever to occur in restless, transitory Kentucky. By mere accident young Lincoln and Davis found themselves thrust into two different sectional settings which in time would force them into political and military rivalry in which the fate of the Union itself would be involved."

It is difficult to think of a state in which pro- and antislavery sentiment, loyalty to the Union and affection for the South were so exquisitely balanced as in Kentucky. Here was a state settled chiefly by Southerners, yet a place where the fabric of society, and the economic situation of the people, was much closer to the North. The lively commerce along the hundreds of miles of Ohio River flank, for instance, made Kentucky just as much a part of the old Northwest as Indiana, Ohio, or Illinois; yet if it was buying manufactured goods from the North, it was generally selling them to the South, and could scarcely afford to imperil its personal and commercial ties to Dixie.

From the start, Kentucky had a significant slave population—in fact, Daniel Boone's trail-blazing party in 1775 had several Negro slaves in its number, two of whom were killed in a raid by the Shawnee Indians. As the Kentucky frontier opened, slaves put in yeoman labor in clearing timber from the fields, erecting the log cabins, building the limestone fences of the central part of the state, and tending the fields. Nevertheless, from the very start there were Kentuckians who saw that the institution of slavery was the very negation of the principles of individual liberty the frontiersmen held most highly. And once the land was cleared, the need for slaves was less in Kentucky than in the steamy black and delta lowlands of states like Mississippi and Alabama. Slaves could be, and were, used by the big farming operations in the Bluegrass and Purchase regions, but on the whole Kentucky's growing season was too short to make feasible the production of cotton, the crop for which slaves were most needed.

Thus Kentucky was to become both a hotbed of abolitionist sentiment and a chief marketplace for slaves to be used in the new cotton states to the south. There were infamous slave markets in Lexington and Louisville— "repulsive enough," Clark noted, "to turn the heart and stomach of even the most rabid slaveholder." Kentucky's abolitionists, though often harassed, agitated continuously against the slave trade. A law passed by the legislature in 1833, forbidding the importation of slaves from Virginia or Maryland to be resold further south, was a point of fierce controversy and the issue of countless election campaigns until the Civil War. There was even an American

Colonization Society, headed by Henry Clay (himself a slaveholder), which advocated returning slaves to Africa. The atrocities sometimes practiced on slaves, and the brutality of families divided in the slave trade, were catalogued by Kentucky's Theodore Weld in his book *American Slavery as It Is: Testimony of a Thousand Witnesses*. Cassius M. Clay, who had fallen under the influence of William Lloyd Garrison and other abolitionists when he studied at Yale, returned to publish a weekly emancipator newspaper, *The True American*. Proslavery forces were all the more enraged with Clay because his father was a large slaveholder, and they eventually ran him out of the state. Then there was Harriet Beecher Stowe of Cincinnati, who learned just enough about Kentucky slavery and the heartrending aspects of the slave trade to write *Uncle Tom's Cabin*, one of the most powerful documents of social protest in the history of literature.

Most Kentuckians, however, were not abolitionists, and in fact thought the movement a grave offense against the South. One reason for this was that they had generally observed a more paternalistic form of slavery than the lurid conditions described in abolitionist literature. Though most did not own slaves, they invariably knew people who did. (Despite the sale of Kentucky blacks to more southerly states, the slave population of the state rose steadily from 40,000 in 1800 to 225,000 on the eve of the Civil War.)

In the election of 1860, it is worth noting, not a single county in Kentucky went for Lincoln. The governor at the time, Beriah Magoffin, was as strong for slavery as he was against any moves that would dissolve the Union. And so when the war began, Kentucky officially declared its neutrality. And when President Lincoln ordered Kentucky to send four regiments to the Union Army, Magoffin wired back: "I say, emphatically, Kentucky will furnish no troops for the wicked purpose of subduing her sister Southern states." Yet in the 1861 elections, a General Assembly consisting of 93 Union sympathizers and 35 favoring the States Rights cause was elected.

The struggle for Kentucky's loyalty was soon to be won by the Union, a development for which the Confederacy was chiefly responsible because it moved rapidly to blockade the Mississippi River with a mile-long chain and to seize the Cumberland Gap, a site considered the Gibraltar of the West. The legislature, over Magoffin's veto, called for an unconditional withdrawal of all Confederate armies and, when that demand was not met, officially ended Kentucky's neutrality and aligned the state with the Union, authorizing the War Department to draft 40,000 Kentuckians to drive out the Confederates. Far more than Jefferson Davis and the Southern leaders, Lincoln understood the political situation of the Border States, and Kentucky in particular. As Edward Cronan Smith wrote in *The Borderland and the Civil War*:

If [Lincoln] had based his policy upon the rights of a downtrodden race, as another Republican President might have done, he would have had the North with him, but he would have lost the Borderland and with it, all hope of reestablishing the Union. He was extremely careful not to make this the issue. Instead, he risked having only the lukewarm support of the North by appealing, from the beginning of his administration, almost solely to the nationalist sentiments of all the people.

That policy, of course, was bound to have powerful appeal in the land of Henry Clay, the fierce nationalist and great compromiser on North-South issues. Smith also noted of Lincoln:

> In his relations with Kentucky, he conceded points, he tacitly recognized an assumed neutrality, and he delayed important military operations, all out of deference to the feeling of States' rights which existed there. He showed such a disinclination to favor emancipation as to provoke an abolitionist gibe that "Mr. Lincoln would like to have God on his side, but he must have Kentucky." The Southern leaders, on the other hand, utterly failed to grasp the essential nature of the situation. They adopted an intractable and dictatorial policy, finally ending in a foolish invasion of the state which turned it toward the active and powerful support of the federal government.

By the end of 1862, after the Confederates had launched a bloody but ultimately unsuccessful attempt to reach the Bluegrass and establish a provisional government on Kentucky soil, the South was so weakened that it was never again equipped to seize or hold significant areas of Kentucky.

The Legacy of Violence

In terms of physical devastation, Kentucky suffered relatively little in the Civil War—in stark contrast, for instance, to its neighbor to the South, Confederate Tennessee. But the state was to pay a gruesome price for this fratricidal conflict. Young hotheads of the Bluegrass and Purchase areas, understanding little of the fundamental issues, marched off to join up with the Confederacy. Mountain boys from eastern Kentucky, used to physical hardships, bored with the monotony of life in the intermontane fastness, tended to sign up for the Union Army. The overwhelming fact was the division of every area between Southern and Northern allegiance. Cousins divided, and so quite often, did fathers, sons, and brothers. At first the divisions might be amicable enough, but as the casualty reports came back from the bloody battlefields of Virginia, and as raids and brigandage began to spread across the Kentucky countryside, differences hardened into bitter hatreds. The ill-regulated Kentucky Home Guard included many men willing to settle old grudges and open new feuds under the guise of public authority. Union and Confederate troops alike were guilty of thousands of guerrilla raids, and guerrillas appeared in almost every county.

The recorded costs of the war were grave enough: 76,000 Kentuckians sent to fight on the Union side, 26,000 to the Confederacy, Kentuckians killing each other from Shiloh to Sherman's last march. Ten thousand died in battle, another 20,000 of disease and exposure. Approximately half the Kentuckians who reached manhood between 1850 and 1860, according to Clark's history, were either destroyed or disabled by war. "Kentucky blood spilled in the war," he wrote, "was bitter and black. Hatreds and enmities ran deep—and ruins, spiritual and physical, crippled at least two future generations emotionally."

Nowhere were the results more appalling than in the east Kentucky mountains. From every valley, Harry T. Caudill noted in *Night Comes to the Cumberlands*, came both Union and Confederate men. And they did not spill their blood on the battlefields alone. From trifling incidents grew carnage on an incredible scale:

Men were killed [Caudill wrote] as they left their cabins in the early dawn. They were ambushed on the trails and shot from the sheltering forests. Sometimes a cabin was attacked under cover of darkness and set afire, and the family shot as they fled the flames. Still children of the frontier, with traditions of warfare acquired in the cruel border struggles, they fought each other now with the same brutality and disregard of chivalrous restraints with which their grandsires had fought the hated Cherokee, Shawnee and Choctaw.

Caudill was not writing dry history. A story from his own family, which had its grisly parallel in hollow after hollow across the hills, illustrated the point:

As a child I heard my paternal grandmother tell countless tales of her wartime childhood. She was eleven when the conflict began, and when her Confederate father rode away to join General Lee in "Old Virginny." In 1864 he came home on a "crop leave"—to plant corn and vegetables for his family. One day while he was at work in his field a half-dozen pro-Union guerrillas swept down on him. Seeing that escape was impossible and resistance futile, he attempted to surrender. But the guerrillas were implacable and riddled him with bullets. His teen-age daughter held his shattered head while his brains ran out onto her apron lap. To the day of her death she was an unreconstructed Rebel, and her eyes glinted and her lips tightened into a thin line at the merest mention of even the grandchildren of her father's killers.

And then there was the account of Frank Wilkeson, a Union veteran who recounted, in *The Recollections of a Private Soldier,** what he had seen in a federal camp for victims of the carnage in the Southern highlands:

At Stevenson [Alabama] there was a large refugee camp, where many women and children and a few crippled or age-enfeebled men had sought refuge from attacks by murderous bands of guerrillas. . . . These pretended soldiers, it mattered not which uniform they disgraced by wearing, were, almost without exception, robbers and murderers, who sought to enrich themselves by plundering their defenceless neighbors. They rode through the Southern highlands, killing men, burning houses, stealing cattle and horses. To-day a band of guerrillas, alleged Unionists, ravaged a mountain district. They killed their personal enemies, who they said were Confederate sympathizers, and destroyed their property. Tomorrow other guerillas burned Union men's houses, and shot so-called Union men to death. This relentless mountain warfare was exceedingly hard on women and children. Agriculture was suspended in the highlands. No man dared to till his lean fields for fear that some hidden enemy might kill him. No stack of unthrashed grain or garner of corn was safe from the torch. The defenseless women and children were starved out of their homes, and they sought safety and food within the Union lines. Our government established extensive camps for these war-stricken Southerners.

Curious to see these people I spent a day in camp at Stevenson. I saw hun-

* Published by G. P. Putnam's Sons in 1886.

dreds of tall, gaunt, frouzy-headed, snuff-dipping, pipe-smoking, unclean women. Some were clad in homespun stuffs, others in calico, others in bagging. Many of them were unshod. There were hundreds and hundreds of vermin-infested and supremely dirty children in the camp. Some families lived in tents, some in flimsy barracks. All lived in discomfort. All drew rations from the government. All were utterly poor. It seemed that they were too poor to ever again get a start in life. Haggard, wind- and sun- and storm-burnt women, their gaunt forms showing plainly through their rags, sat, or lolled, or stood in groups, talking drawlingly. Their features were as expressionless as wood, their eyes lustreless. I talked to many of these women. All told stories of murder, of arson, of blood-curdling scenes. One, gray-eyed, bony, square-jawed, barefooted, forty years old, clad in a dirty, ragged, homespun dress, sat on a log outside of a tent sucking a corncob pipe. Her tow-headed children played around her. She told me that before the war she and her husband owned a mountain farm, where they lived in comfort; that they owned horses, cattle, and pigs, and raised plenty of corn and tobacco. One day her husband, who was a Union man, was shot dead as he stood by her side in the door of their house. She buried him in a grave she dug herself. She and her children tended the crops. These were burned shortly after they gathered them. Then her swine were stolen, and her cows and horse driven off. Finally her oldest son, a boy of fourteen, was shot dead at the spring, and her house and barn were burned in broad daylight, and she and her children were left homeless and without food on a desolate mountain side. Many of her neighbors had been burned out the same day. They joined forces and wandered down the mountain, hungry, cold, with little children tugging at women's dresses, to a Union camp. From there they had been sent to Stevenson. Long before this woman had finished her story she rose to her feet, her face was white with intense passion, her eyes with fire, and her gaunt form quivered with excitement as she gesticulated savagely. She said that if she lived, and her boys lived, she would have vengeance on the men who had murdered her husband and son, and destroyed her home. As she talked so talked all. These women were saturating their children's minds with the stories of the wrongs they had endured. I heard them repeat over and over to their children the names of men which they were never to forget, and whom they were to kill when they had sufficient strength to hold a rifle. The stolid manners, the wooden faces, the lustreless eyes, the drawling speech of these people, concealed the volcanoes of fire and wrath which burned within their breasts. . . . It was easy to foresee the years of bloodshed, of assassination, of family feuds, that would spring from the recollections of the war, handed from widowed mothers to savage-tempered sons, in the mountain recesses of Georgia, Tennessee, Alabama, and Kentucky. And long after the war closed rifles continued to crack in remote mountain glens, as the open accounts between families were settled.

Indeed, some of the darkest chapters of American history were to be written in the mountains of Kentucky and the other Southern highlands over the next half century. The storied battles of the Kentucky McCoys and West Virginia Hatfields had their origin in the Civil War. There were the less familiar but equally bloody struggles of the Bakers and Whites in Clay County, the Tollivers and Martins in Rowan County, and the Frenches and Eversoles in the Kentucky River hills around Hazard. If any reader has taste for a blood-curdling tale of cruelty and murder, on a scale rarely approached in any nation in any time of history, he should read Thomas Clark's account of the war between the Hargises and their neighbors the Cockrills and their kin and countless bystanders in east Kentucky's Breathitt County between 1890 and 1910. Hired assassins struck down leading citizens in broad daylight in Jackson, the county seat, and within the very walls of the county court-house. Yet even when the law finally began to put some of the murderers behind bars, they did not remain there long because the Hargises had a friend in Governor J. C. W. Beckham, who pardoned no less than 37 Breathitt County hoodlums. Such feuds could not be dismissed as the excesses of illiterate backwoods families. Lawyers, judges, sheriffs, and merchants fought so bitterly that even their casual associates were often slain in revenge. According to writer Bill Surface, author of *The Hollow* (Coward-Mc-Cann, 1971), some 2,800 persons in Kentucky's mountains died from vendettas that resulted only in an occasional conviction.

The pattern of murder and mayhem that infected Kentucky political life was laid out for the nation to see in episode after episode, all the way down to recent times. In 1899, for instance, Democrat William Goebel, a machine candidate from Covington, ran for governor in a vitriolic campaign aimed against the moneyed interests and the Louisville & Nashville Railroad in particular. William S. Taylor, the Republican nominee, was declared the winner by a narrow margin, but the Democrats controlling the legislature up-set the returns and declared Goebel the winner instead. The L & N Railroad people, anticipating just such a contingency, transported a thousand angry, armed, and frequently intoxicated Republicans from the hills to the state capital at Frankfort. Goebel was shot down in the Frankfort streets, but as he lay dying he was sworn in as governor. Beckham, his lieutenant governor, took over on Goebel's death, and for five weeks Kentucky had two governors. Finally the courts decided against Taylor; not long after, choosing discretion over valor, he fled Kentucky.

The fruits of political violence were apparent in the 1904–1908 period when Governor Beckham, reelected in a tumultuous election in 1903, refused to lift a finger to stop the nightraiding and beatings of Kentucky's infamous "Black Patch War." The trouble was started by farmers of the dark tobacco belt in western Kentucky, who were up in arms about the machinations of the "tobacco trust" they held responsible for prices that were driving them to the point of starvation. When some farmers refused to join them in their boycott of the trust, they rode through the countryside at night, destroying crops, burning barns, and whipping recalcitrant farmers. The violence did not subside until tobacco prices rose and a new governor declared martial law in Calloway County, bringing several of the terrorists to trial.

In the early 1930s Kentucky society again seemed on the verge of anarchy as gunfire cracked across the coal fields of Harlan and Perry County in the decisive struggle of the United Mine Workers to organize the coal mines there. Old mountain hatreds, excessive partisan politics, and the abuses of the legions of armed company police and deputy sheriffs all compounded a human tragedy in which 56 men, women, and children were killed in Harlan County alone in 1933. There were dynamitings, murders, and pitched battles in Harlan and Perry.

Even to this day, Kentuckians practice such an intense brand of politics that fatalities, especially in the eastern hills, are not uncommon. Brothers have been known to kill brothers, and shootings have occurred over such offices as school board positions. In 1971, at Goose Creek in Clay County, the Democratic and Republican election judges got involved in a gun battle watched by observers peering through the windows of the polling place, in an elementary school. When the smoke had cleared, the Democratic judge, James Smith, had a bullet hole through his hand. The Republican, 74-year-old John Mills, a retired schoolteacher, lay dead on the floor.

Kentucky Politics: Style Over Substance and the Spoils of Office

Style, rather than substance, has been the most important thing about Kentucky politics over the years. In what other state under the Stars and Stripes, one asks, is politics such an all-engrossing game? Kentuckians like politics so much they have elections every year, choosing national officials in even years, state and local officials in the odd. In this nonstop political theater, there is never a dark night—and scarcely enough respite between elections for Kentucky officeholders to get down to the serious business of governing.

And in what state, one may ask, have personalities and political oratory —from the thunderings of Henry Clay to the humor and partisanship of Alben Barkley to the bluntness and malarkey of a "Happy" Chandler—so engrossed the public? And again, in what state have spoils politics been played so intensely, so constantly, with so much skulduggery, to the general exclusion of serious issues? Again, few competitors spring to mind.

Strong and independent political parties have never been a hallmark of the Kentucky scene, but a word should be said about partisan balances. In the decades preceding the Civil War the Whig party, controlled by the Bourbon slaveholders of the Bluegrass in coalition with the poorer folk of the mountain areas, won most elections. The Whigs' opponents were the Jacksonian Democrats, chiefly farmers of the Outer Bluegrass and western Kentucky. After the Civil War, Reconstruction forced the ex-slaveholding Whigs into the Democratic party; led by a series of "redeemer" politicians, many of them ex-Confederates, they formed a winning coalition by assembling the poorer farmers on their side. But the Republicans, with strong support from the eastern mountain areas that had sided with Lincoln in the Civil War, as well as the newly enfranchised Negroes, were strong enough to get about 40 percent of the vote in most elections for governor. The Democratic majority began to disintegrate in the 1890s when western Kentucky farmers, upset about high freight rates and depression, broke with their Bourbon allies to vote Populist. The result was the election of the first Republican governors since the Civil War; Republicans were able, in fact, to win five of nine governorship elections between 1895 and 1927, their vote swollen by the rapidly expanding population of the eastern Kentucky coal-producing counties, plus substantial support in the growing cities. The state went Republican for President in 1924 and 1928, and a period of solid Republican control seemed possible.

The Depression and the New Deal changed that. The Negro vote went Democratic, and the coal miners—under the influence of the United Mine Workers—went Democratic too. So the Republicans remained a distinct minority, and Democrats won all crucial elections, until well after World War II.

The Democrats became so confident of their majorities, however, that they luxuriated in fierce and often quite senseless factional disputes. This gave the Republicans an opportunity to recoup. Once the Republicans carried Kentucky for Dwight Eisenhower and three times for Richard Nixon. They won virtually all the U.S. Senate elections between the late 1940s and the late 1960s. At one point the state had a Republican governor, two Republican U.S. Senators, Republicans in control of three of the seven U.S. House seats, and Republican control of Louisville. In elections for the legislature and most state offices, however, the Republicans remained a distinct minority—as they have in party registration, which was 66.6 percent Democratic and only 30.6 Republican in 1973. Kentucky in recent times has been said to have a three-party system—two Democratic factions of constantly changing composition, plus the Republicans living off the patronage crumbs thrown them by the Democrats and occasionally closing in to win the governorship or other major local offices when the Democratic factional fighting becomes too ferocious or divisive.

Only a foolish man or woman, however, would predict automatic Democratic dominance of Kentucky politics in the years to come. The state shares, with all others, the breakdown of traditional party loyalties. Relatively speaking, this is a fairly conservative state, especially in matters economic and social. But on race issues it is not a conservative state; otherwise, blacks would not have enjoyed, for so long, unhampered access to the ballot box. It is worthy of note that in 1968 George Wallace got only 18 percent of the Kentucky vote, not a great deal more than his national average of 13.5 percent and certainly far less than the 34 percent he received in neighboring Tennessee, a member of the old Confederacy.

Thus by all outward standards, there is no more reason that Kentucky today should be a "normally Democratic" state than Ohio, for example, or Indiana. But Kentuckians themselves continue to vote generally Democratic in the manner of people born into a religion who continue to conform to its rituals even after the light of true faith has flickered out.

Over the span of Kentucky's history, its vivid politics were in large measure a fruit of the state's isolation, its poverty, and its low levels of education. The isolation made the people look inward and derive much of their entertainment from political campaigns. Now television is minimizing that, broadening people's horizons and also reducing the hours spent at political rallies or discussing candidates in country stores and courthouses. Increasing income levels mean that fewer people must claw for patronage jobs as their sole hope of a decent paycheck. And as people get more and better years of schooling, they become too sophisticated to swallow the old political buffoonery or to tolerate corruption to the extent they used to.

Still, many of the old forms hold on, even if in reduced measure, and they go far toward explaining the uniqueness of Kentucky civilization, past and present:

The Counties and Their Rings. Kentucky inherited the county system from England by way of Virginia, and ever since old Fincastle County was organized in 1774, the county has been the essential unit of government in the state. The number of counties, in fact, continued to multiply until the present number of 120 was reached in 1912. The ostensible argument for each new county was usually how far it was to the nearest courthouse, the idea being that the trip should never take more than a day on muleback. The real reason was that county governments afforded splendid and multitudinous opportunities to get close to the public trough. The hungry office seekers had a wonderful array of jobs open to them as each new county formed, and one can still drive through Kentucky and see countless highway posters proclaiming the merits of various candidates for county judge or jailer, coroner or county clerk, sheriff or member of the county school board. Each county has the full complement of these offices, even though there are now 34 counties with less than 10,000 people, and one with only 2,163. Ask a Kentuckian where he comes from, and unless it is Louisville or Lexington, he'll usually name his county, not his town.

The whole system seems to smack of an outmoded, agrarian past. As Thomas Clark wrote, the rural Kentucky courthouse adorns main squares of towns across the state, sometimes sitting astride main roads. "It is used and abused with equal vengeance. In many places the temples of justice long ago become king-sized spittoons. They give off odors of unwashed bodies, tobacco juice, and public toilets. It takes a lot of loafing and the passage of time to produce the mellow aroma of a rural Kentucky courthouse."

Yet the county is where essential power resides. Each governor has his man or small committee—a local county "ring"—in simple relationship to him. The administration man or his crowd is expected to "deliver" the county on election day. In return, all state patronage—jobs, contracts, and assorted other favors—is surrendered to the local boys. "The courthouse gangs can defeat anything," a group of rather bitter Louisville civic leaders told me one evening. As a prime example they pointed to a new model constitution, including various valuable innovations, on which the voters had to decide in 1966. The courthouse rings saw a peril to their jobs, and the constitution failed to win approval in a single county.

Spoils. This leads us to a fuller look at patronage, the mother's milk of Kentucky politics. The power to dispense jobs and government business is particularly awesome in the poorer counties. The school superintendent often controls the largest payroll, decides who will be hired as a teacher, coach, or bus driver, determines who supplies food, oil, maintenance, and insurance for the schools, and in recent years, often who gets relatively lucrative positions with the federal antipoverty program. Through the cumulative power of their offices, Bill Surface observed, some school superintendents had perpetuated themselves or their relatives in office for 30 to 42 years. Their kinfolk and friends were also in an excellent position to win other county offices.

Clan, in fact, plays a stunning role in Kentucky county life. Sons, daughters, wives, cousins, and nephews show up on public payrolls by the score. And family ties are immensely important in getting elected in the first place. Several years ago, when a man named Oscar Haggin was running for jailer of Breathitt County, he ran an ad in the county seat newspaper in which he announced:

> Among those to whom I am related by blood or marriage are the following families: Bach, Lovelys, Allens, McQuinns, Pattons, Landrums, Stampers, Watts, Watkins, Manus, Crafts, Calhouns, and the Nichols. My wife was a Crawford which makes our relation to the Jetts, Johnsons, Combs, Griffiths, Terrys, Amburgys, Bowmans, Heralds, Spences, Lawsons, Hargises, Days, Haddixes and Evans and many more.

In both Republican and Democratic sections of east Kentucky, a number of the old machines based on patronage and clan still hold on in the 1970s. In other parts of the state, where patronage has not been so much a life-and-death matter, the machines have dwindled but important power still lies in the hands of the administration man and the incumbent courthouse ring. The biggest break with the old pattern has occurred in the cities and suburban areas where affluent middle-class people have found the old machine politics an anachronism and a bar to their own political advance. Attorney Edward Prichard, Jr., a canny observer of Kentucky politics of whom we will have more to relate later, noted that in metropolitan areas the Goldwater campaign of 1964 brought in a group of dedicated, reasonably prosperous political activists who were not motivated by the old concerns about patronage and faction. "Even if they were not sea-green, uncorruptible Goldwaterites," he said, this Jaycee, station-wagon set perceived that if they tried to advance on the Democratic side, they would have had the "old-fashioned corner tavern-keepers hanging around to obstruct them." They found more congenial associations in the Republican party and, by their frequent successes, disrupted the old order.

The spoils system is as prevalent at the statewide as at the local level, and at times in Kentucky history has led to horrendous scandals. The worst case of all time was that of James William Tate—"Honest Dick," as his compatriots called him—who served as state treasurer from 1868 to 1888. An obliging man in every way, Tate craftily accepted worthless promises of some future payment from hard-pressed constituents, knowing that their fear of exposure would make them his eternal political allies. Eventually a group of freshman legislators, not yet "instructed and obligated," started an investigation. Tate panicked and fled Kentucky, and to this day no one knows where he went. He left behind $100,000 in uncollectable debts and, to make his own future life easier, took a cool quarter-million dollars of public funds with him.

To bar against any repetition of "honest Dick's" exploit, the state constitution was amended to prevent any official from succeeding himself. On occasion, this has led to absurd job-hopping by professional politicians. But the reelection bar, even if it forces good men to leave office, also forces out those who may be benefiting personally from office. Two governors of recent times—Democrat Happy Chandler and Republican Louie Nunn—fit that pattern, and we will say more of them later.

The four-year limit obliges governors to put through all salient or controversial elements of their programs (if they have any) during the first year or two in office, before they become political eunuchs. In the meantime, they control, in fact if not in law, thousands of patronage jobs. A model civil service law was passed by the legislature in 1960, after years of pressure by the League of Women Voters and other good-government groups. The legislation put 16,000 of Kentucky's 20,000 positions under the merit system. Nevertheless, when Republican Louie Nunn ran for governor in 1967, the officeholders were warned they had better campaign to keep the Democrats in office or lose their jobs. And not long after taking office, Nunn did indeed fire 6,000 state employees for alleged political activities. They were, of course, replaced by loyal Republicans.

When Democrat Wendell Ford succeeded Nunn in 1972, he instituted a "reform" involving the transfer of all patronage operations from the governor's office to the Democratic state headquarters. He insisted that the merit system would be used for all state workers except those in top policy-making positions and, far down the income scale, for common laborers like highway workers. Yet one wonders if the Kentucky tradition of governors handing out positions to droves of hungry job-seekers can really be broken. The governor's anteroom has traditionally been filled with supplicants seeking, for themselves or relatives or friends, every conceivable type of post from state park guard to designation as a Kentucky Colonel. The people simply expect it. Thomas Clark told the story of a revered old governor who said to a group of intimate friends at a meeting of the Kentucky Club in the nation's capital that there were two things he never wanted to have again—gonorrhea and the governorship of Kentucky.

Honest and thorough application of the merit system, of course, would do wonders for the quality of state government. Politicians might devote more energies to solving Kentucky's grave problems in fields like poverty and education, rather than concentrating their efforts on political jobs. As it is, the overriding concern of the "outs" is on getting "in," and of the "ins" on staying "in"—with too little regard for fundamental issues of government. The system can even corrupt the minority party, as occurred in 1958 when Republican legislators seemed to abandon any principles or programs they had in return for Governor Happy Chandler's promises of jobs and rural roads for their counties. Finally, an applied merit system would minimize the appointment of political hacks to sensitive middle-level positions of state government which cry out for professionalism and continuity in the application of policy. But even that would not do the job unless Kentucky began to pay its professional state officials—people with managerial, accounting, legal, and engineering backgrounds—much higher salaries. As it is, the pay is so low that the turnover is immense.

An interesting custom, shared by Kentucky, its neighbor Indiana, and a few other states, has been the systematic assessment of state employees to enrich the coffers of the party in power. Alexander Heard, researching his book *The Costs of Democracy*, was informed several years ago that about two-thirds of the campaign money raised by an administration in power in Kentucky came from state employees. If true, Heard noted, that would have made Kentucky more dependent on political assessments than any other state. The assessments, Governor Ford told me, had alternatively been set at 2 percent of an official's salary or put on a sliding scale from $15 to $500. He claimed he had eliminated the practice altogether.

The source and disposition of privately collected campaign funds remains something of a mystery in Kentucky politics, despite a seemingly comprehensive reporting law and the establishment, in 1967, of the country's first independent election finance reporting agency. In a striking parallel to the earlier merit system law for state employees, the reform forces in Kentucky were obliged to wage a massive lobbying campaign to get a reluctant legislature to pass the election finance registry law—only to see the new legislation grossly violated. In fact, the registry law was repealed by the 1968 session of the legislature and saved only when the governor vetoed the repealer. And the registry turned out to be a toothless tiger indeed. In 1973 the Louisville *Courier-Journal* reported that the registry had never prosecuted a violator of the law it oversees. In fact, it had not once investigated any violations, issued subpoenas, or held public hearings, as it was empowered to do. Nor had it used its powers to bar a candidate from office for violating the reporting law. The ostensible reason: the legislature had never appropriated enough money for appropriate enforcement. Another reason, according to the chairman of a legislative committee looking into the problem, was that commonwealth's attorneys were reluctant to take cases to court. "It's just a matter of local politics," he said. "They just don't want to make any enemies." In Kentucky, it appeared, *plus ça change, plus c'est la meme chose.* But in the post-Watergate atmosphere of 1974, the legislature did tighten up the reporting requirements of the law and inserted tough language giving the administrator of the elections registry all the authority he ought to need to obtain compliance.

The Sovereign Electorate and the Tragedy of Edward F. Pritchard, Jr.

One of the more pernicious and persistent features of Kentucky politics, at least until the recent past, was what John Fenton delicately described as "taking certain liberties with the vote of the not-so-sovereign electorate." Election-day irregularities were reported from most parts of the state, but most frequently from the poor mountain counties and precincts of Louisville and some of the other cities. The reason was quite elemental: too many people depended on the spoils of politics for their livelihood. It was quite usual, according to a study of a century of Kentucky elections by J. B. Shannon and Ruth McQuown, for 10 percent more votes to be recorded in a county than it had in the way of adult residents. "In the fat old days," John Gunther reported, "the bosses did not bother with anything so crass or rudimentary as mere stuffing of ballot boxes, and precinct captains did not rummage around to fabricate single names. They simply certified as cast, *en bloc,* the grand total of votes they needed." Numerous observers of Kentucky politics authenticated that report with lively stories of election clerks trying to find out, on election night, just how many votes they had to fabricate so that their candidate or cause would succeed.* As late as 1963 the Republican party conducted a confidential study and found that both parties were stealing votes with impunity.

Today, thanks to voting machines and electronics, vote theft seems to be largely a matter of the past. The first voting machines were introduced in the Louisville area in the 1940s; now they are used statewide. The system is so efficient, in fact, that Kentucky, with its 6 P.M. poll closing, generally reports full election returns before any other state on election day. As everyone knows, it was much easier to stuff a ballot box than it is to tamper with a voting machine. The Nirvana of spotless honesty may never be achieved, but a computerized, statewide registration system, enacted into law in 1973, may propel Kentucky in that direction.

An episode of the late 1940s, involving one of the great personal-political tragedies of modern American state politics, had a great dampening effect on ballot box skulduggery in Kentucky. Edward F. Prichard, Jr., possessing the most brilliant mind in Kentucky politics and every credential to become a governor of the state, was convicted of stuffing 254 ballots—all but one marked straight Democratic—into the boxes of his native Bourbon County. Before President Truman granted him clemency, Prichard had served five months of a two-year sentence in the federal prison at Ashland, Kentucky.

Marked as a prodigy in grade school, Prichard graduated at an early age from Princeton and Harvard Law School and was then selected to clerk for Supreme Court Justice Felix Frankfurter. From there he went on to become a bright young man in FDR's brain trust, served in several important executive branch positions, was an assistant to Kentucky's Frederick Vinson (then Secretary of the Treasury, later to be Chief Justice), and was chosen counsel of the Democratic National Committee. Then he returned to Kentucky to set up his own law firm and prepare for a race for governor. Brilliant, magnetic, dynamic, corpulent, witty—Prichard seemed literally to have Kentucky at his feet. But then came his fatal error of 1948, which some said was the

* Ironically, several of the most beneficial amendments to the state constitution appear to have been passed in this manner. Until the postwar years, for instance, Kentucky was hobbled by a constitutional provision that barred paying any state official more than $5,000 a year. One result was that the state couldn't recruit college presidents or professors. Governor Earle Clements backed a constitutional amendment to repeal the limit, and there were rumors that the Clements machine had to fiddle with the vote to get the right returns. The vote from eastern Kentucky, a veteran newspaperman told me, "took the longest time to count."

result of a wager or a dare to prove that Washington had not made him too good for Bourbon County politics.* Prichard won the wager but lost his political life. Actually, his conviction of ballot theft might have been reversed by the Supreme Court, since the only solid evidence was offered under duress by an old family friend and lawyer in alleged violation of the attorney-client privilege. But the Supreme Court refused to hear the case because no less than four Justices—Frankfurter, Vinson, Tom Clark, and Stanley Reed —had been friends of Prichard and therefore disqualified themselves.

Two years after his release from prison Prichard was able to resume the practice of law, and in time his unparalleled talents as a storyteller and political strategist made him a trusted adviser to a number of governors. Among other things, he developed the skill of predicting, with uncanny accuracy, the election returns in all 120 Kentucky counties. He was also Kentucky's best speechwriter and an expert writer of legislation that bore the names of lesser men. Frank Browning quoted editor Don Mills of the Lexington *Herald* as saying of Prichard: "I don't think any individual in this state has had more influence on two and maybe three of the last four governors. Most Kentuckians look on Prichard as merely a shrewd dealer, a political strategist, and they fail to recognize the tremendous influence he's had on things considered right and good government—especially higher education and teacher salaries. Prichard was the same way in human rights during the struggles in the early '60s. He was always standing there advocating the right thing in that area."

I sensed the same thing in a talk with Prichard. We were talking in his modest apartment near Frankfort (he maintains a bigger spread at his home in Versailles), and after many questions "Prich" would lean back in a big overstuffed chair, his eyes closed and seemingly asleep, until he had decided on a carefully worded reply characterized both by perspicacity and an essential grasp of what is right in human affairs. To think that Kentucky and the country were robbed of this man's services by 254 lousy faked ballots is still enough to make one weep.

Who Runs Kentucky?

When you ask "who runs Kentucky," the answer is never "the people." Some political personality of the moment may be named, but soon the talk gets back to "the interests" who have bought governors and legislatures and directed the vital affairs of the state from time immemorial. Around the turn of the century, Thomas Clark noted, the vital powers included the railroad companies, of which the Louisville & Nashville Railroad traditionally exercised the most clout; the tobacco trusts, whose excesses were soon to trigger the Black Patch War; the whiskey distillers; the Jockey Club, symbolizing the

* For some details of this account I am indebted to Frank Browning for his article "After the Scandal: Picking Up the Pieces," in the *Washington Monthly* for October 1973. I chose deliberately not to discuss the matter in my own interview with Prichard, feeling—rightfully, as it turned out—that there was too much else of fascination about Kentucky politics to learn from the old master.

racing interests; schoolbook and insurance companies; and the then rising coal mining companies.

John Gunther, after talking to some Kentucky sages at the end of World War II, modified the list—but not too greatly. The swashbuckling days of the Louisville & Nashville Railroad were past, he noted, but the line still interlaced the commonwealth so tightly that it had to be reckoned a great power. The Jockey Club remained high on the list, as did the liquor interests. Gunther also included the Kentucky Education Association, the Louisville *Courier-Journal* ("a splendid liberal force"), the Kentucky Utilities Company, and in the realm of declining powers, the coal companies.

Gunther was right, at the time, in downgrading coal's influence, but subsequent economic history has elevated coal once more to the level of a mighty force in Kentucky life. Coal is mined in 55 of the 120 counties, and in many it is so central to the local economy that the industry would be viewed as a major power even if it abjured politics. The fact is that the coal companies, by means devious and direct, do provide a major source of campaign money, and see to it that their properties are lightly taxed and their activities lightly regulated. (We will have more to say of this in the subsequent discussion of eastern Kentucky.) However, it is worth noting that Kentucky belatedly passed strip mining control legislation in 1966, and that for the first time in the state's history, a severance tax was recently placed on the production of coal.

By contrast, back in 1923, when Alben Barkley—as John Fenton put it— "came charging out of the grassy fields of western Kentucky to do battle with the racetrack, liquor, and coal buzzsaw," urging among other things a production tax on coal, he was defeated by the efforts of the so-called "Bi-Partisan Combine" which held Kentucky in an iron vise in those days. The principal leaders of the Combine hailed from the Bluegrass, the cities, and the coal counties, and they were intimately tied to the racetrack, coal, and liquor interests, for whom they fought many political battles. The word "bipartisan" in the Combine's title had nothing to do with "good government," and certainly nothing to do with an interest in either of the political parties. The Combine's leaders came from both parties, their interest was in seizing power for themselves, and the "interests" financed the operation. The attitude of the economic powers had once been summed up eloquently by a president of the Louisville & Nashville Railroad when he said: "Damn the Republicans. Damn the Democrats. We are not office holders, we are not office seekers."

The modern-day power structure is more variegated and less coordinated, but the intent to manipulate public policy for private ends remains unchanged. The coal, horse, and whiskey people are still active and influential, and one cannot ignore the burley tobacco interests, who have virtually all members of the congressional delegation championing their interests in Washington. Governor Earle Clements, in his latter years, went off to Washington to head the Tobacco Council and try to fend off the notion that cigarette smoking had anything to do with cancer. Kentucky continues to have one of the lowest cigarette taxes in the country. Tobacco's political clout is magnified by the fact that the weed is grown in *every* county of the state and accounts for $350 million in sales each year.

The Kentucky Education Association, mentioned by Gunther, has grown into a huge and powerful lobby that gets candidates for governor to grovel for support. Its chief objective is higher teacher salaries, a cause that often puts it in conflict with the older "interests" who are most concerned with lower taxes.

An interesting reversal took place in the utilities industry in recent years. Under J. R. Miller, a Mississippi transplant who became the key man in the rural electric cooperative movement in Kentucky, the co-ops used their offices in every town of any size to become potent political powers and put friendly candidates in as presiding officers of both houses of the legislature and into the governorship itself. Miller even served several years as Democratic state chairman. "Miller and his people," one of my press friends said, "have driven the Kentucky Utilities Company practically back to the bushes."

The *Courier-Journal*, considered as a power factor, presents a curious case. Its national recognition has been little less than overwhelming. Over the years it has won many Pulitzer prizes; a 1970 survey of American newspaper publishers ranked only the New York *Times* and Los Angeles *Times* ahead of the *Courier-Journal* on such criteria as independence and impartiality; and *Time* magazine in the early 1960s and again in 1974 rated it as one of the 10 best daily papers in the United States. Much of this is due to the outstanding leadership provided over many years by publisher Barry Bingham, and in the more recent past by his son and personable successor, Barry Bingham, Jr. *Time*, in its 1974 review, noted that the *C-J* often got "measurable results" from its state coverage and was the first daily in the country to hire a full-time editorial ombudsman to monitor the paper's fairness and accuracy. Yet the *C-J* has failed spectacularly in some of its major efforts, including an all-out campaign to win approval of the proposed new state constitution in 1966.

The *Courier-Journal* enjoys an odd relationship with Kentuckians. "The people of the state," Ed Prichard said, "have an ambiguous feeling about it. There is a tendency to scourge the *Courier-Journal* because it seems too judgmental to them. More important, it has a little too much class and a degree of austerity in its judgments. But the notion that it colors its news is absurd. The truth is that many politicians have known that if the *Courier-Journal* is for you editorially, it may well lash you with scorpions in its news columns." In the intensely personal world of Kentucky politics, where loyalties come before issues, the *C-J* remains the odd man out. And it has to be sobered by the opinion of many rural and small town Kentuckians, as related by Bill Surface, that on the local level it is "no equal to one of the state's 146 weekly or semiweekly newspapers."

A Cavalcade of Personalities

Thundering Henry Clay, brilliant of mind and forceful of phrase, as much at home championing a culprit in a courtroom as whipping up passions at a political rally or debating the profound issues of the day in state legislative chamber or Congress, set the style of colorful political personalities that would mark Kentucky politics down to our day. As John Bradford wrote in the Lexington *Gazette*, Clay had "all that becomes an American Republican—[he has] a sacred reverence for the public liberties; love of country, and ardent zeal, tempered with prudence and wisdom for its honor and welfare. His soul is Roman but his oratory is that of Demosthenes."

Clay had a contemporary, John Jordan Crittenden, governor and United States Senator, less colorful in personality but as hard-working as Clay at trying to hold the Union together in the early 19th century. The more frequent pattern in Kentucky leaders, sad to report, was to emulate Clay's oratory without his substance. Thomas D. Clark has provided us with a captivating list of them. There was John C. Breckinridge, United States Senator, Vice President, and Confederate General, who "had the oratorical gift and bearing to arouse a tipsy, burgoo-stuffed audience to the point of weeping over the lost cause in the immediate postwar years." Later on James ("Gentleman Jim") Bennett McCreary, twice governor, got the extra name of "Bothsides" in honor of his adeptness at straddling issues; as smooth in demeanor as Bourbon whiskey, he dispensed the essence of cheer from the Elkhorn bottoms at the Centennial Exposition in Philadelphia. Clark wrote:

McCreary, like an Oriental father offering a daughter in trade, described the virgin resources of Kentucky which awaited the ravaging hands of the exploiter with money. What Governor McCreary did not tell the people gathered in Philadelphia was that he and his predecessors had swept under the commonwealth's rug enough unsolved problems to sink the state. They had ignored education, correctional institutions, the penitentiary, highways, corporations, and almost everything else that could be put out of public view. Oratory and anecdotes were substituted for social planning, and congeniality substituted for foresight and sound administrative policy.

A politician who at least professed concern about substantive issues was the assassinated William Goebel, to whom I referred previously. Born in Pennsylvania, the son of an immigrant German cabinetmaker, Goebel had once killed one of the most prominent ex-Confederates in a duel. Yet he was also a champion of the people: a free silver Democrat, hostile to the railroads and corporations, for free textbooks, workmen's compensation, and cheap freight for farmers. This violent commoner was also the first Kentucky politician of modern times to build a statewide organization on a personal basis—thus setting a pattern of functional leadership that has characterized Kentucky politics ever since.

Public life in the state took such a bitter and vengeful tone with Goebel's assassination that politicians took on a more somber hue for some years.

The scene brightened up around the time of World War I with what Clark called a new crop of "glorious stump speakers," the primest cock of which was the Democrat Augustus Owsley Stanley of Henderson, "bald as a turnip, with piercing dark eyes, brassy and courageous, and possessed of a foghorn voice" so formidable that when Stanley was fired up with Old Crow, "he could almost make himself heard across the narrow waist of Kentucky." His stiffest competitor was Edwin P. Morrow, a mountain Republican, also eloquent and a master of words of sweet nothingness. One of Morrow's biggest "issues" was the dog tax which the Bluegrass sheep raisers had imposed on the mountain men; to Morrow, of course, the tax was an unspeakable offense to the hill people and the hounds who graced their hearths and shared their sport in squirrel season. According to Clark,

Stanley and Morrow bemeaned each other on the stump, traveled together, slept together, and drank generously out of the same bottle. On one occasion they appeared on the same stage. Stanley had eaten too much burgoo and had washed it down with too much from the "spring," and became nauseated and vomited before the crowd. When his time came to speak he apologized profusely for this unforgivable act, but, he explained, every time he heard Ed Morrow make a speech it made him turn so sick to his stomach that he lost control of himself.

Kentucky's most famous politician of modern times was Alben W. Barkley, a native of Paducah on the state's western tip. Few states have ever produced a more genial, witty, durable, and gallant campaigner, and few national political conventions have ever been as enlivened as was the Democrats' 1948 meeting in Philadelphia through the old warrior's fiery keynote speech. That speech, bringing a semblance of unity to a badly divided party, led directly to Barkley's nomination and subsequent election as Vice President. Few American politicians have been held in such affection as Barkley during his years as "the Veep" under Harry Truman. Barkley had been in the Senate from 1927 up to the time he became Vice President, serving as majority leader from 1945 onwards. Even after his Vice Presidential term, the old charger wanted no rest, returning to the Senate until his death in 1956.

A Don Quixote challenging the vested interests early in the '20s, Barkley by the 1930s had become a master of political patronage, putting the resources of the Works Progress Administration in Kentucky against his political foes. But the Kentucky reverence for Barkley has been dimmed somewhat by revelation that he had failed for several years to pay income taxes on his lecture fees of $1,000 to $5,000 an appearance. Barkley had $8,000 in cash on his person when he died and large sums of cash in his apartment and in a lock box. Three-quarters of his estate was consumed in paying deficiency assessments and fraud penalties on unpaid federal taxes, and his widow was obliged to go to work to support herself.

History shows that the reform forces Barkley first symbolized—chiefly the farmers and other rural folk of western and central Kentucky—were never to win control of the state government. In 1927, for instance, former Governor Beckham remounted the bloodied reform horse from which Goebel had been shot and Barkley rudely removed and actually won the Democratic gubernatorial nomination. But the "Bi-Partisan Combine" of which we spoke before, depending on the Bourbon Democrats of the Bluegrass, the city machines, and the easily bought Republican counties of eastern Kentucky,* funneled enough money to election officials to assure the election of a "safe" Republican instead. The Jockey Club, fearful of the elimination of pari-mutuel betting, put $500,000 into the campaign. And so Kentucky, as John Fenton wrote, was "left safe for bourbon, horses, and coal. . . . Since 1927, no candidate has presented himself who has seriously challenged the position of the ruling oligarchy of the state."

With every thought of serious grass-roots revolt safely behind it, Kentucky was then free to play personal and factional politics with a vengeance from the 1930s up to recent times. For years the chief protagonists, either in person or through intermediaries, were Albert B. "Happy" Chandler and Earle C. Clements. Their rivalry stemmed from childhood, and it produced the bitterest primary feuds of modern times, dividing families and leaving wounds that remain to this day. Historically, Chandler drew on support from the silver wing of the Democratic party, Clements from the gold wing. But it was personality, not issues, that marked the vital difference between them. Chandler was brilliant, effusive, superstitious, given to bragging and colorful campaigning that at once amused and enervated the boys at the branch heads. Clements, by contrast, was a political boss type who got elected. Those who observed him closely over the years described him to me as introspective, devious, relentless—a cold and calculating man but also one with a towering temper, much like Lyndon Johnson. "Earle," in the words of veteran Kentucky newsman Hugh Morris, "didn't care who was governor as long as he could run him. Happy didn't care who ran things as long as he could be governor; in fact he was out of the state half the time he held the office."

Chandler drew the first blood in engineering, as lieutenant governor, a shift in the state's election law to get himself elected governor in 1935. And that first administration was vital for Kentucky, because the state government had been creaking along with patched-up agencies and personnel of the 1880s and '90s. Chandler brought in a crew of bright young men who were the first real innovators in state government in some 40 years. In those days he combined Populist notions with fiscal conservatism: he was against sales taxes as regressive but for a "pay as you go" fiscal policy and against the type of bonded indebtedness that makes possible modern highway networks, community colleges, and other costly civic improvements.

In his first gubernatorial term, Chandler unabashedly mobilized the state employees into a political organization of immense power. He made the mistake of challenging Alben Barkley for the Senate and turning sharply to the right, however; Barkley had the support of President Roosevelt, the United Mine Workers, and the resources of the WPA in Kentucky, and easily

* Eastern Kentucky was ever malleable for the interests because coal called the tune for Republicans there and the Democrats of the region, generally excluded from county-level patronage, depended on the state administration for political spoils. There was a clear parallel in the way that Tennessee's Democratic Boss Crump enticed strongly Republican East Tennessee into voting his way so often in Democratic primaries.

defeated Chandler. Chandler did go to the Senate in 1939, remaining until 1945 when he resigned to accept a higher salary as commissioner of major league baseball. When he was dismissed from that job six years later, he was prepared to return to his Versailles, Kentucky, home, and reenter the political wars.

Earle Clements, in the meantime, had assembled a powerful county-by-county organization that enabled him to win election as governor in 1947. He proved to be one of the hardest-working and most competent men ever to hold that office, learning an incredible amount of detail about the workings of state administration, upgrading the state police, pushing a rural highway program that opened up many hitherto inaccessible areas, and introducing the whole concept of economic development as a responsibility of state government. Kentucky's splendid state park system, the basis of its modern tourist industry, also got its start under Clements.

Clements was also able to install a follower as governor in the early '50s, and went off to serve in the U.S. Senate himself. By 1955, however, Chandler was ready to upset the Clements applecart. Running for governor again himself, Chandler concentrated on the county courthouse circuit, clasping hands and asking: "Plenty of meat in the smokehouse?" Then, facing the crowd, he would say: "Not enough meat and too many bugs and taxes? Well, we're gonna fill your smokehouse and get the real bugs up there in Frankfort out of all our smokehouses." This seemed to be the kind of profundity the voters wanted, and Chandler beat Clements' man. A year later Chandler withheld enough normally Democratic support from Clements so that his old opponent lost a reelection race for the U.S. Senate to Republican Thruston B. Morton. The second Chandler administration exceeded even the first in purging state employees of his enemies' faction and installing his own flunkies. Major questions remain to this day as to how much Chandler benefited personally from his governorship. Ed Prichard, a Clements ally, insists that Chandler was essentially in the game for money and "would steal a copper cent off a dead man's eye."

(Clements, it should be noted, was also accused of financial improprieties and in fact once was forced to pay substantial back taxes, with fines, by the Internal Revenue Service. His friends claim he was never on the take, but rather collected a lot of money for his political friends and even mortgaged his home for notes for the campaigns of others.)

Even after his second term, Chandler tried three times again for governor—in the 1963 and 1967 Democratic primaries, and as a rather lonely and pitiful minor candidate in 1971. He was to lose each time, finally acknowledging after the 1971 defeat that "those who want to write my political obituary are free to do so because I don't ever intend to be a political candidate again." Chandler's defeats could be traced to voter fatigue with his antics, advancing age, and the fact that a "hot" orator of his style was peculiarly unsuited to make the "cool," cautious appeal that comes across best on a television tube.

As for Clements, things seemed to be going well for him when his hand-picked man, east Kentuckian Bert Combs, won the governorship in 1959. Combs made Clements his highway commissioner, a position from which Clements undoubtedly hoped to run the whole show of state government. But then a truck scandal erupted in the highway division and Clements had to resign. Combs ran a tight, efficient ship, and in 1963 installed *his* man, Ned Breathitt, as governor. That race is interesting because an embittered Clements backed Happy Chandler for the job, a final uniting of the childhood protagonists.

Both Combs and Breathitt were reasonably activist, able governors. Combs revived the sales tax that Chandler had killed in the 1930s, producing funds for roads, a major expansion of the park system, and important forward steps in higher education. Breathitt waged a strong, successful battle for air and water pollution control legislation, got enactment of strip mining control in 1966, and pushed through Kentucky's first 20th-century civil rights legislation in the fields of fair employment and public accommodations. Ed Prichard, working behind the scenes in both administrations, deserved some of the credit for these achievements.

The saga of Clements and Chandler was not quite ended, however. Having achieved a kind of senior statesman status, Clements was made chairman of the commission which wrote a new state constitution in 1966. Though the voters rejected it, the document was an outstanding one, likely to be revived in part or whole in future years. Chandler's last real punch was on the negative side. He and his embittered allies lay behind the log, waiting for revenge against the Combs-Breathitt faction. They got their chance in 1967 when they contributed to the election of Louie Nunn, a Republican, as governor.

If the reader feels a bit exhausted by the story of factional machinations in Kentucky politics, he can perhaps sympathize with the poor Kentucky voters expected to keep up with the plottings through all these years. The only bright note, perhaps, is that factionalism is much less prominent now— that the clear-cut, fiercely antagonistic factions that dominated Kentucky elections from the 1890s to the late 1960s now seem to be waning. One reason for this is the Republican rise, which forces some more unity on the Democrats; the other is television, which creates a much more volatile electorate, less susceptible to manipulation and fast deals worked out in the back rooms of the 120 county courthouses. In 1971, for instance, Bert Combs resigned a federal judgeship to return to the political wars, fully expecting to win another term as governor. But a much younger man, Wendell Ford, defeated him for the Democratic nomination. It was sad for Combs, everyone agreed, but the fact that one of the old factions had pulled a coup on the other no longer excited the populace as it might have a few years before.

A word about Louie Nunn, interesting to us because he was Kentucky's first Republican governor in some 20 years. A young man who had been elected the first Republican county judge ever in Barren County in south central Kentucky, Nunn proved his political adeptness by managing successful GOP Presidential and Senate campaigns in the state in the 1950s and early '60s. Other factors in his rise were the ambitions of his wife and, even more importantly, his scheming brother Lee Nunn, a veteran Republican campaign strategist and fund-raiser on the national scene. Lee returned to Kentucky to help Louie run his first race for governor in 1963, and the result was an innuendo-packed, racist campaign in which Louie promised, if elected, to revoke an executive order by Governor Combs that sought to open public accommodations to members of all races. Louie barely lost to Breathitt that year, and four years later he tried again, running a rough-and-tumble primary campaign against Marlow Cook of Louisville. Lee Nunn, the man of many hates, was the evil genius of the primary season, issuing a series of anti-Negro, anti-Jewish, and anti-Roman Catholic statements in Louie's name. After the primary, however, Lee was sent off to Washington and Louie ran a much more respectable general election campaign, winning with 50.7 percent of the vote.

When Louie Nunn took office he proved a pleasant surprise, even for some of his bitterest enemies. For one thing, he installed a group of bright and very young "whiz kids" in major state administrative posts—the first governor to have done that since Chandler in the 1930s. He also defied his segregationist image by signing an open-housing law passed by the legislature. A sales tax increase—from 3 cents to 5 cents on the dollar—made possible important improvements in education and in the mental health field. The tax increase broke a campaign pledge, but most thoughtful people in the state agreed some revenue hike was needed to correct glaring deficiencies in state services.

By the end of Nunn's term, however, people were more apt to characterize his record as mediocre than as excellent. Either venality, or lethargy, or both, overtook his administration. The "whiz kids," seeing their brightest ideas pigeonholed, began to drift away until at the end of Nunn's term few were left. And then there was a host of questions about the handling of political money. Not a man of great personal wealth, Nunn finished up four years as governor at a $30,000 annual salary by going out and purchasing for himself a Lexington house worth (with contents) $169,000 and paying off the mortgage within six months. Rumors flew thick and fast about people making regular cash payments to bagmen in the governor's office, and two dismissed state employees filed affidavits charging they had been required to collect $35,000 from state employees and turn it over to Nunn's personal assistants. A year and a half after Nunn left office his top aide, Jim Watson, committed suicide, reportedly in the midst of an IRS investigation. While Nunn was in office an appreciation dinner was held for him. About $700,000 was raised; some of it was included in later campaign spending reports, but the disposition of more than half of it remained a mystery. In 1971 the tidy sum of $100,000 was channeled to Kentucky by the Nixon administration's great money courier, Herbert Kalmbach, with Louie Nunn handling the cash. One source said he had seen the $100,000 turned over to the treasurer of the Emberton campaign, but another responsible official in the Emberton entourage said he never heard of the money. In any event, it was never reported, as required by law. At least one coal operator was asked by Nunn, "I've treated you fellows pretty well, haven't I?" When the answer was "yes," Nunn was said to have replied, "I want $10,000." And the cash was allegedly turned over. Edward Prichard, Jr., said it was his opinion that "Nunn and his people organized a systematic milking of everything connected with government on a highly effective and personal basis, and they kept a lot of the money." *

By contrast, John Sherman Cooper seemed to have occupied the Olympian heights of probity, intelligence, compassion, and disinterested public service during the 20 years that he represented Kentucky in the U.S. Senate. Cooper, of course, was no stranger to the fractious world of Kentucky politics; a mountain man and native of the southeastern Kentucky town of Somerset, he was descended from a settler who came through the Cumberland Gap in 1790 and never let his Yale college education and Harvard law degree stand in the way of competing with the local boys to win election as a county judge and state representative in his early years. People still call him "the Poor Man's Judge" in memory of his early service as a circuit judge. After World War II, Cooper won three special Senate elections and lost two regular elections in between, one of them to Alben Barkley. During the Eisenhower years he was Ambassador to India and Nepal and a delegate to the United Nations, and in 1960 and 1966 he won landslide victories for full Senate terms.†

Cooper rose to be the ranking Republican on the Senate Public Works Committee and helped gain bipartisan backing for a number of important environmental laws. And despite the primarily rural nature of his state, he was instrumental in gaining Senate approval for permitting the cities to use the highway trust fund for rail transit. Over the years he was known as a strong supporter of civil rights legislation and the TVA. Yet it was in the realm of foreign affairs, seeking to sustain and enlarge the Senate's influence in matters of war and peace, that Cooper did his most distinguished work. He helped lead the fight to curb the deployment of the ABM system, and as he became increasingly anguished about American involvement in the Vietnam war, he sought again and again to extricate the United States from that struggle and coauthored the Cooper-Church amendments which prohibited the use of American ground troops in Laos and Cambodia. His overall voting record was well to the left of his party; in fact, early in his career, when reproached for going against the regular Republican line, Cooper had replied: "I reckon I'll vote as I see fit." Kentucky voters responded warmly to his

---

* Not wishing to engage in guilt by association, I still think it is worth noting that two guests at a party given by Nunn at Frankfort on Derby Day in 1971 were the then Attorney General, John N. Mitchell, and Mrs. Dita Beard, the lobbyist for the International Telephone and Telegraph Company (ITT). Mrs. Beard, who was drinking heavily that day, accosted Mitchell repeatedly about ITT's antitrust problems and ended up collapsing in a stupor on the floor of the governor's mansion.

† President Eisenhower, generally thought to have taken little interest in state elections, felt so strongly that Cooper should be elected to the Senate in 1960 that he sent in a five-man team of professional campaign consultants, headed by one of his own aides, Frederick H. Sontag, to spend an entire year working on campaign strategy, fund raising, and media work for the Cooper campaign.

independence and enjoyed having a man of his stature in the Senate. If he had not chosen to retire in 1972, he doubtless could have won another term with ease. In retirement, Cooper continued to be consulted as one of the nation's most prestigious elder statesmen. But his career was not really ended: in September 1974 President Ford appointed him the first U.S. Ambassador to the German Democratic Republic (Communist East Germany).

Thruston B. Morton, Cooper's Senate colleague for several years, was a political moderate but made no effort to assume Cooper's almost nonpartisan stance. A former House member and Assistant Secretary of State for Congressional Relations, Morton was an early Eisenhower backer and served as Republican National Chairman in 1959 and 1960. He had strong backing among delegates for the 1960 Republican Vice Presidential nomination, but Nixon chose Henry Cabot Lodge instead. Morton had been considered a strong contender for the Senate Minority Leadership after Everett McKinley Dirksen of Illinois, but in 1968, at the age of 54, he decided to retire and return instead to his native Louisville, where the Mortons are one of the wealthiest and most influential families. His brother, Rogers C. B. Morton, served as a Maryland Congressman and became Secretary of the Interior in the Nixon administration.

There is a sort of accepted Kentucky tradition that regardless of parties, one U.S. Senator should represent the rural areas of the state and the other the urban areas, especially Louisville. Cooper, of course, was the "rural man." and so is his successor, Walter (Dee) Huddleston, a moderately liberal Democrat who made his mark by repealing, in the legislature, the sales tax Louie Nunn's administration had put on food. The issue enabled Huddleston to defeat Nunn himself in the 1972 Senate race, despite Nixon's landslide victory (63.4 percent) in Kentucky.

The "urban" seat was held by Thruston Morton for 12 years and then fell to another Louisville Republican, Marlow W. Cook. Cook was one of the least predictable of Republican Senators, sometimes voting an administration line, sometimes going against it, sometimes straddling the fence until the last minute. He was floor manager of the unsuccessful nomination of Clement Haynsworth to the Supreme Court, for instance, but some months later held off taking, until the last minute, a position on the nomination of G. Harrold Carswell, finally casting what many observers considered the decisive vote to defeat Carswell in one of the Nixon administration's biggest defeats. Before going to the Senate, Cook established a fairly progressive image as judge (administrator) of Jefferson County, which encompasses Louisville. In Washington, despite his unpredictability on many issues, he never failed to stand up squarely for Kentucky's tobacco, thoroughbred horse, and mining interests. Yet in the early 1970s, when Nixon and John Mitchell were pushing the new Republican "Southern strategy," Cook attacked their stand as "morally wrong" because it wrote off any support of black people. Cook's prickly independence (except where "vital" Kentucky interests are involved), combined with his gruffness, directness, and occasional breakthroughs to astounding thoughtfulness and disinterested patriotism, made him one of the most interesting Senators to watch—until Governor Ford took his Senate seat away from him in the 1974 elections.

Cook's Roman Catholicism might have stopped his advancement to statewide office in Kentucky, a state of fervid Protestantism, but he was also blessed in 1968 by the fact that his able opponent, Katherine Peden, a former state commerce commissioner, was a woman. The story was told of the day that Cook, campaigning in eastern Kentucky, met a mountaineer and asked for his vote. "Young man," the reply came, "you're a *Roman* Catholic and you're from Louisville and you ran in that primary [for governor in 1967] against our Louie Nunn, and you ain't getting my vote." Cook said he was sorry, that the mountaineer would have to vote for his opponent. "Who you runnin' against?" the man asked. "Miss Katherine Peden." "Who?" "Miss Katherine Peden." "She a woman?" "Yes," Cook replied. "Son," the mountaineer said, "you just got my vote."

In terms of substantive influence on national legislation, no Kentuckian has played a greater role since World War II than Carl Dewey Perkins, Congressman from a poor Appalachian district in the eastern part of the state and (since 1967) chairman of the House Education and Labor Committee. The shape (and very existence) of federal aid-to-education programs, of antipoverty efforts, and a host of bills ranging from school lunches to "black lung" benefits to the Coal Mine Health and Safety Act have been due in no small part to the intense efforts of Carl Perkins. Taking over the Education and Labor Committee after the tumultuous reign of New York's Adam Clayton Powell, Perkins "democratized" it by placing no time limits on witnesses, instituting open committee mark-up sessions, and allowing a fair share of funds to be used for staffing by the Republican minority.

Perkins the personality is equally interesting. He is an incredibly hardworking man, up at the break of dawn and often working until the late night hours. He has worked hard to channel funds into rural areas, and his impoverished district in particular, but he is scrupulously honest and not a penny of the millions of federal benefits appears to have flowed into his own pocket. The loyalty to their Congressman of Perkins' Kentucky mountaineer constituents has few parallels in American politics. All of this goes well beyong the charms of Perkins' mountain twang and rustic personality. Ivan "Red" Swift, now an aide to Perkins and formerly a Louisville *Courier-Journal* correspondent and staffer for John Sherman Cooper, points out that Perkins gets back to eastern Kentucky close to 50 weekends each year. "You can't take the mountain out of these people. Once a mountaineer, always a mountaineer." Perkins has a difficult job in getting Education and Labor bills passed by the House, Swift said, because they tend to be very controversial (minimum wage or legal services, for example), and the committee's membership lacks diversity. It has few Southerners, for instance, who can mobilize support from that part of the country. Thus Perkins is often obliged to compromise—to accept something less than he would like to get a bill through at all. "But," Swift insisted, "Perkins won't deal or swap off—that goes against his grain. He fights things out on their merits. On occasion, this can hamper legislation, because Perkins has no guile. This comes back to the mountaineer psychology. People from that part of the state have always had to struggle harder than folks from the Bluegrass or Louisville, for example. They're used to taking risks, and they're used to plugging."

The other Kentucky Congressman who has risen to national notice in recent years is William H. Natcher, representative of a T-shaped district that includes Bowling Green, Owensboro, Fort Knox, and vast stretches of rural central Kentucky stretching from the Ohio River to the Tennessee line. Natcher matches Perkins in tenacity and loyalty to his district but not in breadth of vision. Back in Bowling Green, Bill Natcher told his neighbors from the age of 16 onwards that he wanted to go to Congress; later he worked his way through law school, got himself a reputation by successfully defending an accused murderer, and started up the local political ladder that would land him in Congress in 1953. The power on the Hill, he knew, lay in the Appropriations Committee, and he directly importuned Missouri's old Clarence Cannon, then head of that committee, to get appointed to it as a freshman. Over the years, he proved amazingly successful at getting dams, river navigation, and flood control projects for the district.

Yet few people outside of Kentucky would have taken much notice of Bill Natcher if he had not become, in the early 1960s, chairman of the Appropriations subcommittee which passes on the budget for the District of Columbia. It was in that post that Natcher fought tooth and nail to prevent construction of Washington's long-sought subway system until the complete local freeway network had proceeded "beyond recall." Natcher may have been prompted by his belief in highways—he had been born in the heyday of the Good Roads Movement, when the Louisville & Nashville Railroad held Bowling Green at its mercy, and the farmers all about were struggling to get "out of the mud." A second motive could have been to court favor with the Public Works Committee, which was backing the freeways and also had authorization power over pet projects for Natcher's district. But the most important reason that Natcher, over several years, stood up against the howls of protest of the Washington press and blocked the subway singlehandedly, was his reverence for Congress as an institution. Congress had ordered the freeways, therefore they must proceed, no matter what other problems—environmental or otherwise—might arise.

The House power structure stood firm with Natcher in holding the subway system hostage, but by 1971 the pressures in the other direction had become so formidable that the House membership, in a 196-183 vote, decided to go ahead with the Metro subway system, Bill Natcher's objections notwithstanding. As a Washington *Star* reporter commented, the vote "probably will serve as a bitter reminder of a cardinal rule in Congress. That rule is: When it comes to raw power, the House giveth, and the House taketh away."

State Government: Governors, Legislatures, Taxes, and the Educational Albatross

Considering Kentucky's hyper-partisanship and factionalism, its ante-diluvian constitution, its all-pervading patronage system and low salaries for government officials, it is surprising that the state government has been as adequate as it is.

Few of Kentucky's governors, for instance, have been brilliant, luminary leaders, but since the first administration of "Happy" Chandler, back in the 1930s, the state has had an outstanding fiscal and budget system. Chandler, in fact, deserves major credit for this because he recruited Professor James W. Martin of the University of Kentucky to be the state's first commissioner of revenue and the chief architect of the state's fiscal system. Martin brought in many bright young men who remained in Kentucky state government for years on end. Martin's recommendation of an income tax on individuals and corporations was pushed through the legislature by Chandler, and the state gradually developed one of the best balanced and most progressive tax systems in America. Much of the credit for this was due to William G. Herzel, who became director of research in the department of revenue in 1939 and remained on the scene until 1973. Because expertise was so vital to any administration, there was virtually no patronage turnover in the revenue department. As each new governor entered office, usually burdened with the problem of making good on expensive promises he had made to pressure groups, he naturally turned to Herzel for counsel. Herzel would give the new governor a list of options for raising more revenue—of which the income tax was usually the least risky choice politically. Herzel gained such a glowing reputation that he was called upon to set up tax systems for such far-flung places as Nicaragua, Ecuador, and the new state of Israel.

Chandler did do Kentucky a great disservice, however, by repealing the state's sales tax (one of the first in the United States) in 1936 and then campaigning against it, year in and year out, for a quarter of a century afterwards. No governor, until Bert Combs took office in 1960, had the courage to reenact the sales tax—and, even then, the unpopular tax got through only because it was tied to a popular veterans' bonus. As soon as it went into effect, the state budget almost doubled, and since that time Kentucky has enjoyed a vigorous government-inspired renaissance. State expenditures for higher education—such a long neglected area that the state's most promising young men and women often went elsewhere for their college educations—rose 397 percent between 1960 and 1968, a rate of increase matched only by New York and Maine. To supplement the interstate roads, most of which cross Kentucky on a north-south axis, an impressive series of toll roads were built, chiefly on an east-west axis, opening up many previously inaccessible portions of the state to economic development. Many new manufacturing plants were built along the toll roads, which have to be funded, at least in part, through general highway fund revenues. (Some suggest Kentucky has ended up overdoing the toll road bit; as one leading state politician noted, "A road is like a status symbol. Every community is entitled to its toll road, whether it carries any traffic or not. We might lease them for bicycle riding—people seem to assume a road has some other function than to carry traffic.")

Kentucky is still paying the price for the years between 1936 and 1960, when the absence of a sales tax and the prevalence of Chandler's pay-as-you-go philosophy stopped almost every kind of public construction in its tracks. It was in those years that Kentucky dropped to the bottom of the list of states in education and many other fields, depriving itself of a generation of growth necessary to give its people decent incomes and a chance to compete in the latter-20th-century national economy. Even with a hefty sales and income tax in recent years, the state has continued to lag badly in revenue raising because it has practically the lowest property taxes in America.* The results, in parsimonious public services, are clear to see. Kentucky in the early 1970s ranked only 43rd among the states in per capita spending for health and hospitals, 42nd in police protection, and, most serious of all, only 46th in its spending for local schools. Only in two areas rich with political boodle—highways, ranking 17th in the country, and welfare, ranking 23rd —did Kentucky compare favorably with the rest of the country. The combined tax collections of Kentucky's state and local governments were $144 a person less than the national average, ranking 45th among the states. Even when one calculated Kentucky's taxes as a percentage of personal income, which is well below the national average, the tax effort ranked only 38th among the 50 states.

If they know how to use it, Kentucky governors can wield great power, with relative independence from the legislature. It is up to the governor to call the legislators into special session; he functions under a constitution that makes it virtually impossible to override his veto; and his powers of appointment, as we noted before, are immense. Governor Wendell Ford, a Democrat elected in 1971, was not considered a powerful personality, but nonetheless began the most thoroughgoing reorganization of state government since Chandler's first administration. When he took office, Ford said, the executive department labored under an unwieldy structure of 60 departments and agencies and 200 boards and commissions. Ford undertook to consolidate the state government into a manageable number of program departments and cabinets, with single secretaries in charge of finance and administration, natural resources and environmental protection, transportation, development, education and the arts, justice, and human resources. The human resources cabinet, for instance, included health, manpower, welfare and unemployment services under unified direction. To help citizens in their dealings with gov-

---

* Kentuckians hate property taxes so much that the legislature, since 1966, has frozen them at the rate they had then. Yet the state is severely restricted, by the constitution, in ways it can give financial aid to the hard-pressed local governments.

ernment, Ford also created an ombudsman within that department. Ford also said he hoped to combine state regulatory bodies, boards regulating everything from watchmakers to dentists, under a single cabinet for consumer protection and regulation.

Kentucky's legislature has improved a lot in decorum since the 1930s when, according to John Gunther, guns were pulled in the chamber seven times during a robust debate over Chandler's proposal to kill a sales tax. Firearms were seen on the house floor again around 1950, when the sergeant-at-arms tried to force an unruly legislator to take his seat. In recent years, many young people, better educated and some of them quite zealous about improving state government, have been elected to the legislature, and in recent sessions the decorum has been close to impeccable. The legislature is also far less at the mercy of the governor than it used to be. Up to establishment of a legislative research commission in 1948, for instance, the only sources of information for legislators were lobbyists and the governor. The average legislator was ill equipped to be anything more than a rubber stamp. The legislative research commission still lacks enough staff to fill the information gap completely, and legislators lack individual offices and a number of other minimal services. Nevertheless, the situation is like night-and-day compared to times past.

If Kentuckians are dissatisfied with their legislature, they really have no one to blame but themselves. In 1966 they voted down the proposed new constitution that would have hauled Kentucky government out of the horse-and-buggy age, and in 1973 they rejected a proposal to permit the legislature to hold annual sessions instead of the wholly inadequate 60 days every other year permitted under the antiquarian state constitution. The legislators tried to get around the problem, at least in part, by authorizing interim committees starting in 1968. But, in the words of Hugh Morris, assistant director of the Legislative Research Commission and former *Courier-Journal* reporter, "the legislature's biggest problem—to be fully informed, and to be independent of the executive branch—will never be licked until they get annual sessions so that they can become, in effect, full-time legislators."

That the legislature does relatively well for itself, despite constitutional obstacles, was made clear in the 1972 session when this rather impressive array of laws was passed—a bill creating a department of environmental protection, designation of wild rivers, Kentucky's first severance tax on coal, a board of ethics for legislators and some financial disclosure requirements, a comprehensive consumer protection law, a new state penal code including a statewide public defender system, voting rights for students on college and university boards, authorization of $200 million in revenue bonds for low-cost housing, and the state's first Presidential primary (to start in 1976). A new order of legislative sophistication was indicated with directions to the legislative research commission to conduct a study of the comparative public policies required in considering the balance between economic development and environmental concerns. An ad hoc action council was also created to facilitate the transfer of scientific and technological information from federal, state and private organizations to all levels of government in Kentucky. The resulting project, funded by the National Science Foundation, was the first of its kind in the United States.

Any suggestion that Kentuckians are using public policy to develop an enlightened society must be tempered by the state's continued lag, despite dramatic efforts since World War II, in public education. The state's dereliction in matters intellectual is not new; in fact it goes back to the very origins of Kentucky, and one might even say to the essential character of the people. The men who wrote the first Kentucky constituion, Bill Surface has noted, failed to make any mention of a public school system, and it was not until 1838, when a survey showed only 22 percent of the state's children were attending school, that the legislature passed a public school act. Another 55 years passed before the counties were required to set up public school systems. As Thomas Clark wrote of conditions at the start of the 20th century,

> Education was Kentucky's cross. From the rugged eastern mountains to the fastness of the Mississippi River bottoms money had to be found to build and maintain schools. A high crime rate, a poor political performance, a lack of capital and industry, and the absence of liberality of points of view reflected severe educational needs. It was difficult indeed to persuade a self-satisfied rural population to act when it was unschooled, afraid of taxes, wedded to the idea that to raise more money for public purposes only served the interests of venal officials, and, finally, convinced that what was good enough for the past generation was good enough for the future.

In 1908, Clark noted, less than half the state's children kept up regular attendance for meager five-month school terms, and the per capita expenditure for education was a trifling and reluctantly granted $5. Some dedicated educational leaders campaigned for longer school terms, compulsory attendance, and the consolidation of one-room schools, but even in the 1940s some 37 percent of Kentucky school children never finished elementary school.

Most of the necessary reforms came after 1950, and especially in the 1960s, when the combination of state appropriations and federal assistance rose from $62 million to $226 million, enabling many poorer counties to replace small and poorly equipped schools with more modern consolidated buildings. Local school taxes rose so rapidly that there were threats of "taxpayers' revolts." Yet even as dollar outlays went up, serious observers questioned the quality of the secondary education offered. Many county school systems, instead of attracting more talented teachers, simply increased the salaries of their patronage-appointed teachers and administrators. Responding to a call from the Kentucky Education Association, the National Education Association conducted an investigation of the state's schools and threatened to impose national sanctions. Many schools in Kentucky, the NEA reported, lacked kindergartens; the schools had an average of just seven library books per child, compared to the national average of 20; and the per child expenditures were $146 a year below the national average. As investigators toured the state, writer Bill Surface reported "they alternatively found gleaming new schools and those where holes were patched with chewing gum or cardboard, where students fired the coal-burning stoves, or rats and mice were seen periodically in assembly rooms." The NEA hearings brought out allegations ranging "from overcrowding in northern Kentucky to coal companies in one southeastern Kentucky county being able to mine $30 million worth of coal a year without paying enough taxes to underwrite 10 percent of the county's school budget."

The 1970 Census showed that Kentucky stood absolutely last among the states in the median number of years of school completed by its adult population—9.9 years compared to the country's average of 12.1 years. More than 9 percent of the adults had so little schooling that they could be classified as functional illiterates. Kentucky was shown to be 48th in the nation in the percentage of its people who had graduated either from high school or college.

Kentucky has sought to compensate for these deficiencies with such measures as vocational-technical schools within commuting distance of all residents of the state. Its school expenditures are rising. But it will be years —perhaps another generation or two—before the state can work off the debilitating effects of its historic neglect of basic education.

Perhaps the only bright note was the speed and ease with which Kentucky integrated its public schools following the 1954 *Brown* decision of the U.S. Supreme Court. In contrast to many other Southern and Border State governors, Kentucky's Lawrence Wetherby said his state would obey the law. Thanks especially to some sound planning by school boards and administrators in Louisville and Lexington, centers of a major portion of the black population, Kentucky did just that. There was temporary foot-dragging in some rural counties, but Kentucky's obsession with basketball helped to solve the problem as many a local high school eagerly snapped up the rangy, skillful black basketball players, happily swallowing any racial inhibitions in the process.

In higher education, as we noted before, Kentucky's hitherto parsimonious approach was abruptly altered in the 1960s. The University of Kentucky enjoyed unprecedented growth in enrollment and construction, and the state's five regional colleges were upgraded to the status of universities. In addition, 13 state-supported community colleges were built. The faculty at the older institutions must have felt that a whole new day had dawned; in the words of Thomas Clark, who had taught at the University of Kentucky since 1928, that institution had been "starved" for funds by the legislature clear up to the early 1960s. With the turnabout in the budget situation, better quality in education was apparent; UK, for instance, now has a very adequate medical school and a number of outstanding departments. Other bright developments on the academic front were the establishment of a combined University Press of Kentucky, with an unusually strong publications program, and almost phenomenal advances in libraries and the state archives.

All the advancements in higher learning, Clark suggested to me, have to be seen in the light of the past. "We have had an awful lot of catching up to do," he said. "I've been teaching a long time. I'm teaching grandchildren and maybe some great-grandchildren of my first students. But I see these kids coming in reflecting the same weaknesses their mothers and fathers had when they were students. It's not just the secondary schools—it's the whole educational system, and the basic attitude of people toward learning, that still needs revising."

Economy and Geography

Kentucky is a curiously advanced and retarded, rich and poor, exquisite and environmentally ravaged state. The contrasts are everywhere to be seen. Handsome thoroughbreds graze on the luxuriant fields of the Bluegrass while not far to the east life at subsistence levels is eked out in the poverty-stricken hollows of Appalachia. The coal industry, which once used 65,000 men to mine 70 million tons in a year, now with automation employs only 30,000 to produce 125 million tons, worth more than $1 billion. Manufacturing industries, producing widely diversified goods valued at $4.4 billion a year, employ 280,000 people; yet the per capita income of Kentuckians, while rising in dollar terms, still ranked only 41st among the 50 states in the early 1970s. The men working in Kentucky's famed distilling industry could easily be tempted to return to moonshining in the hills when one considers their wages: barely over $100 a week. (The bourbon makers employ only 7,000 people, though the value of their shipments is a robust half billion dollars a year.) Horse raising is associated in the public mind with the fanciest affluence, yet the people it employs earn a lot less than the workers in Kentucky's machinery, metals, chemical, and tobacco plants. Out-of-state tourists deposit close to $500 million in Kentucky each year, and the state park system is deservedly recognized as the best in America; yet in eastern and western Kentucky one can witness the gruesome high walls and spoil banks of unfettered strip mining. Of America's 500 largest corporations, 192 do business in Kentucky; yet in manufacturing as well as mining, the great bulk of ownership is outside of Kentucky itself.

Low personal income is the economic counterpart of Kentucky's educational malaise. In 1929 the state's per capita income was only 56 percent of the national average; in 1960 it was 71 percent; in the following decade it almost doubled, but it was still only 80 percent of the national figure at the start of the 1970s. Government projects suggest the income figure will still be only 83 percent of the national figure in 1990. Several reasons could be named. One is surely the presence of deeply depressed areas in Kentucky, the southeastern counties in particular. Another is the higher number, in comparison to other states, of blue collar and farm jobs, and the relative shortage of professional and other types of white collar employment. Among the 50 states, for instance, Kentucky ranks 46th in the proportion of scientists to the total population (only Alabama, South Carolina, Mississippi, and Arkansas are worse off). One might say that Kentucky, once the nation's frontier and seedbed of the West, has simply become too inward-looking, too inbred. It has exported close to a million of its sons and daughters to other parts of the nation since the eve of World War II, in fact.* But relatively few Americans from other states have moved into Kentucky; in fact the 1970 Census identified only three other states with such a low proportion of residents born elsewhere. In short, Kentucky desperately needs fresh blood, and the new ideas and directions that come with that stimulus.

No matter what economic innovations arise in Kentucky in the next years, there may never be a day when bourbon whiskey will cease to be its most famed product for home-state ingestion and distribution to the world. The beginnings of bourbon—especially the chain of events that suggested storing corn liquor in charred white oak kegs to give the spirit its amber tone and bouquet—remain somewhat shrouded in history. We do know that from the days of the first settlers, wherever a corn mash could be concocted, liquor was the result. The Kentucky colonel-mint-julep legends, fused with notions of the state as a place of fast horses and quick pistols and old South gentility, developed right along with the bourbon industry in the past century. By 1880, there were 400 distilleries at work in the state, and they produced 85 percent of the bourbon whiskey in America. Today there is stiffer competition from distilleries located everywhere from Pennsylvania to California, but Kentucky still produces more bourbon than all of the others put together.

Yet Kentucky was also the state that gave Carrie Nation to a country in need of redemption from the corner saloon, and Kentuckians have remained ever ambivalent about their famous product. As Thomas Clark noted: "They drink heavily, talk even more loudly about liquor, support their schools and institutions to a significant degree from liquor taxes, and vote more than 90 of their 120 counties 'dry.'"

For a century and three-quarters, Kentuckians made for themselves an overwhelmingly agrarian society, and to this day farming remains the state's most prevalent though not its most profitable industry. Tens of thousands of rural families, even if their breadwinners head off for industrial jobs during regular working hours, still raise enough foodstuffs to make them partially self-reliant. They will have a vegetable garden and perhaps a small orchard, raise a few cows or hens, or even a sow who produces a litter each year. Some remnants of the old barter economy linger on; according to Bill Surface, for instance, farmers in bib overalls meet once a month behind the old tobacco barns in the county seat of Glasgow "to swap anything from sledgehammers to hunting dogs."

Tobacco remains the omnipresent crop, because the government-guaranteed price makes it so profitable. It is grown everywhere from the flatlands to the hills, on corners of thoroughbred farms and on hardscrabble farms alike, everyone jealously guarding his poundage allotment. The noxious weed has been the base of Kentucky agriculture since the last century, when the coming of the warehouses prompted the farmers to cultivate burley and sev-

---

* Through natural increase the state's population grew by 373,000 over the three decades, to a 1970 figure of 3,218,706. But the rate of increase was only a third of the national average.

eral other tobacco varieties. Even members of fundamentalist churches which associate smoking with sin cheerily raise the stuff. Each year's tobacco crop now brings in more than $300 million, second only to North Carolina. But the rise of other crops, like soybeans, and particularly the growth of the livestock industry, has reduced tobacco's share of overall Kentucky farm output from 50 percent to 30 percent.

The small-bore scale of Kentucky agriculture is illustrated by the comparison of the value of its farm products ($1 billion a year, ranking 20th in the country) and its number of farms (120,000, the fourth highest number among the states). Even so, the number of farms is now less than half what it was before World War II. Just between 1960 and 1970, agriculture declined from 26 to 14 percent of the total employment in the state. One could in fact argue, as Thomas Clark has done, that Kentucky began to lose its bucolic soul as long ago as the depression of the 1890s, when so many members of the rural aristocracy met economic ruin. The smaller farmer has met his nemesis in modern times, just as the bulldozer has replaced the mule and the machinery shed the barn. "No longer," Clark wrote, "can a rugged yeoman farmer with a stout back and legs, a clean mind, and a willing young wife build a modest house on the land and begin farming with the expectation that he will prosper. Successful farming in Kentucky bears more resemblance to banking, market speculation, and installment financing than to the historic past of a self-sufficient rural economy."

The modern, expansive, industrial Kentucky is more localized geographically than its agrarian predecessor. One can take a line on a map, going from Ashland in the northeast, through center-state a ways south of Lexington and Louisville, and then along the Western Kentucky Parkway all the way out to Paducah, northernmost city of the Jackson Purchase. And from there north to the Ohio River you have a "frontier" of population concentration and industrial growth in Kentucky today. Significantly, it is a river frontier. It is also an urban frontier, because of the metropolitan complexes within its borders. Of Louisville and Lexington, the two greatest, we will have more to report in separate subchapters. Ashland (population 29,245) bespeaks big industry—most particularly Ashland Oil, the only Kentucky corporation among America's largest 100. The visitor sees huge oil tanks and the vast refining complex that receives natural gas from the Big Sandy field to the south. There are also blast furnaces, railroad yards, and as a scenic exception to the industrial profile, lovely homes on the ridgetops.

All along the river, in fact, the atmosphere reminds one more of the nation's industrial heartland than classic pastoral Kentucky. Ashland shares a metropolitan area designation with factory-studded Huntington, West Virginia. The Covington-Newport area is directly across the river from Cincinnati, the home of a quarter million suburbanites, factory workers, and their families. Back in the 1920s and '30s, Newport was one of the biggest gambling centers of America, featuring plush casinos run by huge syndicates. Parlors of pleasure also offered an intimate touch of flesh for Cincinnati's "tired businessmen," labor leaders, and assorted visitors. The last important elements of this hoodlum-dominated activity were driven out by the local people after World War II, though the nightclub scene is still lively, with some illegal gambling on the side. Still, as Ed Prichard put it, "most Kentucky people view that area with some embarrassment—as a sort of sinful place where people talk different." (Prichard also observed that the Covington-Newport area, with its substantial share of Catholic ethnic stock, gave Jack Kennedy a small vote in 1960 "because they thought he was pinko." The *Kentucky Post and Times Star*, published in Covington, has recently given the state its first taste of old-style "yellow" journalism. The paper's readers must be convinced that everything in Kentucky is scandals and swindles—though the material, however highly colored, generally has a germ of truth. The paper's Frankfort coverage is said to have given the governor "fits.")

Along the Ohio's flank west of Louisville is Owensboro (population 50,329), not far from Indiana's industrial city of Evansville and itself a town of oil refineries, distilleries, and assorted factories. Owensboro is the largest city in the dozen-odd counties of the western Kentucky coal field.

Three major Kentucky regions, lying largely outside the orbit of the northern river frontier, merit attention. To the east, there is the hilly Appalachian area, a region so fascinating and problematic that I will treat it in a separate section. Then there is the Pennyrile or Pennyroyal (named after a variety of prevalent wild mint), which encompasses the major chunk of central Kentucky, from the mountains on the east to the Bluegrass on the north and the Tennessee River on the west, running for miles along the Tennessee border on its southern flank. Finally, there is the Jackson Purchase, or Mississippi delta region of the state's extreme western extension.

Most of the Pennyrile today consists of rural backwater counties, declining in population. The soil is generally of middling quality, and the farming thus less than robust. Here one finds Kentucky's interesting limestone belt (site of Mammoth Cave and many others) and lots of water impoundments, natural lakes, and several state parks, which support a significant tourist industry. To the north, the Pennyrile overlaps with the western coal fields and includes Fort Knox, home of the nation's largest armor training center and of course the famed U.S. Bullion Depository, where half a million gold bricks are stored under awesome security conditions. There is one real growth center in the modern Pennyrile: Bowling Green (population 36,253). Traditionally known as the trading center for a small but fertile corn, tobacco, and dairy cattle area, Bowling Green now has a regional university and several thriving industries.

Along the Cumberland and Tennessee Rivers in western Kentucky, which generally separate the Pennyrile from the Purchase, two gigantic power-generating dams were built—TVA's Kentucky Dam and the U.S. Corps of Engineers' Barkley Dam. Taken together, the two lakes formed by the dams are the world's largest man-made body of water. They have some 300 miles of recreational shore and encircle the Land Between the Lakes, a prime recreational area run by TVA.

The Purchase strikes one as a piece of Mississippi or Arkansas, located accidentally in Kentucky. After the first settlers there cleared the luxuriant groves of poplar, hickory, and gum, and started to plant crops, they discovered the alluvial soil laid down by the rivers over millennia provided them with a superb natural asset. This riverbottom territory has historically produced high yields of corn, tobacco, and cotton, and especially in recent times, soybeans. But now industries—chemical, rubber, textile, and other kinds of plants—are increasing in noteworthy numbers. The largest town is Paducah (population 31,627), a placid city at the confluence of the Tennessee and Ohio Rivers. Among other things, Paducah lives off the payrolls of an AEC gaseous diffusion plant, which native son Alben Barkley snared back in the 1940s. Politically, the Purchase lands are a piece of the Old South. They are located only some 110 miles from Memphis and were once big slaveholding territory. Back in the days when being a Democrat and holding black people in "their place" were synonymous, these lands were known as Kentucky's "Gibraltar of Democracy." The federal government in the 1930s brought an indictment against landowners in two Purchase counties for peonage. The lingering racism, plus a touch of Populism that Barkley himself exemplified, later made this strong territory for George Wallace.

The Bluegrass, Horses, and Lexington

The Bluegrass has forever been the jewel of Kentucky's kingdoms, some thousand square miles of spring-fed and gently rolling land unmatched anywhere on earth for the nurturing of fine livestock. Here one finds the 300-odd horse farms, nurturing grounds of some 200,000 thoroughbreds, standardbreds and show animals who graze on placid meadows divided by miles of white plank fences—as perfect an example as one can find anywhere of man's manicuring of nature. Great chunks of the Bluegrass, of course, are given over to more mundane forms of agriculture, and Lexington, the central city of the region, has of late been expanding at a giddy rate—presenting at once the best hope of an advanced Kentucky economy and a dire threat, by virtue of the bulldozer and the subdivision, to the farms and the natural setting of the Bluegrass.

Yet the horse farms, for the most part, have remained unmolested, and steps are being taken to protect their future. Protection is well advised, because the horse means more for Kentucky than one can easily encapsulate in a sentence. First, there is history. Dr. Thomas Walker, Christopher Gist, and Daniel Boone and his long-rifle-hunting party broke the trails into early Kentucky on horseback. A great many of the state's most illustrious early citizens, including Henry Clay and John Breckinridge, were avid horse breeders and racers. Since the Gilded Age following the Civil War, when fabulously wealthy Eastern business moguls began to buy up Bluegrass horse farms and race their prime specimens, the indigenous Kentucky aristocracy has generally taken a back seat in the expensive, exciting horse business. But the exclusion has by no means been total; many of the wealthy outside families who gravitated to the Bluegrass for breeding lines and pasturage stayed on and intermarried with Kentuckians; and it is the rare Kentuckian of any economic class who does not take some vicarious pleasure from the horsing scene.

A second benefit to Kentucky is economic. Close to 12,000 Kentuckians make their living off the horse industry. Trainers, grooms, jockeys, exercise boys, veterinarians, harness makers, track attendants, auctioneers and horse brokers, pedigree searchers, bookies, writers for such Lexington-based publications as the *Thoroughbred Record* and the *Daily Racing Form*—the list of horse-related jobs is almost endless. And visitors to the horse farms and race tracks around Lexington, and of course to the Kentucky Derby at Louisville's Churchill Downs each May, account for a major chunk of Kentucky's immense income from out-of-state visitors.

Finally, the horse gives Kentucky identity rivaled only, perhaps, by Bourbon whiskey. The state seal might well be redrawn to show the profile of a noble steed; this would fit neatly with the state's publicity and be more felicitous than other possibilities, such as a bottle of bourbon, a tobacco leaf, or a lump of coal.

The Bluegrass horse business has come a long way since 1788 when the Kentucky *Gazette*, the first newspaper west of the Alleghenies, ran this advertisement:

The famous horse Pilgarlic, of a beautiful colour, full fourteen hands three inches high, rising ten years old, will stand the ensuing season at the head of Salt River at Captain Abe Irvins, Mercer County, and will cover mares at the very low price of ten shillings a leap. . . .

The stallions of that day were nothing of the quality that would develop over time, however, as English thoroughbreds with Arabian blood were brought in from Virginia or directly from England. One of these was the great horse Buzzard, foaled in New Market, England, and purchased by Henry Clay for $5,500 in 1806. In addition to thoroughbreds, Kentucky specialized in the standardbreds (trotters and pacers), and cross-bred those two types to produce the American Saddle Horse, a strain famed for its intelligence and show qualities. Generations of selective breeding, as Lexington freelance writer Mary Jane Gallaher noted, "make the offspring of the thoroughbreds and standardbreds a wonder to see, each possessed of a *joie de vivre* that washes over every living thing around." One can visit any of the famous farms of Bluegrass country—Castleton, Spendthrift, Pebblebrook, Calumet, Darby Dan, Greentree, and countless others—to see the famous horses and perhaps a glimpse of their pedigreed owners.

Horse racing has, of course, become an incredibly expensive business. As a yearling, Man o' War was bought for $5,000; yet in 1973, one yearling was bought at Lexington for $600,000. That same year a record $6,080,000 was paid by a syndicate for Secretariat, born three years before in Virginia (though sired by Bold Ruler of Kentucky's Claiborne Farm). The investment proved to be a good one, as Secretariat went on to sweep the Derby, the Preakness, and the Belmont—the first horse to win all three since Citation in

1948. The sale of blood horses in Lexington each year has reached monumental proportions, even affecting America's balance of payments. In the 1973 sales, for instance, well over a third of the $20 million spent came from abroad, led by the Japanese, who were buying horses with such fervor that the average price went up 40 percent per animal over the previous year, which itself had been a record-breaker.

The Bluegrass orbit includes not only gracious countryside but old and interesting cities. Toward Louisville lies Frankfort (population 21,356), a picturesque, hill-set town rightly described by the late Allan Trout as "a flawless cameo of Kentucky history." It was the first state capital west of the Alleghenies; it is the burial place of Daniel Boone; and in their time it was visited by such luminaries as Jefferson, Burr, Madison, Monroe, Jackson, and Theodore Roosevelt. Between Frankfort and Lexington is Versailles, named in honor of French help in the Revolution; more northeasterly is Paris, the county seat of Bourbon County, where some historians would have it that the first bourbon was distilled by Jack Spears in 1790. Among Paris's present-day residents is Seth Hancock, the brilliant young man who, at the age of 24, put together the syndicate deal for Secretariat.

The major interest, inevitably, turns to Lexington, a town both intensely old an new. It was named for the Battle of Lexington, only a few weeks after that event, and following permanent settlement in 1779 became the chief commercial and cultural capital of the old frontier. At one end of Gratz Park, a charming wooded square near the city's center, stands Transylvania College's Morrison Hall, built in 1833, where Abraham Lincoln first heard Henry Clay speak. Historic houses stand all around the park's periphery; in fact, Lexington has more old homes than any other Kentucky city. At the far end of Main Street is Ashland, Henry Clay's home, where he bred horses and in 1825 held a great reception for the visiting Marquis de Lafayette.

Over the years Lexington prospered as a farm center, the site of great tobacco auctions, and of course as a focal point of the horse industry. The first race path in Kentucky was marked out near the town in 1790, and today it has The Red Mile (the world's fastest harness track) and, even more important, Keeneland, a private racetrack of studied informality, greenery, and immaculateness, where Kentucky's most important race meetings and yearling sales are held. Today Lexington has an immense variety of activities, including large veterans' and public health facilities, the sprawling buildings of the University of Kentucky (which more than doubled its enrollment in the past decade), large manufacturing plants (all of IBM's electric typewriters are made in Lexington, for instance), Kentucky's leading economic research organization (Spindletop Research), and the national headquarters of the Council of State Governments. Some Lexington boosters believe the town is becoming the regional office center for the Upper South between Atlanta and Cincinnati. (Discounting the competition, one local businessman wrote me, "Louisville and Cincinnati are Midwestern cities; Nashville is oriented westwards, and Knoxville and Charleston are just not very attractive.") In addition, one gets the impression that just about any east

Kentucky coal operator who strikes it rich deserts the mountains for the sophisticated and monied world of Lexington.

All of this has created some serious growing pains. The population of the old core city, which includes some black slum areas, has held relatively constant,* but suburban subdivisions have been marching out across the Bluegrass. The combined population of the city and surrounding Fayette County, which was 78,899 in 1940, soared by 121 percent, to 174,323, by 1970. Until the early 1960s, there were pitifully few controls on this expansion. Highways and subdivisions began to gobble up much of the green space around Lexington, including some of its treasured horse farms. The last decade has seen some effort to dampen the helter-skelter urbanization. Such restrictive zoning and development rules were adopted, in fact, and land prices rose so steeply that not a single new industry employing more than 100 people was located in Lexington for 10 years. But the university, IBM, and other local enterprises expanded so rapidly that trailer parks began to proliferate on the Lexington side of the surrounding rural counties, where land-use controls were lax or nonexistent. Many outside industries which had thought of locating in Lexington found the costs and controls so tight there that they went instead to satellite cities like Paris, Georgetown, or Versailles, or to cities in Indiana or central Kentucky.

Lexington's methods for slowing growth could well be instructive for other rapidly expanding cities around the country. The greatest single deterrent, according to H. Foster Pettit, mayor of Lexington, was almost accidental —the inability to build sanitary sewer systems fast enough and in the place industries and developers wanted. This was backed up in the mid-1960s when the Fayette County health board decreed that no septic system could be installed on any plot of land less than 10 acres in size. Strictly enforced, the regulation stopped many of the smaller and tackier developments. Concurrently, Fayette County for several years has decreed an urban service area of some 75 square miles, beyond which it will not extend police, fire, or sewer services. That leaves 225 square miles, including the entire area north of Interstate 75 where the bulk of the horse farms are located, where it is virtually impossible to get zoning or essential services for new developments. There are no horse farms at all within the urban service district, and there are 23,000 presently undeveloped acres within the district, largely south and southeast of the city, where growth can take place over the coming years. So it would seem—unless political pressures cause a reversal in the future— that the Lexington area, its postwar growth notwithstanding, has taken adequate measures to protect the remainder of its greatest asset, the Bluegrass farms. But the protections do not extend to the surrounding counties, a problem to which the state legislature, if it has its wits about it, should address attention in the immediate future.

Pettit said that those in Lexington oriented to the traditional "growth is

* Downtown Lexington is ugly as sin physically, but it is slowly being rebuilt and counts on a massive civic center as a catalyst to higher-grade development.

good" psychology had been the older bankers and chamber of commerce types, plus a few of the big horse farmers not completely opposed to the idea of selling their land for $6,000 an acre if they can go out further in the Bluegrass and buy land at $1,200. The Lexingtonians most dedicated to controlling growth are its relative newcomers, the people who have witnessed the evils of urban sprawl elsewhere and don't want to see it in their new community. "Old Lexington people," Pettit said, "are not as impressed with its uniqueness as those who've lived elsewhere."

The Lexington area in the early '70s made an historic advance to a merged city and county government. Historically, there had been severe antagonisms between city and county officials, many of whom would not even speak to each other at times. At the same time Lexington-Fayette had probably the most crazy, patchwork city-county boundary of any of the 30 communities in the country which have tried for metro government in the years since World War II. The results were absurd misunderstandings about which fire or police department should respond to calls, plus gross waste and inefficiency. Civic groups including the chamber of commerce, the Rotary, the Jaycees, and the League of Women Voters had nurtured the idea of consolidation for 20 years, but it did not become a realistic possibility until 1970 when enabling legislation was pushed through the state legislature by two Fayette County representatives. The good government forces then assembled, with little difficulty, the required petition signatures to create a merger commission to draw up a new charter. The commission for several months was snagged on the shoals of political opposition in the city of Lexington. But in November 1971 Foster Pettit and a city council pledged to merger were elected, and in a six-month period of around-the-clock marathon sessions an imaginative and well thought out plan was drawn up. The leadership was in the hands of William E. Lyons, a political scientist at the University of Kentucky who had been involved in merger attempts in at least 20 other communities. (Pettit called him "a realistic professor.")

The proposed metro charter provided for a strong mayor-council form, districting of the council to allow for adequate representation of the various communities (a provision which generated support from the black community in particular), and such innovations as a citizen's advocate or ombudsman, a federal programs director, and a code of ethics. It also contained flexible guidelines for taxing of various parts of the county at levels accurately reflecting the levels of urban service afforded them. The charter advocates had some lucky breaks, including a pending city annexation of built-up areas on the fringe of Lexington, which residents feared would mean new taxes without services. Essentially it was the vigor, planning, and concerted campaign of the merger advocates which carried the day, however. They secured the backing of practically all the elected officials of the county, got the support of the business community and civic groups, and organized a citizen's group to campaign for the charter, using a full-scale precinct organization, publications, television and radio. Ample financing for the campaign was arranged. The opposition, by contrast, was fragmented and unorganized. The result was a 69 percent favorable vote in November 1972—the second time in U.S. history (Jacksonville, Florida, being the other case) when a merger was accomplished on the first vote.

Some individual politicians played interesting roles in the merger fight. One was a chief opponent, Lexington Mayor Pro Tem Thomas Underwood, who had been elected on a preposterous promise to eliminate the sewer-service tax, controlled most officials of the old commission government, and was responsible for a major part of the city-county dissension. Underwood was indicted on bribery charges in connection with building permits, and though he was later acquitted, the incident helped Pettit and his reform slate to take control of Lexington in 1971 and turn the city's support to merger. Another vital figure was the county judge (chief executive), Robert Stephens, who at an early point threw his full support behind merger, even though it meant his own position would fade to a mere shadow of its prior power. Finally, Foster Pettit played a fascinating role. He campaigned for merger, even though it meant his own four-year term as mayor of the city, which began in 1972, would be cut in half. Then, in 1973, he announced for mayor of the new metro government and was considered an almost sure winner. But Pettit campaigned poorly and, instead of getting the big mandate he had expected, emerged the victor by a margin of only 54 votes, after a recount and a court test. (The near winner was James Amato, an old-line "courthouse crowd" Democrat who had initially opposed the merger.) With Pettit, however, the voters chose a majority of progressive pro-merger councilmen, and the prospects for Lexington's governmental innovation seemed bright.

Low-Key Louisville

The city of Louisville, more than a century past its days as a brawling frontier riverfront town, is a comfortable, low-key place, generally a follower rather than a leader among America's urban centers. For years on end, it may seem to slip into total lethargy—I remember well a Louisville newspaper writer telling me a few years ago that his home town was "a dull Midwestern city, a good place to embalm a dog." Then, as in a number of past eras, including one which began around the turn of the 1970s, the old town bestirs itself and lunges forward with political innovation or a new spurt of building. "We wait and see how things work elsewhere," said Barry Bingham, Jr., of the *Courier-Journal*. "Then maybe we try them if they have proven themselves. If we don't have big population and growth pressures, why hurry?"

That go-slow-and-do-it-right attitude should not be interpreted as reaction, even if it leaves some problems unresolved beyond their time. It simply bespeaks the temper of a city graciously balanced between the South and the North, a city that fosters a civility between people and groups often lacking in American society these days, a city where the fun of a Kentucky

Derby or the old grace of the *Belle of Louisville* all alit on the river of a summer eve suggests one might do best to savor what is all right about the way things are now. Tomorrow serious problems can be solved—and usually are.

These themes appear again and again in Louisville life, as we shall see. Consider the economic scene, for instance. In times past, Louisville had about 40 important home-owned industries—the fruit of the fabulous boom it had enjoyed as the supersalesman to the post-plantation South after the Civil War, when the city was rightfully viewed as one of the country's most important commercial and industrial centers. But after 1900, except for the boomtimes of the '20s, the economy languished. In 1930 James B. Brown's Bank of Kentucky was obliterated by the Depression, and the great banking, railroading, and industrial families of Louisville never regained their power and influence. One by one, the Louisville-owned businesses sold out to national concerns, until only a handful were left in the wake of World War II. The families of the old magnates, come down to the second, third, and fourth generations, with frequent intermarriage between them, felt little need to perform. A lot of the downtown land fell into the hands of trusts, and the owners—often absentee—took a dark view of any interruption in their income. For years, there was scarcely any downtown construction, and the banks were renowned for their timidity. Only the arrival of some big out-of-state firms—most notably General Electric, which came in 1954 to open its largest U.S. appliance plant, with an eventual payroll of 19,000— prevented severe unemployment in the postwar years. Of the few home-owned industries which remained, the most notable were the Brown-Forman and Glenmore distilleries. The city basically thought of itself as a branch town, with big payrolls from firms like GE, American Standard, International Harvester, Brown & Williamson, Phillip Morris Inc., a number of synthetic rubber manufacturers including Goodrich and DuPont, and later a large Ford truck assembly plant.

Over the course of the 1960s, however, some local entrepreneurs, mostly younger men, began to move in a big way. One was John Y. Brown, Jr., who acquired for a song the formula for Kentucky Fried Chicken from Col. Harland Sanders, a London, Kentucky, restaurateur, developing it into a worldwide operation before he sold out to Heublein. (In 1972–73 Brown was the driving force behind the national Democratic Telethon programs, which proved highly successful in erasing the party's debts.) Another successful entrepreneur was Stanley Yarmuth, a native of Passaic, New Jersey, who moved to Louisville in the late 1940s and, though he had some good connections, got his start there as a used car salesman. By the late 1960s Yarmuth had advanced to ownership of the lot, to control of the Life Insurance Company of Kentucky, to a full-blown conglomerate mogul. His National Industries—"the Kentucky Conglomerate"—owned a large string of companies in such fields as food products, retailing outlets, furniture and toy manufacturing, located throughout the U.S. Total sales were $320 million by 1968. The next year Yarmuth made a brash move to buy a controlling interest in

Churchill Downs and ran straight into the horse set, which had to pay a high price to keep him out. I talked with Yarmuth, an intense and aggressive young man preoccupied with his Jewish identity, a short time after the Churchill Downs effort. He made it clear that he held the old Louisville establishment in utter contempt.

The success of Brown and Yarmuth and the young executives in firms like Extendicare, another arrival of the 1960s, inspired scores of other young entrepreneurs in Louisville. Some of the older, more established businessmen cooperated actively; others continued in their old ways. Louisville evolved what some called an "unstructured power structure" in which no single group held death-and-life power over new projects. By the late '60s the two biggest Kentucky financial establishments, Citizens Fidelity Bank & Trust and First National Bank-Kentucky Trust Company, had caught the new spirit and announced plans for new downtown buildings in the 30-40-story range. The Louisville Trust Company and others joined in the building splurge, which created more than 100 floors of rental space for corporate offices. Louisville had itself a new skyline, and a lot was going on at ground level as well. Sparked by Louisville Central Area, Inc., a civic and business group, the city built the nation's third largest pedestrian shopping mall to rejuvenate downtown retailing, and simultaneously constructed Plaza/Belvedere, a handsome park over a parking garage on the riverfront where crumbling warehouses and auto wrecking yards had stood.

The tie to the past in Louisville's latter-day development is greater than meets the eye. Visitors in the early '70s could see construction underway on a major civic center and convention center, just west of center-city, without knowing that a quarter century of planning had gone into it. Wilson W. Wyatt, Louisville's outstanding mayor of the 1940s, told me that two major freeways were decided on during his administration, but they were not completed until 1970. The pedestrian mall for downtown had first been proposed when Wyatt was mayor, too, but work on it was not finished until 1973. One of the men responsible for the mall's actual construction was Wyatt's son, Wilson Jr., a 29-year-old former state representative and executive director of Louisville Central Area, Inc. (Wilson Wyatt, Sr., of whom John Gunther wrote glowingly in *Inside U.S.A.*, later served as lieutenant governor and remains an active citizen today, serving in the presidency of the National Municipal League.)

The change in Louisville is even discernible in its clubs. The blue-ribbon old aristocracy still congregates at the ultra-exclusive Pendennis Club, which to this day has refused to admit a black or Jew to membership. But the atmosphere is somewhat looser at the River Valley Club on the Ohio's banks northeast of town, where the third and fourth generations meet to play cards at night. And in 1971 an alternative prestige business club, the Jefferson, was opened atop one of the downtown skyscrapers, open from the start to members of minority racial groups.

Louisville rarely excites much national news these days, but there is of course one great exception—the Kentucky Derby, run at doughty old Churchill Downs on the hallowed first Saturday of every May, just as it has been every year since 1875. The event is quintessential Kentuckiana—who could doubt it as he hears the hawkers offering mint juleps and the strains of *My Old Kentucky Home* as the horses hit the track? But it is also quintessential Americana; once having seen those twin spires of Churchill Downs and the 100,000-plus crowd stomping on the wooden stands as the cream of horsedom's three-year-olds charge around the track, American writers are prompted to their best. Fred Russell of the Nashville *Banner* penned these lines: "The start of the Kentucky Derby is perhaps the most electrifying moment in sports and Churchill Downs on the first Saturday of May exudes more carnival spirit than any other show." The late humorist Irvin S. Cobb wrote: "If I could describe it, I'd have a larynx of spun silver and the tongue of an anointed angel. . . . Unless you go to Kentucky and with your own eyes behold the Derby, you ain't been nowhere and you ain't never seen nothin'." Dwight Chapin of the Los Angeles *Times*, who assembled those quotes, offered his own: "It's not the richest, nor the best race but it's the best known—by about a million furlongs." And then he added this contribution from his colleague Jim Murray, which I like the best:

Derby Day is like no other day in American sports. For 23 hours and 58 minutes, it is as noisy as a Saturday night in Italy. It is people drinking booze with weeds in it, it is rich men pouring off private planes and poor guys dropping off freights. It is dames who never saw a horse race before in their lives, and dames who have lugged the rent money into the track or to the bookie for so many years they have to shoplift to stay even. It is college kids on a beer lark and bankers sipping martinis in the Matt Winn room. It is hot pants and Salvation Army lasses, guys with holes in their shoes and guys who need a tailor to make their clothes and a valet to help put them on. It is Gaudy Saturday, as American as Stephen Foster, stud poker, and the girlie show.

The Derby is also the occasion of one of the biggest party scenes in America, spread across the landscape from Louisville to Lexington (where the real horse aristocracy hangs out, of course). It is a great rip-off for the Louisville hotels, which double their rates and require one to pay for three nights minimum. And it helps keep Louisville solvent. A chamber of commerce man was asked what the financial impact of the Derby was on Louisville. "What's the impact of the snow at Aspen?" he replied.

Obviously it had to be off the record when a prominent Kentucky politician broke every canon to remark: "What a comment on Louisville that its greatest publicity comes from Derby Day—which is a big bore."

The fact is that there's a lot more to Louisville culture than horses. The city has, in fact, a proud literary and intellectual history, rooted in the early 19th century and enhanced by the broadminded and intelligent Germans who poured in during the 1840s. The University of Louisville, formed in antebellum days, was the first municipally owned university in the United States. The distinguished Louisville Symphony, however, was in danger of going under several years ago. It was then that Mayor Charles Farnsley came forward with the innovative idea of a Louisville Fund for the Arts, which over the years grew to attract thousands of givers who contribute more than a quarter million dollars each year. The symphony flourished, starting an imaginative program for performance of works by new composers that caught on in many other U.S. cities. The city seems to have more than its share of cultural activities, including a children's theater, ballet, opera, Bach society, youth orchestra, dance council, and junior art gallery.

The performing arts got no help, however, from Louisville's biggest giver to charity in modern times. He was J. Graham Brown, an ascetic and shy capitalist who made news in hotels and timber all over the South, running nine distinct corporations. A small group of Louisville leaders gathered at the home of lawyer Rucker Todd one evening described Brown to me as "short, fat, round, incredibly ugly, and taciturn," a man so obsessed with commercial interests that he breakfasted at 6:30 each morning and worked until 10 at night, never married, and had only one hobby in his lifetime— raising horses. He was the largest single stockholder in Churchill Downs. During his life, Brown gave millions to such charities as the Louisville Zoo and a Red Cross blood bank for the city. When he died in 1969, at the age of 87, he left the bulk of his $100 million estate for charitable, educational, and religious purposes. But he forbade using a penny of the estate for the performing arts. It appeared that Brown had once had a tiff with the managers of a theater he owned and wanted to tear down for a parking lot. What's more, theatrical people and all their carryings-on offended the old man's puritanical sensibilities.

(The same group of Louisvillians at Rucker and Ann Todd's home carefully described for me the major geographic sections of Kentucky, somehow omitting their own city. When I asked the reason, they replied: "We're part of Kentucky only once a year—and that's at tax time.")

One of the most fascinating Louisville stories surrounds Carl Braden and his wife Anne, two of the most dedicated and persistent social activists —critics would say agitators—that Kentucky has ever seen. Operating out of a ramshackle old house in the West End, they directed for years the activities of the Southern Conference Educational Fund, an outgrowth of the Southern Conference for Human Welfare that was founded at a 1938 conference attended by Eleanor Roosevelt and Aubrey Williams. Reared in a Eugene Debs-Socialist environment and a worker for the early CIO, Braden was a newspaperman for many years in Louisville, Cincinnati, and, during the bloody labor wars of the 1930s, in Harlan, Kentucky. In the mid-1950s, while working in Louisville as a copy editor for the Louisville *Times*, he purchased a house for a Negro family in a white suburb. The house was dynamited and Braden imprisoned for sedition (until the U.S. Supreme Court reversed his conviction). The Bradens then took over the SCEF, which moved its offices to Louisville from the more hostile atmosphere of New Orleans. Not long after Braden was sentenced to a year in prison for contempt of Congress after he told the House Un-American Activities Committee, which wanted to know the names of his fellow civil rights workers, "My beliefs and my associations are none of the business of this committee."

SCEF, operating with a paid staff of 30 and numerous volunteers, has the avowed aim of helping "the powerless people of the South, white and black, organize themselves for new forms of joint political action that can bring them the power to control their own government, their economic resources, and the conditions of their lives." That means support for black militants and other unpopular types, and also involves a challenge to many established powers; it has also made the organization and its workers a handy target for unscrupulous politicians like Louie Nunn, who promised as a candidate for governor to use his executive power "to run the type of organization the Bradens head out of Kentucky." It was a promise Nunn never made good on. But his 1967 running mate, Thomas Ratliff, commonwealth's attorney for Pike County in eastern Kentucky, did stage a raid on the home of SCEF organizers Alan and Margaret McSurely, who were agitating against strip mining. Ratliff, who had netted about $3 million from strip mining ventures, accused the McSurelys of harboring Communistic literature and got them convicted on a sedition charge which Bert Combs, then a federal judge, quickly invalidated. But the McSurely home was dynamited and they were driven out of eastern Kentucky; later Senator John McClellan got them convicted of contempt of Congress when they defied a subpoena of his Senate subcommittee—a conviction also reversed on appeal.

The thing that impresses one about the Bradens and their associates is that they are invariably exonerated—if not by the courts, then by history. The "radical" things they stand for in one decade look moderate enough in the next. After a long talk with Carl Braden one day, I came away convinced that he was a decent man, deeply disturbed by social injustice and anxious to see American society redeem itself. Kentucky is probably unfortunate not to have more like him.

Residentially, Louisville is divided into three general parts. The East End is the section of the affluent, where gracious homes and mansions house the families of Louisvillians who made their fortunes (recently or long ago) from whiskey, tobacco, banking, or commerce, with a modern admixture of the corporate branch chief types. (Steep, lovely parks, and some grand blufftop views characterize this part of the city.)

The South End, by contrast, is overwhelmingly blue collar and includes many modern-day immigrants from rural Kentucky. And the West End, overwhelmingly white back in the days when black people made up only 15 percent of the city's population, is now largely a black ghetto, with all the familiar problems ranging from overcrowding and joblessness to poverty and inadequate community services. Not long after the 1968 riots in the West End, in which hundreds of people were arrested and two killed, Anne Braden wrote:

A few years ago some of us who are white had dreams of creating in the West End of Louisville a sort of model community—where black and white would work together to the mutual benefit of all. We formed an organization, the West End Community Council, to try to bring this about.

Today, as I ride through the area and see burned buildings, boarded store

windows, and glass-littered streets—silent documentation of the recent disorders—
I see how miserably we have failed.

All that sounds like the familiar scenario of Northern cities, but some
caveats are in order about Louisville's black-white scene. "We've had less
change in our racial composition than most cities," Wilson Wyatt pointed
out. "We have the same race-oriented problems as the rest of the country,
but at lower cadences." A *Courier-Journal* poll in the late '60s found that
61 percent of Louisville's blacks favored nonviolent protest as the best way
to effect change, and that 51 still preferred to be called "Negro." Only 8
percent wanted to be known as "black." Even the 1968 riot was mild compared to what most other large cities experienced.

Although blacks were household slaves in antebellum Louisville, the
record shows a relatively enlightened public policy afterward. Public education created a quite literate Negro populace within a few decades of the Civil
War. Rigid segregation in schools and all sorts of public accommodations continued right down to the 1940s, but blacks were free to vote and there was a
flourishing culture of black-owned stores, hotels, restaurants, theaters, and
newspaper publishing houses. Black home ownership up to World War II
was relatively high, albeit in mostly substandard units. Louisville sent a
Negro representative to the state legislature in 1934, elected its first black
alderman in 1945, and chose its first black state senator—a personally delightful and politically astute woman, Georgia Davis—in 1967. The first desegregation in Louisville began well before cities further south, as blacks in the
late 1940s were admitted to many municipal facilities on an equal basis with
whites. In 1951 they were first admitted to the University of Louisville, and,
as we noted earlier in this chapter, school desegregation after the 1954 Supreme Court decision went quite smoothly.

Politically, Louisville for years had been balanced about 2–1 for the
Democrats. The East End was predictably Republican; the working families
of the South End were mostly Democrats; and the West End blacks, since
FDR's day, had voted Democratic. But by the start of the '60s the Democrats
had become stale, offering for office run-of-the-mill businessmen sponsored
by the entrenched Fourth Street Democratic Organization. In the spring of
1961 the Democratic-controlled board of aldermen turned a cold face to
Negro demands for a human relations commission and an ordinance to open
up restaurants and other public accommodations to black people. This gave
the Republicans a golden opportunity, which they seized that fall by electing
two bright young men in their 30s—William O. Cowger and Marlow Cook
—as mayor and Jefferson County judge (executive) respectively. Cowger and
Cook talked about reviving Louisville's sluggish economy and spirit, but the
vital political turn was their ability, in the face of a segregationist-type campaign by the Democratic mayor, to snare over 60 percent of the black vote.
Soon afterwards a comprehensive accommodations law was passed, and the
human relations commission set up. The Republicans provided such generally outstanding administration of local government that even in 1965, when
their black vote slipped badly, they were still able to reelect Cook with 64

percent of the vote, install their chosen candidate to succeed Cowger as mayor, and win most of the 24 state legislative races in the county. Cowger ran for Congress in 1966 and 1968, winning a strong Louisville vote, just as Thruston Morton and John Sherman Cooper had for several years.

On the local scene, however, things did not go well for the GOP after 1965. Kenneth Schmied, Cowger's successor in city hall, turned out to be a very pedestrian leader and let many important local projects languish. After Schmied resisted open-housing demonstrations in 1967, the Democrats swept back to control of the board of aldermen (and promptly enacted an open-housing ordinance). The next year Cook left to go to the U.S. Senate, and in 1969 the Democrats won both the mayoralty and county judgeship. Newsman William Greider quoted a local Republican officeholder as saying: "It took the Democrats 28 years, but we managed to blow it in only eight." Moderate Republicans charged that Schmied and the other Republicans had turned their backs on political moderation, an untenable position in an urban area with a central city 24 percent black. In 1970 Cowger took the low road, accusing his Democratic opponent of radical connections, and was narrowly defeated for a third term in Congress. The GOP was virtually obliterated in the 1973 city and county elections, when the Democrats won by landslide proportions.

Harvey Sloane, Louisville's mayor for the 1974–79 period, may turn out to be one of the more significant political personalities of the next decade. Born in Virginia in the late 1930s, he graduated from Yale and Cleveland's Western Reserve School of Medicine. Rebelling against his family, he became a hobo for a while, sleeping in boxcars, getting to know different kinds of people around the United States. Before he actually "settled down," Sloane found time to work on an oil rig in the Gulf of Mexico, to pick celery with migrant Mexicans in California and strawberries with Indians in Oregon, to be a construction worker in western Canada, to join an international survey team studying hunger in Malaysia, to serve as a medical volunteer for Vietnamese civilians, and to visit medical facilities in Peru and the Soviet Union. In the mid-1960s he worked for two years in a health program in Appalachian Kentucky. Family wealth helped make some of these exploits possible, but still, on meeting Sloane, an unprepossessing though affable young man, one has to be amazed.

In 1966 Sloane chose Louisville as a place to live—because "It enjoys the benefits of a large city while still having a small-town atmosphere. Its problems are solvable; it's not a Newark or a Cleveland, and America's future depends upon the future of its cities." Sloane established and made a great success of an OEO-funded neighborhood health center which cares for some 15,000 of Louisville's poor and near-poor. After six years as its director, he resigned to run for mayor. His Democratic primary opponent, ironically, was another physician, Carroll Witten, a conservative and favorite of the old-line organization Democrats. Among the issues on which the two clashed was medical-care delivery, with Witten warning about the dangers of socialized medicine while Sloane argued: "If we as a country cannot care for our people but can only subsidize such inept railroads as the Penn Central and airplane companies as Lockheed, then our future is dim indeed."

Sloane's biggest problem was to win the Democratic primary. A poll in late 1972 had shown his name recognition among Louisvillians was only 15 percent, and Witten, his adversary, was well known as president of the city's board of aldermen. Sloane hired a professional campaign manager, put $135,000 of his own money into the primary (out of a total budget of $188,000), and concentrated on coffee hours with small groups and a lot of door-to-door canvassing. Before the campaign started, an alderman had dismissed Sloane as "a loopy liberal" with no chance of success. But Sloane, through his contact with citizens, crystalized a set of issues that put that label to rest. He came down strong for law and order, urging more police district substations and more foot patrols. He put a lot of emphasis on supporting and strengthening the individual neighborhoods of the city. To all of this he added a populist theme of less taxes and a better break for the poor man. And in the year of Watergate Sloane made the well advised move of disclosing all his financial holdings early in the campaign and insisting that all contributions to his campaign, however small, be made public, even those below $500 which the law did not require reporting. He ended up winning the primary with a majority in all 12 wards of the city.

The momentum from the primary virtually assured Sloane's general election victory over a rather weak Republican opponent, C. J. Hyde, former police chief of the city. Sloane agreed to spend only $3,000 of his own money at this stage, out of a campaign budget of about $90,000. He conducted a well publicized 250-mile walk through the Louisville neighborhoods, producing invaluable word-of-mouth, neighbor-to-neighbor campaign endorsements. The theme was strictly upbeat—that Louisville was a good place to live and could be made even better, by good law enforcement and equalizing city and county tax loads. The final returns showed Sloane the victor by a margin of better than 2–1, the biggest plurality in any mayoralty election in Louisville history. The same election also resulted in a landslide reelection victory for the liberal Democratic Jefferson County judge, 33-year-old Todd Hollenbach, who was aiming at an early race for the U.S. Senate or governor.

Harvey Sloane's mixture of pragmatism and energy could well furnish what Wilson Wyatt told me had been missing for a long time—"any real leadership from City Hall." But Sloane would be faced with the same dilemma that his immediate predecessor, former Democratic Congressman Frank Burke, and all recent Louisville mayors had been obliged to grapple with—whether the city, within its existing boundaries, could cope adequately with its problems. During the 1960s the population of the city proper declined by 7.5 percent, to 361,472, the lowest figure in a quarter century. In the meantime the suburban ring in Jefferson County went up 51 percent, to 333,583. The number of suburban cities mushroomed from 30 to more than 70 in a hodgepodge of small, jealously guarded little principalities. There were some advances toward ostensibly more rational government as the city and county merged or pooled a number of previously separate functions, ranging from parks and library services to sewer and water facilities. But former Mayor Charles Farnsley claimed that the terms of merged services had bled the city white. "The white middle class moved out and tried to get the people inside the city to pay the bills," he said. "All power—and services —flow to the rich districts. The taxes are all set up to bleed the poor of the city for the benefit of the rich outside. Louisville simply doesn't get a fair share. It loses perhaps $200 million net a year to the county and the state, yet it's the area that needs the money." (Farnsley, perhaps the angriest ex-mayor I encountered anywhere on my travels, also said of the ghetto conditions: "I'm one jump from a riot myself. I'm mad. The blacks would be even angrier if they knew what was happening to them." He also dismissed the value of urban renewal and highways because "they have driven people from their homes and destroyed their churches.")

The essential point of Farnsley's complaint about fiscal inequalities boils down to taxation. When water and sewer rates are set at so much per gallon, for instance, or a suburban community pays just what the cost of an extended service to it may be, Farnsley sees the system as "cruelly regressive" because the affluent are not paying enough to subsidize the costs to the poor, for whom each dollar paid in taxes or fees is more burdensome.

Up to now, the political climate has been hostile to any kind of merger that would effect the kind of income redistribution critics like Farnsley urge. Even more limited proposals have come to naught. A proposal for Louisville to annex 46 square miles of urbanized land in the county was approved by city voters but overwhelmingly rejected by voters outside the city limits in 1955. Under a more recent amendment to the state constitution, Louisville could expand to include areas in the county, setting tax rates appropriate to services rendered. At the start of the '70s a bipartisan task force of the area chamber of commerce, headed by Wilson Wyatt and Thurston Morton, recommended that Louisville be expanded to take in all unincorporated areas in the county. But even that modest proposal has yet to win enough political support to make significant headway.

Like many other innovations in Louisville, the idea of piecemeal annexation, or even completely consolidated government for the metropolitan region, will probably have to bide its time. Sloane said he was leery of annexing reluctant suburbs and saw a more fruitful avenue in consolidating more county-city functions, especially the police, and working toward a fairly loose confederation of localities under a metropolitan umbrella, like the Dade County-Miami model. Cautious Louisville will probably weigh a lot of possibilities, will watch to see how the Lexington metro government works out, and then debate and think some more. Finally, it will probably act. But not precipitously.

In the meantime, those who want change can take heart in the infusion of youth—the rising generation symbolized by Sloane and Hollenbach, Barry Bingham, Jr., John Y. Brown, Jr., and Wilson Wyatt, Jr. There are other youthful innovators, like Newman Walker, who has done much to rejuvenate the city school system, and George T. Underhill, Jr., a onetime Goldwater Republican who got a livewire program called "Action Now" organized in the late 1960s to aid poor people with housing, jobs, and economic development. The youth wave is even apparent in the arts: Jorge Mester, the conductor of the Louisville Symphony, and Jon Jory, producing director of the Actors Theater, are both under 40. The yeast of change has obviously been slipped into the Louisville brew; now the question is how long the fermentation will take.

East Kentucky: Perennial Problem Child

Outside of a joke about bloodlines and relating that mountaineers can spit burley juice ten yards in a crooked line, John Gunther had barely a paragraph to report about the whole region of East Kentucky in his *Inside U.S.A.* With hindsight, one can be a little shocked about the short shrift given this vast and most troubled of Kentucky territories; yet in fact until the late 1950s and early '60s, only isolated incidents—like Harlan's bloody mine wars of the 1930s—ever reached national notice.

Then, in the late 1950s and early 1960s, East Kentucky suddenly emerged in the public consciousness as a place where the human and ecologic crises of Appalachia reach their climax, a case study of rural poverty in America. Two natural calamities, crippling floods in 1957 and again in 1963, helped focus attention on the region, and John Kennedy's 1960 primary campaign in neighboring West Virginia dramatized the problems of all of the southern Appalachians. (Today in East Kentucky mountain homes one is likely to find three pictures on the wall—Jesus Christ, Franklin Roosevelt, and John Kennedy.) These were the years of heavy layoffs in the coal mines, throwing tens of thousands of men out of work in a region with no effective relief programs. Then, in 1962, Americans began to learn in depth about East Kentucky through Harry M. Caudill's *Night Comes to the Cumberlands*, one of the most poignant and compelling accounts ever written on the woes of an American region, and certainly the best ever on Appalachia.

Before long, reporters, sociologists, social planners, federal bureaucrats, and, on one occasion, even President Lyndon Johnson were descending upon this problem child of state and nation, observing and prescribing solutions for everything from its dire poverty and isolation to its coal-mine-ravaged landscape. The plight of East Kentucky was to lead directly to establishment of the Appalachian Regional Commission and contribute significantly to Washington's decision to launch the Great Society's "war on poverty." And the need was real enough, for as the Census showed there were few other American regions in which income levels were so abysmally low, where so much housing was dilapidated, where illiteracy was such a pervasive problem.

Yet as Harry Caudill himself observed, in a talk we had one morning between cases he was handling as an attorney for his trouble-prone mountain neighbors in the Letcher County Courthouse—

East Kentucky always leads the nation. We are a pioneer territory.

We were the frontier—the West—back in the 1780s, and to an amazing extent we blazed the way for the nation.

We taught the nation the consequences of land exhaustion and too many people. When you read the projections of the Club of Rome [about a crisis point in the next century when the world will lack enough resources for its population] you realize you're reading what happened to East Kentucky before the Depression, when the land wore out and the people became too numerous, and society broke down for a lack of resources.

We also taught the nation, through our experience with coal, what can happen when an industry is mechanized too rapidly. The coal catastrophe sent people out of these mountains after World War II and struck them with the same kind of idleness and bitterness one has seen around the air and space centers with the collapse or near-collapse of such giants as Lockheed.

Finally, we led the nation with environmental ills. To a big extent, the nation became aware of environmental problems through the strip mines and burning coal heaps, the polluted streams and devastated forests of East Kentucky.

We are the nation's perennial problem child.

What makes East Kentucky the way it is? The answer seems to lie in the peculiar convergence of people, land, and resources in this ragged backwoods of eastern America. The first settlers who came down through the Cumberland Gap found a land of sharp hillsides and small valleys, intricately compartmentalized. The whole was covered with great virgin hardwood forests; the waters were flashing clean; from streams and woodlands came fish and game plentiful for a settler's needs. Properly cultivated, some have suggested, this might have been as pleasing and prosperous a province as Switzerland, a land of not very dissimilar topography.

Yet from the very start, the devastation of the Cumberland Plateau began. The frontiersmen viewed the wilderness as a place to be conquered, not to be preserved. They used farming methods that would seriously erode and deplete the soil before their grandchildren reached maturity. They hunted the once copious game virtually to the point of extinction of many species. Late in the 19th century came the great logging boom. With casual abandon, the great aboriginal forests of black walnut and chestnut and white oak and sugar maple were decimated in an orgy of felling and cutting. Sometimes logs of four to ten feet would be taken out, but the idea of planned reseeding never seemed to occur to the loggers. Out of these forests came wood for houses and ships, for tobacco hogsheads, for cooperage for whiskey, and finally a basic supply of the next era of exploitation: props for the coal mines. Left behind were denuded hillsides where new growth would take decades to develop. With the natural cover decimated, floods became an ever more serious problem. Then the coal barons completed the destruction, turning East Kentucky into a ravaged land.

Caudill suggests that the uncultured, rough people who settled East Kentucky, and then lived on there in splendid isolation, simply lacked the skills or intelligence to nurture their land and protect it from outside domination. One generally looked in vain for men of letters or distinguished familial lines, skilled tradesmen or craftsmen or merchants, among those who came to occupy the hills. Rather it was the castoffs of 18th-century society, English and Scotch-Irish, those who had been street orphans or debtors or prisoners in Britain, despised by the motherland and sold into forms of indentured servanthood, who chose the frontier and spread "along every creek bed and up every hidden valley."

The Appalachian frontiersman, Caudill wrote, was "an uncouth brawler, wholly undisciplined and untamed." He made up for his lack of skills through his adeptness as a fighter; he had hated the crown, and now in America "any manifestation of government was abhorrent to his lawless soul." In 1799, after Kentucky had joined the Union, 16,000 square miles of East Kentucky were designated as Floyd County. Yet 16 years would pass before Floyd's courthouse, a log structure 22 feet on a side, was built. The night it was dedicated it was burned by parties unknown; apparently there were mountaineers who saw it as a symbol of oppression. They simply wanted no government. During the Civil War practically every courthouse in East Kentucky was put to the torch, many by the indigenous population, and to this day the region remains a big one for school burnings. The attitude seems to be that if there have to be schools, and if they are poor ones, and if the government refuses to build better ones, the best way to solve the problem is by sending the old ones up in smoke.

For East Kentuckians the tradition of independence and violence was built by event after event, starting with the bitterly fought Indian wars, continuing to struggles against the federal government when it tried to impose taxes on whiskey, through the Civil War, and then down to this century with guerrilla warfare and clan blood feuds. Scarcely a tenth of the people, at the turn of the century, had experienced enough schooling to sign their names with any more sophisticated mark than an "X." They were easy prey for the timber and coal men who paid pittances to exploit their land. They sought work in the coal mines, risking life and limb for what seemed to be decent enough wages; thousands, however, were maimed if not killed as they worked in the bowels of the earth. As the mines discharged half and more of their workers, the stage was set for arrival of the welfare system, sapping the last bit of the mountaineers' independence. What was left, Caudill wrote, was a population "listless, hopeless, without ambition." Another conclusion, not too different, was reached by John Fetterman of the Louisville *Courier-Journal*, who described the mountain people to me as "fundamentalist, fatalistic, literal Bible-reading folks who believe that if you're going to be poor, you're going to be poor."

Yet what is true for the mass may be false in the particular. Fetterman, for instance, has also described a sharp diversity of mountaineer types. "Each hollow," he wrote in a *National Geographic* article, "has its moonshine peddlers and loose women and lazy men and complaining women. And each hollow has its courageous men and determined women who battle hopeless odds to bring their broods to a better life." In many a mountain family Fetterman found qualities of innate honor and curiosity and loyalty to friend and kin that could put many other American families to shame. He has written of farm men and women of a charm and warmth that defies every description of the taciturn, suspicious hillbilly. I liked his account of a Memorial Day spent at a neatly tended cemetery south of Hyden as the roads up the hollow were crowded with cars from Detroit and Chicago and Cincinnati, the expatriates returning to decorate the graves of kinfolk and reestablish their tie to the mountains. "Being here is being somebody," a young Vietnam veteran said. "You don't have to buy your spot to be buried in. I want my children to always come see this place. It's beautiful and the people are that way. I can remember Grandma. She was so gentle that wild birds would eat out of her hands."

Caudill's view, by contrast, is that the isolation and depression of mountain life, the lawlessness and lack of opportunity, have driven out the most talented and promising sons and daughters of the region, those who might have built independent and self-reliant institutions on their own home soil. The drain of human talent has been going on for close to a century now, he said. He spoke of his mother's brother, who was given 35 cents by his mother one day in 1901 and sent down the creek to a little country store to buy a box of soda and a box of baking powder. But instead of coming hime, his uncle—who was only 11 years old at the time— kept that 35 cents in his pocket and kept on walking, on to Whitesburg, across Pine Mountain; he slept under a cliff and then kept on going until he reached a railhead in Virginia, where he hopped a train, and got to Arkansas. He eventually landed in New York and there, in time, married an English-woman and amassed a fortune of a million dollars. Predictably, he never returned to East Kentucky.

"Consider my high school class," Caudill said. "One of my classmates is a tax commissioner in the District of Columbia, and another is a traffic commissioner there. One is a vice president of Chrysler Airtemp. Another is a vice president of the Bank of America, the head of their computer program. Another is in charge of security for a big Ford plant in Los Angeles. They all came off these East Kentucky creeks. But the bloodstream is thinned now by intermarrying, and we won't have another class like that for a long time."

Who is left in East Kentucky? Caudill's view is dreary in the extreme. Primarily, he asserts, it is the ignorant and the weak, the kind of families who have 10 or 12 children, unable to care for any of them adequately. There are schools in East Kentucky, he said, where the IQ level goes down an average of a point a year, year after year. "The big industry in East Kentucky," he insisted, "is checks—signing up for, getting qualified for, mailing out, receiving, cashing, spending welfare checks. We have a myth our economy is based on coal. It isn't; it's based on poverty." The result, Caudill believes, is to make citizens very timid, "a kept population" with little capacity for asserting its own rights or stopping corruption in government.

The best thing that could happen to the mountains, Caudill thinks, would be for the Army to put in a big base, thus introducing some new genes into the people's bloodstream. "Send in some of those eager boys, because these mountain girls will cross with anybody. They do love to consort, and that would be good for the country. Many of the problems of East Kentucky that they're spending money on are insoluble until you get in new genes."

To understand the gene problem, one has to recall how East Kentucky people live—crowded together in hollows, which are isolated from each other. It is an incredible picture of density of a thin population. John Fetterman explained well the milieu of the "hillbilly" in his 1967 book, *Stinking Creek:*

> A hillbilly rarely lives upon a hill. He lives in a hollow. All hollows are basically the same: high mountain walls thrown up on either side by a whimsical nature millions of years ago; at the bottom of the fold in the land runs a stream that drains the watershed. . . . Along these streams, with the mountains soaring both behind and before him, the hillbilly dwells.
>
> In Appalachia there are thousands of such hollows, each with its own winding stream. All the hollows have two things in common: the streams become larger as they near their rendezvous with the larger streams they serve as tributaries, and the people at the mouths of these larger hollows and streams are more affluent. As you walk farther and farther up the hollow, both the size of the stream and the standard of living decline steadily. . . .
>
> So in judging the social, political and financial status of the hillbilly, it is not enough to ask, "Are you a hillbilly?" One must also ask, "How far up the hollow do you come from?"

Fetterman's descripton of the hollows remains universally true in East Kentucky. The region today is criss-crossed with the impressive new roads of recent years, many the work of the Appalachian Regional Commission, cutting unbelievably deep gashes through the ragged hills and in fact materially reducing the isolation of the region. Yet if one turns off anywhere, the roads up the hollows can be found. I investigated several, some on the tips of friends, others at random. And always the picture was the same: fairly sturdy and well-tended houses at the bottom of the hollow, and then near the top the broken-down, ramshackle cabins, surrounded by abandoned autos and heaps of junk and old furniture, as often as not with half-clad little children looking blankly at the intruders into their remote corner of the world. My own children came along on some of those expeditions, and they made the inevitable comment of today's city-reared youngsters: "But we thought only black people are poor."

One of the areas in which Appalachian Kentucky has made some headway of late, is in beginning, however tentatively, to solve its egregious problem of unsightly mounds of trash thrown along practically every roadway of the region. Traditionally, not a single county of East Kentucky had a publicly run trash removal service; as a result, when the refuse was not thrown into rivers and creeks, there to cause hideous pollution problems, it was simply dumped beside the highways—old wrappers and tin cans, bottles and disintegrating mattresses, rusting bed springs and the carcasses of generations of cast-off trucks and cars. Rats, flies, and smoldering fires followed in due course, and it seemed as if no one in the region cared. The refuse problem continues today, but the worst of it is seen only up the hollows. Along the main roadways trash receptacles are being installed, county trash removal systems are appearing, and if federal dollars to assist in solid waste removal—East Kentucky always needs federal money to attack any problem—are not cut off in the next years, the mountain folk may finally learn to stop despoiling their own environment.

Unlike most regions of America, Kentucky has the huge bulk of its people living in such rural settings. Outside of Ashland, at the region's far northeast corner, only 15 percent of the region's 600,000 people live in towns or cities of more than 2,500 people. Storied whiskey and mining towns like Harlan, Hazard, Whitesburg, and Pikeville, though they are county seats, represent a small share of the county's population.* And even the cities, such as they are, are exhibitions of incredibly intertwined family lines. In the thin little Whitesburg phone book, I looked up Harry Caudill's number and found 167 families of the same surname. There were 203 Adamses in the same book, and extraordinary numbers of such blood-lines as Sexton, Stallard, Boggs, Combs, Fields, Kinker, Profitt, and Shepherd.

Harry Caudill's harsh view of his fellow mountaineers jarred me, and I made an effort to test his theory of interbreeding and genetic problems with other thoughtful people in the mountains. William Hambley, a physician and mayor of Pikeville, said there were instances of genetic disasters, like a hollow in his county where brothers have married sisters and the like and "the whole clan are virtually idiots." But enough traveling salesmen came into his area, Hambley said, to give the cross-breeding process a healthy thrust. The greater problem, as he saw it, was cultural confinement. "When someone here uses a word with an unfamiliar inflection," Hambley said, "people know he doesn't belong. They become suspicious and say, 'He's an outsider.' You find this among the educated as well as the uneducated. Part of this cultural confinement is used by those who know better as a means of controlling the people." As for breeding, Hambley said, it has only to do with the fact that large families are more likely to be narrowly confined in their culture. He agreed with Caudill that many of the smartest were leaving, and that the welfare contingent, ill-educated and unadaptive to new thoughts, posed a grave problem for the region. "But our people are very intelligent if they get a chance," Hambley said. "And among those who do remain here, to run businesses and services, there will be many competent people."

If one wants to find an example of creative local initiative in East Kentucky, Hambley's Pikeville is about the best one can find. Many local people have been involved in developing the fantastically ambitious and ex-

---

* The 1970 Census showed 25,714 people in Perry County, for instance, but only 21 percent of them—5,459—in Hazard, Whitesburg's 3,624 people were only 16 percent of the Letcher County population. Harlan's 3,318 represented only 9 percent of the county total. And Pikeville, with 4,576 inhabitants, made up only 7 percent of the population of Pike County.

pensive plans for this forlorn-looking little city on a fork of the Big Sandy River in the East Kentucky mountains. But Hambley himself, a human dynamo and intellectual of no mean proportions (if unchecked, he will regale a visitor for hours about his own complex and quite brilliant system of metaphysics and explanations of human behavior throughout history), is the chief reason there is now hope in a city and county that seemed to have the cards stacked against it in every imaginable way.

Pikeville is the county seat of sprawling Pike County, the largest in Kentucky, which has few equals in the production of coal. Born in Pikeville in 1914, Hambley went off in 1935 to enter Notre Dame University (where he made the Irish football team), with M. D. and Master of Science degrees from Northwestern University, and complete highly successful internships and residences in Illinois. When Hambley returned to practice in Pikeville in 1953, he found the area plunged into a great coal mining depression that would push unemployment to 14 percent, force a third of the people to desert the area of their birth, and oblige half those remaining to struggle along on poverty-level incomes. "From 1953 to 1962 I couldn't make $10,000 a year, even though I had a big practice," Hambley said. "Seventy percent of my practice was charity. Every third house in Pikeville was empty. Those were such grim years that people offered me unbelievably valuable coal lands in trade for medical services. One man offered me a 1,000-acre tract of coal land for $75,000; I couldn't raise the money, and he has since sold the property for more than $1 million."

Pikeville in those years, Hambley found, suffered from "isolation, cultural confinement, depreciated human values, and underdevelopment of its greatest asset—its people." In 1955 Hambley decided he wanted to do something to solve the problem, and he gave himself 20 years to put through what would eventually become a grand—some would even say grandiose—program of physical and human renaissance. Not long after he was elected to the city council and in 1961 became mayor. Two examples suggest what he had been able to achieve by the early 1970s. When he took the oath as mayor, the city was terribly in debt with an $86,000 unsecured note at the bank and two payrolls that couldn't be met. "You couldn't buy a damned nut or bolt on credit," Hambley said. "Our general fund budget was $112,000, and 50 percent of that was property tax. We altered the fiscal policy to make it a growth policy, establishing a payroll and net profits tax which I consider a marvelous monitoring system for what's happening in your economy." By 1973, the city budget had gone over $600,000 a year. When Hambley took office, the city had only two acres of recreational land, and there were only one and three-quarter acres of land for the schools. He eventually got 20 acres for the elementary school, and the city bought four acres for a new high school adjacent to a new 11-acre ballfield. Such amenities seem commonplace in most American cities, but the crowded valley-sites and shortsighted early planning of Appalachian Kentucky make them great innovations there.

By the mid-1960s Pikeville had succeeded in selling $2 million in revenue bonds for a modern water and sewage system, built a new $800,000 elementary school, spent $100,000 for street improvements, and begun an $8.5 million urban renewal plan. These were some of the reasons the National Municipal League and *Look* gave Pikeville an All-American City award in 1966.

Hambley was not content, however, to rest on those laurels. He had some massive projects in mind for Pikeville, and perceived a chance to get a vital increment of federal support through two developing Great Society programs—the Appalachian Regional Commission and Model Cities. For an impoverished community like Pikeville, both programs were potential godsends because they could supply the local share required to qualify for most federal grant-in-aid programs. To get that kind of boot-strap aid, however, Pikeville needed to demonstrate broad citizen participation. Therefore a community services commission was formed to bring in representatives from the city's civic clubs, churches, youth, and low-income population. Hambley's close associate and fellow Pikeville native, Homer Robinson, became chairman of the human services commission, which was to provide a way for the city to adopt "the planning discipline as a basis for community growth and development."

Pikeville applied for a grant to plan its future under Model Cities, and in November 1967 the city's name was on the list of 63 chosen for the first round of grants under the program. The fact that Pikeville was in Carl Perkins' district doubtless helped in its selection as the smallest of all communities picked for Model Cities, but Hambley's salesmanship was probably even more important.

Pikeville's peculiar physical and human problems set the framework for the array of programs which began to develop through Model Cities and ARC aid. The city was already the medical center and the legal and the educational center for a regional population of 200,000 mountain people, but it was severely restricted in growing to meet its full potential as a chief regional service center. The chief drawbacks were isolation, occasioned by the inadequate roads coming in through the mountains, and critical overcrowding in the city proper. The isolation problem started on its way to solution when the ARC began to improve four major highway corridors through this part of Appalachia—all of which happened to converge in Pikeville.

The overcrowding problem was much thornier. Pikeville had been built in the 19th century on a mountainous neck of land formed by a horseshoe curve in a fork of the Big Sandy River. Around the curve, crowded right into the downtown section, came U.S. Route 23 and the lines of the Chesapeake and Ohio Railroad. The river and the railroad took up 50 percent of the level space, and both were disruptive factors: the river because of periodic flooding, and the railroad because it competed for space with automobiles and pedestrians and caused occasional wrecks. Passenger traffic on the railroad was long since past anyway, so it was just hauling coal through the city. The situation in downtown Pikeville's narrow streets was so severe that traffic piled up for six or eight blocks, parking space was almost impossible to find, and the flow of autos came to a virtual standstill on the day each month the welfare checks were given out. Attracting new industries or service facilities under those conditions was a near impossibility.

Various types of federal and state aid would have been available to build a highway bypass, or to tunnel the railway through the mountains and get it out of town, or perhaps even to divert the river through a cut in the mountains. The genius of Hambley and his associates was to propose a single, 1,000-foot-wide cut-through that would accommodate all three—the highway, the railroad, and the river itself. The single cut-through, far more attractive on a cost-benefit analysis, required the coordination of a plethora of government agencies. But Pikeville finally got them all to agree, pooling Model Cities, ARC, urban renewal, and Corps of Engineers funds to pay the total $22.5 million cost of the cut-through. Pikeville had to mortgage itself for $1.25 million, a big cost for the city but a minor part of the total. The excavation for the cut-through, which will have the highway on one side and the railroad on the other side of the new river channel, will involve digging up 16 million cubic yards of mountain—half again the solid volume of the Grand Coulee Dam and nearly a tenth of the digging for the Panama Canal. The landfill will be dumped into the obsolete horseshoe bend of the river, thus creating some 250 acres of level land, directly adjacent to the city, an immense new asset in a region so rugged that level acreage for economic development is as hard to find as water in Death Valley or mountains in Louisiana. Among the facilities to be built on the drained riverbed will be two vital to Pikeville's regional center role—a one-stop medical service building for the surrounding counties and a one-stop social services building for welfare recipients.

As dramatic as the cut-through may be, Dr. Hambley insists it is secondary to improved education, "the crux of our entire program and the only way to break out of our cultural confinement." At his instigation Pikeville has tried to create a model of educational process development, ranging from preschool through vocational and postgraduate training. Again, he has played crafty fundsmanship, obtaining hundreds of thousands of dollars, often through Model Cities, for improved college-level training, the Teacher Corps, vocational education, and a plethora of smaller programs.

Hambley has also been a leading force in the Big Sandy Development District, one of the 15 into which Kentucky was divided by the state legislature, and since the early '70s the chief funnel for federal funds flowing into the localities. John Whisman, states regional representative for the Appalachian Regional Commission, named Big Sandy as a model for the type of substate regional planning groups which the ARC has sought to foster throughout Appalachia. Not only in Pikeville but also in Prestonburg and Paintsville, the other important towns of Big Sandy, one sees today new health facilities, new low-cost housing, and the germs of a wave of industrial development that could one day be the salvation of these hard-pressed coal counties. Dr. Hambley sees industrial diversification as an essential ingredient of "breaking the monopolistic, single-industry economy of coal," so that there will be a broadened management base, employment options for the people, and a better chance to develop a democratic society.

The threat to miners' health posed by pneumoconiosis or black lung— discussed more fully in the West Virginia chapter of this book—has become a major public issue in Kentucky in recent years. In some counties black lung checks have replaced welfare or food stamps as the most important support of the local economy. But Dr. Hambley said that as a chest specialist he had also become alarmed by the high incidence of silicosis among coal miners caused by the high-speed cutting equipment used in the mines today. (There are streaks of sandstone, even in the highest-quality coal seams, Hambley said, producing fine silica dust, and thus almost inevitably disabling cases of silicosis.) Hambley said he had such little faith in the coal industry's desire, or even its technological capacity to control the silica dust, that he looked to a future agreement among the coal firms and the unions to work out a system for transferring each worker to a safer, new industry at the earliest signs of disability. That solution, however, would have to wait arrival of the alternative industries, and they are still few and far between in East Kentucky today. And unless the cultural and educational environment of the region can be made more attractive, Hambley noted, the wives of the executives and scientists of potential new industries would never agree to move to East Kentucky.

The type of solutions Hambley has sought for his city and the Big Sandy Region involve a close orchestration of the efforts of multitudinous government bodies, ranging from the local to the federal, and very ambitious physical and social planning. As we noted in the introduction to this book, there are many mountain people who consider this a rather dangerous type of social engineering that can and often does eclipse the right of the highlanders to decide their own destiny. The Big Sandy district has been severely attacked on occasion for refusing to put more "plain people"—especially poor ones—on its board. Critics say development district control inevitably falls to the "Main Street crowd"—county and town officials, the merchants, lawyers, and undertakers. The other side of that argument is that development districts, through the people they pull together in common endeavor, can function as agents of good will, overcoming the traditional and deep-seated suspicions and hostilities that exist from county to county and even hollow to hollow.

Big Sandy's difficulties are minor compared to those of the Kentucky River Development District, which encompasses eight utterly poverty stricken counties further to the southwest, the "lowest of the low" in any type of standard-of-living index in any part of Appalachia. The Kentucky River District, ever since its inception, has been entangled in bitter personal disputes among its leaders and with elements of the indigenous population. Yet it was the grueling poverty conditions of the Kentucky River area in particular that created the publicity which led to formation of the Appalachian Regional Commission in the first instance. Attacking the development district leadership, one prominent citizen of the Kentucky River region said: "In terms of representation, the ARC provides tokenism, and hardly that. They work with elected officials. Oh, sure, that leaves us where we've been for 200 years. No one worth two cents ever runs for public office in East Kentucky. We buy and sell county judges every day, and we hold mayors in contempt, and we're not about to respond to their leadership."

If the reader finds that kind of statement incomprehensible in view of the relative success of the neighboring Sandy River district, he can put it down to classic East Kentucky orneriness and differences of view—and probably be right. Consider, for instance, this view of conditions in Hazard, the biggest town of the Kentucky River area, as related in 1970 by *Business Week*:

> Hazard is a grimy mining town crouched along a winding valley. It is cursed by a dearth of local leadership, fierce jealousies, and a sadly dispirited populace. Big coal trucks rumble along dusty, narrow streets adding layers of soot to the squat, 19th-century brick buildings. Railroad coal cars bang and bump along the narrow stream valley below shacks set precariously on hillsides. The town's residents wear the classically hollow, forlorn look of every boom-bust mining town from Pontyberem, Wales, to Shenandoah, Pennsylvania.

Hazard's Mayor Bill Morton was quoted as saying that "coal and the dole are sapping vitality." I went to look at Hazard for myself three years later and found things a bit brighter than the 1970 report—but not much.

Just north of Hazard lies Breathitt County, the scene of incredibly bloody feuds in earlier times, where one of East Kentucky's handful of remaining true-blue political machines—the Turner family dynasty—remains in power. The old county judge, Ervine Turner, the kindly dispositioned but immensely political, astute patriarch, died in 1968, but his wife Marie, herself a veteran of many political wars who built a base for many years as the outstanding and powerful county school superintendent, remains vital and active in her seventies. The Turners, John Ed Pearce of the Louisville *Courier-Journal* wrote, "rose to power in the hard days of the New Deal, when poverty lay heavy in the mountains. . . . In the classic pattern of Kentucky politics, they channeled money and jobs down to needy people, and the people in turn sent back votes that increased their power and their access to money and jobs."

Today holding power is becoming more complicated, because of fissures in the next generation. On one side has been the Turners' son, John Raymond, a controversial figure given to "telling people off" on occasion, and their daughter, Treva Turner Howell, for several years head of the poverty program in a multicounty area. Governor Louie Nunn vetoed a $177,000 OEO grant for Treva's program but got his fingers burned when Treva went off to Washington and excoriated him before Carl Perkins' committee in a speech written for her by Ed Prichard. The veto was overridden by Washington, but when Treva ran against her brother John Raymond for state representative in 1973, John Raymond won. One reason may have been that Treva Howell, in running the poverty program, had raised enough feathers to get the banks, the coal companies, the school superintendents, and most of the local politicians—including her matriarch mother Marie Turner—lined up against her. But she is a charming and indefatigable woman who may yet win out and be a bridge to a better era.

One sign of progress in Breathitt is that when a onetime Turner ally turned on the clan and called them "the biggest bunch of trash I ever saw," no gunfire cracked across the hills.

In 1973–74, however, threats of violence reappeared in "Bloody Harlan" County where the reformed United Mine Workers of America and the Eastover Mining Company, a subsidiary of Duke Power Company of Charlotte, North Carolina, were locked in a prolonged strike. The UMW, which had organized the area's mines after the protracted, murderous struggles of the 1930s, had lost much of its membership there during the slack times for coal in the 1950s. After winning an organizing vote at the Eastover mine in 1973, the UMW was determined to win a contract conforming to the nationwide 1971 Bituminous Wage Agreement—including a 75-cent a ton royalty payment to the union's hard-pressed Welfare and Retirement Fund. Another issue was the UMW's insistence that union miners accompany safety committees inspecting conditions in the mines. Eastover's settlement offer was substantially less favorable than the national agreement, and the strike wore on for 13 months as the UMW tried to focus the issue on "outside" exploitation of East Kentucky by firms like Duke Power (which has assets of $2.5 billion and provides electric power for 3.6 million consumers in the Carolinas) and on unsafe conditions in the mines. The union poured about $1 million into the strike, hoping for a victory that would provide an opening wedge in organizing the 15,000 non-UMW miners among East Kentucky's 21,000 coal miners.

One of the great victories of the UMW's history was achieved in August 1974 when Duke Power finally capitulated, agreeing to all the union's demands. UMW president Miller said the agreement meant "the beginning of the end for nonunion coal in this country." A price in blood was paid, however: the shotgun murder of a UMW picketer, 23-year-old Lawrence Jones, at the hands of a company foreman the day before the strike ended.

Young Jones' death recalled Harlan County's "Battle of Evarts" 43 years before, when at least five men died. Such sacrifices scarcely reflect what some call the region's slothful welfare society. Nor are East Kentuckians' achievements writ in blood alone. Consider the observations of Pat Gish, the head of an OEO housing project and wife of a Whitesburg editor. Pat Gish's program hires mostly older men to repair the homes of welfare recipients and is also involved in a prefab factory project for modest new homes. Despite relatively low base wages, she said, the mountaineers working in the project were offered hospitalization, insurance, and a guarantee of year-round employment. And that cross-section of the bottom-tier unemployed people showed up, worked steadily, and recorded virtually no absenteeism. "It's a plain old business of opportunity and proof that if you treat people well, you get results," Pat Gish said.

Little glimpses of the same human potential have been apparent in these hills for a long time. Back in 1899, in the little village of Hindman at the juncture of two forks of Troublesome Creek, rumors began to seep in of two "fotched-on" women who were doing fine things with basic education in Hazzard. And so Uncle Solomon Everidge, an 80-year-old pioneer always concerned about schooling, walked 22 miles barefoot to Hazard to learn first-hand of the activities of Miss May Stone and Miss Katherine Pettit. Not long after, according to an account in the *Mountain Eagle*, the young teachers chose Hindman as the place for their major effort. Assisted by the mountain folk, the Hindman Settlement School has grown and prospered over the years, teaching local youngsters every skill from the three "R's" to home nursing, sewing, weaving, and basketry. The Settlement school tries to supplement, not replace, the local public schools, and is forever developing extension projects of various kinds that it perfects and then spins off to the community. Many students have gone on to universities and the professions.

Another fascinating case is that of Mary Breckinridge, the daughter of a famous Kentucky patrician family who decided, in 1925, after the death of her own two children, to devote the rest of her life to the medical and nursing care of children in the remote backwoods areas of Leslie County.* "In 1925," Mrs. Breckinridge once wrote, "the territory in the Kentucky mountains was a vast forested area inhabited by some 10,000 people. There was no motor road within 60 miles in any direction. Horseback and mule team were the only modes of travel. Supplies came from distant railroad points and took from two to five days to haul in. . . . There was not in this whole area a single state-licensed physician—not one." In time, her Frontier Nursing Service was bringing medical attention to the people in a 1,000-square mile area. Mrs. Brekinridge died in 1963, at the age of 84, but her work has been carried on with special emphasis on birth control work. In the first half of the 1960s, 1,944 babies were born in Leslie County; in the following five years, only 1,278 were born. The superintendent of schools, in an interview with Kenneth Reich of the Los Angeles *Times*, gave full credit for this to the Frontier Nursing Service. "They've introduced birth control services. Families that were having 12 children now are having only one or two." The birth control effort, I heard, is catching on all over East

* The Breckinridge family line is awesome to behold. Mary Breckinridge's father was Clifton Rhodes Breckinridge, six terms a Congressman from Arkansas and minister to Russia under Grover Cleveland. She was 13 when the family moved to Russia. Until then her life had been a whirl of childish adventure between Pine Bluff, Arkansas, Washington, D.C., Ontario, Canada, where her father fished, Moa Oasis Plantation in Mississippi, the ancestral seat of her maternal grandfather, and Hazelwood, the fabulous estate of her great aunt in New York. She went to school in Switzerland and New York, England, Scotland, and other places on the continent. Her grandfather was John C. Breckinridge, Vice President of the United States, 1856–60; her great-grandfather was Joseph C. Breckinridge, U.S. Secretary of State and speaker of the Kentucky house of representatives; her great-great-grandfather was John Breckinridge, U.S. Senator from Kentucky, U.S. Attorney General under Thomas Jefferson and founder of the great, patrician Breckinridge family in Kentucky. She began her backwoods nursing career after a summer spent visiting Kentucky relatives and riding in the mountains. She was related, of course, to the present U.S. Rep. John C. Breckinridge of Lexington, former attorney general of Kentucky.

Kentucky, with the big families everywhere declining almost as rapidly as in Leslie County. One physician had 400 to 500 women on pills by 1973. And school enrollment in the lower grades was dropping off a little more each year. The trend seemed to indicate that mountain people had earlier been propagating at such an impracticable tempo out of ignorance, not preference. Again, given a chance, they seemed to be making the intelligent decision about family size.

Though the bulk of East Kentucky's most talented sons and daughters have fled the region, the exodus has not been total. Bill Hambley and Harry Caudill themselves are proof of that, and so are Tom and Pat Gish, Caudill's friends and neighbors in Whitesburg, the shabby and poverty-stricken county seat of Letcher County. Tom Gish grew up in a coal camp about 10 miles from Whitesburg, where his father was general foreman for the Southeast Coal Company. (It was, Gish said, one of the better constructed and more humanely run of the early coal camps.) Gish was fortunate enough to go off to the University of Kentucky, where he majored in journalism, a background that prepared him to become the United Press correspondent in Frankfort from 1947 to 1957. Pat Gish at the same time was a reporter and city editor for the Lexington *Herald*. But they tired of their jobs and decided to return to Whitesburg and buy the *Mountain Eagle*, a 50-year-old weekly with the wonderful motto, "It Screams." (The slogan runs directly beneath a drawing of a great eagle in flight.)

Two big surprises awaited the Gishes. "The leisurely life of country editors" they had anticipated turned out to be "sheer myth" as they put in 60, 70, even more hours to get the paper out regularly. The pressures eventually contributed to a serious heart attack which Tom Gish suffered in the early 1970s, and the profits from the paper turned out to be so slim that Pat Gish eventually took her OEO job to provide a steady income for Tom and herself and their five children.

The other surprise had to do with gathering news. Accustomed to the relatively open news sources and objective-style reporting of Frankfort and Lexington, the Gishes started about gathering news as they were accustomed. But they rapidly discovered that "no one had ever been to city hall or county meetings as a reporter" in Letcher County. "We found ourselves fighting the issues of freedom of the press and freedom of speech we thought had been settled a long time ago." And it took several years, over the bitter opposition of the fiscal court, the school board, and other legal government bodies to get the right to send a reporter to their sessions. One county official threatened Gish's life if the paper published an audit of his accounts, but Gish went ahead anyway. To this day, people still appear in his office to ask how much it "will cost" to put a story in the paper.

The *Mountain Eagle* also plunged into controversial issues, publishing pictures of destructive strip-mining operations, revealing the environmental desecrations caused by exploration for oil and gas, urging a TVA-like public power authority for East Kentucky which enraged the Kentucky Power

Company, criticizing organized medicine and questioning powerful anti-poverty officials and Appalachian Regional Commission programs. Accumulating enemies through such coverage was easy, and in 1974 an arsonist set fire to the paper's offices, destroying much of its equipment and library about East Kentucky. Gish had to set up temporary office in his own home.

The *Mountain Eagle*'s success is based on getting close to the mountain people. It carries several pages of community news each week, written by residents of the towns in the county. "At first," Gish said, "we were dumb enough to cut down their reports and edit the opinions out. Now we give complete freedom to each community correspondent, so that his or her column becomes a kind of community focus, a medium of information even within the community itself." The columns mirror the vivid language of the hills, the philosophy and value of the plain people, and they build fierce reader loyalty.

The *Mountain Eagle*'s circulation, by 1973, had reached 5,400—of which 4,000 went to subscribers in Letcher and surrounding counties, about 1,200 to expatriates of the hills settled mostly in the Midwest, and some 200 to a subscriber group unique for a local weekly—outside media, campus libraries, and such government agencies as TVA and the Interior Department. Gish's main frustration was that he lacked money to hire reporters. He benefited from the help of young volunteers, many from outside the area, some former VISTA workers and the like, who were attracted to the *Mountain Eagle*'s unique enterprise. But he had money enough for only one part-time paid editorial employee, with the result that "vast areas go unreported."

The thought of leaving their native mountains, of going somewhere else where the pay would be better and life easier, is one that the Gishes do not seriously entertain. "We couldn't turn our backs on it," they insisted. "This has never been a boring place to be." In fact, they drove me in the twilight hours of a summer evening to a spot a few miles out of town where they had purchased several hundred acres of land, including an exquisite little valley where a farmhouse had once stood. There they hope to build a home, in one of the most idyllic settings I have ever seen.

Intellectually, the Gishes have come to a position of fierce defense of mountain people's right to self-determination—to be free of the depredations of the coal companies but also of the well-intentioned big government planners. People in the Appalachian Regional Commission and other government bodies, they said, have often come to the conclusion that East Kentucky has been offered every conceivable kind of aid program, and since nothing had succeeded, it might be time to use force to move people out of the hollows into designated "growth centers," or to create, as Gish put it, "a kind of BIA [Bureau of Indian Affairs] lifestyle." Gish said he had detected "alarming signs of that from federal and state planners. As a result, some of us find ourselves fighting planning—things we would really support otherwise—because it becomes so dictatorial, and because there is no real provision for participation of the people." One detects here a resurgence of the old mountaineer independence and desire to be left alone, yet coming now from highly educated and perceptive native people, not from an unlettered hillbilly.

(And yet again, one wonders about the grisly consequences of letting the mountaineer live the totally independent and frontier-oriented life that may be his wont. Is he never to be disturbed, to be left blissfully alone at the top of some hollow where sanitary sewers and school buses and medical care may not make it until well into the 21st century—if ever? Is it worth it if the mountaineer never has the satisfaction of a fulfilling job, if his wife loses her teeth by the time she's 35, if his children are afflicted with worms and rarely make it to school? That remains the pattern in thousands of mountain families, and it is hard to see how the pattern can be broken without some degree of coercion.)

A man who has long celebrated the life of East Kentucky people as it is, expounding the beauties, the tragedies, and the mordant humor of the mountaineers long before Caudill or the poverty wars emerged, is writer Jesse Stuart. Since the early 1930s Stuart has written 43 books, more than 2,000 poems, and hundreds of short stories and magazine articles—all reflecting, in one way or another, his upbringing in the hills and the life he sees around him at W-Hollow, Greenup, Kentucky. Stuart does not believe the mountain culture is about to fade away. Appalachia, he told an interviewer not long ago, "is the only region of this country with a real culture. It came to us from the British Isles—the music, the dances, the humor, the writers—but now it's ours, and I think we'll keep it."

The record of that culture is being preserved at Berea College, in the Cumberland foothills, which now has the largest collection of literature on Appalachian life, history, music, and crafts ever assembled anywhere. The collection was begun in earnest in the 1920s and today includes some 6,000 books of fact or fiction by or about the people of the Southern mountains, the original manuscripts of some of the most famous books ever written on the region, works on the English and Scottish ballads whose descendants are mountain songs still sung today, tape recordings and records of mountain balladeers, newspaper clippings, and photographs.

The history of Berea College itself is a fascinating one. It was founded in 1855 by native Kentuckians drawn together by their abolitionist sympathies to form a church school—originally housed in a single, humble log building—in which poor whites and Negroes could study together. The purpose was to develop a college "under an influence strictly Christian, and as such opposed to sectarianism, slaveholding, caste, and every other wrong institution or practice." Irate slaveholders drove the founder and his 33 faculty and students out of Kentucky in 1859, but they returned after the war and within a year had an attendance of 96 Negroes and 91 whites. The college enrollment remained about half black until 1904, when a mountain legislator capitalized on the racial prejudice of the time to put a bill through the legislature forbidding biracial education. Berea raised $400,-000 to start a new institution for Negro education, Lincoln Institute, near

Louisville. But when the law was amended in 1950 to permit biracial education above the high school level, Bera again opened its doors to black students, who in recent years have comprised about 10 percent of an enrollment of 1,400.

Since 1892 Berea has not charged admission but rather required its students to participate in a work program. They may work in the Boone Tavern Hotel, or the university's stores or farm, or as janitors or dormitory monitors; or they may put in several hours a week in the unique student industries—woodworking, fireside weaving, broomcraft, or needlecraft. More recently, they have had another option: to work as tutors for dropped-out or turned-off children and adults in nearby rural communities, teaching them basic literacy. Since 80 percent of Berea's students come from mountain backgrounds themselves, this provides an opportunity to reach the isolated and suspicious people in the Appalachian hollows through young people who "speak the same language" and have a much better chance of being accepted than volunteers for VISTA and similar government-run programs, who were often regarded as rank outsiders.

An even smaller institution, Alice Lloyd Junior College at Pippa Passes, has had remarkable success in pioneering the concept of Appalachian youth in service to their communities. Founded in 1923, Alice Lloyd—like Berea—has imbued its students over the years with the idea that they have an obligation to return and serve in Appalachia once they have garnered their professional degrees in such fields as law, medicine, or teaching. A program called ALCOR (Appalachian Leaders in Community Outreach) was begun at Alice Lloyd in 1969 and soon thereafter expanded to a consortium of six community colleges, operating in 22 mountain counties. It is basically a summer project in which the students, who earn both money and academic credits for participation, fan out into the hollows to live in the homes of the people and become involved in their life. The typical approach has been to start with a children's arts-and-crafts or recreation program and then work into reading workshops, social activities—perhaps cookouts that draw in the adults as well as children—and finally nutritional programs and help for the people with the help of ALCOR's medical volunteers. The reason for these summer programs in such spots as Beefhide, Backwoods, Buffalo, and Huntin' Fork is not just immediate care for the people; it is to help East Kentucky to develop its own doctors in a physician-short area, and other professionals. Raymond K. LeRoux, ALCOR's president, was quoted as saying: "The hero in eastern Kentucky is the high school dropout who went off to Detroit, got a job, and came back in a fourth-hand '64 Chevy with a case of beer in back and the radio turned up. We were trying to show the youngsters an alternative."

The most important person behind ALCOR, according to a report in *Business Week*, was Benny Ray Bailey, who was only 22, and the assistant dean of students, when the program began at Alice Lloyd. Bailey came from Spewing Camp, Kentucky, a locality harboring 76 of his first cousins. With a country twang, a muscular frame, VISTA experience; and serious intent as a sociology instructor, Bailey got ALCOR started and then peformed with his colleagues the minor miracle of lining up several hundred thousand dollars in support from foundations and corporations.

With success stories like that, it is hard to believe that the future of East Kentucky's people is totally dark. Yet ultimately satisfactory solutions to this area's problems of private poverty and public misfeasance will probably have to await, as Harry Caudill suggested some years ago, a Southern Mountains Authority or some other agency cloaked like TVA with federal prestige, an authority with the power to influence and direct the entire resource base and ecosystem of the Cumberland Plateau and neighboring regions of Appalachia. Thoughtful East Kentuckians today are so horrified at what strip miners are presently doing to their mountain fastness to feed the furnaces of TVA that they dismiss TVA as just a big utility and look for more modest solutions. Thus the real issues—the futility of fragmented recovery and development, the need for massive infusions of money, the interesting potentialities of direct citizen involvement in choosing the leaders of a regional authority, and the possible nationalization of the coal industry (a latter-day corollary of TVA's preemption of power production) —tend not to be discussed. Until they are, East Kentucky's advances are likely to be tentative and inconclusive, while more generations of mountain people lose the opportunity to lead less blighted, less fearsome, and more rewarding lives.

Coal: The Curse of Kentucky

Hundreds of millions of years ago the land now called Kentucky was part of an immense swampland in which trees and ferns the size of trees grew over cons, decomposing into organic deposits that would create the state's greatest geologic asset—and its curse: coal. Two great deposits formed. One was in an area now covered by several counties of western Kentucky, a gently rolling land where the coal lies below the surface in bowl-shaped horizontal layers. It was here, actually, that coal was first commercially mined in Kentucky. Yet the greater fame—and pathos—was to come to the East Kentucky counties where the cataclysm of the building of the Appalachians, some 200 million years ago, thrust the great coal seams upward to run through the mountains in some of the most rugged territory of eastern America.

In all, Kentucky was endowed with 30 to 35 *billion* tons of recoverable coal. The quality varies: in the west, one finds a variety relatively high in sulfur, ash, and moisture content; in the east, it is uniformly high-quality bituminous coal. The methods of mining differ as well. Surface mining dominates in the west, where the gigantic steamshovels of recent times remove the overburden in fantastic bites (each the size of several houses), exposing the coal for removal. This technique is called pit mining; when it is finished, the terrain is covered with series of 100-foot-wide spoils, resistant to reclamation because of the acidity of the exposed soil and rock. Natural drainage is also disrupted, with the result that pockets of water form, in which mosquitoes breed. (In some places in western Kentucky the black marsh mosquitoes are so thick that people can't sit outside or leave their cattle outside.)

Most of the coal mines in western Kentucky are big producers using strip methods; there are, however, a number of underground mines, generally of the slope type.

East Kentucky's hilly terrain presents quite different mining problems. The underground method, historically the one used to mine the vast bulk of the region's coal, involves the digging of great horizontal tunnels along the seams. "Into the mines" go thousands of miners, in earlier days with pick and shovel, now with highly automated equipment, to dig away the bowels of the mountain. There are still close to 1,000 such mines in East Kentucky, compared to only 35 underground mines in the western part of the state.

Strip mining in eastern Kentucky is a quicker, cheaper way to get at the coal, but it only reaches that close to the surface. Bulldozers uncover the seams in great and unsightly gashes around the mountainside; often huge drills work their way into the hill and claw the coal out to the deepest penetration they can manage, a technique known as auger mining. Sometimes the strippers use an alternative method of scooping off the whole top of a mountain, where the seam lies that high.

Kentucky competes with West Virginia as the state that produces the most coal (about a fifth of the national total). It also has the dubious distinction of being the largest producer of surface-mined coal in the United States. The King Kong technology of monster bulldozers, immense shovels, and the highlift have made this possible. As recently as 1960, only 33 percent of the state's coal production came from surface mines; in 1972, by contrast, the figure was 53 percent, or 68 million tons out of a statewide production total of 120 million tons. The movement to strip mining has been caused by its economies—the production per man day of labor, for instance, is three times greater in surface than in deep mines. Western Kentucky, heavily weighted to surface mining, produces 43 percent of the state's coal with just 27 percent of the coal labor force. Another important factor has been the set of safety regulations for deep mines prescribed by the 1969 Coal Mine Health and Safety Act, which made strippers of many deep mine operators. The trend to surface mining was also accelerated by TVA's ever increasing demands for Kentucky coal. Even when Congress in 1974 moved toward federal controls on acceptable methods of strip mining, it seemed likely that the pressures for increased use of the method would continue through the 1970s and into the following decade.

For all its environmental problems, stripping is less dangerous to human life than deep-coal mining. The carnage from Kentucky mine explosions, roof falls, electrocutions, and other underground mishaps over the years must be one of the darkest pages in the history of any state. There is no way that adequate excuse could ever be made for the long roster of maimed bodies, of widows and orphans left in the coal towns over the years and even up to our time. There have been recent years, Harry Caudill said, when the kill rate in small mines in East Kentucky was more than 20 times what it had been in Dutch mines, mostly under the sea, in 1952. Yet withal, one can see a trend for the better, coinciding with better engineering and safety methods, and the replacement of marginal underground mines with stripping operations.

Kentucky Coal Production and Fatalities by Decades

Years	Employment Range	Production (millions of tons)	Fatalities
1890–99		34	95
1900–10		83	274
1910–19		223	754
1920–29	57,000–65,000	507	1,614
1930–39	40,000–58,000	420	1,203
1940–49	53,000–77,000	688	1,328
1950–59	38,000–76,000	696	659
1960–69	24,000–36,000	853	451
1970	28,000	125	89
1971	31,000	119	41
1972	31,000	120	29

Kentucky's infamous broad form deed, the device which clever outside interests used around the turn of the century to gain control of the mineral riches beneath the soil of East Kentucky, remains one of history's most vivid cases of the duping of an unsuspecting and backward people.

Pikeville Mayor William Hambley said he had talked to a lot of the oldtimers about the era of the deed granting. Coal company agents would visit a mountaineer who held land, saying: "You have some coal under your ground here. We'd like to buy it. We won't be taking it out for a long time. If we do, we won't be bothering your land much. All we want is the right to take the coal out. We'll dig a hole in the hill and take it out —we won't disturb anything else." If the highlander agreed, the agent would return soon afterwards with the deed, drawn up by an attorney. For a fee averaging some 50 cents an acre, the highlander—who generally knew neither how to read nor write—would convey title to "all coal, oil, gas, stone, salt and salt water, iron, ores and all minerals and metallic substances whatsoever" under his land. The deeds were written broadly enough to let the coal companies do anything *they* might deem necessary—including the moving of buildings, or accummulation of slate and slag heads, or whatever—in the mining of the minerals. And not only was the immediate owner of the property bound by the terms of the deed; rather it applied specifically to his "heirs, successors and assigns forever." "The broad form deed," Dr. Hambley noted, "is the damnedest monstrous thing I've ever seen in my life." By the time the deed-signing splurge was finished, the ownership of 94 percent of the mineral wealth of East Kentucky had been sold to corporations with their headquarters in such faraway places as London, Philadelphia, Pittsburgh, New York, and Baltimore.

Among the long-term effects of the broad form deeds was an undermining of the mountain people's willingness to raise taxes to cope with their most excruciating problem, inadequate education. As Pikeville Mayor Hambley put it, "If you try to pass a school tax or bond issue in this county, it would be killed. The people look around and see the coal companies with their wealth of holdings in minerals. And they say: 'You want to put all the assessment on my surface and make me pay all the taxes, when the broad form deeds give the coal companies the right to come in with a bulldozer and rip it all up.'"

The 1910s and 1920s brought an incredible surge of railway building and coal camp building in the once inaccessible backwoods of the Cumberland Plateau. Black people and fresh immigrants from Europe were imported to build the railways and the towns and to work in the mines, but the bulk of employment was of the rawboned mountaineers, most earning the first decent wages of their lifetimes. Perhaps the most compelling chapter of Harry Caudill's *Night Comes to the Cumberlands* is the one which deals with the construction of "the alabaster cities," the company-built and -owned coal towns, almost 200 in number, which sprang up in the coal counties in less than 20 years, changing forever the complexion of the region.

Despite ups and downs, the deep-coal mining industry continued to bring steady employment from the 1920s straight down to the years following World War II. Then came the mechanization of the mines, acquiesced in by the United Mine Workers. In place of the old pick and shovel approach came such advanced modern methods as continuous mining, short-wall mining, mechanized equipment handling, and the like. Tens of thousands of miners, who had never known any other productive labor in their lives, were suddenly thrown out of work; now too old or sickly or ill-educated to learn anything new, they were often destined to live on welfare until they died. Rotting coal tipples and weed-grown railway lines by broken-down miners' shacks gave evidence to a radically altered economy and the human wreckage left behind. The young and able-bodied, perceiving no future in East Kentucky, deserted it in droves. Between 1950 and 1970, the population of Harlan County dropped from 71,751 to 37,370, that of Letcher County from 39,522 to 23,165, Perry County from 46,566 to 25,714. Overall, the number of people in the eleven major coal-producing counties of East Kentucky had dwindled by 35 percent, from 390,490 to 256,107. Yet the better-run mines turned in good profits, and the UMW workers lucky enough to hold on to their jobs after mechanization became what Harry Caudill called "a favored class, a sort of blue-collar royalty amid a population of industrial serfs."

Then came the shift to surface mining, and the descendants of the mountaineers who had signed the broad form deeds half a century or more before began to realize the horrible price of those cheaply bought pieces of paper. True, the underground mines had involved unsightly coal tipples and monstrous slate dumps. But all that was as nothing compared to the desecration that came with strip mining. The surface mine operators, until they were brought under some control by a reclamation law passed by the Kentucky legislature in 1966, simply pushed over the mountainsides the earth they removed to get at the coal seams. When rains came, the hollows would be inundated with silt or, even worse, monstrous landslides. As Caudill testified before a congressional committee in 1971:

I lament the utter ruination of the hills of my own homeland and the assault surface mining has made on people of my blood and name. I have seen once clear streams choked with mud, and lawns and gardens layered with foul sediments from the spoil heaps. And I have seen wells that once brimmed with crystalline water filled to the top with yellow mud flecked with coal. I have visited the homes of widows and work-worn old men whose basements and cellars reeked of sulfurous slime from the spoil banks. I have seen the shattered roofs, the broken gravestones and the fences that tell of the blasting that "cast the overburden" from coal seams. I saw the sad, disbelieving face of one-armed Herman Ritchie of Clear Creek in Knott County, Kentucky, after he came home from a federally sponsored vocational school and found his house knocked from its foundations by a massive landslide. I was attorney for Roosevelt Bentley of Jenkins, Kentucky, a paraplegic ex-coal miner whose house was severely damaged by washouts from a mine operated by Bethlehem Steel Corporation. And I sat by the desk of Governor Edward Breathitt when eighty-year-old Mrs. Bige Ritchie—a neighbor of Congressman Carl D. Perkins—told the governor how she stood on the front porch of her home and saw the bulldozers come to her family cemetery after coal for the Tennessee Valley Authority. She shouted to them that the graves of her children lay in front of them, but they ignored the pleas of an old, impoverished and helpless woman.

Some legitimate East Kentucky folk heroes emerged from the battle to hold off the strippers. One was Ollie Combs of Knott County, known to everyone as Widow Combs, who held off the bulldozers by sitting in their path. For this transgression she had to spend Thanksgiving Day of 1965 in jail, but her land was saved. Another was Dan Gibson, who picked up his rifle and stopped the strippers by telling them: "I'll give you a minute to get in that machine and get out of here. Somebody's going to get hot steel in 'em if you come in here again."

In a way, the mountaineers had no other choice, because the state courts in the postwar years had abandoned their earlier protective attitude toward people whose land was harmed by mining. At the end of World War II a coal company in Pike County stripped away virtually the whole top of a mountain on a fork of Ferrells Creek, leaving 10 acres of loose earth and rocks and tree stumps exposed. When a flash flood hit, the rubble came cascading down the creekbed, sweeping all the homes in the valley before it. The local inhabitants sued and won damages from a local jury, but the state appeals court reversed the decision, claiming that the mass of rubble had been harmless until set in motion by water, and that since the cloudburst was an act of God, the coal company had no responsibility. Later a mountaineer claimed that a coal company had plowed up his mountainsides, so that rubble covered his bottomland and his well had gone dry. The trial judge dismissed the case, telling the distraught highlander: "I deeply sympathize with you and sincerely wish I could rule for you. My hands are tied by the rulings of the Court of Appeals and under the law I must follow its decisions. The truth is that about the only rights you have on your land is to breathe on it and pay the taxes. For practical purposes the company that owns the minerals in your land owns all the other rights pertaining to it."

This type of travesty of justice was confirmed by the highest court of Kentucky in 1956, when it ruled—under heavy political pressure from the coal industry—that a landowner who signed away mineral rights to his property had no grounds whatever for complaint when his land was chewed to pieces or otherwise defaced unless he could prove the destruction was "wanton or malicious." The specious reasons given: the property destroyed was not of much value in any event, and a contrary decision might harm the coal industry, which at the time was in a mild depression.

Through the outcries of Harry Caudill, the Louisville *Courier-Journal*, and other conservationist leaders in Kentucky, the legislature in 1966 finally passed a fairly strong strip mine control and reclamation law. Caudill, for one, was disdainful of the way in which the law was applied, declaring in 1971: "When it comes to restraining strip-mine operators, the Division of Reclamation is as worthless as a cupful of cold spit."

I was anxious to find out for myself, however, and my break came one day when I looked up H. Combs, the colorful buccaneer who owns several strip-mine sites in Letcher County and runs the incongruously named Suburban Motel in Whitesburg. Combs was having a cup of coffee with the area mine inspector, David Dykes, a bright young native of West Virginia who had majored in landscape architecture at Clemson. Dykes invited me to climb in his jeep and examine a cross-section of strip-mine sites—the "good" and "bad" ones alike. Most of the "bad" ones turned out to be orphan or outlaw mines; when he discovers an operation going on without a permit, Dykes said, he turns in the offender, who in turn is fined—though no state funds are available to repair the damage he may have done. Dykes showed me some places where huge dirt slides of 150 feet or more had taken place when an operator pushed too much dirt out in his contour mining operation, thus desecrating a whole valley.

The "good" strip sites were those where the operators were keeping their digging back from steep slopes. Dykes prefers a system in which there is a barrier between the high wall and the slope. As a job is worked, he makes frequent, unannounced inspections and can hand out "noncompliances" where there are violations. But the "noncompliance" device, something akin to and rarely more injurious to the operator than a speeding ticket, does not work very well. Dykes prefers to work with the operator from the start of a strip site, suggesting preventive measures that will avert later problems. Silt dams are required below each operation to prevent muddy runoff, and if tests show acid water coming from a dam, the strip operator is required to treat the water and take steps to cover up any poison soil. The operator must also put up a bond—averaging $500 an acre —which will not be released until there is satisfactory grass or tree cover on the site. Dykes showed me some locations with fairly satisfactory grass cover and seedlings of walnut or other species getting underway, but it was a wonder to me that the raw, rocky soil left after mining could prove very hospitable for any kind of vegetation.

There was no question about the sincerity of David Dykes, who at 25 years of age had already been offered his share of bribes and knew how to turn them down. In theory, one has to sympathize with those who say that strip mining is so rife with evils—not only the ugly headwalls and hazardous mudslides but the perhaps unbeatable problem of some acid drainoff—that it should be banned from the mountains altogether. David Hawpe, an East Kentucky native and writer for the Louisville *Courier-Journal*, put it well when he told me: "The difference, most of the time, is not between good and bad in strip mines—just between bad and worse." As just one example of the possibly inevitable consequences of stripping, he mentioned a 1973 GAO study showing that Fishtrap Reservoir, a huge Corps of Engineers Project in Pike County built at the cost of $56 million, was being silted up, and thus having its prospective life shortened, *seven times* faster than had been expected. The reason: 280 mines above the reservoir, many of them strip operations, which had been allowed to operate at will.

Governor Wendell Ford, however, said the energy crisis had diminished if not obliterated the outlook for a total abolition of strip mining in the mountains, the solution favored by the conservationists. "Our improvement of strip mining regulation since 1971 has reduced the hue and cry," Ford said. He named several steps taken to tighten the regulations and their enforcement. "We're trying to eliminate the irresponsible operator and to improve our relationship with the responsible operator," he added. "You can fly over East Kentucky and see what's happening since early 1972 and you see a great deal of improvement."

Yet even when one talks with as engaging and sincere a man as David Zageer, division superintendent of Beth-Elkhorn Corporation at Jenkins, a subsidiary of Bethlehem Steel, perhaps the most "responsible" of all East Kentucky's coal operators, one wishes stripping were not necessary. "We live here and we have as much interest in the land as the next person," Zageer said. "Even back in the early 1960s, when we were surface mining and there were no laws, we reclaimed the land because it was ours and we wanted it protected." His staff, Zageer said, included an agronomist, a forester, and a photographer to document all work done before, during, and after reclamation efforts. But there are gashes of ugly, exposed earth around some of the most carefully reclaimed Beth-Elkhorn strip mines. With Zageer I looked over the deep and picturesque valley of Jenkins from a nearby mountaintop park, and even while he spoke enthusiastically of land actually being "improved" by surface mining, I saw the scars of past activity in the hills all about. Beth-Elkhorn on occasion has been accused of misleading national advertising about its capability to restore strip-mined land for recreational use, and of causing streams running off its property to turn so bitter cattle won't drink from them. Though the bulk of the company's operations are in underground mines, it plans to strip no less than 3,000 acres of Letcher and Pike Counties in the next several years. One can only cross his fingers and hope that the cumulative damage will not be too great. (In the meantime, if I had to pick a modern "coal camp" to live in, I would pick Jenkins. The site is a pleasant one, and Beth-Elkhorn's paternalism extends to providing at nominal cost a splendid country club and golf course for the use of its employees.)

It is possible that all the controversy over strip mining may divert attention from other grave environmental threats in East Kentucky. Riding up through the hills with David Dykes, I saw huge slag heaps beside underground mines, streams dammed up by activity around sites where exploration for natural gas was going on, and severe damage from logging. There was nothing Dykes or his fellow inspectors could do about those ravages, because no state law yet covers them.

The essential problem of regions like East Kentucky remains, as has so long been the case, their colonial status. "Coal is the only significant economic factor of East Kentucky," the late Fred W. Luigart, Jr., president of the Kentucky Coal Association, said. "Almost everyone makes his living off it. The only other thing is some timbering and a little limestone quarrying." And who owns the coal lands and the coal companies? In the 1950s, many small family-type operators were still at work. But in the last several years the smaller operators have declined sharply in number and significance. The big operators in the West and East Kentucky coal fields are now either subsidiaries of big American steel corporations (Bethlehem, U.S. Steel, National Steel, etc.) or owned by nationally run energy conglomerates (Island Creek, a subsidiary of Occidental Petroleum, for instance, or Pittsburgh & Midway, a Gulf Oil subsidiary). Peabody Coal, an especially important operator in the western Kentucky coalfields, is a subsidiary now of Kennecott Copper. No matter where the ultimate ownerhip lies, it is not in Kentucky itself.

David Hawpe said he had "known some responsible coal operators and seen some responsible coal operations," but that in general he thought coal "the most venal, destructive industry imaginable, run by a callous bunch of people who control politicians and corrupt the courts." If one asks why the people of Appalachia have never risen up, Hawpe said, the reason is that they "don't control the wealth—the minerals—of their region. So they lack the opportunity or the firepower to shoot the industry down." An occasional victory is won—reclamation legislation, for instance, or the first Kentucky severance tax on coal, passed in 1972, largely due to pleadings by Harry Caudill and the Louisville *Courier-Journal* over the years. (At last report the new tax was netting the state treasury $36 million a year, not too much of a burden on a billion-dollar-a-year business, but at least a beginning of serious taxes on an industry which has usually paid laughably little to the region from which it extracts such immense wealth.)

Groups to fight strip mining rise up out of the indigenous population at times. One of the most colorful anticoal leaders of recent years, for instance, has been Joe Begley, a mountain type who runs a general store at the little hamlet of Blackey in Letcher County. Begley formed a group of mountaineers to fight strip mining in the courts (with Harry Caudill as attorney), and he has testified before a congressional committee as well. Not everything Begley says is totally consistent, but there's no question where his heart is. Here are some nuggets I picked up one summer afternoon:

Strip mining is a malicious attack on the people. They issue strip permits up there in Frankfort and it reminds me of a hunter who turns his dog loose on people and says, "You go kill, I don't care how many people or when."

We were all taught wrong. I was taught from the time I was a little boy to shine my shoes, wear a necktie, salute the flag. It's not easy for a man 50 years old to stand up and say, "Hell no, you've done it wrong. This is not right."

I see people living in misery. I see malnutrition all over the place. We're sitting on a gold mine of minerals here, but we're starving to death. And the churches are not doing a thing, the school system and the Jaycees and the forestry people are all avoiding the issue.

A lot of people here are afraid to speak out. The reason is very simple. Remember what happened when the United Mine Workers tried to organize. The people are afraid what the industry can do to them in the ways of gunslingers.

The schools here keep the children so busy playing basketball—basketball is Jesus Christ—that they have no time to sit down and reason out what we really are and where we're going. But some children are saying today—"My daddy sold out. My daddy ain't gonna do nothing. We want to do it different."

There's no such thing as strip mine reclamation. When you dig up billions of tons of rock and spread it out in the hollows and down the rivers, the Gulf of Mexico is going to fill up.

We want deep mining. We want some decency. We have 500 or 600 years of coaling.

When we try to organize we find we're dealing with old people and sick people and poor people. And what the hell can you get out of them?

And so it goes in the mountains of America's most heavily stripped state. By its very nature, the mining of coal seems to have baleful consequences. Few indeed are the places on earth where it has ever been done without profoundly negative effects, human and environmental. The best argument against a beneficent Deity, it was once suggested, was that he made man so dependent on energy, and above all on coal. "Even the people who've made their fortunes on it are never very happy," Ed Prichard noted. Alluding to the pressures to accelerate production in the 1970s, Prichard predicted: "I suppose we will have a great period of 'prosperity' in the coalfields, followed by a devastation of a third of Kentucky that will make the deserts of the Oriental potentates look like rose gardens."

TENNESSEE

FRONTIERS OLD AND NEW

COLLECTIVELY AND CONSCIOUSLY, gathered at the state capital in Nashville, Tennesseans have never been very progressive or innovative in the management of their society. There are few states in America, for instance, which tax the poor so heavily and the rich so lightly.

But in two eras of its history—its first half century or so of existence, and the years since World War II—Tennessee has contributed a lot to the United States. The state epitomized the frontier society and some of the best and worst American traditions in its early years—Jacksonian Democracy, Indian exile, and the first glimmerings of manifest destiny.

The latter years are just as interesting. Tennessee has given us national leaders like Estes Kefauver and Howard Baker, Jr., the court case that revolutionized the legislatures of America, a splendid example of metropolitan government, a thriving poor people's labor union made great by the martyrdom of Martin Luther King, Jr., and music from the hearts of the people (country music centered in Nashville, the blues from Memphis). It is the principal state of the Tennessee Valley Authority—a phenomenon of such continuing national importance that I will devote a separate chapter to it. And at Oak Ridge, in the East Tennessee hills, much of the vital research in nuclear energy has been underway since the secretive wartime years; now Oak Ridge's horizons have been expanded to a total energy laboratory to deal with one of the most pressing American and international problems of the later 20th century. No single factor puts Tennessee at the forefront of American states, yet the sum of the parts of the cultural phenomena and societal experiments underway there makes it the most important of the Border States and a vital member of the Union in our time.

Until a recent governor decided the slogan was too divisive, the highway signs welcoming a visitor read: "Welcome to the Three Great States of Tennessee." The reference was to the three Grand Divisions—East, Middle, and West Tennessee—which are officially recognized in the state constitution and represent lesson one of any Tennessee primer. Geographically, the Grand Divisions are about the only way to make sense out of a long, rectangular state (sometimes likened to a license plate) which seems to have been flung violently onto the map without regard to natural boundaries like mountains or river valleys. Historically, they explain fairly coherently the early settlement pattern from the eastern highlands to the Mississippi lowlands. Politically, they divided in the Civil War (East for the Union, Middle and West for the Confederacy), and the process of reunification is only now being accomplished. Economically, they divided in antebellum days (independent yeomen in the East, slaveowners in Middle and especially West Tennessee); industry then flourished first in the population centers of the East, while the other sections remained predominantly agricultural—an imbalance not to be corrected until the mid-20th century.

We will return later to the three states theme and the complexion of Tennessee's constituent parts today. First, however, it is appropriate to look into Tennessee's unique early history—the key to its character, past and present.

Years of Glory

Tennessee began as a western mountain offshoot of North Carolina; in fact, many of the early settlers were fleeing the oppressive colonial government to the east. A varied lot they were: hunters and traders, adventurers and land speculators, missionaries and outlaws and outcasts. But timid they were not; one could not afford to be that and face log cabin life and precipitous mountain trails and the ever present danger of Indian ambush. Out of the crucible of frontier life and Indian wars and the American Revolution, which coincided with the first wave of serious settlement of the territory, there emerged a tough folk stream, a society of sturdy self-reliance and hair-trigger passions and fervent evangelism.

The exploits of that early era still glow in the pages of history. In 1772,

Tennesseans like to recall, the first independent government of white men in the New World was created by a compact of isolated mountaineers of the Watauga Settlements of northeastern Tennessee. That was the era when the Long Hunters penetrating into central Tennessee brought back enticing stories of the fertile lands and abundant game beyond the mountains. Pioneer James Robertson, "the Father of Tennessee," moved on to the Cumberland Valley to found the first English settlement in Middle Tennessee. Personally he headed an overland party in the fall of 1779, driving a herd of horses, cattle, and sheep to create the outpost at "French Lick," where Nashville now stands. Another party, headed by the Scotch-Irish pioneer John Donelson, brought the women, children, and household goods to the new settlement on 30-odd flatboats. Their incredible water course carried them down the Holston River from northeastern Tennessee, over the length of the Tennessee River past the present sites of Knoxville and Chattanooga and Muscle Shoals and northerly to where the Tennessee joins the Ohio on the present Kentucky-Ohio border, and then east again on the Cumberland River to French Lick—in all, a distance of more than 900 miles. Braving extreme cold, treacherous shoals, hunger and smallpox and hostile Indians, they made the trip between December 1779 and April of the next year. Thousands of other pioneers experienced hardships almost as severe before the roots of civilization could be firmly planted in this rough transmountain area.

In 1780 a ragtag regiment of Tennessee settlers in buckskin, backed up by a contingent of Virginians, mustered to meet a British force of some 1,200 men raiding westward from their bastion in South Carolina. At King's Mountain on October 7, they met and decimated the splendidly uniformed and trained soldiers of the King in a battle that Thomas Jefferson later called "the joyful annunciation of that turn of the tide of success which terminated the Revolutionary War with the seal of our independence."

The American leader in that battle was the robust early leader of the mountain people, John Sevier, a veteran Indian fighter, described by an early Tennessee historian as "fluent, colloquial, and gallant. . . . Of books he knew little. Men, he had studied well and accurately." Twice married, the father of 18 children, Sevier instructed his instant soldiers at King's Mountain to use the Indian tactics they knew so well, creeping from tree to tree, sniping at the British. In 1784 the settlers of the Tennessee country bristled at a "land grab" by the North Carolina legislature and formed the would-be State of Franklin, with Sevier their governor. "Franklin" lasted only three years, but when Tennessee was actually admitted to the Union in 1796, Sevier was made governor. (The name Tennessee was derived from Tenase, the name of a Cherokee village on what is now the Little Tennessee River.)

Though circuit riders of Methodist and Presbyterian and Baptist allegiance rode their wiry ponies through the wilderness traces of early Tennessee, the brawling frontier was not conducive to organized religion, and many churchmen agreed with Lorenzo Dow, the somber Methodist Savonarola, that Tennessee was "a Sink of Iniquity, a Black Pit of Irreligion." Then, in the early 19th century, came the "Great Revival" of camp meetings which, accord-

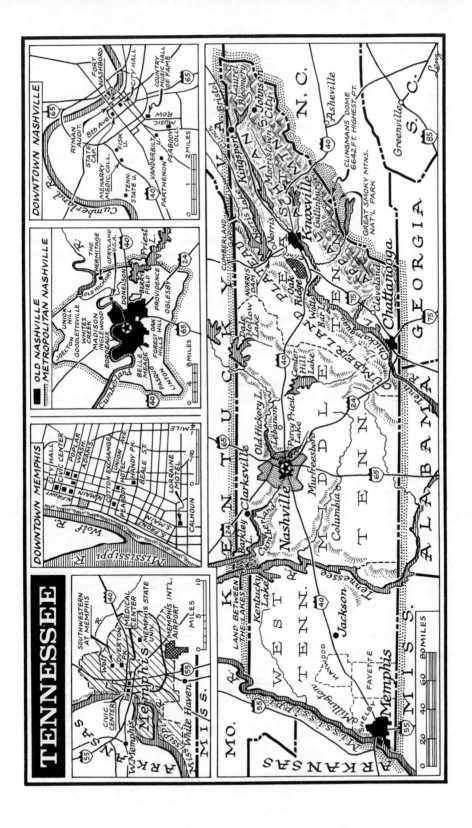

ing to one history, "swept the state like a wind-driven grass fire and thousands of converts came singing and shouting to the mourners' bench." The Methodist doctrine of John Wesley, that all men are equal and each the master of his own destiny, fitted perfectly with the democratic philosophy of the frontier people and took special root.

In the political realm the egalitarianism of the frontier—its peculiar contribution to American life—was most perfectly embodied in Andrew Jackson, seventh President of the United States. Born of Irish immigrant parents in South Carolina in 1767, Jackson was orphaned at an early age, served as a mounted courier (at the age of 13) in the Revolution, studied law in North Carolina, and in 1788 followed the crude Cumberland Road to Nashville, remaining a Tennesseean until his death in 1845. Variously a Congressman, Senator, and judge of the Tennessee superior court, Jackson won national fame as the victor in the Battle of New Orleans in 1814–15. Americans revered him as the rough-hewn military leader of indomitable will and courage, but support also gravitated to him because of his personal magnetism, his pride and hardy frontier individualism, and because he spoke for the common man. Martin Van Buren, Jackson's successor in the White House, said later that the people "were his blood relations, the only blood relations he had."

Jackson had his share of faults. Given to fierce hatreds as well as loyalties, he once killed a fellow Nashville attorney in a duel after the man made a disparaging comment about Jackson's beloved wife, Rachel. (An indication of the newness of the Tennessee society was that Rachel had come to Nashville on the flatboat *Adventure*, commanded by her father, John Donelson, during the illustrious pioneer voyage of 1779–80.) Jackson and John Sevier clashed and almost fought a duel once. Jackson had the frontiersman's disdain for the Indians; retaliating against a Creek Indian massacre of Indians in Alabama in 1813, for instance, Jackson led a force of recruits from the "Volunteer State" that attacked the Creeks at Horseshoe Bend and slaughtered them. As President, Jackson personally ordered the Army to evict the Cherokee Indians from their ancestral homelands in the southern Appalachians, in accordance with an ill-advised treaty of removal some Cherokee leaders had signed. The result was the long trek to Oklahoma, "The Trail of Tears" in which 4,000 of the 15,000 Cherokee perished—one of the greatest blots on our national history.*

Nevertheless, Jackson made an immense contribution to the vitality of democracy in America. Thwarted in his run for the White House in 1824, he won overwhelmingly against John Quincy Adams in 1828 and Henry Clay in 1832. Aristocrats gasped when he admitted the unwashed masses to the White House on his inaugural day, and they attacked him for instituting a spoils system in government. The monied powers of the East bristled at his attacks on the Bank of the United States. But when Southern interests raised the issue of nullification over the tariff, it was Jackson who embodied national

* The story of the Cherokees' removal, and their subsequent life in Oklahoma, was related in a previous book in this series, *The Great Plains States of America*, pages 248–253.

power and prevented dissolution of the young Union. As Wilma Dykeman and James Stokley wrote in the regional volume of the Time-Life Library of America:

"Old Hickory" would not permit civil war during his administrations. By threat, by reason and by the use of the power of his own personality, he held the United States together—the wilderness West he knew in his blood, the financial East he distrusted by instinct, the plantation South he would not palliate and the industrial North he could not court.

The concept of "Jacksonian Democracy" was to dominate American politics until Jackson's death and to form a major ideological base of the modern Democratic party.

Politically and economically, Tennessee was the most important state of the mid-South in the decades following Jackson's inauguration. Wealth came to Middle and West Tennessee by virtue of cotton, wheat, and the steamboat, and Nashville became the permanent capital in 1843. At the same time, thousands of restless Tennesseans pushed on westward and into the Ohio country, Arkansas, Alabama, Mississippi, and especially Texas. Tennessee furnished a majority of the volunteers who fought in the Mexican War. It was Sam Houston—the greatest of Jackson's frontier captains and a former Tennessee Congressman and governor—who led the Texas armed forces in their victorious struggle for independence from Mexico. Davy Crockett, Tennessee politician and Congressman, later surrounded by fabulous myth and storytelling about his prowess as a bear and 'coon hunter, marksman, wit, lover, and mighty drinker, was in the band of Texans annihilated by Santa Anna at the Alamo.

Houston became the first president of the then independent Republic of Texas, represented Texas for 13 years in the U.S. Senate after it joined the Union, and as governor ended his public life in a lonely struggle against secession in 1861. In retrospect, Houston's achievements seem even greater than those of the second Tennessean who became President of the United States, Jackson follower James K. Polk (1845–49). But it was during Polk's administration that Texas joined the Union, and California too, thus completing the territorial expansion of the United States across the continent to the Pacific. From being the frontier itself in the years just before and after 1800, Tennessee in a remarkably short span of time had become the seedbed of the ever westward-moving American frontier.

The Civil War Century: From Secession to Crumpism

When Tennessee's interior and exterior frontiers were reached, when the seed of Jacksonian Democracy had been planted (to reappear again and again in our national experience), the state receded in national importance. Tennessee's geographic position, which had made it such a prominent frontier state, made it an exposed border state and the scene of particularly bloody battles in the Civil War years which followed. It would take Tennessee almost a century to recover from the physical and spiritual devastation of the War Between the States, and the vestigial scars are still there today.

Slavery was introduced into Tennessee by some of its first settlers and became a vital economic factor in the rich farmlands of Middle and West Tennessee. In 1790 there were only 3,800 slaves in the state, representing less than 10 percent of the total population; by the eve of the Civil War there were 435,000—almost 25 percent of the state's people. Some Tennesseans treated their slaves almost as part of the family; others subjected them to beatings and abuse. Montgomery Bell, the state's leading antebellum industrialist, abused his slaves and frequently called for the forced return of those who fled. Abolitionist sentiment—especially in mountainous East Tennessee, where slavery was light—flourished until the 1820s but then died out. Most Tennesseans wanted to maintain the "peculiar institution" but wanted to stay in the Union too. Even after John Brown's raid on the Harper's Ferry arsenal had fed the flames of secessionist sentiment, a first statewide referendum in February 1861 produced a vote of nearly four to one against secession. It was only when Fort Sumter fell and President Lincoln demanded 75,000 volunteers for the Army that Governor Isham G. Harris stated that Lincoln had "wantonly inaugurated an internecine war" upon the people of the South and the tide in Tennessee turned to secession, ratified in a June 1861 referendum. Even then, a decided majority of the people in East Tennessee wanted to remain in the Union, and several counties there tried to withdraw from Tennessee and cast their lot with the North.

Back and forth, the war raged across Tennessee soil. Vulnerable to attack along the Tennessee and Cumberland Rivers, both broad highways to the South's heartland, Tennessee was a major battleground of the West and suffered more from the war than any state except Virginia. In all, there were an estimated 300 to 700 engagements in the state. In 1862 a little church near Corinth lent its name to one of the goriest clashes of the entire war, the Battle of Shiloh. It was to prove a vital turning point for the Union side in the West. At Murfreesboro some months later, there was a terrific struggle in which each side lost about a third of its troops. At Chickamauga in 1863 "the pale river of death ran blood"; in that battle the Confederates were victorious, but soon, in the Chattanooga campaign highlighted by the struggle at fog-shrouded Lookout Mountain, "the Battle above the Clouds," the entire Mississippi Valley was assured to the Union. Later, at Franklin, a desperate Confederate counterattack cost the South several generals and 6,000 men.

In 1862 President Lincoln appointed Andrew Johnson—a former Tennessee Congressman and governor, later to be Vice President and then President—as military governor of the state. A former slaveholder, but always loyal to the Union, Johnson was denounced as a traitor to the South but in reply excoriated secessionists and hinted they should be executed. In 1865, when Johnson left for Washington, he was replaced as governor by the acid-tongued Knoxville editor and preacher, William G. (Parson) Brownlow, who warned that continued Southern rebellion might trigger a second civil war in which the Union should completely destroy the South, making "the entire Southern Confederacy as God found the earth when he commenced the work of creation, 'Without form and void.' " The urge for vengeance among Brownlow's Radical Republicans was soon matched on the other side by the Ku Klux Klan, formed by Confederate veterans at Pulaski, Tennessee. The Klan resorted to all manner of violence and intimidation in its effort to subdue the Negroes, drive out Northern agitators and carpetbaggers, and restore conservative Southern white rule.

These public struggles were copied in thousands of street fights and ambushes between Union and Confederate veterans, by communities and even families torn asunder by the passions of the great conflict. And whether Northern or Southern in loyalty, the returning soldiers found a scene of incredible devastation, summarized this way by Tennessee writer Fred Travis:

> Everywhere the land had been laid waste by the ravages of war: farm buildings and homes burned; livestock killed or confiscated; railroads, built at such great expense before the war, now virtually useless. Food, medicine and clothing were scarce and even nonexistent in places. Civil authority had collapsed so that thieves and bandits preyed mercilessly upon the people.

Recovery, political or physical, was slow indeed. When Reconstruction ended with Brownlow's departure for the U.S. Senate in 1869, the resurgent Democrats were so anxious to undo the works of his regime that they abolished the public school system and anti-Klan laws for which he had been responsible. Illiteracy, alarmingly increased during the disruptive war years, was a terrible problem; even after an 1873 law that laid the basis for a modern school system, it was decades before the legislature appropriated enough money to make it a reality. Tennessee agriculture remained overwhelmingly centered on cotton, the evils of a one-crop economy compounded by the sharecropper and crop-lien system, slavery's unattractive successor. There was a lot of talk of industrialization, centered in cities like Chattanooga where the floats in an 1878 parade proclaimed, "Cotton Was King," "Iron is King Now," and "Coal is Prime Minister." But until the turn of the century, the pace of industrialization and economic diversification was slow indeed. Even in 1929, just before the Depression, Tennesseans' per capital income was only $377 a year—barely more than half the national average.

Tennessee politics seemed particularly barren, compared to the lively ferment of the early 19th century. A patchwork state constitution, ratified in 1870, would last 83 years and become the oldest unamended state constitution in the country. Under it, the Democrats were restored to control of the governorship and legislature and Tennessee languished under rarely interrupted one-party rule for almost a century. Conservative Bourbon Democrats, mostly former Confederate officers, dominated the political scene for many years. The big issue of the 1870s was the huge state debt occasioned by the free spending and almost incredible corruption, principally in railroad bonds, of the Brownlow regime. Then for decades the dead-end street issue of Prohibition seemed to be the biggest problem of public life. Begun on a limited basis in 1877, the dry laws were constantly expanded as politicians exploited the Prohibitionist fervor in one of the most Baptist and Protestant of all American states. The hypocrisy of the issue was underscored in 1908 when Edward Ward Carmack, a fiery and hard-drinking editor and former Senator, ran for governor on a platform demanding total suppression of liquor. Carmack sometimes fortified himself with several swigs from a jug before mounting the platform. He barely lost and later was killed in a street corner shootout with the son of a political enemy toward whom Carmack had directed sarcastic editorials; the incident led to a seemingly watertight statewide dry law. But moonshine liquor continued to flow from the East Tennessee hills, and speakeasies thrived along the Memphis waterfront and Printers Alley connecting the newspaper offices in Nashville. Not until 1939 were package stores permitted, and then only on a local option basis. Liquor by the drink, also on a limited basis, had to wait another 30 years.

In place of substantive new public policies, Tennessee politicians did expose the voters to some lively antics. One of the most colorful political campaigns of American history was waged in 1886 between two brothers, Democrat Robert L. Taylor and Republican Alfred A. Taylor, both seeking the governorship. Traveling together through the state, they stayed at the same hotels and filled the air with oratory, wit, fiddle music, and occasional debate of issues in dozens of joint appearances. Some said it was their father Nathaniel who wrote their speeches and directed their campaigns. On one occasion, Bob found Alf's prepared speech text, committed it to memory, and when introduced as the first speaker, recited the talk his brother was about to give. The Taylors were an old East Tennessee family, and when one of them said they were "roses from the same garden," the race was promptly nicknamed the War of the Roses. It was a great relief from the political bitterness that had plagued the state since the Civil War.

Bob Taylor, a well educated lawyer and kind of self-made hillbilly, won the 1886 race. His ascendancy was especially welcomed by the "wool hat" and agrarian Democrats who had had their fill of stuffy Bourbon rule, and in fact Bob did "deliver" in office with election reform and badly needed extra money for the public schools. In all, he served three terms as governor and once each as Senator and Congressman. Alf was elected three times to Congress but had to wait until 1920 to be elected governor for a term.

For the most part it was private Tennessee citizens, not the elected leaders, who made the greatest contributions in the years from the Civil War to World War II. Tennessee still reveres the memory of Alvin C. York, the hunter and blacksmith who came out of the Cumberland mountains to become—in the words of General John J. Pershing—the outstanding citizen-soldier of World War I. Almost 100,000 Tennesseans enlisted in that conflict, just as the state had made a unique contribution to the war with Spain in the 1890s by dispatching four full regiments—in each case underscoring the Volunteer State tradition begun in the war with Mexico.

Another kind of volunteer, suffragette Sue Shelton White, played a key role in making Tennessee the state that provided the decisive vote of ratification to make the 19th Amendment, granting women the right to vote, part of the Constitution. In a very different realm, it was a 24-year-old school-teacher at Dayton, Tennessee, who lent his name to one of the most important tests of freedom of expression in 20th-century America. A state legislator who belonged to the Association of Primitive Baptists had won approval of a state law outlawing the teaching in public schools of "any theory that denies the story of the Divine Creation as taught in the Bible, and to teach instead that man has descended from a lower order of animals." John T. Scopes disobeyed the law, setting the stage for the famed "monkey trial" of 1925. Few Americans escaped the drama of the confrontation of William Jennings Bryan, the "Great Commoner," acting as a special prosecutor in the waning days of his life, pitted against Scopes' defender, Clarence Darrow of the American Civil Liberties Union. The jury—"unanimously hot for Genesis," as H. L. Mencken caustically reported from the scene—quickly convicted Scopes. The conviction was later set aside on a technicality, precluding a U.S. Supreme Court decision on the issue. Scopes had sat silent through the trial, letting Darrow speak for him. But his name goes down in history with a great deal more distinction than those of the Tennessee politicians who sought in the evolution controversy, as they had in the Prohibition fight, the use of the power of state government to force their private religious and moral precepts on others.*

As capricious as the anti-evolution teaching statute may have seemed to the outside world, it was no accident that the governor of the early 1920s— Democrat Austin Peay, an enlightened administrator who must personally have realized its foolishness—signed it into law. Peay needed the support of the rural legislators, many of them religious fundamentalists, to pass a general education law establishing a teacher salary schedule and an eight-month minimum school term. The evolution law was the price for their support. Peay was the same governor who passed a sweeping reorganization of Tennessee state government into eight operating departments, each headed by a commission appointed by and responsible to the governor. Previously the government had been a veritable administrative jungle, operated by 64 boards, departments, and commissions, each of which negotiated independently with the legislature for money and authority.

Peay's administration was the most outstanding in many decades. It was followed, however, by that of one Henry H. Horton, who fell under the in-

---

* Bryan died five days after the trial, Darrow in 1938, and Scopes in 1970 after a successful career as a geologist for major oil firms. Three years before his death, he authored (with James Presley) a reminiscence of his life and the trial, *Center of the Storm*. In it, he observed: "Today, over 40 years from the trial, it seems incredible that the Dayton controversy rose to such an emotional peak. The war cries of the Fundamentalists sound archaic. Yet they were very serious. The trial itself was a test and a defense of the fundamental freedom of religion. At stake was the separation of church and state. If the state is allowed to dictate that a teacher must teach a subject in accordance with the beliefs of one particular religion, then the state can also force schools to teach the beliefs of the person in power, which can lead to the oppression of all personal and religious liberties."

The law under which Scopes had been convicted remained on the books, though largely ignored, until 1967 when it was repealed under threat of a repetition of the Scopes trial. In 1973 the never-say-die legislature tried again, enacting a law which required that evolution be taught only as a theory and that other theories of creation, including that in Genesis, be given equal emphasis in biology textbooks used in the public schools.

fluence of the flamboyant and conniving publisher of the Nashville *Tennessean*, Luke Lea. Lea was in league with an unorthodox Nashville investment banker, Rogers Caldwell. Through Horton, Lea was able to manipulate well over $10 million in state bank deposits and road construction contracts to banks and firms owned by Caldwell & Co. Governor Horton barely escaped impeachment when Caldwell's banks went under in the 1929–30 crash, costing the state government $6.7 million. Lea ended up in prison. Rarely in American history has a state government been "taken" for such a huge sum of money.

After that, the dominant power of Tennessee politics until the World War II era was Edward H. Crump, the Democratic boss of Memphis. Crump was a Mississippi farm boy who had ridden the train into Memphis in 1893 to begin one of the most tumultuous and successful careers of any big city political boss in American history. In the late '20s, Crump returned to power after a hiatus of a few years occasioned by his enemies' success in turning the power of state government against him. Crump was determined to control the governorship and legislature to protect his own power flank in Memphis. The result was to be a quarter century of unparalleled vituperation and political manipulation as Crump excoriated his political enemies, hand-picked Senators and Congressmen and governors and legislatures, and used them to implement his own plans for the promotion and development of Memphis.

In Memphis, as we will note later in this chapter, Crump provided honest and efficient government by means of a controlled black vote and social terrorism leveled against any and all white opponents. On the state-wide level, the secrets to his power were (1) the one-party system, (2) the poll tax and low levels of voting, and (3) the massive, unitary vote Crump produced in Shelby County, of which Memphis is the county seat. Tennessee's Republicans, V. O. Key noted in *Southern Politics*, numbered about 100,000 voters, mostly in East Tennessee. Since most of them did not vote in the crucial Democratic primary, they were in effect "political eunuchs." Then there was the poll tax and traditional voter apathy, which held down the participation in Democratic primaries to about 300,000 votes—out of a potential electorate of 1,600,000. (The poll tax was not a problem in Shelby County, since Crump by hook or crook got the people on city-county payrolls and local businesses—including bawdy houses—to put up the money for poll tax receipts for virtually everyone in the county, including the largely illiterate black voting group there.)

Since it took only a little more than 150,000 votes to win a Democratic primary, Crump had an immense leg up since he could produce a plurality of as much as 60,000 to 70,000 votes from Shelby County alone. To that he added a big percentage—almost half—of the outstate vote, coming from dissident local factions, county bosses who looked to him for state favors or election-time "boodle," and several thousand East Tennessee Republicans with whom he had a working "arrangement" to provide 10,000 or so votes in the Democratic primary in return for patronage favors. Crump's patronage powers were formidable, including both state government positions and federal jobs steered his way through the U.S. Senators he controlled, Kenneth D. McKellar and Tom Stewart, and his political friend, Franklin D. Roosevelt. (In 1938 some eyebrows were raised when Crump used WPA money to build a heated dog kennel. Crump reassured FDR at a seven-state Democratic rally in the Great Smokies: "It will mean a lot of votes for you.")

Some vote returns of the '30s neatly illustrated Crump's power over the Shelby County vote. When Gordon Browning ran for governor in 1936 with Crump's blessing he got 60,218 votes in Shelby County, compared to 861 for his opponent. But Browning subsequently broke with Crump, and in the 1938 election Crump turned on him as a "Judas Iscariot" and "a bigoted boor [whose] heart had beat over two billion times without a sincere beat." The good burghers of Shelby County got the message and gave Browning only 9,315 votes. Even that total would have been lower if Crump had not become worried that too microscopic a vote for Browning might look suspicious and had the total raised so that the results would "look good and democratic."

Browning had seen his 1938 defeat in the offing and tried to prevent it by a bold plan to undercut Shelby County's influence in state primaries. The device he proposed was a county unit system, akin to Georgia's. Under it, Shelby County's vote would have been reduced from 25 to 13 percent of the total. Browning rammed the scheme through the legislature, prompting Crump to remark that the governor "would milk his neighbor's cow through a crack in the fence." But the scheme was torpedoed when Crump got the state supreme court, on which he had several of his allies, to declare it unconstitutional.

Five years later Crump again used the supreme court, in an even more diabolical way, to invalidate an entirely legal repeal of the poll tax. The three-term governor then in office, Prentice Cooper, was normally a toady for Crump and knew that the boss wanted the poll tax preserved because it depressed the vote outside Shelby County. But Cooper had put a repeal plank in his platform each time he ran for governor, and in 1943 the newspapers chided him mercilessly as a liar and servant to poll-tax-loving Crump. As Alfred Steinberg related the incident in *The Bosses*, Cooper suddenly sprang to life, pushing the anti-poll tax bill through the subservient legislature. But despite the glee of the papers and good-government groups, Crump had the last laugh again. A vacancy suddenly occurred on the supreme court, and Crump persuaded Cooper to appoint the boss's most fawning Memphis aide to the vacancy. The court then voted by a one-vote margin to invalidate the repealer, on the curious theory that the legislature lacked the power to repeal the poll tax law it had passed 53 years before. "Afterward," Steinberg wrote, "the mood throughout the state was one of grim pessimism, that Mistah Crump could not be defeated on any issue."

In earlier years, there had been a mild progressive streak in Crump—when he battled corporate interests, for instance, or demanded public power and cheap electricity for the poor. But in his latter years the boss took on the marks of an aging conservative. He insisted on McKellar's retention in the

Senate despite signs of creeping senility in his old ally. He took such sharp exception to Harry Truman's civil rights program that he backed the Dixie-crat Presidential ticket in 1948. And all along, it had been personal power rather than ideology that motivated Crump and his followers. "His state organization," Key wrote, "was held together largely by the perquisites of office, the desire for office, [and] the disciplinary tools inherent in the control of government and party machinery."

As for the political "outs" of the Crump era, they offered no coherent body of policy alternatives to the electorate. They simply sought to transform themselves into the "ins," to become little Crumps in their own way.

The public policy consequences of this frozen politics were well critiqued in a view from the left by Norman L. Parks of Middle Tennessee State University:

The culture mentality rooted in Southern traditionalism made both [Tennessee] parties fundamentally undemocratic and gave the stamp of inevitability to the established pattern of poverty-plenty, segregation-white supremacy, disfranchisement-oligarchy. It provided a complete rationalization for the need for a continuous supply of cheap labor, the natural "inferiority" of low-income classes, the evils of unionization, the absence of social responsibility, and . . . bland indifference toward the retraining of the state's unemployed and underemployed labor force. . . .

Politically the culture mentality accorded respectability to a non-aristocratic Bourbonism, which, by means of the *modus vivendi* of conservative Democrats and Republicans, controlled the state and county government and protected the interests of the dominant classes against the forces of social change. A major bulwark of defense was the unamendable constitution of 1870, which blocked the creation of a modern tax structure and kept the tax burden on the back of the consumer. On the pattern of resistance to constitutional change, the old orders of planters, bankers, doctors, and manufacturers stood shoulder to shoulder with the latter-day front of insurance executives, industrial managers, and finance capitalists. The absence of a classified property tax, an income tax, or a rational corporation tax [was] evidence of the cohesion of this alliance. Further evidence [was] a compulsory open-shop law [and] the weakest protective labor legislation. . . .

Overrepresentation of the rural counties in the legislature [was] also part of the embalming fluid.

It would take the intervention of outside forces—the leavening influence of TVA, and, even more important, the economic and population changes set in motion by World War II—to disrupt finally the politics without policy debate that had thwarted Tennessee's maturation during its Civil War century.

Postwar Politics: The Fresh Winds Blow

The first signal of change to come was the famed "G.I. Revolt" of 1946 in McMinn County in East Tennessee. For years the area had been in the iron grip of a group of vicious, corrupt Democratic politicians who gouged the local populace and used physical violence and egregious vote fraud to maintain their own power. And they were in league with Crump, giving his candidates close to 100 percent of the local vote (as they counted it). The returning veterans, having battled tyranny abroad, determined not to countenance it at home. With rifles and dynamite—"as nearly justifiable," John Gunther commented, "as political violence can ever be," they overthrew the local bosses and restored a semblance of democracy under the Republican banner.

Crump's downfall and collapse as the dictator of Tennessee politics was to come two years later—but not without appropriate political pyrotechnics. Both the governorship and a Senate seat were up. Seeking the governor's chair from which Crump had ousted him a decade before, Gordon Browning returned from the war and "hit the ground running." Crump alleged in newspaper ads that when Browning was governor before, he had "converted the proud capital of Tennessee into a regular Sodom and Gomorrah, . . . reeking with sordid, vicious infamy." But Browning's counterattacks on Crump seemed to carry more weight with the voters, and he won easily, a stunning defeat for the old boss.

The outcome of the Senate race of '48 was just as significant. Liberal Democratic Congressman Estes Kefauver of Chattanooga entered the three-man race and was making little headway until Crump accused him of Communist sympathies and likened him to a pet coon. "The pet coon," Crump said, "puts its foot in the open drawer in your room, but invariably turns its head while its foot is feeling around in the drawer. The coon hopes, through its cunning by turning its head, he will deceive any onlookers as to where his foot is and what it is into." What Kefauver was up to, Crump suggested, was that he "had a foot in the Communist camp but could pretend it was all very coincidental."

Crump's attack gave Kefauver just the opening he needed. "I may be a coon, but I am not Mr. Crump's pet," he replied. "The coon has rings on his tail but not in his nose. . . . It is one of the cleanest of all animals; it is one of the most courageous. . . . The coon is all American. Davy Crockett, Sam Houston, James Robertson, and all of our great men in that era in Tennessee history wore the familiar ring-tailed, coonskin cap." And so Kefauver, to the delight of Tennesseans, donned a coonskin cap and won the election—becoming, as one of his admirers once said, a "self-made lowbrow." He was on his way to building a coalition of liberals, intellectuals, blue-collar workers, and blacks which would play a substantial role in the postwar era. Outside Tennessee, Kefauver's homespun style was sometimes ridiculed. But it was a legitimate reincarnation of Jacksonian Democracy and enabled Kefauver to project himself into the Presidential arena, to mount his successful investigation of organized crime, and tackle monopolistic practices in the drug and power industries.

The Browning and Kefauver victories, Fred Travis wrote, "demonstrated that the once almost invincible Crump machine was not only vulnerable but a political anachronism." Reelected governor in 1950, Browning was able to eliminate the tools of Crump's statewide power by packing the state election board with his own men, repealing the poll tax once and for all, and forcing the cities to use voting machines instead of paper ballots. An old-fashioned populist, Browning had the opportunity to effect a true reform of Tennessee state government based on the new coalition that Kefauver best symbolized. But while he increased expenditures for education and started a major rural road-building plan, Browning lacked a real sense of progressive government and ended up being defeated by an aggressive newcomer, Frank G. Clement, in the 1952 Democratic primary. Clement had the backing of the old Crump machine, but in the same election Kenneth McKellar's long Senate career was finally terminated by a liberal Congressman and Crump foe, Albert Gore. Two years later Crump was dead and his Memphis organization faded away, as his statewide organization had four years earlier.

From the 1950s into the 1960s, the young Democratic triumvirate of Kefauver, Clement, and Gore rode high in Tennessee—so high that each man was considered a Presidential possibility and the question was whether there would be room on the national stage for the rival ambitions of all three. Liberal Democrats look back almost nostalgically to that era now; as Oak Ridge attorney Eugene Joyce put it: "They were men of real stature— personable, brilliant men, independent and unencumbered. That was a time when the union movement was strong and being a liberal down here wasn't bad, because people were interested in pocketbook issues."

The nation got a view of the three Tennesseans at the 1956 Democratic Convention when Clement gave the keynote address, Gore hoped lightning would strike him as a Vice Presidential candidate, and Kefauver ended up on the ticket with Adlai Stevenson. Kefauver then remained in the Senate until his early death, in 1963, truncated an amazing political and legislative career and also deprived Tennessee liberals of their most effective leader of this century. Gore, lacking Kefauver's homespun manner and appeal to the little man, was defeated for reelection in 1970.

On the state scene, Frank Clement remained a major figure until his death in a 1969 automobile accident. He had been only 31 when he began his first gubernatorial campaign in 1952; courthouse oldtimers muttered "Too young, son," but Clement won then—and in two later campaigns— through a remarkable blend of religious fervor and astute politics. He established a state department of mental health (separating psychiatric hospitals from the prison system) and provided free textbooks for pupils. Most important, he seemed to bring a breath of fresh air into the administration of one of the nation's stodgiest state governments. But Clement did the people a disservice by endorsing (for gubernatorial terms alternating with his own) Buford Ellington, a man of little imagination.*

America may never again produce Clement's equal in Bible-thumping politics. References to the Deity interlaced his public and private pronouncements. Gospel music and quotations from a Bible clutched in his hand were constant features of Clement campaign rallies, which were likened to the

---

* This phenomenon of political "leapfrogging" was a result of a constitutional provision which prohibited incumbent governors from seeking reelection—but did not prevent them from running again after a four-year hiatus.

colorful Chautauqua crusades of earlier times. The speech ending of the early Clement campaigns never varied, as the sound truck crew began softly the Clement theme, "Precious Lord, Take My Hand" and Clement lifted his arm and called on his listeners to stretch their hands with him "to that inverted bowl we call the sky." The volume increased with the finish—"and figuratively say with me Precious Lord, Take our hands, lead us on to better government in Tennessee! Thank you and God bless you, one and all!" When elected, Clement hung a portrait of Jesus in the governor's office; when some objected, he said, "If you can't mix your politics and your religion, then something is wrong with your politics."

For Tennessee, Clement's religiosity was politically impeccable. As James T. Wooten of the New York *Times* wrote after his death: "It was an irresistible technique for the thousands of small-town and farm-oriented Tennesseeans whose lives are so inextricably tied to the socio-religious traditions of the region. . . . His people were the people who still worship in the small churches that dot the back roads of Tennessee—Methodist or Baptist or Church of Christ congregations of farm families whose lives are uncluttered by the urban ills they recognize and condemn in their city cousins."

Clement had high hopes of reaching the White House and believed he might vault onto a national ticket, in Alben Barkley style, through his keynote speech to the 1956 convention. The speech had some good lines, including Clement's definition of the "sordid record" of the Eisenhower-Nixon administration: "the vice-hatchet man slinging slander and spreading half-truths while the top man peers down the green fairways of indifference." But the speech was more remembered for its overdone "How long, O Lord, how long" line and its pure cornpone. It also prompted New York sportswriter Red Smith, who was assigned to cover the convention, to write one of the classic leads of American political journalism: "The young governor of Tennessee, Frank G. Clement, slew the Republican party with the jawbone of an ass here last night. . . ."

After that Clement was never again seriously considered as a national leader, and though he won two more terms as governor, he lost two bids for the U.S. Senate. In a sense, he was becoming an anachronism, even in his own time. The reasons were several but could be summarized in a few words: increasing urbanism (and thus a more sophisticated society), a Republican renaissance, and the implications of a momentous court case that originated in Tennessee, called *Baker v. Carr*. Together with an increased and truly independent black vote, these developments were to change Tennessee politics, within a few years, practically beyond recognition.

One of the first results was a forward surge in Tennessee Republicanism. "Our party's strength," Senator Howard Baker, Jr., said in an interview, "was always bottled up in the eastern third of the state—partly as a result of the Civil War, when most East Tennesseans fought on the Union side, and most Middle and West Tennesseans on the Southern side." The East Tennessee congressional district his father held for many years, Baker noted, had never elected a Democrat, while the other district in that part of the state was statistically the most Republican in the nation. Between the 1890s and 1928, the Republicans had been gaining some strength in Middle and West Tennessee, but they were still far from a majority point when the Great Depression and the FDR-Crump era scuttled whatever gains they had made.

The legendary "working arrangement" of East Republicans with the dominant Democratic factions was quite real and lasted until the death in 1961 of the East Republicans' longtime boss, Congressman B. Carroll Reece (the onetime Republican National Chairman). Norman L. Parks has catalogued the reasons for the alliance: "the permanent minority status of the Republicans at the state level; the Democratic control of the general election commission in every county; the desire of Republicans to run things in their local counties as they wished; the advantages which the *modus vivendi* contributed to individual Republican leaders; the need to have local legislation approved by a Democratic state administration; the state's open primary system permitting unrestricted voting; and election laws toothless enough to make manipulation and skulduggery safe avocations." The only caveat that should be entered is that the East Tennessee vote for Crump candidates in Democratic primaries, especially in close contests, was not as great as generally assumed. But Reece was capable of vengeance toward any insurgents in his own ranks, and for his own purposes quashed the abortive attempt in 1944 of a progressive Republican, John W. Kilgo, to create a coalition of mountain Republicans and liberal Democrats to overthrow Crump. The effort not only marked a deviation from Reece's own brand of Taft conservatism but probably seemed to Reece to be a hopeless adventure that could only end in weakening his own control of the party and the patronage benefits that flowed from that control. "The Tennessee Republican high command," V. O. Key reported in 1949, "contemplates victory in state races with a shudder." *

This "no win" plan, a classic in the annals of American politics, was to be undermined by the very phenomena—urbanism, television, and the decline of the political bosses—which accompanied the decline of straight ticket Democratic voting in postwar Tennessee. An "instructed" vote became less and less practicable, and the troops could not be held in line long when real victory seemed possible.

The prospect for winning was made very real in 1952, when General Eisenhower—whom Reece had opposed for the Republican Presidential nomination—narrowly carried Tennessee over Adlai Stevenson. Except for the Republican clover years of 1920 and 1928, it was the first time a GOP Presidential nominee had carried the state since 1868. It was not, Howard Baker pointed out, an increased East Tennessee GOP vote which made this possible; in fact, he produced from his desk an old almanac showing that the

---

* Reece's control of the Tennessee GOP was a pretty cynical business. Even though he had run unsuccessfully for the U.S. Senate against Kefauver in 1948—"15 years ahead of his time," as Howard Baker puts it—Reece undercut Kefauver's subsequent GOP opposition in return for Kefauver's willingness to let Reece-backed nominees win confirmation in the U.S. Senate during the Eisenhower administration.

heavy Republican percentage in East Tennessee in 1868 set a pattern which was almost identical to that a century later. The vital change was an historic increase in the West and Middle Tennessee Republican vote, permitting the GOP to spring out of its old beachhead.† Since Ike's initial breakthrough, Republican Presidential nominees have carried Tennessee in every election except 1964. In 1966 the Republicans won a U.S. Senate seat; in 1970 they became the first state south of the Mason-Dixon line to have a Republican governor (their first in half a century) *and* two U.S. Senators. They have advanced from distant minority status in the legislature to near-majorities in both houses; in fact, they actually controlled the state house of representatives in 1969–70. And by 1973 they held five of Tennessee's eight congressional seats.

Baker named these factors in the GOP's resurgence:

First, we have come out of the Civil War century. The ancient geographical and historical biases of the Civil War have pretty well receded. Secondly, it appears that the two-party system works from the top and goes down. First one wins for President, then for the Senate, then for governor, and lastly adds more congressmen and comes close to winning the legislature. Finally, we have built grassroots Republican strength and organization in every part of the state. In the last 20 years we have slipped slightly in East Tennessee, but we have gained dramatically everywhere else. Polls show the Democrats' party strength has receded substantially—from 75 percent down to the 30 percent range. The Republicans have even less, but now there is a huge independent vote. Both parties have to scrap for it. Neither gets fat and happy. They have to compete—and that way they stay lean and hungry.

To hear some of the GOP's critics, the party has made its new inroads by appealing to the wealthy, the aspirers, and the prejudiced. Organizationally, a new stream of volunteers fed into the party at the time of the Goldwater movement of the early '60s. As Norman Parks wrote, the Goldwaterites poured into the GOP leadership vacuum created by the passing of the old-line East Tennessee leaders "prepared to exploit the older norms of white supremacy, laissez faire, anti-unionism, and businessman Bourbonism. . . . Politically inexperienced, but deeply ideological and impatient with the supineness of the Old Guard, the New Guard proposed to bring to politics the hard sell, the grassroots drive, and the systematic organization which generated success in the business world." The base of the new Republican order, Parks said, was to be in the cities that had been steadily turning toward the Republicans in Presidential elections. The center was to be Memphis, "long-time political capital of Tennessee under Crump and currently the major center of expanding population in the state." The leaders were "Memphis natives, tristate migrants, and middle and upper management men with branch offices of national corporations," many of whom were "incased in

† The historic record also shows a center of isolated Republicanism in the poor clay hill country along the Tennessee River in the southwestern part of the state, where in antebellum days there were few plantations and the Jacksonian yeomen resented the easy living of the slave-owning Black Belt residents. Those counties voted against secession and have remained steadfastly Republican for more than 100 years—an example of political fealty as unreasonable in the days of TVA and poverty programs (both of great aid to this region) as the continued loyalty of many conservative Tennessee counties to the Democratic loyalties of their fathers.

the old Bourbon insensitivity to social responsibility." With comparable ideological schools in Nashville and Chattanooga, Parks contended, they sought "to reconstitute the Republican party as a lily-white, solidly conservative, business-oriented organization prepared to challenge the Democrats for office at all levels."

There was some evidence to support Parks' description. At the 1964 state convention the dominant Goldwater faction crushed opposition from the traditional East Tennessee Republicans, threw out the appeal of the Lincoln League of Memphis on behalf of George W. Lee, a veteran black Republican leader, and sent an all-white delegation to the national convention for the first time in Tennessee Republican history. By 1972, two of the three congressmen from the Memphis area were strongly conservative Republicans. GOP Congressman William E. Brock played the school busing issue to the hilt to win a U.S. Senate seat in 1970. When President Nixon, in his 1972 reelection race, swept Tennessee with 68 percent of the total vote, his greatest support outside the longstanding Republican areas of East Tennessee came in Memphis, its suburbs, and the rural counties of West Tennessee—the very areas that had given the biggest leads to George Wallace in 1968. The big Wallace vote, 34 percent of the state total, seemed to have moved lock, stock, and barrel into the Republican column. And in the overwhelmingly suburban white collar areas of Tennessee, Nixon by 1972 was winning an astounding 78 percent of the vote.

Modern-day Tennessee Republicanism, however, is more complex than all this might suggest. The most popular Republican in the state in the early 1970s was Howard Baker, Jr., a true son of the East Tennessee hills and a man who melds moderate economic conservatism with a generally liberal stand on race matters. Baker remembers his first and only unsuccessful race for the Senate in 1964, when "the Goldwater onslaught about sunk the Republican party." That year, Baker said, he was on a platform in Knoxville, "the home of the TVA, and watched Goldwater urge that it be sold. I had an intense desire to sink into the dust, which I later did." Two years later, however, Baker bounced back to become the first popularly elected Republican Senator in Tennessee history, defeating no less a figure than Frank G. Clement. In 1972 Baker went on to win reelection with a startling 62 percent of the vote, capturing a majority in every section of Tennessee, even the sections of West Tennessee considered most segregationist in their sentiment. He even came close to beating his Democratic opponent, a strong conservative on racial matters, among the state's Negro voters.

And in 1970, while most attention was focused on Brock's successful assault on liberal Senator Albert Gore, a mild-mannered and affable Memphis dentist, Winfield Dunn, rode into the governorship on the GOP ticket. Dunn's prior political experience had been limited to membership on his party's executive committee and a losing race for the legislature. He "had little to recommend him," Fred Travis noted, "other than a winning smile and a warm handshake." But it was enough, because outgoing Governor

Buford Ellington had left the Democratic organization in a shambles, and Dunn's opponent, a Kennedy-type Democrat named John Jay Hooker, Jr., had acquired a poor public image when a series of his business ventures (most notably "Minnie Pearl Chicken" franchises) turned sour.*

The Republicans won, Democratic attorney Eugene Joyce commented, "because the busing issue overshadowed the pocketbook issue and cracked the unions wide open, and because the Republicans came up with three bright young men—Dunn, Baker, and Brock." The Democrats only had a set of weakened older politicians, he said, "and then Hooker and his chicken business." Governor Dunn agreed with part of Joyce's analysis. The 1968 Wallace vote, he suggested, showed a real sense of frustration on the part of Tennesseans who were tired of the old one-party domination and political bossism. Race tensions, he said, were only part of the picture. "The people were looking for something new and fresh and dependable. Senator Baker, for example, hasn't had any bad habits. But look back on some of our past leadership in Tennessee and you'll see they had bad habits. Albert Gore didn't, but some of them did. Senator Brock and I too, through our personal deportment, have a basically clean and honest image. I think the people enjoy and appreciate us. And television has had a tremendous impact on people, because we've been able to communicate with them."

In office, Dunn was far from the stand-pat conservative one might have predicted in a man out of the antigovernment Republican milieu of Shelby County. He pushed (as we will note later) a number of progressive reforms and even appointed a number of blacks to important state positions. Senator Brock, who had chaired Young Voters for the President in 1972 and hoped to parlay his support among the rightist Young Republicans into a Presidential campaign in 1976, suddenly saw his chances eclipsed in the backwash from Watergate. (It turned out that Brock's chief political operative, Ken Rietz, was involved in political espionage undertaken by the Young Voters organization.) Watergate elevated Senator Baker, on the other hand, to temporary national prominence through his performance on the Senate Watergate Committee. While the Tennessee competition between the moderate and ultraconservative, the traditional and "new" Republicans, was sure to continue, it seemed in 1974 that the moderates were in the ascendancy. As an example, Dunn's designee as Republican state chairman was S. L. Kopald, Jr., a prominent businessman and Jewish leader and member of the board of

* Hooker's political demise was sad in a way, because he was one of the most direct politicians to surface in recent years. He was against capital punishment, and not even afraid to say so to an audience of policemen. He thought the state campaign expenditure limit of $25,000 in a gubernatorial primary was absurd, so he simply filed a statement saying he had spent $785,000 in a first race in 1966—and of course no one dared to do a thing about it, since every candidate had been breaking the law. Hooker was also willing to say, years before most other Tennessee politicians, that until Tennessee's regressive tax system was cracked, "all our solutions will be on a piecemeal basis." When I met Hooker in 1969 in his opulent Nashville office, filled with memorabilia of his contacts with the Kennedys, I found a sartorially elegant but somewhat disheveled man, tall with bushy dark hair, wearing shiny black buckled shoes and talking of his franchise empires in chicken, nursery schools, and hospitals. He was a kind of press agent's dream—but for New York, not Tennessee.

the National Conference of Christians and Jews. Kopald went out of his way to keep the door open to Republicans of all ideological persuasions. The Republicans' 1974 candidate for governor, Lamar Alexander, 33, was apparently cut from the same progressive cloth as Baker and Dunn, whose campaigns he had coordinated, but he was beaten by former Democratic Congressman Ray Blanton.

Bereft of top-level leadership and divided even more deeply in ideology than the Republicans, the Tennessee Democrats faced a very uncertain future. They still held a precarious majority in the legislature, controlled the lion's share of local government posts in the state, and could pray that the school busing issue, their chief nemesis in recent years, might obligingly go away. But a measure of their problem was Tennessee's first Presidential primary, held in 1972.* Riding the busing issue for all it was worth, maverick Democrat George Wallace took 68 percent of the vote in an 11-man primary field. The regular national Democrats were left trailing in the dust—Hubert Humphrey the strongest at a mere 16 percent. But the Wallaceites had every reason to be bitter when blacks, women, and other liberal party forces concentrated their efforts on the local and state party meetings that actually selected delegates, and eclipsed some of the Wallace strength at the national convention.

When I passed through Tennessee in 1973, the regular Democrats were expressing an almost forlorn hope that a new generation of bright young figures in their party, the modern-day counterparts of a Kefauver or Clement, might loom on the horizon. Unfortunately for the Democrats, the party's back benches did not seem packed with talent. Another possibility was that some volatile economic issue, like the tide of inflation rising in the 1970s, would rise to stop the ascendant Republicans.

It was significant, I thought, that none of the Democrats thought they could reassert their power by the kind of manipulations that characterized the Crump era. The old county rings and city machines were but a shadow of their former selves, and the electorate had become much too large and fragmented to be susceptible to control. With a more literate electorate and the death of the poll tax, the number of Tennesseans voting had gone up from half a million in 1940 to 1.2 million in 1968 and 1972. Still, only 44.3 percent of the state's voting age people cast Presidential ballots in 1972—the fifth worst turnout rate among the 50 states. The figures could be reviewed as a dismal commentary on the condition of popular democracy in Tennessee —or alternatively as an indication of a great untapped reservoir of voters that superior candidates, running on more sharply defined issues, could draw to the polls in the next several years. The arrival of a vigorous two-party system seemed almost sure to increase turnouts. The question was whether the Tennessee politicians would simply continue their penchant for *personalismo* politics or would also offer the people some real policy choices about their future.

* Under the primary law, delegates are supposed to vote for the Presidential preference poll winner statewide or in their district. But there is no legal way to force them to abide by the primary results. Tennessee had so many Democratic candidates in the 1972 preference poll because the primary statute (molded after Oregon and Wisconsin) required that the secretary of state put the names of all generally discussed Presidential hopefuls on the ballot.

Urbanism, Baker v. Carr, *and Meager*
State Government

The Tennessee constitution of 1870, which was to last so many decades, was adopted when 93 percent of the state's people lived on farms or in little towns of less than 2,500 people. Up to the eve of World War II, when 65 percent still lived in rural areas, Tennessee was still viewed as one of the least urbanized of all states. The political repercussions were inevitable: the influence of the small county rings, almost inevitable selection of a rural figure as governor, and thorough domination of the legislature by rural and small-town forces. The rural control was offset somewhat by Crump's machinations, but his essential interest was only to keep control of Memphis. There were scarcely any cities in the medium population range, and only four over 100,000—Memphis, Nashville, Chattanooga, and Knoxville. Cumulatively, they accounted for only 24 percent of the state's people.

Tennessee today, Lee S. Greene and Jack E. Holmes noted in *The Changing Politics of the South,* "may still give the impression of rurality to the passing traveler, but its politics are far more urban than the sweeping forests indicate." Only 40 percent of the people now live in "rural" places, and almost half live in the four big cities or their suburbs. A fifth metropolitan area seems in the making in upper East Tennessee around Kingsport and Johnson City.

Growing urban strength in the legislature was reflected in the 1950s in a rather strong new municipal league, a bigger city share of the state sales tax, authorization for supplementary local sales taxes, constitutional home rule, and a strong annexation law that enabled the center cities to expand, even in the face of suburban opposition. The change in the 1960s was to be even more dramatic, as Tennessee's legislative apportionment battle led to a Supreme Court decision profoundly affecting the nature of American federalism.

Despite a state constitutional requirement of legislative reapportionment every ten years, no recasting of district lines had taken place since 1901. The forces which controlled the districting at the turn of the century—the rural, Democratic counties of Middle and West Tennessee, ganging up against the cities and Republican East Tennessee—had obdurately refused to redraw the legislative districts for more than 60 years. As a result, the metropolitan counties had barely half the seats they were entitled to by population. By 1960, house districts ranged from 3,454 to 79,301 in population—a disparity of 23 to 1. In the senate there was a six-fold disparity. When a citizens group asked the state supreme court to intervene, it refused to enforce the state's own constitutional requirement of reapportionment, leading Nashville attorney Z. T. Osborn, Jr., a leader of the pro-apportionment forces, to comment that the court was ignoring the motto on its own seal: "Let justice be done even if the skies should fall." It was the name of a Memphis politician,

Charles Baker, that was immortalized in the federal court case which followed, *Baker v. Carr.** (Joe Carr was Tennessee's veteran secretary of state.) The plaintiffs were able to show that Tennessee had callously disregarded its own law, that relief was impossible through the state political system or courts, and that only federal intervention could break the logjam. The United States Supreme Court sustained the position of the irate Tennesseeans in its landmark 1962 decision, entering the "political thicket" because 14th Amendment guarantees of equal protection of the laws could not otherwise be realized. Within a few short years, the composition of virtually every state legislature in the Union was changed as a result.

Tennessee's legislators made a few fitful and reluctant efforts to comply with the federal decision and then called a constitutional convention in a last desperate effort to avoid compliance. The controlling forces at that meeting, especially the rural people and Farm Bureau, wanted to find a device that would prevent the cities from gaining control of the legislature. They endorsed a "little federal system" that apportioned the house by population and the senate on a geographic basis. That effort was quickly invalidated by the federal courts, however, so that both houses went on to a straight population base of apportionment. The four big metropolitan counties suddenly advanced to control of 14 of the 33 senate seats and 42 of the 99 house seats; with allies from other urbanized areas, they seemed to have a real chance to gain a working majority.

The rural forces had foreseen that possibility and switched the system to all single districts in place of at-large legislative elections in the metropolitan counties. The result was to undermine the cohesiveness of the metropolitan delegations, creating seats for a large contingent of suburban legislators who could be expected to side with the rural legislators against the center-city interests. The single-member district system soon proved to have another consequence of major importance, because it increased the opportunity for Negroes and Republicans to win more seats. The net result was a fragmented, albeit more democratic legislature than Tennessee had ever had.

Another burning issue was the almost dictatorial control which Tennessee governors, through deals with patronage-hungry representatives, had assumed over the legislature. For their labors, legislators had been paid a paltry per diem—only $4 until the first increases were started in 1953—and they had been limited to 75-day sessions every other year. In those short sessions, legislators were inclined to give the governor any program he asked for, in hopes of future favors on roads and the like. Moreover, they were easy prey for the lobbyists. ("During those 75 days," Fred Travis told me, "legislators lived like kings, wined and dined by lobbyists. After the 75 days, lobbyists wouldn't buy 'em a cup of coffee.") The constitutional convention shifted the balance of power by instituting annual legislative sessions and putting the legislators on a higher, regular salary. Afterwards,

---

* Baker was a Democrat, but the suit was bipartisan. One of the complainants, for instance, was the late Hobart Atkins, a conservative Republican state senator from Knoxville.

there were still arguments about the lobbyists' influence in Nashville.* But the legislators did have continuing power and influence, and the governor's power over them declined rapidly. Other legislative reforms followed fairly quickly—a streamlining of the committee system with professional staff, increased power for interim committees, a legislative fiscal review committee to "watch-dog" the state's spending, and private offices for the legislators—the first time they had ever had a place to hang their hats outside the legislative chambers. In 1971 the Citizens Conference on State Legislature ranked Tennessee 26th among the 50 state legislatures in its ability to act in an independent, informed, and functional manner. Except for West Virginia, which ranked 25th, it was the best ranking of any Border State legislature, and miles ahead of Tennessee's Deep South neighbors like Alabama (50th), Arkansas (46th), and Mississippi (42nd).

All this does not mean Tennessee has suddenly acquired a progressive state government. Though state budgets have expanded rapidly (to about $2 billion a year), expenditures for state and local government services still lag far behind national averages. In the early '70s per capita outlays for public schools in Tennessee ranked only 47th in the country—even though the state's proportions of high school dropouts, of functional illiterates, and of young men failing Army pre-induction mental tests have been among the nation's highest. Public kindergartens have only recently advanced beyond the pilot stage inaugurated in 1965. Even Mississippi is ahead of Tennessee in the percentage of college graduates in its adult population, yet Tennessee continues to rank only 37th among the states in its per capita outlays for higher education. The state's per capita expenditures for welfare rank 35th in the country, police protection 43rd, and highways 38th. The only notable exception has been in health and hospitals—a rather high ranking of 13th among the states. Yet in people needs, Tennessee ranks alarmingly low. As Governor Winfield Dunn said in his 1973 budget message:

> We in Tennessee are four million people. A quarter million of us are children, many desperately needing help. Eight hundred thousand of us are old or blind or unable to support ourselves because of physical infirmities. A quarter million of us are slaves to drugs or alcohol and a half million are orphans or are in prison or are mentally incapacitated. Sixty thousand of us have no jobs. A quarter million are under-employed. A quarter million of us are hungry. All of us are diminished by these weaknesses among us.

Compared to most American states, Tennessee was doing precious little to solve those problems. Its tax effort in the early 1970s—state and local taxes measured as a percent of personal income—ranked a dismal 47th in the nation and mitigated against major new or expanded state programs. Governor Dunn did, in fact, try to effect reforms in such fields as corrections, early childhood development, and comprehensive community-based mental and public health. He accomplished some reorganization of the

* The lobbies apparently retain immense power. In 1973, for instance, a score of lobbyists from the American Trial Lawyers Association descended on Nashville to kill, with little effort, no-fault insurance legislation which would have reduced premiums on motor vehicle liability by an estimated 15 percent.

state government, including creation of a department of economic and community development to coordinate growth efforts. By 1973 Tennessee seemed well on its way toward a statewide kindergarten program and passed Dunn's proposal for a housing development corporation to make mortgage money available for less affluent citizens. But Dunn was frustrated in effecting, at least within the time span of his own term, the problem every disinterested observer agreed was the most serious for Tennessee government: reform of the state tax system.

As the report of Dunn's own tax reform commission showed in 1973, there are few other states in which the poor, least able to pay, expend such a high portion of their income in taxes, and the rich are so lightly taxed. Incredible as it may seem, Tennessee families living in dire poverty at $2,000 or less a year were paying 16.4 percent of their income in state and local taxes, *five times* greater than the 3.6 percent burden of families earning upwards of $25,000. The principal reason was Tennessee's excessive reliance on sales taxes. The commission's central recommendation was institution of a personal income tax, which would be far less regressive and would also tap rising incomes more effectively, thus permitting Tennessee to provide much broader services for its people. The income tax solution is forbidden in the existing Tennessee constitution, however, so that constitutional amendment with approval in a popular referendum—perhaps a political impossibility—would be necessary. The Tennessee legislature showed its lack of concern for low-income taxpayers in 1973 by turning down a proposed state minimum wage law and rejecting Governor Dunn's request for a "circuit breaker" plan to give relief to thousands of low-income families hard pressed by high property and sales taxes in an era of rampant inflation.

Tennesseans in Washington: Greats, Near-Greats, and an Old Hack

After its brilliant role in national life in the early 19th century, Tennessee proved unable to contribute leaders of real national stature for practically a full century. A notable exception was Cordell Hull, a Congressman from Middle Tennessee for 22 years, briefly a Senator, and then Secretary of State from the day Franklin D. Roosevelt became President until 1944. During the 1930s Hull did much to implement the "good neighbor" policy toward Latin America, and in 1945 he won a Nobel Peace Prize for his part in organizing the United Nations. Back in Tennessee, Hull had been one of the few statewide politicians Boss Crump could never tame. After his long years in the international field, it was easy to forget what a true son of Tennessee Hull had been. He was born in a log cabin, and his mountaineer father had once murdered a man in a blood feud.

An example of what was wrong with Tennessee politics for so many years was Kenneth Douglas McKellar, who became the state's first popularly elected Senator in 1917 and then spent 36 generally unproductive years in

Washington. Through the inexorable workings of the seniority system, "Kay Dee" McKellar, as he had been called in the early days of his political career in Memphis, rose to immense power as chairman of the Appropriations Committee and President Pro Tempore of the Senate. After Roosevelt's death, in fact, McKellar was President of the Senate and second in line for the Presidency—a situation, John Gunther wrote in *Inside U.S.A.*, "that made political philosophers whistle." Gunther, in fact, devoted several pages to McKellar, describing him as "one of the angriest men alive," "a creature out of another age," and "short, squat, rubicund." McKellar fascinated Gunther in part because he was the only public official to throw the famed interviewer-author out of his office; this happened when Gunther made the mistake of asking McKellar what he should see in Tennessee "aside from TVA."

McKellar rose to power in Memphis municipal politics in 1905 and soon formed an alliance with Ed Crump that was to last half a century. The two were peas in a pod; McKellar, for instance, backed TVA in its early years but then thought nothing of pressing a bill that would have destroyed the agency's independence by making virtually all its officials subject to Senate confirmation—and thus McKellar's personal approval. When Truman became President he invited McKellar, as temporary Senate President, to sit in on Cabinet meetings, a situation which prompted a leading Southern newspaper, the Richmond *Times-Dispatch,* to editorialize: "A hack sits in the Cabinet. . . . Senator McKellar is a vindictive . . . grudge-bearing politician with an incurable itch for spoils . . . a shoddy impresario of the patronage grab."

FDR had sought, in vain, to get Crump to retire "Kay Dee" from the Senate in the mid-1940s, but McKellar, spurning even Crump's advice to step out gracefully, held on until Albert Gore administered the *coup de grace* in the 1952 Democratic primary. By then, senility was the big issue. Presiding over the Senate, McKellar often had little idea of what the debates were about and once had a spell of dizziness that caused him to faint and tumble out of the Vice President's perch. His dotage was so far advanced that he was virtually unable to campaign against Gore.

Gore was as striking a contrast to McKellar as one could imagine—an intellectual, an austere legislator, and a man of such prickly independence that he was once called "an unclassifiable Democrat whose familiar habitat is somewhere off the reservation." No one ever doubted Gore's liberalism, or his courage, as he exposed the Dixon-Yates private power contract of the Eisenhower years, stood up for TVA and the public power cause in general, fought to reduce the oil-depletion allowance, refused (with Kefauver) to sign the 1956 "Southern Manifesto" on school desegregation, and, in a state known for its "Volunteer" military tradition, pressed for arms control and disarmament and opposed the Vietnam war at every turn. When Gore finally lost, to Bill Brock in 1970, some said it was busing and school prayer and gun control and votes against the Nixon administration's Southern strategy Supreme Court Justices that sank him. But the loss also stemmed from Gore's arrogance, from his lack of warmth and consideration for others.

"He rubbed people the wrong way, even when they knew he was right,"
one of Gore's closest Tennessee associates told me. "He was one of the
great public leaders of the South. But he lacked Kefauver's ability to show
the homefolks he still cared, to make up for the gap between his own
advanced beliefs and the state itself. In his first Senate campaign, he went
around with his fiddle and sang songs, and the people loved it. After that,
he viewed himself as some kind of Roman Senator, and we could never get
him to play his fiddle again."

In retirement, Gore became chairman of the board of the Island Creek
Coal Company and a vice president of Occidental Petroleum, Island Creek's
corporate parent. It was, he said, an opportunity to do something about the
energy crisis. It remained to be seen if Gore could and would do something
about Island Creek's mine safety record, the very worst of the 10 largest coal
producers, or the devastation of people's land and homes from the company's crude strip-mining operations.

Once groomed by Sam Rayburn as a potential Speaker (during his earlier years in the House), and in 1956 a serious possibility for the Vice Presidency, Gore seemed quite a tragic figure when he lost his Senate seat while at
the prime of his intellectual power. But the greater tragedy was the death, in
1963, of Estes Kefauver, at the age of 60, when he was just beginning the
golden years when seniority and personal seasoning make it possible for a
Senator to make his greatest contribution in substantive legislation.

From his first years in Congress, Kefauver had shown a startling pre-
science about issues with which the country would have to come to grips in
the latter 20th century. Thirty years before the nation suddenly realized the
dangers of excessive Presidential power, he proposed in 1943 that U.S. Representatives have a right to question Cabinet members, who would have
floor privileges. In 1947 he coauthored a book calling for abolition of the congressional seniority system. Long before most Americans, he saw that the
chief threat to the nation was loss of personal liberties, not internal subversion; thus he took a lonely stand against outlawing the Communist
party and was one of the first to condemn the red-hunting tactics of Wisconsin's Senator Joseph R. McCarthy. In 1959 he suggested a national
"Consumer's Office" to act as a "daily burr in the hides of government
officialdom and get important consumer issues raised" and settled in a way
that would give proper weight to consumer interests. In his later years,
after the disappointment of his unsuccessful tries for the Presidency, Kefauver plugged away in his committee work at problems of excessive concentration of economic power in the United States. In the words of his
biographer, Joseph Bruce Gorman, Kefauver was convinced that "it is only
a step from the loss of economic freedom to the loss of political freedom."
His probes of price-fixing in steel, autos, bread, electric equipment, and
drugs gave Americans their keenest sense of the dangers of monopoly since
the era of Theodore Roosevelt and laid the groundwork for Ralph Nader
and the consumer movement of the latter '60s and the '70s.

A tall and soft-spoken man born in the foothills of the Great Smokies,
Kefauver had served 10 years in Congress from Chattanooga (fighting,

among other things, to save TVA from McKellar's machinations) before his startling 1948 victory over the Crump machine. He may have impressed people as a country bumpkin, but he had a keenly analytical mind and the benefit of a legal education at Yale. He became a national figure through his 1950–51 televised hearings on organized crime in America and its ties to elected officials. A shocked public witnessed the parade of characters like Frank Costello, Joe Adonis, and "Greasy Thumb" Guzik before the cameras, and then watched the heavy political fallout—Tammany's Mayor William O'Dwyer sent in flight to Mexico, Senate Majority Leader Scott Lucas forced into early retirement in Illinois, and public officials (most of them fellow Democrats) stunned by Kefauver's revelations of the crime-politics combines in New Jersey, Chicago, and many other metropolitan centers of the country. The Democratic "regulars" never forgave Kefauver for the embarrassment he caused them, or for such maverick deeds as challenging and defeating President Truman in the 1952 New Hampshire primary. Thus, while he went on to win 14 of the 17 primaries that year, Kefauver was denied the Democratic nomination and was still considered too unreliable to be accorded the honor in 1956.

According to some of his Senate critics, Kefauver was bent on building up a personal following, even at the expense of his party, and contrived an exaggerated image of himself as a noble martyr fighting for the people's interests against the bad political bosses. Biographer Gorman, in a different vein, suggested that Kefauver went as far as he did in national politics because he had "a very special quality, an attraction which won him the support of the mythical common man, who saw in Kefauver an honest, sincere, and unique champion of ideals and values that seemed to be ignored or taken lightly by too many others in public life." Before the terms "alienation" and "going over the heads of the politicians to the people" had become vogue, Kefauver had found a way to deal with the first by doing the latter.

On the surface, there are many parallels between Kefauver and the Tennessee Senator getting the national attention in the 1970s, Howard Baker, Jr. Both went far to change the face of politics in Tennessee in their first Senate races—Kefauver by crushing the Crump machine and showing that a racial moderate could win in Tennessee, and Baker by breaking out of the Republicans' East Tennessee stronghold to win a statewide race on the GOP ticket. Both exhibited first-class intellects and were considered impeccably honest. Both were called brash—Kefauver for running for President as a freshman Senator, without the blessing of the party's elders, Baker for trying twice as a freshman to upset Pennsylvania's Hugh Scott as Senate Minority Leader. Both became known nationally by virtue of televised Senate hearings—Kefauver in the crime hearings, Baker on the Watergate panel. Both had a quality of looking more centrist in their politics than their actual Senate votes indicated—Kefauver by being very liberal and not talking about it, and Baker by casting some very conservative votes and not talking about it.

The parallel, however, should not be taken too far. Because while Kefauver was the apostle of new ideas, indeed a generator of them, and very much the loner, Baker's strength is as a mediator and a team player, a man who can conceptualize problems and find the more workable solutions for them. He is regarded in Washington as a skilled operator in congressional hearings, able to go into a session with a hasty briefing, listen for a half hour or so, and then demonstrate a command of the situation. He is not, in the Kefauver mold, a pioneer in public policy. But my newspaper friend Bruce Biossat, after an intensive survey of people who had dealt with Baker in Washington and back in Tennessee, found a "dazzling pattern" in opinions of the Senator: "brilliance of mind, flashing comprehension, integrity, balance and fairness, a capacity to articulate, and ability to get action leading to solutions."

At the time of the Watergate hearings, however, Tennessee Democratic chairman James Sasser said that Baker, in questioning witnesses, "bore down harder on the spear carriers than he did on the big boys" like John Mitchell, H. R. (Bob) Haldeman, and John Ehrlichman. Some reporters also charged Baker had lied to them in denying contact with the White House shortly after his appointment as vice-chairman of the Watergate Committee. Baker later admitted he had met with President Nixon at that time to discuss the very relevant question of executive privilege. Despite his appearance of impartiality during the Watergate hearings, Baker was privately accused of taking "Nixon's side in executive session every time."

During the early years of the Nixon administration Baker made statements that could return to haunt him in a national campaign. One could argue about Baker's motives—personal loyalty to President Nixon, his friend of 20 years' standing, or desire to gain administration support for his leadership bids, or simply personal conviction. But the fact was that he praised the President at the time of the Cambodian invasion for "a track record for candor and honesty in his representations with respect to Southeast Asia." Later it turned out that both the public and Congress had been deliberately misled on the degree of U.S. commitment. In 1970 Baker also lauded the administration for the "exquisite precision" of its effort to control inflation by "traditional means of fiscal restraint"—shortly before Nixon junked his malfunctioning economic policy, went to a temporary program of mandatory controls, and headed down the road toward the worst runaway inflation of the 20th century.

Baker's Senate voting record was on the whole quite conservative. While supporting the Vietnam war and new weapons systems, he voted for the nominations of Haynsworth and Carswell to the Supreme Court,* opposed

---

* The Nixon administration in 1971 offered Baker himself an appointment to the Supreme Court, but he turned it down. Ironically, the offer was made by then Attorney General John Mitchell, later to be a principal witness before the Watergate Committee. In 1962, during the Kennedy administration, there had been talk of appointing Kefauver to a vacancy on the court. But Kefauver's homespun style was seen as a bit anachronistic in the heady days of the New Frontier. Not only was he distinctly not a member of the high-swinging Washington social set of the Kennedy years, but that administration was not much interested in a lonely Populist fighting the monopolies. The appointment went to a man of substantially less social vision, Byron "Whizzer" White.

establishment of the consumer protection agency (Kefauver's idea of many years previous), voted against no-fault insurance, opposed compulsory school busing, and was against reduction of the oil depletion allowance. He voted against poverty programs and independent legal services for the poor, opposed federal funding for public affairs programs on public television, and stood virtually alone in the Senate supporting the chemical industry position on federal legislation to control toxic substances. A cynic could have likened the latter stand to the fight which Baker's father-in-law, the late Senator Everett McKinley Dirksen of Illinois, waged against Kefauver's landmark legislation to control abuses in the drug industry.

There was, however, a quite different side to Baker's Senate record. He was a supporter of the 18-year-old vote and the equal rights amendment for women, and in 1968 he helped formulate a compromise that won Republican support for open-housing legislation. In 1973 Senate Republicans pulled some of the props out from under the seniority system by adopting a Baker proposal that Republican members of each Senate committee elect their ranking member subject to approval of the full Senate Republican Conference. A member of the Senate Public Works Committee and Joint Committee on Atomic Energy, Baker played a major role in writing the environmental control bills of the late '60s and early '70s, often in close cooperation with Maine's Edmund S. Muskie. Among these were tough air and water control bills and a Baker-proposed provision to make the Atomic Energy Commission conform to the safety standards of the National Environmental Protection Act. Though a friend of TVA, Baker has been concerned about the effects of public works on Tennessee's ecology and has been praised for "taking the strongest regulatory stand of any of the Tennessee Valley Senators." He has also offered legislation to control strip mining of coal (though he owns vast tracts of Tennessee coal and lumber lands himself). He considered passage of the 1972 revenue-sharing bill his greatest legislative achievement.

Notes on other Tennesseans: Senator William Brock has taken a keen interest in youth in politics, and claimed credit for the Nixon administration's support of the vote for 18-year-olds. Aside from this, his record fits precisely the image of a conservative young businessman in politics, more interested in political techniques than the substance of public policy. *Time* described him well as "a super-regular guy, the median of Middle Americans, giant of the jaycees." The son of a bank director, Brock was attacked in 1972 by columnist Jack Anderson for going into a Senate Banking and Currency Subcommittee meeting on fair credit billing legislation armed with a list of anti-consumer amendments prepared for him by a lobbyist for the American Banking Association. Generally, he has left little mark outside his fight against school busing.

Another "New Guard" Republican of strongly conservative stripe is Dan H. Kuykendall of Memphis, a former Procter & Gamble salesman who ran a strong but losing race for the Senate in 1964. He went to the House in 1967 and has won easily since, including a 1972 victory over state senator

James O. Patterson, Jr., the first black man in Tennessee history to win a major-party nomination for Congress. Patterson lost by 19,000 votes (44 percent), but blacks are confident they will be able to elect a Congressman from Memphis by the end of the 1970s.

The leading liberal on the House delegation is Richard H. Fulton of Nashville, a battler for civil rights legislation and early proponent of reassessing U.S. energy resources and the power crisis.

The reapportionment after the 1970 Census reduced Tennessee to nine U.S. Representatives (from a onetime high of 12), and the reshuffling of district lines was one factor in the defeat of the state's most interesting Congressman of the last decade, William R. Anderson. An Annapolis graduate and captain of the *Nautilus* on its historic 1958 voyage under the Arctic ice cap, Anderson until 1970 was known as a moderate Democrat and levelheaded fellow whose biggest achievement was an amendment to expand aid for police training. He had voted for every military appropriation and war measure to come before the House, but in 1970 he experienced a sudden change in heart after he witnessed the tiger cages in South Vietnam's Con Son prison. Returning home, he began to meet people in the peace movement, among them the radical Roman Catholic priests, Philip and Daniel Berrigan. When J. Edgar Hoover charged the Berrigans with a plot to blow up government heating systems and kidnap Presidential assistant Henry Kissinger, Anderson accused the aging FBI director of "tactics reminiscent of McCarthyism" and "scare dramatics rather than due process of law." Anderson said he was convinced that the Berrigans were committed to a philosophy of nonviolence, so that the mad schemes which Hoover (and later government prosecutors) charged them with "would be in complete violation of their code, and the teachings of Christ, whom they feel they are following."

So it was that a man who might have become Chief of Naval Operations if he had stayed in the Navy became a hero of the antiwar forces in the United States. It was an anomalous position for a Congressman from conservative West Tennessee, perhaps untenable under any circumstances. But Anderson's 1972 defeat, by a margin of 17,000 votes, was caused in major part by the addition to his district of 51,000 conservative voters from a Shelby County suburb named, appropriately enough, "Whitehaven."

Notes on the Economy

Tennessee has every reason to be an economically prosperous state. It has immense reserves of coal, millions of acres of productive forests, and an impressive river system offering ample water for industry as well as cheap barge transportation. The vast TVA system of dams and steam plants, the largest integrated power system in the United States, supplies electricity at rates substantially below the national average. Three-quarters of the major markets of the United States are within 500 miles of Tennessee's borders.

Tennessee is also a regional rarity in that it has a very well balanced economy—diversified agriculture, the greatest mix of industries in the Southeast, and contrasting specialties in its big cities. Chattanooga, for instance, is very dependent on steel, iron, and other heavy industry, while Nashville thrives on banking, insurance, and country music. The recreation, tourist, and convention businesses have been providing an increasing stimulus— close to three quarters of a billion dollars annually—to the state's economy. The factories added since World War II have been in every field from chemicals, nylons, tires, leather, and glass to electronic equipment, machinery, aluminum, and furniture. Blue chip firms like DuPont, Ford, Magnavox, Combustion Engineering, and Alcoa have been a factor in a rise of manufacturing employment to almost twice its level in 1950. The value added by manufacturing has multiplied five times over in two decades, and Tennessee factories now turn out more goods than Georgia, the "Empire State of the South." Tennessee would even be ahead of North Carolina, the regional leader in manufactures, if it were not for the Tar Heel state's huge concentration of textiles.

The result of all this has been a relatively strong rise in population, topped off by an increase of 5.2 percent—more than any other Border State— between 1970 and 1973. (The Census estimated the state's total 1973 population at 4,126,000.)

There are some flies in the ointment, however. Tennessee's per capita income has risen at one of the briskest rates in the nation in the last decade, but it still lags 20 percent (and close to $1,000 a year) behind the U.S. average. There are only seven other states where income levels are lower. Although labor union membership in Tennessee is somewhat higher than in the state's Southeastern neighbors, average wages rank in the lowest fifth of the states. The average factory wage is dragged down by the garment plants, the biggest single employer, and textiles, another notoriously low-paying industry. Tennessee has a network of vocational and technical schools and community colleges that teach specialized skills, but there is still a shortage of skilled labor in both urban and rural areas. Nine planning and development districts, covering the entire state, have been established in recent years, but a coherent statewide land-use and economic plan has yet to be developed. The Dunn administration was moving in that direction in the early 1970s, however—as Dunn told me, "so that we can plan for long-term growth, and the proper and rational exploitation of our resources in a way that will give the people of our state what they have not had—an opportunity to earn at a high income level per capita."

Part of the Dunn administration's effort was to get localities to deemphasize textiles, furniture, and apparel, and try to attract more service industries, such as distributorships, and major financial industries. The land-use plan was needed to prevent environmental desecration and to prevent large outside corporations from buying up so much land that they could control the economy and development of large areas of the state. The problem is especially acute in coal-rich East Tennessee, where for example, American

Association, Ltd., a British-controlled land-holding company engaged in strip mining of coal, already owns 64,000 acres in Claiborne County near the Cumberland Gap. The problem also gets back to taxes, and the possibilities that corporations and their executives could exploit Tennessee's human and natural resources without paying much back to the counties or the state. Research sponsored by a student health group in Nashville showed that companies and corporations controlled 34 percent of the land in the five major coal-producing counties of East Tennessee but paid only 3.6 percent of the property taxes. A group called Save Our Cumberland Mountains had been instrumental in getting somewhat more adequate assessments placed on the coal companies and in getting Tennessee's first severance tax on coal approved by the legislature in 1972. But a substantially higher severance tax, uniformly higher property tax assessments on large land holdings, and a state income tax would all be required if the state's common people were to have hope of fair treatment by their own government.

The twin factors of race and rurality help explain why poverty remains a gnawing problem for hundreds of thousands of Tennesseans. About 10 percent of the white families live below the federally defined poverty line, and among blacks the figure is 38 percent. Nearly a quarter of all rural families subsist on incomes below the poverty level, the result in part of a 60 percent drop in farm employment since 1950. Despite the flight to the cities in recent decades, 1.6 million Tennesseans still live on the land or in small towns.

Tennessee may remain encumbered in reaching national income levels as long as the job mix remains as heavily weighted to blue-collar employment as it is today. The state has only a few home-based national corporations or regional headquarters offering major white-collar job opportunities, and the higher pay that goes with them. Despite TVA's staff of 15,000 in the state and the research in atomic energy at Oak Ridge (a town which boasts it has more Ph.D.'s per capita than any other place in the world), Tennessee as a whole ranks only 39th among the states in the proportion of scientists in its population.

While Tennessee factories now dominate the economy with an output of close to $5 billion annually, agriculture is still an important component with products valued at more than $700 million a year. The production of cattle, hogs, and other livestock outstripped crops during the 1960s. Tobacco and soybeans are now the leading crops; cotton, the old king, has dropped to a weak third place because of the competition of synthetic fibers and more economical production in the Far West. Less than 120,000 farms remain now, and only a third of them produce any significant amount of crops or livestock. Much of the interest in affairs pastoral now centers around such phenomena as the thriving Tennessee Walking Horse industry, or the shrubs, evergreens, and fruit trees grown in some of the country's largest nursery centers. But the rural ways die slowly, and thousands of people farm on a part-time basis, commuting each day to factory jobs in nearby towns. The continuing tie to the land is underscored by the fact that food and fiber from Tennessee farms and forests account for a major segment of the manu-facturing employment.

The Population Mix and Black Themes

In its native white population, Tennessee remains one of the most homogeneous of states; in the beginning there was the mixture of Scotch and Irish, English, Germans, and a dash of Dutch and French stock, but the tides of time and intermarriage have erased most of the memory of special origins. A modern-day survey showed only a small percentage of Tennes-seans who could identify their families' origins—some 10 percent Irish and 4 percent German. In 1970 only a half of a percent of the state's people were foreign born, a tenth the national average.

Tennessee's black people remain the distinctive exception to the state's unvaried complexion. In 1970 the Census counted 621,261 of them, repre-senting 16 percent of the total state population. The number of blacks has climbed steadily over the years, but an even greater expansion of the white population has steadily reduced the black share of the total from the peak of 26 percent reported in 1880. The population traces of the plantation system are still apparent in the heavy concentrations of black people in rural counties of West Tennessee and, to a lesser extent, Middle Tennessee. But now two out of every three black Tennesseans live in heavily urbanized areas, and in Memphis blacks account for about 40 percent of the total population.

Legal segregation—in schools, trains, and buses, restaurants and hotels, and in marriage relations—afflicted Tennessee Negroes throughout the Civil War century. Only a few localities had ended Jim Crow voluntarily when the federal government, in the postwar era, stepped in to end the practice once and for all. Not until 1952, and then only as a result of litigation, were Negroes finally admitted to the University of Tennessee at Knoxville or voluntarily to Vanderbilt and the other private universities.

Ironically, the little city of Clinton in overwhelmingly white East Ten-nessee provided the arena for the first big test of school desegregation after the Supreme Court's 1954 *Brown* decision. The local newspaper and civic leaders of Clinton had worked hard to create a spirit of compliance when a federal district court ordered the local high school integrated in 1956. But racial agitators arrived to harangue crowds and incite violence to keep some dozen Negro children out of the previously all-white school. Before it was over Governor Clement had twice called in the National Guard and the disturbances climaxed in a bombing of the school. Clement declared his in-tention to keep Tennessee public schools open, but the segregationist clamor was so high that he went along with the legislature in approving a spate of anti-integration bills—soon declared unconstitutional by the federal courts. Clement's prospective successor, Buford Ellington, did not help mat-ters much by declaring during his 1958 campaign: "Yes, I'm a segregationist;

I am an old-fashioned segregationist. I would not hesitate as governor to close a school down in order to prevent violence and bloodshed. . . . I favor and will propose legislation to avoid the mixing of the races in the public schools of our state." Once elected, however, Ellington had enough common sense to tell his legislative leaders to block drastic proposals on the subject.

School integration then proceeded at a snail's pace until the end of the '60s and start of the '70s, when the federal courts forced substantial compliance across the state and aroused a terrible furor in the big cities by ordering large-scale busing to achieve integration. It was then that the Nashville *Tennessean's* Joe Hatcher, a veteran of many earlier political wars (Boss Crump once honored him with the epithet of "slimy rat") could report: "Busing at the moment is undoubtedly the biggest political, emotional, social, economic, and certainly legal issue in Tennessee. The federal courts are tied up, entangled and struggling on the issue in Knoxville, Chattanooga, Nashville and Memphis. . . . And the issue is so great it is beginning to affect the population picture—even to the point of possibly reversing the trend of movement to the city. . . ." Forgotten in the ruckus, of course, was that back in the 1950s, the black parents of Clinton had brought suit in the federal courts precisely because of busing. They found something wrong in a system that required the busing of black children 50 miles a day—right past the door of the all-white Clinton High School—so that they could attend a *segregated* school in Knoxville.

Tennessee differed from its Deep South neighbors in refraining, for the most part, from actual intimidation of Negroes to prevent them from voting. But for more than half a century, the poll tax served as a severe depressant on black participation in the political process. The intimidation that did occur was mostly in the old plantation counties of West Tennessee. In 1959, for instance, the U.S. Civil Rights Commission reported that "Negroes have not been permitted to register and vote in Haywood County for approximately 50 years. . . . Negroes in the county own more land and pay more taxes than white persons but their rights are strictly limited: They must observe a strict curfew. They are not permitted to dance or to drink beer. They are not allowed near the courthouse unless on business." It was significant that Haywood was one of the two Tennessee counties where blacks made up a majority of the population.

The other was adjacent Fayette, near Memphis on the Mississippi border. There a few blacks were registered, but usually when a black person dared to enroll, the sheriff was informed and he told the Negro's landlord and employer—so that the hapless citizen lost his job *and* his home. A registration campaign in Fayette in 1959 led to a new wave of coercive acts by white landowners, merchants, and bankers. Eviction notices were served on 700 Negro tenant farmers, and some of them set up a tent city on a farm—one of the most daring gestures of defiance in the early stages of the civil rights movement. Later federal antipoverty funds began to crack the relentless poverty of Fayette, then listed as the fourth poorest county in America. The tent city even turned into a neighborhood of cottages built with federal assistance. But even a decade later, a brutal assault by white men on three black women in Fayette resulted in a prolonged black boycott against local white merchants.

The Fayette County disturbances were an overt form of the conflict between black and white that has run as a sinister undercurrent of life in Tennessee ever since the Civil War—the state where black people's greatest leader of modern times, Martin Luther King, Jr., would be slain in 1968. In the electoral arena, however, the traditional form was to use the black man as a pawn in the white man's politics, not to exclude him from the ballot box altogether. The manipulative form reached its zenith in Crump's Memphis. Crump had a classic Mississippi-Confederate attitude toward Negroes, viewing them as childish creatures fit mainly for hard physical labor. But he knew that in official counts, a black vote counted as much as a white vote, and he organized a huge campaign to register blacks and pay their poll-tax receipts. "On occasion," Alfred Steinberg reported, "truckloads of blacks were brought from Mississippi and Arkansas to Memphis, given poll-tax receipts and registration names, and carted through the polling places to cast their votes." The standard procedure after blacks left the polling places was for Crump's agents to treat them to a silver dollar, a barbecue sandwich, a Coke or bottle of red eye whiskey, and a watermelon to take home. There also seemed to be a more substantive payoff in schools and parks built for blacks and hundreds of units of federally financed public housing. In Crump's Memphis, scarcely any Negroes were allowed to rise above the most menial jobs. But by using blacks in his "captive" coalition, Crump firmly established blacks' right to vote in the state's largest city. Thus it was that the Memphis black community, in the post-Crump era, could provide political leadership for Negro voters across Tennessee—and in fact make Tennessee a leading state in the South in opening the franchise to black people.

Relatively few Tennessee blacks registered or voted outside of Memphis until World War II, although there were unique spots like Nashville, where two blacks sat on the city council for many years. From a base of 16 percent of the black voting-age population, Negro registration rose gradually to 29 percent in 1956 and then shot up to 69 percent—a level comparable with whites—by 1964. That dramatic rise came *before* the Voting Rights Act of 1965, which was needed to clear the way to the ballot box for blacks in most Southern states.

Important political consequences flowed from the newly emerged black vote. In 1965 A. W. Willis of Memphis became the first black to sit in the Tennessee legislature since 1887, and by 1973 there were two black senators and seven representatives. All were Democrats, because the few blacks who had not changed their allegiance from the party of Abraham Lincoln to the party of Franklin Roosevelt during the New Deal had been forced out of the Republican party when the Goldwater-Southern strategy triumphed in 1964. The rise of the Republicans in the legislative halls permitted the blacks, in a close two-party situation, to do some intelligent horse-trading. It was the switched vote of a Negro Democrat from Knoxville that enabled the

Republicans to organize the lower house in 1969, when the parties were evenly balanced at 49 seats each. The maverick black got a good committee assignment in return. In the 1971 legislative session, when the Democrats had a narrow majority, the "Black Caucus" in the house withheld support for partisan measures until the last minute and thus won agreement to passage of several bills of major importance to Negroes. A local newspaper called the move "the first effective black show of lawmaking power in modern times" in the South.

By the early 1970s blacks represented 16 percent of the Tennessee voter pool and their vote was potentially crucial in any close Democratic primary or general election. Groups like the Tennessee Voters Council and Tennessee Federation of Democratic Leagues have been effective in "passing the word" to their black followers, but even in the absence of clear advice, the black voters have shown sophistication and remarkable cohesion. The paranoia of fear stemming from the riots after the King assassination, and more recently the busing controversy have polarized Tennessee politics and undermined the coalition of blacks and white blue collar workers that resulted in the election of many moderate-to-liberal Tennessee Democrats up to the mid-1960s. But when and as racial tensions abate in future years, the leaders of the Republican as well as the Democratic party are likely to recognize the importance of the minority vote, giving Tennessee blacks more leverage in Tennessee politics than at any time in the state's history.

Country Music and the People

Back in the 1920s, from the heart of the Southern mountains, out of the soul of the common people and their travail and loves and everyday life, came country music. Really, its roots went far deeper—to the times of the traveling troubadors of old England, to the ballads brought centuries ago by the first settlers to the hills, to such musical forms as the hoedown, jigs, and reels, to myth and story told by hearthsides and then set to the music of a crude string instrument for a family's pleasure. Gospel airs played a big role in early country music—"hillbilly music," as people called it then; in fact, Nashville's funky and famous old Ryman Auditorium, so long the home of the Grand Ole Opry, was built in the 1890s as the union Gospel Tabernacle, and many of the thousands who have gone to Nashville to hear The Opry have participated in all-night singings of Gospel hymns too. (For many folks out of the rural, ultrafundamentalist country background, country music has been about the most secular pastime they admit to openly.) To the country music airs drifting out of the hills of the Carolinas, Tennessee, Kentucky, and Georgia were added French Cajun moods from Louisiana. And out of Memphis and New Orleans and the plantation countryside came the spiritual and blues and rhythm influence of the American Negro.

Country was a little loath to admit to the black inspiration that fed into it, but music has a way of crossing all sorts of barriers without people being quite aware of what is happening. It is true that country, until quite recently, was practically the exclusive property of Southern whites, and the white working classes at that: rooted in rural conservatism ("You got to have smelled mule manure before you can sing hillbilly," Hank Williams, a revered early country star, said), blatantly patriotic, distrustful of wealthy city folks and intellectuals, fundamentalist but loving sweet Jesus, and tolerant (as one observer has put it) of "homegrown vices like boozing and philandering when accompanied by a footnote that they don't come free."

But as in so many things Southern, the link between white and black was greater than met the eye (or in this case, the ear). The Southern musical traditions of the two races, Pat Watters wrote, "have been akin in their shared concreteness, stubborn authenticity of language, vividness of imagery, and most of all, faithfulness to the reality of the human condition, . . . both heavy on the basics of life, of love and all its joys and tribulations, of marriage and child-bearing, of sickness, of death."

The most important date in the history of country music was November 28, 1925, when radio station WSM broadcast the first evening of Grand Ole Opry. As the years wore on, more and more Southerners would huddle around the old family radio each Saturday evening to hear the songs they understood, laugh with the performers who seemed like members of the family, and let a touch of romance enter their plain lives. Hard days were coming: the Depression years, when country was the medium that sang of the hobos and country stores and rattling freight trains and prisons and yet the dreams of everyone. One's miseries and hopes were shared, one's isolation in tens of thousands of rural hamlets across the Southland made more bearable. The boundaries of the South were the boundaries of country music in those days. But a bond of allegiance to one radio program was formed that would carry Grand Ole Opry on the airways northward as people migrated during the war, and after, and would make Grand Ole Opry, as it is today, the oldest continuous show in the history of radio and probably right in its claim to have "the largest single listening audience in the world."

WSM, Nashville's 50,000-watt clear-channel station, carries five hours of the Opry on Saturday nights and four on Friday, and the program is broadcast on a delayed basis by hundreds of stations across the United States.* And it is not just the Opry itself that gets that exposure. Country music is now the fulltime fare on more than 1,000 radio stations in the country, 16 times as many as in the early 1960s. The stations are literally everywhere—even New York City—but the biggest concentrations are in Kentucky, Tennessee, West Virginia, and Texas, in northern Alabama and Georgia, in the western sections of the Carolinas, and southwestern Virginia. (Again, one notes how

* A sponsor, since broadcast number one in '25, has been the National Life & Accident Insurance Company, a firm with almost $10 billion of insurance in force which early acquired WSM ("We Shield Millions") and the Grand Ole Opry itself. By the early 1970s, all were owned by NLT Inc., a holding company.

closely the Bible Belt equals the Country Music Belt, although the biggest country music station in the U.S., with 1.2 million listeners, is New York City's 50,000-watt WHN.)

Country music, in its early days, was pretty unpolished stuff. Paul Hemphill (author of *The Nashville Sound*) described it as a "scratchy, undisciplined, backwoodsy cacophony of grating fiddles and twanging guitars and singers with head colds." It smoothed out as the years rolled by, becoming, for one thing, much less nasal and twangy. Yodeling became less popular, fewer religious songs were heard, drums were finally admitted to the Grand Ole Opry, and more and more amplification was heard, an egregious departure from old bluegrass style. Country music was being "urbanized," some observers lamented; Hemphill suggested that the medium was losing its bared-and-stripped heart, its "unabashed *soul*," and that just like the South itself, it was being flattened out, losing its singular identity "in its feverish grab at the brass ring." Some voices were also heard to say that the poor country boys and girls who came out of the hills and made fantastic fortunes in country music were engaged in a massive rip-off as they bought up Cadillacs (Webb Pierce plated his with silver dollars) and moved into grandiose mansions with guitar-shaped swimming pools—while offering an increasingly mediocre product to their fans, the everyday struggling folk of middle America.

But still, the deep-gut appeal came through in many country stars. Johnny Cash still reflected legitimately the hard times he knew growing up in an Arkansas cotton patch and took many older Americans back to memories of a hard youth with songs of hobos on the road and the clattering railway tracks—while relating to younger people with an authentic interest in prison reform. Roy Acuff, veteran and "king" of the Opry (where he first appeared in 1938), singer of "The Great Speckled Bird" and "The Wabash Cannonball," was still going strong in the early 1970s; he was still great fun to see, balancing a baton and fiddle on his nose and swinging a yoyo, but he knew what he was talking about when he explained the success of many of the oldtimers: "Each of us had a type of cry in our voice." That cry still came through loud and clear in Loretta Lynn, married at 13 and a grandmother at 28, telling the absolute truth when she sang about her Kentucky roots: *Well, I was born a coal miner's daughter/In a cabin on a hill in Butcher Holler.* . . . Loretta never made it beyond the eighth grade, but up in that bleak hollow she acquired a warmth and strength that radiates through every word she sings; straight through her country girl manner and ole-girl accent comes an emotional impact scarcely anyone can ignore, because it is both power and honesty.

In the late '60s Merle Haggard's "Okie from Muskogee," with its attack on hippies and pot smokers and flag-burners, seemed to symbolize the vengeance of lower-class whites who sent their young men uncomplainingly off to war in Southeast Asia. Yet Haggard's most moving songs were about prison and the lonesome road, and as *Newsweek* noted, the full range of his work was that of "a brilliant, soulful writer and singer." Among the thousands at any performance of the Grand Ole Opry, you can usually count the black people on the fingers of one hand. But consider Charley Pride, who used the money he had earned picking cotton at the age of 14 in Sledge, Mississippi, to buy his first guitar and in 1967 was invited to give his first Opry performance. Pride had to make a tough decision in life: "I was part African, part Caucasian, and part Indian. I didn't make this society, I was born into it. So I could just be Charley Pride, genetic man, American. I had enough courage not to deny myself as an individual." Pat Watters reported that when Pride first won fame at the Opry, white fans would grudgingly tell record store clerks: "Gimme that album by that nigger country singer." By the early '70s Pride was superstar enough to be chosen to present Loretta Lynn with her Entertainer-of-the-Year award on television. Loretta was reportedly advised to take her prize "but don't touch him, just back off." But Loretta, who is part Cherokee Indian, hugged Charley instead. Watters wrote: "It is unlikely that all the combined forces of civil rights organizations, church, government, or even integrated athletics had worked as much good for race relations on the whites of the South most in need of it as had Country Charlie."

Things have even changed so much in Opry country that in 1970 the Country Music Association gave its Song of the Year award to "Sunday Mornin' Comin' Down"—the creation of a long-haired, pot-smoking hippie type named Kris Kristofferson who also happened to be a former Rhodes Scholar and novelist. In recent years young country boys and girls hoping to strike the big time have been pouring into Nashville as they used to assault Hollywood in the '20s and '30s. They come with guitars on their backs and songs in their pockets, the odds always heavily against them, and even if they begin to make it, the chance of ripping themselves apart in a scene of pills and booze and the crazy lust for Cadillac and ranch-house success. But some have leveler heads and form a kind of Nashville underground that fights the prevailing mores of the Opry world, and Kristofferson, like Johnny Cash, having survived some severe personal crises himself, was seen as the underground guru of the early '70s.

It was the late 1950s before cutting records got off the ground as a serious business in Nashville, but since then an industry grossing well over $100 million a year has flowered in recording, record manufacturing, music publishing and licensing, and film making for theater and television. In 1973 Nashville agencies handled 14,832 songwriters and booked appearances worth $100 million for country and Western artists. There were 5,396 music publishers centered in the city, and 15,877 recording sessions were reported. "Record Row," a small section west of downtown where old homes were converted into publishing houses, talent agencies, and small record companies, had flourished spectacularly. Its profit-making instincts were a major reason that the music out of Nashville began to diversify into folk, pop, rock-n-roll, soft rock, acid rock, rhythm-and-blues, and each new music form as it appeared. A central figure in Music City's growth was Chet Atkins, a brilliant guitarist whom RCA Victor discovered in the late 1940s and subsequently put in charge of its Nashville office. As RCA's top artist and repertory executive in the city, Atkins matched dozens of artists and song material and became possibly the most respected artist in Nashville. (His own albums of country have sold in the millions, but he is versatile enough to have also played with symphony orchestras.) Himself a country boy from the Tennessee soil, Atkins had the right instincts to pull the best out of the budding young musicians from the hills, who were high on soul but low on reading musical notes. The free, natural, open feeling of "Nashville sound" was the result. His own comment on Nashville's new musical diversity: "Since I've been around, music has kinda merged. But country music is still the one with the message."

An example of the many who have made fortunes in the new scene is Jack Stapp, a former associate of Bert Parks and onetime manager of the Opry, who started Tree Publishing back in the 1950s and by '70 had more than 100 writers working for him and a multimillion-dollar operation that even extended overseas. "Here you start out with country music," Stapp said—"that's your backbone. But we know lots of it will go pop-pop-pop." Stapp brought out rhythm-and-blues and psychedelic music in Memphis, for instance, and when I talked with him had just started promoting Joe Tex, a black Louisianan, a writer who combined country and blues music.

Nashville's Music Row is a positively relaxed, calm place compared to New York or Hollywood, and the music that comes from it is renowned for its improvisation and informality. Stapp defined the "Nashville sound" this way:

To me it goes back to what happens in the Nashville studios compared to what happens with musicians in a New York or Chicago or California studio. In New York, for instance, the musicians might go in because they have an assignment to record from 12 noon to 3 P.M. When it gets to be 12, they sit down, they pick up their fiddles, and the sheet music with the fly specks on it, and the conductor gets up there, and off they go. It's cold. Here everybody works as a team and the musicians from the beginning have fought for one thing, to make Nashville the number one recording center of the world. Even though they're unionized, and under the same rules as musicians elsewhere, they try to contribute to the recording session. And it's done in a relaxed atmosphere. The bass player might say, "Hey, why on this next chorus, instead of my playing it this way, why don't I slap it, and why don't you do such and such on the piano?" You know, they would never think of doing that in the big cities. Everybody's making suggestions and working, and they may carry on to all hours of the night until they have a recording just right. Even the engineer, he gets into it and discusses things with the various musicians, and with the conductor, and they're all trying to do one thing—to do the best, and to come out with a sound that people are going to say, "Hey, that's Nashville!" That's my definition of the Nashville sound.

Stapp's definition sounded like chamber-of-commerce stuff, but the record sales seem to show the music fans agree.

A visitor in search of the soul of the Border South could do no better than spend a Saturday night at the Grand Ole Opry. There are the excited crowds, who will have heard Opry on the radio for years and will now have traveled an average of 450 miles *one way* to see the performers in person.

Someone figured out the average fan might be a 29-year-old blue-collar worker who had written for tickets months in advance but still had to wait in line for an hour or more. The fans come armed with hundreds of instamatics, and they are forever thronging the aisles to get good shots in a constant barrage of flashes. At the old Rymer Auditorium, the stage was incredibly cluttered with people—the performer of the moment, others waiting for their numbers to begin, assorted managers, hangers-on, and guests. I spotted a group holding an animated conversation behind the piano while someone else sang, and a drummer chewing gum to the rhythm of the songs. Then there were the big backdrop ads for the radio sponsors—National Life, of course, but also Martha White Hot Rize Flour and others. (Most of the price sponsors, ranging from Coca-Cola to Trail Blazer Dog Food, have advertised on the Opry for more than 20 years.)

Some of the performers were wearing iridescent blues and purples, some tricked up with rhinestone patterns in the shape of red lips, covered wagons, guitars, alligators, or frogs and ferns. Most of the female performers do their thing under layers of heavy makeup, topped off by hair it must have taken hours to tease into shape. Others have outfits as simple as a plain business suit or subdued Western garb. Variety is the key word—from a Miss Skeeter Davis, fixed up in a dazzling silver pants suit and long, blonde hair, to a Bill Monroe, doing pure country stuff with a line of patter that is pure Southern politico. Some of the biggest, national country stars are there for each performance, and many lesser lights too. A fixture for years was the indomitable comedienne Minnie Pearl, who performed in a hat decorated with vegetables and a $1.98 price tag; the audience would hoot with laughter when she threatened to sing a song, and of course she would back off, saying, "I used to sing a lot down home, but it made the dogs howl so bad."

Until early 1974, the Ryman Auditorium with its churchlike wooden pews, thick with the aroma of sweat and Juicy Fruit and tobacco renewed each Saturday night for 33 years, was an inextricable part of the Opry scene. A monstrous gallery overhung the scene—officially named "the Confederate Gallery," because it had been added in 1897 to accommodate the remnants of the Confederate Army when it assembled there. (Captain Tom Ryman, whose name the hall bore, was a riverboat reprobate who had run vessels of pleasure and then got religion and built the hall to the glory of God. At Ryman's funeral, the man who had converted him, a Methodist minister named Sam Jones, had suggested the name be switched officially from Union Gospel Tabernacle to Ryman Auditorium.)

The Opry managers finally tired of the old auditorium's limited seating (3,300 places), the complaints of poor view from many spots in the hall, the fire danger, and the numbers of heat prostration cases in a place the experts said couldn't be air-conditioned. Another drawback, as they saw it, was the honky-tonk atmosphere of the part of downtown Nashville where the hall was located. So they moved to a spanking new Grand Ole Opry House that cost $12 million and was said to be the largest radio-television studio in the world. President Nixon was on hand for the grand opening in March 1974, playing the piano, spinning Roy Acuff's trademark yo-yo, telling some jokes, and trying desperately to build support with the Opry constituency for the impeachment battle which lay before him. George C. Wallace and three other governors, two Senators, 13 Congressmen, and, according to one report, "virtually every known candidate for governor of Tennessee" were on hand as well. But much of the VIP audience was a culture gap away from the less pretentious Opry friends who had been on hand for a teary farewell to the Ryman Auditorium the night before. The new Opry hall is part of a new amusement park six miles from the Nashville Airport, the Disneyland of country music called "Opryland U.S.A." The owner of the park, of course, is NLT, which also owns National Life. The place is billed as "The Home of American Music" and includes rides of all sorts, steam engines and a German carousel, an animal ravine and crafts exhibit, and five big musical areas with continuous sound—"Opry Plaza," "Hill Country Area," "New Orleans Area" (featuring jazz and blues), "America West Area," and "Music of Today Area." The whole park is forested and clean as a whistle and militantly red-white-and-blue Main Street America. It is tastefully done and will make a lot of money. But it implicitly rejects the themes of hard times, of beer joints and prisons and human frailty ensconced in joyful-mournful melody that made country music what it is today.

As for the Ryman Auditorium, National Life wanted to tear it down and use the bricks to build "The Little Church of Opryland" at the new amusement park. Preservationists pounced on the issue, saying Ryman should be saved for its Ruskinian Gothic style and because the thousands of performances there had made it a veritable shrine of the music of Americans, 20th century style.

East Tennessee Folkways and Oak Ridge

East Tennessee is a land of high mountains, heavily forested foothills and narrow valleys, until the 1930s one of the most remote areas of America. The Scotch-Irish, British, and Pennsylvania Germans built their log cabins deep in the ridges when Tennessee was not yet named, and some of those enclaves remained scarcely touched by civilization for well over a century. Here touches of Elizabethan English and ballads carried from the Old World can still be heard, and one finds such strange ethnic manifestations as the Melungeons, a swarthy hill folk of mysterious beginnings whose historic memory of their own origins has been erased by their years of isolation and illiteracy.* East Tennesseans were traditionally some of the most stub-

---

* By varying theories, the Melungeons are either survivors of a Portuguese fleet dispatched in 1665 to capture Cuba from the Spanish, a lost tribe of Israel, descendants of Phoenician sailors who fled the Roman sacking of Carthage, or simply the result of cross-breeding of white pioneers with Indians and black slaves. Several other theories have also been advanced, but the fact is that only 100 or so now survive in their chief place of residence, the Clinch Valley.

bornly individualistic, reserved people in any state, often called hillbillies and the butt of malicious jokes and stories. But mostly they were simply unknown. When Horace Kephart, a St. Louis librarian, decided to go into the Great Smoky Mountains region in the early years of the 20th century, he could not find even "a magazine article, written within this generation, that described the land and its people." In his classic book, *Our Southern Highlanders*, Kephart wrote of a people "beleaguered by nature, . . . ghettoed in the midst of a civilization that is as aloof from them as if it existed . . . on another planet." But the mountaineers—farmers and moonshiners and feuders and hunters alike—befriended Kephart, and he returned the favor by describing them as a "people of keen intelligence when they can see anything to win."

"When I got to this part of the country in the 1930s," former Knoxville *Journal* managing editor Steve Humphreys told me, "I thought it was the most clannish, the coldest, most reserved place I'd ever gotten into. I came from Kansas where you took strangers at face value. But here—they looked at you as if you were a damned foreigner. They distrusted any outsider." But then, Humphreys said, the old clannishness and reserve of the Scotch-Irish and other folk of East Tennessee began to fade. The reasons were complex and intertwined but formed a common pattern of adjustment to the life of the nation as a whole. The Great Smoky Mountains National Park, established in large part through Horace Kephart's inspiration, began a tourist thrust that brought in travelers from afar. The mountaineers, Humphreys noted, "realized the outsider had money, and they could take his money by being nice to him." (Some of the manifestations of the tourist boom are an offense both to nature and the true mountain culture. The worst example is the town of Gatlinburg, at the entrance to the Great Smoky Mountains Park, once a pleasant resort of stately old hotels. Now it has turned into a hurdy-gurdy of overpriced, plastic hostelries and gaudy signs to snag the tourist's dollar. Matters of taste aside, however, each tourist attraction does reduce the isolation of the mountain people.)

It would be difficult to overestimate the importance of TVA and its great system of dams and steam plants. The agency's early resettlement of bottomland farmers to make way for the dams tore cruelly at the old social order of East Tennessee, but TVA did introduce a fresh stream of formally educated and more liberal people into the region. Then came Oak Ridge and its scientific community, gradually interacting with the mountain people. Roads began to pierce the intermontane wilderness, and finally there were interstate highways too. Radio and television brought in the voices, and then the faces, of the outside world. And then there was the discovery that being a "hillbilly" could be an asset. Country music is a direct outgrowth of hillbilly music; Tennessee Ernie Ford and Roy Acuff and Chet Atkins and many other country music entertainers came out of East Tennessee and offered no apologies for it.

World War II and its aftermath brought a strong, fresh wave of industrialization, not only in Knoxville and Chattanooga but such places as

Kingsport (electronics, chemicals, book printing), Bristol (computing equipment), Morristown (textiles, furniture, electronics), and Maryville (aluminum). Many East Tennessee counties are being stripped for coal. Creative cottage industries—like the lovely Iron Mountain Stoneware made by 60 craftsmen in a tranquil village in the most northeasterly corner of the state—are relatively rare. The future of East Tennessee, Senator Howard Baker, Jr., said, seems to lie in more and more heavy industry.

Still, desperate poverty afflicts many East Tennessee counties. And there remain pockets of incredible isolation. In Oak Ridge one evening, I had a talk with Peter Cohan, a sophisticated educator who has carried programs in science to some of the most remote hollows of the region. Like Horace Kephart before him, Cohan made many friends. While we talked, he suddenly produced a mountain dulcimer made of wormy chestnut and played some of the sweet tunes he had learned from the mountain people. And this was the story he told:

I can take you through time. We'll take a truck and move up into those hills. You'll sense you've moved out of current time to another time. Back in Stony Fork and other places in those hills, a man gets to be a school principal by his physical strength. The question is—can he beat the 17-year-old boy, and maybe his father? Teachers sometimes walk around with a huge oak paddle.

You just have to accept that there are very different value systems from what we know. Many mountaineers, for instance, have had religious experiences that give them strength and very strong convictions. They disagree strongly with science. I've been in little one- and two-room schools and heard teachers insist that everyone knows we haven't been to the moon. They're fiercely independent and critically suspicious of things that affect their religious beliefs or the religion of their children. They may have all the NASA literature about the moon landings, but they just don't believe it, or what they see on television.

There's a lot of drinking out in the hills—but it's a covert way of drinking, out behind the barn. And there's still a big problem with guns. There's little verbal conflict. It's not talk—it's shoot. Lots of killings and maimings result.

But the mountaineers can judge people very well. They have an old saying about a man they admire: "He ain't got much book learnin', but he's got common sense."

Many people born into that mountain environment now work in Knoxville or Oak Ridge. There is a successful Knoxville lawyer who remembers that he arrived there on foot, wearing his sister's borrowed shoes. All of this creates what Cohan calls "a tremendous disparity in time phase." Some of his coworkers, he said, were born "in log cabins with dirt floors and no electric power. Yet today East Tennessee has a place like Oak Ridge, with its nuclear laboratories. That's how far we've moved in the lifetime of those people."

From the North Carolina border moving westward, East Tennessee has the Great Smokies, which are covered with snow during the winter months and offer spectacular shows of flowering shrubs and trees in springtime and changing leaves in autumn; the Great Valley of East Tennessee, which runs clear from Virginia to Alabama and is home for most of the region's people and industries; and finally the Cumberland Mountains, with rich coal deposits and spots of fertile farmland.

Oak Ridge does offer one of the most fascinating case studies anywhere of the sudden intrusion of an advanced scientific-technological community into a pristine, isolated agrarian society. It all began on a spring day of 1942 when three men on a top-secret mission stood atop a peak and looked over the hill-locked valleys with little communities peopled by simple farm folk who could trace their past to 1792 when pioneers came from Virginia, by way of the Cumberland Gap. To the north rose the foothills of the Cumberlands, to the southeast the peaks of the Smokies. The government men were agents of the Manhattan District, the code name for the secret wartime project to build man's ultimate weapon, the atomic bomb. They were looking for a place to produce enough uranium-235 for the bomb, and the site they found—along a crest known as Black Oak Ridge—fitted their specifications perfectly. It was close enough to a major city (Knoxville), rather sparsely settled, well watered, and supplied with abundant electric power from TVA's nearby Norris Dam. The terrain of ridges and valleys, it was thought, would provide natural separation between several plants and buffers "if anything went wrong" with the nuclear experiment.

By September 1942 the decision had been made final to build America's largest atomic city on this site. The government purchased 58,880 acres, paying the owners $45 an acre and ordering them off by the first of January, 1943. Into the area poured the Army Engineers, countless private contractors, thousands of construction workers, mechanics, and scientists of world renown. High fences went up, the severest wartime security measures were ordered, and the scientific work got underway with startling rapidity. Between two peaceful ridges some three miles from the center of the new town the so-called Y-12 complex (a name derived from the map location) was built to produce uranium-235; simultaneously in a wooded area near the western limits of the city the enormous K-25 plant was constructed for the separation of isotopes of uranium by means of a new gaseous diffusion process. The original research laboratory, K-10, rose at the same time, including the famed graphite reactor (now a national historic landmark) for production of fissionable material by the "pile" process. Enrico Fermi, who had supervised the world's first nuclear chain reaction at Chicago less than a year before, directed loading of fuel slugs into the graphite reactor on November 3, 1943. W. E. Thompson, one of the wartime scientists at Oak Ridge, later observed: "We can only feel amazement at the boldness with which the wartime atomic energy projects were planned and the speed and success with which they were carried out."

The growth of the town, which would soon be called Oak Ridge, was almost as phenomenal. In one of those few instances in human affairs when haste has made for excellence, the architectural-engineering firm of Skidmore, Owings and Merrill was given a topographical map of an unidentified area and miraculously came up with a new community plan which it submitted to the Manhattan District within 72 hours. In the wartime rush, one might have expected cheesebox subdivisions of houses lined up in monotonous rows. And indeed, there were a lot of barracks-like dormitories and primitive shelters called "hutments," devoid of glass windows, running water, or winter heating. (Most of the black labor force brought into Oak Ridge was confined to hutments, a fact which still embarrasses Oak Ridgers.) Oak Ridge in the wartime years had the appearance of an enormous, constantly muddy construction camp. But the roads planned by the Skidmore firm, even if initially sidewalkless, did follow the contours of the terrain. The houses were gracefully sited along the natural contours, with picture windows facing the woods. Cutting of trees was kept to a minimum. At war's end the temporary barracks and hutments were demolished, leaving one of the most tastefully laid-out towns in the country. The most undistinguished parts, it would turn out in later years, were the Downtown Shopping Center and the Oak Ridge Turnpike, the connecting line of a city nine miles long and two miles wide, slightly larger than Manhattan.*

Within the wartime context, the Manhattan District's objectives had certainly been met. By mid-1945 the Oak Ridge plants (then assigned the cover name of "Clinton Engineer Works," after a nearby town) employed a peak of 82,000 persons, and the town of Oak Ridge had a population of 75,000. Within two and a half years, it had become the fifth largest city in Tennessee, though more than half the population departed shortly after the war.

In 1945, with the dropping of the atomic bomb over Japan, the secret of what had been happening at Oak Ridge and the other wartime atomic towns —Los Alamos (where the atomic bomb was actually designed and built) and Hanford (the principal location for the production of plutonium)— became known to the world.† Two years later, the Manhattan District, including all the operations at Oak Ridge, were transferred to the new Atomic Energy Commission, and in 1949 there arrived the historic day when the fences came down and Oak Ridge was "opened" to the world. The X-10 plant became the Oak Ridge National Laboratory, one of the world's largest nuclear research centers. Since 1948, the Union Carbide Corporation has operated the three government plants in Oak Ridge under contract with the AEC; the research policies, however, are determined by the laboratory management in direct collaboration with the AEC.

Oak Ridge since the 1940s has remained at the forefront of nuclear research in America with an array of activities that range from basic research

---

* Eden Ross Lipson, in a delightful set of letters about Oak Ridge written for the Institute of Current World Affairs, has characterized "downtown" Oak Ridge as "an uninspired, profitable, and unmistakable bit of Americana circa the mid-1950s." Despite an impressive civic center, I noted that the Oak Ridge Turnpike had evolved into the kind of gaudy and commercialized affair that sophisticated people like Oak Ridgers are supposed to abhor. But the commercial development, it should be pointed out, has been the responsibility of Oak Ridge's business interests, not its technical community.

† The Los Alamos story was related in an earlier book in this series, *The Mountain States of America* (pages 271–272), and that of Hanford in *The Pacific States of America* (pages 262–263).

in exotic elements to the production of weapons components and the development of new reactor concepts. As in wartime, the laboratory still directs the operation of the AEC's several gaseous diffusion plants for the production of enriched U-235. In recent years the focus of the nuclear research has been on the perfection of the fast breeder reactor, hoped to be a major solution to the country's energy "crisis" of this and the next decades. One of the most awesome sights I have ever seen is the laboratory's high flux isotope reactor, used for research in the creation of heavy elements. In deep water, one sees the deep blue, luminescent glow of cooling reactor shields, symbols of the fearfulness and promise of atomic energy in our time.

Dr. Alvin M. Weinberg, who was director of the laboratory through 1973, said its future lay in the study of energy in its broadest context, with atomic energy only one component. "The laboratory," he told me, "will in fact have important secondary thrusts in environmental studies, in the biomedical sciences, in the basic sciences, and possibly even in social science." The disciplines, he said, turn out to be closely interrelated. "When you realize the major pollution of the air and water is in one way or the other connected with the production of energy, then you realize that if you are to be an energy laboratory, you almost by definition become an environmental laboratory. You realize that environmental impacts affect the incidence of cancer—and in fact the laboratory is now deeply involved in research in the causes of cancer and its cures." A major concern of the laboratory is the safety of nuclear reactors, and also thermal pollution from reactors. There is an aquatic ecology laboratory which uses a computer to control the temperatures in six fish ponds, measuring thermal shock (rapid changes in water temperature) as well as long-range effects of altered water temperatures. The work in aquatic ecology, Weinberg believes, illustrates the great advantage of an interdisciplinary institution such as the Oak Ridge Laboratory, which can integrate at the working level the study of problems which are fragmented when they get started at the Washington bureaucratic level. There are some two dozen Ph.D's working in the environmental sciences division of the laboratory, said to be the largest group of ecologists working under one roof in the country.

Among the more interesting projects of the laboratory are those specifically designed to ease the energy crisis, including the gasification and liquification of coal and ways that electrical power plants, both nuclear and conventional, can be made more efficient. By the early '70s, the laboratory was deemphasizing its earlier projects which involved huge demands for power, such as the desalting of ocean water. "We had thought," Weinberg noted, "that energy was going to be immensely cheap, so that the right direction would be to substitute energy for raw materials. It turned out that we were wrong." Thus the important future directions, he concluded, were in making nuclear and other energy forms more efficient and environmentally benign. An example of the new orientation was establishment in 1970 of an environmental program at the laboratory, with financial support from the National Science Foundation. The program involved various types of social scientists, as well as technicians. While the laboratory had historically been concerned only with the supply of energy, part of the revised focus was on energy conservation.

Oak Ridgers themselves have reason to be concerned about environmentally benign energy production. Within 20 miles of the city are six TVA coal-burning steam plants. Two of them—including the Bull Run Steam plant, whose 950,000-kilowatt capacity made it the world's largest power plant when it went on line in 1966—are cheek by jowl with Oak Ridge itself. With TVA selling more and more electricity to distant spots like New York and Chicago, and with a real air quality problem in the Oak Ridge region, some local people are raising serious questions. "Are we," Peter Cohan asked, "to become a power park for the eastern half of the United States?"

A visit to a plant like Bull Run impresses one with the "giantism" of the power production world. The plant burns 7,800 tons of coal a day, piled in huge mountains beside the railroad right-of-way bringing the fuel in from poor, benighted Hazard, Kentucky. One feels rather awed when he stands beside one of the huge pulverizers, which grind the coal down to powder so fine that it can be blown, like a jet of gas, into 12-story-high boilers with fireboxes that record internal temperatures of 2,600 degrees. Yet for all that modernity, new precipitators have been required at Bull Run because of the fly-ash fallout. G. H. Wheaton, the plant superintendent and veteran of 35 years work for TVA, said he was often besieged with complaints from nearby Oak Ridge houses. When I asked him what he planned to do when he retired, Wheaton replied: "I'll sit by my window and look up to the plant and if I see a whiff of smoke I'll phone the engineer and raise hell."

The contrasts between Oak Ridge's scientific intelligentsia and the East Tennessee mountain folks were and are immense: one highly educated, the other struggling to eliminate illiteracy; the one given to fine wines and classical music, the other to white whiskey and hillbilly; the one given to multitudinous civic organizations ("from the African Violet Society on up," one Oak Ridger commented), the other traditionally ingrown and suspicious. This is not to say there is something intrinsically *better* about the Oak Ridgers; the mountain people, for instance, may enjoy a much better family life than the scientists and their families, who often have severe problems in human relations. But the fact is that in Oak Ridge, family incomes average around $12,000 a year while in surrounding Anderson County, a dirt-poor strip-mining area, there are more than 2,000 families that live below the poverty line with incomes averaging just $2,000 a year. Old style political machines hang on in some of the surrounding mountain counties, while Oak Ridge practices egghead democracy with a city council consisting of 11 AEC or Union Carbide employees, several of them Ph.D.'s, lined up against one lonely carpenter. (The high intelligence level creates a kind of problem, since the councilmen thrash every problem to pieces and are unwilling to take the city manager's advice. The city thinks of itself as liberal Democratic, which is true in primaries because of the intellectual vote and the presence of strong, politically active unions. But the town has voted for most Republican Presidential candidates.)

The early attitude of Oak Ridge's East Tennessee neighbors was far from friendly. "They didn't know what we were or what we were doing down here," Oak Ridge attorney Eugene Joyce commented. "We were all too smart and had no sense and were too liberal. They wanted us to stay inside our fence and keep quiet." Joyce told the story of when he campaigned for Anderson County attorney in the early 1950s:

My wife campaigned with me. We went up and down the country roads. I was a real stranger out there—one of the first guys that every ventured out from Oak Ridge into the country to run for public office. We ran into this old fellow at the drugstore opposite the county courthouse.

"Where you from?" he asked.

"Let's face it," I replied. "I'm an outlander. I'm from New York. But I've been down here some 20 years."

Then my wife walked up and the East Tennessean said: "Where's she from?"

In her best Southern drawl, Mrs. Joyce replied: "I'm from West Tennessee, down by the Mississippi."

The old fellow looked at me and said: "She'll take up the slack."

Amazingly, Joyce won the election, and today he thinks only a small part of the old antagonism is left. "We got less brash, and they got to know us." Joyce said there were "thousands of do-gooders in Oak Ridge, learning to use their talents in a more reserved way." Among them, he noted, are wives who do immense good through clubs and churches and projects for the Appalachian poor outside the city. Richard Smyser, editor of the *Oak Ridger*, said most people in the town had become "clawingly appreciative of the natural culture of the Appalachian people."

One of the most amusing and perhaps important incidents in Oak Ridge's history was a visit in the early 1960s by the famed anthropologist Margaret Mead, who castigated Oak Ridgers for taking too little interest in their mountaineer neighbors. The town reacted defensively and angrily, stepping up efforts—many of which had already begun—to provide rehabilitation for physically and mentally handicapped children and adults of the area, opening Oak Ridge's hospitals and clinics to its neighbors, setting up a pioneering Planned Parenthood League of the Southern Mountains, and a summertime program of communication in the area of arts and crafts. "Overall," Smyser said, "Margaret Mead's coming was a good thing. She should come back." (If she does, one wonders if she would repeat the question Dr. Weinberg said she had addressed to a gathering of Oak Ridge women: "Now tell me, do scientists make good lovers?" Regretfully, I must report that Dr. Mead insists she did not pose that question. "It's just a male nightmare," she told me. She said she had been able to make her painfully incisive comments about Oak Ridge, cataloguing the scientists' sins of omission in relating to the broader community, because one of the scientists' wives had written to her regularly—but secretly—over a period of years to give her the scuttlebutt on the town.)

Weinberg said the laboratory and its highly educated, technical work force were having a real impact on the service workers, mostly native East Tennesseans "who have these rather backward traditions." The broader horizons and stronger aspirations of the technical personnel, whose native cities were all over America and the world, Weinberg suggested, were rubbing off on the local people. "They're not all that satisfied to have their kids do just what they've done. Many of the children of Oak Ridge workers are much more upwardly mobile than the workers who are not associated with Oak Ridge. The workers see what education can do for you."

Ironically, this is happening while the Oak Ridge scientists—veterans and more recent arrivals in East Tennessee's "great, swinging, enlightened city" of the hot and cold war years—feel the first blush of enthusiasm is past. Smyser suggested that Oak Ridge was experiencing a kind of "municipal menopause." With budget cuts in the early '70s, many talented and gifted AEC scientists had lost their jobs and were suffering simultaneous middle age and early retirement. Those sophisticated cocktail-dinner parties, at which Oak Ridgers "sit on the floor and argue like hell until midnight" (Joyce's words) were losing their luster for some people. The cultural opportunities, said to be more appropriate to a city of 250,000 than Oak Ridge's 28,319, no longer proved as irresistible a magnet. One senses a lack of a full sense of community and belonging in Oak Ridge. I asked Smyser, who arrived there 25 years ago to start the *Oak Ridger*, now an outstanding small daily, if he and his family didn't consider Oak Ridge their real home now. We were sitting on the back porch of his tasteful ridgetop home, looking out several miles to lovely mountain ridges in the twilight of a perfect summer day, and I expected an unambiguous "yes." But it did not come. "There are lots of other interesting people and places in the world," he replied.

Knoxville (Still the "Ugliest City"?) and Chattanooga

I suppose I should approach a description of Knoxville, the biggest city of East Tennessee, with a touch of trepidation because of its unhappy experience with outside commentators. John Gunther, in *Inside U.S.A.*, called Knoxville "the ugliest city I ever saw in America," an appellation that still rankles in this Tennessee River town of old red brick factories and office buildings. A Nashville newspaperman told me that "Gunther was probably right." Knoxville, he said, is a "grim industrial city with tough, ultra-personal, and sometimes corrupt politics. And the Knoxville *Journal* is the graveyard of journalism." When it became known, in 1945, that atomic research had been underway at Oak Ridge during the war, there was a joke told around Tennessee that if a bomb went off accidentally, Knoxville would be "the least missed city in the United States."

The indictments and jokes, however, appear a little unfair, especially in view of what has taken place in Knoxville in the last quarter century. Gunther's controversial quote, in fact, helped to jolt Knoxville into some constructive action. The city could not change its history as an ill-planned, ill-conceived country town, but it could—and did—begin to change. "For one thing," a local sage told me, "we had six or seven wonderful deaths." There was some renovation of the center city, with a handsome mall and enclosed shopping area, and even some shiny new high-rise office buildings. TVA's electric power obviated the belching coal furnaces that cast a dark cloud over the city and made it almost as dark as night in the middle of the day. The University of Tennessee, which has the headquarters of its statewide system at Knoxville, shucked its old reputation as a football college and scored advances in physical plant and intellectual quality (despite egregious lapses like opening up its facilities to a 1970 Billy Graham crusade that turned out to be a kind of campaign rally for a visiting President Nixon, with strongarm tactics used against any and all dissenters). A number of university and TVA people became active in Knoxville affairs, further diluting the influence of the city's old guard. Cultural enrichment came via a new coliseum, built over great opposition, which attracts many traveling plays and other events and is one of the most used in the country. From its old concentration on industries like textiles and iron, the town shifted its sights to being a wholesale distribution center for East Tennessee. The Knoxville banks, incredibly stuck-in-the-mud and closely allied to a conservative power structure that resisted unions or threatening new economic enterprises, began to widen their horizons a little.

The downtown banks and mercantile interests, however, were too lethargic to make the center city the focus of Knoxville's really important postwar growth. That occurred some 10 miles to the west, where West Town Mall, an ultramodern, multimillion-dollar office building and shopping center complex was built—depending in large measure on outside capital. West Town Mall sits on Kingston Pike, an example of the gauchest strip development. But while the planning is atrocious, at least there has been the spark of growth there, which people equate with success in this country. And if one leaves some of the major highways, some lovely residential sections can be found. With its choice location in the foothills of the Smoky Mountains, Knoxville *could* be one of the more attractive cities of the country.

One of the Knoxville deaths that caused private rejoicing in some quarters was that of Guy Lincoln Smith, editor from 1936 to 1938 of the *Journal*. Smith for many years was Republican state chairman and a close ally of Carroll Reece. He was a strong-minded man who thought that not just the editorial pages but also the news columns should reflect his archconservative convictions. The paper condemned all progressive causes and periodically discovered Communism, subversion, and immorality in the hills of East Tennessee. The *Journal* lost some of its bite after Smith died, but it had already given up its Sunday edition and fallen in circulation far behind the blander but mediocre *News-Sentinel*, a Scripps-Howard paper. Steve Humphreys, retired managing editor of the *Journal*, said of the *News-Sentinel*: "They're broadminded. We never pretended to be broadminded."

Another declined power is former Knoxville mayor and Republican political boss Cas Walker, a wealthy owner of a string of grocery stores who had a pretty free hand in deciding, for many years, who got elected and who didn't in Knoxville. Democrats attacked Walker as a man who played skillfully on people's emotions to discredit his opposition, but I also heard that blacks liked him because he got job opportunities for many of them and put some of his stores in black areas, keeping prices lower there than in his other outlets. Now in his seventies, Walker's influence has subsided with the new, open spirit in Knoxville.

Knoxville by 1970 had 174,587 people, with 225,750 more in its metropolitan area. Chattanooga, the other big East Tennessee city, counted 119,082 souls in its center city and 185,854 in the metropolitan area (including some 80,000 in suburban Walker County, Georgia). Not much more than a village until after the Civil War, Chattanooga was peopled by ex-Union soldiers and industrialists who hoped to make the town a Pittsburgh of the South. It remains, first and last, a heavy industry town, turning out vast quantities of iron castings, brake drums, boilers, and pressure vessels. The city is the 10th most industrialized in the country and has had to pay a heavy price in air pollution; indeed one reading in the mid-1960's indicated Chattanooga had the third most polluted air in the United States. Since then some $15 million in smoke control equipment has effected a dramatic reduction in the sooty fallout, one of America's most notable victories over air pollution.

Chattanooga has had its share of race problems, including a fierce controversy over school busing and a 1971 riot that brought death for one Negro and scores of injuries before the National Guard could restore calm. Efforts to consolidate the city with its suburban hinterland have failed twice in the past decade, but the city's liberal young mayor, Robert Kirk Walker, has been fighting hard for major structural reform in what he calls Chattanooga's "horse and buggy commission form of government." Walker and his predecessor pioneered in a "human services management information system" to coordinate all social services, including welfare, with efficiency and positive benefits for poor citizens equalled by few other American cities. (A computer, for instance, keeps track of a welfare client's total problem and needs, making it possible to get disparate agencies working together to help him or her, rather than at cross purposes.) The project, originally funded as a pilot project by the federal government, is indicative of the advanced government service systems likely to be adopted in hundreds of U.S. communities within the next several years.

In a manner of speaking, Chattanooga was the birthplace of the New York *Times* because Adolph S. Ochs bought the Chattanooga *Times* there in 1878 and ran it for several years before going on to make his mark in New York. Over the years the two papers not only enjoyed overlapping ownerships but very similar typography. The Chattanooga *Times* is strongly liberal by Tennessee standards, compared to the starchy conservative philosophy of the competing *News-Free Press*.

Considerations of space have generally obliged me to omit the origin of place names, but Chattanooga's is especially interesting. It is derived from "Chat-to-to-noo-gee," a Creek Indian word for "rock coming to a point." And indeed, Lookout Mountain, with its picturesque incline railway, remains, as it has always been, the city's most distinctive physiographic feature.

Middle and West Tennessee Overview

Middle Tennessee, with its Nashville, has developed rapidly in recent years as the governmental-financial-intellectual center of a progressing state, and one would no longer think of it first, as John Gunther did, as "mint-julep, big-plantation, old-Southern aristocracy" territory. This Grand Division is hemmed in by the looping Tennessee River on both its eastern and western flanks, and most of it is gently rolling Bluegrass country. In fact, Tennessee has more Bluegrass territory than Kentucky and produces some of the finest blooded horses in America. This is also a prime area for tobacco. It has attracted a lot of light, clean industry in recent years, and in general its income levels are higher than those of East or West Tennessee. Middle Tennessee has also been the most politically stable area of the state since World War II. Its normal complexion is moderate-to-liberal Democratic, though Wallaceism and Republicanism have made some inroads. Political scientists Lee Greene and Jack Holmes noted that the "homogeneous and stable" Democratic counties of Middle Tennessee were the most prone in the state "to support the civil weal in the form of a clean courthouse, new school buildings, or even a library, despite the attendant necessity of new taxation."

Finally, we come to West Tennessee, the generally flat, alluvial plain bordered by the northerly flowing Tennessee River on the east, the great Mississippi on the west. With its rich valleys and black bottoms, this is the most productive agricultural area of the state. Soybeans and livestock are rapidly replacing cotton, and there are a goodly number of big old plantation style farms mixed in among the smaller units. West Tennessee in many ways is simply an extension of Mississippi's Delta region, of which the great river port of Memphis is the real capital. Like the Delta, West Tennessee has a big black population—30 percent of the total, compared to 13 percent in Middle Tennessee and only 6 percent in East Tennessee. And in typical Deep South style, it has a lot of apparel plants, many of the sweatshop variety. Larger industries are now intruding, though; in the late 1960s, for instance, Goodyear Tire and Rubber built a $100 million plant there. Outside of Memphis, which now counts a population of 623,530, the only city of any size is Jackson, with about 40,000 people. Long a railroad center and the home of Casey Jones, Jackson has recently shaken off some of its lethargy and gone industry hunting with modest success.

West Tennessee has some egregious rural poverty and, as we will note later, a large black ghetto population in Memphis. Race tensions help to keep the area Tennessee's most conservative. That used to mean an Old South-style Democracy; these days it can mean voting Democratic, Wallaceite, or Republican, just as long as a candidate can sell white voters on his eagerness to keep blacks in their place.

A note on population: the three Grand Divisions are remarkably equal in population—Middle and West Tennessee each about 1.2 million, East Tennessee (with its larger number of cities) just ahead at 1.5 million. I cannot think of another state where the major regions are so delicately balanced in population—or political power.

Metamorphosis in Mistah Crump's Memphis

Edward H. Crump has been a-moulderin' in his grave lo these 20 years now, but it is hard to resist a flashback to the days when the boss ruled the old river town so long and so absolutely.

> Oh, the river's up and the cotton's down
> Mistah Ed Crump, he runs this town!

Roustabouts on the Mississippi waterfront, Alfred Steinberg wrote in *The Bosses*, used to chant those lines as they did their work back in the 1930s. Memphians of the early 20th century, Steinberg observed, had come to know Mistah Crump as a colorful dresser, a good family man, the munificent giver of free picnics and fairs and boat rides, and a figure as courtly as a planter out of the Confederacy. All the public façade obscured Crump the dictatorial boss, who would destroy any friend or foe's dignity just to prove his own powers. In his office, Crump viewed visitors through cynically half-closed eyes; out on the street to meet the people, by contrast, he was always popeyed in eager attention to those he encountered. Steinberg caught the spirit of old Memphis in his description of

Crump's recognizable walk—a strut on the balls of his feet with slightly flexed knees—[as] it carried him down cotton-oil-smelly Front Street to the Mississippi; or past the Poplar Avenue station, the starting point of Casey Jones' ill-fated trip in Cannon Ball Engine No. 382 in April, 1900; or onto Gayoso Street, known as the "street of shame" because of its 20 to 30 bawdy houses. The walk might take him through the lobby of the Hotel Peabody ("The South's Finest") where, said an observer, he approached "friends with pastoral dignity and like an elder statesman."

If Crump were today granted a reincarnation and transported back to "his" city, he might rub his eyes in amazement. There would be points of familiarity, of course. Standing on the Chickasaw Bluffs by the Father of Waters, heavily parked and verdant, Memphis remains a great port city, the true capital of the Mississippi Delta region and a great land area extending over West Tennessee, eastern Arkansas, and the northeastern section of the state of Mississippi. In many ways it is quintessentially Southern: not so much because it sprang into being in 1819, as the South was being formed, when three Nashville real estate developers, Andrew Jackson among them, picked it as a site for a town to handle the river traffic, but because its people over the years were, and are, refugees from the Delta and other farmlands of a region long agrarian by very definition. Yet Southern as it is, Memphis also has a hint of the West: the atmosphere of those vast glazed skies, the bustle, the raw energy.

What would shock Crump the most would be to see how his city, belittled in times past as a backwater river town, has burgeoned into a vast metropolis in anarchic sprawl across the Delta lands. Huge freeways have devoured an inordinate amount of land; a six-lane monolith would even have plowed through proud old Overton Park, the 342-acre respite of greenery and peace in the city's heart, if Memphis conservationists had not carried their battle all the way to the U.S. Supreme Court and finally got a decision against the road by Secretary of Transportation John A. Volpe. Today soaring skyscrapers have dwarfed the downtown Ed Crump knew, and a massive new convention center was opened in 1974. There are nostalgic touches still in the city's heart, like the colonnaded bandstand on Court Square, but shiny newness is the theme now. The gleaming Medical Center has become a vital center of activity; out to the east, where fields of cotton bloomed in Ed Crump's lifetime, tall office buildings poke at the sky, not far from the monolithic buildings of fast-growing Memphis State University. The suburbs are pushing out in every direction they can (which means every way except west, where the river blocks the way); some are scruffy affairs, but especially east and south of the center city are expensive suburban developments. An example is Whitehaven, in the southern part of Shelby County, filled with wealthy and middle class conservatives who fled the city and created an environment hot with Citizen Council activity.

Back downtown, even old Beale Street, where W. C. Handy gave birth to the blues around the turn of the century, where Memphis lowlife hit its zenith with strutting dandies, gamblers, and voodoo practitioners, where there used to be the smell of ribs or blue cat cooking over wood fires, and some splendid soul food restaurants, and flocks of loan sharks, is being modernized and commercialized by a new plan. The old buildings have fallen victim to the wrecker's ball; now there is to be a "blue light" district of night spots, shops, and restaurants that will try to memorialize Beale Street as it was back at the turn of the century. Travel writer David Butwin has attacked the plan as "a plastic 1970s model of the old scene," but the jury is still out on what the final result will be.

Another odd thing Ed Crump would note if he looked around Shelby County today: a dozen look-alike motels with great flashing signs called "Holiday Inns." For Memphis is the world headquarters of the fabulously successful chain founded 25 years ago by Memphis businessman Kemmons Wilson with a first motel on the city's eastern fringe. (The corporate name was taken from a 1942 Bing Crosby film and Irving Berlin song, while the "Great Sign," whose gaucherie is now visible in 50 states and 42 other nations, was inspired by a movie marquee.) Operating chiefly by the franchise route, Wilson and his associates had 1,500 Holiday Inns in operation by 1973 and a firm aim of 3,000 by 1980. The number of rooms is approaching a quarter million, and revenue is about $1.8 billion a year. The Holiday Inn executives discovered the power of positive thinking before they ever heard of Norman Vincent Peale; they are Southern Protestants who have even hired a corporate chaplain but blend faith and capitalistic prowess in a happy combination for themselves. The oft-quoted statement of Wallace Johnson, one of the cofounders of this remarkable organization which has brought so much efficiency and plastic sameness to the American inn business: "I don't have problems; I have only opportunities." *

The agrarian base of old Memphis is still distinguishable in its role as a cotton center and the largest hardwood market in the nation. But with the Holiday Inns and scores of other enterprises, the economic base changed fundamentally during the 1950s and '60s: from rural- to urban-based industries, from cotton to industry, and from industry to commerce and distribution. From the Mississippi Delta to the "bootheel" of Missouri, the chamber of commerce boasts, live 3.3 million people who look to Memphis as a center of trade, service, and finance. The Cotton Carnival, a kind of weak imitation of New Orleans' Mardi Gras featuring balls and parades and socially appropriate figures assuming the names of Egyptian deities, still takes place each year. But cotton has declined in importance with the increased use of man-made fibers and the substitution of soybean oil for cottonseed oil as a major ingredient of plastics and processed foods. Diversification is the theme of Memphis industry now—in chemicals, machinery, rubber goods, pharmaceutical products, and electronic equipment. And as new industries are snared these days, the Memphis chamber of commerce has shown some sophistication in encouraging them, behind the scenes, to go into smaller towns outside the heart of the metropolitan area, where they can get cheaper labor and cause fewer environmental problems for the city. Still, they remain dependent on Memphis for track, rail, or barge transportation and for supplies. The city itself is more interested in corporate headquarters and branch offices, together with more warehousing and distribution facilities.

All of this means a lot of money for Memphis, but it is worth reminiscing about what the river city once meant to its hinterland—espeicially the Mississippi Delta. David L. Cohn, the talented Delta writer, summed it up in a delightful way in his book *Where I was Born and Raised:*

> The Mississippi Delta begins in the lobby of the Peabody Hotel in Memphis and ends on Catfish Row in Vicksburg. The Peabody is the Paris Ritz, the Cairo Shepheard's, the London Savoy of this section. If you stand near its fountain in the middle of the lobby, where ducks waddle and turtles drowse, ultimately you will see everybody who is anybody in the Delta and many who are on the make.

* By way of comment, one might add that one opportunity Mr. Johnson and his colleagues were passing up was the chance to beautify—or should we say decontaminate—the American landscape by voluntarily scaling down that cultural excrescence of the 1950s, the Holiday Inn "Great Sign." The Holiday people could well design something of more modest proportions and less flashing lights, and then use their dominant position in the industry to persuade other motel chains and fast-food joints and maybe even the oil companies to do the same.

(Who, one wonders, will ever be able to write that way about a Holiday Inn?) Cohn continued:

Memphis is the metropolis of the Delta. It is its financial, social, and cultural capital. Many of its citizens grew wealthy by lending money at exorbitant rates of interest to Delta planters. . . . Other Memphians founded their dynasties in lumber. They leaped from cypress to Cezanne in one generation. Some of them brought fortunes to Memphis from Arkansas. They had lived on land which "wasn't fitten fur a houn' dawg." But oil sprouted underneath their feet. On the whole, however, Memphis draws its sustenance from its immense surrounding territory. . . .

But back to the Peabody Hotel, in an incarnation not to be forgotten:

Here come the business men of the Delta to make loans, sell cotton, buy merchandise, and attend conventions. For a day or two the lobby of the Peabody is filled with ice-cream men and their ice-cream wives. They suddenly melt into nothingness and are succeeded by anti-exterminators bent upon destroying the termite, which, like the politician, is blind but destructive. Then the undertakers appear. They discuss embalming by day. By night they dance delicate dances macabre with their necrophilic ladies under the scared and disapproving eyes of the Negro waiters. Finally they vanish into the outer darkness from which they came, giving way to hay-and-feed men who year long have cherished harlequins in their hearts now to be released in this place of bright carnival. . . .

In Memphis the stern [Delta] business man shows the world his other soul-side. . . . Here he goes in search of frail women, human, all too human, who live in houses with shades perpetually drawn, or he stumbles perhaps with a sudden gasp of delight upon some peripatetic beauty strolling sole-eyed and lost in the soft darkness of the hotel mezzanine. Sin, a hydra-headed monster at home, becomes in Memphis a white dove cooing in the shade of tall cathedral columns.

(The ducks, incidentally, waddle about in the Peabody's lobby. But the hotel, although renovated in the late 1960s, is not quite the glamorous spot it once was.)

Modern Memphis has a lively world of "high" culture, sparked by a fine art gallery and school, symphony and opera, and several local theater groups. (A Memphis arts council subsidizes several of these activities.) Far better known nationally are the offbeat cultural activities in Memphis. The city boasts that it is hot on the heels of Nashville as a major music and recording center. There is said to be something called the "Memphis Sound," which blends white country music and black soul; it has especially deep historic roots on the black side, because of Beale Street and W. C. Handy's invention of the blues there. Handy's music reflected the culture of the blacks from the cotton fields, yet in the early 1950s the white component began to develop with once poor whites like Elvis Presley and Jerry Lee Lewis leading the way. The dollar value of the Memphis recording industry was close to $100 million a year by the early 1970s.

About the same time, national business reporters were amazed to note that Memphis had become the nation's third largest market for tax-free municipal bonds, after New York and Chicago. At least three dozen Memphis bond firms, employing hundreds of salesmen, were reported in operation, placing some $2.5 billion worth of bonds each year. But the Wall Street *Journal* charged that "because many Bond Daddies are dishonest," they had also made Memphis "a national center of fraud and shady dealings in municipal bonds."

In Ed Crump's Memphis, of course, questionable businessmen would have found themselves leaving town on the next train. But in a perverse way, one can even rejoice about the freedom to engage in some questionable business dealings in this city. In the Crump era, the financial as well as the political decisions were left, in the last analysis, to the boss, and there were stories of Memphians who made the slip of one irreverent comment about the leader who suddenly lost their livelihoods and found it wise to seek another city in which to live. (It was, for instance, considered an act of incredible apostasy, and a sign that the old order was beginning to crumble, when a group of Memphis businessmen in 1948 dared to make a public announcement of support for the old man's political enemy, Estes Kefauver.) When Crump died, there was a yawning leadership gap, simply because no one else in Memphis was trained to see the big picture or assert a leading role. In the words of Lewis R. Donelson III, a city councilman and Republican leader: "We raised an entire generation of people who simply did not have any say about their community." And for more than a decade after Crump's death in 1954, no one emerged to lead.

Riding on its old momentum, the Crump machine held power for five years in Memphis after the boss's death, finally meeting defeat in 1959 when political reformers captured the mayoralty and control of the commissioners. "The key word," according to local Democratic leader William W. Farris, "became 'machine.' Whenever a strong leader began to emerge, his opponents used the key word to weaken him politically. It was hard for one man to become strong enough to unite or bring all the people together." Thus from an excess of control, the Democratic party went to the other extreme, its leadership fragmented in many little clusters. This created the opportunity for the Republicans, who had been largely a Negro fringe body in Memphis for many decades, to change in character (to a conservative white organization) and gain strength. The GOP's big breakthrough came in 1966, when Dan Kuykendall was elected from Memphis to the U.S. House. The GOP rise was of more than incidental importance. As Barney DuBois wrote in the *Commercial-Appeal*, "Memphis arrived as a two-party town and issues, instead of personalities, became more important." The new situation was, of course, the antithesis of Crumpism. Kuykendall himself said his party's emergence meant that "the Democratic party can't run bums anymore. (Kuykendall, a friend of Richard Nixon, was to be defeated for reelection in 1974 by a 29-year-old black state legislator, Harold E. Ford.)

Another vital change was the shift in government which occurred in 1968. Since Crump's early days, Memphis had been ruled by a five-commissioner government—a form ideal for manipulation and control by the boss. But after his demise, it was clearly outmoded. New political voices, including Republicans and blacks, were crying for representation, and the now leaderless commissioners fell into severe bickering among themselves. Thus support developed for a strong mayor form of government, with a city council large enough to include a real cross-section of the community. The very process of gathering support for the strong mayor-council form was healthy for Memphis, because it required getting such disparate groups as business, the two parties, blacks, the newspapers, religious leaders, and women's groups, all working together for the first time in living memory. "The drive," DuBois wrote, "was the first successful community effort . . . since 1954. It brought new awareness to leaders, previously with little practical experience in the science of community organization and leadership."

As Memphis was taking these forward steps, the cataclysm of the assassination of Martin Luther King, Jr., intruded on the scene. Viewing Memphis's history, a racial conflagration of some type was almost inevitable. Here was a city of explosive racial-cultural components: the receptacle over decades of the displaced white tenant farmers and black plantation hands of its hinterland (a folk movement that reached a crescendo with 160,000 rural refugees during the 1960s). And race conflict had always been present, even when the standard histories spoke of other things. The years after the Civil War, for instance, are generally remembered for the onslaughts of yellow fever epidemics that felled thousands, made Memphis into a lawless pesthole, and obliged the city to surrender its charter to the state. But it was also true that in 1866 a police riot resulted in the death of dozens of freedmen living in squalor on Memphis's south side. The histories of Ed Crump's rise to power recall the hellish conditions around the turn of the century: 600 saloons, drunks in gutters everywhere, more gambling joints than grocery stores, prostitutes numbered in the thousands, dope for 10 cents in the drugstores, and a murder rate much worse than any other city in America. But it was also true that Memphis had registered so many public lynchings in the 1890s that it had, as one observer put it, "an international reputation for white barbarity." Straight down to the 1960s, Memphis blacks were treated much the same way they had been on the plantations from which they or their ancestors came.

Crump's Memphis had been the epitome of the urban plantation, and the condition of life for blacks remained appalling for years after his death. The 1960 Census found black family income only 44 percent that of white family income in Shelby County. Blacks lagged four and a half years behind whites in average schooling. The vast majority of black housing was classified as deteriorating or dilapidated. All but a handful of blacks were consigned to the most menial and unskilled labor. Among 181 federal contractors surveyed in the county in 1966, there were 10,500 white-collar jobs held by whites—but only 145 held by black people. In the city government, it took a magnifying glass to find a handful of token blacks scattered through the ranks of thousands of white collar workers. Police brutality against blacks was rampant, and in 1967 the U.S. Civil Rights Commission was warned by the Rev. Samuel B. Kyles of the Memphis NAACP that Negro distrust and fear of the police was so serious that the situation was ripe for a major urban riot.

There was, of course, one kind of employment considered most appropriate for blacks: picking up the garbage. And then there were the peculiar circumstances of 1968. As historian Lerone Bennett, Jr., has written:

> Because of the rain, which fell on Memphis on January 31, city officials made a decision which would lead, web by web to the martyrdom of Martin Luther King Jr. They didn't plan it that way. But a pattern of racism, as old as the slave ships which brought King's ancestors to this country, worked in them and through them. It was this pattern which spun the first web of death. It was this pattern which led Memphis officials to separate garbage collectors on the basis of race, sending the black workers home with two hours' pay and keeping the white men for a full day's work. This decision, which would change so many lives, which would lead to so many graves, angered the black garbage collectors who held a meeting and decided to go out on strike. The strike catalyzed the black community of Memphis and sent ripples of red across the land.

The strike had begun on February 12, when 1,375 workers, affiliated with the small and officially unrecognized Local 1733 of the American Federation of State, County, and Municipal Employees walked off their jobs. The racist mayor of the time, Henry Loeb, stonily refused recognition of the union. Then came the marches through the streets, to which King lent his presence and prestige. And at 6:01 P.M. on April 4, a bullet severed his spinal cord as he stood on the balcony of the Lorraine Motel. One may omit here the complex debates over the motive of the once-confessed slayer, James Earl Ray, and whether he was a paid agent; the best judgment seems to be that Ray was a race-crazed man, a failure in all he had done in life, reaching for a moment of fame, though we may never be sure that others were not involved. (Ray pleaded guilty to the murder charge in 1969 but subsequently sought a new trial and permission to change his plea to innocent. A federal court in January 1974 granted Ray's request for a review of his case, opening the possibility of a new trial and further revelations.)

It is worth recalling the hauntingly prescient words King uttered in his last speech, addressing a mass meeting of 2,000 people in Memphis's Mason Temple Church of God in Christ the night before he was felled:

> Well, I don't know what will happen now. We've got some difficult days ahead. But it really doesn't matter with me now. Because I've been to the mountaintop. I won't mind.
> Like anybody, I would like to live a long life. Longevity has its place. But I'm not concerned about that now. I just want to do God's will.
> And he's allowed me to go up to the mountain. And I've looked over, and I've seen the Promised Land.
> I may not get there with you, but I want you to know tonight that we as a people will get to the Promised Land.

There were interesting parallels between the Dallas of 1963, where President Kennedy met his death, and Memphis of 1968. In both cases the political fanatics seemed to have gained the upper hand over men of decency and moderation in the frame of time before the bullets flew. In both cases there were those who said the assassinations were only accidentally events of the cities where they took place; indeed a Memphis judge proclaimed: "Memphis has been blamed for the death of Dr. King, to me wrongfully and irrationally. Neither the decedent nor his killer lived here, their orbits merely intersected here." In both cities, the reactions of the populace ranged from ill-disguised glee to horror and contrition. Among white Memphians, there were said to be two schools: those who were genuinely sorry that King was killed, and those who were only sorry that it happened in Memphis. One can reach his own conclusions about Mayor Loeb, who was asked three years later by writer James Conaway for his opinion of the influence on Memphis of King's death. Loeb sucked on an empty pipe for fully ten seconds and then said through his teeth, "I don't *have* an opinion." During the spring that King was killed, Loeb carried a loaded gun around on his person—and bragged about it at parties.

To carry the Dallas-Memphis analogy a bit further, it can be said that the assassinations had a deep effect on the life of the two cities. Memphis did not, as Dallas did, install an outstanding mayor like Eric Jonsson to bind up the wounds. But it was obliged to back down and grant Local 1733, 12 days after King's death, effective recognition as the bargaining agent for its members. Since then the local has blossomed into the most aggressive and effective public employee union in the South, inspiring similar successful bids for recognition by hospital workers in Charleston, South Carolina, and for other sanitation workers in such cities as Mobile, Alabama, and Pascagoula, Mississippi. Memphis sanitation workers now earn more than twice the $1.10 hourly wage they had been receiving for the previous 15 years. For the first time, they have been granted sick pay, vacations, and grievance procedures. And Local 1733 won an unprecedented contract agreement which requires the city to fund a "career ladders" program to enable sanitation men to train themselves for more skilled and better paying jobs.

Outside of the 1,500 garbage collectors, Local 1733 has 4,500 other members, including hospital and education workers; it has also become very active in elections, both through political education programs and cold cash investments in candidates sympathetic to its goals. Only grudgingly did Memphis finally agree to name a stretch of freeway after Dr. King, but that is probably not important: his real monument, for Memphis blacks, is the union.

They need that confidence, for their lot is still an unhappy one. Unemployment in ghetto areas was estimated at 28 percent in 1973. The number of blacks in the skilled trades has remained negligible. The most blatant police brutality has subsided, but it is still a very force-prone and trigger-happy department. (When a new police director took over and reviewed the shambles of his force, he publicly asked a group of businessmen: "How did you let it get this bad?") As Maxine A. Smith, leader of the Memphis NAACP, said five years after King's death: "The few changes secured have come about not because of Dr. King's death or because white people have recognized their racism, but because black people have continually pushed and pushed." As an example, she pointed out that it took a boycott of 67,000 black school children to get three black members appointed to the school board. But the pushing has achieved something for the blacks: by 1973 they not only had that toehold on the school board but had three members on the 11-man city council and four on the 13-person county governing body called the county court. And state judge Otis Higgs, an outspoken black in his mid-30s elected to the bench with Local 1733's help in 1971, helped effect some real changes in the criminal court system.

Even broad school desegregation involving large-scale busing, the chief issue that polarized the races and dominated political rhetoric in the years following King's assassination, was accomplished with remarkable calm in January of 1973. The price of desegregation was a mushrooming of church-sponsored private schools for whites and an alarming increase in the black percentage in the public schools—from 45 percent in 1960, when separation of the races in the Memphis system was absolute and the NAACP Legal Defense and Education Fund first sued to force integration, to 68 percent in 1973–74. The court-ordered plan actually left 25 all-black schools in the system, a feature which the NAACP protested—in vain—all the way up to the U.S. Supreme Court. By the spring of 1974, there were 105 private schools in Memphis, many of them havens of white flight. They had an enrollment of 33,000, compared to 119,000 in the public schools. John P. Freeman, the Memphis school superintendent, told me "the question of whether we will have a biracial public school system in the next years" still hung in the balance, but the loss of many top teachers to the private schools, plus recurrent racial disorders in some of the public schools, led some observers to believe that question had already been settled in the negative. The city's all-white Briarcrest Baptist School System, Inc., a coordinated group of schools operated by churches affiliated with the Southern Baptist Convention, already had an annual operating budget of some $2 million.

The bright side of all this was that despite the organized resistance of antibusing groups and rumors of violence, the big court-ordered pupil transfer plan had gone into operation without incident. There were no bus burnings on the model of Pontiac, Michigan, or Denver, Colorado; indeed the only person known to have suggested that he would destroy buses was turned over to police by the antibusing group to which he made the offer. As Southern writer John Egertson reported to the Southern Regional Council:

> In a very real sense the Memphis story is a success story, a success hammered out in tough and realistic sessions between the opposing forces, a success brought about against a background of much turmoil, citizen misunderstanding, all in a city . . . which too often in the past had seemed wedded to the past. . . .
> In all of the intricate and convoluted maneuverings that have gone on in public and behind the scenes in Memphis, there has been enough emotion to elate and depress and exhaust everybody. That no overt violence has occurred . . . can only be seen as a hopeful indication that this city, however divided, has had its fill of violence.

Indeed, it had been the chamber of commerce that took the initiative in mobilizing major public support for a smooth transition to school desegregation in 1972–73. Businessmen were showing an increased willingness, on issue after issue, to lean hard on the city's politicians to find compromises on racial issues before they reached an explosive point. Without business intervention, it is doubtful that the city's elective officials would have gone as far as they did by the early 1970s to include the once ignored black community in vital decisions for Memphis.

King's death was the principal reason for the new business attitude, though there had been glimmerings of change before April 1968. Among other things, some major business leaders were worried about the chamber of commerce, which at that time limited its scope to counting new smokestacks and issuing "bigger and better" propaganda about the city. A businessmen's junket to Atlanta, to see how that Cinderella city was succeeding on the social as well as the economic front, had been organized in 1967, and early in 1968 a multimillion-dollar "Greater Memphis Program" was initiated to modernize the chamber of commerce's approach. Not until King's death, however, did the effort get underway. As its chief executive, the chamber attracted David W. Cooley, who had played a major role in the consolidation of Jacksonville, Florida, with its surrounding county. A prominent sociologist was also hired to evangelize with local businesses for more black hirings and high-level black placements. Some real successes were chalked up, including establishment of a black-owned and -run shopping center and loans for a number of new black-run businesses. But these advances hardly scratched the surface of black people's economic disadvantage in Memphis, and by the early 1970s it was apparent that the chamber's black enterprise and employment program was running out of steam. (Significantly, both Cooley and the sociologist left for more promising positions in other cities.) The Greater Memphis Program was also unable to create enough momentum to get approval of a charter consolidating Memphis government with that of Shelby County; in 1971, in fact, the voters turned down the merger idea, already proven so successful in Nashville, for the second time in a decade.

Finally, the Greater Memphis Program fizzled out altogether and the chamber of commerce replaced it with an incredibly hucksterish and amateur "Believe in Memphis" program, geared to jingles in radio commercials and the like. The head of the new effort, not surprisingly, was Wallace Johnson of Holiday Inns.

In 1970, in a classic series on the Memphis power structure for the *Commercial Appeal*, Barney DuBois had written that in place of the one-man rule of Crump's days, Memphis had developed a leadership group consisting of "a fluid, frequently competitive, almost structureless combination of political, commercial, and professional people," diverse in their backgrounds and thinking alike. Three years later, he told me that the city's leadership was even more in flux than in 1970—an "incredibly pluralistic" and undirected group. Occasionally, as on the school issue, some business leaders would stir themselves to prevent the worst, but creative long-range planning seemed beyond their scope. On the political front, Wyeth Chandler, the mayor elected to succeed Loeb in 1971, was prone to rabble-rousing on the school busing issue and seemed to offer Memphis more opportunism than principle in high office. None of the business or other civic leaders seemed interested in stirring themselves to elect a leader of stature, like Ivan Allen, Jr., in the Atlanta of the 1960s, who might help to make the old river town a real city of distinction.

Nashville: Going Metro and Doing Well

Nashville enjoys a string of assets that make it one of the most vibrant and promising cities of the Border South. It is Tennessee's state capital and an important enough center of higher education, the arts, trade, and finance that the slogans "Athens of the South" and "Wall Street of the South" cannot be dismissed as mere hyperbole. The inner city has been revamping its tired old physical plant through sweeping urban renewal programs. There is a rich historic tradition, going back to Captain James Robertson's first settlement in 1779 and the days of Andrew Jackson, whose lovely home, the Hermitage, has been restored and furnished almost exactly as it was when Old Hickory lived there. Of the new phrase "Nashville sound" and the thriving music industry behind it, I wrote earlier in this chapter. And the city's metropolitan form of government, inaugurated in 1963 when Nashville was merged with surrounding Davidson County, has created a climate of confidence enhancing economic growth. Clashes between the inner city and suburbs, for instance, have subsided under "Metro" because Nashville no longer has to worry about losing taxpaying enterprises to its surrounding area. The Metro plan also consolidated the city and suburban school districts, a step which other widely heralded consolidation plans, like that in Indianapolis, have not included. But partly for that reason, the political furor over school busing to achieve integration has been of peculiar intensity in Nashville, the latest evidence of a recurrent hostility between the races that has plagued the city over most of its history.

Nashville did not adopt Metro government without reason or without a hard battle. In the early 1950s, when the battle for consolidation got underway, the city of Nashville encompassed 22 square miles with a static population of 170,000 people. Surrounding Davidson county had a rapidly growing population of some 260,000 in 511 square miles. It was a classic example of fiscal and legal imbalance in urban America: a city government bearing practically the full responsibility for facilities used by the whole metropolitan community, including the airport, library, hospitals, and parks, while the county government lacked legal authority to perform many essential services in the suburban area. There were expensive duplications of services and constant buck-passing between the jurisdictions.

The effort to consolidate the two governments took 12 years, an amendment to the state constitution, legislation in three sessions of the legislature, and the defeat of a first proposed consolidation charter in 1958. Metro might never have been resurrected if Nashville had not then set out on a process of annexation that brought tens of thousands of suburbanites under the city, obliging them to pay city taxes but without accompanying municipal services. As the suburban vote shifted to Metro, for fear of more annexations, the idea gained momentum and was finally approved by the voters in 1962.

A principal campaigner for the new form was the head of the old Davidson County government, Beverly Briley. When the two governments were finally merged in 1963, Briley became the first mayor of the metropolitan government—a position he still held in the early '70s. He artfully fused the two old governmental empires, in part by bringing in new top officials from elsewhere, so that it seemed neither local faction was winning out. The merger created a feeling of stability in local government, because it was much easier to assign responsibility for good or bad municipal services. Consolidation did not, as proponents had advertised it would, provide *less* expensive government. But it did slow down the rate of growth in taxes so that Nashville's effective tax rate, the highest in Tennessee before consolidation, slipped to the lowest within a few years as the cost of local government accelerated across the state. Combined administration of general government and the schools saved money for the taxpayers; a consolidated sewer system was pushed forward rapidly, thus stemming the tide of small, uneconomical water and sewer districts in suburban areas; and the Metro government was able to set aside hundreds of acres for parks and open space outside the old city borders before the subdividers and developers acquired all the vacant land.

One secret of Metro's success was the charter provision dividing the county into two tax districts, one the "urban services" area including the area of the old inner city and the other a "general services" district encompassing the whole county. The urban services district could set a higher tax rate appropriate for a densely populated area providing garbage collection, fire protection, storm sewers, heavy police protection, and the like. But all county residents and businesses had to pay taxes to the general services district, which was made responsible for general government functions, schools, libraries, parks, the court system, hospitals, welfare, and the human resources development services in general. Thus a rational taxing system was adopted, and because it was rational, it worked and helped gain constantly increasing public acceptance of Metro.* Within six years, polls showed that up to 90 percent of the people approved of the new government form. Local government officials from all over the country were visiting Nashville to see if it held a model for solving their own problems.

The Metro charter was criticized for providing a rather unwieldy 40-man council, but in practice the big body, with 35 members elected from separate districts, helped to offset the remoteness of a single county government by giving citizens local representatives they could turn to. The multidistrict system also guaranteed center-city blacks, who feared losing voting power, sev-

---

* Suburban residents, of course, complained at times about paying for services for the inner-city poor. Robert H. Horton, fiscal director in the Metro mayor's office, cited the example of people from the affluent areas saying, "We don't use General Hospital—why do we have to pay so much for it?" Horton's answer to them: "Who provides for your maid when she is sick? Do you buy her a Blue Cross policy?"

eral council seats. (The black population, 34 percent in the old city, slipped to 20 percent in Metro Nashville.) Some blacks were bitterly critical of the Metro government, complaining it had shown little concern when an interstate road sliced through heavily black north Nashville, splitting the community in half, wrecking a major portion of the black business district, and destroying homes. They charged that the Capitol Hill urban renewal project had uprooted many black families to make way for a commercial development. Mrs. Curlie McGruder, a black community leader, complained that "Metro always wants to dominate—it's not willing to come halfway." But Robert E. Lillard, a former black councilman who opposed Metro when it was first proposed, said he had come to favor it because of the efficiencies in eliminating dual school systems and dual law enforcement efforts. In a way, Metro has both enhanced and hindered black political power. In 1971 Lillard ran for vice mayor and lost by almost 30,000 votes, even though 28,000 whites joined 15,000 blacks in voting for him. Blacks would definitely have preferred retiring Briley as mayor that year, but when Briley ended up in a runoff with a virulent white busing foe, black voters provided the critical margin necessary for his reelection.

The fact of Metro made a real difference when federal judges began to order a broad program of school busing to achieve full integration. If the school districts of city and county had still been separate, it would have been much more difficult to order and enforce broad-scale busing. Unhappy with the situation, some whites were even moving their residences to neighboring counties while they continued to commute to jobs in Nashville.

Economically, Metro gave Nashville a strong forward impetus. "Prior to consolidation," Briley told a reporter for *Business Week*, "the business community was fed up. The downtown was dying and many of our leading businesses were preparing to leave. I believe there is a direct relation between Metro and the revitalization that downtown Nashville is experiencing." The Metro effect apparently was threefold—psychological (a general feeling of forward movement in the city), financial (because the cost of municipal services was spread countywide, investors in downtown Nashville were given the security of more stable tax rates than in many other cities), and functional (an easier government to deal with).

A very direct result of Metro, in fact, was the decision of one of Nashville's biggest employers, National Life and Accident Insurance Company, to stay in the city. Before consolidation, National Life had already bought land for a move away from the Nashville area. "We had a very bad political climate—two tax assessors, two equalization boards, two of everything. We were ready to move," the firm's president, William C. Weaver, Jr., recalled later. But when Metro was passed, National Life changed its mind and instead built a 31-story, $25 million headquarters in downtown Nashville.* That started a building spurt that resulted, in a few years, in new skyscraper

---

* An equally important factor in the company's decision to stay was a court-imposed requirement that the state government implement a property tax equalization. This deprived the firm of opportunity to deal with neighboring rural counties for favorable tax treatment for its headquarters.

buildings put up by the city's major banks and a dramatic downtown urban renewal project covering 10 square blocks. Work began in the late 1960s to clear away more than 100 deteriorating buildings and replace them with public and private office buildings, a convention hotel center, new streets and walkways. In effect, the whole core of the old center city was scooped away and replaced. Together with several other renewal projects, the downtown effort promised to alter forever the image of Nashville as a low-silhouetted, rather unkempt city of dingy two- and three-story brick buildings.

Nashville had, in fact, led all other Tennessee cities in urban renewal, starting with the pioneering Capitol Hill redevelopment project shortly after World War II. Capitol Hill, as a local business leader told me, "had been surrounded by one of the biggest, swingingest, piano and jukebox red light brothel districts in the United States." Military commanders had threatened to put Nashville off limits unless the red light district was closed. The houses themselves were shut down, but the old buildings, occupied mostly by poor blacks, remained an eyesore, and the decision was made to clear the whole mess away and create a proper setting for the handsome Grecian style Capitol and nearby state office buildings. It remained for the 1960s, however, to provide the right climate for renewal massive enough in scope to assure the city's future.

An even later innovation was the nation's first facility for burning garbage to create both steam for heating and cold water for air conditioning. The big thermal transfer plant opened in 1974 on a site not far from where the city began as Fort Nashborough. It was designed to receive half of the 720 tons of garbage picked up in the city each day and provide heating and air conditioning for 30 downtown buildings at 30 to 40 percent the cost of conventional fuel. Thus everyday garbage, which otherwise would have to be buried in sanitary landfills at great cost in manpower and land resources, would create power equivalent to 71 million kilowatt hours of electricity each year. Plans for the $16.5 million plant had begun in 1970, before the energy crisis was apparent in the U.S., but the plant's 1974 opening proved to be fortuitous indeed.

Nashville's position as a regional trade center is easily explained by its location in the heart of Middle Tennessee. It is the chief city of the Cumberland River, providing barge transportation via the Tennessee River to the Ohio and thence to the Mississippi. Three interstate routes (40, 65, and 24) intersect at Nashville, providing easy highway access to Midwestern, Eastern, and Deep South markets. Why the city has traditionally been a finance center of the Middle South is harder to explain, except the fact that it developed a number of extremely wealthy families which fostered insurance companies of national renown (National Life, Life and Casualty) and big banks that lent money in a generally capital-scarce region. "This is an old son-in-law town in which concentrations of wealth, power, and influence have come down through families," a chamber of commerce official said. John Siegenthaler, publisher of the Nashville *Tennessean*, reminded me of Rogers Caldwell, who started an investment banking firm in Nashville early in this century. Caldwell joined with Luke Lea, publisher of the *Tennessean*, and between 1915 and 1928 they developed a huge financial empire.* "Caldwell," Siegenthaler said, "was a bit of a sharp operator. But he was a financial genius. His motto was 'We Bank on the South.' In the crash, he went under and was indicted in Kentucky. Lea went to prison in North Carolina for bank fraud. But Caldwell's impact as an inventive financier has lasted, to the financial welfare of the Nashville area. Today there are still people in investment houses, insurance, or banking who were associated with Caldwell or whose daddies or fathers-in-law were."

Today diversity is the recurring theme of the Nashville economy. State government provides more than 8,000 jobs. There are many federal offices. There is a huge printing industry. The whole music scene is there (Opryland, Country Music Hall of Fame, and all the recording and publishing houses). One finds corporations as different as Genesco (with worldwide headquarters in Nashville), du Pont, Ford, and Avco. Entrepreneurs of every description are active. One even thought up the idea of a high-rise mausoleum and began to build it in the early 1970s—a 20-story structure, crypts seven-deep on each floor, space for 130,000 bodies. (The same number would require almost 200 acres of normal cemetery land.) The builder promised "the finest burial anywhere in the world—as fine as the Taj Mahal."

Then there is the whole nexus of religious-oriented activities that spawned another Nashville slogan, "the Protestant Vatican." Here one finds the headquarters of the big, powerful Southern Baptist Convention and its Board of Publications, the Board of Education of the Methodist Church and the Methodist Publishing House, the central offices of the Gideons, and the archives and library of the Disciples of Christ. The ultrafundamentalist and often intolerant Church of Christ treats Nashville as its little Jerusalem, though the sect lacks a central governing body. All of this adds up (especially when one counts religious publishing) to a tremendous amount of human and financial activity centered in Nashville and spreading chiefly through the famed Southern Bible Belt.

Dr. Emory S. Bucke, book editor of the United Methodist Church, said the Bible Belt was heaviest in South Carolina, Tennessee, Alabama, West Virginia, and Kentucky, with strong pockets in Georgia, Mississippi, and Virginia. (By contrast, he said, it was quite weak in Louisiana, and only moderately strong in North Carolina.) In descending order of influence, he listed the Church of Christ ("the loudest"), the Southern Baptists ("the largest—generally conservative but with some very forward looking leaders today"), the Southern Presbyterians, and then a plethora of little sects including such phenomena as the "Two Seed of the Spirit Predestinarian Baptists." East Tennessee is a citadel of the snake handlers, who sometimes die trying to prove that faith will immunize them against the reptiles' venom. Throughout the territory one finds faith healers and those who speak in tongues.

---

* The political machinations of Caldwell and Lea, who fleeced the state government of millions of dollars, were alluded to on page 298.

In practically any Protestant denomination, Dr. Bucke pointed out, the Southern branch is more conservative than its counterpart in the North. "The general rule is this: the more fundamentalist a group is, the more conservative it is on social issues." But as insularity breaks down, as television, TVA, interstate roads and new industries move in, the church hold on people's social values begins to fade. Prohibition dies a slow death, it gets harder and harder to stop the schools from teaching about evolution, dancing seems less evil than some sects used to say it was, and of course the old issue about the sinfulness of watching movies became a dead letter with the arrival of television. Yet the membership figures of several Dixie-based denominations, the rapidly growing Southern Baptists in particular, suggest that the essential faith remains a very vital part of the lives of the region's people, an anchor to windward in very unsettling times.

For all their organizational strength in Nashville, the Protestant churches have not controlled the community mores. Nashville is actually the most progressive of Tennessee cities, for which there are a variety of reasons. It has a large contingent of enlightened, progressive businessmen. The religious community is not as monolithically conservative as it might appear at first glance, because there are strong liberal elements among the Methodists and the socially attuned dioceses of the Roman Catholic and Episcopal Churches. Then there is the influence of the state labor movement, which has its headquarters in Nashville. To all of this one must add two other vital factors: Nashville's feudin' newspapers and its large university community.

I suggest the newspaper struggles as a reason for the progressive climate simply because the two dailies, the *Tennessean* and the *Banner*, have saved Nashville from the monotony of single viewpoint which deadens public debate in so many Southern cities and across the country. The two papers have shared production facilities, but until recently they detested each other so thoroughly that each used to black out news of the other's pet projects. Once there was a local dispute about daylight saving time, which the *Tennessean* favored and the *Banner* opposed. When the city voted to adopt daylight saving, the *Tennessean* set its clock outside the joint newspaper building ahead an hour. The *Banner*'s clock, on the other side of a back-to-back sign, obstinately stayed on standard time. All this was based in major part on the personal antagonisms of the families which owned and ran the two papers— the Evans family, owners of the *Tennessean*, and the Stahlman family, owners of the *Banner*. Fred Travis correctly depicted the papers as "the two last bastions of personal journalism."

The story on the *Banner* side went back to the years after the Civil War, when the Louisville & Nashville Railroad, anxious to have a mouthpiece to take its stand in a controversy over state bonds, established the paper and gave title to it to Major E. B. Stahlman. When the L & N finished its bond fight, it wanted to liquidate the paper, but Stahlman held on and became a major political figure in Tennessee, distinguishing himself—among other things—by allying himself with Boss Crump in opposing Austin Peay, one of Tennessee's most outstanding governors. Stahlman finally died in

1930 and passed on the paper to his grandson, James G. Stahlman, who was sole owner until he finally sold out to the Gannett chain in 1972. The *Banner* remained a fierce voice of Southern conservatism, backing local and state Democrats of that persuasion but pumping just as enthusiastically for Republican Presidential candidates,* including President Nixon in all his races and Barry Goldwater in 1964. The Gannett chain installed Wayne Sargent, a professional newspaperman and for many years veteran of work for the UPI, as its publisher, and the paper quickly calmed down its editorials and abolished a long string of taboos on news coverage. (Some disfavored families, for instance, had never been mentioned in news columns, while Stahlman's friends' achievements were written up in bold headlines.)

The *Tennessean* evolved from the merger of several papers and won special notoriety in the years that Luke Lea used it to milk the state government for funds. When Lea went to prison, the paper went into bankruptcy and was eventually acquired for $750,000 by Silliman Evans, Jr., a Texan with ties to politicos of that state who was able to engineer the deal through a big loan made through a Nashville bank by Texan Jesse Jones, head of the Reconstruction Finance Corporation in New Deal days.

Under Evans and his son Amon, who eventually took over in his stead, the *Tennessean* became a fiery liberal Democratic paper. It was Crump's fiercest enemy, and its circulation into the hamlets of Middle Tennessee helped make that region Crump's most hostile territory in elections. Some cynics questioned whether the Evans' liberalism was as sincere as it looked or really just opportunism. The idea of the Newspaper Guild organizing the *Tennessean* brought apoplectic reactions from the Evans family (and in fact it was never accomplished), and the story was told that when Silliman Evans once felt obliged to fire a liberal editorial writer, he privately said he had no regrets about firing that "radical s.o.b." but that he would have to hire someone equally liberal. "I'm running a liberal Democratic newspaper," he said. "I have to hire someone to write those editorials because I don't think that way myself." Amon Evans hired John Siegenthaler, a man out of a liberal Catholic background with true liberal feelings, as his editor. Siegenthaler, who was close to the Kennedys, was elevated to publisher in 1972, but the Evans family kept ultimate control. Among other things, the *Tennessean* can be credited with building up public support for the Metro concept in Nashville.

I might add that some of the most objective, reliable reporting anywhere about the South and its integration struggles of the past two decades has come from the Race Relations Center (formerly Southern Education Reporting Service), located on the edge of Nashville's George Peabody College. Established by a group of prescient Southern educators and journalists after the Supreme Court's 1954 school decision, the organization provided an amazingly accurate, continuing count on the process of school desegregation. Some described its reports, read by all sides, as a small miracle in "mili-

---

* There was one exception, in 1948, when the *Banner* proclaimed "in Dixieland we take our stand" for Thurmond and Wright.

tant objectivity." The organization had to close down operations, stopping publication of its periodic *Race Relations Reporter,* for several months in 1972, and its future foundation support remained unsure—even as it began to branch out into detailed coverage of Indian and Mexican-American rights developments and race questions in the Northern cities as well as the South. But the basic record it made of the South's second Reconstruction would be an historic treasure for centuries to come.

The Nashville tradition of excellence in higher education goes back to the years following the Civil War when three institutions, destined to play a vital role in the modern Southland, were formed. Vanderbilt University, founded in 1873 by the Southern Methodist Church and endowed by the eccentric Commodore Cornelius Vanderbilt and his family, gave the postwar South its first institution with an academic standard comparable to that of the better northern universities. Eventually Vanderbilt extricated itself from Methodist control, seeking an intellectual freedom that has remained a vital part of its tradition.

While Vanderbilt led the region in higher white education, Fisk University, founded in 1866 at the instigation of a Union officer, General Clinton B. Fisk, did the same thing for black Southerners. It was and has remained a relatively small institution dedicated to quality learning, and its graduates have included such preeminent black leaders as W. E. B. DuBois, probably the most celebrated scholar black America has produced; A. Maceo Walker, the millionaire Memphis banker and insurance executive; John Hope Franklin, chairman of the history department at the University of Chicago; and Frank Yerby, the successful novelist.

Meharry Medical College, founded in 1874 by one of five abolitionist brothers, is America's only privately sponsored, predominantly black medical school, and has filled the indispensable role of training more than half the Negro physicians and dentists in the country. Meharry never won a reputation for scientific distinction, but it pioneered—long before the concept was even considered elsewhere—in the field of community medicine, trying to reach all black Americans, wherever they lived, with decent medical care. By the 1970s eight out of ten of its graduates were practicing in urban or rural poverty areas.

In all, Nashville has 14 universities and colleges. Included are George Peabody College, a widely recognized teacher-training institution; Tennessee State University, a land-grant college established by the state government in 1912 to provide educational opportunities for Negroes; and a much newer but fast expanding branch of the University of Tennessee. Theoretically the two state-supported institutions, TSU and the UT branch, should be merged, a proposal which has triggered a complex court case and posed major sociological problems.

Each of the Nashville schools has been struggling in recent years over problems of finance and self-identity. Fisk, which sends two-thirds of its 200-odd graduates on to graduate or professional schools, has been challenged by militants to purge the whites on its faculty and become a *black* institution in every sense of the word. The idea is resisted by the administration and most of the students who want Fisk graduates equipped to excel in a biracial society. (As one student was quoted as saying, "You can't create power out of no power. You get power by being associated with power.") At Meharry, there has been a desperate scramble for funds alleviated only in very recent years as money-granting foundations and government agencies have discovered the relevance of the community medicine concept. And at Vanderbilt, Chancellor Alexander Heard had to face severe abuse from some parts of the community when riots broke out on nearby black college campuses after Stokely Carmichael was permitted to speak at Vanderbilt in 1967. Heard replied that the university existed "not to protect students from ideas but rather to expose them to ideas."

Heard, in fact, emerges as one of the most outstanding university administrators anywhere in the United States in the last several years. He is also a nationally influential figure as chairman of the board of trustees of the Ford Foundation. Born in Savannah, he still cultivates a soft Tidewater accent and gentle approach to problems which belie a top-notch mind, exceptional administrative talents, and dedication to racial integration.* He was so successful in keeping lines of communication open at Vanderbilt during the difficult years of the 1960s that the late Winthrop Rockefeller of Arkansas described him to me as a master of "preventive medicine on student unrest." Heard knew hundreds of students by name, for instance, and dealt with all in a cordial but not overly familiar fashion. He was one of the first college administrators to put students on the board of trustees. (The move was particularly welcome at Vanderbilt, whose board was threatened by hardening of the arteries by a rule giving lifetime status to any member who reached the age of 72.) In 1969 Columbia offered Heard its presidency. All segments of the Vanderbilt community—students, faculty, deans, alumni, and board members—urged him not to go, a rather unusual honor for any college president in those years. Heard finally turned down the Columbia offer, saying he thought he could do more at Vanderbilt to help solve "the unique important and tenacious problems of our biracial society."

A year later, in the wake of the Cambodian invasion and Kent State and Jackson State killings, President Nixon made Heard his adviser on campus problems. Heard bluntly told the President that the administration did not face a transitory "student crisis" but rather an outpouring of pent-up frustration and dissatisfaction in a student community that was assuming real self-identification, and power, within American society. Students, he told a President prone to see much human activity in the win or lose terms of the football field, did not think of the war in terms of winning or losing. They simply wanted to "stop the killing," Heard said. "Student behavior that to some seems 'unpatriotic,' " he added, "may be intended by the stu-

* A political scientist by trade, Heard had already distinguished himself before his selection as Vanderbilt's chancellor in 1963 through several major books, including *A Two Party South?* and *The Costs of Democracy.* The latter, a seminal work in the problem of American campaign financing, led to his appointment as a chairman of President Kennedy's commission on campaign spending.

dent as the highest form of patriotism." Many students, he warned the President, viewed the Kent and Jackson killings as an expression of increasingly repressive quality in the American system, a feeling exacerbated by "sledgehammer statements by public officials impugning the motives of dissent."

Heard believes that university centers, rather than isolated institutions of higher education, are "the shape of the future," and has said that the Nashville University Center, which provides for exchange of faculty, students, and resources among the city's colleges and universities, offers "the components for one of the important educational concentrations of the world."

One of the most stimulating sessions I had anywhere in preparation for these books was spent one Sunday morning with Heard in the sun-flooded solarium of the chancellor's beautiful estate on a wooded tract in Belle Meade. The United States, Heard said, faced a different order of crises from those in the past, a situation imposing much greater strains on the national decision making process. The American black, he said, had reached a stage in his aspirations in which he had thrown off fear and become ambitious and demanding, creating "a situation which is psychologically demanding for everybody." The method of protest against the Vietnam war, he suggested, presented a parallel situation of unprecedented challenge to American institutions—all coinciding with "the problems of hugeness, of a technological and dehumanized society." The result, he said, was "a sense of doubt about our ability to work out of our own problems—for the first time since the early 1930s, a vacant feeling in the stomach, a deep anxiety about the nation's future."

Heard proposed no heroic solutions for the national anxieties. He did stress the need for basic governmental reforms and for releasing the energies of business to work on social problems. And he laid great emphasis on the need for preserving a sense of community. "Consensus is still a good word. The problem of governing, both for cities and for universities, may be beyond hope unless we can work on shared assumptions of basic goals. If everyone is simply out for himself alone, the situation is almost impossible, because you can't govern by technique alone. We have to look for new ways to undergird the sense of community." In that connection, Heard suggested that my books on the states, while not skirting problems and failures, also be in part a list of the really meaningful *success* stories of present-day American society. It was good advice, and I have tried to follow it.

TVA

STILL OUR BEST MODEL?

MORE THAN A quarter century ago, only 14 years after the Tennessee Valley Authority had been spawned in the first blush of the New Deal, John Gunther wrote in *Inside U.S.A.* that "the TVA idea is the greatest single American invention of this century." Oddly enough, Gunther observed, TVA was more bewondered by foreigners than by Americans—a condition still true today. Gunther also listed the great advantages of TVA as America's first experiment in coordinated development of a great natural region. It had superb leadership, it had autonomy that saved it from the depressing hand of a distant bureaucracy, it was decentralized—reaching the people where they really lived—it made its appointments exclusively on the basis of merit rather than politics, and while it was a public agency deeply involved in the economy, it functioned without prejudice to private enterprise.

Amazingly, practically all Gunther said about TVA is still true today. For while most of the personalities and political machinations Gunther wrote about have now passed into history, TVA remains. It is not just a fossil of the New Deal but rather an active organism, a generator of fresh ideas, and—with some exceptions of which we will take note—a beneficent influence for the people of the Tennessee Valley and millions beyond it.

Even TVA's present-day critics revere its past. Author Harry M. Caudill observed:

TVA took over the valley when it was washed down to bedrock. The saddest spectacle I ever saw in my life was the Tennessee Valley when I crossed it as a boy with my dad. It was just worn out; it looked desolated and hopeless. Then TVA came in, and for years and years, it gave away loads of fertilizer to anyone who'd come and get it. They got seedling trees and then persuaded people to plant them. Now they've filled in those ugly gullies, and the eroded hills have been reclaimed and made green and fertile once again. And the dams tamed that turbulent river, and capital came in, and it wasn't a decade after TVA started that the valley of the Tennessee was the showplace of the nation.

From the start, TVA generated controversy. It cut across zones as sensitive as states' rights, the sanctity of private property, political patronage, and the utilities industry. Vetoing a forerunner bill to TVA in 1931, President Herbert Hoover called the idea "the negation of the ideals upon which our civilization is based." Two years later, during Franklin D. Roosevelt's "first hundred days," the TVA Act did indeed become law. For years afterwards, however, business spokesmen attacked TVA as a pernicious experiment in domestic socialism. Finally they gave up because private enterprise was benefiting so much from cheap electricity and other TVA-created opportunities.

Now, in a day when the perils to the ecosystem from man's helter-skelter and polluting activity is recognized as never before, TVA stands out as the finest (and really the only) program of integrated regional planning and development ever undertaken in this country.

But still, it remains controversial. Most of the opposition now comes from the environmentalists, who look to the agency's massive reliance on coal for its many steam generating plants and accuse TVA of becoming the prime despoiler of the Appalachian landscape. Critics also say TVA has become a diehard builder of marginal dams to keep its engineering staff busy and assert that its power rates are tipped too far to the advantage of the Atomic Energy Commission and private industry. (In 1973 the rates averaged 5.86 cents per kilowatt hour for the AEC, 6.31 to industry, and 7.18 to the rural and municipal cooperatives which distribute TVA electricity to homes and other nonindustrial consumers.) Perhaps everyone would agree with the late Gordon Clapp, a TVA director, who said "We're controversial because we're consequential."

The Early Years: Fortune Smiles on the Infant Child

The development of the great Tennessee, America's fifth largest river, had been discussed almost from the time the first settlers ventured west of the Appalachians to discover the river's prime location—and its treachery. On its southern loop, the Tennessee came close to cities like Atlanta and Birmingham, which were to become population centers of the South; on the north, it emptied into the Ohio River, forming a natural water link to the nation's developing heartland. But at low water there were places where the river had a depth of no more than a foot or two; the

Chattanooga area offered special navigational hazards, and near Muscle Shoals, in Alabama, there was a shallow stretch, dotted with boulders, where the river fell 130 feet in a distance of only 37 miles. During World War I the potential for multipurpose development of the Tennessee was demonstrated when the government started to build Wilson Dam at Muscle Shoals, with a lock providing free movement of river traffic and a power house to generate electricity for use in making nitrate for explosives in a nearby plant built by the government at a cost of nearly $100 million. After the war, many bills were introduced in Congress to sell the nitrate plant. One which passed the House would have released it to Henry Ford for $5 million.

Ironically, it was not any member of Congress from Tennessee or Alabama who stepped in to block the giveaway of the nitrate plant or who first saw the possibilities for coordinated development of the entire Tennessee Valley. Instead it was a prairie Populist, Senator William George Norris of Nebraska, who became the father of the Tennessee Valley Authority. Norris, a bitter enemy of monopolies and vested private interests, was determined that the hydroelectric potential of the valley—which the private utilities could not and would not develop on a coordinated basis—would not be handed to them on a piecemeal basis. He also wanted the Tennessee Valley's power potential to be developed on a public basis so that there would be a yardstick to measure the fairness of rates charged by the private power companies around the nation.

With Roosevelt elected President and private business thoroughly discredited through the Depression experience, Norris had his opportunity. He and FDR decided on the broadest conceivable charter for TVA—an authority that would not only produce low-cost electricity but be responsible for flood control, soil conservation, reforestation, industrial diversification, improved navigation, and demonstration farming with cheap fertilizer. The sweeping mandate was spelled out in Roosevelt's message to Congress submitting the proposed legislation, an authority "charged with the broadest duty of planning for the proper use, conservation, and development of the natural resources of the Tennessee River drainage basin." It would be a corporation "clothed with the power of government but possessed of the flexibility and initiative of a private enterprise." And its headquarters would be placed in the region, rather than Washington, to make it easier to work with state and local governments, farmers, and businessmen.

Norris had been worried that the old phobia about "socialism" might sink the TVA bill, and he asked FDR, "What are you going to say when they ask you the political philosophy behind TVA?" Roosevelt jauntily replied, "I'll tell them it's neither fish nor fowl, but whatever it is, it will taste awfully good to the people of the Tennessee Valley."

Roosevelt's hope was that TVA would provide a model for regional development in America. But there has yet to be a second TVA, and it may be that the prototype was only launched—and kept alive—by the fortuitous timing of New Deal days and the absolutely exceptional leadership which it enjoyed during its first, tumultuous years. There was Arthur E. Morgan,

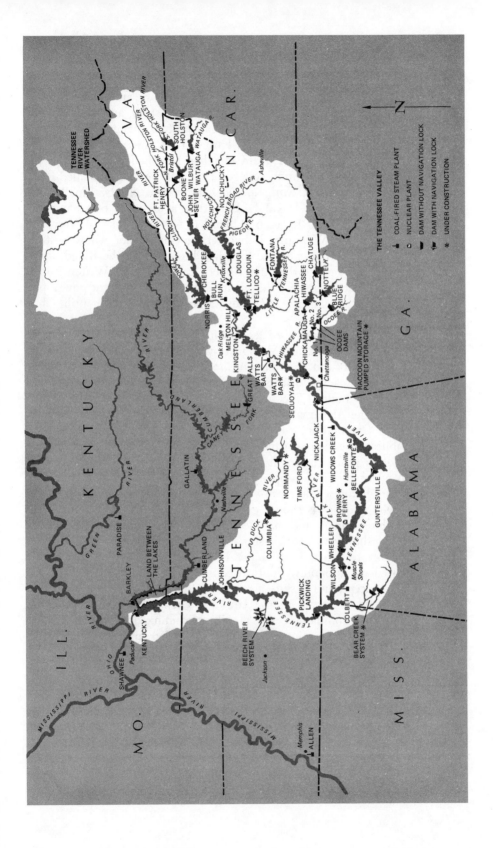

TENNESSEE
RIVER
WATERSHED

THE TENNESSEE VALLEY

- COAL-FIRED STEAM PLANT
- NUCLEAR PLANT
- DAM WITHOUT NAVIGATION LOCK
- DAM WITH NAVIGATION LOCK
- ✳ UNDER CONSTRUCTION

N

ILL.

KENTUCKY

VA.

N. CAR.

MO.

TENNESSEE

MISS.

ALABAMA

GA.

MISSISSIPPI RIVER

OHIO RIVER

GREEN RIVER

CUMBERLAND RIVER

TENNESSEE RIVER

CLINCH RIVER

POWELL RIVER

HOLSTON RIVER

FT. PATRICK HENRY
N. FORK HOLSTON RIVER
S. FORK HOLSTON RIVER
SOUTH HOLSTON

Bristol

BOONE
JOHN
WILBUR
SEVIER WATAUGA
WATAUGA

NOLICHUCKY
NOLICHUCKY R.
FRENCH BROAD RIVER
Asheville
PIGEON R.

CHEROKEE
BULL RUN
Knoxville
DOUGLAS
NORRIS
FT. LOUDOUN
TELLICO ✳
LITTLE TENNESSEE R.
FONTANA

Oak Ridge
MELTON HILL
KINGSTON
GREAT FALLS
WATTS BAR
WATTS BAR ✳

HIWASSEE R.
APALACHIA
HIWASSEE
CHATUGE
NOTTELY
BLUE RIDGE
No. 2
No. 3
OCOEE R.
OCOEE DAMS

Chattanooga

RACCOON MOUNTAIN
PUMPED STORAGE ✳

SEQUOYAH ✳

Shawnee

Paducah

SHAWNEE

Kentucky

LAND BETWEEN THE LAKES

BARKLEY

PARADISE

Nashville

GALLATIN

JOHNSONVILLE

CUMBERLAND RIVER
CANEY FORK
DUCK RIVER
ELK RIVER

NORMANDY ✳

COLUMBIA ✳

TIMS FORD

NICKAJACK
WIDOWS CREEK
Huntsville
BROWNS ✳
FERRY

WHEELER
WILSON
Muscle Shoals
COLBERT

PICKWICK LANDING

BEECH RIVER SYSTEM

Jackson

KENTUCKY

BEAR CREEK SYSTEM ✳

BELLEFONTE ✳

GUNTERSVILLE

Memphis

ALLEN

CHICKAMAUGA

TVA's controversial first board chairman, a talented hydraulic engineer who directed the staff of top-notch engineers TVA was able to hire to design its dams during the Depression years. Morgan was also a dreamer, who thought in terms of coordinated regional planning, new industries, and new communities for the people. And he kept political appointees out of TVA, resisting even the blandishments of a James A. Farley. Then there was Harcourt A. Morgan, another original TVA board member, who had been dean of the University of Tennessee's strong college of agriculture and propelled TVA forward, through extension work, in soil conservation efforts. Finally, and most important, there was David E. Lilienthal, a founding board member and chairman from 1941 to 1946. Lilienthal was a brilliant lawyer and former member of the Wisconsin Public Service Commission whose hostility to the corporate monopolies of the time had brought him the friendship of such men as Felix Frankfurter and Robert LaFollette, Jr. Writer Robert Sherrill has described him as "the giant of the TVA's electric-power program, a master at waging the intricate warfare of the electric utility business."

TVA needed that quality of leadership, because every effort was made to strangle the infant. During TVA's first five years, private power companies instituted 57 lawsuits and 26 injunctions to stop the agency from developing its hydroelectric capacity, distributing the electricity once the dams and powerhouses were built. (The most celebrated case of all was lodged by stockholders of the Alabama Power Company, a holding of Commonwealth and Southern Corporation, whose head, Wendell Willkie, was to be the 1940 Republican Presidential candidate.) TVA won all those court battles, but it had other problems. In the valley, it had to fight the resistance of a very independent breed of people worried about a big federal agency controlling their destiny. There was even opposition from religious fundamentalists who said floods should go unhindered, because they were God's way of punishing sinners, and that electricity and modern conveniences were the "works of the devil." In Washington, Interior Secretary Harold Ickes tried repeatedly to bring TVA under his department, a step that would have destroyed its autonomy. Political conservatives continued to fight the whole TVA concept, and despite a respite in that opposition during World War II, it broke out again in the late '40s when TVA wanted to build steam plants to accommodate the rapidly expanding demand for electric power. The private power interests almost succeeded in truncating TVA's growth at that point, but TVA won a close battle in Congress.

President Eisenhower was no friend of TVA. During the 1952 campaign he had felt constrained to make a carefully hedged commitment of support, but the whole idea of socialized power did not sit well with him. In an early Cabinet meeting, Ike exclaimed: "By God, if ever we could do it, before we leave here, I'd like to sell the whole thing, but I suppose we can't go that far." Eisenhower did propose to cut TVA's budget to the bare bones, eliminating money for everything but power and basic water control. But Alabama's Senator Lister Hill saved the authority from emasculation by restoring nonpower developmental funds in a crucial Senate vote.

Not long after that the Dixon-Yates scandal broke wide open—an under-the-table effort of the Eisenhower administration to force TVA to buy power from private utilities to meet the expanding demands in its territory. The clear intent was to create a precedent for reentry of the private utilities into the Tennessee Valley market area. Dixon-Yates became too much of an embarrassment for Eisenhower and was dropped.

In the later Eisenhower years, when congressional funds for new steam plants were not forthcoming, TVA's friends in Congress waged a hard fight for a self-financing plan which would permit the authority to finance new power facilities on Wall Street, like any private utility. The bill passed Congress—albeit at the price of an amendment, backed by Congressmen friendly to the private utilities, which forbade expansion of the geographic area served by TVA electricity. President Eisenhower threatened to veto the bill but was dissuaded after a private meeting with the man he had selected to be chairman of the TVA board, Herbert D. Vogel. Eisenhower had picked Vogel, a brigadier general in the Army Corps of Engineers, with the expectation that Vogel would either dismantle the agency or whittle it down to size. But Vogel, after learning about TVA's activities and potential, had become an enthusiastic backer of the agency—"more Catholic than the Pope." Vogel helped persuade Eisenhower to sign the self-financing bill, and since then TVA's growth has never been seriously challenged in Washington.

Costs and Benefits

An assessment of TVA's meaning for the valley's people must be as multifaceted as the agency itself. In gross economic terms, the impact has been nothing short of stupendous. Before TVA, the Tennessee Valley was the country's most poverty-stricken river basin. In 1933, the year Congress created the authority, the per capita income in the area was $168 a year, a mere 45 percent of the national average. Fifteen of the 201 TVA area counties did not have a single manufacturing plant. Underemployment and unemployment were chronic; there were counties in which more than half the people were on relief. Many people, Arthur Morgan noted when he first arrived in the valley, were "on the verge of starvation." The people were so desperate for jobs that 38,000 men turned out for TVA job examinations the first year, and 98,000 the second.

Within 20 years, TVA had given employment in dam building and service jobs to more than 200,000 men and women. When there was no town near a dam site, TVA sometimes built one. The most famous of these was Norris, the town named after the Senator; laid out with tree-lined streets and a town center and commons reminiscent of England, it provided not only decent housing but health care, library facilities, adequate schools, and recreation facilities—amenities that many rural valley people had never known before.

By the early 1970s, the per capita income in the 201 Tennessee Valley counties had increased 20 times and was up to 75 percent of the United

States average. The level was not much different from that of the rest of the South, but one has to consider what might have happened without TVA. Former TVA Director Frank Smith, the onetime Mississippi Congressman, points out that in 1933 southeastern Kentucky had much in common with East Tennessee. Both were Appalachian country grubbing very little out of coal, timber, and tobacco. Southeastern Kentucky's per capita income was 36 percent of the national average, East Tennessee's 45 percent. By 1970, a generation later, southeastern Kentucky remained impoverished with incomes only 40 percent of the U.S. average, but in East Tennessee the figure was up to 65 percent. Since 1940, practically all the counties of southeastern Kentucky have suffered a continuous, heavy population loss. In East Tennessee, all but a handful have gained population. Neither in East Tennessee nor in the valley as a whole has population increase come near to the annual average, and only a strong birth rate has outbalanced the heavy outmigration—especially of farmers displaced from the land. But outmigration from the valley, which hit a peak of 701,000 between 1950 and 1960, tapered off in the early '60s and a slight inmigration has been recorded in the last few years. From 6.7 million in 1970, the population in the 201-county Tennessee Valley region is projected to grow steadily to just under 10 million in the year 2000.*

TVA has never been a typical pork barrel operation. The federal government has spent $1.4 billion on the authority's power system, but practically all of it will eventually be repaid to the Treasury, with interest.† In principal or interest, payments of more than $1 billion have already been made, with another $815 million, plus interest, due before the books are presumably cleared in the year 2014. There have been federal appropriations, since 1933, of $1.25 billion for TVA's non-power projects. But overall, the Tennessee Valley has not been treated with special munificence by Washington. Federal expenditures for all purposes in the valley between 1934 and 1970 were $11,000 per person, compared to a national average of $16,800 per person.

Dams and the Land

Physically, the greatest impact of TVA on the valley was the monumental series of dams to control the flow of the river over the 1,000-odd

---

* The region is defined as the 125 counties within the Tennessee River watershed, plus 76 other counties in which TVA power is distributed by locally owned municipal and cooperative electric systems. The reversal of the valley's population outflow in the 1960s, incidentally, may be due to the fact that it has a low Negro population. Other Southern areas with few blacks, such as the Ozark-Ouachita upland region centered in Arkansas, also showed remarkable population stability in the 1960s, without the benefit of a TVA.

† In 1974, however, TVA's friends in Congress began pushing for a bill permitting TVA to deduct the total cost of air and water pollution control facilities for its power plants from its annual payment to the Treasury—in other words, a 100 percent subsidy that might amount to $150 million a year. The bill was opposed by the Treasury Department, whose general counsel commented: "Unavoidably, [the bill's] effect would be to shift to the general public expenses which otherwise would be borne by consumers of electricity produced by the TVA, and we have to regard this as an undesirable precedent for federal absorption of pollution controls generally."

miles of water between the valley's easternmost brooks, which are actually in Virginia, to Paducah, Kentucky, where the Tennessee empties into the Ohio River. The authority pioneered in building the first system of multiple-use dams and locks that created a navigable waterway all the way from Knoxville to the Ohio. In addition, high dams were built on the major tributaries of the upper valley to control flooding and provide the bulk of the hydroelectric power. In all, there are 34 dams controlled by TVA (including six actually owned by the Aluminum Corporation of America). Behind them are more than 600,000 acres in reservoirs so vast they have been nicknamed "the Great Lakes of the South." Most of the dams were built in the early years of TVA, rushed to completion to meet wartime electricity demands in the 1940s. The Tennessee is in effect "dammed out"; while some new dams are now under construction or contemplated on the tributaries, they will not increase the water base or hydroelectric capacity significantly.

TVA omits the point in all its literature, but there was an immense social cost in the dam building. To make way for the dams and reservoirs, thousands of families farming the riverbottoms—the richest and most productive land in the valley—were forced to give up their land. Some got excellent land in trade, but many ended up with hill country sites, much of it with ledge rock outcroppings, a lot still covered by timber. The riverbottom farmers had no idea what they faced in terms of land erosion problems on their new land, and most lacked the skills to cope with the new situation. The displacement process also broke up the riverbottom settlements, each with its own ties of blood and community. Small wonder that when the sharp TVA lawyers arrived and told the people they had to move, many of them just sat down and wept. TVA technical help in farming their new lands eventually alleviated some of the sorrow. But the experience left indelible scars in people's attitude toward TVA and government in general.

The hydroelectric dams, extolled in TVA's early years as *the* magic key to cheap electricity and better lives, had a remarkably short life as the center of the TVA system. Starting in World War II, steam power generating plants were added to the system so rapidly that by 1955 they had surpassed the hydro dams as the chief source of TVA power. The hydro share of TVA's electricity output was down to 20 percent by the start of the 1970s and due to dip to 15 percent by the early 1980s. Already, hydro capacity is used mainly for reserve power in peak demand periods.

Nevertheless, the dams brought electricity to the Tennessee Valley when most of its homes were still mired in the kerosene era. And the other benefits from their construction have been immense. Consider navigation, for example. In 1933, before TVA, about a million tons of mostly local shipments moved along the river. But by the early '70s the figure was approaching 30 million tons a year, most of it interregional movements to ports along the 21-state waterway system of mid-America which connects with the Tennessee. Each year, for instance, millions of tons of Tennessee coal move out of the region, while millions of tons of grain—the base of the Middle

South's booming poultry and beef industry—move in. The brawny tow-boats, which can move a string of barges the size of a city block, offer the cheapest form of commercial shipping and also tend to depress, through competition, the rates offered by railroads and truckers. And without the dams, one would certainly not see any semblance of the $2.1 billion worth of industrial plants, providing jobs for some 40,000 people in the chemical and metal and other industries, which have been built along the Tennessee waterway. For who would have made that investment on a flood plain of a scarcely navigable river?

Flood control has been one of TVA's greatest boons. The cumulative flood damages averted because TVA dams were in place have now exceeded $1 billion in the Tennessee Valley and the lower Ohio and Mississippi River basins. The city of Chattanooga, situated on a low flood plain, has benefited especially. In the past it suffered many floods, including one in 1867 that went 28 feet above flood stage. In the early spring of 1973 there was another flood, 22 feet above flood stage, that resulted in $35 million damage at Chattanooga. But without the TVA dams the damage to the city would have come to a staggering half billion dollars.

Then one has to consider the fact that the two most dynamic centers of government spending in the Tennessee Valley—the Oak Ridge National Laboratory in East Tennessee and the Redstone Arsenal and Marshall Space Flight Center in Alabama's Huntsville—are only where they are today because the government chose those sites for major World War II installations, cheap TVA power being a major point in the decisions. The influx of scientists in military, atomic, and space technology has made the valley very much part of the mainstream of American life in the past several decades and tangentially creates the opportunity for the valley's people to participate in the work and profits of a future post-industrial era.

TVA's man-made lakes have been a boon to recreation—a word not even mentioned in the original TVA Act, because no one thought of it in those hard times. The reservoirs have become immensely popular places for boating, fishing, and swimming. TVA built demonstration parks, donated stretches of shoreline to local governments for parks, and put the TVA states in the forefront of public recreation in the United States. Recreation has meant dollars for the local economy—in fact, $350 million has been invested by private interests and public agencies other than TVA in recreation facilities and improvements on TVA lakeshores.

There had been predictions that TVA's reservoirs would be biological deserts, but quite the opposite occurred. The reservoirs now teem with fish—at least 50 times as many as the river held before TVA. Each year sport fishermen catch some 15 million pounds of bass, crappie, walleye, and other game fish, and commercial fishermen take another 3,500 tons of such rough fish as catfish and carp. TVA's biologists work to increase the fish population by various techniques—but not, TVA officials insist, by crude "put and take" operations for the benefit of sportsmen. Another point is that waterfowl, almost nonexistent in the valley 40 years ago, now abound.

Some 400,000 ducks and geese, for instance, summer on the high plains and then come to refuge and management areas on the shores of TVA's reservoirs.

TVA's dams helped to revolutionize the valley's agriculture in two ways. First, the authority *cared* about getting electricity, and cheap electricity at that, to every isolated farmstead in the region. This was a task the private utilities, who preferred to service the high-density, profitable urban centers, had previously scorned, but TVA took the job seriously. The lights began to flicker on along once remote ridges and valleys, humanizing the life of the farmer's wife and providing him with many helps in his daily work. When TVA began, only one in 28 farms had electricity; today the job is virtually completed.

Before TVA, the valley's farmers had concentrated on row crops, a practice that led to terrible washouts and gullies on hilly land. A million acres of valley were idle and eroding, and the average farm earned only $300 a year. But when TVA came along, it took over the government chemical plants that had been built at Muscle Shoals to produce munitions, converting them into a national fertilizer development center. Using TVA power, the plant began to produce highly concentrated phosphates and nitrates. TVA teamed up with state agricultural colleges and their county agents to spread the word of fertilizer use and its possibilities throughout the valley. The result today is stunning: in place of the old row crops, the hills and meadows are thick with grass. Livestock grazes on pastures established with the help of fertilizer and lime, and the grains come in by barge from the Midwest. Production per man hour on the farms has increased 30 times over; the valley's farm products now have a value of $1 billion a year.* Muscle Shoals remains the country's only full-scale center for fertilizer research, sharing its findings in constantly improved methods both with valley farmers and agricultural circles across the country. Among other things, the TVA facility is working on forest fertilization, greenhouse production, products with higher nutrient content, and new nitrogen fertilizers that pose less hazard of stream pollution.

Alongside its work in agriculture, TVA has worked a minor miracle in forestry. It supplied hundreds of millions of seedlings which farmers and other owners used to cover the guttered mountainsides of yesteryear, and there is simply no comparison between the quality of the valley's forests now and in 1934. Through educational efforts and intensive forest control programs, the authority has virtually eliminated the threat of major forest fires. (The valley's woodlands had been like a tinderbox in pre-TVA days, due to exploitive logging and people's burning of their own land to get forage for livestock.) The average value of an acre of timber in the valley has risen

* TVA believes the value of farm products could be tripled again if valley farmers would exploit already proven farm innovations. The authority has experimental "resource management" and "rapid adjustment" programs for farmers who want to move ahead rapidly. The programs require farmers to follow very rigidly defined techniques on their land, a hard step for strong-willed and independent valley people to take. But neighboring farmers are learning from the positive results of the few hundred farmers who have participated.

from $6 to $76; the volume of annual timber production has about doubled; yet with the improved quality of the forests, the Tennessee Valley is now growing more wood each year than it harvests. There is a work force of 50,000 people directly related to wood products in the valley.

The Power System and the Coal Controversy

If George Norris were alive today, he would probably be delighted to see how TVA's "yardstick" function in measuring reasonable electricity rates has helped to depress power costs for consumers across the nation. He would surely have been gratified to see how, in the 1960s, TVA publicized identical bids and thus put an end to a price-fixing conspiracy by the manufacturers of electrical machinery. In his lifetime he had seen how the model of cooperatives distributing TVA power had helped to launch the Rural Electrification Administration. But viewing the America of the 1970s, Norris might be a little appalled to see how the TVA, his creation, had become in the view of some critics "just another big, aggrandizing utility."

"Big" is certainly an appropriate word for the TVA power system. In fact, the authority's 22 million kilowatts of installed generating capacity make it the largest system in the United States, half again as large as the runner-up, the Southern Company. TVA now generates about 100 billion kilowatt-hours a year, compared to about 1.5 billion in 1933. The power is sold directly to some large industries and government installations like the Oak Ridge Atomic Energy Commission facilities, and then indirectly through 160 local electric systems to more than two million consumers. The authority's power revenues are climbing rapidly toward three-quarters of a billion dollars annually.

The residential power users of the Tennessee Valley have every reason to be delighted. In the early 1930s they were paying over 5½ cents a kilowatt-hour, but with the advent of TVA the rates in the valley plummeted to less than a penny an hour during the 1960s. Even with a 50 percent increase since the mid-1960s, the TVA residential rate is still only one quarter what it was in 1933, and not much more than half the national average.* TVA figures, for instance, that the annual bill for an all-electric home in the valley (24,000 kilowatt-hours) at only $292, or not quite $25 a month.

As soon as TVA went into operation in the '30s—in some cases even before—utilities in adjoining areas of the Mid-South began to cut their rates, fearful that socialized power might gobble them up. The rates of the neigh-

---

* TVA's price increases of recent years stem from escalating coal prices, interest on the massive capital needed for expansion, and heavy outlays of pollution-control equipment. Its rates are now well above those of regional authorities mainly dependent on water power, such as the Bonneville Power Authority in the Northwest. TVA power consumers, accustomed to the authority's dirt-cheap prices, began to complain in the early '70s. The unrest was especially high among industrial users, whose rates were hiked 69 percent between 1967 and 1973. Although TVA was still selling electricity to industries at rates far below the national average, a couple of phosphate and aluminum plants, which consume massive amounts of electricity, actually fled the valley.

boring utilities are still well below national averages (a fact, some cynics suggest, that might not be entirely coincidental). Traditionally, private utilities have complained that TVA has an automatic leg up on them because it pays no federal taxes, as private utilities must on their profits. If they wished, of course, the "investor-owned" utilities could emulate TVA by plowing a much larger share of their profits back into their systems.

The reason TVA can produce electricity so cheaply, it would appear, is that it has had extremely talented and dedicated leaders in its power division (a far cry from the inefficient bureaucratic ways said to be part and parcel of "socialistic" enterprises), and also that the authority has had the courage, and the financial capacity, to pioneer in larger and larger, and thus more economic, generating units. When the valley's hydro capacity reached its limits in the '40s and '50s, TVA overcame political opposition to move strongly into steam generation. In the late 1960s the authority decided that practically all its future growth should be in nuclear plants and began construction of a 3.5 million-kilowatt nuclear plant at Browns Ferry in Alabama and the 2.4 million-kilowatt Sequoyah atomic facility near Chattanooga. Then, in 1972, the Atomic Energy Commission announced that the United States' first large-scale breeder reactor demonstration power plant would be built on the TVA system near Oak Ridge.* The breeder reactor holds out special hope for solving long-term energy problems because it is expected to produce more nuclear fuel than it consumes, thus extending the life of economically recoverable uranium for centuries. In addition, light water reactors capture only some 2 percent of the energy available in uranium, while the breeder reactor is expected to capture 60 to 80 percent. The breeder will also pose fewer problems with thermal pollution, because its thermal efficiency will be higher.

By 1982, according to TVA's projections, the system's generating capacity will have risen to about 41 million kilowatts, with 15 million of that figure furnished by nuclear plants. Some 6 million kilowatts will be furnished by hydro plants, slightly above the present figure. But the bulk of generating capacity will remain in coal-powered steam generating plants—the bane and blessing, and the principal point of controversy, surrounding TVA in our day.

The critics' case centers on the damage done to the green hills of Appalachia through strip mining for coal. From a base of about 1 million tons in the early 1950s, TVA's coal consumption has risen to some 35 million tons a year in the 1970s—a total of some 725 carloads of coal *each day*. TVA has thus become the largest consumer of coal in the United States, absorbing about 5.5 percent of the national production. About half the amount it uses comes from underground mining, a process that can raise serious problems with unsightly slag heaps and acid drainage. The other half comes from

* The pilot breeder reactor will be built jointly by TVA and the Commonwealth Edison Company of Chicago, under a unique financing arrangement that involves support of the Atomic Energy Commission and the nation's electric utility industry—not only public power groups but also the private power companies, TVA's old enemies. The total price was expected to be about $700 million.

strip mining, an even more destructive process of blasting, gouging, scraping, and quarrying that leaves an indelible mark on the natural landscape. In the words of West Virginia's Congressman Ken Hechler,

George Norris dreamed of a Tennessee Valley Authority that would produce public power and provide unified planning for an entire river basin, so that the soil, forests, hillsides, and streams would be protected for future generations. [Those dreams] are being shattered as the hills of Kentucky and Tennessee are gouged by strip miners to satisfy the insatiable thirst of the Tennessee Valley Authority's steam plants for coal. In particular, the Cumberland Mountains of eastern Kentucky are being devastated by the escalating demands of TVA for strip-mined coal. TVA, the nation's biggest producer of electricity, is turning its back on one of its original objectives—to preserve the land—in order to generate vast quantities of power.

The charge that TVA is despoiling the landscape of Kentucky—in areas mostly outside of the Tennessee Valley, and thus receiving few benefits in return from the authority—seems especially valid. Almost 70 percent of TVA's coal comes from the fields of western and eastern Kentucky, with the worst ecologic damage inflicted in the mountainous east. Silted and poisoned streams, unsightly "headwalls," and massive slides from thousands of acres of "orphan mines" still dot the eastern Kentucky landscape, as well as parts of East Tennessee itself. Many of the scars will be visible for centuries to come.

TVA started using strip-mined coal in the early 1940s, and for years afterward reclamation was essentially ignored. The agency was, in fact, responsible for the creation of more than 20,000 acres of "orphan" strip mines. Imbued still with the cheap-power psychology of its early days, TVA drove such hard bargains with its coal suppliers that the companies had every incentive to shift from underground to the more destructive method of strip mining, and no funds left for reclamation even if their hearts had been softened to the fate of the land. In 1963, at the same time that TVA Chairman Aubrey J. Wagner was telling the press that "cheap TVA power was vital to the whole Appalachian region," there were reports of parts of whole hamlets in eastern Kentucky being inundated by mud slides caused by strip mines.

In the words of TVA's own former director, Frank E. Smith, the authority "was an environmental delinquent in not establishing until 1965 a reclamation provision in its contracts with suppliers of strip-mine coal." Though claiming that more than 16,000 acres were "reclaimed" in the next half decade through that mechanism, TVA implicitly admitted the insufficiency of the 1965 reclamation provisions by adding strengthening provisions, taking out several loopholes, and providing for tighter enforcement, in 1968, 1970, and 1971. The amendments were much more specific about what lands might be strip-mined and exactly how reclamation should be carried out; they also provided a 2 percent holdback in the agency's contract payments to a supplier, payable only with completion of the required reclamation work. Instead of putting the reclamation enforcement in the hands of its power division, TVA assigned that responsibility to a division with a different constituency—forestry, fisheries, and wildlife. Dr. Thomas H. Ripley, director of the latter division, told me "we are power's conscience in seeing that reclamation is carried out. We delete whole mountains from stripping for aesthetic reasons or because of danger to the local streams. In several cases, where our inspectors have found violations, we have suspended deliveries or stopped mining altogether. We're not window dressing." Ripley also insisted that the TVA board had been "completely responsive" to the proposals of the forestry and wildlife environmentalists, even to the extent of taking adverse action with large suppliers that could negatively affect coal supplies, and thus the cost of power.

To those who believe that strip-mining, especially in mountain territory, is of necessity so ruinous that it should never be permitted, TVA's reassurances have a hollow sound. TVA has such an omnivorous hunger for coal, they argue, that the agency sometimes negotiates short-term coal purchases under conditions that make reclamation controls problematic at best. The contour line in the mountains, critics say, can never be restored to its prior condition.* The terrain is too steep, they say, to copy the European reclamation method of carefully separating the strata (topsoil, subsoil, rock, and slate) and then putting them carefully back into place after extraction of the coal, with ample fertilization and planting of the topsoil as a last step. In any event, TVA says the topsoil layer in Appalachia is too thin for separation, so strip mining is permitted on hills with a slope of up to 28 degrees; an effort is made to contain the dug-up overburden so that it will not slide down the slopes; sedimentation basins are required to cut down on the runoff of sediment into the streams; and seeds and trees must be planted on the exposed, rocky "soil" that is left. The technology is still quite crude, as TVA's forestry division implicitly acknowledged in a 1972 report that urged application of engineering skills to a whole range of unsolved problems—appropriate handling of the spoil material, analysis of the overburden to realize maximum reclamation success, better water control during and after strip operations, and improved planting methods, to name a few. Somewhat belatedly, the TVA working paper also said the authority should study the impact of strip-mining on people and their communities.

Officially, TVA still maintains the "let George do it" position on strip-mining reclamation and control which it adopted in the early 1960s. The authority argues that standards for regulation of the mining, including supervision of reclamation work, should be set by the state or federal governments, and it has fiercely opposed proposals that all strip-mining operations must return the land to its original contours. TVA fears such a provision would virtually eliminate strip-mining in central Appalachia at the very time when it is having difficulty getting enough coal to feed all its steam-generating plants. (TVA officials argue that leveling off of very hilly areas may be beneficial, allowing future housing or industries; the environmentalists, pre-

---

* The steep grades are one reason for this. Another is that uprooting of mountain soils increases the volume of dirt and rock to be replaced by 30 percent, so that spoil and fill operations are practically inevitable.

dictably, take umbrage at this idea.) TVA also argues that direct federal appropriations should be used to reclaim the huge number of orphan mines left behind by private coal, phosphate, and sand and gravel mining companies, including TVA's own suppliers in preregulation days. (There are close to 70,000 acres of destitute orphan mines in the Tennessee Valley alone, but federal budget makers have stoutly resisted the idea that national money should be used to repair the damage.) By the late 1960s, most states of the valley had adopted strip mine reclamation laws, albeit of uncertain efficiency. One of the worst laws was Tennessee's, revised in 1971 with few of the new safeguards that environmentalists had recommended. The Tennessee conservation commissioner at that time, William L. Jenkins, allegedly lobbied to keep the provisions weak. The Knoxville News-Sentinel said the revised legislation was "written by strip-miners." Jenkins later assigned a fairly meager staff, including one person who owned strip-mined area himself, to enforce the legislation. Early in 1972, after a three-day tour of East Tennessee, Pennsylvania's chief of strip-mining reclamation, William E. Guckert, commented: "Strip-mining devastation in Tennessee is a disgrace to the nation. I've never seen such irresponsibility on the part of coal operators anywhere." Only a few months later, however, President Nixon appointed Tennessee's Jenkins to a nine-year term on TVA's board.

In autumn 1974 Congress was on the brink of passing national strip-mining controls that would obviate 90 percent of the harmful effects. The legislation banned stripping on the steepest slopes and required that the highwall be completely covered, thus returning the land to approximately original contour. The revegetation period of liability was extended to five years. To avert another Buffalo Creek disaster, strict standards were set on impoundments. And a large fund was established to reclaim orphan mine sites. The legislation promised to get TVA off the hook in its most embarrassing problem area.

The present-day argument over strip-mining boils down to one of competing value systems. On the one hand there is the official TVA position that getting cheap power for homes and high-paying industries (like aluminum) is the first consideration, provided intolerable desecration of the landscape can be avoided. The environmentalist critics, on the other hand, charge that cheap power is an obsession with TVA; that the mountains are Appalachia's gift from nature, to be preserved inviolate wherever possible; and that strip-mining poses a simply unacceptable risk to the habitat and livelihood of the mountain people. The charge that it is ecologically insensitive stings TVA officialdom to the quick. One is quickly reminded that the Tennessee River itself is now much cleaner than it was in 1933; that the whole face of the woodlands and farmlands was enhanced by the agency's work; and that TVA takes clean air problems so seriously that it has spent $270 million to clean up emissions of fly-ash from its coal-fired steam plants. (The electrostatic precipitators are gradually licking the fly-ash problem, but no satisfactory way has yet been found to remove sulfur dioxide from the steam plant emissions. TVA has resorted to two stop-gap solutions while research continues. The first has been installation of extremely high stacks which disperse the gas and minimize harm to humans and plant life. The second has been development of a computer-based meteorological monitoring system which allows cutbacks in generation during periods of low air quality.)

The environmental movement has unquestionably had a major effect on TVA's thinking and approaches, and today one would not hear the agency's reclamation director proclaim, as he did in 1965, that "strip-mining is part of the American way of life." David E. Lilienthal, still energetic and combative at the age of 74, in 1973 made his first trip back to the valley in 10 years and came away convinced that "the balance" between power generation and humanistic programs had "been restored" under Chairman Wagner.*

Aubrey Wagner does, in fact, personify the drawbacks and also the immense strengths and potentialities of the Tennessee Valley Authority as it passes its 40th anniversary. He has been working for TVA precisely that long, having come aboard as an $1,800-a-year engineer with the first crew of brilliant young professionals the agency was able to attract from all over the country in Depression times. Wagner was involved in survey work for the first dams, and he knows the Tennessee Valley like the palm of his own hand. By the 1950s he was general manager and a crucial figure in converting General Vogel, the Eisenhower administration's planner destructor, into an evangelist for the TVA cause. Thus having given his entire professional life to TVA, and having saved it once from a dire fate, Wagner tends to be fiercely defensive and overprotective about the agency. He personifies the extreme dedication of the senior personnel who labor on, in a kind of hangover from New Deal idealism, at salaries far below national industry standards. There is probably no agency of the United States government today with comparable *esprit de corps*. Some close observers of the agency believe that since its engineers and lawyers and administrators tend to be drawn now more from Tennessee, Kentucky, and Georgia universities, with less of an influx from outside the region, that the excellence and breadth of vision of the early years cannot be maintained. But the younger TVA personnel with whom I spoke all had the sense that they were working for a very special organization, with a glowing history. They said there was inspiration in working for a common purpose with a staff of such a wide range of skills—as one of them put it, "map surveyors, civil engineers, city planners, foresters, architects—you name it—a fantastic array of people of many trained disciplines, all together under one roof, all obliged to consider how what they might do in their particular field affects the rest of the agency."

There is a question of whether the ideas of the progressive, idealistic younger staff members are actually reflected in TVA policy. Some see a deadening hand in the Presidentially appointed directors, who in recent years have lacked the social vision and courage of Lilienthal and his col-

* Lilienthal, in a New York *Times* interview, did say TVA had been too concerned with buying coal cheaply, at the expense of environmental considerations. "I doubt whether mountain strip-mining ever will be compatible with environmental considerations," he said. "They can be met by companies that are big enough and have long-term contracts. They can't be met if you go peckerwooding around trying to pick up coal on short-term from necessitous sellers."

leagues. (One proposal is to have the directors elected by the people of the valley, a device that would make them more accountable—and responsive as much to people as to the industrial interests that have come to the area.)

The tough priority questions TVA faces in the 1970s are illustrated by the debate over ever increasing electricity output versus environmental and human values. Wagner and some of the older professionals, especially those in TVA's power division, still remember "when the lights went on," and how the lives of the valley's people were enhanced by inexpensive electricity. The idea of seriously deemphasizing growth of TVA's generating capacity is very hard for them to accept, because since their youth electricity has been equated with good. At the instruction of the TVA board, the power division has looked into the problem of energy conservation, and particularly since 1969 TVA has used its influence to put a crimp in the manufacture and use of shoddily insulated mobile homes and to educate architects, builders, and FHA offices in the valley about energy-saving insulation techniques in new home construction. The agency has also pressed the manufacturers of heat pumps to turn out more energy-efficient products. TVA has a program to show industrial engineers how they can save money, and in 1969 it eliminated the "promotional block" in its retail rate structure.

But shifting focus from energy use to energy conservation has been a wrenching, slow process for TVA's leadership and its power division in particular. One problem is the frequently expressed fear of TVA power officials that they might price themselves out of the market on industrial rates. Aubrey Wagner reflected the same point of view when he condemned suggestions for inverted power rates, or other adjustments in the rate structure to increase costs to large industries. Such change, he said, would put "our factories" in the Tennessee Valley "at a disadvantage in competition with those in other parts of the country."

TVA's critics suggest that Wagner's view is entirely too parochial for a federally chartered agency that has the capacity for broad-ranging social experiments. TVA's energy conservation program, in the words of Dr. Jack Gibbons, a longtime resident of the Tennessee Valley and director of the Interior Department's Office of Energy Conservation, "is way the hell underdone." There are several private utilities, he said, that have moved well ahead of TVA by converting their whole marketing groups to the reduction of unnecessary energy usage. (Among the most advanced utilities on energy conservation, according to industry sources, are Pennsylvania Power and Light, New York's Con Edison, Southern California Edison, and TVA's neighbor, Carolina Power and Light.) "With its public charter," Gibbons said, "TVA should be leading the pack, not following it. The TVA power marketing group and Wagner himself concentrate on the cheapest possible electricity. But keeping energy cheap means you waste it. They should spend their time helping people save energy, not to use more. We're past the era of electrifying the old hand-pumped well." Gibbons also pointed out that TVA's environmental statements on dams and new power projects have never spoken about energy conservation. "It's time," he said, "that some healthy external pressure be applied on TVA. The TVA board should be providing leadership, but it isn't. TVA's public education efforts in saving power are tiny compared to the agency's gross revenues and its capacity to innovate in a massive energy conservation program."

Aubrey Wagner, a redhead known for the strength of his passions, responds to such assertions by saying that the critics just "don't know what's going on in TVA."

I did find some internal inconsistencies in TVA's energy policies. Thomas Ripley, from the viewpoint of his forestries division, pointed out that it takes only 400 kilowatt-hours of electricity to harvest, process, and prepare a ton of wood for use. For steel, the figure is 2,700 kilowatt-hours. And for aluminum, a metal produced in large quantities in the valley because of TVA's inexpensive electricity, the figure is 17,000 kilowatt-hours a ton. Thus to conserve electricity, TVA would have every reason to urge wood in place of aluminum sidings on houses, as an example. But wages in the aluminum industry are much higher than those in wood products, and when I asked David Patterson, chief of TVA's planning staff, if the authority would turn down a high-paying, high-electricity demand industry for the valley—even at the environmental cost of more power generation—he replied it certainly would not.

TVA managers do recognize that they are dealing with a far more complex world than their predecessors of the 1930s, whose job was simply to raise the Tennessee Valley out of the mire of deep depression. As David Patterson put it:

The trade-offs we have to deal with—wages versus the environment, for instance—are a serious problem. We're trying to handle them in a best of all worlds way. We say we can have industrial growth and also enhance the environment. From now on we'll be walking a tightrope between those two values. The question is—can we industrialize this valley, and have it end up being something more attractive than New Jersey today?

There is risk in all development. The nuclear power plants are the latest case in point. We'd never have any if only zero risk were acceptable. But we will take reasonable risks to bring in, for example, high-paying industries to an area of the valley where everyone's working in a socks factory now.

Managing the Ecosystem and Reaching the Grass Roots

TVA's greatest contribution to American government has been an integrated systems approach to regional development. But a systems approach does imply control. And TVA officials, whatever their other differences may be, line up solidly against the school of thinking that suggests that people and the natural world are best served by being left alone. As Ripley said:

I'm attracted to the notion of spaceship earth. To view the biologic systems of this world—oceanic, terrestrial (tropical, subtropical, temperate, or arctic) and the fresh-water aquatic systems in terms of an aboriginal condition—and their capability of supporting life as we know it now—is just absolutely ridiculous. Unless you choose to dispose of 90 percent of humanity, I know no way to do it. And yet that's at the root of the present-day environmentalist movement.

There's no question that man has exploited nearly every resource on this planet. And he continues to do so at an alarming rate. The solution, though, is not to go back to the mussel-eating campground Cherokee vision of pre-Colonial times.

We do need to preserve in wilderness form in some cases vast parts of the marine, aquatic, and terrestrial base. But generally, the answer is for man to control his populations. And then to learn to manage in a closed-cycle fashion the biological systems, because we're absolutely dependent upon them.

On a somewhat more mundane level, Patterson noted that some people took a "neo-noble savage view of the mountaineers," suggesting that they didn't need all the amenities of an advanced civilization and that if they wanted them, they should move north. The TVA idea, he said, is that people should have the option to live well, to have a decent education and a decent future in the Tennessee Valley.

Has TVA, however, created a really closed ecosystem, a truly integrated systems approach that would be a 21st-century model? Compared to any other part of the United States, the answer is that it is well down the road. In absolute terms, though, the answer is certainly no. The Tennessee Valley region extends over parts of seven states, covering thousands of local government units. TVA can propose to, negotiate with, and cajole local government officials, but rare have been the occasions when it has had either the desire or the legal authority to force them to do anything. The authority has not even drawn up a proposed land use policy for the valley.

It has, however, had an integrated approach to very real activities, in every field from fisheries to fertilizer to flood control. And it has expanded its activities of late in some fascinating ways. Some of the best examples are provided by the agency's so-called "tributary area development" program. TAD, as it is familiarly called, began in 1961 after TVA's regional planners and economists took note of a disturbing imbalance in the valley's development. Robust economic growth and diversification were apparent in the major metropolises as well as the smaller riverside cities for which TVA had supplied the first impetus for modern development, such as Huntsville and Decatur. But practically all those growth centers were situated on the main channel of the river. By contrast, the rural "outback" and the tributary areas in general were suffering from the typical ills of Appalachia—high outmigration, lack of income opportunities, and the beginnings of rural slums.

The TAD program was designed to meet the problem by providing a kind of miniature TVA for any area that wanted advice and assistance. In effect, it is a personalized version of the original TVA charter, developing the resources of the tributary areas by seeing them singly and uniquely, taking the strong point of each (whether forest, water, human resources, or whatever), and then applying the range of TVA consultative skills to solve the most pressing local problems—in the environment, economy, education, or health. The program is carried out cooperatively with local communities through existing watershed associations, state agencies, citizens' organizations, or the planning and development districts that began to spring up across the South in the 1960s. Sometimes the local areas bring their problems to TVA, asking for help; sometimes officials of the TAD division go to the local areas with suggestions. But the programs are "all carrot, no stick," studiously avoiding any element of coercion from TVA.

TAD's activities have touched so many aspects of life in the valley that the program's thrust can only be understood by illustration. Unsightly roadside dumps and rusting car hulks along the rights of way, for instance, have polluted the Appalachian landscape for years, and localities have lacked either the money or the will to do anything about the problem. TAD began to work on the dump problem by advising several areas in how to set up cooperative type garbage collection agencies jointly financed (and thus affordable) by a number of counties. When, in the late 1960s, local officials in Tennessee's Anderson County asked TVA for help on clearing away their thousands of junked automobiles, the TAD division replied that it might help on a demonstration basis. It put together a demonstration vehicle—a standard wrecker modified so that it could get into ravines, fence rows, and other hard-to-get-at places. The contraption was an instant success, and TAD subsequently supplied the vehicles for some 30 other demonstration junk car removal programs. In each case, however, the local authorities had to commit themselves to insuring the wrecker, providing the manpower, and making arrangement for disposal of the car hulks once they were gathered at a central collection site. (TVA subsequently put together a "how-to-do-it" brochure on junk cars and received 1,300 requests for it, from every state of the Union plus six provinces of Canada and the Virgin Islands. The city of Philadelphia even copied the wrecker after borrowing a prototype from TVA.)

The TAD division was approached for help of quite another sort by officials of a planning district in a 1,400-square-mile Appalachian coal-mining region of western Virginia which was plagued by high unemployment and had such hilly terrain that it was hard to find sites for any new industries. TVA engineers surveyed the area and found one riverbottom location, near the town of Duffield, which the local people had not regarded seriously. A 981-acre industrial park was built there with TVA's counsel, made safe from flooding by TVA flood protection work. By 1973 two industries had moved in, and eventually the area was expected to gain 5,000 new industrial jobs and $33 million in annual payrolls. The development program at Duffield has involved a multitude of agencies, including TVA, the local planning district commission, the Appalachian Regional Commission, and the economic development administration of the state of Virginia. But the impetus was local; as Paul Holmes of the TAD division put it, "If we'd approached those Virginia counties and told them we had all the answers, the local people would have said 'No' right off." (When I asked Holmes if he has encountered the traditional stubborn and independent quality of Appalachian people, he replied: "Yes, but once they like you, they're loyal to you, and they trust you. And you have to remember we're dealing with far more sophisticated, educated people in the Tennessee Valley than in the destitute 1930s. The personal skill of local leaders is one of our major resources.")

Local communities have turned increasingly to TVA for help on getting new factories and jobs, and the authority has responded by pulling together all its economic studies to see what kind of industry would match the resources of an area. The communities are saved much anguish in chasing down the wrong leads, since TVA's research papers show just what kind of resources (water, power, labor skills, etc.) each type of industry needs, and can advise each locality on what type of prospects it should pursue.

It is not always industries that TVA advises localities on recruiting, however. Some communities have been encouraged to develop recreation facilities to exploit their tourist potential; others have been helped in developing family gardens to alleviate local hunger problems; others have been assisted in setting up educational cooperatives, mobile health clinics, and computer cooperatives to service local governments.

No dramatic master plan emerges from all of this. But the generalized goal is as vital as one could imagine: to foster the valley's human and physical resources so that its people can make the change from an agrarian, often isolated life to an existence in which they can enjoy the benefits of a modern and industrialized society without losing their individuality or despoiling their environment. The TAD program, Paul Holmes said, reflected a "national feeling to personalize things—an outgrowth of the period when people thought governments were too big, too depersonalized, not responsive enough." His own program, he thought, was an example of cutting the red tape and offering responsive answers to local and particularized needs. TVA is uniquely well equipped to approach that ideal, another official of the authority said, because "with our range of expertise, we can tackle practically any task." The chances of success are much greater than in the typical setting of American government, where multitudinous agencies must be coordinated. It also makes it easier for TVA, because it does speak with a single voice, to get other agencies of federal, state, and local government to cooperate with it.

TVA in recent years had been putting forward the challenging argument that the population growth patterns it has fostered in the valley, especially the growth of "satellite cities" some miles removed from the cores of the metropolitan areas, are an antidote to the "density disease" in the United States. Echoed frequently in talks with TVA leaders, the case was stated with remarkable fervor in the agency's 1972 annual report:

> The nation has been too long coming to the realization that the giant city, the cramming of too many people into too little space, is as obsolete as the dinosaur. . . . There can be no doubt that the large metropolitan area as we know it is hemorrhaging badly, inundating precious quantities of land, air, water, trees, and open space. There is strong evidence that the overwhelming majority of Americans feel the good life is to be found outside the metropolis, even as more and more of them find themselves trapped within it. . . .

The Tennessee Valley today has the opportunity to offer a viable alternative to the continued headlong rush to the congested, polluted, unstabilized super-cities of tomorrow. In the valley, planned industrial growth is helping disperse population, countering the national trend. Eighty percent of the region's new industrial jobs and two-thirds of all nonfarm employment opportunities are being created outside the major metropolitan centers. The people who are filling these new jobs still have access to open space, to green fields and forests and lakes and streams.

To back up its point, the agency points out that in 1930 there were only a dozen cities in the region with populations of 10,000 to 50,000 people but that by 1970 there were 42 within that medium range. Such metropolitan areas as Knoxville-Oak Ridge, Chattanooga, and the Tri-Cities (Bristol, Kingsport, Johnson City) serve as the nucleus for a host of medium-range communities like Morristown, Greeneville, Cleveland, and Athens. Huntsville's sphere of influence extends across north Alabama and into nearby Tennessee. The satellite cities around all these centers, TVA argues, mean it is "no longer necessary for people to migrate to the major urban centers of the valley or to other parts of the nation to find employment." The Tennessee Valley is thus said to offer "a viable alternative to traditional concepts of growth for 'growth's sake,' or conversely, to the utopian proposals which advocate a return to some forgotten pastoral existence."

The point may be somewhat overdrawn, because the Tennessee Valley is certainly not alone in having metropolitan areas with thriving satellite cities that are independent employment centers on their own, even while drawing on the larger cities for capital, wholesaling facilities, and the like. But it does mean that TVA is devoting more and more of its time to urban problem solving, with a special emphasis on smaller and middle-sized communities—and, most recently, to new towns. Again, the forms of assistance a regional authority can offer are rather rare in the country today. The agency's city planners are available to medium-range communities which could rarely afford their own professional planning staffs, and the skills of TVA engineers, industrial and recreation development experts, foresters and health personnel can easily be tapped. For the smaller communities there is TVA's "Operation Townlift," helping solve a multitude of short-term problems within the context of long-range plans.

The authority is working on an array of plans for "new towns" of varying populations. For those who like a real country setting, for instance, TVA's regional planners are fostering a set of "rural new communities" beginning in the Elk River region of northern Alabama and neighboring Tennessee. The new communities, of about 1,000 people each, will be for workers who commute to jobs in Huntsville, Decatur, and Athens. The residents will be able to work on "minifarms" in their off hours or perhaps live in mobile homes in cluster developments. But unlike many unplanned, "instant" mobile home settlements on the outskirts of metropolitan areas, these towns will be designed with environmental considerations in mind and with early and adequate provision for schools and other municipal services. "We see an orderly development of these rural communities all over the valley in the next 20 years," James L. Gober, TVA's chief regional planner, said. The authority would also like to turn some strip-mining operations from environmental curse to asset by instructing the strippers, before they dig their first shovelful of earth, how to rearrange the overburden and reshape the land contour so that it would be suitable for new residences and town sites later on.

TVA's biggest and most dramatic "new town" proposal is for a city of 35,000 people to be built on the shores of the 20,000-acre reservoir which will rise in the foothills of the Great Smokies, some 30 miles southeast of Knoxville, when the authority's Tellico Dam is completed in the late 1970s. The dam, being constructed at the confluence of the main Tennessee and the Little Tennessee Rivers, was originally conceived as a normal flood control, power, and navigation project. But the TVA regional planners, noting the high unemployment in the area, conceived of a new city with some 9,000 manufacturing and 2,000 recreation-related jobs that could stem outmigration from the territory and also be a model new city of the later 20th century. They believe that Timberlake, as they propose to name the new town, could fit into the series of satellite cities around Knoxville and brighten the economic future of the area on the order of another Oak Ridge.

Having conceived the Timberlake idea, TVA planners took it to a local planning council that included representatives from the three counties and 10 municipalities which would be directly affected. The planning council became enthused about the potentialities for new jobs, homes, and recreation, and asked TVA to design a model community. TVA then formed a task force to do a thorough feasibility study and in 1969 began to look for a possible private developer. A representative of the Boeing Company, which was then in an employment downspin in Seattle and looking for diversification opportunities, saw a news item about the project in the Huntsville paper. Boeing soon became deeply involved, and while other developers were invited to submit proposals, most seemed to be looking for a quicker turnover of their money and a more dynamic area than the Appalachian foothills near Knoxville. The TVA-Boeing plan, as it evolved, called for carefully separated residential, recreation, and industrial areas along the reservoir. The site, in all, would be 40,000 acres, but much of it would be left in open spaces. On the west bank, a chain of small, planned communities of 1,100 people each was envisaged as the residential heart of Timberlake. The industry would be confined to a 5,000-acre site with deep-water navigation facilitating low-cost transportation.

Independent surveys showed the people of the three-county area favored the Tellico-Timberlake project by a margin of about three to one, but opposition did arise. First there were objections from trout fishermen, who feared reduction in size of a stretch of the Little Tennessee that provides some of the best fishing in the state. (The area grows unusually large trout because of cold water from TVA's upstream dams, but it is a "put and take" operation because the trout cannot reproduce there.) After TVA showed that the length of the Little Tennessee suitable to fishing would not be substantially reduced, the opposition seemed to die down and money was appropriated to build the dam.

In 1971, however, the Environmental Defense Fund and some of the local trout fishing interests filed a suit against TVA to stop the Tellico Dam and thus Timberlake. They claimed that the massive water impoundment would endanger species of fish and rare waterfowl and destroy "a recreational, aesthetic and ecological resource that is increasingly rare." Great emphasis was also laid on the point that Chota, the sacred old capital of the Cherokee Nation, would be immersed. The waters would also threaten Tuskegee Town, birthplace of Sequoyah, the great Cherokee leader who invented an alphabet for his tribe. And they would drown the site of Tenassee, the Indian village from which the state of Tennessee took its name. No Cherokees now live in the area, however. The case went on trial in autumn 1973 and TVA won the case at the district court level.

The difficulties over the Tellico-Timberlake project are indicative of the increasingly troublesome problems TVA faces in trying to manage the ecosystem of the Tennessee Valley. Another example may be taken from the area in which the authority seems to have quite wide latitude—in scientific management of the valley's wildland base. The Tennessee watershed, forestries director Ripley noted, "sits in the middle of one of the world's largest hardwood regions and one of the few temperate hardwood regions anywhere." The oak, maple, cherry, walnut, poplar, and other choice hardwood of the valley could, in the years ahead, provide the base of an expanding valley hardwoods industry, relieve national timber shortages in the years of scarcity ahead, and provide a prime export material to help the country's position in international trade.

The problem is that only 17 percent of the region's 21.6 million acres of forests are in public hands. There are 356,000 individual property owners who have all the rest, mostly in holdings of less than 100 acres. Collectively, Ripley pointed out, the small owners sit on an enormously valuable natural resource in its capacity for wood production, wildlife, and recreation. Few of them have ever given much thought to the scientific development of their woodlands. In the past, the small owner's management decision about the land has generally been limited to hip-pocket advice from some adviser who has walked through the woods with him, kicked a few stumps, and said, "Joe, you should . . ." The counsel rarely took into account the owner's tax and income situation, soil or watershed conditions, or the real timber potential.

To solve the problem, TVA is building a computer-based information system aimed at the small forest owner. It will help him to identify his goals for the land, taking into account his financial position, the productive capability of his forest, his own ideas of use of it for recreation, housing, or whatever. As Ripley put it, "the objective is to help the owner direct the ecological succession on his land so that the products which flow from it are in concert with his personal objectives and financial capabilities." If the system works, of course, it could be a model for woodland management across the United States.

Yet at the same time, if the environment is to be protected while timber production is maximized, more work will have to be done in complete tree utilization, forest fertilization, and irrigation of the woodlands. On steep slopes, ground logging will have to give way to aerial methods (balloon, helicopter, skyline, etc.). Coordinating that operation with 350,000 separate owners will provide a rather severe test of TVA's ingenuity.

The Public Model

New towns, pure waters, creating clean energy, raising people's income, finding enough recreation space for a valley population headed toward 10 million—TVA's problems seem to roll on and on. But each is being dealt with and, despite the authority's obvious failings, on a more efficient and human basis than anywhere else in the United States.

One is reminded of President Roosevelt's message in sending the TVA Act to Congress in 1933: "If we are successful here we can march on, step by step, in a like development of the other great natural territorial units within our borders." But the fact is that this controlled experiment in better living has not been copied anywhere else in America—not in the other areas of Appalachia that cry out for it, not in the valley of the Arkansas River with conditions so similar to those of the Tennessee, not in the Missouri or Columbia River Valleys. Yet one can look abroad and see regional agencies in such widely spread nations as India, Colombia, and Iran, all modeled on TVA. "Only in its homeland," writer Peter Barnes has observed, "'is TVA an overlooked relic of another era."

Yet with appropriate changes, some version of TVA would seem applicable to every region of America, urbanized or not. "If FDR's vision had been fulfilled," Robert Sherrill wrote, "how much more rationally we could be handling our problems—with community planning, transportation, health and recreation, neither dictated from Washington nor bungled by cities and counties and states." Under Roosevelt's image, he suggested, the country would be divided into a number of TVA-units, large enough to contain a meaningful pool of resources but small enough to be manageable. The basic theme would be *public*—public power, public resources, public planning. But, as the TVA experience proved, private enterprise can flourish in that environment.

Why, one asks, has TVA not been copied? In the '30s and '40s, when real efforts were made to duplicate it, the effective resistance came from old-line federal agencies, jealous of their prerogatives, as well as from the private utilities. (These forces, for instance, defeated the proposed Missouri Valley Authority, as well as several others proposed in Congress.) When I asked Aubrey Wagner about the possibility of new TVAs in the 1970s, he replied that "if you tried to move from one valley to another, dividing the country up into eight or ten regions as people proposed in Roosevelt's day, you simply couldn't do it. The interests, government and private, would stop it." Another problem, of course, is that a TVA may have been best suited to development, from the ground up, of a depressed area. A new authority would be much less welcome in areas already filled with development, no matter how ill-conceived and poorly coordinated that development may be.

Wagner said any new kind of TVA would be different from the original. Yet he did see some promise in forming regional agencies, whether centered on watersheds or not, that might try to implement the basic secret of TVA's success—a coordinated approach to all resource problems, physical and human, using the multiple technical and social skills of the coordinating agency. Beyond that general and rather loosely defined concept, Wagner had not developed further his ideas on new TVAs. He seemed to feel that TVA did better to concentrate all its energies on doing a good job in the Tennessee Valley, letting others, if they chose, look to it as some kind of a model.

Clearly, the present TVA leadership lacks the foresight or evangelizing skill of the Lilienthals and Morgans of the first years. Yet it would be within the power of future Presidents of the United States to infuse TVA with that kind of revitalized leadership, to give the authority a mandate to spread its word across the country, and to instruct the departments of the federal government to cooperate in devising new and experimental forms for similar regional authorities.

As this book was completed in 1974, it looked even more likely that the other part of TVA's innovative first charter—public development of energy sources—might become more popular in the wake of spiraling oil and gas costs in an arena totally dominated by private industry. Several members of Congress were urging creation of a federal oil and gas corporation to explore for, produce, and possibly even to market the oil and gas lying untapped under federal lands. Senator Adlai Stevenson of Illinois said a government corporation in the energy business would provide "a spur, a yardstick, an incentive, and competition" for private companies. Among the several proposals was one for a TVA-like authority to develop the oil shale resources of the American West.

The demand for regional authorities was far more muted. Yet if the day ever comes when rational integrated regional development is accepted as a way for solving the nation's problems, the model will be there. For in the humble valley of the Tennessee River, a forgotten backwater of early 20th-century America, in the area of this country where people have been more suspicious of government than anywhere else, a pilot form of the grand experiment has been tried. And it has worked.

PERSONS INTERVIEWED

THE FOLLOWING PERSONS kindly agreed to interviews with the author in the preparation of this book. Affiliations shown are as of the time of the interview.

ALEXANDER, James H., Governor's Staff Director, Staff Division for Industrial Development, Nashville, Tenn.

AUTRY, George B., President, North Carolina Manpower Development Board, Chapel Hill, N.C.

BAKER, Howard, U. S. Senator from Tennessee

BARNES, Clifford, Council of Independent Kentucky Colleges and Universities, Lexington, Ky.

BASS, Jack, Fellow, Institute of Policy Sciences and Public Affairs, Duke University, Durham, N.C.

BEGLEY, Joe, Proprietor, Caudill's General Store, Blackey, Letcher County, Ky.

BINGHAM, Barry, Sr., former Publisher and Editor, Louisville Courier-Journal, Louisville, Ky.

BINGHAM, Barry, Jr., Editor and Publisher, Louisville Courier-Journal, Louisville, Ky.

BISHOP, Dr. C. E., Vice President for Public Services, Consolidated University of North Carolina, Chapel Hill, N.C.

BLACKFORD, Staige D., Press Secretary to Governor Linwood Holton, Richmond, Va.

BOETTNER, John L., Jr., Attorney, Appalachian Research and Defense Fund, Inc., Charleston, W. Va.

BRADEN, Carl, Director, Southern Conference Educational Fund, Louisville, Ky.

BUCKE, Emory Stevens, Book Editor, The Methodist Publishing House, Nashville, Tenn.

CALDWELL, James, Director, WAVE Radio, Louisville, Ky.

CALVERT, Lawrence L., Washington Representative, Tennessee Valley Authority, Washington, D.C.

CARLSMITH, Roger, National Science Foundation Environmental Project, Oak Ridge National Laboratory, Oak Ridge, Tenn.

CARPER, Julian F., President, Virginia State AFL-CIO, Richmond, Va.

CAUDILL, Harry M., Author and Attorney, Whitesburg, Ky.

CAVETT, Van, Editorial Writer, Louisville Times, Louisville, Ky.

CHILTON, W. W. III, Publisher, Charleston Gazette, Charleston, W. Va.

CLARK, Thomas D., Distinguished Professor of History (retired), University of Kentucky, Lexington, Ky.

CLEGHORN, Reese, Editor, Editorial Pages, Charlotte Observer, Charlotte, N.C.

COHAN, Peter, Executive Director, Cooperative Science Education Center, Inc., Oak Ridge, Tenn.

COMBS, H., Strip Miner and Owner, The Suburban Motel, Whitesburg, Ky.

COMSTOCK, Jim, Editor, The Hillbilly, Richwood, W. Va.

CRONIN, Ralph M., Vice President–Corporate Communications, National Industries, Inc., Louisville, Ky.

CROWE, John, Chief, Eastern Band of Cherokee Indians, Cherokee, N.C.

CUMMING, Joseph B., Jr., Southern Correspondent, Newsweek, Atlanta, Ga.

DAVID, Paul T., Professor of Government, University of Virginia, Charlottesville, Va.

DAVIS, Georgia, State Senator, Louisville, Ky.

DeBRUHL, Claude, State Representative, Candler, N.C.

DeVRIES, Walter, Associate Professor, Institute of Policy Sciences and Public Affairs, Duke University, Durham, N.C.

DiTRAPANO, Rudolph L., Democratic State Chairman of West Virginia, Charleston, W. Va.

DOSTER, Joe, Managing Editor, Winston-Salem Journal, Winston-Salem, N.C.

DuBOIS, Barney, City Desk, Memphis Press-Scimitar, Memphis, Tenn.

DUNN, Winfield, Governor of Tennessee

DYKES, David, Mine Inspector, Division of Reclamation, Kentucky Department for Natural Resources, Whitesburg, Ky.

EBERSOLE, Gordon, Executive Director, Congress for Appalachian Development, Sheperdstown, W. Va.

ECKL, Christopher E., Information Office, Tennessee Valley Authority, Knoxville, Tenn.

EISENBERG, Ralph, Professor of Government, University of Virginia, Charlottesville, Va. (deceased)

ESSER, GEORGE, Executive Director, Southern Regional Council, Atlanta, Ga.

EVANS, Paul L., Director of Information, Tennessee Valley Authority, Knoxville, Tenn.

FARNSLEY, Charles, Former Mayor, Louisville, Ky.

FETTERMAN, John, Writer, Louisville *Courier-Journal,* Louisville, Ky.

FITZ, J. D., Publisher, Morgantown *News Herald,* Morgantown, N.C.

FITZPATRICK, Joseph T., Democratic State Chairman of Virginia, Norfolk, Va.

FORD, Wendell, Governor of Kentucky

FORGY, Lawrence E., Jr., Deputy Commissioner, Kentucky Department of Finance, Frankfort, Ky.

FRANKLIN, Ben A., Correspondent, The New York *Times,* Washington, D.C.

FREEMAN, John P., Superintendent, Board of Education, Memphis City Schools, Memphis, Tenn.

FRIDDELL, Guy, Special Writer, Landmark Communications, Inc. (*Virginia Pilot* and other papers), Norfolk, Va.

GIBBONS, Dr. John H., Director, Office of Energy Conservation, Department of the Interior, Washington, D.C.

GILLESPIE, David, Director, Southern Growth Policies Board, Research Triangle Park, N.C.

GILLIS, Richard S., Jr., Executive Director, Virginia State Chamber of Commerce, Richmond, Va.

GISH, Pat (Mrs. Thomas), Director, OEO Housing Program, Whitesburg, Ky.

GISH, Thomas, Editor, *The Mountain Eagle,* Whitesburg, Ky.

GOBER, James L., Chief, Regional Planning Staff, Division of Navigation Development and Regional Studies, Tennessee Valley Authority, Knoxville, Tenn.

HAMBLEY, William, M.D., Mayor of Pikeville, Ky.

HARDEN, John, Author and Textile Executive, Greensboro, N.C.

HAWKINS, Dr. R. A., Civil Rights Leader, Charlotte, N.C.

HAWPE, David, Editorial Page Writer, Louisville *Courier-Journal,* Louisville, Ky.

HAYS, Brooks, Former Congressman from Arkansas, Washington, D.C.

HEARD, Alexander, Chancellor, Vanderbilt University, Nashville, Tenn.

HECHLER, Ken, U. S. Representative from West Virginia

HERZEL, William, Director of Research, Kentucky Department of Revenue, Frankfort, Ky.

HINSLEY, Jay, Political Writer, Asheville *Citizen,* Asheville, N.C.

HODGES, Luther, Former Governor of North Carolina, and Chairman, The Research Triangle Foundation, Chapel Hill, N.C.

HODGES, Luther, Jr., Vice President, North Carolina National Bank, Charlotte, N.C.

HOFFMAN, Harry, Editor, Charleston *Gazette,* Charleston, W. Va.

HOLMES, Jack, Professor of Political Science, University of Tennessee, Knoxville, Tenn.

HOLMES, Paul H., Tributary Area Development Office, Tennessee Valley Authority, Knoxville, Tenn.

HOLSHOUSER, James E. Jr., Governor of North Carolina

HOLTON, Linwood, Governor of Virginia

HOOKER, John Jay, Jr., Performance Systems, Inc., Nashville, Tenn.

HOWARD, A. E. Dick, Assistant Dean, University of Virginia Law School, Charlottesville, Va.

HOWELL, Henry, Lieutenant Governor of Virginia

HUMPHREYS, Steve, Former Managing Editor, Knoxville *Journal,* Knoxville, Tenn.

JENKINS, Dr. Leo, President, East Carolina University, Greenville, N.C.

JONES, Eddie, Executive Secretary, Nashville

Area Chamber of Commerce, Nashville, Tenn.

JONES, Walton, Acting Dean of University Extension, University of North Carolina, Raleigh, N.C.

JOYCE, Eugene, Attorney, Oak Ridge, Tenn.

KARNES, Eric, Businessman, Lexington, Ky.

KAUFMAN, Paul, Former State Senator and Founder, Appalachian Research and Defense Fund, Inc., Charleston, W. Va.

KELLER, Ernest, Staff Division for Industrial Development, Nashville, Tenn.

KLINE, Sheldon, Bureau of Labor Statistics, Department of Labor, Washington, D.C.

LATIMER, James, Political Writer, Richmond *Times-Dispatch,* Richmond, Va.

LEAK, Robert E., Administrator, Office of Industrial, Tourist & Community Resources, Raleigh, N.C.

LEWIS, John, Chairman, Voter Education Project, Atlanta, Ga.

LUIGART, Fred W., Executive Director, Kentucky Coal Association, Lexington, Ky. (deceased)

MARSH, Don, Political Writer, Charleston *Gazette,* Charleston, W. Va.

McATEER, J. Davitt, Solicitor for the Safety Division, United Mine Workers of America, Washington, D.C.

McCAULEY, Joseph L., Executive Director, Big Sandy Area Development Council, Prestonburg, Ky.

McCONNELL, Mitchell, Jefferson County Republican Chairman, Louisville, Ky.

McCUTCHEON, Andy, Assistant to Lt. Governor J. Sargeant Reynolds, Richmond, Va.

McDOWELL, Charles, Washington Correspondent, Richmond *Times-Dispatch,* Washington, D.C.

McKNIGHT, C. A., Editor, Charlotte *News and Observer,* Charlotte, N.C.

McGRUDER, (Mrs.) Curlie, Civil Rights Leader, Nashville, Tenn.

MILLER, Andrew P., Attorney General of Virginia

MILLER, Arnold, Miner, Ohley, W. Va. (Subsequently President, United Mine Workers of America)

MILLS, Fred M., Jr., State Representative, Wadesboro, N.C.

MILNER, Hudson, President, Louisville Gas & Electric Company, Louisville, Ky.

MONROE, Jefferson, Office of the President, West Virginia Institute of Technology, Montgomery, W. Va.

MOORE, Herman A., State Senator, Charlotte, N.C.

MOORE, Stanley, Editor, Morgantown *News Herald,* Morgantown, N.C.

MORGAN, Ray, Acting Director, Research and Planning Division, Kentucky Department of Commerce, Frankfort, Ky.

MORRIS, Hugh, Associate Director, Legislative Research Commission, Frankfort, Ky.

MORTON, Hugh, Owner, Grandfather Mountain, Linville, N.C.

NADER, Claire, Associate Director, National Science Foundation Environmental Project, Oak Ridge National Laboratory, Oak Ridge, Tenn.

NEELY, Charles B., Jr., Attorney, Raleigh, N.C.

PARKER, Jerome, Assistant to the Chief, Eastern Band of Cherokee Indians, Cherokee, N.C.

PARRIS, John, Contributing Editor, Asheville *Citizen,* Sylva, N.C.

PATTERSON, David A., Chief, Planning Staff, Office of the General Manager, Tennessee Valley Authority, Knoxville, Tenn.

PEARCE, John Ed, Writer, Louisville *Courier-Journal,* Louisville, Ky.

PETTIT, H. Foster, Mayor of Lexington, Ky.

PEYTON, Angus, Business Leader, Charleston, W. Va.

PHILLIPS, James, Government Affairs Writer, Washington, D.C.

PLEMMONS, William, President Emeritus, Appalachian State University, Boone, N.C.

PNAKOVICH, L. J., President–District 31, United Mine Workers of America, Fairmont, W. Va.

PRICHARD, Edward, Jr., Attorney, Frankfort, Ky.

PROTAN, John, Department of Agriculture, West Virginia, Charleston, W. Va.

RAMSEY, Liston B., State Representative, Marshall, N.C.

RATCLIFF, Ray E., Jr., Attorney, Appalachian Research and Defense Fund, Inc., Charleston, W. Va.

REYNOLDS, J. Sargeant, Lieutenant Governor of Virginia (deceased)

RIPLEY, Thomas H., Director, Division of Forestry, Fisheries, and Wildlife Development, Tennessee Valley Authority, Norris, Tenn.

RITCHIE, John, Assistant to Governor Linwood Holton, Richmond, Va.

ROBERTSON, Dr. Jack, Director, Division of Business Administration and Economics, West Virginia Institute of Technology, Montgomery, W. Va.

ROCKEFELLER, John D., IV, Secretary of State of West Virginia

ROEBUCK, James, Student Council President (1969–70), University of Virginia, Charlottesville, Va.

ROUNTREE, H. Horton, State Representative, Greenville, N.C.

SANFORD, Terry, Former Governor of North Carolina and President, Duke University, Durham, N.C.

SHANDS, The Rev. Alfred R., Alfred Shands Productions, Louisville, Ky.

SHIDLER, Atlee, President, Washington Center for Metropolitan Studies, Washington, D.C.

SHUMAKER, James, Editor, Chapel Hill *Weekly*, Chapel Hill, N.C.

SIEGENTHALER, John, Publisher, Nashville *Tennessean*, Nashville, Tenn.

SINCLAIR, Lewis S., Chief, Economic Research Staff, Division of Navigation Development and Regional Studies, Tennessee Valley Authority, Knoxville, Tenn.

SINGER, Richard G., Attorney, Raleigh, N.C.

SITTON, Claude, Editor, *The News and Observer*, Raleigh, N.C.

SLOANE, Harvey, Mayor of Louisville, Ky.

SMYSER, Richard D., Editor, The *Oak Ridger*, Oak Ridge, Tenn.

SNIDER, Reitzel, Insurance Executive, Charlotte, N.C.

SNOW, Brewster, Secretary-Treasurer, Virginia State AFL-CIO, Richmond, Va.

SPEARMAN, Robert, Attorney, Raleigh, N.C.

SPONG, William, Former U. S. Senator from Virginia

STAFFORD, Thomas F., Clerk, U.S. Court, Northern District of West Virginia, Elkins, W. Va.

STANLEY, Miles C., President, West Virginia Labor Federation, AFL-CIO, Charleston, W. Va. (deceased)

STAPP, Jack, President, Tree International, Nashville, Tenn.

STEVENS, H. Hugh, Jr., Attorney, Raleigh, N.C.

SUNDBERG, David, Director of Public Information, Oak Ridge National Laboratory, Oak Ridge, Tenn.

SWIFT, Ivan, Office of Representative Carl Perkins (Ky.), Washington, D.C.

TAYLOR, Charles J., Director, Research Department, Federal Reserve Bank of Atlanta, Atlanta, Ga.

TAYLOR, Livingston, Frankfort Bureau Chief, Louisville *Courier-Journal*, Frankfort, Ky.

THORNTON, William S., P.D.M., Chairman, Crusade for Voters, Richmond, Va.

THORSELL, Richard, Edison Electric Institute, New York, N.Y.

TODD, Rucker, Attorney, Louisville, Ky.

TRAVIS, Fred, Chief, Capital Bureau, Chattanooga *Times*, Nashville, Tenn.

TUNNELL, James S., Political Writer, Louisville *Courier-Journal*, Louisville, Ky.

UNDERHILL, George T., Jr., Executive Director, Action Now, Inc., Louisville, Ky.

WAGNER, Aubrey, Chairman of the Board, Tennessee, Valley Authority, Knoxville, Tenn.

WALLS, Dwayne, Correspondent, Charlotte *Observer*, Charlotte, N.C.

WEINBERG, Dr. Alvin, Director, Oak Ridge National Laboratory, Oak Ridge, Tenn.

WHEATON, G. H., Superintendent, Bull Run Steam Plant, Tennessee Valley Authority, Oak Ridge, Tenn.

WHITT, Wayne, Correspondent, Nashville *Tennessean*, Nashville, Tenn.

WILKINSON, J. Harvey, III, Author and Assistant Professor of Law, University of Virginia, Charlottesville, Va.

WILLIAMS, Cratis D., Dean of the Graduate School, Appalachian State University, Boone, N.C.

WILLIAMS, Norman, Staff Consultant, House Interior Subcommittee on Mines and Mining, Washington, D.C.

WYATT, Wilson W., Former Mayor of Louisville, Ky.

YARMUTH, Stanley, President, National Industries, Inc., Louisville, Ky.

YOUNG, John, Edison Electric Institute, New York, N.Y.

ZEGEER, David A., Division Superintendent, Beth-Elkhorn Corporation (subsidiary of Bethlehem Steel), Jenkins, Ky.

BIBLIOGRAPHY

In ADDITION TO THE EXTENSIVE INTERVIEWS for these books, reference was made to books and articles on the individual states and cities, their history and present-day condition. To the authors whose works I have drawn upon, my sincerest thanks.

NATIONAL BOOKS

Barone, Michael, Ujifusa, Grant, and Matthews, Douglas. *The Almanac of American Politics—1972,* and *1974.* Boston: Gambit Publishing Co., published biennially.

Birmingham, Stephen. *The Right People—A Portrait of the American Social Establishment.* Boston: Little, Brown, 1968.

Book of the States. The Council of State Governments. Published biennially, Lexington, Ky.

Brownson, Charles B. *Congressional Staff Directory.* Published annually, Washington, D.C.

1969 Census of Agriculture, Bureau of the Census, Washington, D.C.

1970 Census of Population, Bureau of the Census, Washington, D.C.

CBS News Campaign '72 handbooks—Democratic National Convention, Republican National Convention, various primary states, and general election. New York: CBS News, 1972.

Citizens Conference on State Legislatures. Various studies including *The Sometime Governments: A Critical Study of the 50 American Legislatures,* by John Burns. New York: Bantam Books, 1971.

Congress and the Nation, 1945–64, and Vol. II, *1965–68.* Congressional Quarterly Service, Washington, D.C., 1967 and 1969.

David, Paul T., *Party Strength in the United States, 1872–1970.* Charlottesville: University Press of Virginia, 1972.

Editor and Publisher International Year Book. New York: Editor and Publisher. Published annually.

Employment and Earnings—States and Areas, 1939–71 U.S. Department of Labor, Bureau of Labor Statistics, Washington, D.C., 1972.

Encyclopedia Americana. Annual editions. New York: Americana Corporation. (Includes excellent state and city review articles.)

Farb, Peter. *Face of North America—The Natural History of a Continent.* New York: Harper & Row, 1963.

Fodor-Shell Travel Guides U.S.A. Fodor's Modern Guides, Inc., Litchfield, Conn. (In several regional editions, the best of the travel guides.)

From Sea to Shining Sea—A Report on the American Environment—Our National Heritage. President's Council on Recreation and Natural Beauty, Washington, D.C., 1968.

Gunther, John. *Inside U.S.A.* New York: Harper & Row, 1947 and 1951.

Jacob, Herbert, and Vines, Kenneth N. *Politics in the American States: A Comparative Analysis.* Boston: Little, Brown, 1971.

Life Pictorial Atlas of the World. Editors of *Life* and Rand McNally. New York: Time, Inc., 1961.

McPherson, Harry. *A Political Education.* Boston: Little, Brown, 1972.

The National Atlas of the United States of America. Geological Survey, U.S. Department of the Interior, Washington, D.C., 1970.

Phillips, Kevin H. *The Emerging Republican Majority.* New Rochelle, N.Y.: Arlington House, 1969.

The Quality of Life in the United States: 1970, Index, Rating and Statistics, by Ben-Chieh Liu with Robert Gustafson and Bruce Marcy. Kansas City, Mo.: Midwest Research Institute, 1973.

Rankings of the States. Published annually by the Research Division, National Education Assn., Washington, D.C.

Ridgeway, James. *The Closed Corporation—American Universities in Crisis.* New York: Random House, 1968.

Saloma, John S. III, and Sontag, Frederick H. *Parties: The Real Opportunity for Effective Citizen Politics.* New York: Knopf, 1972.

Sanford, Terry. *Storm Over the States.* New York: McGraw-Hill, 1967.

Scammon, Richard M., ed. *America Votes—A Handbook of Contemporary American Election Statistics.* Published biennially by the Government Affairs Institute, through Congressional Quarterly, Washington, D.C.

Scammon, Richard M., and Wattenberg, Ben J. *The Real Majority—An Extraordinary Examination of the American Electorate.* New York: Coward-McCann, 1970.

Sharkansky, Ira. *The Maligned States: Policy Accomplishments, Problems, and Opportunities.* New York: McGraw Hill, 1972.

State and Local Finances. Published periodically by the Advisory Commission on Intergovernmental Relations, Washington, D.C.

State Government Finances. Published annually by The U.S. Department of Commerce, Bureau of the Census, Washington, D.C.

Statistical Abstract of the United States. Published annually by the U.S. Department of Commerce, Bureau of the Census, Washington, D.C.

Survey of Current Business. U.S. Department of Commerce, Bureau of Economic Analysis, Washington, D.C., monthly. April and August edition contain full reports on geographic trends in personal income and per capita income.

Thayer, George. *The Farther Shores of Politics.* New York: Simon & Schuster, 1967.

These United States—Our Nation's Geography, History and People. Reader's Digest Assn., Pleasantville, N.Y., 1968.

Tour Books. Published annually by the American Automobile Assn., Washington, D.C.

Uniform Crime Reports for the United States. Published annually by the U.S. Department of Justice, Federal Bureau of Investigation, Washington, D.C.

Who's Who in American Politics (New York: R. R. Bowker Co., published biennially).

Williams, Joe B. *U.S. Statistical Atlas.* Published biennially at Elmwood, Neb.

The World Almanac and Book of Facts. Published annually by Newspaper Enterprise Assn., Inc., New York and Cleveland.

REGIONAL BOOKS AND SOURCES

The Border South (as distinct from the Southern region as a whole) has been the subject of few major works. The single volume I found most useful was *The Border South,* by a Newport, Tennessee, couple, Wilma Dykeman and James Stokley, written as part of the Time-Life Library of America (New York: Time Inc., 1968). Among historic works, Edward Conrad Smith's *Borderland in the Civil War* (New York: AMS Press, 1927), and *The Southern Highlander and His Homeland,* by John C. Campbell (Chapel Hill: University of North Carolina Press, 1921), were especially valuable. Several of the individual states' politics were perceptively analyzed in V. O. Key, Jr.'s *Southern Politics in State and Nation* (New York: Alfred A. Knopf, 1949), in John H. Fenton's *Politics in the Border States* (New Orleans: Hauser Printing Co., 1957), and more recently in *The Changing Politics of the South,* edited by William C. Havard (Baton Rouge, La.: Louisiana State University Press, 1972).

Numerous works touching on the general character and development of the modern South were cited in the bibliography of *The Deep South States of America,* the preceding volume in this series. Among those which proved most relevant in the study of the Border States were: *A History of the South,* 4th ed., by Francis Butler Simkins and Charles Pierce Roland (New York: Alfred A. Knopf, 1972); *The South and the Nation,* by Pat Watters (New York: Pantheon, 1969); *Human*

Geography of the South, by Robert B. Vance (Chapel Hill, N.C.: University of North Carolina Press, 1935); *You Can't Eat Magnolias,* edited by H. Brandt Ayers and Thomas H. Naylor, publication of the L. Q. C. Lamar Society (New York: McGraw-Hill, 1972).

The Mind of the South, by W. J. Cash (New York: Alfred A. Knopf, 1941); *The Burden of Southern History,* by C. Vann Woodward (Baton Rouge, La.: Louisiana State University Press, 1960); *The Southern Strategy,* by Reg Murphy and Hal Gulliver (New York: Scribner, 1971); and *The Emerging South,* by Thomas D. Clark (New York: Oxford University Press, 1961).

Report of the United States Civil Rights Commission—1959 (Washington: Government Printing Office). Includes the best review of state laws restricting the right to vote in the post-Civil War period, voting registration figures in the 1950s, and a good review of various states' reactions to the 1954 Brown decision of the U.S. Supreme Court. *Climbing Jacob's Ladder: The Arrival of Negroes in Southern Politics,* by Pat Watters and Reese Cleghorn (New York: Harcourt, 1967); *Negroes and the New Southern Politics,* by Donald R. Matthews and James W. Prothro (New York: Harcourt, 1966); *Plantation Politics: The Southern Economic Heritage,* by J. Earl Williams (Austin, Texas: Futura Press, 1972); *State and Local Taxes in the South, 1973,* by Eva Glambos (Atlanta: Southern Regional Council, 1973).

APPALACHIA

The following sources were most helpful as background for the general discussion of Appalachian problems included in the regional introduction of this book: "Pockets of Appalachia," by Funson Edwards, *The Appalachian South,* Spring & Summer, 1967; "O, Appalachia!," by Harry M. Caudill, *Intellectual Digest,* April 1973; "Appalachian Pictures," by Edward Abbey, *Audubon,* September, 1970; "Appalachia Could Have Wealth Coming Out of Its Ears!," by Harry Caudill, *The West Virginia Hillbilly,* June 22, 1968; and *American Mountain People,* photographs by Bruce Dale (Washington: National Geographic Society, 1973).

Annual Reports and other releases from the Appalachian Regional Commission, Washington,

D.C.; "Appeal of Regional Commissions: Politics and Extra Federal Money," by Prentice Bowsher, *National Journal,* Sept. 22, 1969; "Can Ralph R. Widner Save New York, Chicago, and Detroit?" by John Fischer, *Harper's Magazine,* October 1968; "The Big Regions," by Melvin R. Levin, *Journal of American Institute of Planners,* March 1969; "U.S. Plans to Redirect Aid to Poor in Appalachia," by Ben A. Franklin, New York *Times,* June 22, 1970; "In Appalachia: Vast Aid, Scant Relief," by Ben A. Franklin, New York *Times,* Nov. 29, 1970; "After Six Years, The Appalachia Commission Says It Still Has Not Reached the People," by Phil Primack, *The Mountain Eagle,* Aug. 26, 1971; "Appalachia After Six Years," by

Ralph R. Widner, *Appalachia*, November–December 1971; "Appalachia Guinea Pig: Hidden Traps of Regionalism," by Phil Primack, *The Nation*, Sept. 24, 1973; "Appalachia Turns into Growth Region," by Bill Williams, *The Christian Science Monitor*, Dec. 20, 1973; "The Gray Woman of Appalachia," by Hariette Simpson Arnow, *The Nation*, December 28, 1970.

"New Strategies for Appalachia," by Si Kahn, *New South*, Summer 1970; "Southern Mountains: Changes in Council Continue in the Effort to Fight Effectively for Rights of People," by Dwayne Walls, *South Today*, September 1973; "Ideal of Unity Stirs Appalachian Poor," by George Vecsey, New York *Times*, April 23, 1972; "Home in the Hollows: Many Former Workers in the War on Poverty Settle in Appalachia," by Thomas Lindley Ehrich, *The Wall Street Journal*, March 15, 1971; "Council of Southern Mountains Has Conference," The Hazard *Herald*, Aug. 22, 1973; "The Mountaineer Minority," by John Egerton and Frye Gaillard, *Race Relations Reporter*, March 1974.

"Coal: Roaring Again!," by Brian Dittenhafer, *Federal Reserve Bank of Atlanta Monthly Review*, March 1972; "Strip Mining: Scourge of the Land," by Ward Sinclair, *The Progressive*, August 1973; "Appalachia—Like the Flayed Back of a Man," by James Branscome, The New York *Times Magazine*, Dec. 12, 1971; "Coal: It's Cheap, but Dirty and Hard to Dig," by Ben A. Franklin, New York *Times*, June 16, 1974.

VIRGINIA

The Old Dominion is blessed with a multitude of studies of its past and present. Among those I found most useful were: *Virginia in Our Century*, by Jean Gottmann (Charlottesville, University of Virginia Press, 1955 and 1969); *Virginia: The New Dominion*, by Virginius Dabney (Garden City, N.Y.: Doubleday, 1971); *Virginia: A New Look at the Old Dominion*, by Marshall W. Fishwick (New York: Harper, 1959); *What Is It About Virginia?*, by Guy Friddell, (Richmond: The Dietz Press, 1966); *Virginia: A Guide to the Old Dominion*, compiled by the writers of the Writers' Program of WPA (New York: Oxford University Press, American Guide Series, 1940); *Harry Byrd and the Changing Face of Virginia Politics 1945–1966*, by J. Harvie Wilkinson III (Charlottesville: University of Virginia Press, 1968); *The Byrds of Virginia*, by Alden Hatch (New York et. al.: Holt, Rinehart, and Winston, 1969); *Virginia: Bourbonism to Byrd, 1870–1925*, by Allen W. Moger (Charlottesville, University of Virginia Press, 1968); "Virginia: A Sense of the Past," chapter in *States in Crisis: Politics in Ten American States, 1950–1962*, by James Reichley (with James Latimer) (Chapel Hill: University of North Carolina Press, 1964); "Virginia: The Emergence of Two-Party Politics," by Ralph Eisenberg, chapter in *The Changing Politics of the South*, ed. William C. Havard, (Baton Rouge: Louisiana State University Press, 1972); "Virginia: Political Museum Piece," chapter of *Southern Politics*, by V. O. Key, Jr. (New York: Random House, 1949).

STATE GOVERNMENT "State Reorganization: The Virginia Experience," by Weldon Cooper, *The University of Virginia Newsletter*, March 15, 1970; "The Governor of Virginia as Legislative Leader," by L. Tucker Gibson, Jr., *The University of Virginia Newsletter*, Jan. 15, 1969; "The Case for a Cabinet," editorial in *The Virginian Pilot*, Nov. 16, 1973; "Virginia's Sales Tax: Its Origins and Administration," by Michael S. Deeb and Stuart W. Connock, *The University of Virginia Newsletter*, April 15, 1970; "Massive Resistance Propaganda Experiment Comes to Quiet End," by James Latimer, Richmond *Times-Dispatch*, Jan. 1, 1969; "The Governor of Virginia," by Carter O. Lowance, *The University of Virginia Newsletter*, Feb. 15, 1960; "Fugate Is Ogre in Northern Virginia but a Hero Elsewhere in the State," by Jay Mathews, Washington *Post*, Oct. 19, 1972; "Modernizing Government for a New Virginia," by Kathryn H. Stone, *The University of Virginia Newsletter*, Dec. 15, 1965; "The Virginia Cabinet: A Preliminary Assessment," by T. Edward Temple, *The University of Virginia Newsletter*, Nov. 15, 1973; "Virginia Still Low in Tax Revenue, Says Researcher," Richmond *News Leader*, May 13, 1970; "Va. Leads in Payments to Civil War Families," by Lew Wheaton, AP dispatch in Washington *Post*, Aug. 12, 1973.

"Rural Bloc Beats Deadline," "Historic Virginia Assembly May Never Be the Same," and " 'New Breed' In Assembly: Young Va. Legislators Challenge Hallowed Traditions," by Helen Dewar, Washington *Post*, March 8, 1970, June 6, 1971, and Feb. 7, 1972; "Virginia: Session Hectic, but Productive in Areas of Court Reform, Education, Environment, and Fair Housing," by George Bowles, *South Today*, October 1973; "Lobbyists Report Expenses—$320,000 Spent During Session," by Kenneth Bredemeier, Washington *Post*, April 27, 1974.

"Virginia Colleges' Waste Put at $80 Million," by Kenneth Bredemeier, Washington *Post*, Jan. 23, 1974; "6 Prison Officials Indicted in Virginia," by Kenneth Bredemeier, Washington *Post*, Jan. 26, 1974; "Godwin Stresses Schools, Prisons, Transit: Penal System Reform Urged," by Paul Edwards, Washington *Post*, Jan. 15, 1974.

POLITICS *Virginia Votes, 1924–1968*, by Ralph Eisenberg (Charlottesville: Institute of Government, University of Virginia, 1971); "Gubernatorial Politics in Virginia: The Experience of 1965," by Ralph Eisenberg, *The University of Virginia Newsletter*, March 15, 1969; "The 1964 Presidential Election in Virginia; A Political Omen?," by Ralph Eisenberg, *The University of Virginia Newsletter*, April 15, 1965; "1966 Politics in Virginia: The Democratic Senatorial Primary," by Ralph Eisenberg, *The University of Virginia Newsletter*, Jan. 15, 1967; "1969 Politics in Virginia: The Democratic Primary," by Ralph Eisenberg, *The University of Virginia Newsletter*, Feb. 15, 1970; "1969 Politics in Virginia: The General Election," by Ralph Eisenberg, *The University of Virginia Newsletter*, May 15, 1970; "The Coalition of the Future," by Michael S. Lottman, *Ripon Forum*, July–August 1970; "Virginia Faces Major Party Realignments," by Dr. Donald J. Senese, *Human Events*, July 8, 1972; "A New Look at the Old Dominion," by John T. Schell, *New South*, Winter 1973; "A Sharp Right and a Hard Left in Virginia," Washington *Post*, June 15, 1972; "McGovern's Plight in Virginia," by Helen Dewar, Washington *Post*, September 17, 1972.

"Virginia's Howell-Godwin Campaign Holds Ramifications Beyond the State," by Jonathan Cottin, *National Journal Reports*, Nov. 3, 1973; "Mr. Hot Henry Howell Against Mr. Cool Mills Godwin," by Charles McDowell, *Washingtonian*, September 1973; "What Happened in Virginia," by Jack Bass, *New South*, Fall 1973; "Godwin

Voters: Rich, White, Conservative," by Helen Dewar and Paul G. Edwards, Washington *Post*, Nov. 8, 1973; "3 Howell Errors Said to Cost Him Election," by Helen Dewar, Washington *Post*, Dec. 17, 1973; "Black Vote May Decide Race," by Helen Dewar, Washington *Post*, Oct. 25, 1973; "Busing: The Word that Won for Mills E. Godwin," by Philip W. Smith, *Race Relations Reporter*, Jan. 28, 1974; "The Politics of Nostalgia: The Byrd Legacy in Virginia," by Thomas C. Ward, *Harvard Political Review*, Winter 1974.

CONSTITUTION "History Hangs Over Charter Changes," by James E. Clayton, Washington *Post*, Jan. 12, 1969; "The Virginia Constitution," Washington *Post*, Jan. 13, 1969; "The Constitution: State Document Is Blend of Innovation, Continuity," by A. E. Dick Howard, Richmond *Times-Dispatch*, June 27, 1971; "How Virginia Succeeded When So Many Failed," by A. E. Dick Howard, Roanoke *Times*, July 4, 1971; "Now Virginia's Up to Date," by A. E. Dick Howard, Washington *Post*, June 27, 1969; *Commentaries on the Constitution of Virginia*, by A. E. Dick Howard (Charlottesville, University of Virginia Press, 1974); "Constitutional Revision: Virginia and the Nation," by A. E. Dick Howard, *University of Richmond Law Review*, October 1974; "The 1971 Revised Virginia Constitution and Recent Const:tution-Making," by Albert L. Sturm, *State Government*, Summer 1971.

LEADERS "The Byrd Dynasty of Virginia," by John H. Cline (book review), Washington *Evening Star*, Dec. 2, 1969; "A Gathering of Governors: Virginia's Chief Executives of the Twentieth Century," by Guy Friddell, *The Commonwealth*, January 1969; "Reynolds: Limitless Future Cut Short," by Helen Dewar, Washington *Post*, June 14, 1971.

"The Godwin Years," by J. Harvie Wilkinson III, *The Commonwealth*, November 1969; "Bipartisan Legislative Group to Steer Godwin's Program," by Helen Dewar, Washington *Post*, Dec. 2, 1973; " 'Godwin Years' a Time of Catching Up," by Helen Dewar, Washington *Post*, Jan. 4, 1970.

"The Achievements of Linwood Holton," Washington *Post*, Jan. 11, 1974; "Gov. Holton Opposes Busing Amendment," by Helen Dewar, Washington *Post*, March 31, 1972; "Holton's Achievement: Building Bridges Between Va. People," by Helen Dewar, Washington *Post*, Jan. 2, 1974; "Governor Holton's Foreign Policy," Washington *Post*, June 21, 1970; "The Men and Why They Run," by Alice Neff, *The Commonwealth*, Oct. 1969.

CONGRESSIONAL DELEGATION Ralph Nader Congress Project Reports on Harry F. Byrd, Jr. (by Mimi Cutler), William L. Scott (by Daniel Epstein), and Joel T. Broyhill (by Duncan Spelman) (Washington: Grossman, 1972); "Confident Scott Had No Doubts," by Kenneth Bredemeier, Washington *Post*, Nov. 9, 1972; "Congressman William Scott. . . . Nobody Likes Him but the Voters," by Jack Linpert, *Washingtonian*, March 1970; "Toughest Fight Won by Broyhill," by David R. Boldt, Washington *Post*, Nov. 9, 1972; "The Ten Dumbest Congressmen," by Nina Totenberg, *New Times*, May 1974; Nov. 9, 1972; "Virginia Congressmen (Broyhill)," Washington *Post*, Nov. 1, 1970; "Why Did Poff Shun Chance at Court?," by Paul G. Edwards, Washington *Post*, Oct. 12, 1971; "Sponge Returns to Portsmouth," by George M. Kelley, *Virginian-Pilot*, Sept. 16, 1973.

POPULATION, ECONOMY *Virginia's Population: A Decade of Change—Socioeconomic Characteristics*, by William J. Serow and Michael A. Spar (Richmond: Tayloe Murphy Institute, University of Virginia-Graduate School of Business

Administration, January 1974); *Virginia's Urban Corridor: A Preliminary Inquiry*, by A. E. Dick Howard *et al.* (Charlottesville, Va.: The Center for the Study of Science, Technology, and Public Policy, March 1970); "Once Leary Virginia Officials Now in Love with Travel Slogan," by Kenneth Bredemeier, Washington *Post*, Jan. 14, 1973; "Upper South's Industry Poses Special Challenges," by Dale Patrick, *Southern Growth: Problems & Promise*, (publication of Southern Growth Policy Board, Research Triangle Park, N.C., 1973); "Breeding and Care Grooms Va. Hogs for World Trade," by Helen Dewar, Washington *Post*, May 10, 1971; "Mt. Vernon Losing Out to Walt Disney," by Robert Brakdoll, Los Angeles *Times*, June 6, 1973.

TIDEWATER "Virginia Ports and Winds of Change," by William Shands Meacham, *The Commonwealth*, December 1969; "Shipping Advance Transforms Va. Gateway to the Sea," by Carl Bernstein, Washington *Post*, August 8, 1971; "The New Vitality at Portsmouth," by Ed Grimsley, *The Commonwealth*, January 1969; "Dates with Destiny Bespangle History of Shipyard," by Wilford Kale, Richmond *Times-Dispatch*, April 28, 1968; "Whites Quitting Norfolk School System," by James Mathews, Washington *Star*, Oct. 25, 1971; "Money Cuts, New Rules—Hard Times for Public Housing," *U.S. News & World Report*, March 26, 1973.

"Flight Little Island," by Joseph O'Keefe, Washington *Star*, Jan. 31, 1971; "Barge Hits Va. Span, Closes It," by Helen Dewar, Washington *Post*, Sept. 22, 1972; "Heart of Dismal Swamp Now Refuge," by Hank Burchard, Washington *Post*, Jan. 18, 1973; "Industry Steps in to Save the Land," *U.S. News & World Report*, March 19, 1973; "By the Sea, By the Sea," by Frank Sullivan, *The Commonwealth*, September 1969; "Busch Is the Magic Word in James City," by John Kinnier, Richmond *Times-Dispatch*, April 26, 1970.

SOUTHSIDE "Surry County: Virginia's Last Outpost of Massive Resistance," by William Winn, *South Today*, November 1971; "New Era in Virginia: Blacks Control County," by Carl Bernstein, Washington *Post*, Jan. 2, 1972; "Court Cases Knock Down At-Large Voting Barrier," by Armand Derfner and Joe Taylor, *Focus*, July 1973; "Black Mayor Elected in Petersburg," by Helen Dewar, Washington *Post*, July 5, 1973; "Plantation Justice in Lynchburg," by Michael L. Dorman, [*MORE*,] June 1973; "Anatomy of a Black Victory," by Carey E. Stronach, *The Nation*, Aug. 27, 1973; "That Old-Time Religion," *Newsweek*, July 24, 1972.

RICHMOND "Richmond Progress—Reported by the Greater Richmond Chamber of Commerce," Richmond *Times-Dispatch*, Jan. 26, 1969; "City-Suburb Dispute Grows," by Ken Ringle, Washington *Post*, Jan. 28, 1971; Richmond Debates Busing Editorials," by Ken Ringle, Washington *Post*, Aug. 16, 1970; "Richmond Pins Future to Schools," by Ken Ringle, Washington *Post*, May 27, 1973; "Media General's Fortunate Misfortune," *Business Week*, Nov. 1972.

NORTHERN VIRGINIA "Forecast 70: Focus on Northern Virginia," (remarks of Frederick A. Babson, representing the jurisdictions of Northern Virginia, to the Governor and Members of the General Assembly at Northern Virginia Community College, Jan. 24, 1970); "Washington Area's 'Real Central City' Now Includes Arlington and Alexandria, Key Indicators Show," *Metropolitan Bulletin* (Washington Center for Metropolitan Studies), January 1974; "What's a Nice Place Like Arlington Going to Do with All Those People?," by Jack Fraser, *Washingtonian*, May 1971; "Alexandria Blacks Jubilant Over Win," Washington

Star, June 10, 1970; "Alexandria Shore Revival Gleams," by Paul G. Edwards, Washington *Post*, July 30, 1970; "Alexandria Riverfront Bill Eyed," by Joanne Omang, Washington *Post*, March 10, 1973.

"Zoning: The Quiet Revolution," by Thomas Grubisich, Washington *Post*, Dec. 22, 1973; "Mc-Lean: Itself After 200 Years," by Robert Alden, Washington *Post*, Nov. 27, 1969; "Fairfax's Full-Time Chairwoman Stays Busy," by Donald Nunes, Washington *Post*, June 25, 1973; "Restrictions in Fairfax County Will Halt Development by 1975," by Ron Shaffer, Washington *Post*, Feb. 20, 1973; "Suburbia Down the Drain?," by Stewart Udall and Jeff Stansbury, McLean *Globe*, Feb. 18, 1971; "Land Use Program Adopted in Fairfax," by Joseph D. Whitaker, Washington *Post*, July 24, 1973; "County Acts to Control New Building," by Kenneth Bredemeier, Washington *Post*, June 22, 1972; "What's a Poor County to Do?," by James M. Perry, *National Observer*, March 31, 1973.

"Reston Adds Low-Income Units to the Mix," by Wolf Von Eckardt, Washington *Post*, April 6, 1970; "Bright New Town but Not the Heavenly City," by Rem Rieder, Philadelphia *Evening Bulletin*, Dec. 8, 1970; "Reston at 7 Years: New

Town Loses Its Innocence," by Ken Ringle, Washington *Post*, Aug. 16, 1972.

VALLEY AND WEST "Sales Boon Rockets Shenandoah Land Values," by William Nye Curry, Washington *Post*, June 29, 1971; "Park Shortage? Recycled Land Is the Answer," by Robert J. Donovan, Los Angeles *Times*, Dec. 3, 1971; "Shenandoah, I Long to Hear You," by Mike W. Edwards, *National Geographic*, April 1970; "Land Rush Changes Massanutten Life," by Ken Ringle, Washington *Post*, Sept. 4, 1973; "The Making of Moonshine in Franklin County, Va.," by J. Y. Smith, Washington *Post*, April 24, 1969.

"Pollution and Power in a Small Mill Town, [Covington]" by Shelby Coffey III, Washington *Post-Potomac Magazine*, Jan. 26, 1969; "Two-State City Government: Bristol, Virginia-Tennessee," by C. P. Curcio, *The University of Virginia Newsletter*, Dec. 15, 1972; "A Town's Jobs Go Abroad," by Helen Dewar, Washington *Post*, April 30, 1973; "Black Lung Benefits: New Life for Miners," by Paul G. Edwards, Washington *Post*, Dec. 6, 1972; "The Homestead," *Life*, July 16, 1971; "Coal Mine Beatrice a Fickle Mistress," by Brian Kelley, Washington *Star*, June 20, 1971.

NORTH CAROLINA

Among the books which furnished the best background for the statewide scene were *North Carolina: The History of a Southern State*, by Hugh Talmadge Lefler & Albert Ray Newsome (Chapel Hill: University of North Carolina Press, 1954); *North Carolina: A Guide to the Old North State*, compiled by writers of the Writer's Program of the WPA (Chapel Hill: University of North Carolina Press, 1939); "North Carolina: Progressive Plutocracy," chapter in *Southern Politics in State and Nation*, by V. O. Key, Jr. (New York: Random House, 1949); "North Carolina: Bipartisan Paradox," by Preston W. Edsall & J. Oliver Williams, chapter in *The Changing Politics of the South*, ed. William C. Havard (Baton Rouge: Louisiana State University Press, 1972); and *North Carolina Politics: An Introduction*, by Jack D. Fleer (Chapel Hill: University of North Carolina Press, 1968). Major economic data was found in *North Carolina Data File 1973-74* (North Carolina Dept. of Natural and Economic Resources, Raleigh).

STATE GOVERNMENT, POLITICS *Schools and Taxes in North Carolina*, by Betsy Levin, Thomas Muller, and William Scanlon (Washington: Urban Institute, 1973); "2nd Med School in the Works?" by Gene Marlowe, Atlanta *Journal-Constitution*, Sept. 2, 1973; "Carolina Senators Reject Equal Rights Amendment," by Pamela Owens, *The Southern Patriot*, March 1973; "Lobbying Pays Off, Budget Shows," by Paul Bernish, Charlotte *Observer*, May 13, 1973; "Gov. Scott Angers Teachers on Pay Boost 'Promises'," by Joe Doster, Atlanta *Journal-Constitution*, Jan. 31, 1971; "North Carolina Enacts $1.80 Minimum Wage," *AFL-CIO News*, June 2, 1973; "Organizing Labor in North Carolina," by Elizabeth Tornquist, *New South*, Spring 1970; "GOP Hopes Riding on Holshouser," by Joe Doster, Atlanta *Journal-Constitution*, Nov. 21, 1971; *North Carolina Statewide After-Election Study*, by De Vries & Associates (January 1973); "Morgan Is Leading in N.C. Senate Bid," by Ferrel Guillory, Washington *Post*, May 8, 1974; "Turning Back the Political Clock in the South," by Rowland Evans and Robert Novak, Washington *Post*, March 21, 1974.

CONGRESSIONAL DELEGATION Ralph Nader Congress Project report on Sam J. Ervin, Jr., by Stephen Klitzman (Washington: Grossman, 1972); "Sen. Ervin vs. 'Information Power'," by David C. Anderson, *Wall Street Journal*, Feb. 8, 1971; "Ervin Suggests Penalizing Aides of Nixon Who Balk," by John M. Crewdson, New York *Times*, March 19, 1973; "Old Words Haunt Senate Candidate," [about Jesse Helms], by Gene Marlowe, Atlanta *Journal-Constitution*, Oct. 15, 1972; "Riding the Airwaves to Washington," by Mark Pinsky, [*MORE*], March 1973; "Ex-Rep. Carl Durham Dies; Fought for Creation of AEC," Washington *Star-News*, April 30, 1974; "The 10 Dumbest Congressmen," by Nina Totenbeg, *New Times*, May 15, 1974; "Sen. Scott Assails Article," Washington *Star-News*, May 23, 1974.

RACE RELATIONS "Black Insurance: From a Barber Shop to a Billion $$$," by Bernard Garnett, *Race Relations Reporter*, May 1972; "Negro 'Apartheid' Seeps into N. Carolina Colony," by Bruce Biossat, *Newspaper Enterprise Association*, May 19, 1969; "N. Carolina Loses Youth in Annual Migration North," by Bruce Biossat, *Newspaper Enterprise Association*, May 13, 1969; "Soul City, N.C., Is Moving from Dream Stage to Reality," by Wayne King, New York *Times*, Jan. 4, 1974; "U.S. Backs McKissick's Soul City Plan," by Austin Scott, Washington *Post*, July 3, 1972; "Bond Sale to Free Soul City Funding," by Claudia Levy, Washington *Post*, March 20, 1974; "Farewell to the Grand Dragon," by Luisita Lopez and Frye Gaillard, *Race Relations Reporter*, November 1973; "Portrait of a Klansman: The Prophetic Voice of C. P. Ellis," by Edward McConville, *The Nation*, Oct. 15, 1973; "North Carolina Justice" and "At Justice's Expense," by Colman McCarthy, Washington *Post*, March 5 and April 9, 1974.

CITIES AND REGIONS "Mr. Charlie's Town: Powerful C. A. Cannon Rules Kannapolis, N.C., but He Faces Challenge," by Neil Maxwell, *Wall Street Journal*, April 29, 1969; "The Passing of Mr. Charlie," *Forbes*, July 15, 1972.

"School Busing: Charlotte, N.C.," by Frank Barrows, *Atlantic Monthly*, November, 1972; "Busing No Longer Bothers Charlotte," by Howard

Maniloff, *South Today*, January-February, 1973; "Two Carolina Banks for High Stakes," *Business Week*, Nov. 10, 1973.

"Are Outer Banks Doomed?" by Gene Marlowe, Atlanta *Journal-Constitution*, Sept. 9, 1973; "Wreck of the Monitor Is Reported Found," by B. Drumond Ayres, Jr., New York *Times*, March 8, 1974.

"Western North Carolina Since the Civil War, by Ina W. Van Noppen and John J. Van Noppen (Boone, N.C.: Appalachian Consortium Press, 1973); *These Storied Mountains*, by John Parris (Asheville, N.C.: Citizen-Times Publishing Company, 1973); "The Appalachian States: North Carolina," by Roy Parker, Jr., *Appalachian Review*, Summer 1966.

GRAHAM "Graham Criticizes Nixon, Old Friend, On Judgment," by R. W. Apple Jr., New York *Times*, Dec. 23, 1973; "Rev. Graham and the Bombing: Still No Critical Comment," by Clayton Fritchey, Washington *Post*, Jan. 20, 1973; "Billy Graham Sees Nixon 'As Great President— if . . .' " by Clive Lawrance, *Christian Science Monitor*, Dec. 31, 1973; "Billy Graham: His Only Goal Now Is Heaven," by Jack Thomas, Boston *Globe*, Jan. 6, 1974.

WEST VIRGINIA

An especially useful resource was *West Virginia*, by Otis K. Rice of the West Virginia Institute of Technology, a manuscript prepared in 1970 for the New York *Times'* abortive series of books on the 50 states. Also consulted were *West Virginia: The Mountain State*, by Charles H. Ambler & Festus P. Summers (Englewood Cliffs, N.J.: Prentice-Hall, 1958); *West Virginia: A Guide to the Mountain States*, compiled by workers of the Writers' Program of the WPA (New York: Oxford University Press, American Guide Series, 1941); and *Bloodletting in Appalachia: The Story of West Virginia's Four Major Mine Wars and Other Thrilling Incidents of Its Coal Fields*, by Howard B. Lee (Morgantown: West Virginia University, 1969).

Some of the most insightful overall articles on the West Virginia scene included "West Virginia Wonderland," by William C. Blizzard, *The Appalachian South*, Spring and Summer 1966; "The Strange Case of West Virginia," by Roul Tunley, *The Saturday Evening Post*, Feb. 6, 1960; and "Poor Rich West Virginia," by Paul J. Kaufman, *The New Republic*, Dec. 2, 1972.

"The Exemplary John Brown," by Robert Merideth (book review), *The Nation*, May 7, 1973; *The Old Man: John Brown at Harper's Ferry*, by Truman Nelson (New York: Holt, Rinehart, and Winston, 1973).

POLITICS *The Primary that Made a President: West Virginia 1960*, by Harry W. Ernst (Eagleton Institute: Cases in Practical Politics— Case 26) (Rutgers, 1962); *Politics in the Border States*, by John H. Fenton (New Orleans: Hauser Press, 1957); *Politics, Party Competition and the County Chairman in West Virginia*, by Gerald W. Johnson (University of Tennessee: Bureau of Public Administration, 1970); "West Virginia Establishment: The Affluent in Total Control," by Curt Brown, Charleston *Sunday Gazette-Mail*, Feb. 7, 1971; "The Challenge in Mingo County," by Michael Adams, Washington *Star*, April 30, 1968; "Mingo Voting Wrongs Told by Watchers," by K. W. Lee, Charleston *Gazette*, May 28, 1968; *"They'll Cut Off Your Project": A Mingo County Chronicle*, by Huey Perry (New York: Praeger, 1972).

The Presidential Candidacy of John W. Davis, by Franklin Rhodes Cook (unpublished Master's thesis, Pennsylvania State University, 1973); "Marland Joins Horse Racing Firm," by Don Marsh, Charleston *Gazette*, April 9, 1965; "Cab-Driving Marland Again Ready for World," by Don Marsh, Charleston *Gazette*, March 13, 1965.

"Moore Tab $170,000 with Tax, IRS Says," by James A. Haught, Charleston *Gazette*, July 18, 1973; "Gov. Moore's Tax Case 'Turkey,' Not a 'Fix'," by James A. Haught, Charleston *Gazette*, May 10, 1973; "Mitchell Ignores Party Label," by Jack Anderson, Washington *Post*, May 29, 1970.

"West Virginia Indicts 47 in Payoffs," by Philip D. Carter, Washington *Post*, Jan. 6, 1970; "West Virginia: The Governor Tooketh," by Mary Walton, *The Washington Monthly*, February 1972.

ROCKEFELLER "Jay Rockefeller: Tall Talent for the New Democrats," by Anthony Wolff, *Look*, April 29, 1969; "John Rockefeller 4th, Who Didn't Run, Is West Virginia Victor," by R. W. Apple, Jr., New York *Times*, May 14, 1970; " 'We Want Jay!' They Shout," by Stuart Auerbach, Washington *Post*, Oct. 14, 1972; "A Break for West Virginia," by W. E. Chilton III, *The Nation*, Oct. 25, 1971; "Rockefeller 4th Will Seek State Ban on Strip Mines," by Ben A. Franklin, New York *Times*, Dec. 31, 1970; "Rockefeller Finds Shanghai," by J. V. Reistrup, Washington *Post*, Nov. 5, 1972; "Rockefeller Gild Fades Off Town," Detroit *Free Press*, June 29, 1969; "Strip Mining Wins a Victory," by William E. Watson, *New South*, Winter 1973; "West Virginia Race Cost $2.2-million," New York *Times*, Dec. 11, 1972.

STATE GOVERNMENT "How a State with Lots of Poor Is Getting People Off Welfare," *U.S. News and World Report*, Oct. 1, 1973; "West Virginia Tries to Make Aid Work," Atlanta *Journal-Constitution*, Nov. 14, 1972.

"Higher Education Behind Bars: A West Virginia College's Prison-Education Program," *Appalachia*, April, 1972; "Moundsville Prison: Cruel and Unusual," by Bernard D. Nossiter, Washington *Post*, June 14, 1971; "West Virginia's Penitentiary Is Plagued by Shakedowns, Robberies and Violent Deaths," by Walter Rugaber, New York *Times*, July 12, 1971.

CONGRESSIONAL DELEGATION Ralph Nader Congress Project reports on Jennings Randolph (by Anne Millet), Robert C. Byrd (by Dane Pullen), Harley O. Staggers (by Cherrill A. Anson), and Ken Hechler (by Gregory L. Diskant) (Washington: Grossman, 1972); "Randolph Scored by Nader on Bill," by Ben A. Franklin, New York *Times*, May 16, 1973; "Sen. Randolph: Key to Highway Trust Fund," by Mary Russell, Washington *Post*, April 16, 1973; "Senator Jennings Randolph—The Sunday Gazette-Mail's West Virginian for 1964," by Thomas F. Stafford, Charleston *Gazette-Mail Magazine*, Jan. 3, 1965.

"Senate Whip Bob Byrd: From Poverty to Power," by Jack Anderson, *Parade*, April 25, 1971; "Byrd's Rise: Butcher to Senate Whip," by John H. Averill, Los Angeles *Times*, Feb. 6, 1972; "The Embodiment of Poor White Power," by Robert Sherrill, New York *Times Magazine*, Feb. 28, 1971; *Hustlers and Heroes: An American Political Panorama*, by Milton Viorst (New York: Simon and Schuster, 1971); "Kennedy Foe Once

High in Klan," by David Wise, New York *Herald-Tribune,* April 21, 1960; " 'Your Faithful Whip' " *Newsweek,* April 2, 1973.

COAL, MINE WORKERS "The Curse of Coal," by Peter J. Bernstein, *The Nation,* Sept. 3, 1973; "Ole King Coal—What's Going on in Appalachia," by Des Callan, *The Mountain Eagle,* Oct. 28, 1971.

"Coal's Toll Since 1907—87,850," by Morton Mintz, Washington *Post,* Nov. 22, 1968; "78 Trapped in Mine by Blasts and Fire," by Ben A. Franklin, New York *Times,* Nov. 21, 1968; "The Human Cost of Production," by Steven Haft, *Ripon Forum,* July 1972; "Blood on the Coal," by Duane Lockard, *The Nation,* Feb. 15, 1971; "W. Va. Mine Conditions Assailed," by Philip D. Carter, Washington *Post,* July 26, 1970; "Bureau May Blame Miners in Death," by Jack Anderson, Washington *Post,* June 9, 1971; "Politics Disclosed on Mine Safety Unit," by Ben A. Franklin, New York *Times,* Feb. 12, 1972; "Mine Safety: Reform or Reversion?" (editorial) Washington *Post,* May 18, 1972; "Specter of Disaster Still Haunts Mines," by Lawrence E. Taylor, St. Louis *Post-Dispatch,* Jan. 31, 1972; "Coal-Mine Study Shows Record Can Be Improved When Firms Really Try," by John V. Conti, *Wall Street Journal,* Jan. 18, 1973; "New U.M.W. Chief Vows to Enforce Mine Safety," by Ben A. Franklin, New York *Times,* Dec. 4, 1973; "Who Will Pay for Black Lung?" by Jerry Landauer, *Wall Street Journal,* June 21, 1972; "The Black Lung Rebellion," by Robert G. Sherrill, *The Nation,* April 28, 1969.

"Stanford Report: It Bores in on Facts," by Mary Walton, Charleston *Sunday Gazette-Mail,* Feb. 20, 1972; "Debate Rages on Strip Mining Bill," by John Fialka, Washington *Star-News,* March 19, 1973; " 'Pot' Luck in Reclamation," by Mary Walton, The Charleston *Gazette,* Sept. 28, 1970; "The Pittston Mentality: Manslaughter on Buffalo Creek," by Thomas N. Bethell and Davitt McAteer, *Washington Monthly,* May 1972; "Bureaucracy of Disasters," by Tom Nugent, *The Na-* *tion,* June 18, 1973; "After the Flood," by Mary Walton, *Harper's Magazine,* March 1973; "Fading Hope for Saving the Land," by Pat Furgurson, *Mountain Eagle,* Nov. 4, 1971.

Death and the Mines: Rebellion and Murder in the United Mine Workers, by Brit Hume (New York: Grossman, 1971); "UMW Rebellion Erupts in Wildcat Strikes," by J. Y. Smith, Washington *Post,* Aug. 10, 1970; "West Virginia Hard Hit by Long Coal Strike that Idles Almost 10% of State's Workers," by Bob Harwood, *Wall Street Journal,* Nov. 11, 1971; "West Virginia: Vortex of Whirlpool in the Coalfields," by James A. Haught, Charleston *Sunday Gazette-Mail,* Jan. 2, 1972; "The UMW Starts to Clean House," *Business Week,* Feb. 3, 1973; "Miller vs. Boyle: Revolt in the Coal Fields," by James Humphreys, *New South,* Winter 1973; "Closing in on Tony Boyle," and "Problems of a New Broom," by Phil Primack, *The Nation,* June 19, 1972 and Jan. 5, 1974; "Coal and the Mine Workers," by John Hoerr, *Atlantic,* March 1974.

ECONOMY " 'Wild, Wonderful West Virginia,' Shocked by Exodus of People, Seeks to Woo Industry and Hold Young," by Homer Bigart, New York *Times,* August 3, 1970; "West Virginia Moves to Overcome Its Image of Poverty," by Tom Miller, *Southern Growth—Problems and Promise* (report of Southern Growth Policies Board, Research Triangle Park, N.C., 1973); "Union Carbide," *Mountain Life and Work,* November 1973; *Natural Resources of West Virginia,* prepared by the United States Department of the Interior, Office of the Secretary, Division of Information (Washington: Government Printing Office, 1964); "West Virginia Town Lifts Union Carbide Tax Ceiling," by Ben A. Franklin, New York *Times,* Dec. 5, 1970; "Union Carbide's Tax Raised 400%," by Colman McCarthy, Washington *Post,* Dec. 5, 1970; "West Virginia, Nearing Heaven?" by Wendell Rawls, Jr., Philadelphia *Inquirer,* April 9, 1974; "The Escalating Cost of a People Mover," *Business Week,* March 16, 1974.

KENTUCKY

Two outstanding modern-day books on Kentucky provided immensely valuable background —*Kentucky: Land of Contrast,* by Thomas D. Clark (New York: Harper & Row, 1968), and *Night Comes to the Cumberlands: A Biography of a Depressed Area,* by Harry M. Caudill (Boston: Little, Brown, 1963). Other books of interest on the state and its regions include *Kentucky: A Guide to the Bluegrass State* compiled by writers of the Writers' Program of the WPA (New York: Harcourt, Brace, American Guide Series, 1939); *Stinking Creek,* by John Fetterman (New York: E. P. Dutton, 1967); *Jesse Stuart's Kentucky,* by Mary Washington Clarke (New York: McGraw-Hill, 1968); *The Hollow,* by Bill Surface (New York: Coward McCann, 1971); and *My Land is Dying,* by Harry M. Caudill (New York: E. P. Dutton, 1971).

POLITICS AND GOVERNMENT Politics in the Border States, by John H. Fenton (New Orleans: Hauser Press, 1957); *Kentucky Politics,* by Malcolm E. Jewell and Everett W. Cunningham (Lexington: University of Kentucky Press, 1968); "Toothless Tiger Watches Campaign Laws," by Charles R. Babcock, Louisville *Courier-Journal,* Aug. 28, 1973; "Politics Keeps Merit Law an Unfulfilled Promise," by Livingston Taylor, Louisville *Courier-Journal,* Dec. 6, 1971; "After the Scandal: Picking Up the Pieces," by Frank Browning, *Washington Monthly,* October 1973; "Happy Chandler Steals Kentucky Political Show," by William Greider, Washington *Post,* Nov. 1, 1971; "Kentucky Agencies Reorganized," *State Government News,* October 1973; "Kentucky's All-Pervasive Spoils Politics," by Gladys M. Kammerer, *Good Government,* July–August 1958; "Kentucky Taxes Coal for the First Time," *State Government News,* May 1972; "Ex-Governor Tells Senators of ITT Lobbyist's 'Stupor'," by Sanford J. Ungar, Washington *Post,* March 8, 1972.

CONGRESSIONAL DELEGATION Ralph Nader Congress Project reports on Marlow W. Cook (by David Ignatius), Carl D. Perkins (by Lora Jane Glickman), and William H. Natcher (by Lenore Cooley) (Washington: Grossman, 1972); "John Sherman Cooper: The Senate at Its Best," Washington *Post,* Jan. 7, 1973; "Cooper Won't Seek Re-election: Served 20 Years in the Senate," by George Vecsey, New York *Times,* Jan. 22, 1972; "Rep. Natcher: Bowling Green's Congressman Keeps Manning the Roadblocks," by Jack Eisen, Washington *Post,* July 20, 1969.

COAL *The Employment and Expenditure Effect of the Kentucky Coal Industry in 1970,* by Darrell Gilliam and David Whitehead (Lexington: Spindletop Research, 1972); *Kentucky Coal Mining Industry: Economic and Employment Data, Underground and Surface Mining* (Lexington: Kentucky Coal Association, 1972–73); "Major Battle Shaping up as a Result of Growing Efforts to Ban Strip Mining," by Tom Bethell, *Mountain Eagle,* May 20, 1971; "Technology Fosters Boom in Coal but Safety and Environment Suffer," by Richard Harwood & Laurence Stern, Louisville *Courier-Journal,* Feb. 4, 1970; "Critics of Strip Mining Are Stepping Up Resistance," by Ben A. Franklin, New York *Times,* May 10, 1970; " 'The Whole Country Will Be Stripped'," *Newsweek,* June 28, 1971; *Industry's Attitude Toward Strip Mining,* speech by David A. Zegeer, Lexington, Ky., June 19, 1973; "New Mines Create a Boom—and a Bane," by Mark R. Arnold, *National Observer,* July 20, 1970.

BLUEGRASS REGION "Historic Kentucky Bluegrass Country," by David Lowe, *Americana,* May 1973; "Horse Watching," by Mary Jane Gallaher, Louisville *Courier-Journal & Times Magazine,* May 4, 1969; "Superhorse—Secretariat," by Pete Axthelm, *Newsweek,* June 11, 1973; "Frankfort," by Allan M. Trout, Louisville *Courier-Journal and Times Magazine,* May 4, 1969; "Kentucky's Treasured Horse Country Is Feeling the Impact of an Advancing Population," by George Vecsey, New York *Times,* April 20, 1971.

"Lexington Sends Out Shock Waves," by Beverly Fortune, Louisville *Courier-Journal,* March 30, 1969; "Lexington Charter Approval Analyzed," by W. E. Lyons, *National Civic Review,* March 1973; "Merger in the Bluegrass," by Florence Zeller, *New County Times,* Dec. 15, 1972; "Pettit Is Mayor on High Court 6-to-0 Decision," by William Peeples, Lexington *Herald,* Jan. 16, 1974.

LOUISVILLE "Cosmopolitan or Rural? Louisville Appears to Be Undecided," by George Vecsey, New York *Times,* Feb. 8, 1971; "Revival Time for Louisville," *Business Week,* Sept. 8, 1973; "Estate of $100-Million Was Left to Charity by Man in Louisville," New York *Times,* April 9, 1969; "Lover of the 'Big Deal' . . . Yarmuth's Hobby Is National Industries," by Mike Kallay, Louisville *Times,* March 3, 1969; "Louisville Group Urges Expansion," *National Civic Review,* March 1970; "It's a Tough Job, Being the Chief," by Robert Schulman, Louisville *Courier-Journal and Times,* Jan. 12, 1969; "The Ten Best American Dailies," *Time,* Jan. 21, 1974.

"Cook's Rise Points Up Spectacular Changes in Jefferson," by James S. Tunnell, Louisville *Courier-Journal,* Jan. 6, 1969; "Louisville Voters Expected to End 8 Years of GOP Rule," by William Greider, Washington *Post,* Oct. 25, 1969; "Kentucky: A Right Turn Spells Disaster," *Ripon Forum,* January 1971; "Young Dr. Sloane," by W. E. Chilton III, *Nation,* Jan. 20, 1973.

"My Old Kentucky Derby Home," by Dwight Chapin, Los Angeles *Times,* May 4, 1973; "About that Derby," by Robert Shulman, Louisville *Courier-Journal & Times Magazine,* May 4, 1969.

"Carl Braden: Shadowy Figure of Controversy," by Howard Kercheval, Louisville *Courier-Journal & Times,* May 18, 1969; "The Organizers

—An Interview with the Controversial Bradens," *Vantage Point* (Centre College, Danville, Ky., Winter 1969); "Nunn Asserts Cook 'Coddles' Agitators," Louisville *Courier-Journal & Times,* May 7, 1967; "The Great Pikesville Bolshevik Beachhead," by Peter A. Iseman, *Ripon Forum,* April 1969.

EAST KENTUCKY "Natives Pouring Out of Jobless Eastern Kentucky," by Kyle Vance, Louisville *Courier-Journal & Times,* June 28, 1970; "Plant in Paintsville Is Luring Workers Back to Mountains," by David Hawpe, Louisville *Courier-Journal & Times,* June 28, 1970; "In the Valley of the Shadows: Kentucky," by Bruce Jackson, *Trans-Action,* June 1971; "An Appalachian Author Describes His Life Style," by Betty Garrett, *Appalachia,* December 1972–January 1973.

A Brief History of Berea College (Berea: Berea College, undated); " 'I Never Thought of College—But Here I am Weaving'," by Wilma Dykeman and James Stokely, New York *Times,* May 17, 1970; "Southern Appalachian Mountain Lore: Berea College's Weatherford-Hammond Mountain Collection," by Alvin H. Perrin, *Appalachia,* April–May 1973; "Appalachian Students Reach Out to Help Mountain Neighbors," by Kenneth G. Gehret, *Christian Science Monitor,* Jan. 6, 1973.

"Appalachia as a Developing Nation," *Business Week,* July 18, 1970; Appalachia Gets a Program It Trusts," *Business Week,* Oct. 16, 1971; "Pikeville's Splendid Dream," by Don Ridings, Louisville *Courier-Journal,* Dec. 22, 1968; "A Kentucky Community Undertakes a Far-Reaching Plan," *Appalachia,* June–July 1969; "Kentucky Town Awaiting Growth Through $22-Million Mountain Excavation," by Ben A. Franklin, New York *Times,* Oct. 11, 1970; "A Dynastic Family at the Crossroads—The Turners of Breathitt County," by John Ed Pearce, Louisville *Courier-Journal and Times Magazine,* Aug. 30, 1970; "Controversy Grows in Kentucky Over Antipoverty Control," by Ben A. Franklin, New York *Times,* March 29, 1970; "Hearings Open Today in Tense 7-Month-Old Miners' Strike in Harlan County, Scene of 1931 Shootout," by Ben A. Franklin, New York *Times,* March 11, 1974; "The Simmering Second Battle of Harlan County," by John Ed Pearce, Washington *Post,* March 18, 1974.

"Two 'Fotched-On' Women, Aided by Local Residents, Began School, by Lois Campbell, *The Mountain Eagle,* Dec. 24, 1970; "Highly Praised Nursing Service Cuts Rural Kentucky Birth Rate," by Kenneth Reich, Washington *Post,* Dec. 28, 1971.

"The *Eagle* Speaks in the Language of Kentucky Hill Folk," *Audubon,* July, 1973; "A Country Editor's Life: Hectic," by Ben A. Franklin, New York *Times,* April 17, 1971; " 'Crusader' Internships," *Columbia Journalism Review,* Summer, 1970; "The Alternative Press Turning to Muckraking," by Robert A. Jones, Los Angeles *Times,* Oct. 28, 1973.

TENNESSEE

In preparing the Tennessee chapter, I was fortunate to have access to an excellent unpublished manuscript on the state by Fred Travis, ஸief of the Nashville Bureau of the Chattanooga *Times.* Other reference works of value included *Tennessee: A Short History,* by Stanley J. Folmsbee, Robert E. Corlew, and Enoch L. Mitchell (Knoxville: University of Tennessee Press, 1969); *The Tennessee Citizen,* by William E. Cole (Norman,

Oklahoma: Harlow Publishing Corp., 1964); *Dimensions of Voting in the Tennessee House of Representatives in 1967,* by Harry F. Kelley, Jr. (Knoxville: University of Tennessee Bureau of Public Administration, 1970); "Tennessee: A Politics of Peaceful Change," by Lee S. Greene and Jack E. Holmes, chapter of *The Changing Politics of the South,* ed. William C. Havard (Baton Rouge: Louisiana State University Press, 1972);

"Tennessee: The Civil War and Mr. Crump," chapter of *Southern Politics in State and Nation,* by V. O. Key (New York: Random House, 1949); *The Bosses,* by Alfred Steinberg (including a chapter on Memphis' Crump) (New York: The Macmillan Company, 1972); *Mr. Crump of Memphis,* by William D. Miller (Baton Rouge: Louisiana State University Press, 1964); and *Kefauver: A Political Biography,* by Joseph Bruce Gorman (New York: Oxford University Press, 1971).

STATE GOVERNMENT *Summary Report of the Tax Modernization and Reform Commission* (Nashville, September 1973); "Tennessee: Budget Plans Don't Live Up to Oratory in Behalf of Poor," by Dana-Ford Thomas, *South Today,* March 1973; "Legislature's Ranking: A Thing to Crow About," by Joe Hatcher, Atlanta *Journal-Constitution,* Feb. 28, 1971; "Tennessee: Major Legislation Enacted, but No-Fault, Minimum Wage, Tax Relief, and Health Left for Next Session," by Dana-Ford Thomas, *South Today,* October 1973.

POLITICS "Tennessee Politics Since Kefauver and Reece: A 'Generalist' View," by Norman L. Parks, *Journal of Politics,* February 1966; "Tennessee Group Loses Reform Bid," New York *Times,* April 8, 1956; *Money as a Campaign Resource: Tennessee Democratic Senatorial Primaries, 1948–1964,* by William Buchanan and Agnes Bird (Princeton, N.J.: Citizens' Research Foundation, 1966); "Too Much Talent in Tennessee?" by Wilma Dykeman, *Harper's,* March 1955; "Clement May Hit Snags on Road to the Senate," by Gene S. Graham, Louisville *Courier-Journal,* Aug. 18, 1963; "Loyal Tennesseans Bid Good-by to Frank Clement, 'God's Man'," by James T. Wooten, New York *Times,* Nov. 7, 1969; "Tennessee GOP Plans Strong 1970 Bid for Major Offices," by Neal R. Peirce, *National Journal,* Dec. 27, 1969; "Close, but No Cigar," by Michael S. Lottman, *Ripon Forum,* July–August 1970; "Scopes of 'Monkey Trial' Is Dead at 70," by Alden Whitman, New York *Times,* Oct. 23, 1970.

CONGRESSIONAL DELEGATION Ralph Nader Congress Project Reports on Howard H. Baker, Jr. (by Steven Saferin), William E. Brock III (by Helene Lexar and Catherine Bell), and Richard H. Fulton (by Arthur Levine and James Burkhardt) (Washington: Grossman, 1972).

"Estes Kefauver Is Dead at 60 After Heart Attack," New York *Times,* Aug. 11, 1963; "A Public Servant Worth His Hire," by Ernest Gruening, *The Nation,* Jan 17, 1972; "Estes Kefauver and Greatness," by Morton Mintz, Washington *Post,* Nov. 29, 1971; "Maverick Kefauver," by Russell B. Nye, *The Progressive,* March 1972.

"Gore's Lost Cause," by Gene Graham, *New South,* Spring 1971; "The End of a Populist," by David Halberstam, *Harper's,* January 1971; "The Old Gray Fox of Tennessee," editorial in Washington *Post,* Nov. 6, 1970.

"Howard Baker: GOP's Post-Watergate Leader?" by Mark R. Arnold, *National Observer,* June 16, 1973; "Tennessee's William Brock," *Time,* Nov. 16, 1970; "Baker Moves Quietly to Left," *Human Events,* Sept. 19, 1970; "Baker for President in '76? His Critics Are Hard to Find" and "Once Too Shy to Wave, Baker Draws Strength from His Roots," by Bruce Biossat, *Newspaper Enterprise Association,* Aug. 3, 1973; "Baker Seen Emerging as '76 Contender," by Louis Harris, Washington *Post,* Aug. 2, 1973; "Sen. Howard Baker Caught in the Middle," by Lloyd Shearer, *Parade,* July 29, 1973; "The Howard Baker Boom," by Robert Walters, *Columbia Journalism Review,* November/December 1973; "Watergate's Lancelot," by Jack Waugh, *The Christian Science Monitor,* June 7, 1973; "Politics: Profiles—Howard Baker, Jr. and Bill Brock," *Ripon Forum,* September 1973.

"Banking Lobby Invades the Senate" (regarding Senator Brock), by Jack Anderson, Washington *Post,* April 4, 1972; "Congressman Anderson's Daring Deed," by Norman C. Miller, *Wall Street Journal,* Dec. 18, 1970; "Mr. Anderson's Conscience: The Greening of a Politician," by James M. Perry, *National Observer,* Feb. 1, 1971.

RACE RELATIONS "Clinton, 1956: The Dooming of 'Deliberate Speed'," by George McMillan, Washington *Post,* March 26, 1972; "Fayette Protest an Anachronism," by Jon Nordheimer, New York *Times,* Oct. 12, 1969; *Racial Protest in the South–1969 Style,* by John Egerton (Nashville: Race Relations Information Center, 1969).

ECONOMY "Tennessee Is Counting on Manpower Skills," by Reginald Stuart, *Southern Growth Problems and Promises* (publication of Southern Growth Policies Board, Research Triangle Park, N.C., 1973); "Tennessee's Economy Building Up Momentum for Further Gains," by John M. Godfrey, Federal Reserve Bank of Atlanta *Monthly Review,* November 1972; "Higher Appalachia Coal Taxes Asked," by Reginald Stuart, New York *Times,* June 22, 1974.

COUNTRY MUSIC "Country Fiddles," by Paul Hemphill, *South Today,* February 1970; "Kris Kristofferson Is the New Nashville Sound," by Paul Hemphill, New York *Times Magazine,* Dec. 6, 1970; "Lookin' at Country with Loretta Lynn," by Pete Axthelm, *Newsweek,* June 18, 1973; *The Nashville Sound, Bright Lights and Country Music,* by Paul Hemphill (New York: Simon & Schuster, 1970); "Country Queen," *Newsweek,* Dec. 4, 1972; "Country Music," by Christopher S. Wren, *Look,* July 13, 1971; "Hard-Times King of Song," by John Frook, *Life,* Nov. 21, 1969; "Another Version of the Dream," *Esquire,* November 1971; "The Grand Ole Opry," by Larry King, *Harper's,* July 1968; "Listen to Jingle, Grumble and Roar—Opry Movin'," by Howell Raines, Atlanta *Journal and Constitution,* June 18, 1972; " 'Opryland, U.S.A.'," by Morris D. Rosenberg, Washington *Post,* June 11, 1972; "Grand Ole Opry Is Yielding to Change," by Roy Reed, New York *Times,* May 29, 1970; "Tin Pan Alley—Country Style," by Haynes Johnson, Washington *Post,* March 7, 1971; "The Grand Ole Opry Ain't Po' No Mo'," by Jeanette Smyth, Washington *Post,* March 18, 1974.

EAST TENNESSEE *This Is Oak Ridge* (League of Women Voters of Oak Ridge, 1968); "Clinton Laboratories—The War Years," by W. E. Thompson, Oak Ridge *National Laboratory Review,* Spring 1973; "A Cumberland Incongruity," by Charles Thornton, Memphis *Commercial Appeal Mid-South Magazine,* April 27, 1969; "Oak Ridge, Or, Birth of a City," and "Oak Ridge Faces Life," by Eden Ross Lipson, Newsletters of Institute of Current World Affairs, New York, April 13 and May 20, 1967.

"Appalachian Stoneware for America's Dinner Tables: The Iron Mountain Story," by Andy Leon Harney, *Appalachia,* October–November 1972; "Mysterious Hill Folk Vanishing," by Jon Nordheimer, New York *Times,* Aug. 10, 1971; "Chattanooga Cleans Air and Keeps Industry," by John Dillin, *Christian Science Monitor,* Oct. 20, 1972.

MEMPHIS "Memphis," by James Conaway, *Atlantic Monthly,* November 1971; "The Power Structure," series of five articles by Barney DuBois, Memphis *Commercial Appeal,* Sept. 20–24, 1970; "Memphis: A City that Wants Never to Change," by Jon Nordheimer, New York *Times,* Jan. 26, 1973; *Where I Was Born and Raised,* by David L. Cohn (South Bend, Ind.: University of Notre Dame Press, 1967).

"Crump's Passing Shows Dangers In One-Man Rule Over Electorate," by Virginia E. Lewis, Washington *Post*, Oct. 24, 1954; "Ring-Tailed Tooter," *Time*, May 27, 1946.

"Memphis Lets New Industries Locate Nearby; Feels City Profits and Remains More Livable," by Roy Reed, New York *Times*, July 22, 1973; "The Hospitality Crusade," by Marylin Bender, New York *Times*, Aug. 26, 1973; "Memphis Blues: City Becomes a Center of Municipal Bonds—And Also Shady Dealing," by David McClintick, *Wall Street Journal*, Dec. 3, 1971; "Memphis Hopes Boom in Recordings Will Aid Local Racial Harmony," by Paul A. Bernish, *Wall Street Journal*, March 30, 1970; "Steamin' Up The River—I: Redbud Time in Blues Town," by David Butwin, *Saturday Review*, May 29, 1971.

"Bad Day in Memphis," by Nicholas C. Chriss, *The Nation*, Dec. 20, 1971; *Memphis—Promise of Progress*, by John Egerton (Atlanta: Southern Regional Council, 1973); *Employment, Administration of Justice, and Health Services in Memphis-Shelby County, Tennessee*, (by the Tennessee State Advisory Committee to the U.S. Commission on Civil Rights, August 1967); "Memphis," *Black Enterprise*, May 1971; "Memphis Garbagemen March," by Austin Scott, Washington *Post*, April 5, 1973; "Five Years After: The Garbage Workers, Memphis and Dr. King," by Jack Slater, *Ebony*, April 1973; *In Memphis: One Year Later*, by Pat Watters with J. Edwin Stanfield, (Atlanta: South-

ern Regional Council, 1969); "Memphis: Municipal Union Now a City Force," by Roger Williams, *South Today*, July–August 1970; "In South, Enrollment in Private Schools Continues to Climb," by Richard A. Shaffer, *Wall Street Journal*, Dec. 17, 1973.

NASHVILLE "The Nashville Story," by T. Scott Fillebrown, *National Civic Review*, May 1969; "Nashville Thrives on a City-County Merger," *Business Week*, Sept. 25, 1971; "Metro Eases City vs. Suburb Conflict," by Ralph D. Olive, Milwaukee *Journal*, April 15, 1970; "The Nashville Sound: A Paradox of Black Urban Politics," by Lester M. Salamon, *V.E.P. News*, July–September 1971; "Integration's Bible," *Newsweek*, April 24, 1972; Nashville to Begin Testing Thermal Transfer Plant, Designed to Convert Garbage into Heating, Cooling," by Fred Travis, Chattanooga *Times*, Nov. 4, 1973; "Nashville's Choice: Six Feet Under—Or 20 Stories Up," by David Brand, *Wall Street Journal*, June 12, 1973.

"Black Medical School Finds It Was Ahead of Its Time," by Nancy Hicks, New York *Times*, Nov. 29, 1970; "Voices of Fisk '70," by C. Eric Lincoln and Cecil Eric Lincoln, New York *Times Magazine*, June 7, 1970; "Chancellor Alexander Heard: Firm and Fair," by Jacque Srouji, *Nashville Magazine*, November 1969; "Straight Talk," *Newsweek*, Aug. 3, 1970; "Campus Communicator: George Alexander Heard," New York *Times*, May 11, 1970.

TENNESSEE VALLEY AUTHORITY

"More Power and Energy to the People," by Robert Sherrill, *Lithopinion*, Summer 1973; "TVA After 40 Years: A Mixed Blessing," by Peter Barnes, *New Republic*, Nov. 10, 1973; "Whatever Happened to TVA?" by Gordon Young, *National Geographic*, June 1973; "Big Users Balk at TVA Rates," *Business Week*, March 10, 1973; "President to Decide Role TVA Will Play in Future," by Marquis Childs, Washington *Post*, April 28, 1969; *The Politics of Conservation*, by Frank Smith (New York: Pantheon Books, 1966).

"Today's T.V.A. Is Assailed as Threat to Environment," by Edward Cowan, New York *Times*, Aug. 5, 1973; "T.V.A. Sets Policy for Strip Min-

ing," by Ben A. Franklin, New York *Times*, Dec. 7, 1971; "TVA Ravages the Land," by Ken Hechler, *National Parks and Conservation Magazine*, July 1971; "Power Corrupts," by Osborn Segerberg, Jr., *Esquire*, March 1972; "TVA and Strip Mines," *New Republic*, Jan 20, 1973; "Cherokees' Ancestral Home Threatened with Flooding," by Sanford J. Ungar, Washington *Post*, Aug. 12, 1971; "A 'TVA' for Energy?" *Business Week*, Nov. 17, 1973; "Improving the Southern Environment," by Frank E. Smith, *New South*, Fall 1970; "Pollution Funds for TVA Backed," by E. W. Kenworthy, New York *Times*, March 19, 1974.

INDEX

Scale of Miles

100 200 300 400 500

CAN

WASH.

Seattle

Olympia

Spokane

MONT.

N.D.

Portland

Salem

Eugene

ORE.

Helena

Butte

Billings

Bismarck

S.D.

Aberdeen

IDAHO

Boise

YELLOWSTONE
NATIONAL
PARK

WYO.

Pierre

CALIF.

NEV.

Great
Salt Lake

Pocatello

Casper

NEB.

Ogden

Reno

Carson City

Sacramento

UTAH

Salt Lake City

Cheyenne

COLO.

Denver

KAN.

Oakland

San Francisco

YOSEMITE
NAT'L. PARK

Mt. Whitney

Las Vegas

Colorado
Springs

Santa
Barbara

GRAND
CANYON
NAT'L. PARK

Farmington

Wicha

Los Angeles

ARIZ.

Santa Fe

Okla
Ci

Amarillo

San Diego

Albuquerque

Phoenix

N.M.

Wichita
Falls

Pacific
Ocean

Tucson

Lubbock

Fort Wort

El Paso

TEXA

U.S.S.R.

Kotzebue

ALASKA

Nome

Fairbanks

CANADA

Austi

San
Antoni

U.S.S.R.
U.S.

Anchorage

Juneau

MEXICO

Bering
Sea

MILES

200 400 600